INTERNATIONAL CRIMINAL LAW

International Criminal Law

DOUGLAS GUILFOYLE

OXFORD
UNIVERSITY PRESS

OXFORD
UNIVERSITY PRESS

Great Clarendon Street, Oxford, OX2 6DP,
United Kingdom

Oxford University Press is a department of the University of Oxford.
It furthers the University's objective of excellence in research, scholarship,
and education by publishing worldwide. Oxford is a registered trade mark of
Oxford University Press in the UK and in certain other countries

Published in the United States of America by Oxford University Press
198 Madison Avenue, New York, NY 10016, United States of America

British Library Cataloguing in Publication Data
Data available

Library of Congress Control Number: 2015953854

ISBN 978–0–19–872896–2

Printed in Italy by
L.E.G.O. S.p.A.

Preface

The purpose of this book is to provide a reasonably concise and accessible introduction to international criminal law. It emerges from my own experience of teaching and studying the subject. International criminal law as a body of law and collection of institutions has grown rapidly since the early 1990s. So too has the volume of relevant literature and the length of specialized texts in the field. What seemed to me to be missing was a shorter and deliberately accessible introduction of the kind that could easily be read by someone new to the subject, including non-lawyers. This book is also self-consciously written with teaching in mind and includes a number of teaching-oriented features explained in the next section ('About this book'). There are numerous larger works (and many excellent articles) which go into more technical detail on specific aspects of the subject. A selection of these are indicated in the 'Useful further reading' at the end of each chapter.

There are many approaches one could take to the teaching of international criminal law including social, historical, anthropological, and critical perspectives. The focus of this volume is largely on presenting a doctrinal account of the law. This is not intended to exclude other approaches but stems from a belief that if one is going to analyse the law from an external perspective it is best to first have a reasonably solid understanding of the law itself. Nonetheless, a number of historical and theoretical points are made along the way. Also, as a matter of teaching methodology the aim of this book is to be, where possible, illustrative rather than exhaustive or overly technical. A number of important points are made by way of detailed examinations of a particular case rather than a survey of case law. This is also a field that engenders substantial scholarly debate and conflicting views. A number of these debates are presented in 'Counterpoint' features.

The book is organized in four parts. The first two chapters concern general topics of public international law which assume a special significance in relation to international criminal law: the doctrines of sources and jurisdiction. If you are coming to international criminal law without a previous background in public international law (or indeed without a background in law) these are important topics. They deal with how we identify a rule of international law and the rules governing when States can exercise criminal jurisdiction, in particular to prosecute extra-territorial acts or the acts of foreigners. Even if you have previously studied international law, these chapters may be worth reviewing. The doctrine of sources, in particular, operates slightly differently in relation to international criminal law than other international law subjects.

The second part of this book concerns international criminal tribunals and the prosecution of international crimes (before both national and international courts). In particular, it examines in some detail the varying jurisdiction and powers of international criminal tribunals and provides an overview of the increasingly complex field of procedural law before such tribunals.

The third part consists primarily of four chapters addressing each of the 'core' international crimes which have been prosecuted before international criminal tribunals. These are, of course, war crimes, crimes against humanity, genocide, and aggression. However, this part begins with a short but important chapter (Chapter 7) designed to introduce a number of key issues relevant to all four crimes, including the required mental states for international crimes. One of the difficulties in studying international criminal law is that it necessarily borrows concepts from a variety of legal traditions and systems. This can create a degree of confusion or even inconsistency, especially regarding such matters as what mental state a defendant must have in order to be found guilty of an international crime.

The fourth part addresses a number of topics related to the liability of a defendant for international crimes and potential barriers to prosecution. One of the distinctive features of international crimes is that those most responsible for their being committed are often high ranking leaders: such leaders, however, may be structurally and physically removed from the individual acts of killing or other atrocities carried out by their foot soldiers or subordinates. Connecting the actions of leaders with subordinates in a manner that allows them to be described as having committed an international crime is now a substantial, complex, and controversial area of the law. It is thus examined in some detail under the heading modes of participation in international crimes. Two further chapters deal with legal defences (which preclude a finding of criminal liability) and immunities under international law (which may preclude prosecution, at least for a time or before certain courts).

As to case-law references, I have generally used a simplified form of citation rather than adopt the often confusing and complex notation which is used by the various international criminal tribunals. Generally, my references are to final judgments of Trial or Appeal Chambers unless otherwise noted. In each case I have provided sufficient information to locate the original on the relevant tribunal website. Direct links to key documents are also contained in the Online Resource Centre which accompanies this volume.

Finally, thanks are due to the numerous people who have assisted this project in various ways. They are many but some must be singled out. The idea that I might write some teaching materials on this subject was first suggested to me by James Busuttil and Linda Cox of the University of London International Programs and this book has grown from that early suggestion. Lucy Read at Oxford University Press is due thanks for being a patient and meticulous editor who commissioned several rounds of exceptionally useful reports from peer reviewers. Thanks are obviously due to those anonymous reviewers and the rest of the OUP team as well.

Finally, one does not learn or teach a subject in isolation. I was very fortunate to begin my teaching career at University College London where I taught a course in international criminal law initially alongside Håkan Friman and Elizabeth Wilmshurst. Both were warm and generous colleagues and I learnt a great deal from them, as well as from cohorts of wonderfully talented and engaged students. I myself was first taught international criminal law by Roger O'Keefe and later had the privilege, briefly, to teach it alongside him. I am indebted to him in particular for his helpful comments on an early draft text of what eventually became this book. I was also exceptionally fortunate to have the research assistance of my former students Eleni Antoniadou, Melissa Bale, Christopher O'Meara, Michele Tedeschini, and Alejandra Torres Camprubí towards the end of this project. Ross Dunn also assisted with proofreading. While I owe all of these people—and others—substantial debts of professional gratitude, any errors in the final text remain, of course, my own.

This book is dedicated to Zoë and Jamie who were always there, wherever 'there' happened to be at the time.

Douglas Guilfoyle
31 July 2015

About this book

International Criminal Law by Douglas Guilfoyle is written with the student in mind. Its user-friendly style will ensure you gain a sound understanding of the subject area, but the text also includes features throughout which will help you to consider the latest debates and reflect upon the issues at hand.

This guide shows you how to use those features so that you can get the most out of your studies.

 Learning aims

By the end of this chapter you should be able

- how a rule of customary international l (or formed) by an international court or
- the concept of *jus cogens*;

Learning aims

Each chapter starts with a bulleted list of the main concepts and ideas you will encounter. These provide a helpful signpost to what you can expect to learn from the chapter.

 Counterpoint

Are defence counsel at a systematic dis

It is a frequent, and to some extent fair, critici als that the resources available to the Prosecu teams.[59] Ambos, while noting that things have of the ICTY:

Counterpoint

These boxes highlight criticisms of the law or areas where there are conflicting viewpoints. Use these boxes to develop an understanding of the problems within the subject area, and the latest debates around these issues.

 Pause for reflection

How would you apply the law to the following sc
Alpha is a military commander in the State of Ent armed group. The armed group is led by Zeta. Th the State of Dystopia.
Zeta orders his men to split up into small three–fi

Pause for reflection

These boxes will often include questions, encouraging you to reflect on the law described. Use this feature as an opportunity to stop and consider the wider implications of the law.

Example

Was Russia's 2014 intervention in Crime

In the period November 2013–February 2014 th
resulting in Ukrainian President Viktor Yanukov
22 February 2014. Mr Yanukovych then fled t
increasing evidence of Russian military interv

Examples

Carefully-chosen examples, sometimes using historical context, show how the law has developed. These real-life examples are designed to help you gain a practical understanding of how the law operates.

13.11 Summary and conclusions

This chapter has provided an outline of one of the national criminal law: the extent to which a defenda are circumstances excusing or justifying what will i a preliminary matter, we noted that while the dist excuses is known in a number of national legal sy to international criminal law. The distinction does, thinking about defences as either raising a plea th

Summary and conclusions

Ideal for assessing your own understanding and particularly useful at revision time, these sections at the end of each chapter can be used to re-cap on what has been covered.

Useful further reading

R CLARK, 'The Mental Element in International Criminal Law: The International Criminal Court and the Elements of Offences' (200 Forum 291.
One of the most important articles written on these questions, which be accessible style—as well as providing insights into the process of negotia from the point of view of a delegate.
S FINNIN, 'Mental Elements under Article 30 of the Rome Statute of the I Court: A Comparative Analysis' (2012) 61 International and Comparati
An exceptionally clear and useful treatment of the concepts involved in i
D PIRAGOFF and D ROBINSON, 'Article 30: Mental Element' in O Triffte on the Rome Statute of the International Criminal Court: Observers'

Useful further reading

Broaden your knowledge by using these reading suggestions to find sources of further information. The author explains what is covered in each source and why it is useful, meaning that this feature is much more than a simple list.

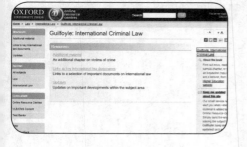

Online Resource Centre

This book is accompanied by an Online Resource Centre offering links to important international criminal law documents, allowing you to locate and read for yourself the basic sources of law. The Online Resource Centre also hosts an additional chapter on victims of crime and updates on significant developments in the subject area. See www.oxfordtextbooks.co.uk/orc/guilfoyle.

Contents

Detailed Contents

Part III The Core International Crimes

Table of Treaties and International Instruments

NATIONAL LAWS

Australia

Canada

France

Israel

New Zealand

UK

USA

Table of Cases

LEIPZIG TRIALS

NUREMBERG INTERNATIONAL MILITARY TRIBUNAL

PERMANENT COURT OF JUSTICE

SPECIAL COURT FOR SIERRA LEONE

OTHER CASES AND REPORTS

PART I

Foundations

1

The sources of international criminal law

1.1 Introduction

Before we commence our study of international criminal law as a body of rules, practices, and institutions we have to have a basic grasp of where those rules, practices, and institutions come from. That is, in any system of law there must be a rule that allows us to identify what the law is; this is known as the doctrine of sources. (If you have studied jurisprudence you might also think of it as HLA Hart's 'rule of recognition'—the rule that tells you which rules have the force of law.[1]) In the common law world, the sources of national law are usually statute (a written law enacted by a regular parliamentary procedure and assented to by the head of State) and common law (unwritten rules of judge-made law declared and modified by the courts over time); in some jurisdictions one might add other sources such as a written constitution or aspects of European Union law. The essential point to note is that a legal system may include both written and unwritten forms of law.

As international criminal law is a branch of public international law, this chapter introduces the basic sources of international law and some of their complexities. It is often thought by students new to international criminal law that it should be one of the easier branches of international law. After all, criminal law is just a question of looking up the rule and applying it to the facts. In fact, a moment's reflection will reveal this is much too simple a conception of criminal law. Criminal law at the national level is a complex field of study. Ideas of guilt, innocence, who should be counted as having committed or participated in a crime, the role of punishment in a society, and so on are all important concepts which are much more complex than 'looking up the rules', and will affect how those rules are applied. International criminal law inherits these complexities of national criminal law and the complexities of public international law as well. In international criminal law our first challenge is to *identify what the substantive rules of international criminal law are*. To do this, we must know where to look for them.

This chapter is thus intended to provide a brief introduction to the two main sources of public international law, treaty law and customary international law (which may also

---

[1] HLA Hart, *The Concept of Law* 2nd ed (Clarendon 1994) Chapter 5. For a useful account of the idea and its critics see: SJ Shapiro, 'What is the Rule of Recognition (and Does it Exist)?' in M Adler and K Himma (eds), *The Rule of Recognition and the U.S. Constitution* (Oxford University Press 2009). A version of the Shapiro paper is also available at: www.law.yale.edu/documents/pdf/Faculty/Shapiro_Rule_of_Regulation.pdf.

be called 'custom' or 'general international law'). It will also consider the special role of 'general principles of law' in international criminal law. It is necessary that you have a good basic grasp of the concepts involved in order to follow the debate over whether certain rules of international criminal law exist, how they should be defined and what their limits may be.

 Learning aims

By the end of this chapter you should be able to discuss or explain:

- how a rule of customary international law is formed, and how such rules will be discerned (or formed) by an international court or tribunal;
- the concept of *jus cogens*;
- the relationship between treaty law and customary international law;
- the benefits and disadvantages of treaty law and customary law as sources of criminal law rules; and
- whether there is a hierarchy of sources of law in international criminal law.

Following on from these aims, the chapter is structured as follows:

- Section 1.2 introduces the sources of public international law in some detail.
- Section 1.3 provides a basic overview of the law of treaties, and will briefly cover the special status of obligations arising under the United Nations Charter.
- Section 1.4 outlines the key features of customary international law.
- Section 1.5 examines the relationship between treaty law and customary international law.
- Section 1.6 revisits the idea of whether there is a hierarchy of sources in international law, and how conflicts between international law norms are to be resolved.
- Section 1.7 provides a brief explanation of the relationship between international criminal law and other branches of international law.

1.2 The sources of public international law

1.2.1 Introduction

The sources of international criminal law are those of public international law. Textbooks normally begin by referring to Article 38(1) of the Statute of the International Court of Justice, which reads:

The Court, whose function is to decide in accordance with international law such disputes as are submitted to it, shall apply: (a) international conventions, whether general or particular, establishing rules expressly recognized by the contesting states; (b) international custom, as evidence of a general practice accepted as law [better understood as the general practice of States as evidence of customary law]; (c) the general principles of law recognized by civilized nations; (d) . . . judicial decisions and the teachings of the most highly qualified publicists of the various nations, as subsidiary means for the determination of rules of law.

These sources are introduced below, with a particular focus on treaty and custom later in the chapter. A few points should be noted at this stage. The first is that there is obviously a preliminary question in any system of law as to *why* rules are binding on a subject of a legal system. The usual answer given by modern international lawyers is: 'A State is bound by the rules of international law to which it has consented.'[2] This is called the *positivist theory* of international law—the law is a thing that has been made (posited) by the will or consent of States. Sometimes that consent is presumed, or is at best theoretical, but this remains the dominant modern theory applied by international courts and tribunals.

The second point to note is that Article 38 is not a *hierarchy* of sources. Treaties are not a superior form of law that inherently trump custom to the extent of any inconsistency, for example. Article 38 is simply a list of sources of law a court might refer to when deciding a dispute between two States. In international criminal law, international courts or tribunals will have a statute setting out the law that the court or tribunal may apply. That statute may include a hierarchy stating the order in which the court *must* apply those sources of law. Such a hierarchy is binding *only* upon that court under its statute.

Third, Article 38 contains the idea of 'subsidiary sources': these do not have the status of formal law, but are merely evidence of what the law is. Looking to Article 38(1)(d), judicial decisions and the writings of 'publicists' (usually eminent textbook authors) are simply listed as a 'subsidiary' form of evidence that a rule exists. The important idea is that the decisions of courts (including national courts) and the writings of publicists are not able to *make* new law in a formal sense (as States may do by concluding a treaty), their decisions or views are only treated as *evidence* of what the law already is. In practice, as we will see, the decisions of courts and judges have played a much greater role in the development of international criminal law than the formal status of judicial decisions might suggest.

Fourth, there is no hierarchy between courts or doctrine of precedent in international law. Decisions of the International Court of Justice (ICJ) do not bind other international courts and tribunals, they do not even—technically speaking—bind future decisions of the ICJ itself. That said, it is very common for international courts and tribunals to cite each others' decisions where relevant. Thus, even where courts are not bound by the decisions of other courts they will often treat them as at least persuasive. For example, where a decision of the International Criminal Court

---

[2] V Lowe, *International Law* (Oxford University Press 2007) 19; compare the statement of the Permanent Court of International Justice in: *Lotus Case* [1927] PCIJ Ser. A No. 10, 4, 18.

departs from the approach taken to similar issues by the International Criminal Tribunal for the former Yugoslavia, that decision will commonly state why it has taken a different approach. (The origins of both the International Criminal Court and the International Criminal Tribunal for the former Yugoslavia are discussed in Chapter 3.)

Let us turn briefly to consider each of the sources listed in Article 38(1), before returning to treaty and custom in more detail.

1.2.2 **Treaty law**

A treaty is a legally binding agreement reached between two or more subjects of international law with recognized treaty making capacity (i.e. States and some international organizations), in written form.[3] Treaties can be used to create new rules of law relatively quickly and have the advantage of certainty (even if a treaty rule is vaguely drafted it has at least been reduced to writing). However, the fundamental principle of treaty law is that a treaty *binds only the parties to it*. Treaty rules thus operate only within their membership (*inter partes*) and can have only very limited effects for a non-party without that non-party's consent.

1.2.3 **Customary international law**

Customary international law (or 'custom' or 'general international law') is a form of unwritten law which is binding upon all States. Rules of customary international law have to be deduced from what States do and say. A rule of custom is evidenced by consistent State practice (i.e. behaviour) coupled with *opinio juris* (a subjective belief held by States that this behaviour is required by law, and is not merely followed as a matter of courtesy or convenience). A rule of customary international law has the advantage of general application—it binds all States and escapes the *inter partes* limitation of treaty law. However, it faces difficulties of proof (especially as to precisely when the rule in question became established); and has the potential disadvantage of a lack of specificity. Unwritten rules are by their nature likely to be somewhat more vague or general than written rules. One can thus have long arguments about whether an unwritten rule exists, when it came into existence, and its precise content (i.e. wording). In the case of a written rule arguments will generally be about interpretation and application.

1.2.4 **General principles**

General principles of law derived from the world's major legal systems ('general principles' for short) can be a difficult source to conceptualize, but one way of

---

[3] Strictly speaking, unwritten treaties are possible but they are rare: J Crawford, *Brownlie's Principles of Public International Law* 8th ed (Oxford University Press 2012) 371.

putting it is that in the courtroom an international court may be faced with questions that treaty and customary international law do not answer—such as which party should bear the burden of proof on an issue. In most international law cases between States the idea of general principles will go to rules of procedure: these will be rules stipulating what a State is allowed to plead (or must plead) or may rely on court.

In international criminal law the concept may be used rather differently. Sometimes it may be relied upon as a secondary argument for deriving or deducing the elements of a crime or the elements or limits of defences, where no other source of law is available to 'fill the gap'. For example, it was quite clear in international criminal law for a long time that rape was a war crime. What was less clear was whether there was a definition of rape at international law that an international court could use. A survey of national legal systems had to be undertaken by the International Criminal Tribunal for the former Yugoslavia (ICTY) on this point in 1998, in the *Furundžija* case, in order to sufficiently define the crime for the purposes of an international prosecution and trial.[4] However, this use of general principles is always strictly subsidiary—only after the sources of treaty and custom had been exhausted could it be turned to fill a gap in the law. This point will be returned to in Chapters 12 (dealing with modes of liability) and 13 (dealing with defences).

One may also suggest that several important general principles of criminal law form a part of international criminal law, including:

- the principle of legality or *nullum crimen sine lege* (discussed below at 1.4.4);
- the presumption of innocence (discussed in Chapter 6); and
- the principle of interpretation that any ambiguity should be construed in favour of the accused or *in dubio pro reo* (discussed below at 1.3).

1.2.5 'Eminent publicists' and judicial decisions

As already noted above, scholarly writings and judicial decisions form only a subsidiary means of determining the law. Thus, strictly speaking, scholarly writings provide only evidence of a rule of international law, not a formal source by which new rules of international law may be created. It is important to note, however, the role of the United Nations International Law Commission (ILC). The ILC is a body of 34 independent international law experts elected for five year terms by the UN General Assembly. They are tasked with the *codification* and *progressive development* of international law. Their work proceeds through extensive research and debate on specialized international law topics, which usually concludes with the adoption of a set of 'Draft Articles', or simply 'Articles', in a form suitable for adoption as a treaty (which sometimes occurs). These ILC draft articles are made available with detailed explanatory 'commentaries'. As international law becomes

---

[4] See: *Prosecutor v Furundžija*, ICTY Trial Chamber 1998, paras 177–82.

more developed and detailed, international courts and tribunals refer to eminent publicists increasingly rarely. Nonetheless, ILC reports, draft articles, and commentaries are still often referred to as persuasive evidence of the law on a topic. It is important to note, however, the distinction between codification (compiling a statement of the law as it is, *lex lata*) and progressive development (setting out rules which do not yet clearly form a part of international law but which either appear to be emerging or which represent a good idea for the law's future development, *de lege ferenda*). In international criminal law, 'guidance' documents or studies issued by the International Committee of the Red Cross may perform a similar role to the work of the ILC—although as the Red Cross is an organization dedicated to ensuring the maximum protection for vulnerable persons in times of armed conflict its studies are sometimes criticized on the basis that they blur the distinction between the law as it is (*lex lata*) and as it should be (*de lege ferenda*). This is not to suggest one cannot look to Red Cross studies, but they must be treated with the same caution one would treat any academic source.

 Counterpoint

When it comes to judicial decisions we should note Dapo Akande's words of caution that despite being formally 'subsidiary' to other rules they play 'a deceptively important role' in international criminal law. He notes that in a system where many of the rules are unwritten or unclear judges play a role in 'determining precisely what the law is':

> Despite the allegedly subsidiary status of judicial decisions, they play a deceptively important role in international law and [international criminal law]. In a system where much of the rules are unwritten, judges play the important role of determining precisely what the law is. They assess the extent to which State practice and *opinio juris* support an alleged rule of customary law. They also decide on what the general principles of law are. Once those customary rules or general principles are identified…they provide an 'off the shelf' assessment…[5]

Such an 'off the shelf' assessment is likely to be accepted in later cases, unless those who disagree with it present convincing evidence that the law is otherwise.

1.2.6 *Jus cogens*

In addition, we should briefly note one particular type of customary international law rule not expressly referred to in Article 38(1) of the ICJ Statute: *jus cogens*. *Jus cogens* rules of customary international law are rules from which no derogation is possible and which can invalidate any other rule found to be in conflict with them. *Jus cogens* rules are thus a higher form of law which 'trump' all other international law. They are

---

[5] D Akande, 'Sources of International Criminal Law' in A Cassese (ed), *The Oxford Companion to International Criminal Justice* (Oxford University Press 2009) 53.

thus sometimes called 'peremptory norms of general international law'. The existence of such rules is acknowledged in Article 53 of the Vienna Convention on the Law of Treaties.[6] This provides that:

A treaty is void if, at the time of its conclusion, it conflicts with a peremptory norm of general international law... [being] a norm accepted and recognized by the international community of States as a whole as a norm from which no derogation is permitted and which can be modified only by a subsequent norm of general international law having the same character.

This same principle is taken to apply to rules of customary international law and to general principles of law. *Jus cogens* is thus, as noted above, a 'higher' form of international law.

The definition of *jus cogens* norms as being those 'accepted and recognized by the international community of States as a whole' as having this special character fits the positivist theory of international law discussed above. That is, States have *recognized* the existence of such norms and have *consented* to being bound by them. Notably, however, this does not tell us which norms are *jus cogens* or what happens if two norms of *jus cogens* conflict.

Despite the Latin title, the idea of *jus cogens* was not widely accepted before the 1950s and its scope (i.e. the number of norms having this status) remains unclear. The few uncontroversial candidates in international law for *jus cogens* status are the prohibitions on genocide, slavery, torture, serious violations of the laws of armed conflict, and the prohibition on aggression (i.e. certain serious, illegal uses of force by a State as discussed in Chapter 11).[7]

The danger inherent in the idea of *jus cogens* is that it becomes an easy rhetorical tactic—if you assert that the norm that you are arguing for is *jus cogens* then by definition you have won the argument. As a student it is always useful to be wary of academics who argue on the basis of *jus cogens*; such arguments should only be accepted where there is persuasive evidence that the norm has been widely accepted as having *jus cogens* status. ICJ judgments or ILC reports or commentaries to draft articles are a good starting point.[8]

We now proceed to consider treaty and customary law in more detail, before turning to how these sources of law may interact. Before doing so, we should reiterate one entirely practical point. A court created by a statute (whether it has its origins in a treaty, a security council resolution, or a national law) will be bound to apply the terms of its own statute first. In practice, then, the rules of international law described here will be subordinate to the terms of the statute of the court in question. Of course, where such a statute does not provide a clear answer, courts will have no option but to refer to general international law concepts.

---

[6] Vienna Convention on the Law of Treaties 1969, 1155 UNTS 331.
[7] ILC, 'Fragmentation of International Law', UN Doc. A/CN.4/L.702 (2006) para. 33; *Armed Activities (DRC v Rwanda), Jurisdiction and Admissibility*, (2006) ICJ Reports 6, 32.
[8] Ibid.

Pause for reflection

1. *Positivism.* Under the positivist conception of international law a State is bound by those rules of international law to which it has consented. It is possible to consider treaties as containing express consent, and to consider the idea of customary international law as involving implied consent (arising from *opinio juris*) which binds all States unless they object (the persistent objector theory). It also explains why treaties cannot directly bind third parties (they have not consented). However, is that consent more apparent than real in some cases? The difference between judges discerning and making rules of custom may seem rather thin in international criminal law, and consent does not perhaps fully explain the concept of *jus cogens.*

2. *Does the ICJ Statute contain a complete list of the sources of international law?* One might note that the ICJ Statute omits *jus cogens* as the idea of *jus cogens* arose after it was drafted. However, as *jus cogens* is a form of customary international law, one could observe that the Statute is formally complete.

3. *Is there a hierarchy among the sources of international law?* The sources of international law are: *jus cogens*, treaty, custom, and general principles. The only hierarchy is that *jus cogens* 'trumps' or prevails over all other obligations. (We will see in section 1.3 below that obligations arising under the UN Charter prevail over all other international law obligations, with the exception of *jus cogens*.) Judicial decisions and the writings of publicists are only evidence of the law (rather than a formal source of law) and therefore are considered inferior to the formal sources of law (but see point 5, below).

4. *The role of general principles of law.* General principles of law derived from national legal systems may be relied upon as a secondary argument for deriving or deducing the elements of crimes or defences (i.e. 'filling gaps') where no other source of international law stipulates their content. For example, it was quite clear that rape was a war crime, but the International Criminal Tribunal for the Former Yugoslavia had to turn to general principles of law to deduce a definition of rape at international law.

5. *The role of the decisions of judicial bodies in international law.* Technically, judicial decisions are only a subsidiary source of law to be used as persuasive evidence that a rule exists. This status is reinforced by the lack of a hierarchy of courts or any formal doctrine of precedent in international law. Akande, however, notes that this formal statement may be misleading.[9] Judicial decisions will include a reasoned statement of what the relevant international law is and an assessment of the evidence supporting that conclusion. If another court is to disagree, it will have to give its reasons why. Thus prior judicial decisions might not be binding, but they will have to be taken into account in practice.

1.3 The law of treaties

Several critical features of the law of treaties have already been noted:

- The fundamental definition of a treaty is that it is an agreement intended to create binding legal relations (some legal-looking documents concluded in international

---

[9] D Akande, 'Sources of International Criminal Law', 53.

relations are intended to be binding only as a matter of political commitment and *not* in law).

- They are typically concluded in writing.
- They may be concluded only between entities holding legal personality at international law (a category effectively limited to States and some international organizations).
- They create obligations only as among or between parties to them, and as a consequence they do not bind or create rights for non-parties without that non-party's consent (a rule sometimes referred to in Latin as *pacta tertiis nec nocent nec prosunt* or simply *pacta tertiis*).

A few further points should be noted:

- It is *not* important what a treaty is called (be it Convention, Statute, Accord, or Pact), or how it is worded, it is the intention to create legal relations that is key.
- There is usually a distinction between *signature* (signing a treaty text normally only indicates agreement that this is the final text), and *ratification* (signalling consent to be bound when the treaty enters force, usually following a national political or legislative process), and when a treaty *enters force* and therefore becomes binding (entry into force normally requires a specified minimum number of ratifications).
- Importantly, *signature* creates only very limited legal obligations not to undermine the object and purpose of the treaty before it enters force.[10]
- There is an obligation upon all parties to implement the treaty in good faith.

As with all international law, it is never an excuse that national law prohibits or does not allow a State to comply with its treaty law obligations domestically.

The most important issues of treaty law for the present course are two-fold. First, the scope of the *pacta tertiis* rule. Second, the rules of treaty interpretation as applied by courts and tribunals. On the first point, just because a treaty cannot bind non-parties without their consent does not mean they can have no consequences for non-parties. For example, what happens to a State's nationals is normally thought to affect that State's interests. However, if a national of a non-party to the Suppression of Unlawful Acts against the Safety of Maritime Navigation Convention (SUA Convention) hijacks a ship under the flag of a State party to the SUA Convention party, the hijacker's State of nationality cannot object to the prosecution on the basis that it is not also a SUA Convention party. Similarly, the United States is not a party to the International Criminal Court (ICC) Statute (which is a treaty) but if a US national commits an offence under the ICC Statute in the territory of a party to the statute, that person can in principle be prosecuted before the ICC.

The *pacta tertiis* rule can, however, give rise to quite complex problems. For example, the rule in Article 27 of the ICC Statute that denies a defendant the ability

---

[10] Article 18, Vienna Convention on the Law of Treaties 1969.

to plead immunity based on his or her official position (such as being a head of State) should, as a matter of treaty law, be binding only *inter partes*. Such a rule should not, in principle, be able to have the effect of stripping the head of State of a non-party of their immunity, thereby allowing an ICC State party to surrender him or her to the Court and the Court to prosecute him or her. Nonetheless, the Court is directed by its Statute that such a plea is *not* available in proceedings before it. So, in practice, it may be that the ICC would have to disregard such immunity (at least once a defendant was before it), even if that resulted in a breach of international law.

A different provision, Article 98 of the ICC Statute, appears to direct States parties *not* to surrender the officials of non-State parties to the ICC in violation of applicable immunities under international law. One would then expect that complying with Article 98 would prevent problems under Article 27 arising. The position is actually rendered much more complex after the findings of the ICC in the *Al-Bashir* case. The point is returned to in Chapter 4, section 4.4 on the ICC.

Second, we should note the rules of treaty interpretation, as they play a major part in the development of international criminal law. Broadly, there are two schools of textual interpretation:

- the *literal approach* (one construes the written words in the context of the document and by reference to their ordinary meaning); and
- the *teleological approach* (one should construe the words by reference to their object and purpose, that is what they were intended to achieve).

One could also attempt to approach the question of treaty interpretation as a matter of original intent, by asking: 'What did the drafters intend these words to mean?' This would be an historical question, involving an examination of the negotiating record, draft documents (showing what words were rejected), and any records of debates. Such preparatory materials in international law are often referred to by the French term, *travaux préparatoires*.

The key rule of treaty interpretation in international law is found in Articles 31–32 of the Vienna Convention on the Law of Treaties (VCLT).[11]

Article 31: General rule of interpretation

1. A treaty shall be interpreted in good faith in accordance with the ordinary meaning to be given to the terms of the treaty in their context and in the light of its object and purpose.

   ...

3. There shall be taken into account, together with the context:
   (a) Any subsequent agreement between the parties regarding the interpretation of the treaty or the application of its provisions;

---

[11] Vienna Convention on the Law of Treaties 1969, 115 UNTS 331.

(b) Any subsequent practice in the application of the treaty which establishes the agreement of the parties regarding its interpretation;

(c) Any relevant rules of international law applicable in the relations between the parties.

4. A special meaning shall be given to a term if it is established that the parties so intended.

Article 32: Supplementary means of interpretation

Recourse may be had to supplementary means of interpretation, including the preparatory work of the treaty and the circumstances of its conclusion, in order to confirm the meaning resulting from the application of article 31, or to determine the meaning when the interpretation according to article 31:

(a) Leaves the meaning ambiguous or obscure; or

(b) Leads to a result which is manifestly absurd or unreasonable.

Several points should be noted here:

- International law endorses *both* the literal and teleological approaches to interpretation: ordinary meaning, context, and object and purpose are all referred to in Article 31(1), VCLT.

- What States subsequently do under a given treaty may help interpret the meaning of a treaty (this gives priority to what the States understood their obligations to entail).

- While the rule on *travaux préparatoires* seems to suggest one should only refer to them where the ordinary interpretative approach leads to an ambiguous, obscure, absurd, or unreasonable result—in practice, courts can always refer to them under the heading of 'confirming the interpretation' (which may also cover *rejecting* the ordinary interpretation).[12]

It may be that a further consideration is applicable in the context of international criminal law, the principle of *in dubio pro reo*. This principle holds that when in doubt, the interpretation should favour the accused. As the ICC Statute puts it: '[i]n case of ambiguity, the definition [of a crime] shall be interpreted in favour of the person being investigated, prosecuted or convicted.'[13]

A final point to note is that a State's treaty obligations are, as a general rule, of equal status. Nothing prevents States entering treaties with obligations which have the potential to conflict later on: if a conflict arises in practice, a State will simply have to choose which obligation to breach and suffer the consequences under the law of treaties and State responsibility for that breach. There is one possible exception to this. The United Nations has 193 member States,[14] representing almost every recognized State in

---

[12] JD Mortenson, 'The *Travaux* of *Travaux*: Is the Vienna Convention Hostile to Drafting History?' (2013) 107 American Journal of International Law 780.

[13] Art 22(2), ICC Statute.

[14] With the admission of South Sudan on 9 July 2011: www.un.org/en/members/growth.shtml.

existence. All UN members are bound by the United Nations Charter 1945 (the Charter). The Charter is treated as having a special status, due to two provisions: Articles 25 and 103. Article 25 provides that UN members 'agree to accept and carry out the decisions of the Security Council'. Article 103 further provides that in 'the event of a conflict between the obligations' of UN member States under Charter and 'their obligations under any other international agreement, their obligations under the present Charter shall prevail.' In particular, these provisions render compulsory decisions taken by the UN Security Council to maintain or restore international peace and security under the powers given to it by Chapter VII of the UN Charter. We thus speak of Security Council Resolutions under Chapter VII as having compulsory force. This is relevant when we come to consider the founding of the International Criminal Tribunals for the former Yugoslavia and Rwanda.

We may sometimes have to ask, however, precisely which parts of a Security Council resolution bind member States. This is because such resolutions may often simply encourage certain courses of action by member States and do so using language such as 'calls upon', 'invites', or—obviously—'encourages'. Where the Security Council has only called upon, invited, or encouraged States to do something it can hardly be said to have *decided* that States *will* do something. The key word in Article 25 is 'decisions'; so the key word to look for in Security Council resolutions will be 'decides'. This is a point we return to in later chapters.

 Pause for reflection

Establishing an international criminal tribunal under Chapter VII of the UN Charter. As we shall see in later chapters the UN Security Council has established international criminal tribunals under its Chapter VII powers. What would be the advantage of this approach, rather than by a new treaty?

A resolution adopted by the Security Council under Chapter VII of the UN Charter is binding upon all UN members. Thus, if: (a) the statute or constituent instrument of an international criminal tribunal is adopted by the Security Council pursuant to a Chapter VII Resolution; *and* (b) the Security Council decides in the same (or any subsequent) resolution that member States shall co-operate with the tribunal in the exercise of its powers under its statute; then (c) State co-operation with that tribunal will be compulsory. In such a case any powers or jurisdiction given to that international criminal tribunal are thus binding on all 193 UN member States. In addition, obligations under Chapter VII prevail over any other inconsistent obligations of international law such as the inviolability from arrest of foreign heads of State.

By contrast a new treaty establishing an international criminal tribunal would bind only its members and could have only limited effects in relation to non-members. In addition, a new treaty would not necessarily automatically prevail over other potentially inconsistent rules of international law or other treaty commitments. If a State was put in a situation where its obligations conflicted, it would have to choose which obligation to honour. In relation to the obligation breached it would simply have to suffer the consequences of its internationally wrongful conduct under the law of State responsibility.

1.4 Customary international law

1.4.1 Introduction

As noted above a rule of custom arises from consistent State practice (i.e. behaviour) coupled with *opinio juris* (a subjective belief held by States that this behaviour is required by law). The element of *opinio juris* allows us to distinguish between regular behaviour that follows a rule and regular behaviour that is simply a matter of courtesy or convenience. Vaughan Lowe gives the example of rolling out a red carpet at airports for visiting heads of State: this happens as a widespread and consistent State practice, but no State believes it to be a legal requirement, it is simply a courtesy.[15]

This section will examine briefly the elements of State practice and *opinio juris*, before considering the strengths and weaknesses (and controversies) of custom as a source of international criminal law. First, however, a few special features of customary international law should be noted:

- The persistent objector rule: a State that has always and consistently objected to being bound by a rule of customary international law from the time it first emerged is not bound by the rule.[16] This is a strict test that is hard to satisfy. A State may not persistently object to a rule of *jus cogens*.

- Newly emergent States: at the time a new State first comes into existence (such as the States that emerged from the dissolution of Yugoslavia in 1991–1995) it is bound by all existing customary international law at that date. It cannot pick and chose the customary rules by which it will be bound. This would appear inconsistent with the idea that international law is based on State consent, but may be thought of as a case of deemed consent or a requirement of the law of statehood (or simply the price of admission to the club of sovereign States).

1.4.2 State practice

The starting point in establishing a customary rule is to identify consistent State practice. But what counts as State practice? Textbooks typically list as examples: concrete physical or military acts; the decisions of national courts; national legislation; diplomatic correspondence; official legal positions; statements and voting patterns in international organisations; and even treaties. (In fact, it was argued by some States before the ICJ in the *Nuclear Weapons Advisory Opinion* that even *abstention* from acting may be State practice.)[17] The categories are thus wide and may include both physical and 'speech' acts. Relevant practice can be generated by all branches of government,

---

[15] V Lowe, *International Law* (Oxford University Press 2007) 38.
[16] Crawford, *Brownlie's Principles of Public International Law*, 8th ed, 28.
[17] *Legality of the Threat or Use of Nuclear Weapons*, Advisory Opinion, ICJ Reports 1996, 226 at para 65; see also the arguments of France in *S.S. 'Lotus' (France v Turkey)*, Judgment, PCIJ Series A No 10 (1927), 28.

even by relatively minor officials otherwise lacking the ability to enter into binding legal agreements.

Historically, State practice tended to emerge over long periods of time. It was acknowledged by the ICJ in the *North Sea Continental Shelf Cases* that while long historical practice will be useful evidence of sufficient State practice to form a customary rule, it is not necessary.[18] A new rule of custom can arise in a relatively brief time if there is enough practice and it is sufficiently consistent.

This raises the question of *inconsistent* practice. The problem is particularly acute in relation to customary rules of prohibition such as are typically found in international criminal law. For example, while all States may agree that international law prohibits war crimes, torture, and genocide, such acts continue to occur. Does this mean there is *not* consistent State practice and therefore no customary rule prohibiting such acts? The ICJ held in the *Nicaragua Case* that 'absolutely rigorous conformity' of State conduct with the rule is not necessary; general consistency is enough.[19] In particular:

> instances of State conduct inconsistent with a given rule should generally have been treated as breaches of that rule... If a State acts in a way prima facie incompatible with a recognized rule, but defends its conduct by appealing to exceptions or justifications contained within the rule itself, then... the significance of that attitude is to confirm rather than to weaken the rule.[20]

Thus, where breaches of a rule are in fact condemned as breaches, or where States defend their actions as legal by invoking exceptions to the rule (whether such exceptions exist or not), this may serve as evidence of a rule's existence. When it comes to prohibitions, this is the only plausible approach.

How many States must participate in a practice for it to be seen as the basis for a customary rule? The simple, if vague, answer is that unanimity is not required but a simple majority is not enough. Special weight must be given to the practice of those States most affected by a rule: for example, land-locked States will have a limited role in the formation of the customary international law of the sea; and the ICJ in the *Nuclear Weapons Advisory Opinion* held it could not ignore the practice and policies of nuclear-weapons holding States. It will be hard to argue a rule of custom exists that is inconsistent with the practice of those States which are most specially affected.

Finally, ICJ cases such as the *Asylum Case* and the *Right of Passage Case* acknowledge that, in theory and practice, a customary rule may arise between only a group of States or even bilaterally.[21] It would then bind only that group of States. There are, however, no relevant examples for the purposes of international criminal law.

---

[18] (1969) ICJ Reports 3, 43.

[19] *Military and Paramilitary Activities in and against Nicaragua (Nicaragua v United States of America)*, (1986) ICJ Reports 14 at para. 186.

[20] Ibid.

[21] *Asylum Case (Colombia v Peru)*, Judgment, ICJ Reports 1950, 266; *Case concerning Right of Passage over Indian Territory (Merits)*, Judgment, ICJ Reports 1960, 6.

1.4.3 *Opinio juris*

As noted, even if one has evidence of a consistent and uniform practice adhered to by many States this will not prove that the practice reflects a legal rule. A consistent practice might represent simply a commonly-extended courtesy between States, or something that is seen as being convenient but not binding. The further required element is a subjective belief on the part of States that the practice is required by law. This element of subjective belief is called *opinio juris*.

This idea is both undoubtedly a legal requirement of custom and inherently problematic. First, to say a rule is binding because it is believed to be binding is a circular argument. By way of example, at the time of the conclusion of the Geneva Conventions in 1949 it was quite clear that only the limited category of war crimes called 'grave breaches' were subject to individual criminal sanction. Other acts, such as using poisoned weapons, were *prohibited* but *not criminalized*. However, the use of poisoned weapons is now widely recognized as a war crime. At some point between 1949 and now there was a day when this was not a war crime, and a following day when it was.[22] The only difference is a change in States' belief (*opinio juris*). How did such a change come about? The theory almost suggests that the first time a rule comes into being States must be under a mistaken belief (i.e. that this is what the law has always required).[23] Second, where do we locate the governing 'mind' of a State: in the head of State or the executive branch, government departments, the legislature, or the judiciary? The answer is, in all of them. All can create State practice, so the views of all may be relevant to *opinio juris*. However, we know that in real life the branches of government and administration are seldom in one mind. There will be internal differences and struggles on most major issues. What these two problems suggest is that *opinio juris*, as discerned by international courts and tribunals, is objectively tested: it is a legal construction based on the publicly available evidence of what States 'think'.

Some have argued that *opinio juris* can simply be inferred from consistent State practice.[24] The more usual view is that the best evidence of *opinio juris* is found in 'speech acts' or government documents: statements made in the United Nations, official government handbooks on the laws of war, etc may all provide evidence of what States believe the law to be.

1.4.4 **Advantages and disadvantages of customary international law as a source of international criminal law**

The principal advantage of customary international law as a source of international criminal law is generality: it is universally applicable to all persons everywhere,

[22] See further: J Crawford and T Viles, 'International Law on a Given Day' in J Crawford, *International Law as an Open System: Selected Essays* (Cameron May 2002).

[23] J Crawford, *Chance, Order, Change: The Course of International Law* (Hague Academy of International Law 2014) 67; H Kelsen, 'Théorie du droit international coutumier' (1939) Revue Internationale de la Théorie du Droit 253, 263.

[24] H Lauterpacht, *The Development of International Law by the International Court* (Cambridge University Press 1982) 380; quoted by Judge ad hoc Sørensen in his Dissenting Opinion to the *North Sea Continental Shelf Cases* (see n 18 above).

irrespective of whether their State of nationality (or the territorial State where they act) has ratified a particular treaty. The obvious disadvantages of this source of law come from custom's potential for uncertainty or imprecision. What exactly is the content of the rule in question? When exactly did it become binding? In criminal law we have come to expect great precision in the framing of criminal rules. This is based in respect for human beings as reasoning or rational agents: criminal law should be clear enough that people can modify their behaviour to avoid criminal sanction.[25] Just as importantly there is a general presumption in human rights law that criminal law should not apply retrospectively: this is sometimes called the principle of legality or *nullum crimen sine lege*. The International Covenant on Civil and Political Rights expresses it thus:

> No one shall be held guilty of any criminal offence on account of any act or omission which did not constitute a criminal offence, under national or international law, at the time when it was committed.[26]

When a rule of international criminal law is found to be customary international law for the first time by a court, it is potentially open to the accusation of retrospective application. That is, one can make the argument that the rule was (in effect) judicially created and applying it to conduct prior to that judicial decision constitutes punishing conduct that was not criminal at the time.[27] The Nuremberg Tribunal, for example, found that the criminal provisions of its Charter reflected customary international law at the time of the trial in 1945. This, however, did not answer the question of whether these were fully developed rules of custom at the time the defendants' conduct actually occurred.

Further, there is a potential methodological disadvantage or risk in customary international law. As it is proved by state practice and *opinio juris*, one might expect courts to engage on wide-ranging and deeply historical surveys before pronouncing on a rule of custom. In practice this does not occur. All courts are subject to constraints of time and resources. Most judgments pronouncing on customary international law will, at best, be able to identify a limited set of examples of state practice and *opinio juris*. This can leave a finding that a particular rule is part of custom open to accusations that the court selectively chose evidence to fit its argument (so-called 'cherry picking').[28] On the other hand where there is overwhelming evidence of *opinio juris*, identifying only limited State practice is less likely to

---

[25] R Cryer, 'The Aims, Objectives and Justifications of International Criminal Law' in R Cryer, H Friman, D Robinson, and E Wilmshurst, *An Introduction to International Criminal Law and Procedure* 3rd ed (Cambridge University Press 2014) 30.

[26] Art 15(1), International Covenant on Civil and Political Rights 1966, 999 UNTS 171.

[27] For further argument on this point see: A Cassese et al, *International Criminal Law: Cases and Commentary* (Oxford University Press 2011) 53–61, 67–8, and 73–5; and B Van Schaack, 'Crimen Sine Lege: Judicial Lawmaking at the Intersection of Law and Morals' (2008) 97 Georgetown Law Journal 119, 119–133, 161–6, and 189–192.

[28] See e.g.: *Jurisdictional Immunities of the State (Germany v Italy: Greece intervening)*, ICJ Judgment (3 February 2012), Separate Opinion of Judge Yusuf, para 23.

be controversial.[29] For example, on 11 December 1946 the UN General Assembly declared in Resolution 96(I) that genocide was a crime under international law for which individuals were punishable. Indeed, by stating that many instances of the crime had occurred in the past, the wording strongly implied that genocide was already a crime prior to 1946. The resolution was adopted without a vote (i.e. with unanimous approval). While a strict application of the usual test for customary international law might demand we look for prosecutions of the crime of genocide as examples of State practice to support this expression of *opinio juris*,[30] it would seem redundant to do so. There was simply overwhelming consensus in the international community that genocide was a crime no later than 11 December 1946. Nonetheless, the inherent imprecision involved in identifying when a rule becomes part of customary international law brings us back to the question of retroactivity or *nullum crimen sine lege*.

 Pause for reflection

The importance of *nullum crimen sine lege*

Antonio Cassese notes the principle of *nullum crimen sine lege* (or the principle of legality) strictly refers only to the principle that a person may only be convicted and punished for something that was a crime defined under law at the time the conduct occurred.[31] However, the principle or legality has several corollary principles (i.e. they follow logically from the basic proposition): (1) the principle of specificity: the idea that criminal prohibitions must be sufficiently precise to guide behaving; (2) the prohibition on retroactivity: that is, law may not be passed that has retrospective effect, thus providing for punishment for conduct that was not criminal at the time of its commission (this principle is not infringed where conduct was at the time criminal at international law, but not national law);[32] (3) the principle that criminal laws must be construed strictly and ambiguity is to favour the defendant (also called *in dubio pro reo*); (4) The principle that definitions of crimes may not be extended or applied by *analogy* (the prohibition on analogy).[33]

The principle of legality might cause us to question the legality of doing something for the first time. As we shall see in later chapters the law of crimes against humanity was not necessarily clearly established by 1945 at the time of the trial before the Nuremberg International Military Tribunal (IMT). Does this mean that the Nuremberg IMT applied retrospective law in violation of the principle of legality? Cassese notes that the Nuremberg IMT held that *nullum crimen sine*

---

[29] A Roberts, 'Traditional and Modern Approaches to Customary International Law: A Reconciliation' (2001) 85 American Journal of International Law 757.

[30] Indeed, there were very few such cases between 1945 and 1998.

[31] A Cassese et al, *Cassese's International Criminal Law* 3rd ed (Oxford University Press 2013) 22–24.

[32] A principle now enshrined in Art 7, European Convention on Human Rights 1950, 213 UNTS 222; Art 15, International Covenant on Civil and Political Rights; and Art 22, ICC Statute.

[33] See e.g.: Art 22, ICC Statute.

lege was not a principle of law at the time of the Nuremberg trial, but argues it is now more strictly adhered to both as the system of international criminal law develops and in national systems generally.[34]

 Counterpoint

Gap-filling in international law. Cassese may somewhat over-state the importance of the prohibition on analogy in international criminal law. International criminal law judges have often had to engage in expansive interpretation of the law in order to fill gaps. This process may in some cases come very close to analogical extension; further, some crimes inherently require analogical reasoning, such as the war crime of committing 'other inhumane acts' of a 'similar character' to other prohibited conduct.

Beth Van Schaack considers the extent to which the development of international criminal law has required other compromises with the principle of legality.[35] She notes that large gaps in international criminal law have had to be 'filled in' by judges; however, as international law becomes more developed and codified, this will happen less (or it will be more a question of interpreting rules rather than deducing their existence). However, she takes the view that international criminal law is not so different in this respect from the historical evolution of the common law, where judge-made crimes were eventually replaced by statutes or codes. Nonetheless, where international criminal judges have relied on customary international law real questions can be asked about whether they have applied the traditional methodology which requires strict proof of both *opinio juris* and State practice to confirm the existence of a rule. She notes, in particular, that there is a tendency to focus on what States *say* (*opinio juris*) rather than what States *do* (State practice).

Van Schaack further notes the dubious practice throughout the history of international criminal law of presuming that because conduct is *illegal* at international law it must also be *criminal*. As not every wrongful act at international law gives rise to individual responsibility one should look for separate evidence that conduct was not only prohibited but intended to be criminalized. Van Schaack's broad approach appears to suggest that while one could raise real concerns that the principle of *nullum crimen sine lege* has not been consistently respected throughout the history of international criminal law this was to some extent the price of its development and is now a diminishing concern.

Both Cassese and van Schaack appear to agree that as international criminal law develops and becomes more certain there will be less concern about possible breaches of *nullum crimen sine lege*. Both also appear to agree there is an important difference between retrospective application of a substantive criminal norm (i.e. the invention of a new crime) and the interpretation or development or evolution of an existing criminal norm. While the former will violate *nullum crimen sine lege*, the latter will not. There may be a difficult question, however, about where to draw that line.

---

[34] Cassese et al, *Cassese's International Criminal Law* 3rd ed, 25–27.
[35] B Van Schaack, '*Crimen Sine Lege*: Judicial Lawmaking at the Intersection of Law and Morals' (2008) 97 Georgetown Law Journal 119.

1.5 The relationship between treaty law and customary international law

It is worth briefly noting that treaty and custom may interact in three possible ways. That is, a treaty could *codify* custom, the process of treaty drafting could *crystallize* an emerging rule of custom, or a treaty rule could *subsequently become* a rule of custom. Each is now considered in turn below.

1.5.1 Codification

A treaty may codify custom: it may set down in writing rules previously only existing as customary law. This will be first and foremost a question of intention; it will require close examination of the treaty text and negotiating history to ascertain whether the parties thought they were engaged in a codification exercise. (Some treaties usefully state this in the preamble.) Caution must be exercised, however, in that many treaties will contain some provisions that codify pre-existing customary law and some that are completely new rules or progressive developments of the law. The question then must always be when looking at a treaty rule 'did the parties intend this rule to be a codification of custom'? If that is the case, and a large number of States participated in the drafting, or subsequently ratified the treaty, then the treaty may be good evidence of custom.

1.5.2 Crystallization

The very process of treaty negotiation and drafting may allow States to clarify an unclear or disputed customary rule by reaching agreement on what the rule is. After all, the process of treaty negotiation is an action of State practice, and in the course of debates many statements of *opinio juris* might be made. This process could 'crystallize' the emergence of a customary rule, even if the treaty never comes into force. Put simply, if enough States agree in a given forum that a rule is part of custom, then it very likely is a part of custom.

One example of the crystallization process is in the formulation of rules on the immunity of States in proceedings before foreign courts (State immunity). Historically there had been a debate between absolute and restrictive approaches to State immunity. The doctrine of absolute State immunity held that a State was never amenable to the jurisdiction of foreign courts in civil claims without its consent. The doctrine of restrictive state immunity held that a State was in general immune from civil proceedings in foreign courts unless an exception applied. The restrictive theory of immunity was adopted in Draft Articles prepared by the International Law Commission[36] and in the UN Convention on Jurisdictional Immunities of States and their Property.[37] Despite the

---

[36] International Law Commission Yearbook 1991, vol. II(2), 12.
[37] GA Res 59/38, Annex (2 December 2004).

Convention not being in force yet, a number of national courts have taken it to reflect an international consensus in favour of the restrictive theory.[38] Jurisdictional immunities and international criminal law is a topic we return to in Chapter 14.

1.5.3 Subsequent customary status

A treaty may set out a rule that later becomes custom. This may seem a bit baffling, but if a non-party to a treaty follows a specific rule in a treaty—then they cannot be doing so because they are bound by the treaty. The practice of a non-party following the treaty rule must represent *opinio juris*, the belief that the same rule is binding as part of custom. As an example, the United States is not a party to the UN Law of the Sea Convention, that first proclaimed a right to a 12 nautical mile limit territorial sea. The United States has, however, proclaimed a 12 nautical mile territorial sea. This State practice is generally taken as evidence that the treaty rule is also found in custom. Similarly, if a rule of international criminal law is found only in a treaty but it is nonetheless followed by non-parties this will provide persuasive evidence that it may also be a rule of customary international law.

1.5.4 The International Criminal Court Statute: codification or progressive development?

When we come to look at the ICC Statute we will find that the crimes it sets out represent a mixture of codification and progressive development. That is, the drafters had the opportunity to reflect on the case law of earlier international courts, especially the International Criminal Tribunals for the former Yugoslavia and Rwanda and decide whether to incorporate rules from the jurisprudence of those tribunals or not. The Statute may thus, in part, indicate what parties believed international criminal law to be at 1998, the date the Statute was concluded. In this context one should note that the final text was adopted by 120 votes to seven, with 21 States abstaining. The States voting against the adoption of the final text were Iraq, Israel, Libya, the People's Republic of China, Qatar, the United States, and Yemen. Other rules, however, may have been newly stated for the first time in the ICC Statute and may be different from the rule (if any) at customary international law. The question might then arise as to whether these new rules themselves may subsequently become rules of customary international law.

 Pause for reflection

What is the relationship between the ICC Statute and earlier case law?

If a rule of international criminal law was articulated for the first time in an early ICTY case, what would be the significance of finding it adopted (or rejected) in the ICC Statute? Where the

---

[38] *Brownlie's Principles of Public International Law*, 8th ed, 490.

ICTY Statute or early case law has taken a detailed approach to an issue of international criminal law and that same approach was taken in the ICC Statute this *may* indicate it was accepted as stating customary international law. One would still need to ask whether the parties negotiating the Statute thought they were codifying an existing rule.

If the ICC Statute appears to reject an earlier articulation of a rule, then it seems hard to argue that earlier rule is accepted as custom. If all States already believed that this was the correct formulation of a rule of customary international law, why would they exclude it or modify it in the Statute? Such a rejection would strongly appear to suggest that the negotiating States thought that it went further than the relevant customary international law rule. Alternatively, in some cases it might only suggest that the States involved could not agree on the 'outer edge' of the rule, and chose to codify only a narrower interpretation of it. This might still lead to a conclusion that the existence of widespread State support for the proposed rule is at best ambiguous.

How do we know if a rule in the ICC Statute is also binding as a rule of customary law?

In general if a non-party to a treaty accepts a particular rule as stating the applicable international law, that provides a good argument that the rule is custom. As a non-party is not bound by the treaty in question, it could only be following an equivalent customary rule. In the same manner, if a State which is not party to the ICC, or an international court other than the ICC, accepts and applies a rule found in the ICC Statute, that would also suggest the rule is being applied as a rule of customary international law.

1.6 Revisiting the idea of a hierarchy of sources, and conflict between international law norms

Before the twentieth century all international legal obligations had the same status: there were no rules that 'trumped' other conflicting rules and there was no hierarchy of sources. As noted above, it is not the case that a treaty, for example, will inherently prevail over a conflicting rule of custom.

However, we now have in modern international law the idea of 'relative normativity',[39] the idea that some 'norms' or legal sources may prevail over or have stronger effects than others. We have already encountered the idea of *jus cogens*, cardinal rules of international law from which no derogation is permissible and which prevail over all other international law obligations to the extent of any inconsistency. We have also noted that obligations under the UN Charter, including the compulsory decisions of the Security Council, prevail over other legal obligations. Logically, however, the UN may not act contrary to *jus cogens*.[40]

---

[39] The classic article on point is P Weil, 'Towards Relative Normativity in International Law?' (1983) 77 American Journal of International Law, 413–442.

[40] The extent to which the Security Council is bound by other rules of international law, especially human rights law is contentious. See: D Akande, 'The Security Council and Human Rights: What is the role of Art. 103 of the Charter?', EJIL: Talk!, 30 March 2009, www.ejiltalk.org/the-security-council-and-human-rights-what-is-the-role-of-art-103-of-the-charter/.

Further, it is now also common to talk of 'soft law'. There is no accepted definition
of 'soft law' but it usually refers to any international instrument other than a treaty
'containing principles, norms, standards or other statements of expected behaviour.'[41]
It is easy for the novice to dismiss soft law as being by definition of no consequence
or as an oxymoron: if it's not binding, how is it law? The simplest way to put it is that
'soft law' may function in a manner similar to Ronald Dworkin's definition of principles: legal ideas that are not precise enough to be called rules (which either apply or
do not apply to given facts), but which may be weighed in the balance when deciding
how to apply a given rule.[42] For example, it may be a war crime to deliberately attack
a person who is not directly participating in hostilities: but who counts as 'directly
participating'? In answering this question a court might look to the 2009 Red Cross
report *Interpretive Guidance on the Notion of Direct Participation in Hostilities under
International Humanitarian Law*. While at best 'soft law', and controversial in some
aspects, this document might come to have an influence on how 'hard law' is applied.

Taking all this into account a simple hierarchy would look like this:

- rules of *jus cogens*;
- obligations arising under the UN Charter;
- the traditional sources of international law (treaty, custom, general principles);
- soft law,

where each source of law would 'trump' those lower in the hierarchy.

This, however, still leaves most rules of international law 'on the same level'. How is
one to resolve a conflict between two treaty provisions, or between a rule of treaty and
custom? The usual approach is to suggest:

- the rule that comes later in time prevails over the earlier rule to the extent of any
  inconsistency (in Latin: *lex posterior derogat priori*); and
- the rule that is the more specific prevails over the rule that is more general to the
  extent of any inconsistency (in Latin: *lex specialis derogat legi generali*; or simply *lex
  specialis*).

Thus, in practice, treaty rules may prevail over customary rules not because of any
formal hierarchy, but because the treaty rules are likely to be more specific and therefore benefit from the application of *lex specialis*. Nonetheless, one must be careful
in the application of *lex specialis*. It was once widely assumed that the laws of armed
conflict completely displaced human rights law during times of armed conflict, or at
least defined the content of human rights law for the duration of or in the locations
of the conflict. (A soldier's right to life on the battlefield in times of war has a different legal meaning than a civilian's right to life on a city street in times of peace.)
The ICJ in the *Legal Consequences of the Construction of a Wall in the Occupied*

---

[41] D Shelton, 'International Law and "Relative Normativity"' in M Evans (ed), *International Law*, 4th ed
(Oxford University Press 2014) 159.

[42] R Dworkin, *Taking Rights Seriously* (Bloomsbury 2013) 39–45.

Palestinian Territory Advisory Opinion told us, however, that we cannot assume so simple a relationship.[43] In that Advisory Opinion the Court said that 'the protection offered by human rights conventions does not cease in case of armed conflict' and there were three possible ways international humanitarian law (i.e. the laws of war) and human rights law might interact:

> some rights may be exclusively matters of international humanitarian law; others may be exclusively matters of human rights law; yet others may be matters of both these branches of international law.[44]

Therefore in relation to each rule of human rights law we must ask: 'is this rule necessarily displaced by a more specific rule of the law of armed conflict and if so, to what extent is it displaced or modified?' Strictly speaking, unless a criminal sanction attaches to the violation of a particular human right, the continued application of human rights during times of armed conflict will have a limited impact on international criminal law. However, it is worth being aware that the relationship between international criminal law, the law of armed conflict, and human rights law is potentially complex.

Pause for reflection

How is an international criminal court to resolve issues of the hierarchy or inter-relationship of rules?

While we return to study the International Criminal Court in more detail in later chapters, Article 21 of the ICC Statute provides an example of how an international criminal tribunal may approach the question of sources and their hierarchy.

Article 21 – Applicable law

1. The Court shall apply:
    (a) In the first place, this Statute, Elements of Crimes and its Rules of Procedure and Evidence;
    (b) In the second place, where appropriate, applicable treaties and the principles and rules of international law, including the established principles of the international law of armed conflict;
    (c) Failing that, general principles of law derived by the Court from national laws of legal systems of the world including, as appropriate, the national laws of States that would normally exercise jurisdiction over the crime, provided that those principles are not inconsistent with this Statute and with international law and internationally recognized norms and standards.
2. The Court may apply principles and rules of law as interpreted in its previous decisions.
3. The application and interpretation of law pursuant to this article must be consistent with internationally recognized human rights…

The ICC is thus first and foremost a court of statute, and is bound by its constituting instrument. However, it may also resort to 'applicable' treaties and rules of (customary)

---

[43] (2004) ICJ Reports 136.   [44] Ibid, para. 106.

international law. Only where the first two sources fail to provide an answer may it have recourse to general principles of law.

 Pause for reflection

What role may general principles of law derived from national legal systems play in international criminal law in general and under the ICC Statute?

We noted in section 1.2.5 that general principles of law derived from national legal systems may be relied upon to derive or deduce the elements of crimes or defences, in order to fill gaps where no other source of international law stipulates their content. This was done in a number of cases at the ICTY.

Before the ICC it is assumed that there will be fewer gaps. The ICC must first apply its own Statute, Elements of Crimes, and its Rules of Procedure and Evidence. As the ICC has detailed Elements of Crimes these may already stipulate much of the content of crimes to the extent they are at all ambiguous. If gaps remain, the Court must next consider 'where appropriate, applicable treaties and the principles and rules of international law'. Only after exhausting all of these sources may it apply 'general principles of law derived by the Court from national laws of legal systems of the world'. This is subject to the very important qualification: 'provided that those principles are not inconsistent with this Statute and with international law'. General principles cannot be used to modify or contradict the Statute or existing international law.

1.7 The relationship between international criminal law and other branches of international law

International criminal law may be considered as having a relationship to human rights law and international humanitarian law. Human rights law may be thought of as a body of law guaranteeing the rights of individuals against both their own government and the governments of other States. International humanitarian law (or IHL; also called the law of armed conflict or LOAC) on the other hand applies protective standards to:

- persons engaged either in wartime hostilities or in the occupation of foreign territory;[45] and
- civilians (who are protected against certain acts whether committed by foreign forces or their own governments in wartime).[46]

---

[45] E.g. the prohibition on methods and means of warfare which cause combatants unnecessary suffering, through the law regulating the treatment of prisoners-of-war (POW), and through the minimum standards of treatment applicable to those taking direct part in hostilities who are not entitled to POW status. See further Chapter 8.

[46] That is, civilians enjoy certain protection in all forms of armed conflict, in particular, civilians taking no part in hostilities may not be the deliberate object of attack under the law of targeting. See further Chapter 8.

It is common to suggest that international criminal law 'enforces' human rights law or IHL. This is not correct. Only *certain rules* of human rights law or the law of armed conflict attract individual criminal sanction. Thus, international criminal law does not enforce all of human rights law or even all of IHL, only certain provisions. Nonetheless, when we come to study the law of war crimes we will find that a general knowledge of IHL is relevant to the interpretation and application of the law of war crimes. Similarly, certain crimes against humanity—especially persecution—involve issues of human rights law.

1.8 Summary and conclusions

This chapter has outlined the law governing the creation and interpretation of public international law generally. It is not possible to fully understand international criminal law (and its strengths and weaknesses) without understanding how it is embedded in concepts such as customary international law and the law governing the interpretation and application of treaties. We have also noted the potentially deceptive role that judicial decisions can play in the creation of public international law in general and international criminal law in particular. Where the law is uncertain or unclear, it may fall to judges to clarify the law and in doing so further develop it. There is obviously a fine line to be walked here. For international law to grow into a coherent system capable of delivering justice, it must become sufficiently detailed. National systems of criminal law have had centuries to achieve this and, obviously, remain imperfect. Why should international criminal law not follow a similar path? Nonetheless, there are questions to be raised about the legitimacy of a judicial role in the creation of criminal law. Chief among these is the risk of retroactivity: there is substance to the allegation that when judges discern a rule of customary international law for the first time (or 'clarify' treaty law) and apply it in a given case, they are imposing retrospective standards on the defendant in that case. In national legal systems it would also be, generally speaking, impermissible for judges to create new criminal offences as this is normally a role left to legislatures. Nonetheless, the room for such criticisms may be diminishing as international criminal law becomes an increasingly stable and well-developed body of rules.

We have also noted that international criminal law is in itself a difficult body of law to master. It involves overlapping considerations of general public international law, criminal law theory and doctrine, questions of human rights, and international humanitarian law (the law governing the conduct of hostilities in time of war). It will be difficult to find any judge who is a true expert in all four branches of law, and sometimes it may not be possible to reconcile the competing priorities between these different branches of law. For example, international humanitarian law is strongly concerned with the protection of individuals as potential victims of war crimes. If one purpose of international criminal law is justice for victims we might measure its success in terms of convictions. Criminal law and human rights law, on the other hand, embody strong protections for defendants in criminal trials. Where such fair trial guarantees are respected we might expect to see a reasonable number of acquittals. Acquittals, however, may leave victims disappointed. In later chapters on prosecutions, procedure, and evidence—as well as the chapters dealing with the substantive crimes—we will see how some of these difficulties may play out in practice.

Useful further reading

D AKANDE, 'Sources of International Criminal Law' in A Cassese (ed), *The Oxford Companion to International Criminal Justice* (Oxford University Press 2009), 41–53.
An excellent and concise treatment of the issues covered in this chapter.

R CRYER, 'Introduction: What Is International Criminal Law' in R Cryer, H Friman, D Robinson, and E Wilmshurst, *An Introduction to International Criminal Law and Procedure*, 3rd ed (Cambridge University Press 2014) 8–21.
An account of the sources of international criminal law, paying particular attention to its relationship with (and borrowings from) other distinct bodies of law including international human rights law, the law of armed conflict and national systems of criminal law.

B VAN SCHAACK, '*Crimen Sine Lege*: Judicial Lawmaking at the Intersection of Law and Morals', (2008) 97 Georgetown Law Journal 119.
A lengthier examination of the particular problems of, and need for, judge-made law in international criminal law.

2

Principles of State jurisdiction

2.1 Introduction

This chapter addresses the extent of a State's criminal jurisdiction. Despite the growth of international courts and tribunals in the twentieth and twenty-first century, no international criminal court has jurisdiction over all international crimes wherever committed; all international criminal courts are courts of limited jurisdiction (not to mention limited resources). Thus, in practice, international criminal law will largely rely on prosecutions conducted before national courts, making the extent of national criminal jurisdiction a topic of vital importance.

Jurisdiction is therefore a fundamental issue in international criminal law, and worth considering before turning to other aspects of the subject. Unfortunately, however, it can appear rather complex at first. The difficulty in examining this topic is that lawyers trained in a national system of criminal law may often start from two ideas: first, that a State's criminal law should be essentially territorial; and second, that there should be a clear division of powers and responsibilities between different national legal systems. The reality is much more complex. In this chapter we will begin with basic principles of national jurisdiction based on 'links', then consider universal jurisdiction and its controversies, before finally examining alternative forms of jurisdiction provided by treaties containing an 'extradite or prosecute' obligation.

 Learning aims

By the end of this chapter you should be able to:

- differentiate between prescriptive, enforcement, and adjudicative jurisdiction;
- define the different forms of national jurisdiction based on 'links';
- explain the controversies surrounding and put forward a reasoned opinion as to what approach should be taken to universal jurisdiction;
- differentiate between the approaches taken to universal jurisdiction by different judges of the International Court of Justice; and
- compare universal jurisdiction with the 'quasi-universal' jurisdiction created by certain treaties through 'extradite or prosecute' obligations.

The chapter is structured as follows:

- Section 2.2 introduces the different forms of jurisdiction and some basic distinctions.
- Section 2.3 provides an overview of the theory of national prescriptive jurisdiction based on 'links'.
- Section 2.4 outlines the principle of 'universal jurisdiction to prescribe' and its controversies.
- Section 2.5 looks to treaty-based systems of 'quasi-universal' jurisdiction over international crimes.

2.2 Forms of jurisdiction: basic distinctions

Jurisdiction is commonly described as a State's power under international law to make, apply, and enforce rules of national law governing persons, objects, or events.[1] Jurisdiction is an aspect of State sovereignty, but this does not mean that jurisdiction is invariably or even ordinarily exclusive. As we shall see, jurisdiction is often concurrent and overlapping.[2]

Several essential distinctions must be made at the outset between three forms of jurisdiction:

- jurisdiction to prescribe: being the power to make rules of national criminal law;
- jurisdiction to enforce: being the power to take coercive action to ensure compliance with, or punish breaches of, national criminal law; and
- jurisdiction to adjudicate: being the power of national courts to hear a given case.

The most important distinction is between jurisdiction to prescribe and to enforce. Different rules govern when a State can enact a rule prescribing conduct and when it can enforce that rule. All legal systems to some extent prescribe conduct occurring outside their territory.[3] So we can expect to find rules that acknowledge at least some cases where extra-territorial prescriptive jurisdiction is valid. However, States may generally not enforce their laws (e.g. take police action) in another State's territory absent that State's consent.[4] Thus while extra-territorial prescriptive jurisdiction is allowed in a variety of circumstances, extra-territorial enforcement jurisdiction is generally prohibited (with some exceptions).

Jurisdiction to adjudicate is a term often found in the literature, but it is of limited usefulness. If a State can prescribe conduct, its courts will be competent to hear a case

---

[1] C Staker, 'Jurisdiction' in M Evans (ed), *International Law* 4th ed (Oxford University Press 2014) 309.
[2] Mann claimed that, in fact, in international law 'jurisdiction is almost always concurrent': FA Mann, *Further Studies in International Law* (Oxford University Press 1990) 4.
[3] *Lotus Case* [1927] PCIJ Ser. A No. 10, 4, 19.
[4] Ibid, 18; see also: *Case Concerning the Arrest Warrant of 11 April 2000 (Democratic Republic of the Congo v Belgium)*, [2002] ICJ Rep. 3, 169 at para 49 per Judge ad hoc Van Den Wyngaert (Dissenting Opinion).

based on a breach of that rule. Therefore jurisdiction to adjudicate can be thought of as being coextensive (i.e. covering the same ground) as jurisdiction to prescribe. Alternatively, adjudication can be thought of as part of an enforcement process, in which case it is part of jurisdiction to enforce.

Finally, we need to distinguish between

- civil jurisdiction; and
- criminal jurisdiction.

Civil cases concern the rights and obligations of individuals in cases such as tort, contract, family law, administrative law, etc. Jurisdiction in civil cases generally follows the same principles as criminal jurisdiction. Two points only should be noted. First, some doctrines of jurisdiction (as explained in this chapter) apply only in civil cases and so are of little relevance to international criminal law. Second, private international law regulates certain civil cases that have cross-border facts. Private international law contains certain rules about what law to apply ('choice of law' rules), and whether a given court should hear a case or whether some other forum has a better claim to hear the case (the doctrine of *forum non-conveniens*).[5] This feature of jurisdiction in private international law might imply there is a hierarchy or rule of priority between jurisdictions: that one jurisdiction could or should prevail over another in a given case. While this may be true in private international law to some extent, there is no hierarchy of jurisdictions in the international law of criminal jurisdiction.[6] Prima facie all valid claims to exercise jurisdiction give an equal right to prosecute a given case and no State may demand another State cease or defer a prosecution because it has the 'stronger' jurisdictional claim.

2.3 National prescriptive jurisdiction based on 'links'

The most widely accepted theory of prescriptive jurisdiction emphasizes that there must be some 'link' or 'nexus' between the crime and the prescribing State (we will come to debates about the limits of prescriptive jurisdiction below). This is sometimes called the 'principles of jurisdiction' approach, where each 'principle' of jurisdiction describes a particular type of link between the crime and the prescribing State.[7]

The two most intuitive forms of prescriptive jurisdiction are the territoriality principle and the nationality principle. It seems reasonably obvious that a State should be able to apply its laws to events happening within its territory (even when committed by foreigners), or by its citizens (even when they are in foreign territory). However, which State has prescriptive jurisdiction if an Australian murders a Belgian

---

[5] See e.g.: A Reed, 'Venue Resolution and Forum Non Conveniens: Four Models of Jurisdictional Propriety' (2013) 22 Transnational Law and Contemporary Problems 369.

[6] R O'Keefe, *International Criminal Law* (Oxford University Press 2015) 25–28.

[7] Staker, 'Jurisdiction', 315; J Crawford, *Brownlie's Principles of Public International Law*, 8th ed (Oxford University Press 2012) 457–71.

in Canada? A moment's reflection shows each of Australia, Belgium, and Canada could prescribe the conduct. Even if we limited ourselves to the territoriality principle and the nationality principle multiple States could have jurisdiction over the one act. This makes an obvious point that jurisdiction can be, and may even commonly be, concurrent.

The rest of this section introduces in more detail the 'principles' or 'heads' of prescriptive jurisdiction based on links:

- the territoriality principle;
- the nationality principle;
- the effects principle;
- the protective principle; and
- the principle of jurisdiction over State organs and registered vessels and objects.

2.3.1 The territoriality principle (subjective and objective territoriality)

Under the territoriality principle a State may prescribe conduct committed within its territory as a crime. However, what happens when a crime is committed in more than one territory? In the classic example, a gun fired across a border by A, intentionally killing B, could be a crime in both countries. In such a case the State where the punishable act was commenced is the State of *subjective territoriality*. The State where the crime occurred or was completed is the State of *objective territoriality*. This leads us to the conclusion that a single crime can be committed in more than one territory.[8]

The principles of objective and subjective territoriality are equally valid, and there is no rule of priority between the State of objective or subjective territoriality. Either State can prosecute the crime as a whole.[9]

2.3.2 The nationality principle ('active nationality' and 'passive personality')

The nationality principle may be divided into two further concepts: the active nationality principle (prescriptive jurisdiction based on the nationality of the offender) and the passive personality principle (prescriptive jurisdiction based on the nationality of the victim).

Active nationality

It is quite common for States to extend the operation of their criminal law to cover the conduct of their nationals abroad. In practice, prosecutions only tend to follow in the case of serious offences (such as murder or sexual offences) and some States only use

---

[8] E.g.: Article 3(2), UN Convention against Transnational Organized Crime 2000, 2225 UNTS 209.
[9] E.g.: Lord Diplock in *Treacy v DPP* [1971] AC 537, 561–2; approved in *Libman v The Queen* [1985] 2 SCR 178 (Canada).

the active nationality principle to prescribe certain serious offences.[10] It is hard to say whether this just reflects the difficulty of prosecuting minor offences when all relevant evidence and witnesses are abroad, or a belief among States that they may only exercise extra-territorial prescriptive jurisdiction based on active nationality in the case of serious offences. If the latter, this could be evidence of a customary international law limit to the principle (see Chapter 1). However, the evidence is, at best, ambiguous.

An important question for the purposes of the active nationality principle is: 'Who is a national of the prescribing State?' This is a question that will be answered by reference to national law. That is, a person may acquire nationality, *inter alia*, by 'birth, descent, naturalization' or upon the creation of a new State.[11]

It is sometimes suggested that international law requires a 'genuine link' between a person and the State in which s/he claims nationality. The idea of a 'genuine link' requirement arises from the famous *Nottebohm Case* before the International Court of Justice, where it was found that Mr Nottebohm had no 'genuine link' with Liechtenstein.[12] As a result Liechtenstein could not bring an international claim against Guatemala based on wrongs allegedly done to Mr Nottebohm by Guatemala. At best, this is a special rule applicable in cases concerning disputes *between States* and has no relevance to the law of criminal jurisdiction concerning the *liability of individuals*. Even in the realm of inter-State disputes, the *Nottebohm* principle has seldom been strictly applied.[13] Thus it will generally be sufficient to establish nationality jurisdiction that a person is treated as a national by the prescribing State's internal law.

Passive personality

Jurisdiction under the passive personality principle follows from the nationality of the victim. (It would make more sense to call it 'passive nationality' jurisdiction but 'passive personality' is the accepted term historically.) If A, a citizen of Austria present in Austria murders B, a citizen of Belgium, Belgium could assert jurisdiction over the crime. The principle has been considered controversial and is still not recognized by all national legal systems. The argument against it is that if citizens can take their criminal law with them abroad it introduces an element of uncertainty, even arbitrariness, as to which State(s) can prosecute offences. Indeed, an act which is not a crime locally but which is committed against a foreign national could result in a foreign prosecution; or a criminal act affecting a group of victims of diverse nationalities could engage multiple jurisdictions. Such concerns were apparent in some of the Separate Opinions in the *Lotus Case* before the International Court of Justice in 1927, a case concerning a fatal collision at sea.[14] However, by the time the ICJ heard the *Arrest Warrant (Congo*

---

[10] Examples include: ss 9, 57, Offences Against the Person Act 1861 (UK); s 7, Sexual Offenders Act 1997 (UK); s15, Official Secrets Act 1989 (UK); s 51(2)(b), International Criminal Court Act 2001(UK); and the Crimes (Child Sex Tourism) Act 1994 (Australia).

[11] Art 4, International Law Commission Draft Articles on Diplomatic Protection 2006, UN Doc. A/61/10.

[12] *Nottebohm Case (Guatemala v Liechtenstein)*, 1955 ICJ Reports p. 4.

[13] See further: Staker, 'Jurisdiction', 320; but compare R Cryer, 'Jurisdiction' in R Cryer, H Friman, D Robinson, and E Wilmshurst, *An Introduction to International Criminal Law and Procedure* 3rd ed (Cambridge University Press 2014) 54.

[14] *Lotus Case*, 91–93 per Judge Moore (Dissenting Opinion).

v Belgium) Case in 2002, several judges of the court noted that while the doctrine was once controversial, it now meets little resistance.[15]

Passive personality is now commonly listed as an optional ground for asserting prescriptive jurisdiction in most if not all the terrorism suppression conventions including, for example:

- Art 5(1)(d), Hostage Taking Convention 1979;
- Art 6(2)(b), Convention for the Suppression of Unlawful Acts Against the Safety of Maritime Navigation 1988; and
- Art 6(2)(a), International Convention for the Suppression of Terrorist Bombings 1997.

It is hard to believe these widely-ratified conventions could list as *permissible* a head of jurisdiction *prohibited* by international law. It thus seems likely it is now an established principle of jurisdiction.[16]

2.3.3 **The effects principle**

The effects principle is a controversial doctrine. It is commonly said to grant prescriptive jurisdiction to a State where the 'effects' of a crime are felt. The Permanent Court of Justice in the *Lotus Case* said that crimes:

> the authors of which at the moment of commission are in the territory of another State, are nevertheless to be regarded as having been committed in the [prescribing State's] national territory, if one of the constituent elements of the offence, and more especially its effects, have taken place there.[17]

On this basis a fatal collision between two ships at sea could be treated in the same manner as gunshots fired across a border: acts commenced aboard the French ship had culminated in deaths aboard a Turkish ship, and both flag States could claim jurisdiction.[18] Nonetheless, this quote opens up a difficult distinction between the *elements* of an offence and *'effects'*.[19] Where a constituent element of an offence has taken place in the territory of a State we have objective or subjective territorial jurisdiction as discussed in section 2.3.1. Such elements are often described as involving an 'overt act' such as a bullet (or drugs, or mail) crossing a border. A common definition of the 'pure effects principle' then is that it involves: an assertion of prescriptive jurisdiction over conduct occurring outside a State's territory where that conduct: (1) has effects

---

[15] *Arrest Warrant Case*, 77–78 at para 47 per Judges Higgins, Kooijmans, and Buergenthal (Joint Separate Opinion).

[16] The only alternative is to presume the State parties to these treaties have decided to 'contract' out of the usual limits of jurisdiction and any provisions of national law based on passive nationality could only be asserted against nationals of other State parties.

[17] *Lotus Case*, 23.

[18] The status of ships is discussed further at 2.3.5. The result in the *Lotus Case* was reversed by special treaty rules limiting the number of States that could prosecute in collision cases. See now, for example: Art 97, United Nations Convention on the Law of the Sea 1982.

[19] The idea of an elements approach to crimes is discussed further in Chapter 7.

within that territory; and (2) those effects are *not* accompanied by any 'overt act'.[20] Thus, the literature on criminal jurisdiction distinguishes the effect principle from objective territorial jurisdiction on the basis that the effects principle applies in cases where 'no constituent element of the offence takes place within the territory of the prescribing state.'[21]

Some national systems would consider this definition too narrow and contend that where there are 'effects' within territory, those effects 'localize' a crime such that the territorial State may assert prescriptive jurisdiction. However, if those effects involve some tangible over act, then one is simply describing objective territorial jurisdiction.

Outside of such abstract debates, the most obvious cases of effects jurisdiction have arisen in *civil* cases. That is, the doctrine has been used to assert jurisdiction over anti-competitive trade practices occurring outside of the prescribing State's territory but which have economic impacts within that State's territorial jurisdiction.[22] In the *Arrest Warrant (Congo v Belgium) Case* several judges noted that in this sense the effects principle is a doctrine principally asserted by the US and (in a qualified form) by the EU.[23] The application of the principle in such cases does not concern us for the purposes of international criminal law.

2.3.4 The protective principle

Under the protective principle prescriptive jurisdiction may be asserted by a State in respect of acts threatening its 'fundamental national interests' (including but not limited to matters of national security), even when those acts are committed by foreigners acting abroad.[24] The protective principle is thus a seemingly simple rule, but it is of uncertain scope: the categories of interests protected are not closed. While it has long been recognized that a State has jurisdiction to prescribe counterfeiting national of currency, passports, stamps, or other official documents abroad,[25] it is not obvious what other conduct may be legitimately covered by the principle.

The principle may lend itself to very wide assertions of jurisdiction. For example, Israeli Penal Law amendments of 1972 made it a crime to commit an act abroad which would have been an offence in Israel and 'which harmed or was intended to harm the State of Israel, its security, property or economy or its [international] transport or communication links.' Similarly, the Hungarian Penal Code once provided for jurisdiction

---

[20] RK Gardiner, *International Law* (Pearson 2003) 324–25.

[21] O'Keefe, *International Criminal Law*, 16. The difficulty is, of course, that what counts as an element of an offence is defined by national law and may well involve the effects of a course of conduct: C Ryngaert, *Jurisdiction in International Law* (Oxford University Press 2008) 75.

[22] C Ryngaert, *Jurisdiction in International Law* (Oxford University Press 2008) 76–77.

[23] In cases such as: *US v Alcoa* 148 F.2d 416 (1945); *Timberlane Lumber Co. v Bank of America* 549 F.2d 597 (1976); *ICI v Commission (Dyestuffs case)* (1972) 48 ILR 106; *Ahlstrom v Commission (Wood pulp case)* (1988) 96 ILR 148. See: *Arrest Warrant Case*, 77–78 at para 47 per Judges Higgins, Kooijmans, and Buergenthal (Joint Separate Opinion).

[24] O'Keefe, *International Criminal Law*, 12.

[25] L Henkin, 'International Law: Politics, Values and Functions' 216 Recueil des Cours (1989-IV) 9, 288.

over any act affecting 'a fundamental interest relating to the democratic, political and economic order of the…Republic'.[26] Such expansive and indeterminate claims of jurisdiction are often criticized.

Cases concerning a conspiracy to import drugs are commonly described as involving the assertion of either objective territorial or protective jurisdiction. What would be the correct characterization where drugs have not yet entered the territory? The *Liangsiriprasert* case involved a conspiracy abroad to import drugs into the United States.[27] Mr Liangsiriprasert then entered the territory of Hong Kong to receive payment and the US sought his extradition. In extradition proceedings the question was whether Hong Kong would have jurisdiction on the same basis as the US if Mr Liangsiriprasert had gone to Hong Kong to receive payment. It was held that the payment constituted part of the entire illegal course of conduct and therefore objective territoriality applied.

2.3.5 The principle of jurisdiction over State organs and registered vessels and objects

While it may seem of limited relevance to international criminal law it is important to note a few special cases where a State may have jurisdiction to prescribe. First, in respect of ships and aircraft the State of national registration, the 'flag State', has exclusive jurisdiction over events *on the high seas*. This is a special form of jurisdiction, where jurisdictional competence has been allocated to States to prevent the high seas (and airspace over them) being a lawless area. Examples in treaty law include:

- Art 3, Convention on Offences and certain other Acts Committed on board Aircraft 1963 ('Tokyo Convention');[28] and
- Art 92, UN Convention on the Law of the Sea 1982.[29]

This may have relevance in international criminal law. For example, in 2010 the Israeli Defence Force (IDF) boarded a vessel, the *Mavi Marmara*, on the high seas. The ship had intended to run the Israeli naval blockade of the Gaza strip. In the course of the IDF boarding a number of protestors were killed. The question arose as to whether this might constitute a war crime and whether the flag State of the *Mavi Marmara* (Comoros) could refer the incident to the International Criminal Court as a crime which had occurred within its jurisdiction. The International Criminal Court certainly has jurisdiction over events occurring aboard the flag vessels of member States on the high seas.[30] In the event, however, while Comoros did refer the case to the Court, in 2014 the Office of the Prosecutor declined to open an investigation on the grounds that while 'the information available provides a reasonable basis to believe that war crimes

[26] M Akehurst, 'Jurisdiction in International Law' (1972–3) 46 British Yearbook of International Law 145, 158.
[27] *Liangsiriprasert v United States Government* [1991] 1 AC 225.   [28] 704 UNTS 220.
[29] 1833 UNTS 3.   [30] Art 12(2)(a), ICC Statute.

were committed' aboard the *Mavi Marmara* the situation was not of 'sufficient gravity to justify further action by the Court' under Article 17(1)(d) of the ICC Statute.[31] (The *Mavi Marmara* incident is discussed further in Chapter 5, section 5.3.2.)

This principle does not mean that ships and aircraft are 'floating islands' as they become subject to national criminal jurisdiction once they are within the territory (or territorial airspace or territorial sea) of another State. In such cases there may be concurrent jurisdiction over events on board; both the flag State and territorial State could have valid claims of prescriptive jurisdiction.

States also retain jurisdiction over the conduct of members of their armed services stationed abroad. This is separate from the nationality principle, as not all armed services require their members to be nationals of their State. Commonwealth citizens can serve in the UK armed forces and foreigners may enlist in the US Army. Of course, such personnel will also be subject to the criminal jurisdiction of the territorial State in which they are stationed. Thus if a serviceman or servicewoman commits a crime in a foreign State, both their 'sending State' and the local territorial State could exercise jurisdiction, providing another example of concurrent jurisdiction. Which State will exercise jurisdiction over a given criminal act in such cases is usually regulated by treaty-based rules under Status of Forces Agreements (SOFAs).[32]

2.4 Universal jurisdiction to prescribe

2.4.1 Basic definition and the offences covered

Roger O'Keefe offers the simplest definition of universal jurisdiction to prescribe. According to him universal jurisdiction is simply the assertion of a prescriptive jurisdiction not based on any recognized head or link.[33] It usually therefore describes a State prosecuting conduct committed by a foreigner in a foreign territory which does not have any effects within the prosecuting State's territory or upon its nationals or against its vital interests.

States may only invoke universal jurisdiction to prescribe in respect of a limited number of crimes. The least controversial candidates are:

- piracy;
- war crimes;
- crimes against humanity;

---

[31] ICC Office of the Prosecutor, 'Situation on Registered Vessels of Comoros, Greece and Cambodia: Article 53(1) Report', 6 November 2014, executive summary, para 3, www.icc-cpi.int/iccdocs/otp/OTP-COM-Article_53(1)-Report-06Nov2014Eng.pdf. Article 17, ICC Statute is discussed further in Chapters 4 and 5.

[32] See e.g.: Agreement Between the Parties to the North Atlantic Treaty Regarding the Status of Their Forces 1951, 199 UNTS 67; and D Fleck (ed), *The Handbook of the Law of Visiting Forces* (Oxford University Press 2001).

[33] R O'Keefe, 'Universal Jurisdiction: Clarifying the Basic Concept' (2004) 2 Journal of International Criminal Justice 735.

- genocide; and
- (perhaps) the crime of aggression.[34]

Most scholars and judges would accept that these are *the* clear cases where universal jurisdiction is allowed: most, but not all. Several judges of the ICJ in their separate opinions in the *Arrest Warrant (Congo v Belgium) Case* suggested that piracy is the *only* true case of universal jurisdiction.[35] One might ask how there can be contradictory opinions on so basic a point. The answer is that the State practice is far from uniform and much is equivocal. Anyone looking for clear evidence of State acceptance of universal jurisdiction in treaty law will be disappointed. For example, subject to certain limitations, the Geneva Conventions provide universal jurisdiction over only *some* war crimes. Article 6 of the Genocide Convention famously only mentions the jurisdiction of the territorial State and any competent international court; it does not mention universal jurisdiction at all.[36] Universal jurisdiction over genocide, then, must have arisen as a matter of customary international law. No treaty provides in clear terms for the jurisdiction of *national courts* in cases of crimes against humanity or the crime of aggression. There have been national prosecutions for all of these crimes (except the crime of aggression); however, any prosecutions based on the nationality or territoriality principles provide no evidence of universal jurisdiction.

Nonetheless, the list at the beginning of this section can be treated as a generally agreed statement of the crimes attracting universal jurisdiction. On the basis of this list it is sometimes said that universal jurisdiction exists in respect of crimes that are especially heinous or 'shock the conscience' of humanity. It is hard to see that the crimes underlying piracy (robbery, assault, and kidnapping on the high seas) are morally equivalent to war crimes or genocide. Three views are thus possible. Universal jurisdiction exists over these offences because:

- of their unique heinousness (which results in some authors arguing piracy is not really a universal crime, or acknowledging it only as an historical anomaly); or
- these are all crimes that, even if not all equally shocking, affect the international legal order and so are of interest to all States; or
- these are simply the cases where States have, in effect, agreed universal jurisdiction may be exercised (an argument based on State practice and reflecting a 'positivist' approach to international law).

This diversity of views over the basic issue of which crimes are or should be subject to universal jurisdiction illustrates a vital further point. One cannot assume that because a crime is defined as a *jus cogens* or *erga omnes* norm[37] that it attracts

---

[34] 'Report of the Secretary-General on the Scope and Application of the Principle of Universal Jurisdiction', UN Doc A/65/181 (29 July 2010), paras 27–28.

[35] See the Separate Opinions of President Guillaume and Judge Ranjeva in the *Arrest Warrant Case*.

[36] Convention on the Prevention and Punishment of the Crime of Genocide 1948, 78 UNTS 277.

[37] *Erga omnes* obligations are those owed to the whole international community. Thus, if a State breaches an *erga omnes* norm all other States may protest that breach irrespective of whether it affects them. All *jus cogens* norms are also binding *erga omnes*; but not every *erga omnes* norm is necessarily *jus cogens*.

universal jurisdiction. More controversial candidates for universal jurisdiction thus include:

- slavery or the slave trade (when not committed as part of a crime against humanity);
- torture (when not committed as part of a crime against humanity or war crime); and
- 'terrorism' (whatever that term may legally mean).

There are certainly academics who would contend that some or all of these three examples are clear cases where universal jurisdiction is allowed. National courts, however, tend to require clear proof that such jurisdiction has been accepted by other national courts or legislatures. For example, while several treaties provide for some form of universal jurisdiction over piracy, all the nineteenth and twentieth century treaties covering the slave trade by sea appeared to leave prosecution in the hands of the ship's flag State.[38] This raises some doubt as to whether States have ever accepted universal jurisdiction over slavery. Several judges in the *Pinochet Cases* doubted there was universal jurisdiction over torture outside the Convention Against Torture.[39] This is not to suggest that there is not or should not be universal jurisdiction over slavery and torture, only that such jurisdiction is not as clearly established as some writers would contend.

2.4.2 **Is universal jurisdiction permissive or mandatory?**

It is sometimes suggested that because universal jurisdiction exists in respect of an offence, States are obliged to prosecute those suspected of the crime in question. If this were so, most States in the world would be continually in breach of such an obligation. That is, if all States were obliged to prosecute all crimes of universal jurisdiction we would expect all court systems in the world to be dealing with such prosecutions all the time. Manifestly, this does not happen. This is strong evidence that universal jurisdiction is generally permissive not mandatory: States have the power to prosecute, but not a duty to do so.

This general position must be subject to two qualifications. First, some rules of international criminal law may require prosecution where a suspect is found within the territory of a State. Such rules are usually found in treaty provisions (discussed further at 2.5). Second, it is sometimes suggested that universal jurisdiction is limited or conditional—that the power to prosecute universal jurisdiction offences only arises when a suspect is within a State's territory. This is discussed in section 2.4.3 as the debate between conditional and unconditional approaches to universal jurisdiction.

---

[38] RR Churchill and AV Lowe, *The Law of the Sea*, 3rd ed (Manchester University Press 1999) 212.
[39] See *Ex Parte Pinochet Ugarte (No. 3)* [2000] 1 AC 147, 204–205 per Lord Browne-Wilkinson; *Ex Parte Pinochet Ugarte (No. 1)* [2000] 1 AC 61, 79 per Lord Slynn.

2.4.3 Is universal jurisdiction conditional or unconditional?

We have arrived at the position where we can say that universal jurisdiction is only available for a limited range of crimes and is (most likely) permissive rather than mandatory in nature. The next question is whether there are limits on when States may invoke the principle and commence a prosecution.

The basic debate is between conditional and unconditional approaches. In simple terms, advocates of conditional universal jurisdiction suggest a prosecution may *only be* commenced when the suspect is already present within the territory of the prosecuting State. That is, universal jurisdiction is conditional upon presence. Advocates of unconditional universal jurisdiction argue that all States may commence investigations, issue arrest warrants, and seek the extradition of persons suspected of crimes subject to universal jurisdiction, wherever those suspects are in the world. Few advocates of unconditional universal jurisdiction would suggest a trial should commence without the suspect being present (trial *in absentia*), and there are *no* cases where a trial based on universal jurisdiction has proceeded to examine evidence, hear argument, and rule on guilt or innocence in the absence of the accused. Despite this, authors and judges commonly—and confusingly—refer to unconditional universal jurisdiction as 'universal jurisdiction *in absentia*'. In any event, it is far from clear that a trial *in absentia* for a crime of universal jurisdiction would be prohibited by international law.[40] The debate is often conducted using a bewildering variety of terms. Table 2.1 summarizes the terms of roughly equivalent meaning:

Table 2.1 Approaches to universal jurisdiction

Restrictive approaches may be called…	**Broad approaches** may be called…
• conditional universal jurisdiction	• unconditional universal jurisdiction
• universal jurisdiction with presence	• universal jurisdiction *in absentia*
	• pure universal jurisdiction
	• universal jurisdiction 'properly so called'

The major argument for conditional universal jurisdiction is that absent some limiting rule there will be judicial chaos, or that suspects could be hounded through the courts of many States for purely political reasons.[41] Whether such criticisms are realistic will be returned to below.

It is sometimes suggested that advocates of conditional universal jurisdiction have misunderstood or confused the distinction between prescription and enforcement.[42]

---

[40] *Arrest Warrant Case*, 80–81 at paras 56–59 per Judges Higgins, Kooijmans, and Buergenthal (Joint Separate Opinion).

[41] See, for example: H Kissinger, 'The Pitfalls of Universal Jurisdiction', *Foreign Affairs*, July/August 2001, www.globalpolicy.org/component/content/article/163/28174.html.

[42] O'Keefe, 'Universal Jurisdiction', 756; *Arrest Warrant Case*, 169 at para 49 per Judge ad hoc Van Den Wyngaert (Dissenting Opinion).

As noted above and further discussed below, the power of States to enforce their own law is (unless an exception applies) strictly limited to their own territory. However, States are free to prescribe extra-territorial conduct on a range of bases including universal jurisdiction. If a national of Austria is murdered by a national of Bolivia in Bolivia, Austria may obviously open a case, commence an investigation and request that Bolivia extradite the murderer to face trial in Austria. Bolivia may or may not grant extradition according to its laws and treaties in force, but it would be unlikely to suggest that an extradition request was an attempt to enforce the law of Austria in the territory of Bolivia. Nothing makes it illegal for Austria to seek the cooperation of territorial Bolivia to secure the presence of the offender before Austria's courts. Nonetheless, many critics of unconditional universal jurisdiction appear to assert exactly this: that commencing extradition proceedings in respect of universal jurisdiction crimes is somehow an unacceptable interference in other State's internal affairs and an attempt to enforce foreign law within another State's territory. Much of the discussion in the *Arrest Warrant* case before the International Court of Justice seems to involve such a confusion. The case concerned a Belgian arrest warrant circulated through Interpol naming the Congolese Foreign Minister, Mr Yerodia, as being suspected of crimes against humanity. For example, Judge Rezek appeared to suggest that the Belgian arrest warrant was an 'activist intervention' and involved seeking out a suspect 'on another State's territory'.[43] However, the 'international arrest warrant' certainly did not constitute an order by Belgium to all States receiving it that they must arrest Mr Yerodia if he entered their territory. Judge Oda put the point bluntly:

> It bears stressing that the issuance of an arrest warrant by one State and the international circulation of the warrant through Interpol have no legal impact unless the arrest request is validated by the receiving State. The Congo appears to have failed to grasp that the mere issuance and international circulation of an arrest warrant have little significance.[44]

That is, an Interpol-circulated arrest warrant is only a *request* for a State to take action. Any action can only be taken by the State receiving the request under its own national law. Such an act would therefore in no way be an act of Belgian jurisdiction. Judge ad hoc Van Den Wyngaert further explained the point that Interpol arrest warrants have no automatic effect:

> Red Notices are issued by Interpol on the request of a State which wishes to have the person named in the warrant provisionally arrested in a third State for the purposes of extradition. Not all States, however, give this effect to an Interpol Red Notice.[45]

The point to take away from these quotes is that seeking a person's extradition *cannot* amount to an impermissible exercise of enforcement jurisdiction in the State receiving an arrest warrant. It is at most a *request* that a person be arrested.

---

[43] *Arrest Warrant Case*, 93 at para 6 per Judge Rezek (Separate Opinion).
[44] Ibid, 52 at para 13 per Judge Oda (Dissenting Opinion).
[45] Ibid, 181 at para 78 per Judge ad hoc Van Den Wyngaert (Dissenting Opinion) and see also para 2.

→← Counterpoint

Even supporters of broad approaches to universal jurisdiction, however, have sometimes proposed that the principle should be limited in its application. In the *Arrest Warrant Case*, Judges Higgins, Kooijmans, and Buergenthal suggested in their Joint Separate Opinion that any exercise of universal jurisdiction:

- should be preceded by an offer to the territorial State that it prosecute the case;
- initiated only by an independent prosecutorial authority, free of government influence; and
- require some special circumstance warranting the commencement of proceedings in the State in question, such as a complaint laid by victims.[46]

The judges, however, cited no case law or State practice supporting such limitations. Ward Ferdinandusse makes three points in response to these and similar suggestions:

- that territorial States only adequately punish international crimes committed by foreign powers or past governments and will usually shelter those in power or allied to the present governments from prosecution;
- therefore, formulating restrictions on universal jurisdiction only hampers the prosecution of crimes otherwise likely to go unpunished; indeed, universal jurisdiction is unlikely to result in judicial chaos given that courts are generally *inactive* in prosecuting such crimes; and
- there is a risk that setting rules of priority (i.e. there must always be an offer made to allow the territorial State that it should prosecute the case before any other State can commence a universal jurisdiction prosecution) would allow States 'to claim ownership over international crimes committed on their territory' and suggest that ideas such as 'sovereignty and non-intervention' can veto international prosecutions permitted (or even required) by international law.[47]

It should be noted, though, that the trial of complex cases is unlikely to succeed in a foreign jurisdiction without the cooperation of the territorial State, due to the location of witnesses and evidence.

Universal jurisdiction is destined to remain controversial, precisely because those in a position to commit international crimes are likely to be agents of the State and to enjoy its protection. Many or most prosecutions based on universal jurisdiction will thus have an inherently political aspect: they will involve prosecuting past or present heads of government, ministers, senior officials, or military leaders.[48] Many States and individuals will thus claim that third-State prosecution of universal jurisdiction crimes

---

[46] *Arrest Warrant Case*, 81 at paras 59 per Judges Higgins, Kooijmans, and Buergenthal (Joint Separate Opinion).

[47] W Ferdinandusse, 'The Interaction of National and International Approaches in the Repression of International Crimes' (2004) 15 European Journal of International Law 1041, 1049–50.

[48] See further: M Langer, 'The Diplomacy of Universal Jurisdiction: The Political Branches and the Transnational Prosecution of International Crimes' (2011) 105 American Journal of International Law 1.

constitutes interference in national politics or internal affairs. Such political pressure can result in severe diplomatic embarrassment for States which exercise universal jurisdiction. Indeed, States are generally unwilling to conduct universal jurisdiction prosecutions unless there is fairly clear evidence that the international community has already concluded certain groups merit international prosecution (e.g. there is generally little international protest at the prosecution of those accused of participating in the Rwandan genocide or in war crimes in the former Yugoslavia before foreign courts).[49]

As noted, the *Arrest Warrant (Belgium v Congo) Case* involved a prosecution commenced under a Belgian law of the then foreign minister of the Congo. Originally, this law allowed prosecutions to be initiated by the complaints of private individuals. This led to a politically and diplomatically embarrassing situation: dozens of cases, which had no prospect of success, being commenced in Belgian courts against foreign heads of State and senior officials. Complaints were laid in Belgium against a variety of leaders including Saddam Hussein, Fidel Castro, Paul Kagame, Yasser Arafat, Ariel Sharon, George Bush Senior, and others.[50] The serving US defence minister, Donald Rumsfeld, threatened that US officials would have to stop attending meetings at the NATO headquarters in Belgium unless the law was changed.[51] In 2003 the relevant Belgian law was amended to prevent the laying of complaints by private petitioners in cases lacking a link to Belgium and to vest control of such prosecutions in the Belgian Federal Prosecutor, creating a degree of executive oversight.[52] Belgian courts terminated several proceedings as a result. In similar developments elsewhere, the Spanish Constitutional Court found in 2005 in the *Guatemalan Generals Case* that Spanish courts had unconditional universal jurisdiction over certain international crimes; concerned by the implications, the Spanish legislature amended the law in 2009 to require some link between cases being brought in Spain and Spain.[53] However, focussing on these examples overly closely might suggest State practice is moving in an increasingly conditional or restrictive direction. Numerous States still have legislation that appears to support unconditional universal jurisdiction in principle,[54] but prosecutions under such legislation in practice seem either rare or non-existent.[55] While the importance of universal jurisdiction as a principle does not seem controversial among States, its scope, the conditions for its exercise (if any), and its relationship to the question of the immunities from foreign criminal jurisdiction enjoyed by State officials remain controversial.[56] The question of immunities is discussed in Chapter 14.

[49] Ibid.
[50] S Ratner, 'Belgium's War Crimes Statute: A Postmortem' (2003) 97 American Journal of International Law 888, 890.
[51] Ibid, 891.   [52] Ibid, 890.
[53] See: N Roht-Arriaza, 'Guatemala Genocide Case (Spanish Constitutional Tribunal decision on universal jurisdiction over genocide claims)' (2006) 100 American Journal of International Law 207–213.
[54] R Cryer, 'Jurisdiction' in Cryer et al, *Introduction*, 64–65.
[55] Langer, 'The Diplomacy of Universal Jurisdiction'.
[56] See the discussion at meetings of the UN General Assembly Sixth Committee (which deals with legal affairs) as recorded in UN Docs A/C.6/68/SR.12, 13, 14, 23, 28, and 29 (2013) and summarized at www.un.org/en/ga/sixth/68/UnivJur.shtml.

Pause for reflection

What approach did each judge (or group of judges) take towards universal jurisdiction in the *Arrest Warrant Case* before the International Court of Justice?

If we examine the Separate and Dissenting Opinions in the case (readily available on the ICJ website) we can observe the following.

President Guillaume holds that the only true example of universal jurisdiction is piracy. He also refers to 'subsidiary universal jurisdiction' arising under treaties—which is the same as the quasi-universal jurisdiction described at 2.5. He holds against unconditional universal jurisdiction as he can find no example, even after reviewing some national laws and cases, where States have asserted a right to prosecute crimes lacking any link to their State and in the absence of the accused from their territory. He expresses concern that prosecutions on such a basis would result in 'judicial chaos'.

Judge Rezek appears to consider that universal jurisdiction is available for war crimes, but only with the territorial presence of the accused (conditional universal jurisdiction).

Judge Ranjeva also holds that piracy is 'the sole...example where universal jurisdiction exists under customary law'.

Judge Koroma adopts the broad view that 'today, together with piracy, universal jurisdiction is available for certain crimes, such as war crimes and crimes against humanity, including the slave trade and genocide' but does not discuss whether he supports conditional or unconditional universal jurisdiction.

Judges Higgins, Kooijmans, and Buergenthal support *unconditional* universal jurisdiction for war crimes and crimes against humanity, but would subject it to the limitations discussed above.

Judge ad hoc Van Den Wyngaert, concludes that there is *unconditional* universal jurisdiction for war crimes and crimes against humanity. She notes that the fact that States seldom assert unconditional universal jurisdiction is not proof that they consider such jurisdiction to be *prohibited* by international law. Rather, this 'negative practice' may be explained by a range of factors, including practicalities and political convenience.

Judge ad hoc Bula-Bula appears to consider universal jurisdiction as limited to crimes under the Geneva Conventions and 'certain historical curiosities' (i.e. piracy).

2.5 Treaty-based systems of 'quasi-universal' jurisdiction

As we have seen, the customary international law of universal jurisdiction has proved controversial because it:

- lacks any rules of priority or hierarchy of jurisdictions (there is, for example, no requirement that a State may only exercise universal jurisdiction if the territorial State where the offence was committed is unwilling to prosecute); and
- may allow criminal proceedings to be commenced, such as opening an investigation or making extradition requests, when the accused is not present in the

investigating State's territory (although some advocates of conditional universal jurisdiction would contend this is *not* allowed).

These criticisms are clearly overstated. 'Ordinary' principles of jurisdiction (such as passive nationality) do not require a rule of priority and may allow proceedings to be commenced against accused persons who are outside a State's territory. This occurs without creating judicial chaos. Indeed, universal jurisdiction may be criticized as not going far enough: because it is generally permissive and not mandatory it embodies no obligation to prosecute those suspected of what are often heinous crimes. This arguably results in too few universal jurisdiction prosecutions taking place.[57]

One might thus ask whether a system of rules establishing duties to prosecute and some form of a hierarchy of jurisdiction would not be more useful than universal jurisdiction under customary international law. Such a system has in fact been established under a number of treaties, in particular in the Convention Against Torture and various 'terrorism' suppression conventions as well as—in a less elaborate form—in the common provisions of the Geneva Conventions relating to 'grave breaches' of those conventions.

 Example

The 1949 Geneva Conventions

The four Geneva Conventions of 1949 all contain a common, identical provision on 'grave breaches'.[58] That is, while a great range of conduct is prohibited under the Conventions, only a small group of especially serious acts including acts such as wilful killing, torture, or inhuman treatment of civilians or military personnel *hors de combat* were originally criminalized (these crimes are discussed further in Chapter 8). In respect of such grave breaches, the Geneva Conventions provide:

- parties must implement the 'grave breaches' as crimes in national law; and
- each party is under an 'obligation to search for persons alleged to have committed, or to have ordered to be committed, such grave breaches, and shall bring such persons, regardless of their nationality, before its own courts'; although,
- it can also 'hand such persons over for trial to another' State party provided that State 'has made out a prima facie case'.

This clearly creates an absolute obligation upon State parties to seek out suspected offenders on their territory and either: to bring them before its courts; or to hand them over to a State willing to prosecute them.

---

[57] For a survey of actual universal jurisdiction prosecutions see Langer, 'The Diplomacy of Universal Jurisdiction', 8 (identifying 1,051 universal jurisdiction criminal complaints and 32 actual trials in the period 1961–2010).

[58] Art 49, Geneva Convention I; Art 50, Geneva Convention II; Art 129, Geneva Convention III; and Art 146, Geneva Convention IV.

The obvious disadvantage of such an approach is that treaties are binding only on their parties. Therefore any treaty-based system of jurisdiction will not have universal coverage unless every State in the world is a party to the relevant treaty. The Geneva Conventions do in fact have universal membership, but this is relatively rare.

How do treaties of this type work? The treaties generally require State parties to assert criminal jurisdiction over certain defined conduct and then also to investigate and prosecute 'those crimes if they [were] committed by a person found within its territory whom the State does not extradite to another State party having jurisdiction over the crime.'[59] The result is that 'a kind of treaty-based universal jurisdiction is established between the parties.'[60] Thus the treaties have several elements:

- they define certain crimes which parties must make offences under national law;

- in this regard they expressly require States to exercise certain heads of prescriptive jurisdiction (so the offence is prescribed throughout all their territory, when committed by any of their nationals, or one of its ships, etc); and, very importantly,

- the parties to the convention agree that: (a) if a person suspected of an offence under the Convention is within the territory of a State party; and (b) that party does not extradite the suspect to face trial before the courts of another party; then (c) the State in which the suspect is present *must* submit the case to its competent national authorities for the purpose of prosecution; and (d) that State *must* in addition have enacted a law enabling it to assert jurisdiction even if the offence lacks any ordinary link to that State (generally referred to as an 'extradite or prosecute' obligation).

The most common form of such treaties are the 'suppression conventions' sometimes inaccurately called 'terrorism suppression conventions'. These treaties were negotiated to deal with the threat posed to the international community by various crimes associated with terrorism, such as aircraft hijacking. Given the absence of agreement within the UN system on a single universal definition of terrorism, it was easier to conclude 'thematic' (i.e. issue-specific) treaties which criminalized certain acts or tactics associated with terrorism rather than negotiate a single 'universal' terrorism convention. Many of the resulting treaties criminalize particular acts without any requirement of a special 'terrorist' motive. Thus the offences envisaged could equally apply to non-politically motivated crimes. The term 'terrorism suppression convention' can therefore be misleading,[61] and it is better to refer to them as 'suppression conventions' as their aim is to suppress certain defined conduct.

---

[59] V Lowe, *International Law* (Oxford University Press 2007) 180.   [60] Ibid.

[61] Unless one believes, contrary to the rules of treaty interpretation, that a special terrorist motive must be read into every such treaty because of their underlying historical origins. This belief that it is only 'appropriate' to use the suppression conventions in cases of terrorism (whatever that term is taken to mean) is curiously widespread among diplomats and even some international lawyers.

 **Example**

The suppression conventions

In the absence of a single universal definition of terrorism in the period 1963 to 2005 the following treaties were concluded:[62]

- Convention on Offences and Certain Other Acts Committed On Board Aircraft 1963 (The Tokyo Convention);
- Convention for the Suppression of Unlawful Seizure of Aircraft 1970 (Unlawful Seizure Convention or Hague Convention);
- Convention for the Suppression of Unlawful Acts against the Safety of Civil Aviation 1971 (The Montreal Convention);
- Convention on the Prevention and Punishment of Crimes Against Internationally Protected Persons 1973 (Internationally Protected Persons Convention);
- International Convention against the Taking of Hostages 1979 (Hostages Convention);
- Convention on the Physical Protection of Nuclear Material 1980 (Nuclear Materials Convention);
- Protocol for the Suppression of Unlawful Acts of Violence at Airports Serving International Civil Aviation, supplementary to the Convention for the Suppression of Unlawful Acts against the Safety of Civil Aviation 1988 (The Airport Protocol, extending the Montreal Convention);
- Convention for the Suppression of Unlawful Acts against the Safety of Maritime Navigation 1988 (SUA Convention);
- Protocol to the Convention for the Suppression of Unlawful Acts against the Safety of Maritime Navigation 2005;
- Protocol for the Suppression of Unlawful Acts Against the Safety of Fixed Platforms Located on the Continental Shelf 1988;
- Protocol to the Protocol for the Suppression of Unlawful Acts against the Safety of Fixed Platforms Located on the Continental Shelf 2005;
- Convention on the Marking of Plastic Explosives for the Purpose of Detection 1991 (Plastic Explosives Convention);
- International Convention for the Suppression of Terrorist Bombings 1997 (Terrorist Bombing Convention);
- International Convention for the Suppression of the Financing of Terrorism 1999 (Terrorist Financing Convention);
- International Convention for the Suppression of Acts of Nuclear Terrorism 2005 (Nuclear Terrorism Convention);
- Convention on the Suppression of Unlawful Acts Relating to International Civil Aviation 2010.

---

[62] Most of the treaty texts are available at www.un.org/en/terrorism/instruments.shtml.

As regards the covered crimes, the suppression conventions often do not provide for the material and mental elements of the crimes (*actus reus* and *mens rea*) in any great detail and leave these to be further defined in national law.[63] This is the obvious consequence of treaties that have to be negotiated by consensus and flexible enough to be implemented in a variety of national legal systems.

All of these conventions contain an 'extradite or prosecute' obligation, with the exception of the 1963 Tokyo Convention and the 1991 Plastic Explosives Convention. Most tend to follow the formula first used in Article 7 of the 1970 Unlawful Seizure Convention concluded in The Hague, and therefore sometimes referred to as the 'Hague model'.[64] Despite the common term 'extradite or prosecute', the Hague model jurisdictional clause is not contingent on an extradition request being made and denied first; indeed, the purpose of the Hague model was to avoid gaps arising where a suspect might be found in a State party's territory and nonetheless *not* have their case submitted to prosecutors.

The consequence of this approach is that, under such a treaty, a State could conduct a prosecution where it lacked any ordinary link to the relevant crime. This is *exactly* O'Keefe's definition of universal jurisdiction—asserting jurisdiction in the absence of an ordinary link. However, this power arises only under the treaty and as among parties to the treaty: while there does not need to be an ordinary link to the prosecuting State, there does need to be such a link to at least one party to the treaty. It is as if the parties have granted permission to each other to exercise jurisdiction on each other's behalf, thus sharing or pooling their jurisdictional powers. It thus creates within a limited patchwork of States a system closely resembling universal jurisdiction, with the addition of an extradite or prosecute obligation making prosecution *mandatory*. Thus this form of jurisdiction is commonly called 'quasi-universal' or 'treaty-based' jurisdiction.[65] Strictly, it is not an independent form of jurisdiction at all but rather a use of treaty law to coordinate member States' existing jurisdictional powers.[66]

While it is acceptable to refer to these treaty obligations as creating an obligation to 'extradite or prosecute' it is important to note that the obligation is not usually expressed in treaties as an absolute obligation to prosecute, but rather one to submit the case without delay to the competent national authorities for the purpose of prosecution, in accordance with the laws of that State. Thus the obligation is only to submit the case to prosecutors for consideration in accordance with normal procedures. A strict obligation to prosecute would not be compatible with prosecutorial independence. The rule is also sometimes referred to by the Latin phrase *aut dedere aut judicare*, meaning 'either hand over [i.e. extradite] or give judgment [i.e. prosecute]'.

While we have noted above that the 'Hague formula' does not require an extradition request before a State's duty to investigate and prosecute is triggered, there is in fact no general rule: it depends on the precise wording of the treaty. Some treaties impose a duty to extradite those suspected of a crime under the treaty with an

---

[63] See e.g. Article 1, Hostages Convention or Article 3, SUA Convention.

[64] C Kreß, 'Universal Jurisdiction over International Crimes and the Institut de Droit International' (2006) 4 Journal of International Criminal Justice 561, 567–8.

[65] J Crawford, *Brownlie's Principles of Public International Law* 8th ed (Oxford University Press 2012) 469.

[66] O'Keefe, *International Criminal Law*, 319.

obligation to prosecute only arising if extradition is refused. Others impose a duty to prosecute but provide for extradition as an alternative. The first type obviously favours extradition; the second obviously favours prosecution in the State where the suspect is found. Most treaties containing an extradite or prosecute obligation concluded after 1970 follow the second approach,[67] including most of the numerous 'terrorism' or 'hijacking' conventions listed in the 'Example' above. In the end, however, we can only understand how such provisions work through close scrutiny of a particular convention. We shall use the Convention Against Torture (CAT), because of the importance of torture to our understanding of crimes against humanity and war crimes later in this volume.

 Example

The Convention Against Torture

Article 1 of the Convention[68] defines the crime of torture:

torture means any act by which severe pain or suffering, whether physical or mental, is intentionally inflicted on a person for such purposes as obtaining from him or a third person information or a confession, punishing him for an act he or a third person has committed or is suspected of having committed, or intimidating or coercing him or a third person, or for any reason based on discrimination of any kind, when such pain or suffering is inflicted by or at the instigation of or with the consent or acquiescence of a public official or other person acting in an official capacity.

Article 4 requires parties to make torture a crime in national law and Article 5 requires that State parties assert jurisdiction over the offence when committed on their territory (or ships or aircraft) or by their nationals.

Article 6 requires that if a territorial State has information that 'a person alleged to have committed any offence' under the Convention is in its territory then it must:

- first, take that person into custody (if 'the circumstances so warrant'), and 'immediately notify' other States having jurisdiction under the Convention;
- second, 'make a preliminary inquiry into the facts'; and
- third, the territorial State must, after concluding its preliminary investigation, indicate to the other States having jurisdiction 'whether it intends to exercise jurisdiction'.

Article 7(1) provides:

The State Party in the territory under whose jurisdiction a person alleged to have committed [torture] is found, shall in … cases [where any other party to the Convention would have jurisdiction], if it does not extradite him, submit the case to its competent authorities for the purpose of prosecution.

---

[67] See: 'The obligation to extradite or prosecute (*aut dedere aut judicare*): Final Report of the International Law Commission' (2014) para 11. Available via: http://legal.un.org/ilc/guide/7_6.shtml.

[68] Convention against Torture and Other Cruel, Inhuman or Degrading Treatment or Punishment 1984, 1465 UNTS 85.

The important features to note from the CAT are:

- The crime of torture has three elements: (1) severe pain or suffering; (2) inflicted for a prohibited purpose listed in the definition;[69] (3) inflicted by or with the involvement of a public official;
- the Convention makes it clear that the territorial State has an immediate duty to begin an investigation and must then make a decision whether it intends to submit the case for prosecution (Article 6); and
- the only way for a State party to escape the duty to submit the case to its own authorities is to extradite the suspect to another State willing to exercise jurisdiction (Article 7).

Based on a close reading it would seem unsustainable to suggest that under the CAT at least a State party has no power to commence a prosecution until an extradition request is made. What is created is really an 'investigate, then either submit for prosecution or extradition' obligation rather than a strict, sequential duty to either 'extradite or prosecute'. While this framework is closely followed in most of the suppression conventions, and while the Geneva Conventions make a *similar* provision covering at least *some* war crimes, we should note that there is *not* generally an extradite or prosecute obligation covering the other major international crimes. For example, there are no relevant treaty provisions covering crimes against humanity or aggression. The Genocide Convention has a unique jurisdictional regime.

 Example

The Convention on the Prevention and Punishment of the Crime of Genocide 1948

The Convention[70] relevantly provides as follows:

Article 1: 'The Contracting Parties confirm that genocide, whether committed in time of peace or in time of war, is a crime under international law which they undertake to prevent and to punish.'

Article 5: 'The Contracting Parties undertake to enact, in accordance with their respective Constitutions, the necessary legislation to give effect to the provisions of the present Convention, and, in particular, to provide effective penalties for persons guilty of genocide...'

Article 6: 'Persons charged with genocide...shall be tried by a competent tribunal of the State in the territory of which the act was committed, or by such international penal tribunal as may have jurisdiction with respect to those Contracting Parties which shall have accepted its jurisdiction.'

Article 7: 'Genocide...shall not be considered as [a] political crime[] for the purpose of extradition. The Contracting Parties pledge themselves in such cases to grant extradition in accordance with their laws and treaties in force.'

---

[69] Or possibly for similar purposes as the list begins 'such as...'.   [70] 78 UNTS 277.

The key features of the jurisdictional regime created by the Genocide Convention to note are as follows:

- State parties are under an obligation to punish genocide (Article 1), and to have adequate national laws with 'effective penalties' to that end (Article 5);
- Article 6 refers *only* to the jurisdiction of the territorial State or an international court; this might be taken to exclude other 'ordinary' bases of jurisdiction (active or passive nationality) or even 'universal jurisdiction';
- nonetheless, we should remember that genocide is also a rule of *jus cogens* and customary law, and subsequent State practice has shown that at general international law universal jurisdiction does exist for genocide;[71]
- the Convention imposes no strict duty to extradite a person suspected of genocide to a State seeking to prosecute them, only an undertaking 'to grant extradition in accordance with their laws and treaties in force' (Article 7).

The reference to 'political crimes' in the Convention is something of an anachronism. It refers to an increasingly defunct concept in extradition law, that of 'political offences'. This originally existed to cover crimes which were purely or inherently political (such as sedition and treason) and in some cases to cover violent revolutionary acts aimed at changing structures of government in a State. The latter reflected the values of a time which took a rather more romantic view of civil war and often applied a rather more generous concept of political asylum than the present age.

Having surveyed the treaty law we are in a position to ask: how effective are these international arrangements for the prosecution or extradition of those accused of offences under international treaty law? Despite the variations in their approach and drafting, one might expect that such treaty obligations would function much better than universal jurisdiction under customary international law in securing the prosecution of persons suspected of international crimes. For example, in 2015 there were 158 States parties to the Convention against Torture. Unfortunately, prosecution under this and other such conventions remains relatively rare. It is instructive to consider the ICJ proceedings in the Hissène Habré case, *Questions relating to the Obligation to Prosecute or Extradite (Belgium v Senegal)*. Hissène Habré, the former dictator of Chad, is widely accused of torture. He had been living in Senegal for some years. Belgium had requested his extradition under the CAT. Senegal appeared reluctant to see a former African head of State tried before the courts of a former colonial power. It refused Belgium's request, but did not commence a prosecution either—claiming it could not afford to conduct such a complex trial.[72] Belgium argues that if Senegal could not prosecute, it

---

[71] One could also consider this subsequent State practice under the treaty reflecting States' support for a non-exhaustive interpretation of Article 6. See Article 31(3)(b) of the Vienna Convention on the Law of Treaties and the discussion in Chapter 1.

[72] *Questions relating to the Obligation to Prosecute or Extradite (Belgium v Senegal)* (2012) ICJ Reports 422, 437 at para 33 and 460 at para 112.

must extradite under the CAT. The ICJ held in *Questions relating to the Obligation to Prosecute or Extradite* that under the CAT:

- there is an obligation to give the Convention effect in national law and especially to take necessary steps to establish jurisdiction under the Convention;
- Article 7 established an obligation 'to submit the case to its competent authorities for the purpose of prosecution' regardless of whether there has been a prior extradition request; however, extraditing a suspect will relieve the State of this obligation; and
- when a suspect is present within its territory a State party must commence an investigation within a 'reasonable time'.[73]

The ICJ thus found that Senegal had violated its obligations under the Convention 'by failing to make immediately a preliminary inquiry' into the allegations against Mr Habré and had either to submit the case 'without further delay' to its competent authorities or extradite him.[74] Senegal, in cooperation with the Economic Community of West African States (ECOWAS), subsequently established the Extraordinary African Chambers in Senegal to consider crimes committed in Chad in the period 1982–1990. While established under national law in Senegal, the Extraordinary Chambers will be assisted by, and include judges from, other African States. Mr Habré has now been charged before the Extraordinary Chambers. Nonetheless it is open for us to ask whether 'extradite or prosecute' treaties are in practice any better than universal jurisdiction under customary international law if a State can simply ignore its treaty law obligations until pressure is brought to bear through international litigation.

2.6 Summary and conclusions

This chapter has outlined the law governing national jurisdiction to prosecute international crimes. It remains important as, given the limited resources of international courts, most international crimes—if they are prosecuted anywhere—will be prosecuted before international courts. It has outlined the formal law involved and also some of the theoretical and practical difficulties in its application. In particular it:

- began by differentiating between prescriptive, enforcement, and adjudicative jurisdiction; making the important point that States often *prescribe* extra-territorial conduct but their jurisdiction to *enforce* their criminal law is usually strictly territorial;
- outlined the different forms of national jurisdiction based on 'links' (including active and passive nationality jurisdiction and objective and subjective territorial

---

[73] Ibid, 451–2 at paras 74–77, 458 at para 102 and 460 at para 114.   [74] Ibid, 462–3 at para 122.

jurisdiction); it further noted that even the application of these basic principles will often result in multiple States have *concurrent* jurisdiction over the one offence and there are no rules of priority governing such a situation;

- examined the controversies surrounding universal jurisdiction (noting that such jurisdiction is most clearly available in cases of piracy, war crimes, crimes against humanity and genocide) and in particular whether there are any special conditions which must be met before a universal jurisdiction case can be initiated (such as the territorial presence of the suspect);

- contrasted universal jurisdiction with the obligation to 'extradite or prosecute' which arises under certain treaties and which may be said to create a kind of treaty-based universal jurisdiction among the parties; and

- gave close attention to the Convention Against Torture as an example of an 'extradite or prosecute' obligation and how it might work in practice.

You should now be in a position to reflect on whether you consider universal jurisdiction or 'extradite or prosecute' obligations to be useful tools (both in theory and practice) in combating international crimes.

One might ask whether the existence of the International Criminal Court has implications for the extent to which national courts may need to (or choose to) rely on universal jurisdiction in the future. The answer is both yes and no. On the one hand, the International Criminal Court will never have the capacity or resources to prosecute everyone suspected of a crime within its jurisdiction: therefore, national courts will still have to do most of the prosecutorial work regarding international crimes. However, history does not give us much cause to be optimistic that the national courts of States where serious international offences have occurred will necessarily prosecute those suspected of being responsible, or at least not in the short term. If there is ever to be anything approaching a system for the successful prosecution of international offences much of the work will necessarily fall to the national courts of other States exercising universal jurisdiction. We have noted however that there are numerous non-legal reasons why universal jurisdiction may rarely be exercised in practice.[75]

Useful further reading

M LANGER, 'The Diplomacy of Universal Jurisdiction: The Political Branches and the Transnational Prosecution of International Crimes' (2011) 105 American Journal of International Law 1–49.
  An exceptionally useful study of when universal jurisdiction is used, against whom and why.

R O'KEEFE, 'Universal Jurisdiction: Clarifying the Basic Concept' (2004) 2 Journal of International Criminal Justice 735–760.
  An important and analytically clear exposition of the doctrine of universal jurisdiction and the debates surrounding it.

---

[75] Langer, 'The Diplomacy of Universal Jurisdiction'.

C Staker, 'Jurisdiction' in M Evans (ed), *International Law* 4th ed (Oxford University Press 2014) 309.

A clear and accessible introduction to the topic of jurisdiction under public international generally.

Institute of International Law Resolution 'Universal criminal jurisdiction with regard to the crime of genocide, crimes against humanity and war crimes' (2005), www.justitiaetpace.org/idiE/resolutionsE/2005_kra_03_en.pdf

A short document prepared by a prestigious body of international law experts. Much of it is framed as guidance, however, rather than as strict conclusion as to the state of the law.

The Princeton Principles on Universal Jurisdiction 2001, http://lapa.princeton.edu/hosteddocs/unive_jur.pdf, especially Principles 6–10 at 31–33 and commentary at 51–54.

A useful document in explaining some of the controversies surrounding universal jurisdiction, albeit a document aimed at providing guidance rather than a strict statement of the law as it stands.

PART II

Prosecuting International Crimes

3

The prosecution
of international crimes:
The role of international and
national courts and tribunals

3.1 Introduction

It was famously said in the International Military Tribunal (IMT) judgment at Nuremberg against the 'major war criminals' that:

> Crimes against international law are committed by men, not by abstract entities, and only by punishing individuals who commit such crimes can the provisions of international law be enforced.[1]

A key feature of international criminal law is that it concerns the responsibility, and criminal liability of *individuals*—an unusual feature in a system of law that primarily governs the conduct of *States*.

It is very common, though somewhat inaccurate, to portray international criminal law as having truly begun in the mid-twentieth century and as forming a parallel narrative to the rise of human rights law from about the same time. On this account, it is common to see modern international criminal law as beginning with the Nuremberg IMT trial. The trial itself was seen at the time as radical. It is worth reflecting on the Nuremberg IMT at some little length, less because the judgment has had a strong legal influence on subsequent developments (it has not) but because it raises questions that still concern us in studying international criminal law.

The ideals the Nuremberg IMT are now seen as embodying were well laid out by the prosecution. Justice Robert Jackson of the US Supreme Court, chief prosecutor at the Nuremberg IMT, opened the trials in 1945 emphasizing that the crimes being tried were ones which 'civilization cannot tolerate... being ignored'.[2] He further said:

> That four great nations, flushed with victory and stung with injury stay the hand of vengeance and voluntarily submit their captive enemies to the judgment of the law is one of the most significant tributes that Power has ever paid to reason.

---

[1] *Trial of the Major War Criminals before the International Military Tribunal*, Nürnberg, 14 November 1945–1 October 1946 (1947) 223; and *International Military Tribunal (Nuremberg), Judgment and Sentences* (1947) 41 American Journal of International Law 172.

[2] Nuremberg Trial Proceedings, Volume 2 (Wednesday, 21 November 1945), http://avalon.law.yale.edu/imt/11-21-45.asp.

> This Tribunal, while it is novel and experimental, is not the product of abstract speculations nor is it created to vindicate legalistic theories. This inquest represents the practical effort of four of the most mighty of nations ... to utilize international law to meet the greatest menace of our times—aggressive war. The common sense of mankind demands that law shall not stop with the punishment of petty crimes by little people. It must also reach men who possess themselves of great power and make deliberate and concerted use of it to set in motion evils which leave no home in the world untouched.[3]

He called the defendants in the dock 'living symbols of racial hatreds, of terrorism and violence, and of the arrogance and cruelty of power' and symbols of the 'fierce nationalisms and of militarism, of intrigue and war-making which have embroiled Europe'.[4] This dramatic and stirring opening speech captures a number of important points:

- it reflects a belief that law could play a role in preventing war or reducing its cruelty;
- it acknowledged that the proceedings were novel and experimental—indeed, revolutionary;
- one of its most revolutionary aspects was that this would be the trial of *individuals* for what previously would have been thought of as *acts of State*;
- the choice of defendants was highly *selective*, and defendants were chosen in part because of what they *symbolized*;[5] and
- the proceedings were deeply theatrical.

These questions of the position of individuals under international law, the selectivity of international criminal law prosecutions, and international criminal law's symbolic and practical goals remain important.

The aim at Nuremberg was in part to try individuals, but also to try the Nazi State system—and to do so for several audiences: the international community, the German people, and future generations. The trials were conducted with an eye to history and aimed to leave a narrative—a narrative which still has a strong resonance in international criminal law today. That narrative, in a nutshell, speaks to us of the forward march of individual accountability for mass atrocities and tells us that trials are a practical and appropriate way to respond to mass atrocities. One of the questions to bear in mind throughout this book is whether that narrative is an overly optimistic or idealistic one.

 Learning aims

This chapter is intended to provide a brief historical introduction to the rise of individual accountability for international crimes. By the end of this chapter you should be able to:

---

[3] Ibid.   [4] Ibid.
[5] For example, it was thought important to put on trial someone connected with the Nazi propaganda effort. Given the death of Joseph Goebbels, a lesser figure, Hans Fritzsche, was indicted. He had only the most tenuous connection to the key prosecution case that there was a Nazi conspiracy to wage aggressive war. He was unsurprisingly acquitted.

- explain the legal difficulties involved in the Nuremberg IMT trial;

- compare some of the different approaches taken to national legislation implementing individual criminal responsibility and explain some of the difficulties encountered in national trials based on individual responsibility under international criminal law;

- understand the events leading to the creation of the major international criminal tribunals of the late twentieth and early twenty-first century; and

- have some knowledge of the controversies surrounding the purposes or goals of international criminal law and trials before international criminal tribunals.

Given these objectives, the chapter is structured as follows:

- Section 3.2 outlines the history of war crimes prosecutions prior to the Nuremberg Trials.

- Section 3.3 introduces the origins of the Nuremberg IMT, the conduct of the trial of the major war criminals, the legal controversies involved, and other post World War II proceedings.

- Section 3.4 provides an overview of national prosecutions after 1945 and the complexities involved in drafting national legislation allowing such prosecutions.

- Section 3.5 examines the 'rebirth' of international criminal tribunals in the 1990s and early 2000s.

- Section 3.6 steps back to briefly survey the question of what international criminal law is for or what goals it is intended to serve.

- Section 3.7 offers some brief conclusions.

3.2 The road to Nuremberg: origins and precursors

In 1945 the idea of trials at the end of a major war was not completely novel. It had simply seldom worked before. Possible precursors to the Nuremberg IMT include:

- The isolated incident of the 1474 trial in Breisach of Peter von Hagenbach, Governor of the Upper Rhine (Burgundy), for his regime of 'arbitrariness and terror', by 28 judges from city-States in the region.[6]

- It has been argued that the presence of amnesty clauses in peace treaties of the 1700s acknowledged the possibility of individual criminal liability.[7] However, one

---

[6] GD Solis, *The Law of Armed Conflict: International Humanitarian Law in War* (Cambridge University Press 2010) 29; GS Gordon, 'The Trial of Peter von Hagenbach: Reconciling History, Historiography and International Criminal Law' in KJ Heller and G Simpson, *The Hidden Histories of War Crimes Trials* (Oxford University Press 2013) 13–49.

[7] FZ Ntoubandi, *Amnesty for Crimes Against Humanity Under International Law* (Martinus Nijhoff 2007), Chapter 2 especially 16–19; C Damgaard, *Individual Criminal Responsibility for Core International Crimes* (Springer 2008) 90.

can equally suggest this was needed to stop foreign soldiers being prosecuted for the mere fact of participation in a war after the event.

- The 'Hague Rules' annexed to the Fourth Hague Convention Relating to Laws and Customs of War on Land of 1907 contain no direct provisions on individual criminal responsibility. While the rules do set out 'forbidden acts' these were intended as prohibitions on State conduct, not a criminal code.

- There was certainly an acknowledged right for a belligerent to try captured members of enemy forces for war crimes or espionage prior to the twentieth century, but this was something done *during* war to relatively low-level participants.

- In 1915 the term 'crimes against civilization and humanity' was used in a joint declaration by the governments of France, Great Britain, and Russia condemning the massacre of Armenians in Turkey.[8] While the word 'crimes' might suggest a belief in the individual criminal responsibility of the perpetrators it might equally have been a simple rhetorical phrase of condemnation.

- More importantly, treaties at the end of World War I envisaged that the Allies could try individuals 'before military tribunals' for war crimes committed by the forces of the defeated powers.[9] These were to be *national* trials: 'Persons guilty of criminal acts against the nationals of one of the Allied and Associated Powers will be brought before the military tribunals of that Power'.[10] Thus a power was given by treaty to national military tribunals that they might not otherwise have had. No such trials, however, occurred.

- Following World War I, under the Versailles Treaty the Kaiser (the German head of State) was to be 'publicly arraigned' for a 'supreme offence against international morality and the sanctity of treaties'.[11] This was not necessarily to be a *trial* before a *court*, as the article made clear the tribunal was to judge questions of 'international morality' and should 'be guided by the highest motives of international policy'.[12] In the event, the Kaiser was granted sanctuary in the Netherlands and no such arraignment occurred.

- There was a failed attempt in 1937 to negotiate a Convention for an International Criminal Court with jurisdiction over what would now be considered terrorist offences.[13]

Prior to the Nuremberg Trial some war crimes trials had been conducted in Leipzig by the German government itself in 1921–23 ('the Leipzig Trials'), following the First World War. After the war the Allies submitted a list of hundreds of named suspects to German authorities; a list which was revised down to 45 of the most serious cases;

---

[8] K Ambos, *Treatise on International Criminal Law* (Oxford University Press 2014) vol 2, 46.
[9] Arts 228–229, Treaty of Versailles 1919.   [10] Art 229, Treaty of Versailles 1919.
[11] Art 227, Treaty of Versailles 1919.   [12] Ibid.
[13] JA Fernández, '*Hostes Humani Generis*: Pirates, Slavers, and Other Criminals' in B Fassbender et al (eds), *The Oxford Handbook of the History of International Law* (Oxford University Press 2012) Chapter 5, 142.

out of which only 12 prosecutions for war crimes commenced.[14] The Leipzig Trials were marked by judicial bias, 'questionable acquittals', and leniency.[15] In some cases the defendants didn't even bother to turn up. However, there was a significant pair of convictions in the *Llandovery Castle* case.[16] This concerned a German U-boat which sank a hospital ship under the misapprehension that it was carrying troops. Survivors of the sinking were questioned, establishing that there had been no troops aboard. An order was then given by the U-boat commander to fire upon survivors in the life rafts. The order was carried out by a sailor, assisted by two junior officers. The Court accepted that the officers could plead a defence of superior orders, but held that the defence was not available where an order was manifestly illegal. The second order to fire upon (and kill) survivors was manifestly illegal and the junior officers were convicted.

During the Second World War, planning for the Nuremberg trials themselves began well in advance. The UN War Crimes Commission (UNWCC) was established in 1943 as a multinational effort by the Allies to identify those *Germans* who should be charged with war crimes. The Commission was supposed to gather evidence and make recommendations on tribunals and procedures for trying such German criminals. While it amassed a considerable number of files on possible suspects and established a legal committee to give technical advice to national governments on how to conduct prosecutions,[17] probably of more use to the eventual prosecutions at Nuremberg was the evidence gathering conducted by the Office of Strategic Services, a US military intelligence agency.[18]

Also in 1943 President Roosevelt, Prime Minister Churchill, and Premier Stalin (the 'Big Three') signed a declaration at the Moscow Conference on atrocities, vowing to return officers and soldiers who participated in 'atrocities, massacres and executions' to the relevant liberated territories for trial and declared in the case of high officials that 'German criminals whose offences have no particular geographical localization . . . will be *punished* by joint decision of the government of the Allies'.[19] Note the reference to punishment: *trials* were far from inevitable. It was only really the Americans who wanted them. The initial British position articulated by Churchill was to execute the top

[14] GG Battle, 'Trials before the Leipsic Supreme Court of Germans Accused of War Crimes' (1921) 8 Virginia Law Review 1–26; G Hankel, 'Leipzig Supreme Court' in A Cassese (ed), *The Oxford Companion to International Criminal Justice* (Oxford University Press 2009) 407–9.

[15] R Cryer, 'The History of International Criminal Prosecutions: Nuremberg and Tokyo' in R Cryer, H Friman, D Robinson, and E Wilmshurst, *An Introduction to International Criminal Law and Procedure*, 3rd ed (Cambridge University Press 2014) 116.

[16] A translation of the judgment appears in: (1922) 16 American Journal of International Law 709–724.

[17] See the United Nations Archive guide to UNWCC materials at: http://archives.un.org/ARMS/Records-Predecessor-Organizations.

[18] See for example: M Salter, *Nazi War Crimes, US Intelligence and Selective Prosecution at Nuremberg: Controversies Regarding the Role of the Office of Strategic Services* (Routledge 2007) 329 ff; JE Persico, *Nuremberg: Infamy on Trial* (Penguin 1995) 27 and 42.

[19] 9 US Department of State Bulletin 310 (No. 228, 6 November 1943) (emphasis added). Reproduced in R Cryer, *Prosecuting International Crimes: Selectivity and the International Criminal Law Regime* (Cambridge University Press 2005) 36–7.

50 or so leaders, and to try the lesser ranks for war crimes. Stalin's preferred option was to kill 50,000 Germans, 'mainly military'.[20]

As late as 1944 the US also seemed to back a policy of executions. The debate was famously between US War Department Secretary Stimpson who wanted trials and US Treasury Secretary Morgenthau whose plan called for up to 2,500 executions and the 'pastoralization' of German industry, which would have rendered Germany effectively a rural society without an industrial sector.[21] President Roosevelt backed the Morgenthau plan until it became clear US popular opinion would not support such a harsh peace. It was the Stimpson plan that Roosevelt took to the Yalta Conference in February 1945, where it gained unlikely support from Russia and then the consent of Churchill. The Big Three thus agreed to trials, but the details remained to be settled. Further negotiations on the subject were led in London by Supreme Court Judge Robert H Jackson, who eventually became the lead prosecutor at Nuremberg.

3.3 The IMT and the trial of the Nazi leadership, and other post-World War II proceedings

3.3.1 The challenges in establishing the Nuremberg IMT

The negotiations referred to above resulted in the London Charter of the International Military Tribunal of 8 August 1945. This was concluded as a treaty between the four major powers (UK, US, Russia, and France), to which 15 other States adhered. The tribunal was, however, quite clearly a creation of the four powers first and foremost. The IMT was to be composed of four judges, one national from each of the major powers; and four similarly selected alternate judges. Those drafting the IMT Charter had several concerns in mind:

- to define the applicable crimes, rather than give the Tribunal the power to determine the content of international law at the relevant time—an approach having the virtues of certainty and expediency;
- to prove to the world in a public forum the criminality of Germany's conduct of the war;
- to avoid creating martyrs through summary executions;
- to shape public opinion and prepare an historical record—make undeniable the crimes of the Nazi regime (including murder of six million Jews and the murder and mistreatment of communists, gypsies, the elderly, and the disabled); and

---

[20] A Tusa and J Tusa, *The Nuremberg Trial* (Skyhorse 2010) 24; D Scheffer, 'Nuremberg Trials' (2008) 39 Studies in Transnational Legal Policy 155, 157.

[21] See generally: GJ Bass, *Stay the Hand of Vengeance: The Politics of War Crimes Tribunals* (Princeton University Press 2000) Chapter 5.

- to put on trial in symbolic form the Nazi regime and the German State itself through a *representative selection* of defendants.[22]

The question that any prosecution had to answer, however, was: how do you try an entire regime? The US legal strategy had three steps. First, the US favoured a theory of conspiracy alien to European law: 'those who participate in the formulation and execution of a criminal plan involving multiple crimes are jointly liable for each of the offenses committed and jointly responsible for the acts of each other.'[23] This approach allowed the trial of all leaders for all the major crimes, and also prevented a superior orders plea vesting all responsibility in Hitler (i.e. a theory that as everyone took orders from someone higher up, ultimately the only person who could not plead superior orders was Hitler who would then be solely responsible for everything).[24] As Hitler was dead, if such a defence were permitted, it might absolve all others of all guilt. Nonetheless, the US conspiracy approach rested on the legal fiction of a single Nazi criminal plan unchanged from 1933 to the war's conclusion. The historical reality was rather more complex.

Second, the US favoured the creation of a procedure for declaring certain organizations illegal, as a result of their role in the criminal Nazi master-plan. Once such an illegal status was established before the IMT, one could then (in theory) prosecute members for the mere fact of membership in subsequent trials. In practice, the prosecution in those subsequent military trials had to prove that a defendant: (1) was a member of an illegal organization; (2) that membership was voluntary; and (3) the defendant knew of the organization's criminal purpose.[25]

Third, the US strategy also involved selecting for the first major trial only a limited group of leaders who together represented all aspects of the Nazi State (ministers, politicians, propagandists, military leaders, and industrialists).[26] This would be followed by other trials of groups, illegal organizations or of individuals (the so-called 'subsequent trials') conducted before a variety of military courts established by the Allies as the occupation government of Germany.

Nonetheless, in creating an IMT by treaty to try the major surviving Nazi leaders a number of problems were evident:[27]

- reconciling three or four different legal systems and traditions of conducting a trial;

---

[22] See generally: R Overy, 'The Nuremberg Trials: International Law in the Making', in P Sands (ed), *From Nuremberg to The Hague: The Future of International Criminal Justice* (Cambridge University Press 2003) Chapter 1. See also the documents contained in: *Report of Robert H. Jackson, United States Representative to the International Conference on Military Trials* (1945) http://avalon.law.yale.edu/subject_menus/jackson.asp.

[23] 'Memorandum to President Roosevelt from the Secretaries of State and War and the Attorney General', 22 January 1945, Section V, http://avalon.law.yale.edu/imt/jack01.asp. See further: Cryer, *Prosecuting International Crimes*, 309–10.

[24] Overy, 'The Nuremberg Trials', 16.

[25] KJ Heller, *The Nuremberg Military Tribunals and the Origins of International Criminal Law* (Oxford University Press 2011) 290–4.

[26] Overy, 'The Nuremberg Trials', 12–13.

[27] See generally the preface to the *Report of Robert H. Jackson*, at n 22.

- the prospect of the trials being used as a platform for defendants to offer Nazi propaganda from the dock;
- concerns that the applicable international law was not clearly established;[28] and
- concerns held by the other powers regarding the US legal strategy itself.

There were obviously significant differences of view as to trials procedure between the Anglo-American, Continental, and Soviet systems of justice. Much writing on international criminal law contrasts the adversarial common law tradition and an inquisitorial civil law tradition. This involves an oversimplification, as there is obviously great variation within both common and civil law countries on these issues. Put simplistically, though, in the adversarial system a judge neutrally arbitrates between the competing accounts of the parties, and it is the parties who control what material is presented to the court. The adversarial system thus assembles a 'trial truth':[29] it is not the job of a court to conduct its own inquiry into the facts. It also has numerous technical rules of evidence, designed to stop prejudicial material with limited probative value reaching the jury. That is, the rules of evidence are designed to shield from prejudice the legally untrained people who must decide questions of guilt or innocence.

In the inquisitorial system the collection of evidence is supervised by an investigatory magistrate who assembles the 'dossier' (the complete written record of evidence) upon which the trial will proceed. The judiciary is seen as having a leading role in examining witness and as being capable of weighing evidence on its merit without artificial rules. This can be characterized as an inquiry into the 'real truth'.[30]

At the IMT the adversarial model was adopted, in part because evidence was still being assembled, so no *dossier* was possible. However, the trial would be conducted with interventionist judges and without common-law rules of evidence adapted to a jury trial.

The IMT technically had its seat in Berlin, but once proceedings opened moved immediately to Nuremberg where it was hosted by the US army. Nuremberg was symbolically valuable as the place where Nazi race laws had been promulgated, but also—despite having been almost entirely flattened by bombing—had a largely undamaged court-house with ample office space and a jail attached.[31] The trials saw 22 defendants indicted, on four broad counts:

- count 1, the general conspiracy (with the US leading the prosecution);
- count 2, crimes against the peace (UK-led);
- counts 3 and 4, war crimes and crimes against humanity. These were taken together divided for prosecution geographically: the French prosecuted the case arising in the western zone of conflict and the Soviets the eastern zone case.

---

[28] For a critique see: H Kelsen, 'Will the Judgment in the Nuremberg Trial Constitute a Precedent in International Law?' (1947) 1 International Law Quarterly 153–71.

[29] In the phrase of Judge Röling: A Cassese and BVA Röling, *The Tokyo Trial and Beyond: Reflections of a Peacemonger* (Polity 1993) 50.

[30] Ibid.   [31] Persico, *Nuremberg*, 37–41.

Two major contemporary controversies regarding the Nuremberg IMT trial of the 'major war criminals' should be noted. First, whether the IMT was a *legally established* court with authority to try Germans? And second, were the crimes in its statute, in particular aggression and crimes against humanity, *criminal* acts entailing *individual responsibility* when committed? These are addressed in the following sections.

 Pause for reflection

What were the major difficulties faced in prosecuting the Nazi leadership and reconciling different national conceptions of criminal law? What significant advantages did the IMT have nonetheless?

It is worth stopping to reflect on these questions as they recur in different forms in the establishment of each of the modern international criminal tribunals and, in a sense, each time we attempt to prosecute leaders alleged to have directed mass atrocities. A key difficulty in establishing the Nuremberg IMT was devising a legal theory that could capture the responsibility of leaders who planned and directed crimes for acts actually carried out by ordinary soldiers. The approach chosen was a version of the law of conspiracy familiar to lawyers in the US but alien to the civil law tradition. Indeed, imposing the idea of an ordered conspiracy on a more complex historical reality caused the IMT judges a certain amount of hesitation.[32] Nonetheless, convictions were in the end entered on the count of a common plan or conspiracy to wage a war of aggression. As we shall see in Chapter 12, how best to describe in law the responsibility of leaders for international crimes has remained a significant area of debate.

The Nuremberg IMT also had to reconcile two very different traditions of criminal trials: those of common law and civil law systems. In theory, we might conclude that if one objective of an international criminal trial is to establish an historical record then a civil law 'inquisitorial' process might be preferable. After all, a comprehensive investigation directed by judges might well do a better job of uncovering the historical truth than litigation conducted by prosecution and defence counsel each pursuing their own agendas. In practice, as we shall see in Chapter 5, international criminal tribunals have tended to adopt a predominantly adversarial procedure.

Finally, we should note that much of the success of the Nuremberg IMT trial could be seen to follow from the fact that the Allied powers were in occupation of Germany. The prosecution therefore not only had the defendants in custody, but also had complete control of government records and access to witnesses. These very significant advantages are not always present in modern international criminal trials. Indeed, lack of cooperation by the territorial government and lack of access to witnesses and documentary records has become a major issue for the International Criminal Court (ICC).

3.3.2 Was the IMT legally established?

As noted in Chapter 2, a treaty does not create rights or obligations for third parties without their consent. Germany was not a party to the IMT Charter and had not

---

[32] Persico, *Nuremberg*, 372.

consented directly to the treaty having operation in its territory. How did the IMT address the prima facie inapplicability of its founding treaty to German territory? It was said by the IMT in its judgment that the IMT was created by the 'sovereign legislative power' of the occupying powers to which Germany had 'unconditionally surrendered' (namely the US, UK, France, and Russia); and that the right of occupiers to legislate for occupied territories was universally recognized.[33] There are two formal problems with this: (1) nothing was said about individual liability in the instrument of surrender; and (2) while the occupying powers had indeed set up a Control Council as successor to the German government which had the power to legislate for Germany, the Charter was enacted not by the Control Council but by a treaty among the occupying powers themselves. The point being that the while Control Council, as the government of occupation, could have passed a law conferring national jurisdiction upon the IMT it did not. The occupation governments did pass Control Council Law No. 10 which governed the subsequent trials of the lower-ranked defendants conducted by national military tribunals; however, this law did not apply to the IMT trial itself. On one view, held by distinguished commentators at the time such as Hans Kelsen, this was in the final analysis only a formal defect.[34] The occupying powers had the power to set up the IMT, they just did it as an act of private treaty-making outside Germany, not through the use of public power in Germany.

Nonetheless, Article 43 of the Hague Rules on land warfare (and now the Fourth Geneva Convention) require occupying powers to respect 'unless absolutely prevented, the laws in force in the country'. It is not clear that the law of occupation allows re-writing of domestic criminal law during an occupation. The answer to this objection offered by some was that Germany's *unconditional* surrender meant this was not an ordinary occupation subject to the usual rules. On this approach—taken, for example, by Robert Jennings—German sovereignty was effectively in abeyance, the State having been completely subjugated, and the Allies enjoyed complete and supreme authority within German territory.[35]

The other possibility is that the Nuremberg IMT was an 'international court' in the sense that it was 'instituted by one or a group of nations with the consent and approval of the international community'.[36] This view rests on the general absence of protest regarding the IMT trial and its recognition by all 51 member States of the United Nations General Assembly in Resolution 95(I). The suggestion would appear to be that if it was a court established directly under international law the constraints of national law (or even the law of occupation) would not apply to it. However, Resolution 95(I) only '*takes*

---

[33] *IMT Judgment and Sentences* (1947) 41 American Journal of International Law 172, 216.

[34] Kelsen, 'Will the Judgment in the Nuremberg Trial Constitute a Precedent?', 157–70.

[35] This was sometimes referred to as a condition of 'debellatio', though Jennings thought 'subjugation' or 'conquest' more accurate: RY Jennings, 'Government in Commission' (1946) 23 British Yearbook of International Law 112, 135–6; compare CC Shears, 'Some Legal Implications of Unconditional Surrender' (1945) 39 American Society of International Law Proceedings 44–53.

[36] KJ Heller, *The Nuremberg Military Tribunals*, 111 quoting R Woetzel, *The Nuremberg Trials in International Law* (1962) 43.

note of' the IMT Charter, which is rather different from endorsing the IMT as a legally established court.[37]

The precise legal basis of the Nuremberg IMT thus remains potentially controversial. The problem is not an isolated one. Challenges to the legal constitution of international criminal tribunals have not gone away, as we shall see later regarding the International Criminal Tribunal for the former Yugoslavia (ICTY) and International Criminal Tribunal for Rwanda (ICTR).

3.3.3 Were the crimes in the IMT Charter *criminal* acts entailing *individual responsibility* when committed?

Again, the point to bear in mind is that not all acts which are prohibited at international law involve individual criminal sanction, indeed relatively few do. For example, if one State damages another's environment through cross-border pollution then the polluting State (as a collective) is obliged to compensate that loss,[38] but its responsible officials are not liable to criminal sanction. Rules of prohibition at international law are thus usually directed to the State as a whole: just because the State is responsible for preventing its officials from doing certain things does not create rules of criminal liability binding upon the officials themselves.

Prior to 1945 the widespread assumption was that—at the international level—only the collective entity of the State could be responsible. If there was in addition to be individual responsibility then that was a matter for the internal national law of each State. This followed from the fundamental assumption that: (1) international law applied between and was binding only on States; (2) only national law was binding upon individuals; and (3) the role of international law within national jurisdictions was a matter for the constitution of each State (so-called 'monist' States might give effect directly to international law in national law, so-called 'dualist' States might require some legislative act before international law became part of national law).[39] Further it was assumed that where an individual State official committed an act breaching international law: (1) that act was *an act of State* and the only responsible entity was the State; and (2) the official acting under colour of State authority was *absolutely immune* from being prosecuted before foreign courts for that act.[40] Thus, even where one could point to a rule of the laws of war that had been violated by the German conduct of the war, it could still be controversial to suggest that this prohibition directed to the State could result in criminal liability for an individual.

---

[37] See the Resolution at www.un.org/documents/ga/res/1/ares1.htm.

[38] E.g. *Trail Smelter Arbitration (US v Canada)* (1941) 3 UN Reports of International Arbitral Awards 1905.

[39] In practice few States fit the neat labels of 'monist' and 'dualist' and a wide variety of approaches are taken in national legal systems to the role of international law.

[40] For a contemporary view see H Ehard, 'The Nuremberg Trial against the Major War Criminals and International Law' (1949) 43 American Journal of International Law 223, 230–231. For an account of the modern law see J Crawford, *Brownlie's Principles of Public International Law*, 8th ed (Oxford University Press 2012) 487–8, 493–5; and Chapter 14 of this book.

This left an awkward question for the judges of the IMT, how could they prove that such rules now created criminal sanctions binding on individuals? In fact, the Tribunal strictly speaking had no need to ask the question. The judges were bound to apply the IMT Charter as the applicable law. Article 6 provided that the IMT 'shall have the power to try and punish persons who, acting in the interests of the European Axis countries' committed crimes against peace, war crimes, or crimes against humanity. (Note that this list does not include *genocide*.) Nonetheless, the defence lawyers for the defendants at Nuremberg made the obvious argument that—especially as regards the crime of aggressive war—the charges involved retroactive punishment and a violation of the principle *nullum crimen sine lege* (as discussed at 1.4.4). The argument was that no such crime had been defined as at 1939, no penalty fixed for it, and no court set up to try it.[41] The reply of the IMT was that:

> the maxim *nullum crimen sine lege* is not a limitation of sovereignty, but is in general a principle of justice. To assert that it is unjust to punish those who in defiance of treaties and assurances have attacked neighbouring states without warning is obviously untrue, for in such circumstances the attacker must know that he is doing wrong, and so far from it being unjust to punish him, it would be unjust if his wrong were allowed to go unpunished.[42]

Thus the IMT took the view that *nullum crimen sine lege* was not a limitation on law-making power (at least not at international law) but was instead a general rule of justice. The principle thus had no application where defendants must have known their conduct was wrong, even if no law specifically permitted it (this is sometimes called a theory of substantive justice).[43] As noted in Chapter 1, the requirements of *nullum crimen sine lege* in international law are now arguably much stricter. As regards *aggression* (the crime against peace), it is not clear that waging war was a *crime* at 1939, though it had arguably been prohibited by the Kellogg-Briand Pact of 1928 (at least as among the parties) and was certainly in violation of various German non-aggression treaties. However, as noted, breaches of international law had not previously ever been said to result in the criminal liability of individual leaders and statesmen.

Crimes against humanity were also controversial. It had not previously been accepted that there were international law limits on what a State could do to its citizens. A US government report acknowledged that certain Nazi outrages from 1933–1939 were 'neither "war crimes" in the technical sense, nor offences against international law; and the extent to which they may have been in violation of German law, as changed by the Nazis, is doubtful.'[44] This obviously novel category caused some concern, and the IMT Charter was drafted to give the Tribunal jurisdiction only where such crimes were committed in connection with a war crime or crime against the peace.[45] This excluded events prior to 1939 and tended to blur together war crimes and crimes against humanity.

---

[41] IMT Judgment and Sentences (1947) 41 American Journal of International Law 172, 216.

[42] Ibid.

[43] See A Cassese et al, *Cassese's International Criminal Law*, 3rd ed (Oxford University Press 2013) 24–7.

[44] 'Memorandum to President Roosevelt from the Secretaries of State and War and the Attorney General', 22 January 1945, Section IV, http://avalon.law.yale.edu/imt/jack01.asp.

[45] G Boas, JL Bischoff, and NL Reid, *International Criminal Law Practitioner Library: Elements of Crimes under International Law*, vol. 2 (Cambridge University Press 2009) 24–25.

Overall, it is quite clear that aggression and crimes against humanity were novel offences being applied to individuals for the first time. The Nuremberg IMT can thus be seen as a turning point in the assertion of individual responsibility for international crimes, even if the legal basis for that assertion was perhaps questionable at the time.

3.3.4 Assessing the IMT trial

In terms of sentences, three out of 22 defendants were acquitted, 12 were sentenced to death, and seven were imprisoned for terms ranging from ten years to life. The fact that certain individuals and organizations were acquitted was quite controversial at the time; but certainly lends credence to the idea that the trials were—overall—fairly conducted.[46]

The most serious criticisms relate to the inequality of defence and prosecution resources (Jackson had a staff of 600), and the limited access the defence were given to documentary archives and on occasions, their own clients.[47] Similar criticisms are still sometimes made of modern tribunals such as the ICTY and ICTR.

Perhaps its greatest achievement was that which John H. Jackson had envisaged: that it would serve as a practical precedent. One can certainly claim that Nuremberg was not technically a legal precedent: the IMT was not a binding authority at law over any other Court—except perhaps those established in occupied Germany under Control Council Law No. 10.[48] However, in a less formal sense, a precedent is—as Jackson put it—'the power of a beaten path'.[49] The possibility of conducting trials and finding an applicable law had been demonstrated. It had been done once. It had worked. It could be done again.

Finally, some contemporary criticism centred on the consequences of failure to admit superior orders as a defence. The argument was that for international law to impose a duty of disobedience or resistance upon individuals bound by national law was seen as unrealistic. It either required every soldier to be a lawyer or put the soldier in the potentially impossible position of risking punishment at under either national law (for disobedience) or international law (for carrying out an illegal order).[50] We still hear similar criticisms made of international criminal law today, and the role of superior orders as a defence is considered in Chapter 13. In terms of criticisms made of the Nuremberg IMT, however, it is important to note that a duty to disobey manifestly illegal orders had already been articulated by a German court in the *Llandovery Castle* case. The criticism is thus overblown.

---

[46] Cryer, 'The History of International Criminal Prosecutions: Nuremberg and Tokyo' in Cryer et al, *Introduction*, 119.

[47] Ibid; Overy, 'The Nuremberg Trials', 23; *contra* Persico, *Nuremberg*, 267.

[48] See Kelsen, 'Will the Judgment in the Nuremberg Trial Constitute a Precedent?'

[49] He was quoting Justice Cardozo: *Report of Robert H. Jackson*, http://avalon.law.yale.edu/imt/jack63.asp.

[50] On the 'soldier's dilemma' see: Y Dinstein, *The Defence of 'Obedience to Superior Orders' in International Law* (Oxford University Press 2012) Chapter 1.

Pause for reflection

What legal criticisms could be made of the Nuremberg IMT and its judgment in the Major War Criminals *case?*

The major criticisms that could be made of the Tribunal are that it: (1) was not legally established; (2) applied retrospective criminal law; and (3) rejected a defence of superior orders which was generally available in legal systems at the time. The suggestion that it was not legally established rests on the fact that the Charter of the Nuremberg IMT was a treaty to which Germany was not a party. Treaties do not bind non-party States without their consent. Thus the legal foundation for prosecuting crimes committed within Germany and against German citizens is open to question. Arguments based on Germany's unconditional surrender are unconvincing, as the instrument of surrender did not mention individual prosecutions. The fact that the occupying powers could exercise German sovereignty does not necessarily help either, while they had the power to pass new *German* laws (such as Control Council Law No. 10) the IMT Charter was not enacted in national law. However, commentators at the time (such as Hans Kelsen) considered this a purely formal defect: the Allies had the power to enact the IMT Charter as a national law binding within Germany, they just omitted to do so. One could still, however, raise a question whether it was consistent with the rules of occupation to modify national criminal law during an occupation.

The accusation that the IMT applied retrospective criminal law has some substance. While there was a precedent in the Leipzig trials for national courts conducting war crimes prosecutions within Germany, the crime of aggression and crimes against humanity were harder to justify as crimes of individual responsibility. None of the treaties cited by the IMT for the proposition that war was illegal at international law contemplated *individual criminal sanction*. Similarly, there was no commonly agreed definition of 'crimes against humanity' prior to the Nuremberg Trial. Indeed, it had not previously been accepted that there were international law limits on what a State could do to its citizens and Nazi atrocities in the period 1933–1939 were probably consistent with German law (as modified by the Nazis). This probably accounts for the IMT's requirement that 'crimes against humanity' have some connection with a war crime or crime against the peace.

The outright rejection of a defence of superior orders was seen as a necessity if senior leaders (who could all claim to have been acting on Hitler's orders) were to be put on trial. The exclusion of a defence otherwise available in German law might seem unfair. However, in German law the defence was not an absolute defence: the *Llandovery Castle* case had set out a duty to disobey manifestly illegal orders. One could argue either that this criticism is overstated, or that the IMT could have allowed the defence as it could have found the orders involved were illegal in any event.

In addition one could raise a question about whether the US theory of criminal conspiracy underlying the prosecutions was known to European legal systems, let alone international law.

One could answer all of these criticisms as the Tribunal did by suggesting that *nullum crimen* is a principle of justice and there could be no doubt that the defendants knew what they did was wrong. Thus, even if retrospective law is ordinarily repugnant to justice that cannot be the case where the defendant's must have known their conduct was gravely wrong even if not strictly illegal. The approach of the IMT is really based on the theory of substantive or objective justice. Substantive justice—no longer a popular theory—holds that retrospective punishment is justified when an act inflicts great social harm and is abhorred by all society, but has not been expressly criminalized in advance. In such cases the community's interest in just punishment may be thought to outweigh the defendant's right to insist on strict legality, as it would be unjust to allow the defendant to escape punishment.[51]

3.3.5 Other post-World War II proceedings

Very brief note should be taken of other trials that followed in the immediate aftermath of World War II. A second international military tribunal was established in Tokyo: the Military Tribunal for the Far East (MTFE) was established to try the so-called 'Class A' Japanese war criminals.[52] It was probably established on a more secure legal foundation than Nuremberg as Japan had expressly accepted the trial of individuals in its instrument of unconditional surrender. The MTFE Charter was based on the Nuremberg IMT Charter. It was drawn up by the US Chief Prosecutor and issued by Proclamation of General MacArthur in 1946.[53] The MTFE notably has an unwieldy bench of 11 Judges (one appointed by each of the nine signatories to the Japanese surrender plus one representing each of India and the Philippines). All sentences were subject to review by MacArthur, who could reduce them but not increase their severity. The trial ran for more than two years and produced an extremely long judgment. The competence of both the chief prosecutor, Joseph Keenan of the US, and the Presiding Judge, Sir William Webb of Australia, have been criticized heavily.[54] The fairness of the proceedings was also criticized, especially in the judges' inconsistent use of Anglo-Saxon rules of evidence (contrary to the Nuremberg approach) and the lack of access to documents given to the defence.[55] The fact that all 28 defendants were convicted, on at least some if not all counts, tends to call into question the fairness of proceedings. Judge Röling in particular would have acquitted several of the political figures in part on the basis that in his view they had clearly entered a War Cabinet with the purpose of ending or limiting a war, and should not be thought part of a wider conspiracy.[56] Overall, it is less well remembered and less influential than the Nuremberg IMT.

Of more significance were prosecutions before American, British, and French military tribunals established under Control Council Law No. 10. A law passed by the Allies as the occupation government in Germany, Control Council Law No. 10 permitted foreign military courts to operate in occupied Germany and to try the offences set out in the IMT Charter (albeit with some modifications to their definitions). Article 3 of Control Council Law No. 10 authorized the commanders of the respective zones of occupation to establish such tribunals. Therefore, as it was simply a statute giving jurisdiction to the military courts of the occupying powers, military tribunals and

---

[51] See Cassese et al, *Cassese's International Criminal Law*, 24–26.
[52] See, generally, N Boister and R Cryer, *The Tokyo International Military Tribunal: A Reappraisal* (Oxford University Press 2008).
[53] As 'Supreme Commander, Allied Powers' or 'SCAP', MacArthur had near monarchical power in Japan.
[54] Boister and Cryer, *The Tokyo International Military Tribunal*, 76–77 and 82–84.
[55] Ibid, 103–114.   [56] See generally Cassese and Röling, *The Tokyo Trial and Beyond*.

procedures had to be established under the national law of the occupying powers themselves. Procedures varied:

- the UK conducted trials under the Royal Warrant of 1945—this was simply an executive decree made under constitutional powers theoretically vested in the monarch and not parliament;[57] and

- the US proceeded by Military Tribunals, established under an ordinance 'enacted on 18 October 1946 by General Clay in his role as Military Governor and commander of the U.S. zone [of occupation]'.[58]

The 12 US prosecutions under Control Council Law No. 10 are the best known of the 'subsequent proceedings' (i.e. subsequent to the IMT trial), and included the *Pohl Case*, which involved prosecuting a private factory owner for the use of forced labour as a crime against humanity.[59]

Trials occurred in other theatres of the war, including but not limited to:

- British Military Tribunals in Italy;
- US Army prosecution of so-called Class B and C war criminals in Yokahama;
- British trials of Japanese war criminals in Singapore;
- US Army trials of Japanese war criminals conducted in the Philippines; and
- Dutch courts martial in Indonesia.

3.4 National prosecutions for international crimes

While this book focuses on the prosecution of crimes before international criminal courts and tribunals, in practice the majority of trials for international crimes will necessarily occur at a national level. No international tribunal will ever have the resources to prosecute every alleged case of an international crime, even presuming it has jurisdiction. Prior to 1945 if a State chose to criminalize, in national law, breaches of international law, that was a matter for it alone. As we shall see in Chapter 5, there are now a range of treaties imposing an international legal obligation upon States to criminalize certain conduct in national law. Further, we can also see in State practice a number of prosecutions where States exercised universal jurisdiction to prosecute crimes defined at international law in cases having no ordinary jurisdictional connection with the State. These can only be thought of as prosecutions based on a recognition of an international rule imposing direct individual criminal liability in the case of certain international crimes. A selection of such cases is discussed here.

Where prosecution for an international crime occurs under a national law, there are roughly four models for how such a law might be drafted:

---

[57] See APV Rogers, 'War Crimes Trials under the Royal Warrant: British Practice 1945–1949' (1990) 39 International and Comparative Law Quarterly 780, 786–7.

[58] Heller, *The Nuremberg Military Tribunals*, 25 and see also 38–42.

[59] Ibid, Chapters 1, 3, and 4.

- **A restrictive approach**: a State may incorporate the terms of international law into national legislation, even if further elements are added making the national offence narrower or stricter than the international law offence. This is permissible, but means that while all conduct that can be prosecuted under the statute would still constitute an international crime, some conduct that would be criminal at international law will not be punishable under the statute.

- **Giving national offences extra-territorial and retrospective application**: A State may attempt to avoid the difficulties of codifying international law and rely on the relative certainty of domestic legal concepts by giving local criminal law extra-territorial and retroactive application. Such approaches typically involve placing a limitation on national courts' jurisdiction over such offences (such as specifying that such national crimes may only be prosecuted if they occurred in certain European States in the period 1939–1945).

- **Double criminality**: A State may incorporate crimes defined at international law, but limit jurisdiction to cases where it also a crime at national law. Thus the prosecution must prove all the elements of the offence under two systems of law, national and international, to secure a conviction.

- **National laws referring to international law's requirements**: A State may refer to international law by statute and leave it up to the courts to work out how to apply it. Such a law might read: 'War crimes as defined by international law are punishable by life imprisonment.' A number of national legal traditions would probably consider such an approach to be impermissibly vague.

An example of each approach will be given and a case referred to. As regards other more recent national prosecutions based on universal jurisdiction, see the discussion of Belgian and Spanish cases in Chapter 2, section 2.4.3.

3.4.1 National prosecutions based on a restrictive approach to international crimes

An example of this approach is Israel's Nazis and Nazi Collaborators (Punishment) Law 1950 ('the 1950 law'). The 1950 law was entirely retroactive, as it applied only to crimes committed during the Nazi regime and before Israel had become a State. Further, the definition of 'crimes against the Jewish people' is effectively the crime of genocide, but with its application limited to one victim group.

 Example

Attorney General of the Government of Israel v Eichmann, District Court of Jerusalem and the Supreme Court of Israel

The *Eichmann Case* involved a former Nazi official (Adolf Eichmann) who was abducted from Argentina in 1960 and brought to stand trial in Israel for offences under the 1950 Law. Israel's official position at the time was that this abduction was carried out by patriotic volunteers without government sanction. Nonetheless, Argentina protested the abduction as a violation of its sovereignty. As a matter of general international law such an abduction, if carried out by government agents, requires restitution which would in principle involve returning the abducted person.[60] The Security Council implicitly upheld Argentina's complaint when it requested that Israel should make appropriate reparation in respect of Eichmann's abduction.[61] The matter was resolved when Argentina and Israel issued a joint communique stating the two States had 'decided to regard as closed the incident…which [had] infringed fundamental rights' of Argentina.[62]

Defence counsel for Eichmann unsuccessfully argued that his abduction and removal to Israel in violation of international law should prevent his trial (see further Chapter 6, section 6.4 on legality of arrest and detention). This argument was rejected by the Supreme Court on the basis that any right to protest the relevant violation of Argentina's sovereignty lay with Argentina, which had waived its right to do so when it settled its dispute with Israel prior to the trial commencing.[63]

At trial the District Court invoked as bases for its jurisdiction both: universal jurisdiction to punish crimes defined by 'the law of nations'; and the idea that it was the 'specific character [of the crimes covered by the 1950 law that they were]…designed to exterminate the Jewish people.'[64] The latter ground sounds very close to passive personality jurisdiction (i.e. asserting jurisdiction to prosecute crimes against one's citizens),[65] and was recognized as such in the Supreme Court of Israel.[66] However, strictly, it does not meet that definition as at the time of the offences Israel was not a State and so had neither citizens nor other protected interests. As a strict matter of international law, Israel was exercising universal jurisdiction: it had just chosen to restrict its exercise of that jurisdiction to offences involving the Jewish people. In the event, the Supreme Court upheld the finding of jurisdiction on the grounds of universal jurisdiction, passive personality, and the protective principle.[67]

Eichmann was convicted and sentenced to death.

In a later trial under the same law, *Demjanjuk* (1988), the accused was eventually acquitted (in 1993) due to problems with identification evidence.[68] Mr Demjanjuk had been accused of being the notorious Treblinka prison guard 'Ivan the Terrible' but it was found that there was reasonable doubt as to his identity. (He was later convicted in separate proceedings in Germany in 2011 and died before an appeal was completed.[69])

[60] See e.g. R O'Keefe, *International Criminal Law* (Oxford University Press 2015) 41 para 110.
[61] UNSC Res 138 (1960), para 2.
[62] LC Green, 'Legal Issues of the Eichmann Trial' (1962–1963) 37 Tulane Law Review 641, 647.
[63] UNSC Res 138 (1960), para 13(6).
[64] *Attorney General of the Government of Israel v Eichmann* (District Court of Jerusalem) (1968) 36 International Law Reports 59, para 11.
[65] On passive personality jurisdiction see Chapter 2, section 2.3.
[66] *Attorney General of the Government of Israel v Eichmann* (Supreme Court of Jerusalem) (1968) 36 International Law Reports 277.
[67] Ibid, paras 10–13.
[68] See the case note in Cassese (ed), *The Oxford Companion to International Criminal Justice*, 641–2.
[69] See 'Nazi camp guard Demjanjuk dies', BBC News, 17 March 2012, www.bbc.co.uk/news/world-europe-17414127.

3.4.2 Prosecuting international crimes by giving national offences extra-territorial and retroactive application

The Australian War Crimes Act of 1945 specified that certain acts committed outside Australia, during the 1939–1945 war in Europe could be tried in Australia if: (1) they would have been crimes in Australia; and (2) were committed in the course of a war or occupation, or were committed in the course of genocide or the crime against humanity of persecution or within a State at war or under occupation.[70] The law was further limited by the specification that it only applied to Australian citizens or residents, or those who had subsequently become citizens or residents of Australia or a citizen of an allied country during the war.[71] This approach could perhaps constitute an exercise of universal jurisdiction but with its application limited to certain persons. Such under-implementation is not perhaps desirable, but so long as it is not clearly compulsory to prosecute international crimes it must be permissible.

But was the Australian legislation a valid exercise of universal jurisdiction? For example, as we shall see in Chapter 8, while the prohibited conduct element (*actus reus*) of a war crime may include murder (a common national offence) the act must be committed against a 'protected person' under the laws of war. Killing someone who is taking active part in hostilities (for example, an enemy soldier on the battlefield) is not an offence. Can a State validly assert universal jurisdiction over 'murder' (as a war crime) if its national law does not include the 'protected person' limitation?

The majority in the High Court of Australia in *Polyukhovich* found the Australian War Crimes Act 1945 was in conformity with Australian constitutional law.[72] In a powerful dissent, Justice Brennan argued the act was not consistent with international law especially in its definition of war crimes.[73] The difficulty was the Act effectively defined all deliberate killing in war as murder but allowed a defendant to lead evidence that their conduct was *permitted* by the laws of war. However, no rule of the laws of war specifically says 'killing an enemy soldier during combat operations is legal', there is simply a general presumption that combatants enjoy an immunity from criminal law for such killings. (This approach is subtly different from a right to kill as it is based on an *immunity* not a *right*.) The flaw in the Australian Act's approach of allowing a special defence of lawful killing was that in many cases a rule giving a positive permission or justification would be hard to find. This is simply not how the laws of war work. Justice Brennan therefore thought the national law went much further than international law. As the national law could not be said to conform to what international law permitted, it was not a valid exercise of universal jurisdiction.

In the event only three prosecutions were ever initiated under the Act: two of these were dismissed by courts on evidential grounds and one was discontinued due to the poor health of the defendant. Australia now has modern legislation implementing in national law the offences found in the ICC Statute.[74]

---

[70] ss 6 and 7, War Crimes Act 1945 (Commonwealth Act No. 48 of 1945) as amended.
[71] Ibid, s 5.   [72] *Polyukhovich v Commonwealth* [1990] HCA 40; (1990) 95 ALR 502.
[73] Ibid, Brennan J (dissenting opinion), paras 45, 49, and 54.
[74] International Criminal Court Act 2002 (Commonwealth).

3.4.3 Prosecutions based on a national law which incorporates international law, but *limits* jurisdiction to cases where it also a crime at national law

The Canadian Criminal Code as amended in 1987 adopted this approach. In *Finta* it was held that the logical result was that the prosecution had to prove all the elements of the international law crime and then show that a national offence was also made out by the same evidence.[75] Therefore the prosecution had to prove that the accused had not only the mental state (*mens rea*) required under national law, but also any further mental state required as part of the international offence. In the *Finta* case it was not enough to make out the mental state for murder alone, the additional requirement for the mental state of a war crime or crime against humanity also had to be made out.

A similar approach was taken under the UK War Crimes Act 1991. The act only covered offences: (1) equivalent to murder, manslaughter and culpable homicide; (2) where the act was also a violation of laws of war; and (3) committed in Germany or German occupied territory between 1939 and 1945.[76]

Again, both Canada and the UK have now enacted new legislation recognizing the definitions of crimes found in the ICC Statute.[77]

3.4.4 National laws referring to international law's requirements

France was historically a good example of the approach of enacting national legislation that simply referred to international law, though the major trials conducted (such as *Barbie* and *Touvier*) were actually for offences on French territory and so were not universal jurisdiction cases. Law No. 64-1326 of 1964 provided in a single sentence that crimes against humanity, as defined in the UN Resolution of 13 February 1946, and 'taking into account' the Nuremberg Charter definitions, could not become prescribed or statute barred.[78]

This left a number of difficult questions for resolution, including:

- If the 1964 statute first created the offence of crimes against humanity in French law, could it apply to acts committed before 1964, given the strict presumption in French law against retroactive offences?; and

---

[75] *R v Finta* [1994] 1 SCR 701; 1994 CanLII 129 (SCC).

[76] s 1(1), War Crimes Act 1991 (UK, 1991 c. 13).

[77] ss 4 and 6, Crimes Against Humanity and War Crimes Act 2000 (Canada, SC 2000, c. 24); s 50, International Criminal Court Act 2001 (UK, 2001 c. 17). Each incorporates the ICC Statute definitions in different ways into national law.

[78] In many criminal justice systems there is a rule of prescription or a 'statute of limitations' providing that if a person is not charged within a certain time of the offence, a court may not ever hear the case. The best justification for such a rule is pragmatic: cases commenced long after the offence are unlikely to succeed as the quality of evidence, and the memory of witnesses, is likely to deteriorate over time. Commencing prosecutions that are unlikely to succeed would not seem to be in the interests of justice except in very serious cases. Some (but not all) systems of criminal law thus have no 'statute of limitations' for very serious crimes, such as murder.

- Could it apply to French citizens, as Article 6 of the Nuremberg Charter was restricted to Axis war criminals?

Despite these interpretative difficulties, convictions resulted against French citizens for their wartime conduct in the *Barbie Case* in 1987, the *Touvier Case* in 1994, and the *Papon Case* in 1998.[79]

 Pause for reflection

Has the ICC Statute improved the prospects for national prosecution?

It will readily be seen from the issues raised above that national legislation which attempts to avoid the difficulties of clearly defining international crimes can run into real difficulties. In part, though, this approach was understandable as the provisions of the Nuremberg Charter were quite broad and there was not a fully developed international code of crimes to draw upon. A great deal more certainty has been introduced by the ICC Statute (discussed further in section 3.5.4), at least for the parties to it. The ICC Statute contains, as we shall see, detailed definitions of the core international crimes. While not perfect, it represents a considerable improvement on the previous situation and provides much clearer definitions which may incorporated into national law. While not obliged to do so, many State parties have introduced legislation enacting the ICC Statute definitions.

However, the ICC Statute itself is not retrospective and it came into force only on 1 July 2002. ICC parties carrying out prosecutions for offences prior to 2002 will still likely involve extensive enquiries into the definition of crimes at customary international law.[80] This is not an abstract concern. The Extraordinary Chamber in the Courts of Cambodia (ECCC) has had to apply the definition of genocide and crimes against humanity applicable during the rule of Khmer Rouge regime in 1975–1979.[81]

As discussed above, State parties to the ICC Statute are not directly obliged by the Statute to enact relevant national criminal laws, and are free to choose their means of implementation if they do so. Cryer notes possible approaches include:

- direct enactment of Statute crimes in national criminal law where the national law reflects the treaty wording (as has occurred, for example, in new legislation in Australia, Canada, New Zealand, and the UK);

---

[79] See, for example, LS Wexler, 'Prosecutions for crimes against humanity in French municipal law: International implications' (1997) 91 Proceedings of the Annual Meeting (American Society of International Law) 270, 270–276.

[80] Of course, if we conclude that the ICC Statute can be treated in whole or in part as codifying customary international law at the date of its conclusion in 1998, then States could perhaps apply those definitions to events occurring after 1998 (or even before).

[81] See: SR Ratner, JS Abrams, and JL Bischoff, *Accountability for Human Rights Atrocities in International Law: Beyond the Nuremberg Legacy*, 3rd ed (Oxford University Press 2009) Chapters 12–14; and the symposium in (2006) 4 Journal of International Criminal Justice 283–341.

- transforming or translating concepts found in the ICC Statute into the terminology of national legal system (as has occurred in Germany); or

- revising the definitions of 'ordinary' crimes to make sure they also capture international crimes.[82]

In this sense, the ICC Statute has acted as a 'catalyst' for new national legislation.[83]

3.5 The rebirth of international criminal tribunals: the ICTY, the ICTR, and the ICC

The 1990s saw a major resurgence in international criminal law, a field that other than sporadic national prosecutions had lain largely dormant, with a sudden growth in the number of international criminal tribunals. In particular the UN International Criminal Tribunal for the former Yugoslavia (ICTY) was established in 1993 and the UN International Criminal Tribunal for Rwanda (ICTR) in 1994. As they began to start functioning and generating case law, there was a renewed sense of optimism about the possibility of establishing a permanent international criminal tribunal. This led surprisingly swiftly to the conclusion of the Rome Statute of the ICC, a treaty, in 1998. In following years a significant number of other criminal tribunals with 'international elements' were established, normally in post-conflict States (see section 3.5.5). The question for the moment is how this remarkable growth came about.

The revival most obviously begins with the International Criminal Tribunal for the former Yugoslavia and the International Criminal Tribunal for Rwanda.[84] Each was set up by the United Nations to cope with a particular crisis, namely the wars within the territory of the former Yugoslavia in the early 1990s (which saw the break-up of that federal State into a series of smaller entities now recognized as States)[85] and the Rwandan genocide of 1994. Both crises involved crimes of extraordinary magnitude committed principally along ethnic (or religious) lines.

---

[82] R Cryer, 'National Prosecution of International Crimes' in Cryer et al, *Introduction*, 81–82. See also G Werle and F Jessberger, *Principles of International Criminal Law*, 3rd ed (Oxford University Press 2014) 144–163. See further, International Criminal Court Act 2002 (Australia), Crimes Against Humanity and War Crimes Act 2000 (Canada), International Crimes and International Criminal Court Act 2000 (New Zealand), International Criminal Court Act 2001 (UK).

[83] R Cryer, 'National Prosecution of International Crimes' in Cryer et al, *Introduction*, 81.

[84] Although the idea of an international criminal court for drugs trafficking offences had been proposed by Trinidad and Tobago in 1989 and there had been discussion about the creation of an international criminal tribunal to conduct trials of the Iraqi leadership following Iraq's invasion of Kuwait in 1990: Cassese et al, *Cassese's International Criminal Law*, 262; W Schabas, *The UN International Criminal Tribunals: The Former Yugoslavia, Rwanda and Sierra Leone* (Cambridge University Press 2000) 11–13.

[85] The status of Kosovo remains, however, ambiguous. It declared independence in 2009, but it has so far received only limited recognition from other States as being a State in its own right.

The result was the establishment of the first international criminal tribunals since the Nuremberg IMT.

3.5.1 The International Criminal Tribunal for Yugoslavia (ICTY)

Yugoslavia was an artificial federal State created by the post-World War I peace conferences, held together after 1943 by the rule of Josip Tito (first as Marshal and then as President of Yugoslavia). Following his death in 1980 ethnic and nationalist tensions within and between its constituent federal states became increasingly evident. Eventually the constituent federal states began to succeed from Yugoslavia—with Slovenia and Croatia first seeking to leave what they saw as a 'Serb-dominated federation' in 1991—resulting in violence.[86] The ensuing conflict of 1991–1995 was characterized by large-scale criminal conduct against civilians, including sexual offences and various crimes against humanity colloquially described as 'ethnic cleansing' (the underlying crimes of forced deportation, persecution, and murder are discussed in Part III of this book).

The reaction in the UN Security Council to the wars of dissolution in Yugoslavia began with Resolutions condemning the violence.[87] Beyond this, there were conflicting approaches: some governments and non-government bodies favoured the creation of an international criminal tribunal, others saw creating a war crimes court as a potential impediment to a political solution aimed at stopping the violence.[88] UN Security Council Resolution 780 of 1992 established a Commission of Experts to examine reports of war crimes and mass killings. The Resolution was the product of French and US enthusiasm, the US in particular aiming at creating something similar to the 1943 Commission on War Crimes which had gathered evidence paving the way for later prosecutions.[89] The first Commission chairman, however, resigned. In the view of the second chairman, the scholar M Cherif Bassiouni, the Commission was deliberately given inadequate resources so that their work could not interfere with the peace negotiations.[90] Bassiouni found resources outside the UN to allow the Commission to function and it began to assemble a database on violations of the laws of war.[91] The Commission collated a vast mass of evidence[92] and produced an interim report in 1993 calling for the creation of an international criminal tribunal.

In addition to the Commission's recommendation, diplomatic pressure was building in favour of the creation of such a court. The UN Security Council in Resolution 808 called on the UN Secretary General to prepare within 60 days a report on how to establish an international criminal tribunal. His report included a draft tribunal statute and a

---

[86] Schabas, *The UN International Criminal Tribunals*, 13.

[87] UN Doc S/Res/764 (1992) and UN Doc S/Res/771 (1992).

[88] Schabas, *The UN International Criminal Tribunals*, 13–22; MC Bassiouni, 'From Versailles to Rwanda in Seventy-Five Years: The Need to Establish a Permanent International Criminal Court' (1997) 10 Harvard Human Rights Journal 11, 40–41.

[89] Schabas, *The UN International Criminal Tribunals*, 14 and 16–17.

[90] Bassiouni, 'From Versailles to Rwanda in Seventy-Five Years', 40–41.

[91] Schabas, *The UN International Criminal Tribunals*, 17 and n 86.

[92] Bassiouni, 'From Versailles to Rwanda in Seventy-Five Years', 40.

recommendation it be adopted as a Chapter VII Security Council Resolution.[93] The possibility of creating the Tribunal by a treaty had been considered by the Secretary General but was rejected as being both too slow and unlikely to gain ratification from the relevant territorial States.[94] Acting on this recommendation the proposed statute was adopted unanimously by the Security Council in Resolution 827, thus creating the ICTY.[95] Even so, it was not a foregone conclusion that the ICTY would commence work and conduct trials: some commentators certainly consider that it was initially intended, at least on the part of some Security Council member States, largely as a threat to bring warring factions to the negotiating table rather than as a working court.[96] It is generally agreed that the Tribunal made a slow start, initially being hampered by delays in the appointment of a prosecutor, an uncertain budget which was then administered by cumbersome UN procedures, and very limited cooperation from those States whose nationals were being indicted.[97] Nonetheless, within a handful of years it became a thriving and busy institution. This success required not just insistence by the ICTY that cooperation with the Tribunal was compulsory because it was founded under Chapter VII of the UN Charter, but the patient building up of cooperative relationships with governments who could assist its work.[98] Another important factor was, however, the 'considerable economic and political pressure' to surrender suspects to the Tribunal brought to bear by the international community upon the States which had emerged from the dissolution of Yugoslavia.[99]

Finally, at the time of its establishment some questioned whether the Security Council had the power to establish a court.[100] While this echoed challenges to the legality of the Nuremberg IMT, the ICTY stands on much firmer legal ground. The point was tested in the *Tadić* case when defence counsel argued the ICTY had not been legally established. The ICTY Appeals Chamber found it had an inherent jurisdiction to inquire into the legality of its own constitution and held:[101]

- the Security Council clearly has a power to create 'subsidiary organs' under Article 29 of the UN Charter;

- given that the General Assembly had used its equivalent power to create an independent administrative review tribunal, there should be no reason the Security Council could not similarly establish an independent judicial body;[102]

---

[93] Report of the Secretary-General pursuant to paragraph 2 of Security Council Resolution 808, UN Doc S/25704 (1993), para 22.

[94] Report of the Secretary-General, para 19.   [95] Cryer, *Selectivity*, 252–53.

[96] Schabas, *The UN International Criminal Tribunals*, 13–24. Some dispute this strongly: DJ Scheffer, 'Three Memories from the Year of Origin, 1993' (2004) 2 Journal of International Criminal Justice 353.

[97] R Goldstone, 'A View from the Prosecution' (2004) 2 Journal of International Criminal Justice 380–4; R Cryer, 'The Ad Hoc International Criminal Tribunals' in Cryer et al, *Introduction*, 130.

[98] Goldstone, 'A View from the Prosecution'.

[99] Cryer, 'The Ad Hoc International Criminal Tribunals' in Cryer et al, *Introduction*, 133.

[100] E.g. A Rubin, 'An International Criminal Tribunal for Former Yugoslavia' (1994) 6 Pace International Law Review 7–19.

[101] Schabas, *The UN International Criminal Tribunals*, 51–52; *Tadić* (Appeal on Jurisdiction), ICTY Appeals Chamber, 1995, paras 18 and 28–40.

[102] *Effect of Awards of Compensation Made by the United Nations Administrative Tribunal* (1954) ICJ Reports 47, 61.

- that the Security Council in the exercise of its Chapter VII powers to deal with threats to international peace and security enjoys a wide discretion in taking 'measures not involving the use of force' under Article 41 of the UN Charter; and

- the conflict clearly constituted a threat to peace and security justifying the exercise of Chapter VII powers.

There was therefore no legal obstacle to the Security Council establishing a court in the exercise of its Chapter VII powers as a measure taken to restore international peace and security (or to attempt to do so).

3.5.2 The International Criminal Tribunal for Rwanda (ICTR)

The ICTR was established in response to the genocide in Rwanda in 1994. Three months of violence in 1994 is estimated to have left between 500,000 and one million Rwandans dead; observers concluded the violence was largely committed against the ethnic Tutsi minority by ethnically Hutu militias and the country's Hutu-dominated military.[103] On some estimates the genocide involved 'over 800,000 perpetrators—nearly half the adult male population'.[104] The violence was not spontaneous but followed a civil war, and the collapse of a peace process, between the Hutu-dominated government and the Tutsi Rwandan Patriotic Front (RPF).[105] The response in the United Nations followed a similar pattern to that in Yugoslavia: the violence was condemned;[106] an investigatory commission was established;[107] the Secretary General prepared reports;[108] and the Security Council created the ICTR through adopting that statute under its Chapter VII powers.[109] A combination of factors supported this outcome. First, having created the ICTY to respond to a conflict in Europe, the Security Council was sensitive to possible criticisms it did not take the problems of Africa sufficiently seriously. Second, a new government incorporating many RPF members had come to power in Rwanda which supported the idea of an international criminal tribunal to investigate and prosecute the genocide.

Intriguingly, Rwanda was by chance a non-permanent member of the Security Council at the time and, in the end, actually voted *against* the establishment of the ICTR. Despite Rwanda having first called for a UN tribunal,[110] it did not support the final UN Security Council resolution for several reasons:

- the narrow temporal jurisdiction of the ICTR covering only events from 1 January–31 December 1994—the government of Rwanda claimed the genocide involved long prior planning and that the ICTR should have had jurisdiction over earlier massacres in 1990–1993;

---

[103] Ratner, Abrams, and Bischoff, *Accountability for Human Rights Atrocities*, 195.   [104] Ibid.
[105] Ibid.   [106] UN Docs S/Res/912, S/Res/918, S/Res/925 (1994).
[107] UN Doc S/Res/935 (1994).   [108] UN Doc S/1994/640 and S/1994/879 (1994).
[109] UN Doc S/Res/955 (1994).   [110] UN Doc S/1994/1125 (1994).

- in the face of enormous crimes and vast numbers of perpetrators the ICTR consisted initially of only two trial chambers, six judges, and was to share a prosecutor and appeal chamber with the ICTY—which seemed rather modest at best;

- it disliked the idea that those convicted might serve their sentences outside Rwanda; and

- Rwanda expressed concern that nationals from 'certain countries' it believed complicit in the civil war might serve as ICTR judges.[111]

It was also thought that the location of the court outside Rwanda would lessen its educative impact on a culture of impunity in Rwanda; and the unavailability of the death penalty before the ICTR would obviously result in a sentencing disparity—while high leaders on trial at the ICTR could only get a life sentence, lower level offenders tried in Rwanda could be sentenced to death.[112]

3.5.3 The ad hoc Tribunals: a preliminary assessment

The ICTY and ICTR were set up to respond to particular crises, and so are often referred to as the ad hoc tribunals. One advantage of establishing such tribunals under Chapter VII is their compulsory powers: if the resolution that creates the tribunal directs States to cooperate with the tribunal and declares that no immunities will be recognized before it—then these powers bind all UN Members. This follows from the fact that not only are UN members obliged to comply with Chapter VII resolutions, but obligations under the UN Charter prevail over all other international law obligations (other than *jus cogens*).[113] We should also note that if Chapter VII can be used to create a tribunal with powers binding upon all UN member States, then Chapter VII can also be used to grant an existing treaty-based tribunal jurisdiction over a situation in a non-party State, a jurisdiction it would not otherwise have. This power is acknowledged as a possible means of conferring jurisdiction over 'situations' upon the ICC and is discussed in Chapter 4, section 4.4.

The disadvantage of Chapter VII tribunals is that they require political will to establish, and continued political will to fund. We are now entering a period of 'tribunal fatigue'.[114] The international community has come to perceive Chapter VII tribunals as expensive and slow. A 'completion timetable' is now in effect for the ICTY and ICTR and puts a degree of pressure on them to conclude their activities.

---

[111] UN Doc S/PV.3453 (1994), 15. In saying 'certain countries' Rwanda was, allegedly, referring to France: Schabas, *The UN International Criminal Tribunals*, 29.
[112] Schabas, *The UN International Criminal Tribunals*, 29.   [113] Article 103, UN Charter.
[114] Ratner, Abrams, and Bischoff, *Accountability for Human Rights Atrocities*, 252.

→← **Counterpoint**

What are the major achievements and failings of the ICTY and ICTR?

The ICTR is commonly praised for:[115]

- having helped establish the truth of the Rwandan genocide;
- developing the law of genocide, and in particular the legal test of who will constitute a member of a 'protected group' under the Genocide Convention;
- establishing that sexual violence can form the material element of genocide or a crime against humanity;
- establishing a definition of rape for the purposes of international criminal law.

Similarly, the ICTY's achievements are commonly said to include:[116]

- highlighting the role of sexual violence against women in the Balkan conflicts;
- establishing that rape can constitute a form of torture and establishing the elements of rape at international criminal law;
- establishing that genocide can occur without 'country-wide massacres' when there is intent to destroy part of a population;
- elaborating the elements of war crimes and also developing the notion of a widespread and systematic attack as the contextual element of a crime against humanity;
- elaborating legal methods to link 'high level defendants to foot soldier's crimes', both through the doctrine of command responsibility and through 'divin[ing]' in custom a new form of responsibility' joint criminal enterprise (a controversial doctrine discussed in Chapter 12);
- the significant and obvious influence of its jurisprudence on the ICTR, and the drafting of the ICC Statute; and
- its judgments have been cited in national case law in the USA, Australia, and Switzerland, among other jurisdictions.

Zacklin, however, examines a number of the major criticisms of the ad hoc Tribunals.[117] The points made by him and others include:

- the Tribunals have been incredibly costly, and have had at times a combined annual budget of more that US $250 million, representing more than 10 per cent of all UN expenditure;
- both the ICTY and ICTR sit outside the territory of the events they are concerned with: the ICTY in The Hague (in the Netherlands) and the ICTR in Arusha (in Tanzania). They are thus

---

[115] See for example: PJ Magnarella, 'Some Milestones and Achievements at the International Criminal Tribunal for Rwanda' (1997) 11 Florida Journal of International Law 517 or Djiena Wembou, 'The International Criminal Tribunal for Rwanda: Its role in the African context' (1997) 37 International Review of the Red Cross (Issue 828) 685.

[116] Ratner, Abrams, and Bischoff, *Accountability for Human Rights Atrocities*, 222–3.

[117] R Zacklin, 'The failings of ad hoc international tribunals' (2004) 2 Journal of International Criminal Justice 541.

too remote from the victims and affected communities to play a role in national reconciliation, and 'outreach' programmes by the Tribunals to try and bridge this gap have not
succeeded; and

- the perception of the ICTY in the States that emerged from the former Yugoslavia is often
  that it is biased and ineffective, or has been exploited for propaganda.[118]

In addition, severe criticism was levelled at the ICTY Prosecutor for declining to open an investigation into the 1999 aerial bombing of Serbia by NATO and whether that action involved war
crimes, despite the obvious jurisdiction of the Tribunal over any crimes committed in that bombing campaign.

3.5.4 The establishment of the ICC

Occurring in parallel with the development of the ad hoc tribunals for Yugoslavia and
Rwanda, the UN International Law Commission had commenced work on a draft
statute for an international criminal court.[119] It reported on its work and provided
a draft statute to the UN General Assembly in 1994.[120] The timing was obviously
fortuitous, following the establishment of the two ad hoc tribunals it came at a time
of diminishing 'scepticism about the prospects for a permanent International criminal Court' among diplomats[121] and positive enthusiasm for such a prospect among
civil society and non-government organizations.[122] The UN general assembly set up a
Preparatory Committee to translate this draft statute into the draft text of a convention which could be put to a diplomatic conference tasked with negotiating a final
treaty.[123] That diplomatic conference occurred in 1998 in Rome, resulting in what
is now often called the Rome Statute of the ICC. The negotiations were large and
complex, officially involving 148 national delegations as well as the participation of
accredited non-governmental organizations.[124] Two broad approaches to the negotiations were apparent. A group of self-described 'Like-Minded' States (largely led by
Canada and Australia) desired a relatively strong court of 'automatic jurisdiction';
several permanent members of the Security Council (especially the United States,
China, and Russia) wanted a more limited court which would have to defer to the
Security Council on numerous issues (such as when and if an investigation should be
commenced).[125]

---

[118] See further: SK Ivkovich and J Hagan, *Reclaiming Justice: The International Tribunal for the Former
Yugoslavia and Local Courts* (Oxford University Press 2011) Chapter 3.

[119] The International Law Commission was discussed in section 1.2.5.

[120] [1994] International Law Commission Yearbook, vol 2(2), 26–74 (containing the draft statute and
commentary).

[121] E Wilmshurst, 'The International Criminal Court' in Cryer et al, *Introduction*, 148.

[122] See generally: H Durham, 'The Role of Civil Society in Creating the International Criminal Court
Statute: Ten Years On and Looking Back' (2012) 3 Journal of International Humanitarian Legal Studies 3.

[123] UN Doc GA Res 50/46 (11 December 1995).

[124] Over 250 of the latter were invited to participate: Durham, 'The Role of Civil Society', 30.

[125] Cassese et al, *Cassese's International Criminal Law*, 263.

There was thus significant controversy over two issues: the extent of the court's jurisdiction (and especially the relationship between its jurisdiction and that of national courts) and the extent to which it should have a completely independent prosecutor capable of launching investigations *proprio motu* (i.e. on his or her own initiative). The latter, in particular, raised fears in some delegations of the possibility of a 'rogue' prosecutor who might engage in politically motivated prosecutions. Given the scale and complexity of the undertaking, much of the negotiating process proceeded in informal committees and draft texts were negotiated by consensus. That is, compromises often had to be reached on important, technical issues and occasionally in isolation from negotiations occurring on related issues elsewhere. This has two important consequences: the final ICC Statute is not always perfectly internally consistent or harmoniously drafted; and the negotiating process did not leave a comprehensive set of preparatory documents which might assist in interpreting the final text.[126]

In the final days of the conference a number of questions were still proving highly controversial, especially those regarding the jurisdiction of the court. The United States in particular proposed an amendment to the text of the draft Convention which would have required the consent of the State of nationality of the suspect before he or she could be prosecuted before the court, among other limitations. Famously, such last-minute attempted amendments were defeated by a procedural motion moved by Norway which allowed the conference to proceed directly to vote on the text as a whole.[127] The text of the Statute was then adopted by a vote of 120 to seven, with 21 abstentions on 17 July 1998. The Statute entered force on 1 July 2002, and at time of writing there were 122 States Parties to the Statute.

With the Statute's entry into force the world's first permanent international criminal tribunal had been established with jurisdiction over war crimes, crimes against humanity, and genocide. In addition, provision was made under the statute for it to have jurisdiction over the crime of aggression. During negotiations the question of how to define aggression had become so controversial that it was simply deferred. Thus, the Rome Statute entered into force without any operative provisions on the crime of aggression. This gap was eventually filled in with amendments negotiated in 2010, though it will be some time before the Court can exercise its new jurisdiction over aggression due to a series of constraints built into those amendments (as discussed further in Chapter 11). The ICC was also created as a court of complementary jurisdiction. The essence of this concept is that unlike the ad hoc Tribunals the ICC does not have jurisdiction over a case to the exclusion of national courts and authorities. Rather, a case is only admissible before the Court where national authorities are either not investigating or prosecuting the crimes in question or are unable or unwilling to genuinely conduct such investigation or prosecution. The nature of this jurisdiction is considered further in Chapter 4, section 4.4.

---

[126] The role of such *travaux préparatoires* in interpreting treaties was noted in Chapter 1, section 1.3.

[127] RSK Lee, 'Introduction: The Rome conference and its contributions to international law' in RSK Lee (ed), *The International Criminal Court: The Making of the Rome Statute: Issues, Negotiations, Results* (Kluwer 1999), 25–26.

The ICC is now a functioning and busy institution. It has active prosecutions or investigations arising out of situations in Uganda, the Democratic Republic of the Congo, Darfur (Sudan), the Central African Republic, Kenya, Libya, Côte d'Ivoire, and Mali. It has convicted two defendants in the *Lubanga* and *Katanga* trials (discussed in later chapters), and has controversially issued an arrest warrant for the President of Sudan and commenced prosecutions in the *Kenyatta* and *Ruto and others* cases against the serving President and Deputy President of Kenya respectively. (At time of writing, however, the case against Mr Kenyatta has been abandoned due to the difficulty of securing witnesses and their cooperation.) This has led to criticisms that the Court is exclusively focussed on Africa. The merits of such claims are discussed in Chapter 4, but it is notable that the majority of these situations were referred to the Court either by the Security Council or by the States in question themselves. Only a minority of these cases were instigated at the initiative of the ICC Prosecutor.

3.5.5 The establishment of other courts with international elements

The ICC does not represent the end of history for the institutional development of international criminal law. It will always be a court of limited resources and jurisdiction incapable of prosecuting every international offence everywhere. Nonetheless, post-conflict societies in particular will often lack the resources required to bring to justice those accused of serious international crimes. At the same time, the international community now seems wary of the expense of establishing new international criminal tribunals within the UN system.[128] The result has been, as noted above, a proliferation of courts with 'international elements'. These have included, among other examples:

- the UN Special Panels in Kosovo and East Timor in 1999;
- the Special Court for Sierra Leone in 2002;
- the Extraordinary Chambers in the Courts of Cambodia in 2004;
- the War Crimes Chamber in Bosnia and Herzegovina in 2005;
- the Special Tribunal for Lebanon in 2007; and
- the Extraordinary African Chambers in the Courts of Senegal in 2012.

These are extremely diverse institutions and generalizing about their common features may be misleading. Nonetheless, the pattern of most of those listed is that they were established under national law with jurisdiction over both national and international offences and are staffed in part by international judges. The principal exception to generalization is the Special Tribunal for Lebanon, which was established by the UN Security Council under a Chapter VII resolution: it is thus an international tribunal which also has jurisdiction over crimes under the national law of Lebanon. There is not space to discuss all of these tribunals here. However, the Special Court for Sierra Leone

---

[128] On so-called 'tribunal fatigue' see: Ratner, Abrams, and Bischoff, *Accountability for Human Rights Atrocities*, 252.

(SCSL), the Extraordinary Chambers in the Courts of Cambodia (ECCC), and the War Crimes Chamber in Bosnia and Herzegovina all receive some brief further discussion in Chapter 4.

A further development is the 2014 African Union initiative to create a single, regional African Court of Justice and Human and Peoples' Rights (the Merged Court) and to grant it jurisdiction over international crimes.[129] This would make it the world's first regional international criminal tribunal. The proposal is seen by some as having its origins in the African Union's hostility towards the ICC's attempted prosecution of President Al Bashir of Sudan. However, there are a number of obstacles to be overcome before the Merged Court starts hearing criminal cases. First, the Merged Court has not yet been created and the African Court of Justice and the African Court of Human and Peoples' Rights presently remain separate institutions and will do so until the treaty merging them comes into force. Further, even after the merger at least 15 African Union member States will have to ratify the separate amending protocol conferring international criminal jurisdiction upon the Merged Court.

3.6 What purposes are served by international criminal law?

International criminal law has grown very rapidly since the 1990s as both a body of law and practice. The premise of this book is that that body of law and practice is worth understanding in itself. It is beyond the scope of a volume dedicated to providing a succinct introduction to the relevant doctrinal law to engage in an extensive survey of the various purported goals or theoretical justifications for international criminal law.[130] Nonetheless, providing a relatively short account of them here may allow us to better consider whether the present enthusiasm for international criminal law's potential (or disappointment with its concrete achievements) is warranted.[131]

International criminal law often appears to be invoked as a useful or necessary response to atrocities, civil wars, or the collapse of dictatorships. In early 2011 for

---

[129] See generally: 2014 Draft Protocol on the Amendments to the Protocol on the Statute of the African Court of Justice and Human Rights, AU Doc EX.CL/846 (XXV); D Tladi, 'The immunity provision in the AU amendment protocol: separating the (doctrinal) wheat from the (normative) chaff' (2015) 13 Journal of International Criminal Justice 3; A Abass, 'Prosecuting International Crimes in Africa: Rationale, Prospects and Challenges' (2013) 24 European Journal of International Law (2013) 933; C Bhoke Murungu, 'Towards a Criminal Chamber in the African Court of Justice and Human Rights' (2011) 9 Journal of International Criminal Justice 1067; H Mbori Otieno, 'The merged African Court of Justice and Human Rights (ACJ&HR) as a better criminal justice system than the ICC: Are we Finding African Solution to African problems or creating African problems without solutions?' (2014), www.academia.edu/7237572/.

[130] Good extended treatments of these issues include: R Cryer, 'The Aims, Objectives and Justifications of International Criminal Law' in Cryer et al, *Introduction*, Chapter 2; Ambos, *Treatise*, vol 1, Chapter 2; D Luban, 'Fairness to Rightness: Jurisdiction, Legality, and the Legitimacy of International Criminal Law' in S Besson and J Tasioulas (eds), *The Philosophy of International Law* (Oxford University Press 2010), Chapter 28; and A Duff, 'Authority and Responsibility in International Criminal Law' in S Besson and J Tasioulas (eds), *Philosophy of International Law*, Chapter 29.

[131] On current pessimism about the field see: W Schabas, 'The Banality of International Justice' (2013) 11 Journal of International Criminal Justice 545.

example, the Security Council, expressing concern at 'the gross and systematic violation of human rights' and 'the widespread and systematic attacks currently taking place'
during the civil war in Libya referred the situation to the ICC.[132] If it is true that the
international community regards international criminal law as a useful tool in responding to atrocities or international crises, then one might expect that we would have a
good understanding of what we intended to achieve through its use. This is, unfortunately, not necessarily the case. As Damaška has observed, international criminal law
suffers from an overabundance of goals.[133] Some of these goals are discussed below.
We also need to consider, albeit briefly, two classic criticisms of international criminal
law: that its legitimacy is undermined by its selectivity; and, in a variant on the same
argument, that it represents only 'victor's justice'.

3.6.1 The goals or justifications of international criminal law

The possible goals or justifications of international criminal law fall into two broad
groups. First, we have goals or justifications borrowed from theories of criminal justice
at the national level such as deterrence, incapacitation, denunciation or education, and
retribution. Others goals usually considered more-or-less unique to international criminal justice include the promotion of lasting peace, national reconciliation, or the creation of an impartial and incontrovertible historic record. There are significant problems
with each of these. As to deterrence, there is relatively little evidence that criminal law
has a strong deterrent effect at the national level.[134] Given the limited number of international prosecutions presently underway it seems hard to claim that world leaders
have a great deal to fear from international criminal law. President Al Bashir of Sudan,
for example, has been wanted by the ICC since 2009 but remains free and relatively able
to travel within Africa. Incapacitation involves the idea that imprisoning people who
have committed crimes in past will prevent them committing future crimes. This is
generally regarded as morally dubious (because it involves punishing people for things
they have not yet done) and is in any event a consequentialist argument which is impossible to prove.[135] That is, removing leaders does not guarantee removing the structures
of State corruption and criminality which empowered them in the first place and which
may allow others to step into their shoes and commit similar crimes.[136] Denunciation or
education involves seeing international criminal law as essentially a 'moral teacher'.[137]
That is, through trial and punishment international criminal justice should not only
condemn the acts of an individual as heinous but teach the lesson that such acts are

---

[132] UN Doc. SC Res 1970 (2011).

[133] The classic work is: M Damaška, 'What is the Point of International Criminal Justice?' (2008) 83 Chicago
Kent Law Review 329.

[134] J Tasioulas, 'Punishment and Repentance' (2006) 81 Philosophy 279, 293.

[135] S Nouwen, 'Justifying Justice' in J Crawford and M Koskenniemi (eds), *The Cambridge Companion to
International Law* (Cambridge University Press 2012) 338–9.

[136] D Saxon, 'Exporting Justice: Perceptions of the ICTY Among the Serbian, Croatian, and Muslim
Communities in the Former Yugoslavia' (2005) 4 Journal of Human Rights 559, 567.

[137] M Damaška, 'What is the Point of International Criminal Justice?' (2008) 83 Chicago Kent Law Review
329, 345, and 361.

always wrong. This, it is argued, sends a message to the international community and may condition politics to make such crimes less likely in the future.[138] Again, it is difficult to prove that such 'messages' are received by the target audience.

Such educative arguments also face a moral objection from theories of retributive justice. Retributive justice holds, broadly, that it is not acceptable to treat people as a means to an end; it is only acceptable to treat them as reasoning moral agents.[139] Criminal law sets standards in advance and if someone transgresses them then they are deserving of punishment. On this view we should not punish people to teach *others* a lesson, we should punish people only because their *own* actions deserve it.

A further potential criticism of international criminal trials is supplied by 'communicative justice' (a particular theory of retributive justice). This approach argues that the purpose of criminal sanction is moral censure of a wrongdoer by a relevant moral community of which they are a part (and which can claim authority over them) with the aim that the wrongdoer should (ideally) experience remorse and accept the imposed sanction.[140] If this approach is correct, it is not necessarily easy to extrapolate it to *international* criminal law. It is not obvious why defendants should accept the claim of an international criminal tribunal to represent the international community; or why such communicative justice would not be better conducted at the national or even local level.

As regards the unique justifications for international criminal law (peace, national reconciliation, or the establishing an historical record) many of these are also not easy to accept at face value. A commonly made argument is that there can be 'no peace without justice': meaning that in post-conflict or 'transitional' societies unless those who committed atrocities are prosecuted they (or other like them) may come to power to commit such crimes again. The argument is superficially attractive but ultimately un-provable: it assumes *stable* peace always requires prosecutions. There have been no prosecutions for the crime of apartheid in post-apartheid South Africa, for example, and the country remains peaceful. The argument for national reconciliation is also, regrettably, weak. There is little evidence that post-conflict societies accept or internalize the verdicts of international criminal tribunals unless they fit pre-existing prejudices. In particular, the ICTY has shown no ability to shift ethnic or nationalist narratives of the conflict(s) in the Balkan region, where each ethnic/national group predominantly sees itself as the exclusive victim of aggression by other groups (and its own conduct as entirely justified).[141] Indeed, in the words of one former ICTY prosecutor, '[a]mong some national communities (particularly the Serbs and the Croats) the ICTY is widely

---

[138] M Drumbl, *Atrocity, Punishment, and International Law* (Cambridge University Press 2007) 174–5.

[139] Cryer, 'The Aims, Objectives and Justifications of International Criminal Law' in Cryer et al, *Introduction*, 30.

[140] Generally: J Tasioulas, 'Punishment and repentance' (2006) 81 Philosophy 279; A Duff, 'Can we Punish the Perpetrators of Atrocities?' in T Brudholm (ed), *The Religious in Responses to Mass Atrocity* (Oxford University Press 2009) 85 ff.

[141] Compare SK Ivković and J Hagan, *Reclaiming Justice: The International Tribunal for the Former Yugoslavia and Local Courts* (OUP, 2011) 160–1; Saxon, 'Exporting Justice', 568; and Koskenniemi, 'Between Impunity and Show Trials', 35.

despised.'[142] There is thus a 'persistence of denial, hate and anti-tribunal propaganda' in both the Balkan region and Rwanda and some therefore claim the ICTY and ICTR have 'yet to establish their legitimacy in the states for which they were created.'[143] In any event, it is far from clear that a criminal trial process—at least one conducted under an adversarial system—is one particularly well-adapted to uncovering and recording historical truth. As noted in section 3.3.1, the adversarial system relies on the parties to put forward the evidence that best supports their own case. This does not necessarily involve a court conducting an extensive inquiry of its own to determine 'the real truth'.

Gerry Simpson once noted that proponents of international law in general, when asked to justify either its existence or effectiveness, tend to resort to a kind of eclecticism and will shift between different types of arguments according to the issue at hand.[144] Given the 'overabundance' of potentially available goals for international criminal law, it is unsurprising its defenders have also sometimes been accused of a similar 'jumping' between different arguments whenever pressed on difficult questions.[145] However, if it is a weakness of international criminal law that it lacks a fully coherent rationale, then the same criticism may plausibly be made of national criminal law.

3.6.2 Criticisms: selectivity and victor's justice

The classic criticism of the Nuremberg and Tokyo IMT trials (and the subsequent pro-ceedings under Control Council Law No. 10 in occupied Germany) is that they were designed expressly to prosecute only the crimes of the defeated powers. These may thus be criticized as being a form of 'victor's justice', the argument being that criminal law can only be seen as fair and legitimate if it is applied even-handedly. The point has some force in that it makes a moral argument that to the extent that the 'victors' have also committed the same or similar crimes then there is a degree of hypocrisy involved in putting the 'vanquished' on trial. At Nuremberg the defence lawyer for Admiral Karl Dönitz had some success in demonstrating that while his client had been charged with waging unrestricted submarine warfare as a war crime, the US and UK had pursued a similar policy.[146] However, the moral point only goes so far: the Nazi regime had in fact committed appalling acts worthy of punishment.[147]

---

[142] Saxon, 'Exporting Justice', 562.

[143] V Peskin, *International Justice in Rwanda and the Balkans: Virtual Trials and the Struggle for State Cooperation* (Cambridge University Press 2009), 244.

[144] G Simpson 'On the Magic Mountain: Teaching Public International Law' (1999) 10 European Journal of International Law 70.

[145] Nouwen, 'Justifying Justice', 338–42. An unfortunate feature of this argumentative style, as Nouwen notes, is the underlying assumption that several partially convincing arguments may add up to one fully-convincing one.

[146] R Cryer, *Prosecuting International Crimes: Selectivity and the International Criminal Law Regime* (Cambridge University Press 2005) 200–1.

[147] Though one might argue Stalin's Russia had also committed crimes of vast scope: several million people in the Soviet-controlled Ukraine died in 1932–1933 as the result of a preventable famine. The famine is widely considered deliberately inflicted, in which case it would clearly now constitute a crime against humanity or possibly genocide. See, e.g., R Moore, ' "A Crime against Humanity Arguably without Parallel in European History": Genocide and the "Politics" of Victimhood in Western Narratives of the Ukrainian Holodomor'

Nonetheless, international criminal law is inherently and doubly selective: both in the limited acts the international community has defined as 'international crimes' and in the limited range of situations where the international community is willing to support their prosecution.[148] That said, selectivity does not inherently undermine the legitimacy of a system of criminal law. National criminal law systems may embody either prosecutorial discretion as to which crimes are worthy of prosecution or a principle of the strict prosecution of all offences. However, even national legal systems that theoretically embody a strict duty to prosecute all crimes must (as a matter of practicality) make substantial exceptions in practice for minor offences.[149] The question is whether—or at what point—such selectivity becomes unfair. Unfairness is most evident when one is prepared to impose certain (international) standards on other States' nationals but to insist on treatment according to different (usually national) standards for one's own citizens. As Cryer notes, the negotiation of the Rome Statute of the ICC and its ratification by 123 States willing to have it exercise jurisdiction over their own territory and nationals shows an historically extraordinary commitment to universal principles.[150]

A degree of selectivity is still obviously apparent in international criminal law. First, in any context where prosecutions can only proceed with the support of the government of the State in which crimes were committed, it will clearly be difficult to prosecute any crimes those 'victors' may have committed. The ICTR was dependent for its ability to operate on the cooperation of the Rwandan government. When, in 1998, the ICTR Appeals Chamber ordered the release of the defendant in *Barayagwiza* (on the basis that delays by the Prosecutor had prejudiced his right to a fair trial) the Rwandan government cut off cooperation with the Tribunal.[151] Cooperation was only restored when the Appeals Chamber (citing new facts being drawn to its attention) over-ruled its earlier decision and allowed the trial to resume. Further, no member of the Rwandan RPF government has ever been charged with an international crime—despite suggestions that RPF forces may have been involved in war crimes or retribution killings during the Civil War which followed the 1994 genocide.[152] For its part, as noted at section 3.5.3, the ICTY attracted severe criticism when its Prosecutor decided not to open investigation into the possibility that NATO member state forces may have committed war crimes in the course of the bombing campaign over Kosovo in 1999. Similarly, in cases where States have self-referred situations within their own territory to the ICC,

---

(2012) 58 Australian Journal of Politics and History 367; compare D Rayfield, 'The Ukrainian Famine of 1933: Man-Made Catastrophe, Mass Murder, or Genocide?' in LY Luciuk (ed), *Holodomor: Reflections on the Great Famine of 1932–1933 in Soviet Ukraine* (Kashtan Press 2008) 93.

[148] Cryer, *Prosecuting International Crimes*, 191 quoting T McCormack, 'Selective Reaction to Atrocity' (1996–1997) 60 Albany Law Review 681, 683.

[149] Cryer, *Prosecuting International Crimes*, 192.   [150] Ibid, 230.

[151] C Ryngaert, 'State Cooperation with the International Criminal Tribunal for Rwanda' (2013) 13 International Criminal Law Review 125, 129–32. This included barring the Prosecutor from her office in Kigali and preventing the travel of 16 witnesses to the ITCR.

[152] E.g.: Human Rights Watch, 'Action urged regarding non-cooperation with ICTR and ICTY: Letter to Security Council Members', 25 October 2002, www.hrw.org/news/2002/10/25/action-urged-regarding-non-cooperation-ictr-and-icty.

the Prosecutor has not opened any investigations regarding government figures.[153] The purpose of international criminal law would seem called into question if it can never be invoked against those in power.

However, this is too one-sided a picture. It is obvious that international criminal law has been used to attempt to prosecute crimes committed by leaders who are still in office. The most notorious case at present is that of President Al Bashir of Sudan. ICC proceedings were also brought against the President and Vice President of Kenya regarding potential international crimes committed during the post-election violence in 2007–2008. Further, the ICC has historically been criticized for failing to investigate possible war crimes committed by armed forces of the United States, the United Kingdom, or Israel when acting within territory (or spaces) subject to ICC jurisdiction. However, a pre-trial chamber of the ICC has for the first time requested that the Prosecutor reconsider her decision not to open such an investigation in respect of alleged war crimes committed by Israeli Defence Force personnel aboard a ship flagged to Comoros in 2010.[154]

Such developments might be taken as promising indications that selectivity and international criminal law is, perhaps, reducing. However, without independent enforcement machinery, international criminal tribunals remain dependent on the cooperation of States—particularly those States which control access to territory, witnesses, and evidence. This will often be the State with the highest interest in shielding accused from prosecution and non-cooperation may seriously hamper investigations. It has also proven difficult for the ICC to either gain custody of high-ranking defendants, as evidenced by the continued freedom of President Al Bashir, or to prosecute cases without strong support from the relevant territorial government, as shown in the collapse of the case against President Kenyatta of Kenya.[155]

 Counterpoint

The discussion above may seem unduly negative. Certainly, one can question both the theoretical justifications for and the practical effectiveness of international criminal law. This does not necessarily, however, mean the project is not worth attempting or the results have been wholly illusory. While the system may not be perfect, as the late judge and scholar Antonio Cassese put it: 'Half a loaf is better than pie in the sky.'[156]

It is perhaps easy to be cynical and to lose sight of the improvement that achievements like the Rome Statute of the ICC represent 'over what went before'.[157] What went before was, of course, a situation in which international crimes often went entirely unpunished. Indeed, the nearly 50 years between the Nuremberg IMT trial and the establishment of the ICTY international criminal law was 'rarely seen as relevant' by scholars, practitioners or governments.[158] It is now a major

---

[153] See Chapter 4, section 4.4.3 on 'self-referrals'.
[154] See Chapter 5, section 5.3.2.   [155] Noted further in section 5.4.3.
[156] A Cassese et al, *Cassese's International Criminal Law* 3rd ed (Oxford University Press 2013) 260. Quoted in Simpson, *Law, War and Crime* (Polity Press 2007) 108 as 'half a pie is better than no pie'.
[157] Cryer, *Prosecuting International Crimes*, 329.   [158] Cryer et al, *Introduction*, 594.

field of practice, study, and debate. That alone is a significant achievement. Further, we should perhaps be modest in what we expect the ICC, with limited resources, to achieve by itself. As Cryer and his co-authors note, national courts will always have to play a role but may require both international support and the legitimacy conferred by 'an international *imprimatur*' in order to conduct effective prosecutions.[159] The future of international criminal law may thus lie in greater collaboration between international and national institutions.[160]

The creation of law and legal institutions is often not an end in itself but simply a first step, especially when it is part of a process of changing moral and political values.[161] We should, perhaps, not be too hasty to judge the success or failure of international criminal law just yet nor be too dismissive of the extraordinary achievement that the creation and development of international criminal law to date represents.

3.7 Summary and conclusions

The simplest conclusion to draw from this section is that while the concept of individual criminal liability directly arising under international law was controversial prior to 1945 it is now widely accepted. The difficulty inherent in national courts exercising jurisdiction over international crimes is thus not one of principle but one of definition. Even if there is direct individual responsibility, defining with sufficient precision the elements and requirements of international criminal offences between 1939 and 2002[162] as a matter of customary international law will not always be easy. As noted this is not a purely academic point: the Extraordinary Chamber in the Courts of Cambodia is tasked with trying Khmer Rouge offences and so must apply international criminal law as it stood in 1975.

Useful further reading

R CRYER, *Prosecuting International Crimes: Selectivity and the International Criminal Law Regime* (Cambridge University Press 2005), Chapters 1, 2, and 4.

Cryer's book remains the leading study of an important challenge for international criminal justice: that of selectivity. That is, in the aftermath of mass atrocities not everyone who could be charged with an international crime will be. How does international criminal law deal with the fact it will only ever be able to prosecute a selection of defendants? Chapter 1 provides a useful and concise overview of the historical development of international criminal law. Chapter 2

---

[159] Ibid, 593.

[160] Such cooperation is sometimes described as 'positive complementarity'. See, e.g., W Schabas, *An Introduction to the International Criminal Court* 4th ed (Cambridge University Press 2011) 191 and compare 166–7.

[161] See, generally, J Brunee and S Toope, *Legitimacy and Legality in International Law: An Interactional Account* (Cambridge University Press 2010).

[162] State parties to the ICC Statute will, after 2002 be able to rely on ICC definitions: (1) under treaty law at least in respect of crimes committed on the territory of a State party to the ICC Statute or by the citizens of a State party; and (2) in other cases, to the extent the Statute codifies customary law.

provides an analysis of States' rights and obligations in respect of prosecuting international crimes and the applicable law and available mechanisms. Chapter 4 addresses arguments based on selectivity in detail.

R CRYER, 'The Aims, Objectives and Justifications of International Criminal Law' in R Cryer, H Friman, D Robinson, and E Wilmshurst, *An Introduction to International Criminal Law and Procedure*, 3rd ed (Cambridge University Press 2014), Chapter 2.

For those wishing to read a more detailed treatment of the goals and purposes of international criminal law, this chapter provides an excellent starting point.

P SANDS (ed), *From Nuremberg to the Hague: The Future of International Criminal Justice* (Cambridge University Press 2003), Chapters 1 and 2.

Chapter 1 contains a useful and highly readable account of the Nuremberg trial by historian Richard Overy and contains numerous insights into the legal, political, and practical difficulties posed by the trials. Chapter 2 by Andrew Clapham delves further into the complexities of the Nuremberg Trial and relates them to the challenges faced by more recent international criminal tribunals.

G WERLE and F JESSBERGER, *Principles of International Criminal Law*, 3rd ed (Oxford University Press 2014) 144–163.

Werle and Jessberger provide a detailed account of the options for national implementation of international criminal law, examining in particular the relevant national law in Germany.

4

Jurisdiction and structure of international criminal courts and tribunals

4.1 Introduction

This chapter provides an overview of the structure and workings of the different types of international criminal courts and tribunals. It also considers their respective strengths, weaknesses, and limitations. Emphasis will be placed on the International Criminal Court (ICC) as a court of complementary jurisdiction. We will also examine the ICC as a case study of how international criminal courts and tribunals are typically structured and how relevant functions are allocated to each organ of such a court or tribunal.

 Learning aims

By the end of this chapter and the relevant readings you should be able to:

- differentiate types of international criminal courts and tribunals (i.e. those established by UN Security Council Resolutions (UNSCRs) and treaty-based courts);
- differentiate between such international tribunals and internationalized or mixed tribunals (being national courts with varying international elements);
- discuss the respective strengths and weaknesses of each type of court or tribunal;
- compare the temporal, geographic, and subject-matter jurisdictions of the different tribunals and any thresholds of gravity (e.g. only the most serious crimes) or restrictions as to defendants (e.g. 'those most responsible');
- define the concept of complementarity and explain its operation under the ICC Statute; and
- define the roles and powers of the official organs of the tribunals (i.e the presidency and chambers, the registry and office of the prosecutors).

The chapter therefore proceeds as follows:

- Section 4.2 introduces the basic types of international criminal tribunal, and asks you to consider the advantages and disadvantages of each.

- Section 4.3 outlines the forms of jurisdiction and asks you to compare how these are exercised by the major international criminal tribunals.

- Section 4.4 considers in more detail the ways in which the jurisdiction of the ICC may be engaged and the limitations which are inherent in its statute on when it may proceed with an investigation or trial.

- Section 4.5 examines the structure of the ICC as a representative international criminal tribunal, which is internally divided into judicial, prosecutorial, and administrative organs, each performing different functions.

4.2 Types of international tribunal and their features

4.2.1 Basic distinctions

There are now a great variety of criminal courts with jurisdiction over international crimes, and an important first step in understanding them is having some sense of what is meant by an 'international criminal tribunal'. Unfortunately this is not a field where there are necessarily clear-cut definitions. One might view a criminal tribunal as being either international or national on the basis of how it was established. Using this formal approach, an *international* criminal tribunal would be one established by a treaty or by a UN Security Council Chapter VII resolution, and a *national* criminal tribunal would be one established under national law. However, much of what you read about criminal tribunals and international law will be rather more descriptive. As shown in Figure 4.1, this approach tends to place international and national courts at the ends of a spectrum with an area of overlap between them.

Figure 4.1 Potential overlap between national and international tribunals

This descriptive approach contrasts:

- international courts with jurisdiction over crimes defined by international law; and
- national courts with jurisdiction over crimes defined by national law (which could also include international crimes).

It then assumes that there is an area of overlap (in the area of overlap in Figure 4.1) covering tribunals that may be described as 'mixed', 'hybrid', or 'internationalized'. These consist of either:

- tribunals located within national court systems that have international elements (such as international judges, international funding, etc) and jurisdiction over international crimes; or
- international tribunals (established by a treaty or a UN Security Council Chapter VII resolution) that have jurisdiction not only over international crimes (e.g. murder as a war crime, crimes against humanity, or genocide) but that also have authority to prosecute crimes defined by a national legal system (e.g. 'ordinary' murder).

On this basis many textbooks divide criminal tribunals into (i) international, (ii) national, and (iii) mixed, hybrid, or internationalized tribunals. The difficulty with this, as we shall see, is that once one moves from a formal approach (that describes all tribunals as either national or international, depending on their legal origins) to a descriptive approach (grouping tribunals by their common features) problems of classification arise. For example, consider the case of a court established by a treaty with jurisdiction over international crimes committed in one State and that also has jurisdiction over domestic crimes committed in that State. Assume also that the court is staffed by international judges and domestic judges from that State. Is such a court appropriately labelled an international court or is it a mixed, hybrid, or internationalized court? The question arises in particular in relation to the Special Court for Sierra Leone, described by some as an international tribunal[1] and by others as a mixed, hybrid, or internationalized court.[2] This might be thought a merely definitional debate.[3] However, as discussed later, the Special Court for Sierra Leone held that because it was an international court certain rules of State immunity did not apply to it. Irrespective of whether you find that argument convincing (it is considered further in Chapter 14), it suggests how we classify tribunals may have important consequences.

---

[1] E.g. W Schabas, *The UN International Criminal Tribunals: the former Yugoslavia, Rwanda and Sierra Leone* (Cambridge University Press 2006 and 2008 reprint).

[2] E.g. A Cassese et al, *Cassese's International Criminal Law* 3rd ed (Oxford University Press 2013) 263–67; A Zahar and G Sluiter, *International Criminal Law: A Critical Introduction* (Oxford University Press 2008) 12–13; SR Ratner, JS Abrams, and JL Bischoff, *Accountability for Human Rights Atrocities in International Law: Beyond the Nuremberg Legacy* 3rd ed (Oxford University Press 2009) 246–50; DA Mundis, 'New Mechanisms for the Enforcement of International Humanitarian Law' (2001) 95 American Journal of International Law 934, at 936 and 951 (appearing to prefer the term 'mixed' as a *description* of the Special Court's jurisdiction).

[3] And in many senses one might be right: R O'Keefe, *International Criminal Law* (Oxford University Press 2015) 85, para 3.1.

The key point is to be aware of these terms and how different authors use them, but not to become overly confused by such labels. Descriptive terms are only an explanatory aid. In the end, they are not a substitute for understanding each international criminal tribunal on its own terms.

4.2.2 International criminal tribunals established by a treaty

The main example of a treaty-based international criminal tribunal established among States is now, of course, the permanent ICC. The Nuremberg International Military Tribunal (IMT) was also such a treaty-based international criminal tribunal. In addition, the Special Court for Sierra Leone was established by a treaty between the United Nations (an international organization) and Sierra Leone (a State). It may thus be formally considered an international tribunal, and as noted has held itself to be so in its own jurisprudence.[4] Despite this, it is discussed at section 4.2.4 as a practical example of a tribunal of mixed jurisdiction.

An international court established by a treaty may have jurisdiction over either (a) offences committed on the territory of, or by the nationals of, its State parties, or (b) offences subject to universal jurisdiction that any State could therefore prosecute irrespective of any link or nexus between the crime and that State. That jurisdiction covers acts committed on the territory of State parties is significant as it means that a treaty-based tribunal may have jurisdiction over the acts of nationals of a non-State party if those acts are committed on the territory of a member State. This may raise concerns for a State which has chosen not to ratify the Court's constituting treaty. In respect of universal jurisdiction, States may in practice be reluctant or cautious in allowing treaty-based courts to exercise it in order to avoid international legal disputes with non-State parties. This is because views differ as to precisely which crimes are covered by universal jurisdiction or whether there are procedural preconditions to its exercise (as discussed in Chapter 3).

A key limitation of treaty-based courts is, however, that they are not able to compel non-State parties to produce or surrender defendants, witnesses, or evidence. Questions of State immunity will arise regarding officials of non-State parties who are accused of committing crimes. Such questions are discussed in Chapters 5 and 14.

4.2.3 International criminal tribunals established by a UN Security Council Chapter VII resolution

The main examples of international criminal tribunals established by a UN Security Council Chapter VII resolution are the International Criminal Tribunal for the Former Yugoslavia (ICTY) and the International Criminal Tribunal for Rwanda (ICTR). Each

---

[4] *Prosecutor v Taylor* (Decision on Immunity), SCSL Appeals Chamber, 31 May 2004, para 42; *Kallon, Norman and Kamara* (Constitutionality and Lack of Jurisdiction Decision) SCSL Appeals Chamber, 13 March 2004, paras 38–79.

was set up by the UN as a temporary tribunal to cope with a particular crisis as discussed in Chapter 3.

One advantage of establishing such tribunals under Chapter VII is the compulsory effect of the constituting resolution. As discussed in Chapter 2, Chapter VII embodies the compulsory powers of the UN Security Council on matters of international peace and security. Therefore, if the resolution that creates the tribunal directs States to cooperate with the tribunal and declares that no immunities will be recognized before it, then this binds all UN member States. Obligations under the UN Charter prevail over all other international law obligations (other than *jus cogens*). In addition to creating tribunals, Chapter VII can be used to grant an existing treaty-based tribunal jurisdiction over a situation in a non-State party. A jurisdiction that it might not otherwise have.

The disadvantage of Chapter VII tribunals is that they require political will to establish and continued political will to fund. This is problematic as the international community has come to perceive Chapter VII tribunals as expensive and slow.[5] The UN Security Council put a completion strategy in effect for the winding up of the activities of the International Criminal Tribunal for the Former Yugoslavia and International Criminal Tribunal for Rwanda by the end of 2014. This obviously puts a degree of pressure on them to conclude their activities. Concerns have been raised that such pressure might compromise the fair trial rights of defendants, but as some trials and appeals will clearly be permitted to run until at least 2017 these concerns may be overstated.[6] Certain residual functions of the ICTY and ICTR will be administered by the Mechanism for International Criminal Tribunals (sometimes called the 'Residual Mechanism').[7]

4.2.4 Mixed, internationalized, or hybrid tribunals

As noted above, tribunals with jurisdiction over international crimes may have a mixture of national and international elements. They may be established as international courts but given national elements or established as national courts that are to some extent internationalized. In theory, this could bring together the best of both systems. Thus, the neutrality, objectivity, and expertise of an international tribunal may be coupled with the legitimacy, ease of access to witnesses and evidence, and greater impact on local reconciliation and politics of a national tribunal. Whether this has been the result in practice may be questioned. Some examples are given below but, as noted, one must be careful to approach each one on its own terms. They are all unique institutions.

---

[5] Ratner, Abrams, and Bischoff, *Accountability for Human Rights Atrocities*, 252.

[6] See for example the 2014 ICTY Completion Strategy Report in UN Doc S/2014/351 (2014). See the continuing cases at trial and on appeal listed on the ICTY website: www.icty.org/action/cases/4.

[7] The Mechanism was established under UN Security Council Resolution 1966, UN Doc S/RES/1966. See further: G Acquaviva, 'Was a Residual Mechanism for International Criminal Tribunals Really Necessary?' (2011) 9 Journal of International Criminal Justice 789; C Denis, 'Critical Overview of the "Residual Functions" of the Mechanism and its Date of Commencement (including Transitional Arrangements)' (2011) 9 Journal of International Criminal Justice 819.

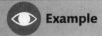

Example

The Special Court for Sierra Leone (SCSL)

The SCSL was established in 2002 by an agreement between the government of Sierra Leone and the UN Secretary General (acting on the authority of the Security Council). It was not part of the Sierra Leone legal system, but it did have jurisdiction over crimes committed during the civil war of the 1990s under both international law (war crimes and crimes against humanity) and the law of Sierra Leone. It had temporal jurisdiction only over crimes committed after 30 November 1996. The majority of the judges who served and the Registrar and Prosecutor were all appointed by the Secretary General. The rest of the judges were appointed by the government of Sierra Leone. It had its seat in Sierra Leone and conducted most of its trials there. The SCSL closed in 2013 following the conviction and imprisonment of former President of Liberia, Charles Taylor.[8] Following its closure, the Residual Special Court for Sierra Leone was established by an agreement between the UN and the Government of Sierra Leone to oversee the continuing legal obligations of the SCSL.[9] These include witness protection, supervision of prison sentences, and management of the SCSL archives.

Example

The Extraordinary Chambers in the Courts of Cambodia (ECCC)

Between 1997 and 2003 there were negotiations between the government of Cambodia and the UN over the establishment of a UN assisted tribunal to try crimes committed during the Khmer Rouge regime. The issue remains politically difficult in Cambodia, as part of the method of defeating the Khmer Rouge had been for the government of the day to absorb many of its defecting leaders.[10] The ECCC is thus under a degree of political pressure to limit the total number of prosecutions it conducts. Funding (by voluntary international donations) to run the trials has also proved difficult to secure and the ECCC's early operations were marred by allegations of corruption.

The Pre-Trial, Trial, and Appeal Chambers each have a majority of Cambodian judges, but can only make certain decisions by a super-majority that requires the concurring vote of at least one international judge. The ECCC operates on a modified inquisitorial process (discussed in Chapter 5, section 5.2), involving two co-prosecutors and two co-investigating judges (in each case one Cambodian, and one an international appointment). In August 2014 the Trial Chamber of the ECCC found Nuon Chea and Khieu Samphan, both senior members of the regime, guilty of crimes against humanity and sentenced them to life imprisonment.

---

[8] For security reasons the trial of Charles Taylor was heard in The Hague. He was sentenced to 50 years in jail on 30 May 2012. His sentence was appealed, but the Appeals Chamber of the SCSL rejected his appeal and upheld his conviction on 26 September 2012.

[9] The Residual SCSL has a useful website: http://www.rscsl.org/.

[10] Ratner, Abrams, and Bischoff, *Accountability for Human Rights Atrocities*, 317. See especially: D McCargo, 'Politics by Other Means? The Virtual Trials of the Khmer Rouge Tribunal' (2011) 87 International Affairs 613, for an excellent account of the political difficulties encountered.

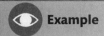 **Example**

The War Crimes Chamber of Bosnia and Herzegovina ('War Crimes Chamber')

The War Crimes Chamber was established in 2005 in the context of the ICTY completion strategy which sets out how the activities of the ICTY will be wound down. It is a national court to which the ICTY can transfer cases involving lower-level perpetrators for prosecution. This occurs under rule 11*bis* of the ICTY Rules of Procedure and Evidence. The War Crimes Chamber was established with international assistance and has international judges at the trial and appeal levels. Their participation is expected to be phased out over time, despite an enormous domestic caseload.

Other tribunals which may be described as hybrids or mixed include:

- the UN Special Panels established in Kosovo and East Timor which were national courts operating with international elements;[11] and
- the Special Tribunal for Lebanon, which is an international court established by a Chapter VII resolution to 'prosecute persons responsible for the attack of 14 February 2005 resulting in the death of former Lebanese Prime Minister Rafiq Hariri and in the death or injury of other persons'.[12] It only has jurisdiction over crimes under the national criminal law of Lebanon.

4.3 The jurisdiction of the major international criminal tribunals

In Chapter 2 we focussed on the principles of prescriptive and enforcement jurisdiction applicable to States. The adjudicative jurisdiction of a court contains elements of both prescriptive and enforcement jurisdiction. For present purposes however, when we think of the jurisdiction of an international criminal tribunal it is best thought of as a separate concept that refers to the limits of a court's power or competence to hear a given case. Adjudicative jurisdiction in relation to an international criminal tribunal thus refers to several types of limitations upon the cases that tribunal may hear. In the first place, such jurisdictional limits will be discerned by interpreting the relevant court or tribunal's statute.

Generally, to proceed to hear a case, an international criminal court or tribunal must have:

(1) jurisdiction over the offence charged, which is called subject-matter jurisdiction or jurisdiction *ratione materiae*;

---

[11] H Strohmeyer, 'Collapse and Reconstruction of a Judicial System: The United Nations Missions in Kosovo and East Timor' (2001) 95 American Journal of International Law 46.

[12] See Article 1(1), Agreement between the United Nations and the Lebanese Republic on the establishment of a Special Tribunal for Lebanon as annexed to UN Security Council Resolution 1757 (2007). See further: F Megret 'A Special Tribunal for Lebanon: the UN Security Council and the Emancipation of International Criminal Justice' (2008) 21 Leiden Journal of International Law 485.

(2) jurisdiction over either (i) the place where the crime was committed, which is called spatial/territorial jurisdiction or jurisdiction *ratione loci*, or (ii) the accused, which is referred to as personal jurisdiction or jurisdiction *ratione personae*; and

(3) both (1) and (2) at the time of the offence, which is temporal jurisdiction or jurisdiction *ratione temporis*.

In addition, there is the question of how such jurisdiction relates to the domestic jurisdiction of States. Broadly, such courts and tribunals will have either:

- primary jurisdiction, where the international criminal tribunal can require a State to defer its own prosecution to the international criminal tribunal and to produce evidence and witnesses; or

- complementary jurisdiction, where primary criminal jurisdiction rests with national courts but where the international criminal tribunal may assume jurisdiction over a case if national authorities are unable or unwilling genuinely to investigate or prosecute a case. Complementary jurisdiction is discussed further at section 4.4.4.

Both primary and complementary jurisdiction assume that the jurisdiction of international criminal tribunals is not *exclusive* but will be *concurrent* with that of national courts. That is, national courts remain competent to prosecute the crimes but under certain circumstances must (or may) defer prosecutions to an international tribunal. Similarly, an international criminal tribunal may refer a case back to a national court system. The existence of one jurisdiction does not therefore preclude the other and there is no single right court before which to prosecute a crime. In practice, however, there will normally be only one prosecution conducted.

A court's statute may further restrain its jurisdiction through:

- language that suggests a threshold level of seriousness before a prosecution should start. This could include references to prosecuting only 'those most responsible'[13] for crimes or to the court having jurisdiction over the 'most serious crimes of international concern'.[14] Note, however, that such thresholds are often *not* strict legal requirements and may be intended to guide rather than limit prosecutorial discretion;

- strict triggers or requirements before a court may assume jurisdiction over a case (as are discussed in relation to the ICC Statute in section 4.4); or

- subtle limitations such as defining the offences over which the tribunal has subject matter jurisdiction more narrowly than is actually required under customary international law.

On the last point, strictly speaking, as we have seen in Chapter 3, defining an international crime narrowly does not mean that a court lacks jurisdiction over the offence, just that it will not be able to prosecute it in cases where the additional requirements set out in the court's statute are not present.

---

[13] See Art 1, Special Court for Sierra Leone Statute ('The Special Court shall...have the power to prosecute persons who bear the greatest responsibility for serious violations of international humanitarian law and Sierra Leonean law').

[14] Art 1, ICC Statute.

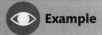 **Example**

The jurisdiction of international criminal tribunals

Articles 1–6, 8, and 9, Statute of the ICTY 1993

The ICTY has:

- jurisdiction over grave breaches of the 1949 Geneva Conventions and violations of the laws and customs of war (i.e. war crimes under both treaty and customary law), genocide, and crimes against humanity (Articles 2–5);

- jurisdiction over the acts of natural persons committed on the territory of the former Socialist Federal Republic of Yugoslavia committed after 1 January 1991 (note that there is no end date to this temporal jurisdiction and that the start date is retrospective) (Articles 1, 6, and 8); and

- primary jurisdiction, meaning that while its jurisdiction is concurrent with national courts, its jurisdiction will take primacy over national proceedings (Article 9).

Article 1 also refers to 'persons responsible for serious violations' of international criminal law. This does not limit the Tribunal's jurisdiction to the *most* serious offences or the persons *most* responsible. Early ICTY cases, such as *Tadić*, involved relatively low-ranking defendants.

Articles 1–5, 7, and 8, Statute of the ICTR 1994

The ICTR has:

- jurisdiction over Common Article 3 of the 1949 Geneva Conventions and of Additional Protocol II (i.e. war crimes committed in a non-international armed conflict),[15] genocide, and crimes against humanity;

- jurisdiction over the acts of natural persons committed between 1 January 1994 and 31 December 1994 (note that this temporal jurisdiction is both retrospective and limited by an end date) on the territory of Rwanda (Articles 1 and 5); and

- primary jurisdiction, meaning that while its jurisdiction is concurrent with national courts, its jurisdiction will take primacy over national proceedings (Articles 7 and 8).

As with the ICTY Statute, Article 1 refers to 'persons responsible for serious violations' of international criminal law.

Articles 1, 5, 11, 12, 13, and 17 of the ICC Statute 1998

The International Criminal Court has:

- jurisdiction 'over persons for the most serious crimes of international concern' (Article 1);

- jurisdiction over genocide, crimes against humanity, war crimes, and aggression (Article 5);

- temporal jurisdiction only over acts committed after the ICC Statute enters into force, which occurred on 1 July 2002 (the jurisdiction is therefore purely prospective and does not cover past acts) (Article 11);

- jurisdiction only in cases where either the territorial State in which the conduct occurred or the State of nationality of the alleged perpetrator is a party to the ICC Statute (Article 12);

---

[15] We encounter the idea of non-international armed conflicts in Chapter 8.

- jurisdiction if a situation involving the apparent commission of multiple crimes under the ICC Statute is referred to the Court either by *any* State party or by the UN Security Council, or where the ICC Prosecutor has initiated his own investigation in accordance with his powers under the ICC Statute (Article 13);

- complementary jurisdiction to national courts, meaning that cases will *not* be admissible in four situations outlined in Article 17(1). In general, the ICC will only have jurisdiction where the State with jurisdiction is unable or unwilling genuinely to carry out an investigation or prosecution; and

- under Article 17(1)(d) the Court must declare inadmissible a case which is 'not of sufficient gravity to justify further action by the Court'.

An observant reader, going over the Statutes, will note that the definition of some offences, particularly crimes against humanity, differ between the various Statutes. Some of these differences may constitute additional limitations not required by customary international law, thus placing an additional limit on the tribunals' jurisdiction. This notion is discussed further in later chapters.

4.4 Features of the jurisdiction of the ICC

The jurisdiction of the ICC is distinct from that of the ICTY and ICTR in that it is complementary to the jurisdiction of national courts and prosecutorial authorities. Strictly speaking, complementarity is a principle that prevents the ICC from *exercising* its jurisdiction. It retains jurisdiction over the relevant offences, but, under the principle of complementarity, it may not exercise it in certain cases. It is thus a rule about the *admissibility of a case* rather than the existence of jurisdiction over an underlying situation or crime.

The exercise of jurisdiction over a situation is normally engaged by one of several 'trigger mechanisms', being: (1) ICC Prosecutor-initiated investigations; (2) a UN Security Council referral; or (3) a referral by one State of a 'situation' occurring in a member State (including so-called 'self-referrals' where a State refers a situation within its own territory). The possibility of non-State parties granting jurisdiction over certain situations to the ICC is also noted below.

Importantly, only 'situation[s] in which one or more crimes within the jurisdiction of the Court appear to have been committed' may be referred to the ICC Prosecutor.[16] That is, a referral may not be limited to certain crimes or individuals but must encompass a 'situation' as a whole. This is intended to prevent politically selective referrals by governments, although much will depend on how widely or narrowly the situation is framed.[17] A 'case' cannot be heard at all if the ICC lacks jurisdiction over the situation from which the case arises.

---

[16] Art 14(1), ICC Statute.   [17] See discussion in section 4.4.3.

Pause for reflection

'Why doesn't the ICC Prosecute Bush and Blair?'

A frequent criticism of the ICC is that it hasn't prosecuted the alleged offences of great powers, such as the US and UK, or their leaders. The usual examples given are the decision by the US and its allies (notably the UK) to invade and occupy Afghanistan in 2001 and Iraq in 2003. At the time George W. Bush was President of the US and Tony Blair was Prime Minister of the UK. Why has the ICC not indicted such leaders?

The first consideration is clearly *temporal* jurisdiction. The invasion of Afghanistan occurred before 1 July 2002. The next is *nationality jurisdiction*: the US is not a party, so the ICC has no jurisdiction over US nationals unless they commit crimes on the territory of a State party. As regards *territorial jurisdiction* Iraq is not a State party and Afghanistan became only in 2003. At best there is: nationality jurisdiction over UK nationals from 1 July 2002 in both Iraq and Afghanistan; and territorial jurisdiction over offences in Afghanistan after 2003.

Further, with what specific crime would one personally charge former President Bush and former Prime Minister Blair? The most obvious candidate would be the crime of waging a war of aggression. However, as we noted in section 3.5.4 the ICC Statute entered force without containing a definition of aggression. While such a definition was added as a result of 2010 amendments (see Chapter 11), it is not retrospective and will not come into force for some time. This creates a further problem of temporal jurisdiction. Clearly, the ICC would have no jurisdiction over former President Bush and former Prime Minister Blair as regards any acts of aggression committed in 2001 or 2003.

However, could not such leaders be responsible for any crimes committed by their national armed forces in Iraq or Afghanistan? The complexities of connecting leaders with crimes committed by low-level subordinates (such as torture) are considered in Chapter 12. Notably, however, the ICC Office of the Prosecutor has re-opened its preliminary examination of information regarding alleged war crimes by UK military personnel in Iraq.[18] It has also opened preliminary examinations in respect of allegations of acts of torture by United States forces in Afghanistan and possible war crimes committed by Russian forces in Georgia.[19] These examinations are not, however, the same thing as opening an investigation. A 'preliminary examination' is just that: a review of available information which could lead to an investigation being opened.

It is best to commence our discussion of ICC jurisdiction by considering how the court may gain jurisdiction over a situation under the three trigger mechanisms. After that, we will consider complementarity, which deals with whether an individual case arising within a situation is admissible before the Court.

---

[18] The Office of the Prosecutor, 'Report on Preliminary Examination Activities 2014', 2 December 2014, www.icc-cpi.int/iccdocs/otp/OTP-Pre-Exam-2014.pdf.
[19] Ibid.

4.4.1 ICC Prosecutor-initiated cases (the first trigger mechanism)

A point of controversy during the ICC Statute negotiations in Rome was the extent of the Prosecutor's powers to initiate investigations without either a State party or a UN Security Council referral (*proprio motu*). Indeed, '[m]any States at Rome objected to giving the Prosecutor' a *proprio motu* investigatory power fearing it might be used to commence 'politically motivated prosecutions'.[20] Nonetheless under the Statute as concluded, the ICC Prosecutor may begin an investigation *proprio motu* on the basis of information received by individuals or organizations, but only if he or she can demonstrate to an ICC Pre-Trial Chamber that there is 'a reasonable basis to proceed'.[21] The possibility of a rogue ICC Prosecutor bringing politically motivated cases has been severely restricted not only by this authorization requirement, but also by the principle of complementarity (see section 4.4.4).

The majority of cases to date, however, have arisen not out of Prosecutor-initiated investigations but out of situations referred by either a State party or the UN Security Council. The ICC Pre-Trial Chambers have, in fact, only granted permission to the ICC Prosecutor to open investigations *proprio motu* in respect of two situations. The first was the situation in Kenya in March 2010 and the second the situation in Côte d'Ivoire in October 2011. A likely explanation for this is that the ICC Prosecutor's chances of gaining access to evidence and witnesses are much greater where States are cooperating voluntarily with the Court. The powers and duties of the ICC Prosecutor are discussed further in Chapter 5.

4.4.2 UN Security Council referral (the second trigger mechanism) and deferral (a blocking mechanism)

As the UN Security Council can establish courts under Chapter VII in response to a situation threatening international peace and security, there is no logical reason why it cannot confer jurisdiction on an existing court under the same circumstances. The ICC Statute acknowledges this possibility in Article 13(b), stipulating that the ICC can exercise its jurisdiction over:

> A situation in which one or more of such crimes appears to have been committed is referred to the Prosecutor by the Security Council acting under Chapter VII of the Charter of the United Nations.

This is not the ICC Statute conferring a power on the UN Security Council, but simply the Statute making provision for powers the UN Security Council undoubtedly possesses. If, however, the UN Security Council extends the jurisdiction of the ICC by referring a situation involving a State that is not a party to the ICC Statute some difficult questions arise. To date, the UN Security Council has referred the situations in Darfur (Sudan) and also the situation in Libya to the ICC. Neither Sudan nor Libya is

---

[20] G Boas et al, *International Criminal Law Practitioner Library*, vol 3 (Cambridge University Press 2011) 71.
[21] Art 15, ICC Statute.

a party to the ICC Statute. To what extent then do these countries become bound by the ICC Statute? For example, does President Al-Bashir of the Sudan lose his immunity from arrest as a head of State as a consequence? Some of these issues are explored in Chapter 14 on jurisdictional immunities.[22]

The Security Council may also make a deferral by requesting that a situation not be investigated for a time. Under Article 16 ICC Statute:

> No investigation or prosecution may be commenced or proceeded with under this Statute for a period of 12 months after the Security Council, in a resolution adopted under Chapter VII of the Charter of the United Nations, has requested the Court to that effect; that request may be renewed by the Council under the same conditions.

The consequence of this wording is that where such a request is made, a failure to renew the request at the end of 12 months opens the possibility of investigation and prosecution. Note also that the drafting could be construed to be broad enough to allow the UN Security Council to require the suspension of a trial that is already in progress, though this has never happened in practice.

A surprising use of Article 16 was made in UNSCRs 1422 (2002) and 1487 (2003). These were both US-initiated resolutions that requested a blanket 12 month deferral of any future exercise of the ICC's jurisdiction over persons who were nationals of a non-State party. These resolutions were clearly intended to be renewed on an annual basis but lapsed in 2004 and have not been renewed since.

Two other Security Council resolutions are worth noting in this context. UNSCRs 1497 (2003) and 1593 (2005) were not Article 16 requests, but instead purported to restrict the jurisdiction of the ICC. UNSCR 1497 relates to UN peacekeeping forces in Liberia and UNSCR 1593 relates to African Union peacekeeping operations in Darfur, Sudan. In both cases peacekeeping personnel who are nationals of non-State parties are subject, according to the relevant resolution, to the *exclusive* criminal jurisdiction of the relevant troop-contributing State. There is debate about the legal effect of these resolutions.[23] The resolutions are certainly binding on UN member States and UN organs, but the ICC is neither a State nor a UN organ. Whilst the ICC cannot be bound directly by such a resolution, it is possible that ICC State parties would be prohibited from complying with an ICC request for the surrender of a suspect to the extent this conflicted with these resolutions. It is also possible that these resolutions would prevent States exercising their own ordinary criminal jurisdiction over foreign nationals covered by UNSCRs 1497 and 1593, e.g. on the basis of passive personality, if a peacekeeper covered by one of the resolutions murdered one of their nationals.

---

[22] See further: D Akande, 'The Legal Nature of Security Council Referrals to the ICC and its Impact on Al Bashir's Immunities' (2009) 7 Journal of International Criminal Justice 333; P Gaeta, 'Does President Al Bashir Enjoy Immunity from Arrest?' (2009) 7 Journal of International Criminal Justice 315.

[23] R Cryer, 'Sudan, Resolution 1593, and International Criminal Justice' (2006) 19 Leiden Journal of International Law 195; DJ Scheffer, 'Staying the Course with the International Criminal Court' (2002) 35 Cornell International Law Journal 47.

4.4.3 State party referral (the third trigger mechanism), including self-referral and non-State party acceptance of jurisdiction

Under Article 14(1) ICC Statute:

> A State Party may refer to the Prosecutor a situation in which one or more crimes within the jurisdiction of the Court appear to have been committed requesting the Prosecutor to investigate the situation for the purpose of determining whether one or more specific persons should be charged with the commission of such crimes.

The view taken in the ICC Rules of Procedure and Evidence appears to be that this is a mechanism for conferring jurisdiction over a situation, such as a particular conflict, and all the crimes arising from it.[24]

Note that such a referral is not restricted to crimes within the territory of a State party or involving the nationals of State parties. Under Article 12(3) of the ICC Statute a non-State party may accept the jurisdiction of the Court 'with respect to the crime in question'.[25] This may suggest a non-State party could confer jurisdiction over, say, genocide (and only genocide) committed by its nationals or on its territory to the ICC. However, an Article 12 acceptance of jurisdiction by a non-State party does not constitute a referral capable of triggering an investigation.[26] Only State parties may make referrals, so some further trigger mechanism (such as the Prosecutor deciding to open an investigation *proprio motu*) would still be required before an investigation could commence. The words 'with respect to the crime in question' are also unlikely to be intended to allow a State accepting jurisdiction to limit the range of offences over which the Court will have jurisdiction, instead they confer jurisdiction on the court over all relevant crimes arising from the situation.[27] Article 12(3) acceptances of jurisdiction have been lodged with the ICC by Côte d'Ivoire and (controversially) by Palestine.[28]

One might presume that State parties would only wish to refer situations occurring in other States. In practice, it has been more common for States to refer situations within their own borders. This practice has become known as 'self-referral'. Self-referral describes a situation where a State party neither attempts to prosecute

---

[24] See: Rule 44(2), ICC Rules of Procedure and Evidence.   [25] Art 12(3), ICC Statute.

[26] Wilmshurst, 'The International Criminal Court' in R Cryer, H Friman, D Robinson, and E Wilmshurst, *An Introduction to International Criminal Law and Procedure*, 3rd ed (Cambridge University Press 2014) 168.

[27] Ibid.

[28] On 21 January 2010 the Palestinian Territories lodged a declaration accepting ICC jurisdiction over events within the Palestinian Territories since 2002. Their status was controversial at the time with many scholars considering they had not attained statehood. Whether a non-State territorial entity may lodge such a declaration is a point of controversy. Some resources and comments on the issue can be found in Marko Milanovic, 'Ronen and Pellet on the ICC and Gaza', EJIL: Talk!, 11 March 2010, www.ejiltalk.org/ronen-and-pellet-on-the-icc-and-gaza/. On 29 November 2012 the UN General Assembly voted to accord Palestine the status of an 'observer State'. For a comment on the impact of this (if any) on ICC jurisdiction see: V Azarov and C Meloni, 'Disentangling the Knots: A Comment on Ambos' "Palestine, 'Non-Member Observer' Status and ICC Jurisdiction"', EJIL: Talk!, 27 May 2014, www.ejiltalk.org/category/palestine/. Subsequently, Palestine submitted a further Article 12(3) declaration on 31 December 2014.

nor to investigate international crimes committed within its territory, but simply refers an entire situation to the ICC. The Democratic Republic of the Congo, Uganda, the Central African Republic, and Mali have all self-referred situations to the ICC. The practice raises a number of issues. The first is the question of whether the ICC *must* accept such self-referrals. This could involve a significant drain on the Court's resources with States 'overburden[ing] the Court with cases they could handle themselves'.[29] There is also the risk that States could attempt to use self-referrals selectively to refer only politically inconvenient cases or the actions of certain groups to the ICC. For example, Uganda originally referred 'the situation of the Lord's Resistance Army' to the ICC: however, the ICC Prosecutor interpreted this as meaning 'the situation of northern Uganda' and the ICC website in December 2015 referred to 'the situation in Uganda'.[30]

An important distinction to bear in mind is that between 'situations' and 'cases'. The mere fact that a situation has been referred does not oblige the Court to prosecute every conceivable case within the situation. The ICC Prosecutor must inevitably, given finite resources, be selective in those cases he or she seeks to pursue. Further, it seems that, at least in the *Lubanga* case, both the Court and the ICC Prosecutor assumed that the ordinary test of complementarity applies in self-referral situations to determine whether or not the case was admissible under Article 17.[31] Thus, this admissibility test might act as a further gate-keeper to exclude some cases where, for example, some State other than the referring State has opened an investigation. This point is explained in the next section.

4.4.4 **Complementary jurisdiction**

The ICC is said to be a court of 'complementary' jurisdiction. Complementarity, in this context is simply the principle that 'regulates the relationship between the ICC and [national] criminal jurisdictions'.[32] While an aim of the ICC Statute is to end impunity for those accused of international crimes,[33] its system of complementary jurisdiction means that ICC member States will generally retain primacy of jurisdiction over core international crimes committed on their territory or by their nationals. The essential

---

[29] Wilmshurst, 'The International Criminal Court' in Cryer et al, *Introduction*, 166. Kleffner, in even stronger language, suggests that the ICC may find itself effectively 'taken hostage' where a State is determined to wash its hands of prosecutions: JK Kleffner, *Complementarity in the Rome Statute and National Criminal Jurisdictions* (Oxford University Press 2008) 222.

[30] E.g. See Wilmshurst, 'The International Criminal Court' in Cryer et al, *Introduction*, 166 or Kleffner, *Complementarity*, 217 and www.icc-cpi.int/en_menus/icc/situations%20and%20cases/Pages/situations% 20and%20cases.aspx (under 'Situation in Uganda').

[31] *Prosecutor v Lubanga, Decision concerning Pre-Trial Chamber I's Decision of 10 February 2006 and the Incorporation of Documents into the Record of the Case against Mr Thomas Lubanga Dyilo*, Pre-Trial Chamber I, ICC-01/04-01/06-8, 24 February 2006, para 40. The PTC concluded that the case was admissible as 'no State with jurisdiction over the case is acting or has acted'.

[32] V Nerlich, 'ICC (Complementarity)' in A Cassese (ed), *Oxford Companion to International Criminal Justice* (Oxford University Press, 2009) 346.

[33] Preamble, ICC Statute.

idea is that the ICC plays a subsidiary role that complements rather than supplants national courts. Under the ICC framework national courts are, in Kleffner's words 'the first line of defence against impunity'.[34] This is a simple necessity. The ICC would never be able to prosecute all possible instances of the crimes within its jurisdiction. On one view, the assumption underlying the ICC Statute was that States would want to preserve the primacy of their jurisdiction. The idea being that the 'threat' of complementary jurisdiction, with the potential for the ICC to step in following State inaction, would provide an incentive for them to conduct investigations and prosecutions themselves.[35] Indeed, 'the underlying premise of the complementarity regime was to ensure that the Court did not interfere with national investigations or prosecutions except in the most obvious cases' requiring international intervention.[36] However, this presumption of State action has not been borne out by the practice of self-referral discussed above.

While the concept of the ICC being a court complementary to national jurisdictions emerged early in the negotiations of the ICC Statute, the detail proved difficult.[37] A permanent international criminal court had to resolve two obvious difficulties. Firstly, the demonstrable fact that national jurisdictions often shield from prosecution those accused of international crimes. Second, the fact that any court founded on State party consent would have to show some degree of deference towards national jurisdictions if it were to expect them to cooperate with it. Even the central idea of the ICC only stepping in where a State was unable or unwilling genuinely to investigate or prosecute was controversial, as it raised the spectre of the Court 'passing judgment on the decisions and proceedings of national judicial systems'.[38]

Article 17(1) of the ICC Statute attempts to resolve these issues:

[T]he Court shall determine that a case is inadmissible where:
(a) The case is being investigated or prosecuted by a State which has jurisdiction over it, unless the State is unwilling or unable genuinely to carry out the investigation or prosecution;
(b) The case has been investigated by a State which has jurisdiction over it and the State has decided not to prosecute the person concerned, unless the decision resulted from the unwillingness or inability of the State genuinely to prosecute;
(c) The person concerned has already been tried for conduct which is the subject of the complaint, ...;
(d) The case is not of sufficient gravity to justify further action by the Court.'

Article 17(2) provides further detail on the concepts of unwillingness and inability. In determining whether a State is *unwilling* the ICC 'shall consider' whether: (a) national

---

[34] Kleffner, *Complementarity*, 96. Ratner and his co-authors call national courts the 'forum of first resort': Ratner, Abrams, and Bischoff, *Accountability for Human Rights Atrocities*, 177.

[35] Kleffner, *Complementarity*, 213.

[36] JT Holmes, 'Complementarity: National Courts versus the ICC' in A Cassese, P Gaeta, and JRWD Jones (eds), *The Rome Statute of the International Criminal Court: A Commentary*, vol. 1B (Oxford University Press 2002) 675.

[37] See, for example, Holmes, 'Complementarity', 672–4.   [38] Kleffner, *Complementarity*, 85.

proceedings 'were or are being undertaken … for the purpose of shielding the person concerned from criminal responsibility'; (b) whether there has been 'an unjustified delay' which is 'inconsistent with an intent to bring the person concerned to justice'; or (c) proceedings either 'were not or are not being conducted independently or impartially' or are otherwise being conducted in a manner 'inconsistent with an intent to bring the person concerned to justice'.[39] In determining *inability* the ICC must consider whether a 'State is unable to obtain the accused or the necessary evidence and testimony or otherwise unable to carry out its proceedings' due to 'a total or substantial collapse or unavailability of its national judicial system'.[40]

Article 17 can be thought of as providing a two-step test. The first step is a 'same case' or 'same conduct' test. The second step is the question of inability or unwillingness. A critical issue will be what constitutes the 'same case'. Essentially, for a case to be the 'same case' it must involve the same person and substantially the same conduct; and this will be determined on a case-by-case basis by the Court.[41]

Where, at the time of an admissibility challenge before the Court:

- *no* State is currently investigating or prosecuting the same case and *no* State has done so in the past; and
- the person concerned has *not* already been tried for the same conduct,

then there is no obstacle to the Court exercising jurisdiction and no further inquiry is needed. This may create difficulties if the State is attempting to address international crimes by non-prosecutorial means or by novel prosecutorial processes which are proving slow to set up. The test under the Statute is that the State is not currently investigating or prosecuting. States will not be able to argue they should be given more time to attempt, for example, to set up a special national court to prosecute serious international crimes.

However, if the same case:

- is being investigated or prosecuted by a State having jurisdiction;
- has been investigated by a State having jurisdiction and that State has decided not to prosecute; or
- the person has already been tried for the same conduct by a national court,

then the case is inadmissible and the ICC is prima facie barred from exercising jurisdiction.

It is notable that the reference here is to 'a State' not, for example, to 'the State where the crimes were committed' or even to 'a State party'. Thus an investigation or prosecution by *any* State in the world could bar the ICC's exercise of jurisdiction. However, what will count as a decision not to prosecute?

---

[39] Art 17(2), ICC Statute.   [40] Art 17(3), ICC Statute.

[41] See *Prosecutor v Saif Al-Islam Gaddafi and Abdullah Al-Senussi* (Decision on the Admissibility of the Case), ICC Pre-Trial Chamber I, 31 May 2013.

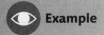 **Example**

The Prosecutor v Jean-Pierre Bemba Gombo (Appeal against Admissibility)

In 2004 a regional court in the Central Africa Republic issued an order dismissing all charges against Bemba. The question for the ICC Appeals Chamber decision was whether this was a 'decision not to prosecute' under Article 17(1).[42] If so, and if the national case covered the same conduct, then the ICC case against Bemba would be inadmissible. The Appeals Chamber dismissed this argument on the basis that two superior courts had later upheld the charges and had also ruled that the case should be referred to the ICC.

The significant factors to note are: (1) the order by the Regional Court was not final as it could be appealed; (2) the charges had in fact not been dismissed, but upheld on appeal; and (3) the government did then refer the case to the ICC. If a lower-level court or official dismisses charges or decides not to prosecute, that is insufficient if the decision is subject to further review at the national level.

Returning to Article 17, we have reached the point where it appears prima facie a case may be inadmissible before the ICC because there is (or has been) an investigation or prosecution at the national level. This is, however, no more than a rebuttable presumption. In such cases, under Article 17(1)(a) or (b) of the ICC Statute, the Court may nonetheless exercise its jurisdiction where the State party is (or was) unwilling or *genuinely* unable to investigate or to prosecute. As noted, Article 17(2) sets out three potentially overlapping categories of domestic cases that demonstrate *unwillingness* on behalf of a State:

- where proceedings are designed to shield an accused from responsibility;
- cases showing unjustifiable delay in a manner inconsistent with an intention to bring an accused to justice; and
- cases being conducted both with a lack of impartiality and independence and in a manner inconsistent with an intention to bring an accused to justice.

 Example

The Prosecutor v Katanga and Chui (Appeal against Admissibility)

In this appeal Katanga argued that the Prosecutor had not shown that the Democratic Republic of the Congo (DRC) was 'unwilling' to prosecute him: the DRC has simply taken a decision it would prefer the ICC to prosecute the case and had handed Mr Katanga over.[43] Katanga

---

[42] *Prosecutor v Jean-Pierre Bemba Gombo* (Judgment on the Appeal against Admissibility), ICC Appeals Chamber, 25 September 2009.

[43] *Prosecutor v Katanga and Chui* (Judgment on the Appeal against Admissibility), ICC Appeals Chamber, 25 September 2009.

argued this was not enough to make the case admissible under Article 17(2) because it was not one of the three types of unwillingness listed above. The Appeals Chamber was unimpressed with this argument. The fundamental principle is that one starts with the same case (or same conduct) test in Article 17(1) and if there is no prosecution or investigation of the same case going on then the case is admissible. Inaction therefore makes a case admissible. To start by asking questions about what may count as inability or unwillingness under Article 17(2) was 'to put the cart before the horse'.[44]

The Appeal Chamber stressed that a case before the ICC is only inadmissible under Article 17(1)(a) where there *is* an investigation at the time of the defendant's challenge. Article 17(1)(b) covers situations where there *has been* an investigation, *followed by* a decision not to prosecute.[45] Here, when he was transferred to the ICC, the investigation into Katanga's conduct was closed without a decision being made regarding whether he could be prosecuted in the DRC. There was therefore no *continuing* investigation at the time of his challenge and no Article 17(1)(b) decision *had been* made because no investigation had been completed.

The Appeal Chamber held that '[i]t follows that in case of inaction, the question of unwillingness or inability does not arise; inaction on the part of a State having jurisdiction (that is, the fact that a State is not investigating or prosecuting, or has not done so) renders a case admissible before the Court, subject to Article 17 (1) (d) of the Statute.'[46] That is, where no State having jurisdiction is investigating or prosecuting, the case is admissible *on that basis alone* under Article 17(1)(a). The ICC does not have to enquire into the *reasons* the State is not investigating or prosecuting.

The point to take away from the case is not to leap to an Article 17(2) analysis before asking whether the same case is or has been investigated or prosecuted before national courts under Article 17(1). If the answer is 'no' then there is no problem and the case is admissible; Article 17(2) is only relevant if there is (or has been) a national investigation or prosecution.

The real potential difficulty with the three Article 17(2) categories of unwillingness is that they all concern situations intended to *benefit* the accused. That is, they all deal with shielding the accused or otherwise acting inconsistently with an intention to bring an accused to justice. Kevin Jon Heller thus argues that Article 17 only permits a finding of unwillingness if legal proceedings at the national level 'are designed to make a defendant more difficult to convict'.[47] In cases where national proceedings 'are designed to make the defendant easier to convict' then Article 17 'requires the Court to defer to the State no matter how unfair those proceedings may be.'[48] However, a convincing argument can been made that some role must be given to the words '*genuinely* to carry out the investigation or prosecution' and 'bring an accused to *justice*' (emphasis added). Thus Frédéric Mégret and Marika Giles Samson argue that at least some violations of fair trial rights might be so egregious that 'one cannot realistically say that there has been a trial at all'.[49] The question then is not one of whether fair trial rights have been

---

[44] Ibid, para 78.   [45] Ibid, para 75.   [46] Ibid, para 78.

[47] KJ Heller, 'The Shadow Side of Complementarity: The Effect of Article 17 of the Rome Statute on National Due Process' (2006) 17 Criminal Law Forum 255, 257.

[48] Heller, 'The Shadow Side of Complementarity', 257.

[49] F Mégret and M Giles Samson, 'Holding the Line on Complementarity in Libya' (2013) 11 Journal of International Criminal Justice 571, 585.

violated but whether those violations have passed a certain threshold of gravity.[50] The question of which approach the Court has adopted will be discussed in the context of the situation in Libya.

Inability is addressed in Article 17(3) which directs that:

> In order to determine inability…the Court shall consider whether, due to a total or substantial collapse or unavailability of its national judicial system, the State is unable to obtain the accused or the necessary evidence or [is] otherwise unable to carry out its proceedings.

It is not entirely clear whether Article 17(3) sets out exhaustively the relevant considerations to determine inability, or whether other considerations may be taken into account.

The correct interpretation of Article 17(2) and 17(3) has been controversial as regards the situation in Libya.[51] The civil war in Libya began in February 2011 and later that same month the United Nations Security Council referred the situation in Libya since 15 February 2011 to the ICC Prosecutor.[52] The new government of Libya wished to see key figures of the former government, indicted by the ICC Prosecutor, put on trial in Libya. Libya thus challenged the admissibility of two cases before the Court: those concerning Mr Saif Al-Islam Gaddafi (said to be acting as de facto Prime Minister) during the conflict and Mr Abdullah Al-Senussi (a colonel in the armed forces).

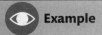 **Example**

The Prosecutor v Gaddafi (Appeal against Admissibility)

In the *Gaddafi* case, Libya was found unable to prosecute Mr Gaddafi on the basis that it could not in practice apply its judicial powers over all of its territory: indeed, it could not take Mr Gaddafi into custody in order to prosecute him because he was being held by rebel forces.[53] On this basis its national judicial system was 'unavailable' in the sense of Article 17(3) and the case was therefore admissible. Further, the Pre-Trial Chamber indicated that the poor security situation in Libya appeared to mean that both an effective witness protection programme could not be run and that a defence lawyer could not be found for Mr Gaddafi.[54] It appeared plain that a trial could not proceed under Libyan law without defence counsel and this clearly went to the ability of Libya to conduct a trial.[55] An important consideration was that the Pre-Trial Chamber assessed the facts in Libya as they stood at the time of the admissibility challenge.[56]

---

[50] Mégret and Giles Samson, 'Holding the Line', 585.

[51] See J O'Donohue and S Rigney, 'The ICC Must Consider Fair Trial Concerns in Determining Libya's Application to Prosecute Saif al-Islam Gaddafi Nationally', EJIL: Talk! Blog of the European Journal of International Law, 8 June 2012, available online at www.ejiltalk.org/the-icc-must-consider-fair-trial-concerns-in-determining-libyas-application-to-prosecute-saif-al-islam-gaddafi-nationally/ (visited 2 October 2014).

[52] UN Doc S/RES/1970 (2011).

[53] *Saif Al-Islam Gaddafi* (Decision on Admissibility), ICC Pre-Trial Chamber I, 31 May 2013 ('*Gaddafi* (Admissibility Decision)'), paras 205–206.

[54] *Gaddafi* (Admissibility Decision), paras 211–13.

[55] Ibid, para 214.   [56] Ibid, para 220.

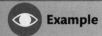 **Example**

The Prosecutor v Al-Senussi (Appeal against Admissibility)

The *Al-Senussi* case, by contrast, involved a suspect held within the custody of the new Libyan government. In this case the Pre-Trial Chamber found the case inadmissible. First, it found the investigation in Libya covered the same conduct. Second, it found Libya was not unwilling or unable to bring the accused to justice. An interesting point to note is that Libya led evidence of its investigations to satisfy the 'same conduct' test (for example, witness statements). Such evidence, however, will also obviously be relevant to the question of *ability* to prosecute. Third, it found that the inability of Mr Al-Senussi to obtain a defence lawyer was: (a) largely brought about by the security situation and therefore not an indication of *unwillingness* on Libya's part;[57] and (b) there appeared no 'concrete impediment' to the 'future appointment' of defence counsel.[58] Despite the concerns of Judge Van Den Wyngaert, the Pre-Trial Chamber held the security situation in Libya was not so bad as to render the justice system *unavailable*.

These seemingly divergent decisions arising from the Libya situation create difficulties. In particular, *Al-Senussi* appears to have misapplied the test that the facts must be judged at the time the challenge to admissibility has been made. At the time of the challenge Mr Al-Senussi had no lawyer. If that fact was relevant to inability to prosecute (and the *Gaddafi* case suggests it is) then it should have been considered rather than set aside because the problem might be resolved in the future. We can, however, observe that both cases consider fair trial rights relevant to the question of *inability* to genuinely prosecute a case. Nonetheless, based on the facts in *Al-Senussi* at least, that would appear to be a high threshold in practice. Finally, one might suggest that the question of the availability of a national justice system might not be an all or nothing proposition. The national justice system was unavailable as regards Mr Gaddafi (who was being held in rebel controlled areas) but available as regards Mr Al-Senussi (who was in government custody).

In the final analysis it would seem undesirable that cases could be admissible before the ICC simply because of human rights or due process breaches in national courts. Other avenues may exist for the accused to vindicate such rights, such as a regional or international human rights body or court. It may be that rights of appeal within the national court system will be sufficient to correct injustices. The violation of fair trial rights should only be relevant to admissibility if the violation is such that it cannot be said that there has been a proper trial at all, thereby revealing an unwillingness or inability on the part of the State in question genuinely to prosecute.[59] This would seem consistent with the result in *Al-Senussi*, if not its reasoning.

---

[57] *Al-Senussi* (Decision on Admissibility), ICC Pre-Trial Chamber I, 11 October 2013 ('*Al-Senussi* (Admissibility Decision)'), paras 292 and 307.
[58] *Al-Senussi* (Admissibility Decision), para 307.
[59] See: Mégret and Giles Samson, 'Holding the Line'.

4.5 The organs of international tribunals: their powers and functions

Generally, international criminal tribunals from the ICTY onwards have tended to comprise three organs, as follows:

- the Chambers and Presidency (i.e. the judges or judicial arm);
- the Office of the Prosecutor (OTP); and
- the Registry.

These organs will be explored using the ICC as an example. One should note that 'the defence' (i.e. the various teams of lawyers representing defendants) is not an official organ of the Court. Even when funded by the ICC Registry, defence teams remain private lawyers retained by an accused person (see Chapter 6). Some defence lawyers suggest this puts the defence at a significant disadvantage as they are excluded from the resources and internal deliberations of the Court both on general issues of Court administration and even on some aspects of the conduct of particular cases.

The specific powers exercised by the Chambers and the ICC Prosecutor are discussed in more detail in later chapters. The following section should be taken as largely an introductory overview. The ICC website also contains a wealth of practical information on the Court's operation.[60]

4.5.1 The Chambers and Presidency

All cases before the ICC are heard by a Chamber comprising of a panel of either three or five judges. The Chambers are further organized into three Divisions:

- the Pre-Trial Division;
- the Trial Division; and
- the Appeals Division.[61]

The judges of the ICC elect, from among themselves, a President and a First and Second Vice-President (collectively, the Presidency) to serve for a three year, renewable term.[62]

The Pre-Trial Division

The Pre-Trial Division is presently composed of six judges sitting in two Chambers. A Pre-Trial Chamber (PTC) has functions before, at the beginning of, and during an investigation by the Office of the Prosecutor. It also has functions regarding the arrest of, and confirmation of charges against, a suspect.

---

[60] See generally: www.icc-cpi.int/en_menus/icc/structure%20of%20the%20court/Pages/structure%20of%20the%20court.aspx and the pages it links to.
[61] Art 39, ICC Statute.   [62] Art 38, ICC Statute.

Briefly, before an investigation opens a PTC may be involved in taking testimony to preserve evidence.[63] More usually, the PTC will be first involved when the ICC Prosecutor seeks to open an investigation *proprio motu*. Before the ICC Prosecutor can open such an investigation, he/she must receive the approval of a PTC. The PTC must authorize an investigation where it finds 'that there is a reasonable basis to proceed with the investigation and that the case appears to fall within the jurisdiction of the Court'.[64] The PTC may authorise an investigation to continue where a State has requested the ICC Prosecutor to defer an investigation, and it may review a decision by the ICC Prosecutor not to open an investigation *proprio motu* on the basis of information received or pursuant to a State party referral.[65] (This procedure can only result in a request that the Prosecutor reconsider his or her decision; the PTC cannot direct the Prosecutor to investigate a situation.) A State or an accused person may also challenge the jurisdiction of the ICC to continue with a case before a PTC.[66] During an investigation the PTC has an obligation to uphold the integrity of proceedings and to ensure that the rights of the defence are upheld.

The PTC may, on the request of the ICC Prosecutor, issue a warrant for a person's arrest where there are reasonable grounds for believing they have committed a crime within the jurisdiction of the Court.[67] On the request of an accused, it may also issue orders or request the cooperation of States to assist the preparation of a defence (e.g. in releasing evidence).[68] It is responsible for supervising the detention of suspects and may order their release if there is an unreasonable delay in bringing a case.[69]

Finally, the PTC is responsible for confirming the charges against an accused. The ICC Prosecutor must present 'sufficient evidence to establish substantial grounds to believe that the person committed the crime charged'.[70] The defence may challenge the inclusion of certain charges on the grounds that there is not sufficient evidence to meet this standard. The PTC thus decides which charges, among those presented by the ICC Prosecutor, will be the subject of the trial.

In practice, Pre-Trial Chambers will have to consider many fundamental questions relating to the Court's operation in its early years. While such rulings are subject to appeal, these decisions may be taken outside the context of an actual trial. A practical example is furnished by Pre-Trial and Appeals Chamber decisions on the extent (if any) of the immunities enjoyed by heads of State from prosecution before the ICC. These issues are discussed further in Chapter 14.

The Trial Division

The Trial Division sits in a chamber of three judges to hear a case (a Trial Chamber). Its functions are:

- to conduct a fair and expeditious trial that respects the rights of the accused;
- to determine the guilt or innocence of an accused; and
- if guilt is found, to sentence that person.

---

[63] Art 56, ICC Statute.　　[64] Art 15(4), ICC Statute.　　[65] Art 53(3)(a), ICC Statute.
[66] Art 19(2), ICC Statute.　　[67] Arts 57(3)(a) and 58, ICC Statute.
[68] Arts 57(3)(b) and 93, ICC Statute.　　[69] Art 60(4), ICC Statute.　　[70] Art 61(5), ICC Statute.

In terms of sentencing, a Trial Chamber may impose a prison sentence of up to 30 years, life imprisonment, or financial penalties.[71] It may also order a convicted person to make monetary or other reparations to victims including making orders for 'restitution, compensation and rehabilitation' of victims.[72]

In general, a Trial Chamber must conduct hearings in public, although it can conduct some parts of a case in closed session if there is a need to protect confidential or sensitive information given in evidence or to protect victims and witnesses.[73]

The Appeals Division

The Appeals Division is composed of the ICC President and four other judges. All five sit as the Appeals Chamber in any case. At any point in proceedings, the ICC Prosecutor or an accused may appeal to the Appeals Chamber on questions of the Court's jurisdiction over, or the admissibility of, a case.[74] The Appeals Division may also decide whether or not the ICC Prosecutor or Deputy Prosecutor should be disqualified in a particular case.[75]

Following a Trial Chamber's verdict of conviction or acquittal, the ICC Prosecutor or the accused may appeal that decision on grounds of procedural error, error of fact, or error of law.[76] An accused may also appeal a sentence on the grounds that it is disproportionate to the crime or a conviction on the basis that new evidence has come to light.[77]

After a convicted person has served either one third of their sentence or 25 years, the Appeals Chamber must review that sentence to see if it should be reduced or not.[78]

The Presidency

The Presidency is a separate organ of the Court alongside the Chambers, the OTP, and the Registry. The Presidency has responsibility for the proper administration of the Court, other than the Office of the Prosecutor.[79] However, 'the Presidency will coordinate and seek the concurrence of the Prosecutor on all matters of mutual concern.'[80]

4.5.2 The Office of the Prosecutor (OTP)

The OTP is headed by the ICC Prosecutor. As will be discussed more fully in the next chapter, the ICC Prosecutor's powers are to review information submitted to him/her suggesting the commission of crimes within the jurisdiction of the Court, to open investigations, to gather evidence and seek arrest warrants, and participate in trials and appeals.[81]

The functions of the OTP are reflected in its three Divisions:

- the Investigations Division;

---

[71] Art 77(1), ICC Statute.   [72] Art 75(2), ICC Statute.   [73] Art 64(7), ICC Statute.
[74] Art 82, ICC Statute.   [75] Art 42(8), ICC Statute.   [76] Art 81(1), ICC Statute.
[77] Art 81(2), ICC Statute.   [78] Art 110(3), ICC Statute.   [79] Art 38(3), ICC Statute.
[80] Art 38(4), ICC Statute.   [81] See generally: Arts 15, 53, 54, ICC Statute.

- the Prosecutions Division; and
- the Jurisdiction, Complementarity and Cooperation Division.

The Jurisdiction, Complementarity and Cooperation Division is 'responsible for ensuring necessary agreements and arrangements are in place to secure full cooperation of states and international organizations' and to maintain contact and engagement with 'civil society' (including non-government organizations that might be able to provide information assisting its work).[82] This reflects the fact that arrests can only be conducted by State officials (ICC officers have no powers of arrest) and that, to a great extent, evidence gathering will be dependent on State cooperation.

4.5.3 The Registry

The Registry is the administrative arm of the Court and is headed by a Registrar. The Registry is 'responsible for the non-judicial aspects of the administration and servicing of the Court'.[83] The Registrar, is therefore, 'the principal administrative officer of the Court'.[84]

The Registry also has a number of specific functions. In relation to the defence of suspects, the Registry runs the programme by which indigent persons may have legal assistance paid for by the Court.[85] As with all legal aid schemes, this will involve a difficult balance between an accused's right to effective representation and the need for efficient use of the Court's limited resources. The Registry has a role in supporting the participation of victims and witnesses in proceedings, including protection and security measures where necessary.[86] It has responsibility for conducting an outreach programme so that affected communities can gain a greater understanding of the work of the Court. The Registrar also has overall responsibility for the running of the ICC detention centre in The Hague, where suspects are held pending and during their trial.

4.6 Summary and conclusions

This chapter has provided a general overview of the jurisdiction and structure of international criminal tribunals, using in particular as its model the International Criminal Court. As a formal matter, most or all international criminal tribunals will have certain structural similarities. They normally consist of a judicial branch (usually called Chambers), an Office of the Prosecutor, and a Registry (concerned with administrative functions). Counsel for the defence are generally *not* integrated as an organ of the court. This gives rise to a number of concerns explored further in Chapter 6.

---

[82] See: www.icc-cpi.int/ (under 'How is the Office of the Prosecutor organized?').
[83] Art 43(1), ICC Statute.   [84] Art 43(2), ICC Statute.
[85] Art 67(1)(d), ICC Statute.   [86] Art 43(6), ICC Statute.

Nevertheless, we should be keenly alert to the significant differences between tribunals. Each must be approached on the basis of its own statute rather than assessing by generalization. We have considered in particular the differences that may arise in subject matter, territorial, personal, and temporal jurisdiction, and whether a tribunal enjoys primary or complementary jurisdiction. A number of points should be noted briefly. First, it is important never to forget there is no court of true 'universal jurisdiction' over international crimes. All are limited in terms of their spatial and temporal jurisdiction, having jurisdiction only over certain events in certain places at certain times. Thus a tribunal may face limitations—often severe limitations—as to which persons and events it may investigate and prosecute. As regards subject-matter jurisdiction, tribunal statutes may define international crimes in slightly (or significantly) different terms. We shall see this in particular we come to examine the law of crimes against humanity in Chapter 9. This may mean that the case law of one tribunal is not readily applicable to the statute of another, or may raise questions about the state of customary international law. A significant difference between the ad hoc Tribunals and the permanent International Criminal Court is that the ad hoc Tribunals were said to have 'primary' jurisdiction while the jurisdiction of the International Criminal Court is said to be 'complementary'. These are not precise terms of art, they are descriptions of the effect of the legal basis on which these tribunals or courts were established. The ad hoc Tribunals, as we have seen (Chapter 3, section 3.5.3), enjoyed certain advantages based on the fact that they were founded by the exercise of the UN Security Council's powers under Chapter VII of the UN Charter. The ICC was deliberately designed to be a court of last resort, taking only the most serious of cases where no national prosecution is occurring, or when national justice systems are unwilling or unable to investigate or prosecute. In practice, the development of the ICC's own law on complementarity will be one of the most important developments in coming years. We have noted in particular the question as to whether the ICC should be able to step in to guarantee that a person accused of serious international crimes receives a fair trial.

Useful further reading

R CRYER, H FRIMAN, D ROBINSON, and E WILMSHURST, *An Introduction to International Criminal Law and Procedure*, 3rd ed (Cambridge University Press 2014).
  Chapters 7, 8, and 9 consider the ad hoc Tribunals, the International Criminal Court, and 'other courts with international elements', respectively.

F MÉGRET and MG SAMSON, 'Holding the Line on Complementarity in Libya: The Case for Tolerating Flawed Domestic Trials' (2013) 11 Journal of International Criminal Justice 571.
  An excellent examination of the arguments as to whether violations of the right to a fair trial should or can be a relevant consideration in admissibility decisions by the ICC.

DA MUNDIS, 'New Mechanisms for the Enforcement of International Humanitarian Law' (2001) 95 American Journal of International Law 934.
  Provides a useful, short account of the mixed or hybrid tribunals for Sierra Leone, Cambodia, East Timor, and Kosovo.

R O'KEEFE, *International Criminal Law* (Oxford University Press 2015).

Chapter 3 considers the distinction between national and international courts in the context of prosecuting international crimes. Chapters 12, 13, and 14 consider the ad hoc Tribunals for Yugoslavia and Rwanda, the Special Court for Sierra Leone, and the International Criminal Court, respectively.

R ZACKLIN, 'The Failings of Ad Hoc International Tribunals' (2004) 2 Journal of International Criminal Justice 541.

A classic and concise account of the limitations of the ICTY and ICTR.

5

Investigations, prosecutions, evidence, and procedure

5.1 Introduction

There is no general law or uniform code of international criminal procedure. Each international tribunal has adopted its own Rules of Procedure and Evidence (RPE). While some similarities are apparent between the ad hoc Tribunals on the one hand and the International Criminal Court (ICC) on the other, this chapter and Chapter 6 on the conduct of trials can provide only a general outline of the applicable procedural law and some of the major issues involved. The principal focus of these chapters will be on the ICC for two reasons. First, it is the one permanent international criminal tribunal. Second, as the International Criminal Tribunal for the Former Yugoslavia (ICTY) and International Criminal Tribunal for Rwanda (ICTR) conclude their work, knowledge of their rules of procedure is less relevant than once it was. However, in focussing on the ICC we should be aware that its law of procedure is still in development and on certain issues (e.g. sentencing) the majority of the experience we have to guide us is provided by the practice of the ICTY and ICTR.

A number of topics relevant to this chapter were also covered in Chapter 4, in particular we have already noted the ICC Prosecutor's power to open investigations *proprio motu*. This chapter addresses a broader range of trial and pre-trial issues including the limited ability of the Prosecutor to conduct territorial investigations without the authorization of the territorial State, as well as the Prosecutor's limited power to receive information confidentially.

 Learning aims

By the end of this chapter and the relevant readings you should:

- understand the basic differences between common law and civil law approaches to criminal proceedings and the impact this has had on international criminal procedure;

- be able to explain the role of both the Prosecutor and Pre-Trial Chamber in decisions to commence an investigation by the ICC;
- be able to discuss the role of the ICC Pre-Trial Chamber in selecting the cases and charges that will go to trial; and
- be able to explain the basic approach to evidence taken in international proceedings.

The chapter therefore proceeds as follows:

- Section 5.2 introduces international criminal procedure and the principal actors, discussing the role of the judiciary, the prosecutor, and the defence.
- Section 5.3 examines the pre-trial phase of proceedings, including criminal investigation, the decision to prosecute and the role of the document specifying the charges (called an 'indictment' by some courts and national systems).
- Section 5.4 provides an overview of the trial phase and examines the role of guilty pleas, evidence (and its pre-trial disclosure) and the conduct of trial proceedings.

5.2 A brief introduction to international criminal procedure and the principal actors

This section will briefly review the origins and nature of international criminal procedural law and the various parties involved in the process (judges, prosecutors, suspects or accused persons, and witnesses and victims).

5.2.1 Questions of procedure and the role of the judge

Chapter 3 discussed the way in which the Nuremberg International Military Tribunal (IMT) had to reconcile different national laws of criminal procedure. In particular we noted that it is common in writings about procedural law in international criminal law to contrast an adversarial common law tradition and an inquisitorial civil law tradition. Put simplistically (because both traditions obviously embody great diversity), in the adversarial system a judge neutrally arbitrates between the parties and the parties control what material is presented to the court. The adversarial system also has numerous rules of evidence, designed to stop prejudicial material with limited probative value reaching the jury (who must decide questions of guilt or innocence). The adversarial system thus relies on the diligence and forensic skills of the parties to obtain evidence and establish the truth. This, among other aspects of the adversarial system, might be thought seriously inefficient and likely to 'paralyse', or at least slow, the progress of 'serious and complex cases'.[1]

---

[1] A Orie, 'Accusatorial v. Inquisitorial Approach in International Criminal Proceedings' in A Cassese, P Gaeta, and JRWD Jones (eds), *The Rome Statute of the International Criminal Court: A Commentary*, vol. 2 (Oxford University Press 2002), 1442.

In an inquisitorial system the collection of evidence is generally supervised by an investigatory or examining magistrate.[2] That magistrate then assembles the 'dossier', the complete written record of evidence for use in the trial. The judiciary has a leading role in examining witnesses and is trusted with examining the totality of the evidence on its merits and without artificial rules.

Antonio Cassese noted that traditionally in the adversarial system the *oral nature* of proceedings prevails: nothing is considered evidence until there has been testimony given in court by a witness.[3] In the inquisitorial or civil law system it is the *written proceedings* that prevail.[4] He also noted that these two systems neither constitute 'watertight categories' nor do they exist in their 'pure' form anywhere.[5] Indeed, it is well understood that the two categories have often intermingled in practice with some traditionally inquisitorial systems adopting adversarial features and vice versa.[6]

At the Nuremberg IMT, as we have noted, an adversarial model was adopted. However, the trial was conducted with interventionist judges who questioned witnesses and without common-law rules of evidence adapted to a jury trial. There was no pre-assembled 'dossier', instead evidence was presented by the prosecution and defence. These observations about the IMT remain broadly true of both the UN ad hoc Tribunals[7] and the ICC: all adopt an adversarial system but one where judges actively manage proceedings and will ask questions of witnesses. A far more detailed law of procedure has, however, grown up in each of the modern international criminal tribunals than existed before the Nuremberg IMT.

The ICTY largely had to develop its own procedural law, having little by way of either precedent or detailed provisions in its Statute to guide it. The judges thus had to develop their own RPEs and these changed significantly over time. In the end, trial procedures at the ICTY were largely adversarial and there is still a strong adversarial element in International Criminal Court procedure. However, the law of international criminal procedure before each of the UN ad hoc Tribunals and the ICC is a unique, hybrid system. National law concepts cannot be easily or safely transposed into an international criminal law context. Further, national systems of criminal procedure are so diverse it would be very difficult to argue there is one 'customary international law' of criminal procedure that tribunals should follow.

Judges in international criminal law will tend to be more interventionist and less 'umpires' than in a common law system. ICC judges, in particular have a defined role in

---

[2] Orie, 'Accusatorial v. Inquisitorial Approach', 1444.

[3] A Cassese, *International Criminal Law*, 2nd ed (Oxford University Press 2008) 358. Although he noted the increasingly use of uncontested witness affidavits (sworn statements) as evidence in common law jurisdictions: that is, written statements by a witness that are not challenged by the party that did not call that witness and which are then submitted instead of oral testimony.

[4] Cassese, *International Criminal Law*, 2nd ed, 358.   [5] Ibid, 353.

[6] Orie, 'Accusatorial v. Inquisitorial Approach', 1441 (giving the example of the adoption of adversarial features into the Italian Code of Criminal Procedure in 1989).

[7] It has been suggested that this result at the ICTY followed to some extent from the fact that both a majority of the UN Office of Legal Affairs lawyers involved in drafting the ICTY Statute and a majority of the first group of judges of the ICTY had common law backgrounds: Orie, 'Accusatorial v. Inquisitorial Approach', 1463–4; G Boas et al, *International Criminal Law Practitioner Library*, vol 3 (Cambridge University Press 2011), 24. The first version of the ICTY Rules of Procedure and Evidence were based heavily on a draft prepared and circulated by the US Department of Justice.

the process of criminal investigation, though a much more limited one than a civil law investigative judge. Such early judicial involvement can lead to tensions between the judiciary and the Office of the Prosecutor (OTP).[8]

5.2.2 **The Prosecutor**

The Prosecutor 'enjoys a high degree of independence' to decide 'on the commencement of the investigation, the conduct of the investigation and any prosecution of a crime' but is subject judicial supervision, especially at the ICC.[9] It is for the Prosecutor to prove at trial that the crimes charged have been committed. The Prosecutor is not, however, entirely free to run a narrow investigation to prove a limited selection of crimes in order to maximize the chances of securing a conviction:

- the Prosecutor has a wider duty to 'establish the truth' and must 'investigate incriminating and exonerating circumstances equally';[10]
- further, the Prosecutor must consider the interests of victims in deciding whether there is a sufficient basis to prosecute;[11] and
- the Prosecutor also has a duty to take 'measures to protect the safety, physical and psychological well-being, dignity and privacy of victims and witnesses' during investigation and prosecution, though such measures 'shall not be prejudicial to or inconsistent with the rights of the accused and a fair and impartial trial'.[12]

5.2.3 **The defendant and defence counsel**

One may refer to a person suspected of a crime and under investigation as a 'suspect' (although the ICC Statute and Rules of Procedure and Evidence avoid the term) and a person against whom charges have been confirmed as the 'accused'. In this book the broad term 'defendant' may be used to cover both cases, but reference to an accused person will always be to a person against whom charges have been confirmed. As in adversarial systems the defendant has a right to be represented by counsel or to conduct their own defence.[13] The existence of separate defence counsel requires the defence to conduct their own investigation, which may be thought to raise issues of 'equality of arms' given the great resources available to prosecutors (an issue explored further in Chapter 6). Several defendants before ICTY have insisted on the right to represent themselves.[14]

---

[8] E.g. R Goldstone, 'A View from the Prosecution' (2004) 2 Journal of International Criminal Justice 380–84.

[9] H Friman, 'Procedures of International Criminal Investigations and Prosecutions' in R Cryer, H Friman, D Robinson, and E Wilmshurst, *An Introduction to International Criminal Law and Procedure*, 3rd ed (Cambridge University Press 2014), 430–1.

[10] Art 54(1), ICC Statute.   [11] Art 53(2)(c), ICC Statute.   [12] Art 68(1), ICC Statute.

[13] Art 14(3)(d), International Covenant on Civil and Political Rights 1966, 999 UNTS 171.

[14] See, for example: *Milošević* (Reasons for Decision on Assignment of Defence Counsel) ICTY Trial Chamber, 22 September 2004; *Karadžić* (Decision on appointment of counsel and order on further trial proceedings), ICTY Trial Chamber, 5 November 2009; *Šešelj* (Decision on Assignment of Counsel) ICTY Trial Chamber, 21 August 2006 (the Tribunal had previously assigned standby counsel). Rule 62(C), ICTY RPE also provides that, if within 30 days of their initial appearance, the defendant has not retained permanent

Ultimately, the ICTY had to conclude that this right was not absolute and imposed counsel (this occurred, for example, in the *Milošević* and *Karadzić* cases).[15] In the *Milošević* case, in particular, the imposition of counsel followed from the disruptive and obstructive conduct of the defendant. Mr Milošević, a politician and former president of Serbia, had little interest in cooperating with what he considered a politically motivated prosecution and used his ability to represent himself to:

- create the impression he was a sole individual pitted against 'an army of foreign lawyers';
- make 'unfettered', political, and 'caustic' speeches throughout the trial which were not restrained by the rules of relevance or those governing cross-examination; and
- repeatedly challenge the legitimacy of proceedings and treat judges, prosecutors, and witnesses in a manner that would 'earn ordinary defence counsel expulsion from the court room'.[16]

In the event, Mr Milošević died before his trial was completed. Nonetheless, imposing counsel on Mr Milošević may also have been necessary to avert the possibility of him undermining his own right to a fair trial through poor management of his own defence. Few lone individuals will be able (even if legally qualified) to conduct their own defence in highly complex trials involving hundreds (if not thousands) of documents and many witnesses. Thus it was suggested by the Special Court for Sierra Leone in the *Norman* case that the right to self-representation is a 'qualified right' and relevant considerations in limiting the right to self-representation include:

- representation by qualified counsel may be a necessary part of a fair trial;
- without counsel judges must explain and enforce basic courtroom rules to and against the defendant;
- given the complexity of such trials allowing the defendant to represent him- or herself risks unfairness;
- self-representation may disrupt the Court's timetable (i.e. by slowing proceedings greatly); and

---

counsel, the Registrar shall appoint counsel temporarily. For cases in which this rule was applied or in issue, see: *Mladić* (Decision by the Deputy Registrar on Assignment of Defence Counsel), ICTY Registry, 22 July 2011 (this involved the temporary assignment of counsel only, an appointment renewed once in a subsequent decision); see also: *Hadžić* (Order on extension of time for the assignment of counsel), ICTY Trial Chamber, 23 August 2011.

[15] G Boas et al, *International Criminal Law Practitioner Library*, vol 3 (Cambridge University Press 2011), 156–61.

[16] MP Scharf, 'Self-Representation of the Accused before International Tribunals: An Absolute Right or a Qualified Privilege?' in BS Brown (ed), *Research Handbook on International Criminal Law* (Elgar 2011), 285. On the potential for a defendant who conceives the trial in essentially political terms to be highly disruptive see: A Zahar, 'Legal Aid, Self Representation, and the Crisis at the Hague Tribunal' (2008) 19 Criminal Law Forum 241.

- in cases with multiple defendants there will be a tension between one defendant's right to self-representation and the rights of his or her co-accused to a fair and expeditious trial.[17]

Both the ad hoc Tribunals and the ICC recognize that defence counsel may have to be provided free of cost to the accused.

5.2.4 Witnesses and victims

International criminal courts may require witnesses to attend and give testimony. Although the judges may call witnesses themselves, in keeping with adversarial proceedings calling witnesses will generally be a matter for the prosecution and defence.

Before the ICC victims have a designated role and rights.[18] At least in theory the ICC Statute thus represents an advance over the ad hoc Tribunal Statutes by giving victims certain expressly defined rights including:

- the ability to have their 'views and concerns' considered in proceedings, in a manner consistent with a 'fair and impartial trial' for the accused (under Article 68); and
- the possibility of receiving reparations from a trust fund funded by voluntary contributions from ICC States Parties and any assets confiscated from convicted persons (under Article 75).

While giving victims a greater role in proceedings than simply being witnesses for the prosecution may seem an inherently good idea, the practical implementation of these provisions has not been without controversy in the early years of the ICC.[19]

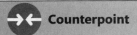 **Counterpoint**

The position of victims before the ICC

Some critics have raised serious concerns about the role of victims and the gap between what the ICC Statute may seem to promise and be able to deliver. Kendall and Nouwen make a number of particularly trenchant criticisms of the role of victims at the ICC.[20] To begin with, victims do not

---

[17] *Norman, Fofana and Kondewa* (Decision on Application for Self-Representation), Special Court for Sierra Leone Trial Chamber, 8 June 2004, para 26; G Boas et al, *International Criminal Law Practitioner Library*, vol 3 (Cambridge University Press 2011), 162.

[18] See Arts 68 and 79, ICC Statute.

[19] See generally: L Catani, 'Victims at the International Criminal Court: Some Lessons Learned from the Lubanga Case' (2012) 10 Journal of International Criminal Justice 905; C Stahn, H Olásolo, and K Gibson, 'Participation of Victims in Pre-Trial Proceedings of the ICC' (2006) 4 Journal of International Criminal Justice 219; H Friman, 'The International Criminal Court and Participation of Victims: A Third Party to Proceedings?' (2009) 22 Leiden Journal of International Law 485.

[20] S Kendall and S Nouwen, 'Representational Practices at the International Criminal Court: The Gap Between Juridified and Abstract Victimhood' (2013) 76 Law and Contemporary Problems 235, available at: http://scholarship.law.duke.edu/lcp/vol76/iss3/.

have a right to their own counsel and may be represented by common legal representatives at the order of the court.[21] In addition, there may be a progressive 'narrowing of the pyramid' as to who will have the status of a victim before ICC. That is, in a war-torn State it may be that the Prosecutor chooses to investigate only some crimes, thus limiting the range of victims who will potentially be involved. The pyramid may be narrowed even further if, for example, the Pre-Trial Chamber does not confirm charges against all suspects. Even where the victims are granted a right to participation and access to counsel (in the form of a common legal representative), those counsel will be operating in The Hague often at great distance from their clients and may not share a language with them or have ready means of communicating with them.

Kendall and Nouwen identify a further risk: that the victims' very identity can be appropriated by the system of international criminal justice. That is, it is easy for prosecutors and judges to claim they are acting to deliver justice 'for the victims' without facing any enquiry as to whether, from an actual victim's point of view, that is the case. The victims thus risk becoming an abstraction; in the authors' term they may become the 'sovereign' of international criminal law—an abstract idea capable of justifying the system and anything it does. International criminal justice can do no wrong, it would seem, so long as it can invoke the victims and their rights irrespective of whether it genuinely helps those victims.

McCarthy raises a different set of concerns regarding the trust fund.[22] The trust fund will never have a great deal of money and court proceedings will never be able to accommodate the individual views of all affected victims. If choices have to be made about how victims participate in proceedings and how limited trust fund moneys should be spent—it would seem important to have a clear idea of *why* victims have any status under the ICC Statute. In particular, it appears likely that the trust fund will only ever have enough money to fund group or community projects as symbols of compensation rather than compensating individual victims. One can therefore say the purpose of victim participation at the ICC cannot be restorative justice—at best it might be to serve a variant of retributive justice (a theory which emphasizes the role of criminal trials in affirming that a wrong has been done to a particular community). However, if this is the purpose of involving victims in international criminal proceedings, and we take Kendall and Nouwen's argument seriously, then the haphazard process of selecting the victims who get to participate in proceedings are selected is potentially problematic.

5.3 The pre-trial phase of proceedings: criminal investigation, decision to prosecute, and the document containing the charges

5.3.1 Introduction

International criminal tribunals will never be able to prosecute everyone who may have committed an international crime within their jurisdiction. The usual strategy,

---

[21] Rule 90(2) and (3), ICC RPE.

[22] C McCarthy, 'Victim Redress and International Criminal Justice: Competing Paradigms, or Compatible Forms of Justice?' (2012) 10 Journal of International Criminal Justice 351.

then, is to focus on those bearing the 'greatest responsibility' for crimes: usually leaders or relatively senior officials rather than foot soldiers. Thus the ICC Office of the Prosecutor has:

> **a policy of focussed investigations and prosecutions**, meaning it will investigate and prosecute those who bear the greatest responsibility for the most serious crimes, based on the evidence that emerges in the course of an investigation.[23]

An exception to this approach was the early prosecutorial strategy of the ICTY, where the first defendants were generally lower-ranking individuals. This had much to do with the availability of defendants: that is, the Tribunal had little choice at first as to which defendants came into its custody. Nonetheless, commencing with less complex trials and lower-level defendants was thought a sound approach by some who saw in it an opportunity for the ICTY to refine its own procedures and to gain practical experience of running trials for international crimes.

5.3.2 Opening an investigation

The Prosecutor may open an investigation into crimes committed by particular individuals in one of three situations:

- a State party has referred a situation to him or her;[24]
- the Security Council has referred a situation to him or her;[25] or
- under his or her own authority (*proprio motu*) 'on the basis of information' received regarding 'crimes within the jurisdiction of the Court'.[26]

In the first two cases, the Prosecutor requires no further authorization to commence investigations. In respect of the third category, Article 15 of the ICC Statute imposes strict limits on a Prosecutor's power to commence investigations *proprio motu*.

In all cases the ICC Prosecutor makes a decision whether or not to initiate an investigation based on the information received (e.g. information transmitted by a referring State, the Security Council, NGOs, or victims).[27] In the case of possible investigations initiated *proprio motu* the Prosecutor 'may seek additional information from States, organs of the United Nations, intergovernmental or non-governmental organizations, or other reliable sources that he or she deems appropriate'.[28] In all cases this process involves a kind of pre-investigation to review evidence that might warrant opening a formal investigation.[29]

---

[23] The Office of the Prosecutor, 'Prosecutorial Strategy 2009–2012', International Criminal Court, 1 February 2010, para 19, www.icc-cpi.int/NR/rdonlyres/66A8DCDC-3650-4514-AA62-D229D1128F65/281506/OTPProsecutorialStrategy20092013.pdf.

[24] Art 14, ICC Statute.   [25] Art 13(b), ICC Statute.   [26] Art 15(1), ICC Statute.

[27] The Prosecutor may receive such information under Art 53(1), ICC Statute.

[28] Art 15(1), ICC Statute.

[29] Cassese called this 'preliminary scrutiny': Cassese, *International Criminal Law*, 2nd ed, 396.

In making that decision the Prosecutor under the ICC Statute 'shall…initiate an investigation unless he or she determines that there is no reasonable basis to proceed' taking into account in making that decision whether:

- the information available provides 'a reasonable basis to believe that a crime within the jurisdiction of the Court has been or is being committed';
- the case would be admissible before the court (as discussed at 5.3.6 and in Chapter 4); and
- despite 'the gravity of the crime and the interests of victims, there are nonetheless substantial reasons to believe that an investigation would not serve the interests of justice'.[30]

Despite the use of the word 'shall' the Prosecutor would appear to have a great deal of discretion (unknown to civil law systems) as to whether or not to initiate an investigation.

By definition, no Pre-Trial Chamber approval is required to initiate an investigation on the basis of a State party referral under Article 14 or a Security Council referral under Article 13(b). However, where the prosecutor decides to initiate an investigation *proprio motu* under Article 15 he or she must seek authorization of the investigation from the Pre-Trial Chamber. The Pre-Trial Chamber must authorize the investigation if it appears there is a 'reasonable basis to proceed' and the case 'appears to fall within the jurisdiction of the Court'.[31] The latter involves a preliminary assessment of jurisdiction, which is without prejudice to future challenges to jurisdiction or contrary determinations of the Court itself (discussed at 5.3.6).

A decision by the Prosecutor *not* to open an investigation is open to review by a Pre-Trial Chamber either: (1) on the application of the referring State or Security Council; or (2) by a Pre-Trial Chamber on its own motion *if* the decision not to commence an investigation was based on the interests of justice criterion.[32] This is an important distinction: in the case of an application to review such a decision of the Prosecutor on the application of the referring State or Security Council the Pre-Trial Chamber may only 'request the Prosecutor to reconsider that decision'.[33] However, in a Pre-Trial Chamber review of a decision by the Prosecutor not to open an investigation based on the interests of justice criterion 'the decision of the Prosecutor shall be effective only if confirmed by the Pre-Trial Chamber'.[34] This strongly suggests that the Pre-Trial Chamber could, in effect, require the Prosecutor to proceed to open an investigation in cases where the Prosecutor has declined to open an investigation *solely* on the grounds of the interests of justice.

---

[30] Art 53(1), ICC Statute.   [31] Art 15(4), ICC Statute.   [32] Art 53(3), ICC Statute.
[33] Art 53(3)(a), ICC Statute.   [34] Art 53(3)(b), ICC Statute.

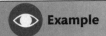 **Example**

Decision on the request of the Union of the Comoros to review the Prosecutor's decision not to initiate an investigation, ICC Pre-Trial Chamber

In Chapter 2, section 2.3.5 we noted that in 2010 the Israeli Defence Force (IDF) boarded a vessel, the *Mavi Marmara*, on the high seas. The ship had intended to breach an Israeli naval blockade. In the course of the IDF boarding a number of passengers were killed. The flag State of the *Mavi Marmara*, Comoros, referred the incident to the ICC as a crime that had occurred within its jurisdiction. In 2014 the Office of the Prosecutor declined to open an investigation on the grounds that while 'the information available provides a reasonable basis to believe that war crimes were committed' aboard the *Mavi Marmara* the situation was not of 'sufficient gravity to justify further action by the Court' under Article 17(1)(d) of the ICC Statute.[35] Comoros sought a Pre-Trial Chamber review of this decision not to open an investigation.[36]

The Pre-Trial Chamber held that in assessing the question of gravity the two key requirements were:

- consideration of whether the group that would be subject to investigation would capture those most responsible for crimes within the jurisdiction of the court; and
- that any assessment of gravity must take into account the 'nature, scale and manner of commission of the alleged crimes, as well as their impact on victims' and such an assessment must be both 'qualitative' and 'quantitative'.[37]

It held that the Prosecutor failed to correctly consider a number of relevant factors including:

- the persons 'most responsible' criterion does not require that the Court would have jurisdiction over senior leaders (implying that the soldiers conducting the boarding could be those 'most responsible'); and
- as regards 'gravity' that evidence of 'ten killings, 50–55 injuries, and possibly hundreds of instances of outrages upon personal dignity, or torture or inhuman treatment' constitutes 'a compelling indicator of sufficient' gravity.[38]

The Pre-Trial Chamber effectively found the Prosecutor had only a very narrow discretion to refuse to initiate an investigation on jurisdictional grounds.[39] While the 'interests of justice' test might provide a broader set of grounds for a decision not to investigate, such a decision must be confirmed by the Pre-Trial Chamber. The combined result would, in effect, subject prosecutorial decisions as to which cases to investigate to close judicial supervision.

The decision of the Pre-Trial Chamber was criticized by Judge Kovács (in a partially dissenting opinion) on grounds including that:

- it was not the job of the Pre-Trial Chamber under the ICC Statute to review decisions of the Prosecutor not to investigate for errors of law as if it were an appeals court;

---

[35] ICC Office of the Prosecutor, 'Situation on Registered Vessels of Comoros, Greece and Cambodia: Article 53(1) Report', 6 November 2014, executive summary, para 3, www.icc-cpi.int/iccdocs/otp/OTP-COM-Article_53(1)-Report-06Nov2014Eng.pdf.

[36] *Decision on the request of the Union of the Comoros to review the Prosecutor's decision not to initiate an investigation*, ICC Pre-Trial Chamber, 16 July 2015.

[37] Ibid, para 21.   [38] Ibid, paras 23 and 26.

[39] Ibid, para 14 (referring to Art. 53(1)(a)(b), ICC Statute as imposing 'exacting legal requirements').

rather it should only intervene 'to make sure that the Prosecutor has not abused her discretion'; and

- if one compared this potential case with the Kenyan situation concerning 'the death of about 1,220 and the serious injury of 3,561 persons in six out of the eight Kenyan provinces' in post-election violence then the violence at issue aboard the *Mavi Marmara* was simply not sufficiently grave to warrant investigation by the Court.[40]

Judge Kovács also noted that the gravity criterion or threshold was designed to prevent the court being 'swamped' with cases not meriting trial at the international level.[41] One should note, however, that Article 17(d) of the ICC Statute refers to the gravity of an individual *case* and not that of the *situation* within which it arises. Judge Kovács' comparison of the *Mavi Marmara* incident with the entire situation in Kenya may thus be somewhat misleading.

Nonetheless, is clear that there was a disagreement between the majority of the Pre-Trial Chamber and Judge Kovács as to how much discretion should be left to the Prosecutor and how far a Pre-Trial Chamber could go without compromising the independence of the Prosecutor. The decision certainly appears to assert that the Pre-Trial Chamber can extensively and closely supervise the Prosecutor's decision-making and would seem to set the gravity threshold very low.

At the time of writing it was unclear whether the Prosecutor would seek to appeal the decision or will instead proceed to reconsider opening an investigation. In the event the Prosecutor again declines to open an investigation, that decision could also be reviewed.

5.3.3 Conduct of the investigation and issuing arrest warrants

The Prosecutor is in charge of the conduct of ICC investigations, which in practice are headed by lawyers ('senior trial attorneys') from the outset. The Prosecutor has a duty to 'investigate incriminating and exonerating circumstances equally'.[42] As we have noted in Chapter 4, in the absence of a police force or coercive powers, the conduct of the investigation will require the cooperation of States and other entities such as peace-keeping forces. Where possible, ICC prosecution lawyers will participate in or conduct the investigations.

As a formal matter, the prosecutor has a range of investigatory powers. In particular he or she may: collect and examine evidence; question suspects, victims and witnesses; seek the cooperation of any State or intergovernmental organization and enter into agreements with them to facilitate that cooperation; and receive information on condition of confidentiality (subject to limitations discussed at 5.4.2 in relation to the *Lubanga* case).[43] States parties to the ICC Statute have wide-ranging obligations to cooperate with the prosecutor in the taking of evidence and conduct of investigations.[44] In theory, then, the Prosecutor issues requests to State and international organizations to gather evidence on his or her behalf. This will often need to be the case as the Prosecutor will lack compulsory powers within the territory of member States: as a matter of national law, he or she is unlikely to be able to obtain warrants or court orders to seize evidence or compel witnesses and must rely on those with local policing and investigatory powers to

---

[40] Ibid, *Partly Dissenting Opinion of Judge Kovács*, paras 7 and 19.
[41] Ibid, *Partly Dissenting Opinion of Judge Kovács*, para 15.   [42] Art 54(1), ICC Statute.
[43] Art 54(3), ICC Statute.   [44] Art 93, ICC Statute.

do so. In practice, a prosecution lawyer may need to examine a public place or take information from people (offered on a voluntary basis) within the territory of a State party. Normally, under Article 99, this is to be achieved through negotiating arrangements with the relevant State party. However, where such negotiations fail the Prosecutor may be authorized by a Pre-Trial Chamber to take such action, even without the consent of the territorial State.[45] The Prosecutor thus has limited powers to conduct non-coercive investigations in a State party's territory even without that State's consent.

The Pre-Trial Chamber has certain functions during the investigatory phase including:

- authorizing certain measures in relation to a 'unique investigative opportunity' to take testimony or preserve evidence (for example, a Pre-Trial Chamber could hear a terminally ill witness before the trial and appoint counsel to represent the interests of suspects who it is anticipated will have charges confirmed against them);[46]

- authorizing the Prosecutor to conduct an investigation in the territory of a State party in cases where the Prosecutor has been unable to secure the cooperation of that State; and

- issuing arrest warrants or summons to appear (for the purpose of giving evidence) or other orders.

The issue of arrest warrants is obviously an important one. The Pre-Trial Chamber may issue an arrest warrant for a person: (1) suspected 'on reasonable grounds' of having committed a crime within the jurisdiction of the Court; and (2) where the Pre-Trial Chamber is also 'satisfied' that the 'arrest of the person appears necessary' on one of three grounds: (a) to ensure his or her appearance at trial; (b) to prevent them obstructing the investigation; or (c) 'to prevent the person from continuing with the commission' of a crime or crimes within the jurisdiction of the Court.[47] On the first limb of this test, the 'reasonable grounds' standard obviously involves some review of prosecution evidence. The second limb is examined in the 'Pause for reflection' below.

  Pause for reflection

***Omar Hassan Ahmad Al Bashir* (Decision on the Prosecution's Application for a Warrant of Arrest)[48]**

(1) On the first limb, on what basis, presuming crimes had been carried out, was President Al Bashir suspected of having 'committed' them?

It was not alleged by the Prosecutor that Al Bashir carried out war crimes or crimes against humanity by personally killing people in Darfur. The Pre-Trial Chamber found there

---

[45] Arts 99(4) and 57(3)(d), ICC Statute.
[46] Art 56, ICC Statute.   [47] Art 58(1), ICC Statute.
[48] Omar Hassan Ahmad Al Bashir (Decision on the Prosecution's Application for a Warrant of Arrest), ICC Pre-Trial Chamber, 4 March 2009, especially at paras 214–217, 221–223, 227–232.

were reasonable grounds to believe that a common plan was formed at a high level of government to carry out a counterinsurgency campaign against rebel factions and that 'a core component of such common plan was the unlawful attack on that part of the civilian population of Darfur' perceived as supporting the rebels.[49] The Pre-Trial Chamber found there were reasonable grounds to believe that, as a person in a position to control the 'apparatus' of State power, Al Bashir either 'played an essential role in coordinating the design and implementation of the common plan' or 'used such control to secure the implementation of the common plan'.[50]

There are thus reasonable grounds to believe Al Bashir had committed crimes as an *indirect* perpetrator: the allegation is that he has committed the crimes *through* using the apparatus of State power and his control of the military and security forces. (The concept of indirect perpetration is further explored in Chapter 12.)

(2) On the second limb, on what grounds was the Pre-Trial Chamber satisfied it was necessary to arrest Al Bashir?

On all three grounds. Given the government of Sudan's failure to cooperate with the Tribunal, the Pre-Trial Chamber considered that his arrest was necessary to secure his attendance at trial. Given this lack of cooperation by the government, and Mr Al Bashir's position as the head of government, it was also reasonable to conclude that if not arrested Mr Al Bashir would obstruct the investigation. The Pre-Trial Chamber noted 'with grave concern that it appears that at least one individual has been recently convicted for the crime of treason as a result of his alleged cooperation with the Court.'[51] It also found that the government of Sudan appeared to be continuing to commit the crimes within the jurisdiction of the Court as alleged in the application for the arrest warrant.

Where a person is arrested and surrendered to the Court they will be placed in pre-trial detention. The Pre-Trial Chamber must periodically review such pre-trial detention and 'ensure that a person is not detained for an unreasonable period prior to trial due to inexcusable delay by the Prosecutor'.[52] In the event of such delay it must consider releasing the suspect.

As soon as the suspect arrives at the Court there will be a 'first appearance': a hearing where the Pre-Trial Chamber will confirm that the person has been served with the arrest warrant and that certain of their rights are being respected.[53]

In practice, however, it is not always the case that a person who is the subject of an arrest warrant will be surrendered to the Court even if State parties are obliged to do so under the Statute.

---

[49] Paras 214–215.   [50] Paras 221–222.   [51] Para 232.
[52] Art 60, ICC Statute.   [53] Art 60(1), ICC Statute.

Pause for reflection

Omar Hassan Ahmad Al Bashir (Decision on the Cooperation of
the Democratic Republic of the Congo Regarding Omar Al Bashir's
Arrest and Surrender to the Court)[54]

**What are the consequences if a member State does not comply with an ICC
Arrest Warrant?**

In 2009 and 2010 the ICC issued to all State parties requests for the arrest and surrender to the
Court of President Al Bashir. On 26 February 2014 the Pre-Trial Chamber issued a specific request
for the arrest and surrender of President Al Bashir to the Democratic Republic of the Congo (the
DRC). This followed from an application made by the Prosecutor based on reports that President
Al Bashir would be attending an international summit in the DRC on 26–27 February. The DRC did
not arrest President Al Bashir, who left on 27 February.

The DRC submitted to the Pre-Trial Chamber that:

- it was impossible to take such serious action in a very short space of time; and
- there was a legal conflict between the DRC's duty to arrest and surrender President
  Al Bashir under the ICC Statute and the DRC's duty to respect President Al Bashir's immunity from arrest as a head of State under general international law.

The Pre-Trial Chamber was not persuaded that there had not been enough time to act and found
there was no conflict between the DRC's various legal obligations largely because a compulsory
Security Council resolution had referred the situation in Sudan to the Court and had also obliged
Sudan to cooperate with the Court. (We shall explore this reasoning in more detail in Chapter 14).
It therefore found the DRC had not complied with its obligation of arrest and surrender under the
Statute. The Pre-Trial Chamber in its reasoning:

reiterate[d] that, unlike domestic courts, the ICC has no direct enforcement mechanism in the sense that
it lacks a police force. As such, the ICC relies mainly on the States' cooperation, without which it cannot
fulfil its mandate. When the [Security Council], acting under Chapter VII of the UN Charter, refers a situation to the Court as constituting a threat to international peace and security, it must be expected that the
Council would respond [and take measures]…if there is an apparent failure on the part of States Parties
to the Statute or Sudan to cooperate…Otherwise, if there is no follow up action…any such referral
would become futile.

Accordingly, the Pre-Trial Chamber decided under regulation 109(4) of the Court Regulations to
report the DRC's non-compliance to:

- the Security Council; and
- the Assembly of State Parties (that is, to the annual meeting of ICC member States).

---

[54] *Omar Hassan Ahmad Al Bashir (Decision on the Cooperation of the Democratic Republic of the Congo
Regarding Omar Al Bashir's Arrest and Surrender to the Court)*, ICC Pre-Trial Chamber, 9 April 2014, especially
at paras 11–34.

Of these two bodies only the Security Council can take compulsory action and, in fact, neither is actually obliged to take *any* action. Indeed, within the Assembly of State Parties there has been considerable controversy as to whether the ICC should ever issue arrest warrants for serving heads of State.

Such non-compliance is not unique in the *Al Bashir* case. The Pre-Trial Chamber has also reported findings of non-compliance against Malawi.[55] In 2015 the government of South Africa allowed President Al Bashir to leave the country, despite the order of a South African court that he not be allowed to depart while an ICC request for arrest and transfer was considered.[56] This latest instance of non-compliance has not yet been the subject of any ruling by the Pre-Trial Chamber.

Does such non-compliance coupled with the failure of the Security Council to take any action render Security Council referrals 'futile' in practice? Does this have implications for cases not based on a Security Council referral?

5.3.4 Decision to prosecute and the commencement of a trial

The ICC Statute contains no duty to prosecute, but does note that the Prosecutor may decide not to prosecute because: there is no sufficient basis to seek an arrest warrant; the case is inadmissible under Article 17; or that the prosecution is not in the interests of justice.[57] A decision not to prosecute may be reconsidered at any time 'based on new facts or information'. Questions of prosecutorial inaction or selection of defendants have been raised before the ICC, but while the Pre-Trial Chamber was, in one early case, prepared to convene 'status conferences' on the progress of investigation into the situation in the DRC, it has not intervened in the exercise of prosecutorial discretion.[58]

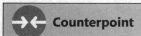 **Counterpoint**

The role of the prosecutor

As we have noted, how much discretion the ICC Prosecutor should have was a source of controversy during the negotiation of the Rome Statute. Indeed, the fact that the statute provided for a highly independent prosecutor was one of the key reasons the United States did not become a State party. Subsequently, the US appears to have dropped much of its opposition to the Court. While it has still not become a party, it has actively promoted the Court's role in certain cases such as the referral of the situation in Libya. The first Prosecutor, Mr Luis

---

[55] *Al Bashir* (Decision Pursuant to Article 87(7) of the Rome Statute on the Failure by the Republic of Malawi to Comply with the Cooperation Requests Issued by the Court with Respect to the Arrest and Surrender of Al Bashir), ICC Pre-Trial Chamber I, 12 December 2011.

[56] 'South Africa denies plot to allow Omar al-Bashir to leave', *BBC News*, 22 June 2015, www.bbc.com/news/world-africa-33221788.

[57] Art 53(2), ICC Statute.

[58] K de Meester et al, 'Investigation, Coercive Measures, Arrest, and Surrender' in G Sluiter et al (eds), *International Criminal Procedure: Principles and Rules* (Oxford University Press 2013), 188–189.

Moreno-Ocampo ascribes this success to 'the strict application of the law' in choosing which cases to pursue.[59]

Professor William Schabas, however, sees at least some evidence that the Prosecutor acted as a diplomat to counter American opposition. The United States' concerns would have been confirmed if the first Prosecutor of the court had been perceived to be an 'irresponsible...human rights activist with an anti-American agenda.'[60] Instead, Ocampo was seen (rightly or wrongly) as sending 'quiet signals' to reassure the US and its allies; including diplomatic reports that claimed that while he was 'looking at the actions of British forces in Iraq' he had privately suggested he would prefer not to mount prosecutions.[61]

Whether this view is accurate or not, it is obvious that the Prosecutor has had to act—to some extent at least—as a diplomat to secure the cooperation of States. We have noted that the accusation that the ICC has an excessive focus on Africa is most convincingly refuted by the numerous self-referrals by African States of situations within their territory to the Court. However, Ocampo himself has said that while he was Prosecutor there was an active policy of inviting or encouraging self-referrals because 'a referral from the territorial state would [be likely to] increase cooperation'.[62] To this end, the Prosecutor made it clear in a statement to the Assembly of State Parties in 2003 that the Court's 'role could be facilitated by a referral or active support from the Democratic Republic of the Congo' but if it was not forthcoming he was prepared to use his *proprio motu* powers.[63] This obviously constitutes an attempt to persuade a State to make a referral. Nonetheless, such interventions seemed initially to be welcomed in much of Africa, so long as they were seen as supportive of a peace process. In Schabas' view the turning point was the indictment of President Al Bashir, as this was seen as potentially 'upset[ting] a delicate peace process'.[64] The response of the Prosecutor was to contend that questions of peace were for the Security Council; he could only be concerned with questions of criminal law defined by and arising under the ICC Statute.[65]

Overall, it is clear that the Prosecutor cannot simply rely on 'strict application of the law' to tell him or her which cases to prosecute. The Court will always lack the resources to prosecute every case which might fall within its jurisdiction and choices will have to be made. That gives the Prosecutor a discretion which, while limited by law, remains broad. Further, successful investigations will clearly require State cooperation which largely relies on the Prosecutor persuading territorial States to cooperate. Inevitably, the Prosecutor must therefore act in part as a diplomat, even if he or she claims 'the diplomatic practice of looking for consensus [is] inconsistent with the prosecutor's independent mandate'.[66]

A trial commences with the presentation of a document containing the charges by the Prosecutor (at the ICC this is called the 'Document Containing the Charges); the

---

[59] L Moreno-Ocampo, 'The Office of the Chief Prosecutor: The Challenges of the Inaugural Years' (2014) 39 Yale Journal of International Law 32, 42.

[60] W Schabas, 'The Banality of International Justice' (2013) 11 Journal of International Criminal Justice 545, 549.

[61] Ibid.

[62] Moreno-Ocampo, 'The Office of the Chief Prosecutor' 42.   [63] Ibid, 42–43.

[64] Schabas, 'The Banality of International Justice' 549.

[65] S Nouwen, 'Justifying Justice' in J Crawford and M Koskenniemi (eds) *Cambridge Companion to International Law* (Cambridge University Press 2012) 327, 340–341.

[66] Moreno-Ocampo, 'The Office of the Chief Prosecutor' 42.

International Criminal Tribunal for the Former Yugoslavia and International Criminal Tribunal for Rwanda used the term 'indictment'). At the ICC the Document Containing the Charges must contain:

> A statement of the facts, including the time and place of the alleged crimes, which provides a sufficient legal and factual basis to bring the person or persons to trial, including relevant facts for the exercise of jurisdiction by the Court.[67]

The document containing the charges is thus a statement of charges and the material facts supporting them. The Document Containing the Charges summarizes what the Prosecutor intends to prove and may read like a narrative or story.[68] For example, a Document Containing the Charges may allege that a certain military/political group in the Democratic Republic of the Congo actively recruited children under the age of 15 in significant numbers and subjected them to military training in its military training camp in certain places at certain times, and that the defendant ordered this. This would form part of the case that a war crime of recruiting child soldiers had been committed. Further, sufficient 'material facts' would have to be alleged which, if proven, would allow a finding that all the elements of the relevant war crime had been made out. This will include 'relevant facts for the exercise of jurisdiction by the Court', such as the requirement to prove the existence of an armed conflict before a war crime can be committed. The Document Containing the Charges must give a sufficiently precise indication of the facts the Prosecution intends to prove so that the defendant can adequately prepare a defence. For example, if the document containing the charges does not clearly specify where and when an offence was committed, a defendant will not be able to assemble alibi evidence that he or she was in fact elsewhere at that time. It is the job of the Pre-Trial Chamber to 'confirm' the Document Containing the Charges and the charges it contains, or to modify it as discussed further in section 5.3.5. Following confirmation proceedings the Prosecutor may only amend the charges with the Pre-Trial Chamber's permission.[69]

The Document Containing the Charges is central in framing how a criminal case will proceed but there may be different views of the extent to which it is binding on the court.

- In common law jurisdictions the court may usually not depart from the *offences* alleged in the document containing the charges and convict for a crime not charged.

- In civil law countries the Court may decide that the *acts and omissions* alleged should be classified as different offences on the principle *iura novit curia* (the court knows the law).

Under the ICC Statute the final judgment of the Trial Chamber 'shall not exceed the facts and circumstances described in the charges and any amendments to the charges'.[70]

---

[67] Reg 52, ICC Regulations.

[68] See e.g. *Lubanga* (Document Containing the Charges), ICC Pre-Trial Chamber I, 28 August 2006, available at: www.haguejusticeportal.net/Docs/Court%20Documents/ICC/Lubanga-Document-Containing-the-Charges.pdf.

[69] Art 61(9), ICC Statute.   [70] Art 74(2), ICC Statute.

However, a Pre-Trial Chamber or Trial Chamber may, under a *iura novit curia* rule, 'modify the legal characterisation' of the facts during the course of proceedings.[71] This power was exercised in *Lubanga* by a Pre-Trial Chamber to change the characterization of the armed conflict in which war crimes were alleged from being a non-international armed conflict to an international armed conflict. As we shall see in Chapter 8, the existence of an international armed conflict requires proof of further additional elements and so substantively changes the case the Prosecutor must run. This has led to some controversy.[72] Even more controversially, the power was used by a Trial Chamber to change the mode of liability alleged against the defendant in *Katanga* after defence and prosecution evidence had closed.[73]

5.3.5 Confirmation of charges

In the ICC confirmation of charges will usually only follow a suspect being surrendered to, or voluntarily appearing before, the Court. However, as obtaining the custody of suspects can be 'a serious obstacle to international criminal proceedings...special confirmation proceedings *in absentia*' may occur under the ICC Statute.[74]

At the confirmation hearing the Prosecutor must present 'sufficient evidence' (usually summary documentary evidence alone although some witnesses may be called) to 'establish substantial grounds to believe that the person committed the crime charged'.[75] The defence is entitled to challenge this evidence, and the result could theoretically be a 'mini-trial'.[76] The case will proceed to trial on the charges that the Pre-Trial Chamber confirms. Any charges that the Pre-Trial Chamber does not find are sufficiently supported will not proceed to trial (and so are effectively 'struck out'). The Pre-Trial Chamber may adjourn the hearing and request the Prosecutor to produce further evidence; and the Prosecutor may request the subsequent confirmation of a previously rejected charge on the basis of additional evidence.

The evidentiary standard required ('sufficient evidence' to 'establish substantial grounds') is higher than that needed for an arrest warrant ('reasonable grounds to believe' a person has committed a crime), but lower than that required for conviction ('beyond reasonable doubt'). The Pre-Trial Chamber also ruled in *Lubanga* that this evidentiary standard was designed to protect the defendant from 'wrongful' and

---

[71] Reg 55, ICC Regulations.

[72] See further: M Miraglia, 'Admissibility of Evidence, Standard of Proof, and Nature of the Decision in the ICC Confirmation of Charges in *Lubanga*' (2008) 6 Journal of International Criminal Justice 489; JC Baker and M Happold, '*Prosecutor v Thomas Lubanga*, Decision of Pre-Trial Chamber I of the International Criminal Court, 29 January 2007' (2007) 56 International and Comparative Law Quarterly 713. It has been suggested this is hard to reconcile with Art 61(7) of the ICC Statute: Friman, 'Procedures of International Criminal Investigations and Prosecutions' in Cryer et al, *Introduction*, 3rd ed, 461.

[73] See Chapter 12, section 12.8 and C Stahn, 'Justice Delivered or Justice Denied? The Legacy of the Katanga Judgment' (2014) 12 Journal of International Criminal Justice 809.

[74] Friman, 'Procedures of International Criminal Investigations and Prosecutions' in Cryer et al, *Introduction*, 3rd ed, 464.

[75] Art 61(5), ICC Statute.

[76] Friman, 'Procedures of International Criminal Investigations and Prosecutions' in Cryer et al, *Introduction*, 3rd ed, 463.

'wholly unfounded' charges.[77] This different standard of evidence from that which applies at trial, and the ability to proceed on written evidence alone (the Prosecutor is clearly *not* required to present all evidence that will be used at trial), perhaps limits the possibility for confirmation proceedings to become a drawn-out 'mini-trial' as feared by some. Indeed, early signs are that the ICC regards confirmation proceedings not as a 'mini-trial' but a filter to make sure that no case goes to trial unless there is sufficient evidence to justify it.[78]

At the ICTY and ICTR the confirmation procedure involved a single judge reviewing the Prosecutor's indictment (the document containing the charges) and supporting material and then confirming each charge or count, dismissing each charge or count, requesting additional material, or adjourning the review to give the Prosecutor more time. The review was *ex parte* and *in camera*: the proceedings were not public and involved only the judge and the Prosecutor; the defendant was not present and the defence had no role. The standard for confirmation was that there must be a prima facie case.[79]

5.3.6 **Jurisdiction and admissibility**

We have already considered the jurisdiction of the ICC and the basis for admissibility of a case before it in Chapter 4. Under the ICC Statute an accused person or certain affected States may challenge the jurisdiction of the Court or the admissibility of the case *once* 'prior to or at the commencement of the trial', unless the Court grants exceptional leave for a later or further challenge or challenges.[80] A challenge to jurisdiction would allege that the court lacked temporal, spatial, or subject-matter jurisdiction over the crimes alleged. A challenge to admissibility may be made on the basis that:[81]

- the case either is being or has been investigated or prosecuted;
- a national investigation led to a decision not to prosecute, and this was not done in such a way as to demonstrate either (a) an unwillingness or inability on the part of the forum state to do so genuinely, or (b) a lack of intent on that State's part to bring the accused to justice;
- the defendant has already been tried for the conduct in question (*ne bis in idem*);[82] or
- the case is not of sufficient gravity to warrant trial before the ICC.

Such a challenge will be heard before other matters (as a 'preliminary motion') and the decision of the Pre-Trial Chamber or Trial Chamber may be appealed to the Appeals

---

[77] *Thomas Lubanga Dyilo* (Decision on the Confirmation of Charges), ICC Pre-Trial Chamber, 29 January 2007, para 37.

[78] See: *Katanga and Ngudjolo* (Decision on Confirmation of Charges), ICC Pre-Trial Chamber, 18 April 2008, para 4; and H Friman et al, 'Charges' in G Sluiter et al (eds), *International Criminal Procedure: Principles and Rules* (Oxford University Press 2013), 400.

[79] See: Boas et al, *International Criminal Law Practitioner Library*, vol 3, 181–3; Art 19, ICTY Statute; and Rule 47, ICTY Rules of Procedure and Evidence.

[80] Art 19(4), ICC Statute.   [81] Art 17(1), ICC Statute.

[82] Note the limited exception to this principle in Art 20(3), ICC Statute.

Chamber.[83] The Court must also 'satisfy itself that it has jurisdiction in any case brought before it' and may do so of its own motion.[84]

5.4 The trial phase: confession, disclosure and evidence, conduct of the trial

5.4.1 Confession or admission of guilt

If the defendant confesses or admits guilt it may be that a full trial does not proceed and a simplified procedure is adopted. Of course, the accused might plead guilty to some but not all charges, in which case a full trial would proceed on the remaining charges. A defendant at the ICTY and ICTR is *required* at their first pre-trial appearance before the Tribunal, after the charges have been read, to enter a plea of 'guilty' or 'not guilty' or to do so within 30 days thereafter.[85] No similar requirement exists at the ICC. For example, in *Lubanga*, no plea was entered in his first appearance on 24 April 2006, one week after his transfer to the Court. The defendant only entered his plea of not guilty at the commencement of his trial on 26 January 2009. Indeed, strictly speaking, the defendant need not enter a plea before the ICC, the Statute only requires that a defendant be given an opportunity to enter a plea at the commencement of the trial.[86]

The ICTY and ICTR, in a manner similar to most common law jurisdictions, treat a confession of guilt as allowing simplified proceedings: the case may move straight to sentencing. This can occur where the guilty plea was 'voluntary, informed and unequivocal' and where there is a sufficient factual basis to make out the crime and the 'participation of the accused in it'.[87] This will involve some review of the evidence, but the sentence may be based on the agreed facts.

The ICC procedure is similar. The Trial Chamber must be satisfied that:[88]

- '[t]he accused understands the nature and consequences of the admission of guilt';
- the admission is voluntary and there has been sufficient time for the accused to have the advice of defence counsel;
- the admission is supported by the facts contained in the charges, any materials supplementing the charges presented by the Prosecutor and accepted by the accused, and any other evidence presented by the Prosecutor or the accused.

If these requirements are met and the admission of guilt, along with any evidence presented, establish 'all the essential facts that are required to prove the [relevant] crime' then it may proceed to convict the accused.[89] Otherwise, it may 'consider the

---

[83] Art 82(1), ICC Statute.   [84] Art 19(1), ICC Statute.

[85] Art 20(3), ICTY Statute; A Cassese et al, *Cassese's International Criminal Law* 3rd ed (Oxford University Press 2013), 371.

[86] Art 64(8)(a), ICC Statute.

[87] Friman, 'Procedures of International Criminal Investigations and Prosecutions' in Cryer et al, *Introduction*, 3rd ed, 470.

[88] Art 65, ICC Statute.   [89] Art 65(2), ICC Statute.

admission of guilt as not having been made' and continue with a trial under ordinary procedures (or remit the case to another Trial Chamber).[90] In the interests of justice, and especially the victims, the Court may require either the presentation of further evidence or it may disregard the admission and proceed with the trial under ordinary procedures (or remit the case to another Chamber).

 Pause for reflection

Is plea bargaining permissible in international criminal law?

These simplified procedures on an admission of guilt may allow some room for 'plea bargaining' as known in some (but not all) common law jurisdictions. Plea bargaining generally takes one of two forms: prosecutorial agreement 'to recommend a lesser sentence in exchange for a guilty plea' (sentence bargaining); or 'the prosecution agreeing to ask the trial chamber to dismiss a count or counts in exchange for the guilty plea' (charge bargaining).[91] The latter may be controversial as it could be considered inconsistent with the truth-finding function of international criminal justice in that it may allow certain allegations to go unexamined or unproven.[92] Plea bargaining was not particularly common at either of the ad hoc Tribunals, largely because any agreement between prosecution and defence was not binding upon a trial chamber. In a number of cases trial chambers were prepared to impose sentences which were significantly higher than that recommended by the prosecution as being appropriate.[93] Unsurprisingly, this did not encourage other defendants to admit guilt.

The ICC Statute does not preclude plea bargaining but it does expressly state that: 'Any discussions between the Prosecutor and the defence regarding modification of the charges, the admission of guilt or the penalty to be imposed shall not be binding on the Court'.[94] On the basis of the experience before the ad hoc Tribunals, therefore, it does not seem likely that plea bargaining will be a common practice before the ICC in the future.

5.4.2 Disclosure of evidence

Disclosure must occur before the trial commences. An accused person cannot adequately prepare their own defence if the prosecutor's evidence is not disclosed to them. Lack of disclosure may jeopardize the right to a fair trial or compromise it fatally. In a civil law system disclosure is in principle straightforward: a single investigation will have compiled a 'dossier' of all incriminating and all exculpatory evidence. The court and the accused have a right of access to the dossier and thus the full evidence available to the prosecution.

In adversarial proceedings, the separate prosecution and defence cases (and investigations) will mean there is no single dossier. Before the ICTY and ICTR the Prosecutor has 'extensive, and continuous, obligations concerning pre-trial disclosure'

---

[90] Art 65(3), ICC Statute.
[91] Boas et al, *International Criminal Law Practitioner Library*, vol 3, 221.   [92] Ibid, 221.
[93] Ibid, 224.   [94] Art 65(5), ICC Statute.

extending to all material supporting the Document Containing the Charges, witness statements, and statements intended to be offered as written evidence in lieu of witness evidence.[95]

Under the ICC Rules of Procedure and Evidence:[96]

- both the prosecution and the defence have a right to inspect evidence held by the other party;
- the prosecutor must provide advance notification the names of any witnesses he or she intends to call and copies of any prior statements they have made; and
- the defence must give sufficient notice of its intention to raise an alibi or a defence (a ground excluding criminal responsibility), but if it fails to give adequate notice it may still raise the issue but the prosecution may be granted an adjournment to adequately prepare its response.

The disclosure rules are subject to provisions on maintaining the confidentiality of certain evidence, in particular the identity of witnesses who might be endangered if their identities were known. The Pre-Trial Chamber and Trial Chamber have powers to order that the Prosecutor disclose information to the defence.[97]

This became a heated issue in the *Lubanga* case and resulted in an order (overturned on appeal) that the trial be suspended and the accused released from custody on the basis that a fair trial could not be conducted while the Prosecutor refused to disclose certain evidence to the defence. The situation arose through the Prosecutor's use of 'intermediaries' (persons who would conduct interviews and take witness statements on behalf of the OTP) working in the DRC and is considered in the example below.

 Example

Prosecutor v Thomas Lubanga Dyilo (Decision on the Disclosure of the Identity of Intermediary 143)

(1) What allegation was made by the defence about the Prosecutors' use of intermediaries?

The defence alleged there were grounds to suspect some of the intermediaries used by the OTP had procured, or attempted to procure, false evidence and that as a consequence they should be called to give evidence.[98]

---

[95] Friman, 'Procedures of International Criminal Investigations and Prosecutions' in Cryer et al, *Introduction*, 3rd ed, 466.

[96] Rules 76–79, ICC RPE.   [97] Arts 61(3) and 64(3), ICC Statute.

[98] *Prosecutor v Thomas Lubanga Dyilo* (Decision on the Disclosure of the Identity of Intermediary 143), ICC Trial Chamber, 8 July 2010, paras 20–21, 27–28, 31; and ICC Appeals Chamber, 8 October 2010, paras 1–3, 32–33, 46–50, and 55–62.

(2) What order of the Trial Chamber had the Prosecutor refused to comply with and why?

The Prosecutor had refused to comply with an order to disclose the identity of Intermediary 143 to a limited group within the defence team. The Trial Chamber held that such disclosure posed no appreciable risk to the intermediary. The Prosecutor refused to comply because in his view he had an independent legal duty under the Statute to 'ensure that appropriate protective measures are taken to protect the safety of victims and witnesses', and that these measures should be in place before he complied with the order.[99] The Prosecutor further argued on appeal that the ICC does not vest control over witness protection in one organ of the Court but establishes a system in which 'all organs share responsibility and must consult and act in a coordinated fashion to provide adequate protection' and thus the Trial Chamber should have consulted the Prosecutor before making such an order.[100] In relation to the Prosecutors' duties in this context one should see Article 68(1), ICC Statute (and note that such measures shall not prejudice a fair trial).

(3) What order was made by the Trial Chamber as a consequence and why?

The Trial Chamber held that 'The Rome Statute framework makes it clear that the Chamber, once seized of the case, is the only organ of the Court with the power to order and vary protective measures vis-à-vis individuals at risk on account of [the] work of the ICC'.[101] It also found that the Prosecutor had adopted the position that, when it came to matters concerning the protection of those witnesses who have had dealings with the prosecution 'the prosecution has autonomy to comply with, or disregard, the orders of the Chamber, depending on its interpretation of its responsibilities under the Rome Statute framework'.[102]

The Trial Chamber found the Prosecutor's actions to constitute an abuse of process and that no 'criminal court can operate on the basis that whenever it makes an order in a particular area, it is for the Prosecutor to elect whether or not to implement it, depending on his interpretation of his obligations'.[103] As it could not secure a fair trial if the Prosecutor would not comply with its orders, it suspended the trial and scheduled a hearing on the question whether the accused should be released. (It did subsequently order his release, but the order was stayed and then overturned by the Appeals Chamber.)

(4) What did the Appeals Chamber consider to be the appropriate course? Did it agree with the position of the Prosecutor? Did it uphold the decision of the Trial Chamber?

The Appeals Chamber considered that the Prosecutor should have complied with the Trial Chamber's order irrespective of his interpretation of his other duties under the Statute. The Appeals Chamber's fundamental holding was that 'when there is a conflict between the Prosecutor's perception of his duties and the orders of the Trial Chamber, the Trial Chamber's orders must prevail. This is a fundamental criterion for any trial to be fair.'[104] However, it found that for the Trial Chamber to have ordered a stay of proceedings was not appropriate: it should instead have first attempted to assert its disciplinary power over the Prosecutor by fining him under Article 71 (the provision also covers other 'administrative' sanctions short of imprisonment).

---

[99] *Lubanga*, Trial Chamber Decision, paras 14–15.   [100] *Lubanga*, Trial Chamber Decision, paras 32–33.
[101] *Lubanga*, Trial Chamber Decision, para 23.   [102] *Lubanga*, Trial Chamber Decision, para 21.
[103] *Lubanga*, Trial Chamber Decision, para 27.   [104] *Lubanga*, Appeals Chamber Decision, para 48.

5.4.3 **Evidence**

As noted above, in an adversarial, common law system it is the parties who control what material is presented to the court. Such common law systems also usually have numerous technical rules of evidence. In the civil law tradition there is a wide approach to what evidence is admissible, as the judiciary is presumed to be capable of weighing evidence on its merit without artificial rules.

While proceedings before international criminal courts are adversarial, and it is largely the parties who control what material is presented to the court (although judges do have powers to call for further evidence or witnesses), the approach to evidence is often 'flexible' and lacking 'technical rules', again based on the assumption that legally trained judges are capable of assessing the reliability and probative value of evidence on their own.[105]

Before the ICC a similar approach prevails:

> The Court may rule on the relevance or admissibility of any evidence, taking into account, inter alia, the probative value of the evidence and any prejudice that such evidence may cause to a fair trial or to a fair evaluation of the testimony of a witness, in accordance with the Rules of Procedure and Evidence.[106]

Under the Rules of Procedure and Evidence the starting point is that a 'Chamber shall have the authority . . . to assess freely all evidence submitted in order to determine its relevance or admissibility'.[107] A number of exclusionary rules should be noted:

- 'communications made in the context of the professional relationship between a person and his or her legal counsel shall be regarded as privileged, and consequently not subject to disclosure';[108]

- a witness has a privilege against self-incrimination and a witness may object to making any statement that might tend to incriminate him or her;[109]

- evidence obtained by means of a violation of the ICC Statute or internationally recognized human rights is not be admissible if it casts substantial doubt on the reliability of the evidence or the admission of the evidence would be antithetical to, and would seriously damage, the integrity of the proceedings;[110] and

- in cases of sexual assault consent to sexual acts cannot be inferred from the silence of, or lack of resistance by, a victim; nor may inferences about a victim's '[c]redibility, character or predisposition to sexual availability' be drawn from evidence of their prior or subsequent sexual conduct and such evidence is not admissible.[111]

---

[105] G Sluiter, 'Evidence' in A Cassese (ed), *The Oxford Companion to International Criminal Justice* (Oxford University Press 2009), 313; see also: Annual Report of the ICTY 1994, UN Doc A/49/342 (29 August 1994), para 72.

[106] Art 69(4), ICC Statute.

[107] Rule 63(2), ICC RPE.   [108] Rule 73, ICC RPE.   [109] Rule 74, ICC RPE.

[110] Art 69(7), ICC Statute.   [111] Rules 70 and 71, ICC RPE.

The ICC Statute shows a clear preference for 'live' witness testimony, but it may also take evidence by video link or pre-recorded testimony.[112]

Before the ICC the evidentiary burden is on the Prosecutor to prove the charges 'beyond reasonable doubt' (see section 5.4.4).[113] The defence is not required to lead any evidence and is entitled to rely on the presumption of innocence and the right to silence (as discussed further in Chapter 6).[114] In contrast to the position in some civil law systems, the accused is entitled to give evidence in his or her own defence.

The issue of exclusion of evidence obtained in breach of human rights was raised in the *Lubanga* confirmation of charges hearing.[115] The question concerned documents seized from a person's home by Congolese authorities in a manner contrary to Congolese law, rendering them inadmissible in national criminal proceedings. The Pre-Trial Chamber ruled that a search and seizure for the purposes of a lawful trial did not constitute a violation of an 'internationally recognized human right', even if it violated national law.[116] One should further note that even if there had been such a violation, the Pre-Trial Chamber ruled that the Court has a 'discretion to seek an appropriate balance between the Statute's fundamental values in each concrete case'.[117] Thus the Court could still have admitted the evidence if it concluded the evidence was reliable and its admission did not damage the integrity of proceedings.

Difficult questions may also arise where evidence is sought from a State but it claims that provision of that information could prejudice national security interests. The essential procedure to be followed before ICC under Article 72 of the Rome Statute is that the State must consult with the defence, the Prosecutor, and the Trial or Appeal Chamber (as the case may be) to seek to agree to resolve the issue. Such measures may include obtaining the information from a different source or provision of the information on conditions such as providing 'summaries or redactions' of documents, placing limitations on disclosure, the 'use of *in camera* or *ex parte* proceedings', or taking 'other protective measures'.[118] Further, under Article 73 of the ICC Statute a State requested to disclose information given to it on terms of confidence by another State or by an international organization need not give that information to the Court unless it can secure the relevant third party's consent.

The issue of the provision of information potentially prejudicial to national security to an international tribunal arose most famously before the ICTY in *Blaškić* when the Tribunal requested Croatia produce certain documents for use in evidence (at the ICTY such a request was called a 'subpoena' when directed to a person and a 'binding order' when directed to a State). In the *Blaškić Subpoena Appeal* Croatia argued that a State could refuse to produce documents to the ICTY on grounds of national security and that it was for the State to determine what its security required. The ICTY rejected this argument in part based on the fact that UN member States were obliged

---

[112] Art 69(2), ICC Statute; Rules 67 and 68, ICC RPE.   [113] Art 66, ICC Statute.
[114] See also: Arts 66 and 67(1)(g), ICC Statute.
[115] *Lubanga (Confirmation of Charges)*, ICC Pre-Trial Chamber I, 27 January 2007, paras 62 ff.
[116] Ibid, para 82.
[117] Ibid, para 84. See further: Miraglia, 'Admissibility of Evidence'.
[118] Art 72(4) and (5), ICC Statute.

to cooperate with it under Article 29 of its Statute and further arguing that in prosecuting cases such as war crimes military documents may obviously provide crucial evidence and to:

> admit that a State holding such documents may unilaterally assert national security claims and refuse to surrender those documents could lead to the stultification of international criminal proceedings... The very raison d'être of the International Tribunal would then be undermined.[119]

However, the ICTY explicitly acknowledged that security concerns could be legitimate, and instituted a system where the documents could be reviewed *in camera* (i.e. in secret) by an ICTY judge. After such a review documents might then be treated as:

- irrelevant to the case and returned to the State;
- relevant to the case, but such that any relevance was outweighed by the need to 'safeguard legitimate national security concerns'—such documents would also be returned to the State; or
- other relevant documents (i.e. where that relevance outweighed legitimate security concerns), which would be filed with the registry, but from which the State might be allowed to redact (black out) certain sections.[120]

In theory the ICTY could rely on the fact that cooperation with it was compulsory as it was established by the UN Security Council in exercise of its compulsory Chapter VII powers. Under the ICC Statute, where a State party refuses to cooperate with the Court the final recourse is for the Court to report that lack of cooperation to the Assembly of States Parties or the Security Council.[121]

5.4.4 Conduct of the trial

All courts have an inherent power to control their own proceedings. The usual course of proceedings before the ICTY and ICTR has been:

- opening statements (by the prosecution and defence if it chooses to do so);
- the calling of prosecution witnesses and introduction of prosecution evidence (be it 'documentary, physical, video' or other);
- the close of the prosecution case (at which point the Court may acquit the defendant if the evidence is insufficient or at which point the defendant may plead guilty);
- the opening of the defence's case in chief, including an opening statement if none was made previously (there may be a break in trial proceedings to allow preparation of the defence case);

---

[119] *Blaškić* (Judgment on the Request of the Republic of Croatia), ICTY Appeals Chamber, 29 October 1997, para 65 (*Blaškić Subpoena Appeal*).
[120] *Blaškić Subpoena Appeal*, para 68.
[121] Art. 87(7), ICC Statute.

- presentation of rebuttal evidence by the Prosecution (only at the ad hoc Tribunals and Special Court for Sierra Leone and only in respect of matters raised for the first time in the defence case-in-chief);
- closing arguments; and
- the Chamber then retires for deliberation (often for a period of months) and then delivers its verdict.[122]

When witnesses are called by the prosecution, the 'the defence may cross examine the witnesses, and the prosecution may re-examine on matters raised during cross examination. The judges may also pose questions to the witnesses at any time, and at the ICC they may allow question by the legal representatives of the victims.'[123] The same procedure applies in respect of witnesses called by the defence. A Trial Chamber may also 'call witnesses on its own initiative', or call on either of the parties to provide further evidence.[124] At the ICC the Presiding Judge may give directions on the conduct of proceedings, and the prosecution and defence may agree on the course of submitting evidence in the absence of directions.[125]

With respect to the examination of witnesses before the ICC, the ICC Rules of Procedure and Evidence provide that:

(a) A party that submits evidence ... by way of a witness, has the right to question that witness [examination in chief];
(b) The prosecution and the defence have the right to question that witness about relevant matters related to the witness's testimony and its reliability, the credibility of the witness and other relevant matters [cross examination];
(c) The Trial Chamber has the right to question a witness before or after a witness is questioned by a participant ...;
(d) The defence shall have the right to be the last to examine a witness.[126]

ICC proceedings are generally to be held in public, but *in camera* (closed) proceeding may be held in certain cases involving evidence relating to victims of sexual assault or where it is necessary for victim or witness protection.[127]

As for the role of the accused, in general trial *in absentia* is prohibited in adversarial systems for the basic reason that the trial is a contest between parties and proceeding in the absence of one would be unfair.[128] In many inquisitorial systems *in absentia* proceedings are permissible as the investigating judge will have gathered all the evidence relevant to both prosecution and defence, and there is a perceived public interest in the trial going ahead even without the defendant being present—as the defendant should not be allowed to thwart justice by fleeing.[129] A trial before the

---

[122] Boas et al, *International Criminal Law Practitioner Library*, vol 3, 278–282.   [123] Ibid, 279.
[124] Ibid, 281.   [125] Rule 140, ICC RPE.
[126] Rule 140(2), ICC RPE.   [127] Arts 64(7) and 68, ICC Statute; Rules 72 and 87, ICC RPE.
[128] Although Orie notes that common-law systems do accept that in exceptional cases trial *in absentia* may be permissible: Orie, 'Accusatorial v. Inquisitorial Approach', 1479. On this basis he finds their prohibition under the ICC Statute odd.
[129] Cassese et al, *Cassese's International Criminal Law*, 337–8.

ICC or one of the UN ad hoc Tribunals, however, may generally not proceed in the absence of the accused.[130] In cases where the accused has appeared before the Court, the trial may exceptionally continue in their temporary absence. The ICC Statute only expressly provides for this where the accused has proved disruptive.[131] Nonetheless, in the *Ruto and Sang* case arising from the situation in Kenya, the ICC Trial Chamber also excused Mr Ruto (the Deputy President of Kenya) from continuous attendance at his trial on the basis that he had significant public duties in Kenya and would nonetheless attend numerous specified sessions of the trial.[132] This was done under a discretion created through the ICC Rules of Procedure and Evidence; however, as the Rules must be consistent with the Statute (which contains no 'public duties' exception) there is the possibility the Rule may later be read down or invalidated by the ICC Appeals Chamber.[133]

In general, international criminal trials have been exceedingly long.[134] In light of the completion strategy, the ICTY in particular has moved towards accepting more evidence in written form without the need for witnesses to testify directly as a matter of efficiency.[135] In such cases the witness will usually be required to be available for cross-examination or questioning by the bench. Whether the ICC will adopt such a practice remains to be seen. The early indications are that 'there has been very little softening of the preference' expressed in its Statute and RPE 'for live testimony'.[136] This proved difficult in the *Kenyatta* case arising out of the Kenyan situation, where the disappearance and withdrawal of witnesses (among other matters)[137] led to the case collapsing in 2015 after the Prosecutor confirmed she lacked sufficient evidence to proceed.[138]

5.4.5 Deliberation and sentencing

At the end of the trial the judges will deliberate in chambers before reaching a verdict, and will give written reasons for that verdict. It is for the judges to find the accused guilty or innocent on each charge. Under the ICC Statute the standard of proof is

[130]   Art 21(4)(d), ICTY Statute; Art 20(4)(d), ICTR Statute; Art 63, ICC Statute.

[131]   E.g.: Art 63(2), ICC Statute.

[132]   *The Prosecutor v William Samoei Ruto and Joshua Arap Sang (oral ruling on attendance)*, ICC Trial Chamber, 15 January 2014. Transcript available at: www.icc-cpi.int/iccdocs/doc/doc1711590.pdf.

[133]   Under Rule 134*quater*, ICC RPE. See further: KJ Heller, 'No, the ASP Didn't Hoodwink Kenya and the AU Concerning RPE 134quater', *Opinio Juris*, 14 January 2014, http://opiniojuris.org/2014/01/14/asp-didnt-hoodwink-kenya-au-concerning-rpe-134quater/.

[134]   See discussion in Chapter 6, section 6.3.3.

[135]   Boas et al, *International Criminal Law Practitioner Library*, vol 3, 353–7. However, for a view that in an adversarial system such statements may be of limited value (because they will be written by the parties and not investigatory police) see: G Sluiter, 'Evidence', 314–315.

[136]   Boas et al, *International Criminal Law Practitioner Library*, vol 3, 356.

[137]   'Claims of witnesses in Kenya ICC trial "disappearing" ', *BBC News*, 8 February 2013, www.bbc.com/news/world-africa-21382339; 'Uhuru Kenyatta: ICC trial witnesses withdraw', *BBC News*, 18 July 2013, www.bbc.com/news/world-africa-23359940.

[138]   See: 'Notice of withdrawal of the charges against Uhuru Muigai Kenyatta', 05/12/2014, ICC Doc. ICC-01/09-02/11-983 and *The Prosecutor v Uhuru Muigai Kenyatta (Decision on the withdrawal of charges against Mr Kenyatta)*, ICC Trial Chamber 13 March 2015.

that: 'In order to convict the accused, the Court must be convinced of the guilt of the accused beyond reasonable doubt'.[139] This follows the approach taken in practice under the RPEs of the ICTY, the ICTR, and the Special Court for Sierra Leone.[140] In UK and US case law this standard does not mean that the Court must acquit if it entertains *any* doubt no matter how remote, fanciful, or improbable; it also does not mean proof is required 'beyond a shadow of a doubt' or which reaches 'absolute certainty'.[141] As Cassese put it: 'the court must find that the accused is guilty without entertaining a doubt that would cause any reasonable and prudent person to hesitate before reaching a definite conclusion'.[142] In one ICTY case a trial chamber was held to have misapplied this standard when it considered that a remote possibility that someone else had killed the victims in question precluded a finding of guilt beyond reasonable doubt.[143] As discussed, proof beyond reasonable doubt does not require an acquittal where a remote possibility casts doubt on the guilt of the accused. In the common law tradition the standard is that the cogency of the evidence 'need not reach certainty, but it must carry a high degree of probability'.[144]

After the judges have given their judgment on guilt or innocence a separate hearing may be held on sentencing, where the parties may make further arguments.[145] After initially holding separate sentencing hearings, the practice before the ICTY and the ICTR has become to hold a single trial and issue a single verdict on both guilt or innocence and sentencing. Such a 'unified trial means that the defendant cannot apply a different strategy for the purpose of sentencing'.[146]

The ICC may order sentences of imprisonment for a specified time of up to 30 years, or a sentence of life imprisonment or a fine or forfeiture of proceedings.[147] In imposing the sentence the Court will 'take into account such factors as the gravity of the crime and the individual circumstances of the convicted person' and in 'imposing a sentence of imprisonment, the Court shall deduct the time, if any, previously spent in [Court-ordered] detention'.[148] That sentence must be reviewed by the Court 'to determine whether it should be reduced' when the convicted person has served either two thirds of their sentence or 25 years (as further discussed at Chapter 6, section 6.6.2).[149]

Sentencing is an inherently discretionary judicial function. It is notorious that the Statutes of international criminal tribunals provide relatively little guidance on sentencing. For example, the ICTY and ICTR Statutes simply direct the Tribunals to have 'recourse to the general practice regarding prison sentences' in the courts of the former Yugoslavia or Rwanda respectively.[150] While the sentencing practice at the

---

[139] Art 66(3), ICC Statute.
[140] Rule 87(A), ICTY RPE; Rule 87(A), ICTR RPE; Rules 87(A) and 98, SCSL RPE. Their respective Statutes were silent on the question.
[141] *Miller v Minister of Pensions* [1947] 1 All ER 373; *Victor v Nebraska* 127 L.Ed.2d 583 (1994).
[142] Cassese, *International Criminal Law*, 2nd ed, 418.
[143] *Tadić*, ICTY Appeals Chamber, 15 July 1999, paras 181–183.
[144] *Miller v Minister of Pensions*, n 141.
[145] Art 76(2), ICC Statute.
[146] H Friman, 'Sentencing and Penalties' in Cryer et al, *Introduction* 3rd ed, 509.
[147] Art 77, ICC Statute.   [148] Art 78, ICC Statute.   [149] Art 110(3), ICC Statute.
[150] Art 24, ICTY Statute; Art 23, ICTR Statute.

ad hoc Tribunals has been criticized as inconsistent, one study into ICTY sentencing practice concludes that certain patterns are discernible in its sentencing practice including that:

- 'high-ranking criminals in influential positions are sentenced to substantially longer prison terms than the ordinary low-ranking offenders';
- 'more extensive criminal activities are punished more severely' than isolated acts;
- crimes against humanity attract longer sentences than war crimes;
- mitigating factors do in practice reduce sentence length;
- instigators of atrocities 'are punished more severely' than other defendants, but superiors 'tend to be punished less severely' (on superior responsibility see Chapter 12).[151]

These factors, however, were found to explain variations in sentence length in only 60 per cent of cases and it is impossible to objectively measure every consideration that might be relevant to sentencing.[152]

At the time of writing only two sentences had been passed at the ICC. In 2012 Thomas Lubanga was sentenced to 14 years imprisonment for war crimes of conscripting children into armed forces over a one year period. In 2014, Germain Katanga was sentenced to 12 years imprisonment for being an accessory to a crime against humanity (murder) and four counts of war crimes (murder, attacking a civilian population, destruction of property, and pillaging). Both *Lubanga* and *Katanga* involved convictions based on a limited number of charges arising out of a broader context of alleged crimes. While it may make sense for a Prosecutor to focus on a more limited number of offences in order to secure a conviction, the Court will only take the offences that have been proven into account in sentencing. For example, while there was evidence of sexual violence against female child soldiers in particular in *Lubanga* it was not among the charges brought against Mr Lubanga and no finding as to his responsibility for such crimes was made.[153]

 Pause for reflection

What factors have the ICTY and ICTR taken into account in sentencing?

As noted, there is no mathematical formula for determining the precise sentence a person should receive. The purposes of sentencing emphasized by the Tribunals have principally been deterrence and more especially retribution (in the sense of objective justice or 'letting the punishment fit the crime'). To this end the gravity or seriousness of the crime should be taken into account

---

[151] B Hola, AL Smeulers, and CCJH Bijleveld, 'Is ICTY Sentencing Predictable? An Empirical Analysis of ICTY Sentencing Practice' (2009) 22 Leiden Journal of International Law 79, 95.

[152] Hola, Smeulers, and Bijleveld, 'Is ICTY Sentencing Predictable?', 95.

[153] *Lubanga*, ICC Trial Chamber I, 14 March 2012, para 913 and see also paras 16, 36, 60, 574, 577, 606, 629–31, 890–96.

along with aggravating factors (warranting greater punishment) and mitigating factors (warranting lesser punishment). As regards the seriousness of the crime, principally a court will look to the quantum (amount) of suffering inflicted.

Aggravating factors may include (according to Barbora Hola, Alette Smeulers, and Catrien Bijleveld):[154]

- the abuse of a superior position/position of power/position of authority or trust;[155]
- the special vulnerability or particular defencelessness of victims;[156]
- the extreme suffering or harm inflicted on victims;[157]
- the very large number of victims or the scale and duration of the crime;[158] and
- the particular cruelty of the crime or its 'heinous' nature.[159]

Schabas would further suggest that acting in an official capacity or having a 'leadership role' may also be an aggravating factor, as may acting with a discriminatory intent (where such an intent is not an essential component of the crime).[160]

Mitigating factors may include (according to Hola, Smeulers, and Bijleveld):[161]

- family and other personal circumstances;[162]
- good conduct in detention;[163]
- expressions of remorse;[164]
- assistance to detainees or victims;[165] and
- voluntary surrender.[166]

---

[154] Hola, Smeulers, and Bijleveld, 'Is ICTY Sentencing Predictable?', 86.

[155] See also: Rule 145(2)(b)(ii), ICC RPE.

[156] *Kristić*, ICTY Trial Chamber, 2 August 2001, para 703; compare Rule 145(2)(b)(iii), ICC RPE.

[157] *Tadić* (Sentencing), ICTY Trial Chamber, 14 July 1997, para 70; *Delalić, Mucić et al (Čelebići)*, ICTY Trial Chamber, 16 November 1998, paras 1225, 1260, 1273.

[158] *Blaškić*, ICTY Trial Chamber, 3 March 2000, para 784; *Erdemović* (Sentencing Judgment), ICTY Trial Chamber, 5 March 1998, para 15; compare Rule 145(2)(b)(iv), ICC RPE.

[159] *Kristić*, ICTY Trial Chamber, 2 August 2001, para 703; compare Rule 145(2)(b)(iv), ICC RPE.

[160] Schabas, *The UN International Criminal Tribunals*, 567–8 and 570. His review of issues involved in sentencing at 563–578 is also useful. On leadership roles as an aggravating factor see: *Tadić* (Sentencing Appeal), ICTY Appeals Chamber, 26 January 2000, paras 55–56; on discriminatory intent see: *Todorović* (Sentencing Judgment), ICTY Trial Chamber, 31 July 2001, para 57; and *Blaškić*, ICTY Trial Chamber, 3 March 2000, para 785; compare Rule 145(2)(b)(v), ICC RPE.

[161] Hola, Smeulers, and Bijleveld, 'Is ICTY Sentencing predictable?', 88. On the role of mitigating factors in sentencing see further: *Todorović* (Sentencing Judgment), ICTY Trial Chamber, 31 July 2001, paras 75–92.

[162] *Erdemović* (Sentencing Judgment), ICTY Trial Chamber, 5 March 1998, para 16; *Delalić*, ICTY Trial Chamber, 16 November 1998, para 1284.

[163] *Strugar*, ICTY Trial Chamber, 31 January 2005, para 472 (although it is noted rather than given great weight).

[164] *Blaškić*, ICTY Trial Chamber, 3 March 2000, para 775; *Kunarac*, ICTY Trial Chamber, 22 February 2001, para 868; *Erdemović* (Sentencing Judgment), ICTY Trial Chamber, 5 March 1998, para 16.

[165] *Delalić*, ICTY Trial Chamber, 16 November 1998, paras 1239, 1270; *Blaškić*, ICTY Trial Chamber, 3 March 2000, para 781; *Erdemović* (Sentencing Judgment), ICTY Trial Chamber, 5 March 1998, para 16. Compare: Rule 145(2)(a)(ii), ICC RPE (referring, narrowly, to 'any efforts by the person to compensate the victims' rather than acts of mercy or assistance in general).

[166] *Blaškić*, ICTY Trial Chamber, 3 March 2000, para 776; *Kupreškić*, ICTY Trial Chamber, 3 March 2000, para 784; *Strugar*, ICTY Trial Chamber, 31 January 2005, para 472.

Friman would add to this list: the 'indirect or limited participation' of the defendant in the crime.[167] Schabas notes that 'substantial cooperation' with the Prosecutor is universally considered a mitigating factor under tribunals' Rules of Procedure and Evidence.[168]

5.5 Summary and conclusions

This chapter has examined the law applicable to the investigation and prosecution of international crimes as being a hybrid of civil and common law traditions. We could ask whether, to some extent, the adversarial system has prevailed. Points to consider in making such an assessment include:

- the role of judges, especially at the ICC and its Pre-Trial Chamber;
- the independence of the prosecutor and the limits of their discretion; and
- the extent to which international criminal trials rely on oral argument and evidence in the common law tradition.

On a balanced view, we might say that while proceedings before an international criminal tribunal have a superficially adversarial character, the system of procedure in international criminal law is ultimately a hybrid with both common and civil law features. Indeed one might argue that the law of international criminal procedure could usefully absorb more from the civil law tradition. In particular we might ask whether the emphasis on oral evidence inherited from adversarial systems is too slow and inefficient for complex international trials. We could also ask whether the requirement of separate defence and prosecution investigations creates problems of equality of arms and disadvantages the defence. We shall explore this question in more detail in Chapter 6.

Useful further reading

JC Baker and M Happold, '*Prosecutor v Thomas Lubanga*, Decision of Pre-Trial Chamber I of the International Criminal Court, 29 January 2007' (2007) 56 International and Comparative Law Quarterly 713.
A short, useful piece which makes the point that the Pre-Trial Chamber's power to confirm or vary the charges brought by the Prosecutor may significantly alter the prosecution's case.

H Friman, 'Procedures of International Criminal Investigations and Prosecutions' in R Cryer, H Friman, D Robinson, and E Wilmshurst, *An Introduction to International Criminal Law and Procedure*, 3rd ed (Cambridge University Press 2014).
This chapter covers the conduct of international criminal investigations and prosecutions in significant detail.

---

[167] H Friman, 'Sentencing and Penalties' in Cryer et al, *Introduction*, 501.
[168] Schabas, *The UN International Criminal Tribunals*, 572 citing Rule 101(B)(ii) of the ICTY, ITCR and SCSCL RPE. See e.g.: *Erdemović* (Sentencing Judgment), ICTY Trial Chamber, 5 March 1998, para 16. Compare: Rule 145(2)(a)(ii), ICC RPE. Obviously, not all cooperation will qualify as 'substantial'.

B HOLA, AL SMEULERS, and CCJH BIJLEVELD, 'Is ICTY Sentencing Predictable? An Empirical Analysis of ICTY Sentencing Practice' (2009) 22 Leiden Journal of International Law 79.

This remains one of very few significant attempts at a thorough survey of sentencing practice in international criminal law.

S KENDALL and S NOUWEN, 'Representational Practices at the International Criminal Court: The Gap Between Juridified and Abstract Victimhood' (2013) 76 Law and Contemporary Problems 235.

An excellent theoretical account of the manner in which international criminal justice risks using victims for its own ends even as it attempts to give them a greater role.

M MIRAGLIA, 'Admissibility of Evidence, Standard of Proof, and Nature of the Decision in the ICC Confirmation of Charges in Lubanga' (2008) 6 Journal of International Criminal Justice 489.

A concise and very useful exploration of the evidentiary standard required in a confirmation of charges proceeding (being the need for 'sufficient evidence to establish substantial grounds to believe' the accused committed the crimes charge) and reflects on procedural questions arising from the Pre-Trial Chamber's variation of the charges brought by the Prosecutor.

A ORIE, 'Accusatorial v. Inquisitorial Approach in International Criminal Proceedings' in A Cassese, P Gaeta, and JRWD Jones (eds), *The Rome Statute of the International Criminal Court: A Commentary*, vol. 2 (Oxford University Press 2002), Chapter 34.

An excellent general overview of common features of adversarial and inquisitorial systems, and analysis of the methods adopted by the Nuremberg and Tokyo military tribunals and the ad hoc Tribunals. It also provides a preliminary assessment of ICC procedures (written before the ICC had commenced hearing cases).

6

Fair trial rights, appeals, and revision and enforcement of sentences

6.1 Introduction

As we have seen, there is no general law or uniform code of international criminal procedure. The International Criminal Court's procedure is still developing, and the ad hoc international criminal tribunals have their own procedural rules. However, defendants before any of the tribunals share certain fundamental fair trial rights. In this chapter, we examine those rights and also examine a defendant's right to appeal against their conviction or sentence.

 Learning aims

By the end of this chapter you should have a solid basic understanding of the issues and be able to:

- identify the rights enjoyed by defendants in international criminal proceedings and discuss how they are secured;
- discuss the grounds for appeal and revision of sentences; and
- explain the general features of the regime governing the detention of convicted international criminals.

In light of these goals, the chapter proceeds as follows:

- Section 6.2 introduces general fair trial rights enjoyed by the defendant.
- Section 6.3 examines in more detail the content of the right to a public, fair, and expeditious hearing.
- Section 6.4 briefly reviews some of the issues concerning legality of arrest and detention (immunity from arrest and detention is considered in Chapter 14).
- Section 6.5 considers the right of appeal.
- Section 6.6 examines the revision and enforcement of sentences.

6.2 Fair trial rights and the position of the defendant

6.2.1 The right to a fair trial in international law and before international criminal tribunals

The right to a fair trial is well recognized in international law, and in the statutes of the International Criminal Tribunal for the former Yugoslavia (ICTY), the International Criminal Tribunal for Rwanda (ICTR), and the International Criminal Court (ICC). The right to a fair trial is actually a collection of procedural guarantees. The most authoritative statements of the content of the right are found in the Universal Declaration of Human Rights passed by the UN General Assembly as a non-binding instrument in 1948,[1] elements of which were subsequently codified in the International Covenant on Civil and Political Rights of 1966 (ICCPR).[2] Certain fair trial guarantees are also found in Common Article 3 of the Geneva Conventions[3] and in the Additional Protocol I of 1977.[4] A brief review of these instruments establishes that certain rights are universally acknowledged as indispensible to a fair trial.

International human rights law

Our survey here will begin with the ICCPR. The majority of protections discussed below are found in Article 14. Crucially, Article 14 of the Covenant recognizes the right to 'fair and public hearing by a competent, independent and impartial tribunal established by law'.[5] Further, everyone has the 'right to be presumed innocent' until proven guilty.[6] Article 14 also recognizes that a defendant must benefit from various other 'minimum guarantees' including: being informed of the charges against him or her in a language that he or she understands; having adequate time and facilities to prepare one's defence; the right 'to be tried without undue delay' and in one's presence; the right to be represented, either by oneself or through 'legal assistance' of one's own choosing; the right to examine witnesses and to call witnesses in one's own defence; the right to an interpreter; and the right not to be compelled to testify against oneself or to admit guilt.[7] In addition, every person 'convicted of a crime' has the right to have his or her conviction and sentence 'reviewed by a higher tribunal according to law'.[8] This does not, however, exhaust the Covenant rights that might be relevant to a fair trial. Other possible 'fair trial protections [found] scattered throughout' the Covenant 'include the right to be promptly informed of the reason for one's arrest (article 9), the right not to be deprived of one's life arbitrarily (article 6), and the right to be free

---

[1] UN General Assembly, Universal Declaration of Human Rights, 10 December 1948, UN Doc 217 A (III). See in particular Arts 9, 10, and 11.

[2] 999 UNTS 171.

[3] E.g. 1949 Geneva Convention (IV) Relative to the Protection of Civilian Persons in Time of War, 75 UNTS 287.

[4] 1977 Protocol Additional to the Geneva Conventions of 12 August 1949, and relating to the Protection of Victims of International Armed Conflicts (Protocol I), 1125 UNTS 3.

[5] Art 14(1).   [6] Art 14(2).   [7] Art 14(3).   [8] Art 14(5).

from torture (article 7).[9] The fundamental importance of these rights is evidenced in the fact that they have been held to be non-derogable: that is, they apply even during states of emergency.[10]

The Geneva Conventions, in Common Article 3, set out minimum fair trial guarantees applicable during non-international armed conflicts. As noted in Chapter 8, these include the prohibition upon 'the passing of sentences and the carrying out of executions without previous judgment pronounced by a regularly constituted court, affording all the judicial guarantees which are recognized as indispensable by civilized peoples'[11] (discussed at Chapter 8, section 8.6.7 as a war crime). Article 75 of Additional Protocol I contains an extended list of fair trial guarantees applicable in international armed conflict including: the right to be informed without delay of the charges against one; the prohibition on retroactive criminal law (discussed at Chapter 1, section 1.4.4); the presumption of innocence; the right to be present at trial; the right not to have to testify against oneself or to confess guilt; the right to examine and call witnesses; and the right to be advised of the judicial remedies available upon conviction and any time limits applying to them.[12]

The position before the ad hoc Tribunals

The Statutes of both the ICTY and ICTR recognize certain rights of the defendant which, in light of the foregoing, should appear familiar. Article 21 of the Statute of the ICTY and Article 20 of the Statute of the ICTR provide first for:

- the equality of all persons appearing before the Tribunal;
- the right to a fair and public hearing, subject to provisions of the Statute dealing with the protection of witnesses and victims; and
- the presumption of innocence.

In addition, both Statutes provide for a list of 'minimum guarantees' an accused person shall enjoy 'in full equality': the right to be informed promptly, in detail, and in a language one understands, the nature of the charge; 'to have adequate time and facilities for the preparation of [one's] defence'; 'to be tried without undue delay'; to be tried in one's presence, and to have the right to defend oneself in person or through counsel of one's own choosing; to have legal assistance assigned to one, 'in any case where the interests of justice so require', or if one lacks 'sufficient means' to retain counsel; to examine and call witnesses; to have the assistance of an interpreter if necessary; and the right not to be compelled to testify against oneself or to confess guilt.[13]

Notably, these provisions set out a list of minimum guarantees. There is no provision expressly stipulating what other aspects of international human rights law might

---

[9] D Weissbrodt and K Zinsmaster, 'Protecting the Fair Trial Rights of the Accused in International Criminal Law: Comparison of the International Criminal Court and the Military Commissions in Guantánamo' in BS Brown (ed), *Research Handbook on International Criminal Law* (Elgar 2011), 264.

[10] Human Rights Committee, General Comment No. 29, States of Emergency (Article 4), UN Doc. CCPR/C/21/Rev.1/Add .11 (2001).

[11] Art 3(1)(d), Geneva Convention I.   [12] Art 75(3)(a)–(j), Additional Protocol I.

[13] Art 21(4) ICTY Statute and Art 20(4) ICTR Statute.

apply. Strictly, the ICTY and ICTR are not bound by any of the major human rights treaties: they are not States and cannot be parties to them. However, both tribunals have made frequent reference to human rights treaties and case law in practice.

The position before the ICC

Article 67 of the ICC Statute provides similarly that the accused has a right to a public and 'fair hearing conducted impartially' and also to certain 'minimum guarantees, in full equality'. The specified minimum guarantees include those found in the ICCPR and ICTY and ICTR Statutes (including the right to be informed of the charge against one, to have adequate time and facilities to prepare one's defence, to be present at trial, to conduct one's defence in person or through legal counsel, including counsel assigned by the Court where the accused lacks means to retain counsel, the right to be tried without undue delay and to call and examine witnesses). Notable variations include:

- the fact that the right to be present is subject to provisions of the Statute on removal from the courtroom for disruptive conduct;[14]

- the right to have a translator extends to the right to have documents translated to the extent 'necessary to meet the requirements of fairness';[15]

- the privilege against self-incrimination is phrased so as to include the right to remain silent, without adverse inferences being drawn from such silence;[16]

- the right to make 'an unsworn oral or written statement' in one's own defence;[17] and

- a prohibition on any reversal of the burden of proof or any onus of rebuttal'.[18]

In addition, certain duties protecting the right to a fair trial are placed upon the ICC Prosecutor. These include the requirement that the Prosecutor must 'as soon as practicable, disclose to the defence evidence' that 'shows or tends to show the innocence of the accused' or which may mitigate the accused's guilt or 'which may affect the credibility of prosecution evidence'.[19]

The ICC Statute, however, goes into even further detail on the question of the rights of the accused and other persons. It contains express provisions on: the rights of persons during a prosecutorial investigation;[20] the rights of the accused on first appearance and during trial;[21] the rights of victims to have a degree of participation in proceedings;[22] among other matters.[23] It can thus be suggested that human rights are given a wider role under the ICC Statute than in the Statutes of the ICTY and ICTR and that the Statute itself goes further in terms of codifying applicable human rights. Further, unlike the ICTY and ICTR Statutes, the ICC Statute expressly provides that the Court in its 'application and interpretation' of the applicable law under the Statute 'must be consistent with internationally recognized human rights'.[24] This obviously not only allows

---

[14] Art 67(1)(d) and Art 63(2), ICC Statute.   [15] Art 67(1)(f), ICC Statute.
[16] Art 67(1)(g), ICC Statute.   [17] Art 67(1)(h), ICC Statute.   [18] Art 67(1)(i), ICC Statute.
[19] Art 67(2), ICC Statute.   [20] Art 55, ICC Statute.   [21] Arts 60, 63, 66–67, ICC Statute.
[22] Arts 68 and 75, ICC Statute.   [23] See for example Art 20, ICC Statute on *ne bis in idem*.
[24] Art 21(3), ICC Statute.

the Court to look to the jurisprudence of human rights courts or human rights bodies, but requires that the Court do so.

6.2.2 Independence and impartiality

As noted, Article 14 of the ICCPR sets out the universally agreed principle that every person accused of a crime 'shall be entitled to a fair and public hearing by a competent, independent and impartial tribunal established by law'. The present question, then, is what are the tests for independence and impartiality?

Independence

The independence of a Tribunal is not compromised by it being subject to the legislative or executive powers of other bodies: for example, both the UN ad hoc Tribunals and national courts are equally reliant on political bodies for matters such as funding. In the case of the UN ad hoc Tribunals the Security Council has never sought to interfere in individual cases, and indeed in the *Tadić case* the ICTY ruled on the legality of its own creation by the Security Council. This followed a challenge by the defence that the ICTY was not a court 'established by law' and therefore the trial was an abuse of human rights.[25] As discussed in Chapter 3, section 3.5.1, the Appeals Chamber (perhaps unsurprisingly) found that the Security Council had the power to create a judicial organ and it was therefore 'established by law'. While the ICC is completely separate from the UN some concerns have been raised about the impact of the Security Council's power to request a deferral of an ICC investigation or prosecution under Article 16 of the Rome Statute.

Impartiality

On the impartiality of judges the ICTY has held that a judge should be disqualified from hearing a case where there is either actual bias or a reasonable apprehension of bias. That is:

> not only [should a judge] be subjectively free from bias, but also there should be nothing in the surrounding circumstances which objectively gives rise to an appearance of bias.[26]

A successful challenge was made on the basis of apprehended bias against President Geoffrey Robertson of the Special Court for Sierra Leone in the *Sesay* case on the basis that he had made highly pejorative comments about the Revolutionary United Front and some of its leaders, several of whom were defendants before the Court, in his book *Crimes Against Humanity*.[27] The allegation was not that he was incapable of being objective or had prejudged the case, but that a reasonable observer could apprehend that he was biased.[28] Similarly, Judge Vaz of the International Criminal Tribunal for Rwanda

---

[25] *Tadić* (Appeal on Jurisdiction), ICTY Appeals Chamber, 2 October 1995.

[26] See: *Furundžija*, ICTY Appeals Chamber, 21 July 2000, paras 189–90.

[27] See: W Schabas, *The UN International Criminal Tribunals: the former Yugoslavia, Rwanda and Sierra Leone* (Cambridge University Press 2008), 417.

[28] *Sesay* (Decision on Defence Motion Seeking Disqualification of Judge Robertson), SCSL Appeals Chamber, 13 March 2004, para 15.

recused herself from the Trial Chamber hearing the *Karemera* case due to apprehended bias (she maintained a close friendship with and lived in the same house as one of the prosecution lawyers).[29]

A detailed provision on point is found in Rule 34 of the ICC Rules of Procedure and Evidence, which provides for disqualification of a judge in an individual case on grounds of apprehended bias where the judge: (a) has a personal interest in the case, including a close family, personal, or professional relationship with any of the parties; (b) was professionally involved in any previous legal proceedings in which the accused person was an opposing party; (c) has performed functions, prior to taking office, in which 'he or she could be expected to have formed an opinion on the case in question'; (d) expresses opinions, that could lead to an apprehension of bias. In such cases not only can a party apply for the judge (or prosecutor) to be disqualified but the judge (or prosecutor) has a duty to ask to be excused from participating in the case where he or she 'has reason to believe that a ground for disqualification exists in relation to him or her'.[30]

The ICC Statute also contains detailed provisions on the independence of judges and prosecutors. Not only is the ICC a treaty body independent of its States parties, but in addition to the fair trial rights of the defendant noted above, the Statute makes provision for:

- the qualifications of judges and their election by State parties;[31]
- the independence of judges, the prohibition on them engaging in activities which might compromise their independence, and their disqualification from hearing particular cases;[32]
- the independence, impartiality, and disqualification of the Prosecutor and Deputy Prosecutors;[33] and
- the solemn undertaking each judge, Prosecutor and Deputy Prosecutor must make in open court 'to exercise his or her respective functions impartially and conscientiously' before taking up their duties.[34]

One can also argue that the 'non-renewable term in office of the judges and prosecutors is one way of ensuring independence and impartiality' as well, as none can hope to benefit from having their appointments renewed.[35] Cassese also suggests that election of judges by a 'parliamentary' body such as the Assembly of State Parties, coupled with their immunities from the jurisdiction of member

---

[29] *Karemera* (Decision on Motions for Disqualification of Judge Vaz), ICTR Bureau, 17 May 2004, para 6.

[30] Rule 35, ICC Rules of Procedure and Evidence.   [31] Art 36, ICC Statute.

[32] Arts 40 and 41, ICC Statute.   [33] Art 42(5)–(8), ICC Statute.   [34] Art 45, ICC Statute.

[35] H Friman, 'Procedures of International Criminal Investigations and Prosecutions' in R Cryer, H Friman, D Robinson, and E Wilmshurst, *An Introduction to International Criminal Law and Procedure* 3rd ed (Cambridge University Press 2014) 438. In order to stagger the terms of judges, the first ever election of ICC judges resulted in appointments of three, six, and nine years duration. As nine years is the ordinary term of ICC Judges, those judges initially elected for three years were allowed to stand for re-election once only. This is an exceptional transitional provision. See Art 36(9)(b), ICC Statute.

States, shields judges from the undue influence of individual States including their national State.[36]

Some, however, have questioned whether the system for appointing judges to international courts works as well in practice as it does in theory. There is a clear requirement that ICC judges possess 'the qualifications required in their respective States for appointment to the highest judicial offices' and *in addition* have either 'established competence in criminal law and procedure' or 'established competence in relevant areas of international law'.[37] In theory, when an ICC State party puts a candidate forward for election as a judge, it must submit a statement explaining how the candidate meets these criteria. In practice, sometimes supporting statements 'set out only very limited information' about the candidate's qualifications or 'are not provided' at all.[38] Thus one early judge of the ICC, a national of Japan who served briefly from 2008–2009, did not even have a law degree.[39] This entirely unacceptable experiment has, fortunately, not been repeated. It does, however, illustrate the dangers of elections conducted through diplomatic forums: politics, vote trading, and 'mutual support' may be more important in securing an individual's election than their qualifications for the role.[40]

6.2.3 Presumption of innocence

It is universally accepted that a person in criminal proceedings has, as set out in Article 14(1) of the ICCPR, 'the right to be presumed innocent until proved guilty according to law'. As noted above, the principle is found in the Statutes of the ICTY, ICTR, and ICC.[41] As Håkan Friman notes, several further principles and rights follow from this:[42]

- A right to remain silent and not be compelled to incriminate oneself or confess guilt—and not to have that silence interpreted as an admission of guilt or have it used to draw adverse inferences against the defendant.[43]

- As a consequence of the right to remain silent, the defendant is under no duty to enter a plea of guilty or not guilty,[44] if the defendant refuses to enter a plea the court must enter a plea of not guilty for the defendant.

---

[36] A Cassese et al, *Cassese's International Criminal Law* 3rd ed (Oxford University Press 2013), 349.

[37] Art 36(3), ICC Statute.

[38] R Mackenzie et al, *Selecting International Judges: Principle, Process, and Politics* (Oxford University Press 2010), 85.

[39] Judge Fumiko Saiga. Afua Hirsch, 'System for appointing judges "undermining international courts"', The Guardian, 8 September 2010, www.guardian.co.uk/law/2010/sep/08/law-international-court-justice-legal. While the judge in question had extensive experience on UN human rights bodies it is hard to understand how she could possibly have qualified for the 'highest judicial offices' in Japan.

[40] Mackenzie et al, *Selecting International Judges*, especially at 85, 97, and 102. See also: Centre for International Courts and Tribunals, University College London, 'Selecting International Judges: Discussion Paper' (2008), www.ucl.ac.uk/laws/cict/docs/Selecting_Int_Judges.pdf.

[41] Art 21(3), ICTY Statute; Art 20(3), ICTR Statute; Art 66(1), ICC Statute.

[42] Friman, 'Procedures of International Criminal Investigations and Prosecutions' in Cryer et al, *Introduction*, 439–40.

[43] Art 67(1)(g), ICC Statute; Art 21(4)(g), ICTY Statute; Art 20(4)(g), ICTR Statute.

[44] Art 64(8)(a), ICC Statute affords the accused 'the opportunity to make an admission of guilt . . . or to plead not guilty' without requiring him or her to do so.

- The general principle that doubt is to be interpreted in the defendant's favour (*in dubio pro reo*) and therefore the prosecutor bears the burden of proving guilt.[45]

Most fundamentally, however, the presumption of innocence means (as noted in Chapter 5) that it is for the prosecutor to prove the guilt of the defendant 'beyond reasonable doubt' and 'if there is a reasonable doubt about the guilt of the accused, he or she is to be acquitted.'[46]

Before the ICTY it was accepted that an accused only needed to present evidence sufficient to suggest a 'reasonable possibility' of innocence in order to raise a reasonable doubt and defeat the prosecution case. For example, an alibi might be raised to prove that an accused was somewhere else at the time they were alleged to have committed a crime in a given place. Thus in the *Delalić* case one of the accusations against the accused was that he had participated in the beating of certain prisoners at a particular time and in a particular place. However, the absence of witness evidence that the accused was present at the relevant time and place meant the prosecution could not 'eliminate the reasonable possibility that he was not there at the time' and no conviction could be made on that count.[47] (On raising an alibi, see the pause for reflection in section 6.5.3.)

Before the ICTY if the defendant raised a defence (as further discussed in Chapter 13), the defendant only had to prove it 'on the balance of probabilities.'[48] It remains to be seen if the ICC adopts such an approach. As noted above, the ICC Statute also contains a separate prohibition on imposing 'any reversal of the burden of proof or any onus of rebuttal' on the defendant.[49]

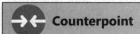 **Counterpoint**

What if the defendant pleads guilty?

Of course, a defendant may admit their guilt and seek a 'plea bargain' as a consequence. Plea bargaining was discussed in section 5.4.1.

6.3 The right to a public, fair, and expeditious hearing

6.3.1 The right to a public hearing

A requirement for a hearing to be public allows public scrutiny and is thus a protection against arbitrary exercises of power.[50] It may also be seen as upholding one of the key purposes of international criminal trials: an 'educational mandate' which necessarily

---

[45] Art 66(2), ICC Statute; Rule 87(A) of the ICTY and ICTR Rules of Procedure and Evidence.

[46] Schabas, *UN International Criminal Tribunals*, 516.

[47] *Delalić*, ICTY Appeals Chamber, 20 February 2001, para 459 and compare para 581.

[48] Ibid, para 590.   [49] Art 67(1)(i), ICC Statute.

[50] Friman, 'Procedures of International Criminal Investigations and Prosecutions' in Cryer et al, *Introduction*, 440.

involves the 'public dissemination of information' concerning the atrocities under investigation.[51] Such goals can scarcely be achieved unless the media and press have access to proceedings. Some exceptions to this general principle may nonetheless be made: for example, closed proceedings might be held to protect vulnerable witnesses. As we shall see the exceptions to the right to a public hearing are wider at the ICTY and ICTR than at the ICC.

The Rules of Procedure and Evidence Rule for both the ICTY and the ICTR provide that a Trial Chamber may exclude members of the press and the public from all or part of the proceedings on several grounds:

- public order or morality;
- the 'safety, security or non-disclosure of the identity of a victim or witness'; or
- for the 'protection of the interests of justice'.[52]

While these exceptions may seem broad, they are consistent with the exceptions set out in ICCPR.[53]

At the ICC, however, under Articles 64(7) and 68 the only two grounds for holding proceedings in a closed session which is not open to the public are:

- protection of the accused, victims, and witnesses; and
- protection of confidential or sensitive evidence (including some evidence related to charges of sexual assault).

The question of sensitive evidence may be an important one to international courts, which may be provided with evidence by cooperating States touching on questions of national security.[54]

6.3.2 **The right to a fair hearing**

A fair trial involves not just formal equality between the parties, but implies equality of arms. The principle of equality of arms requires that 'each party must be afforded a reasonable opportunity to present his case under conditions that do not place him at a disadvantage *vis-à-vis* his opponent'.[55] Notably, equality of arms is a *principle* rather than a strict right: the point is not that the defence must have the same resources as the prosecution, but that it must have an adequate opportunity to prepare its case and not be put at an unfair disadvantage.[56] The principle is thus essentially procedural in nature.[57]

---

[51] S Zappalà, 'The Rights of the Accused' in A Cassese, P Gaeta, and JRWD Jones (eds), *The Rome Statute of the International Criminal Court: A Commentary*, vol. 2 (Oxford University Press 2002), 1333.

[52] Art 79(A), ICTY and ICTR Rules of Procedure and Evidence.

[53] Art 14(1), ICCPR; see further: Human Rights Committee, 'General Comment No. 32: Article 14—Right to equality before courts and tribunals and to a fair trial', UN Doc. CCPR/C/GC/32 (2007) paras 28 and 29.

[54] Zappalà, 'The rights of the accused', 1333.

[55] *Bulut v Austria*, European Court of Human Rights, 22 February 1996, para 47.

[56] A Zahar and G Sluiter, *International Criminal Law: A Critical Introduction* (Oxford University Press 2008), 293.

[57] *Tadić Case*, Judgment on Appeal, ICTY Appeals Chamber, 1999, paras 48 and 50.

Before an international criminal tribunal the duty may go further, as held by the ICTY Appeals Chamber in the *Tadić Case* which said that under the ICTY Statute:[58]

> the principle of equality of arms must be given a more liberal interpretation than…before domestic courts. This principle means that the Prosecution and the Defence must be equal before the Trial Chamber. It follows that the Chamber shall provide every practicable facility it is capable of granting under the Rules and Statute when faced with a request by a party for assistance in presenting its case. The Trial Chambers are mindful of the difficulties encountered by the parties in tracing and gaining access to evidence in the territory of the former Yugoslavia…Provisions under the Statute and the Rules exist to alleviate the difficulties faced by the parties so that each side may have equal access to witnesses.

This clearly contemplates a duty upon an international court to help, in particular, the defence in preparation of its case.

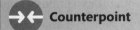 **Counterpoint**

Are defence counsel at a systematic disadvantage in international criminal law?

It is a frequent, and to some extent fair, criticism made by defence counsel in international trials that the resources available to the Prosecutor significantly exceed those available to defence teams.[59] Ambos, while noting that things have improved slightly since, observes that in the case of the ICTY:

> in 2004 while the prosecution…[had] many offices within the ICTY building, well equipped with personal computers, printers, and photocopy machines, the defence counsels [for all cases] had only one room within the ICTY building, sharing one photocopy machine, four computers, and two printers,

and otherwise had to rent office space and equipment outside the building.[60] However, as noted, the principle of *equality of arms* does not extend to requiring *equality of resources* in pre-trial investigations or outside the courtroom. Indeed, the proof of vast and complex crimes to a standard beyond reasonable doubt by the prosecution will necessarily require more resources than gathering sufficient evidence to raise a reasonable doubt on the part of the accused.

Nonetheless, one can make several legitimate observations about the disadvantages typically faced by the defence in international criminal trials. First, defence lawyers in an adversarial process will need to conduct their own investigations. This will involve travel to the country and places where the crimes in question are alleged to have taken place and in practical terms is likely to require the cooperation of the Court or Tribunal's Registry and Prosecution in order to secure the defence lawyers' access to relevant sites (and their ability to inspect documents) and in making arrangements for their safety in what will often be potentially violent post-conflict societies.[61] Indeed, defence

---

[58] *Tadić Case*, Judgment on Appeal, ICTY Appeals Chamber, 1999, para 52.

[59] The American Non-Governmental Organizations Coalition for the International Criminal Court, 'Defending Atrocity Crimes: The Requirements of Defense Counsel before the ICC' (2005), www.amicc.org/docs/Necessary%20Requirements%20for%20Defense.pdf.

[60] Ambos, *Treatise*, vol 1, 21.

[61] S Kay and B Swart, 'The Role of the Defence' in A Cassese, P Gaeta, and JRWD Jones (eds), *The Rome Statute of the International Criminal Court: A Commentary*, vol. 2 (Oxford University Press 2002), 1424.

lawyers may be unwelcome visitors, seen as acting on behalf of the present government's defeated enemies.[62] Second, under the Rome Statute the ICC Prosecutor enjoys one distinct advantage over defence counsel in conducting investigations.[63] Under Article 99(4) of the Rome Statute the Prosecutor may 'directly' conduct investigative activities on the territory of a State party which require no 'compulsory measures' (i.e. orders that the State cooperate) such as taking voluntary evidence from a witness or inspecting a public place. Such activity is, in general, only to occur after consultation with the territorial State party and may be subject to 'reasonable conditions' by the State party.[64] However, where consultations have been exhausted it appears the Prosecutor may simply proceed directly to conduct an investigation in the territory of the State party.[65]

Other 'basic guarantees' benefiting the defendant and forming part of the right to a fair trial, as already discussed, may also reflect the principle of equality of arms.[66] Such rights include:

- the right to be assisted by competent defence counsel (and usually a team of such counsel) and to have them paid for by the court where the defendant is indigent;
- prompt and full particulars (i.e. detailed information) of the charges against him or her;
- disclosure of, and a right to examine, the Prosecutor's evidence;
- access to translators where necessary; and
- the right to call witnesses and to examine witnesses called by the prosecution against him or her under equal conditions.

The right to call witnesses might also be taken to include a right to request the court secure the attendance of reluctant witnesses or grant safe conduct to vulnerable witnesses.[67]

 Pause for reflection

Prosecutor v Tadić (Judgment), ICTY Appeals Chamber

Can the accused claim he or she has been denied a fair trial on the basis of equality of arms?

As we have already seen, in *Tadić*[68] the Appeals Chamber found the principle of equality of arms placed a duty on the Tribunal to assist parties in the preparation of their case, in particular in terms of assisting in gaining access to witnesses. The questions which then arise are what powers of the

---

[62] Kay and Swart, 'The Role of the Defence', 1424.
[63] Zahar and Sluiter, *International Criminal Law*, 294.   [64] Art 99(4)(b), ICC Statute.
[65] Art 99(4)(a), ICC Statute.   [66] Art 67, ICC Statute; Art 21, ICTY Statute; Art. 20 ICTR Statute.
[67] E.g.: *Kupreškić* (Decision on Defence Motion to Summon Witnesses), ICTY Trial Chamber, 6 October 1998 where certain persons were 'reluctant, for reasons of personal security and possible intimidation, to appear as *defence* witnesses' unless compulsorily summoned by the Tribunal. See further: Cassese, *International Criminal Law* 2nd ed (Oxford University Press 2008), 386.
[68] *Prosecutor v Tadić*, ICTY Appeals Chamber, 15 July 1999, paras 43–55.

Tribunal can be used in this regard—and can the accused claim failure to secure equality of arms prevented his or her conviction being fair?

The Appeals Chamber noted that the Tribunal is 'empowered to issue such orders, summonses, subpoenas, warrants and transfer orders as may be necessary for the purposes of an investigation or for the preparation or conduct of the trial.' Such powers included the power to:

(1) adopt witness protection measures, ranging from partial to full protection;

(2) take evidence by video-link or by way of deposition;

(3) summon witnesses and order their attendance;

(4) issue binding orders to States for, *inter alia*, the taking and production of evidence; and

(5) issue binding orders to States to assist a party or to summon a witness and order his or her attendance under the Rules.[69]

The Appeals chamber noted two further powers: (6) the Tribunal may send a request to the authorities of a State asking for their assistance in securing the attendance of a witness; and finally if such measures have all 'proved to be to no avail' a Chamber may (7) 'order that proceedings be adjourned or, if the circumstances so require, that they be stayed.'

The defence submitted that the appellant did not receive a fair trial because relevant evidence was not made available for use in the trial as a result of the lack of cooperation by the government of the Republika Srpska (one of the two territorial entities that makes up Bosnia and Herzegovina) in securing the attendance of witnesses. The defence had to concede, however, that the Trial Chamber 'took virtually all steps requested and necessary within its authority to assist the Appellant in presenting witness testimony' including granting long adjournments to allow witnesses to be traced.[70] The Appeals Chamber held that if a fair trial was genuinely not possible due to the lack of cooperation by certain government authorities, then the defence should have submitted a motion requesting a stay of proceedings until those difficulties could be overcome.[71]

As Zahar and Sluiter note, this argument that lack of cooperation by a territorial government violated equality of arms was never particularly convincing as 'both sides suffer[ed] from this lack of cooperation.'[72]

6.3.3 The right to an expeditious hearing

The right to an 'expeditious' trial may also be thought of as an aspect of the presumption of innocence: defendants in international criminal trials are not usually released on bail, and a person who is not yet proved guilty should clearly be detained for as little time as possible. However, it must be observed that by their nature international trials are factually highly complex and thus take considerably longer than many national trials. Nonetheless, some trials before the ICTY and the ICTR seem shockingly long.[73] One example is the *Bagosora* case before the ICTR.[74] Mr Bagosara was arrested in 1996

---

[69] Ibid, para 52.   [70] Ibid, para 53.   [71] Ibid, para 55.
[72] Ibid, 294.   [73] Ibid, 300.   [74] Ibid.

and transferred to the ICTR in 1997, but the judgment in his case was delivered only in 2008 and appeal proceedings concluded in 2011. Such manifestly slow proceedings inspired efforts by the ICTY and the ICTR to reform their procedures.[75] In particular, the Tribunals attempted to create greater expedition and efficiency through measures such as:

- having a pre-trial judge who could call pre-trial conferences to supervise and set a timetable for the preparation of the case;
- imposing time limits for the filing of procedural or preliminary motions;
- providing for the admission of written evidence, especially witness affidavits; and
- the introduction of *ad litem* judges ('non-permanent, or not-full-time judges, who only sit in one or two cases') to increase the number of cases that can be heard at one time.[76]

It was expected in some quarters that the creation of a system of Pre-Trial Chambers at the ICC should speed proceedings up. Generally, the ICC has indeed proved faster than the ICTY or ICTR. In the *Lubanga* case before the ICC Mr Lubanga was transferred to the Court in 2006, his trial commenced in 2009 and he was sentenced in 2012. In the *Katanga* case Mr Katanga was transferred to the Court in 2007, his trial commenced in 2009 and he was sentenced in 2014. An appeal is pending in *Lubanga*; prosecution and defence appeals were both discontinued in *Katanga*.[77] While progress appears faster than before the ad hoc Tribunals, the *Lubanga* case at least looks likely to span a decade before appeals are exhausted. Whether, having refined its procedural law in these early cases, later cases move faster remains to be seen.

6.4 Legality of arrest and detention

The question occasionally arises in international proceedings as to whether the legality of a suspect's arrest violates their right to a fair trial.[78] If so, should a court decline jurisdiction and release the defendant? The question was considered by the ICTY in *Nikolić*.[79] In *Nikolić*, the accused was abducted from Serbia and Montenegro by persons unknown and transferred to Bosnia and Herzegovina, where international

---

[75] On the difficulties the Tribunals encountered, and on some difficulties of their own making, see: PM Wald, 'ICTY Judicial Proceedings: An Appraisal From Within' (2004) 2 Journal of International Criminal Justice 466.

[76] Cassese, *International Criminal Law* (2nd ed), 389.

[77] 'Press Release: Defence and Prosecution discontinue respective appeals against judgment in Katanga case', International Criminal Court, 25 June 2014; see commentary in: Kevin Jon Heller, 'Why Did Katanga Drop His Appeal? And Why Did the OTP?', *Opinio Juris*, 26 June 2014, http://opiniojuris.org/2014/06/26/katanga-drop-appeal-otp/.

[78] G Boas et al, *International Criminal Law Practitioner Library*, vol 3 (Cambridge University Press 2011), 113–18.

[79] *Nikolić* (Decision on Interlocutory Appeal concerning Legality of Arrest), ICTY Appeals Chamber, 5 June 2003.

peacekeeping forces (known as the 'Stabilization Force' or 'SFOR') arrested him pursuant to an ICTY warrant and transferred him to the Tribunal. There was no evidence that SFOR or the ICTY Prosecutor's Office had been involved in the initial abduction. The Appeals Chamber held that a violation of State sovereignty (i.e. by illegal abduction or arrest) would not be a bar to trying serious crimes of international concern. It did, however, suggest that quite extreme abuses of human rights might merit a court declining jurisdiction. It quoted the ICTR Appeals Chamber in *Barayagwiza* to the effect that a court may decline to exercise jurisdiction in cases 'where to exercise that jurisdiction in light of serious and egregious violations of the accused's rights would prove detrimental to the court's integrity'.[80]

The position before the ICC is untested. However, one may note that before the ICC, as a consequence of Article 21(3), 'breaches of the rights of the suspect or the accused' by national authorities in the course of transferring him or her to the ICC 'may provide ground for halting' proceeding against them.[81] If a trial cannot be conducted fairly, it cannot proceed. Two further points may be noted for present purposes in relation to ICC.

First, an arrest warrant issued by the ICC may be challenged after it is issued but before a suspect has been transferred to the Court, under Rule 117(3) of the Rules of Procedure and Evidence, on the basis that the warrant was not properly issued in accordance with Article 58(1)(a) and (b) of the Statute. This would in effect be a challenge on the basis that either there are not reasonable grounds to suspect the person of a crime within the jurisdiction of the Court or that arrest is not necessary to ensure appearance at trial, to prevent the obstruction of the case, or to prevent continuing commission of crimes within the jurisdiction of the Court. In practical terms, this is likely to occur while a person is in the custody of national authorities awaiting transfer to the Court.

Second, once a person is transferred to the ICC and placed in its detention facilities, a Pre-Trial Chamber must periodically review the detention of suspects in custody and 'ensure that a person is not detained for an unreasonable period prior to trial due to inexcusable delay by the Prosecutor'.[82] In the event of such delay it must consider releasing the suspect.

 Pause for reflection

Is there a customary rule or general principle of law regarding the consequences of a defendant's illegal abduction to stand trial?

If there is a general rule, it could only be deduced from the practice of national courts. A selection of leading cases is reviewed below. Are they sufficiently consistent to give rise to a rule

---

[80] *Nikolić* (Decision on Interlocutory Appeal concerning Legality of Arrest), ICTY Appeals Chamber, 5 June 2003, para 29.

[81] *Thomas Lubanga Dyilo* (Judgment on the Appeal against the Decision on Jurisdiction), ICC Appeals Chamber, 14 December 2006, para 44.

[82] Art 60, ICC Statute.

of custom? Alternatively, is it possible to deduce a single rule from these cases that could be called a general principle?

Attorney-General of Israel v Eichmann (1968) 18 International Law Reports 36 and 277

Eichmann's defence counsel raised before the court his illegal abduction from Argentina to stand trial in Israel to argue that a court should not ground its jurisdiction in an illegality. The Court rejected the argument on grounds that: (1) no rule of international law required a court to decline jurisdiction in such cases; and (2) it was for Argentina to raise the claim that the abduction involved a violation of its sovereignty, and that dispute had been settled diplomatically between Israel and Argentina.

Stocke v Germany (1991) 95 International Law Reports 327

In *Stocke* the German constitutional court reviewed relevant State practice and suggested that a court would generally only decline jurisdiction due to an illegal abduction where another State has protested the abduction.

US v Alvarez-Machain (1992) 31 International Legal Materials 900

In this case US agents abducted a suspect from Mexico. The Supreme Court found this was no bar to a criminal court exercising jurisdiction over the suspect, *even if* the injured State requested the return of the accused. It cited the doctrine *male captus, bene detentus*: illegal arrest may still give lawful custody.

State v Ebrahim (1992) 31 International Legal Materials 888

Ebrahim involved the abduction of the accused by South African officials from another State. The South African court declined jurisdiction on the basis that the State must come to court seeking justice with 'clean hands'.

Bennett v Horseferry Road Magistrates' Court (2003) 3 All ER 138

Bennett involved a person forcibly taken by South African police and restrained aboard a plane bound for London under the pretext of deporting him to New Zealand. This was done with the knowledge of British police who intercepted Bennett at London's Heathrow airport and arrested him. The court found it was an abuse of process for a person to be forcibly brought into the jurisdiction of the English courts in disregard of extradition procedures and with the knowing participation of law enforcement agencies or prosecuting authorities. The later English case of *R v Staines' Magistrates' Court (ex parte Westfallen)* [1998] 4 All ER 210 emphasized that this result will only follow in cases where British authorities have been *actively* involved in violating international law to secure the presence of the defendant. A further case *R v Mullen* [1999] 2 Cr App R 143, however, suggested that the rule might not be applied in the case of particularly serious crimes, given the counterbalancing interest of the community in seeing serious offences tried.

6.5 Appeals

6.5.1 Introduction

We have noted already that an important fair trial guarantee is the right of a convicted person under the ICCPR to have his or her conviction and sentence 'reviewed by a higher tribunal according to law'.[83] Similarly, Additional Protocol I guarantees, in times of international armed conflict, the right of a convicted person to be advised of the judicial remedies available upon conviction and any time limits applying to them.[84] However, the right to appeal may be important not only upon conviction. In practice, appeals are also possible on questions that arise in the course of a trial or even during pre-trial proceedings. These are called 'interlocutory appeals' and are discussed first.

6.5.2 Interlocutory appeals

An interlocutory appeal is one made in order to challenge a decision of a Trial or Pre-Trial Chamber before judgment. It is thus an appeal that arises within the course of the hearing (hence 'interlocutory': it is an interpolated or intermediary discussion) and will usually relate to a question of procedure or the conduct of the case. Interlocutory appeals take time and resources and obviously slow proceedings down. They are therefore usually only allowed on limited issues. Nonetheless, an appeal on jurisdiction is always allowed before the ICTY and ICTR.

Before the ICC the decisions (other than sentence) that may be appealed by either the prosecutor or the accused are any decision: (a) with respect to jurisdiction or admissibility; (b) granting or denying release of the person being investigated or prosecuted; (c) made by the Pre-Trial Chamber to act on its own initiative to preserve evidence; or (d) that involves an issue that would significantly affect the fair and expeditious conduct of the proceedings or the outcome of the trial.[85]

This last ground is obviously wide, and under the ICC Rules of Procedure and Evidence appeals made on this basis may only be made with leave of the Court.[86] That is, the Chamber that made the decision in question must itself grant leave to appeal, on the basis that it considers that 'an immediate resolution' of the issue by the Appeals Chamber 'may materially advance the proceedings'.[87] This power has been used liberally and generously in the early life of the ICC to allow the Appeals Chamber to issue authoritative guidance on developing questions of procedural law before the Court.

6.5.3 Appeals against judgment and sentence and grounds for review

Other than interlocutory appeals, an appeal may be against judgment (i.e. the finding of guilt in respect of a crime) or the severity of the sentence imposed, and will usually be against both. Appeals proceedings in international courts and tribunals are *corrective*: the appellant must identify either 'an error of law so serious as to invalidate the judgment' or 'an error of fact so serious as to entail a miscarriage of justice'.[88]

---

[83] Article 14(5), ICCPR.   [84] Article 75, Additional Protocol I.   [85] Art 82, ICC Statute.
[86] Rule 155, ICC Rules of Procedure and Evidence.   [87] Art 82(d), ICC Statute.
[88] Cassese, *International Criminal Law* (2nd ed), 427.

The appeal is only heard on these limited grounds, the appeal itself is not a new trial.[89] Before the ICC such an appeal can be made either by the accused or the Prosecutor. At the ICC it appears clear that appeals against judgment and sentence are appeals as of right (no leave of the Court is required) and such appeals may not be brought by victims or affected States, only the accused or the Prosecutor.[90]

On appeal the Appeals Chamber may affirm (uphold), reverse (quash), or revise the judgment appealed and, where appropriate, remit the case to the Trial Chamber.[91] It is not uncommon for Appeals Chambers to revise judgments in part by upholding the findings of a Trial Chamber on some questions and overturning or quashing the decisions reached on other points. As a general principle an appellate court may reduce but not increase the sentence imposed. This principle was applied in the ICTY and ICTR, and is formally incorporated in the ICC Statute.[92]

Before the ICC appeals may be brought by the accused on the grounds of:[93]

- procedural error;
- error of fact;
- error of law; or
- any other ground that affects the fairness or reliability of the proceedings or decision.

The ICC Prosecutor may only bring appeals on the first three grounds (errors of procedure, fact, or law). Under Article 83, where the ICC Appeals Chamber 'finds that the proceedings appealed from were unfair in a way that affected the reliability of the decision or sentence, or that the decision or sentence appealed from was materially affected by error of fact or law or procedural error', it may either:

- reverse or amend the decision or sentence; or
- order a new trial before a different trial chamber.

The ICC Statute and Rules of Procedure and Evidence do not make clear what the standard of evidence is on appeal. It is usually sufficient to 'precisely identify the error of law', to present arguments in support of that claim and to explain how it 'invalidates the trial chamber's decision',[94] but appellate courts are traditionally reluctant to review findings of fact. Thus at the ICTY the Appeals Chamber will not overturn a finding of fact unless it was a finding 'which no reasonable trier of fact could have reached'.[95]

---

[89] Although the result of the appeal might be that the case is remitted to a Trial Chamber for determination in accordance with the (correct) law or for re-trial.

[90] G Boas et al, 'Appeals, Reviews and Reconsideration' in G Sluiter et al (eds), *International Criminal Procedure: Principles and Rules* (Oxford University Press 2013), 954.

[91] See: Art 25(2), ICTY Statute; Art 24(2), ICTR Statute; Art 82(1), ICC Statute.

[92] Art 83(2), ICC Statute.   [93] Art 81, ICC Statute.

[94] Boas et al, *International Criminal Law Practitioner Library*, vol 3, 443.

[95] *Tadić*, ICTY Appeals Chamber, 15 July 1999, para 64.

The principal ground for appeal of sentence, and for the Appeals Chamber to vary a sentence, before the ICC is that the sentence imposed in disproportionate to the crime.[96] Either the prosecutor or the defendant may bring an appeal against the sentence.

 Pause for reflection

Zigiranyirazo v The Prosecutor, ICTR Appeals Chamber

Zigiranyirazo[97] involved an appeal on the basis that the trial chamber had not correctly considered certain aspects of the defence case, in particular alibi evidence.

What were the defendant's essential ground(s) of appeal?

Mr Zigiranyirazo argued that he had an alibi for the crimes he was charged with: that he had evidence he was elsewhere at the time they were committed. Mr Zigiranyirazo argued that the Trial Chamber had failed to properly consider his alibi evidence and had imposed a reverse burden of proof (i.e. requiring him to refute or disprove the Prosecutor's evidence as to his location at the relevant time).

Was this an appeal on an error of fact or law?

One might think this was a challenge on an error of fact: where the defendant was and at what time. It was not. The question was whether the Trial Chamber applied the correct *legal standard* in assessing the evidence produced by the defendant. This makes the question one of error of law (even if the error of law may have resulted in an error of fact: a conclusion about where the defendant was at what time).

What was the correct standard for assessing alibi evidence?

When the prosecutor has produced witness evidence that the accused was in a certain place at a certain time, the burden does not shift to the defendant to exclude the possibility that he or she was in that place at that time.[98] The defendant need only 'establish reasonable doubt' that he or she could have been in the relevant place at the time alleged.[99] On the facts of this case it was not necessary for the defendant to prove where he was throughout the entire day. Taken as a whole, his alibi was that he had evidence placing him on the morning (8 am) and afternoon (4 pm) of the crime in a location too far from the scene of the crimes to make the round trip (8–20 hours) in the time available. The fact that he could not prove where he was at every intervening moment was irrelevant if there was a reasonable doubt that he could have reached the scene of the crime and returned in that time.

Was this an appeal on conviction or an appeal on sentence? What was the result?

It was an appeal as to both, but given that the convictions were overturned the sentence did not have to be reconsidered. The defendant was acquitted of all charges and ordered to be released.

---

96 Arts 81(2) and 82(3), ICC Statute.
97 *Zigiranyirazo*, ICTR Appeals Chamber, 16 November 2009, paras 37–52, 75, and 79.
98 Ibid, paras 41 and 42.   99 Ibid, paras 41.

6.6 Revision and enforcement of sentences

6.6.1 **Revision of sentences**

Review proceedings exist to prevent a miscarriage of justice, typically allowing a sentence to be reviewed, especially where new facts come to light after conviction. Under Article 84(1) of the ICC Statute an application may be made to the Appeals Chamber to revise a sentence on grounds that:

- new evidence has been discovered that was not available at the time of trial and is such that, if proved, it would have likely resulted in a different verdict (so long as the unavailability of the evidence was not attributable to the party making application);

- it has been newly discovered that decisive evidence upon which the conviction depended, was false, forged, or falsified; or

- one of the judges who participated in the conviction or confirmation of charges has committed 'serious misconduct or serious breach of duty of sufficient gravity to justify the removal of that judge or those judges from office'.

Returning to the first ground, new or newly discovered facts may show either: that the sentence imposed should be increased or reduced; or, alternatively, that the accused should never have been convicted.

A two-step process follows. First, the Appeals Chamber shall determine whether the application is meritorious or unfounded.[100] Second, if it is meritorious the Appeals Chamber may remit the matter to the original Trial Chamber, or convene a new Trial Chamber for determination, or proceed to hear the matter itself.

Before the ICTY a similar procedure exists regarding a 'new evidence' application for revision of sentence. Although the ICTY requires that 'new' facts were not known to the party making the application (or were not discoverable with due diligence), revision applications have been granted even in such cases to prevent a miscarriage of justice.[101] Such applications are usually then remitted to be heard by the original Trial Chamber.

Before the ICC, where new evidence ultimately establishes that a conviction was wrongful and a miscarriage of justice occurred, the defendant may apply for compensation.[102] In cases where there has been a 'grave and manifest' miscarriage of justice, the Court may award compensation at its own discretion.[103]

---

[100] Art 84(2), ICC Statute.

[101] *Tadić* (Decision on Motion for Review), ICTY Appeals Chamber, 30 July 2002, para 13.

[102] Art 85(2), ICC Statute. In some national legal systems 'miscarriage of justice' would only describe a wrongful conviction following a *legal* error: e.g. *Mraz v R (No. 1)* (High Court of Australia) [1955] HCA 59.

[103] Art 85(3), ICC Statute and Rule 173, ICC RPE.

6.6.2 **Enforcement and review of sentences**

Sentences of imprisonment will have to be served in a State cooperating with the relevant international criminal tribunal, and, as this cooperation is voluntary, conditions may be imposed by the State (such as the numbers of prisoners it is willing to take). The court or tribunal can choose not to accept such conditions, but a State may then withdraw its cooperation. Imprisonment thus occurs under national law and conditions, but under the supervision of the international criminal tribunal in question. The detaining State may not alter the sentence or commute or pardon it.[104] This may lead to complexities where local law allows a prisoner who has served a certain portion of their sentence to certain benefits, such as early release or parole: '[i]f these conditions are not applied to persons convicted by an international tribunal, this might be deemed to constitute discrimination against international convicts' under national law.[105] The essential approach is that international tribunals must be notified of such developments or proposed changes in a prisoner's conditions and may transfer them to another State if such treatment is considered inappropriate.

Features of the enforcement regime under the ICC Statute include:

- the Court designates the cooperating State where a convicted person will serve their sentence and the choice among cooperating States will be guided by certain principles (such as international principles of prisoner treatment, fair burden sharing among State parties, etc); where there is no available cooperating State, the host State of the Court—i.e. the Netherlands—will detain the individual;[106]

- once a convicted person is serving their sentence in a particular State the Court may transfer him or her to another State, and a convicted person may apply for such a transfer;[107]

- the sentence is binding on the State of imprisonment, which may not vary it;[108]

- as noted above, detention will occur under national law and conditions but under the supervision of the ICC; detention must be consistent with international standards of prisoner treatment;[109]

- the convicted person, while they remain in custody, may not be punished, prosecuted or extradited for conduct prior to their transfer without the approval of the ICC;[110] and

- in the case of non-custodial sentences, States parties are obliged to 'give effect to fines or forfeitures ordered by the Court' in accordance with their own national law and procedure.[111]

Review of sentence is thus a matter for the international tribunal in question. Under Article 110 of the ICC Statute the Court must review a sentence 'to determine whether it should be reduced' when the convicted person has served two thirds of

[104] Art 110, ICC Statute.   [105] Cassese, *International Criminal Law* (2nd ed), 432.
[106] Art 103, ICC Statute.   [107] Art 104, ICC Statute.   [108] Art 105, ICC Statute.
[109] Art 106, ICC Statute.   [110] Art 108, ICC Statute.   [111] Art 109, ICC Statute.

their sentence, or after 25 years in the case of life imprisonment.[112] In conducting this review the ICC may reduce a sentence where it finds one or more of the following factors are present:

- 'early and continuing willingness of the person to cooperate' with the Court's investigations and prosecutions;
- the voluntary assistance of the convicted person in matters such as 'providing assistance in locating assets subject to orders of fine, forfeiture or reparation which may be used for the benefit of victims'; or
- '[o]ther factors establishing a clear and significant change of circumstances sufficient to justify the reduction of sentence'.[113]

In the case that the Court determines no reduction of sentence is appropriate, the ICC Rules of Procedure and Evidence may stipulate the intervals at which the question must be revisited.[114] At present, the default rule is that the sentence must be reviewed every three years after the initial review.[115] By way of practical example, in *Prosecutor v Katanga* the accused was sentenced to 12 years imprisonment in May 2014. That sentence was to take into account the nearly seven years Mr Katanga had spent in pre-trial and trial detention. As Mr Katanga has not appealed his conviction, he became eligible for a review of his sentence in late 2015.

6.7 Summary and conclusions

This chapter has discussed the rights of accused persons before international criminal tribunals, the grounds for appeal or revision of sentence, and the general features of the regime governing the detention of persons convicted before international criminal tribunals. Turning to the first of these issues, on the basis of the discussion in this chapter it should be apparent that the two most basic rights that a defendant in international criminal proceedings enjoys are:

- the right to a fair, public, and expeditious trial; and
- the right to be presumed innocent until proven guilty according to law.

Each of these rights gives rise to further principles of criminal law or more detailed substantive rights. From the right to a fair trial follows:

- at the least, the principle of equality of arms, extending to matters such as a right to defence counsel and an opportunity to call and examine witnesses; and
- arguably other rights such as a (general but not unqualified) right to be present at trial and to provisional release if a trial is not commenced within a reasonable time.

---

[112] Art 110(3), ICC Statute.   [113] Art 110(4), ICC Statute.   [114] Art 110(5), ICC Statute.
[115] Rule 224(3), ICC Rules of Procedure and Evidence.

As regards the principle of equality of arms, one should note that while this is generally a procedural right in national courts it may require more active assistance to be granted to the defence by international tribunals. (Whether such assistance is as generous in practice as it is in theory has been questioned by some commentators.[116])

From the right to be presumed innocent until proven guilty according to law, flows (at a minimum) the following rights:

- the right to silence (including a right not to enter a plea and not to have adverse inferences—i.e. of guilt—drawn from that silence); and

- the principle that it is for the prosecutor to prove the case and that the defendant must not be subjected to a reverse onus of proof (i.e. an obligation to disprove or refute evidence led by the prosecutor).

This chapter has also briefly considered grounds for appeal. Appeals may either be interlocutory (i.e. on a question arising during proceedings, usually on an important point of law) or against judgment or sentence. Before the ICC appeals may be made on grounds of procedural error, error of fact, error of law, or any other ground that affects the fairness or reliability of the proceedings or decision. However, appellate courts are usually reluctant to review questions of fact. The most common appeals will allege errors of law by a Trial (or Pre-Trial) Chamber. Before the ICC one must show that such an error 'materially affected' the decision or judgment.[117] Sentences may be reviewed either to prevent a miscarriage of justice (where new evidence tending to show the innocence of the accused has been found) or as part of a Court's procedure to determine whether a sentence should be reduced after a portion of it has been served. Grounds for reducing sentences in such cases might include consideration of whether, while in detention, the convicted person has cooperated with other investigations or prosecutions before the Court.

We have also noted in this chapter that once convicted before an international tribunal an international criminal will have to serve their sentence in the prison system of a cooperating State. This will occur under the supervision of the international tribunal in question. Tensions may arise, for example, where under national law a convicted person might be eligible for parole in a manner not available before or considered appropriate by the international tribunal. In such cases the tribunal may have to transfer the convicted person to another cooperating State.

Useful further reading

G Boas, J Bischoff, and N Reid, *International Criminal Law Practitioner Library*, vol 3 (Cambridge University Press, 2011).
An exceptionally useful and relatively up-to-date account of the practical issues involved in the conduct of international criminal trials.

---

[116] Zahar and Sluiter, *International Criminal Law*, 294–5.   [117] Art 83, ICC Statute.

R MACKENZIE, K MALLESON, P MARTIN, and P SANDS, *Selecting International Judges: Principle, Process, and Politics* (Oxford: Oxford University Press, 2010)

The only authoritative study on how international judges are selected. For a shorter discussion paper summarizing the key findings see www.ucl.ac.uk/laws/cict/docs/Selecting_Int_Judges.pdf.

G SLUITER et al (eds), *International Criminal Procedure: Principles and Rules* (Oxford University Press 2013).

The most comprehensive single volume study on the topic. Its approach is exceptionally detailed, thorough, and historically grounded.

PART III

The Core International Crimes

7

The elements
of international crimes

7.1 Introduction

Part III of this book concerns the 'core' international crimes, those falling within the jurisdiction of international tribunals: war crimes, crimes against humanity, genocide, and aggression. However, before turning to the definitions of those offences some questions about criminal law generally and international crimes in particular need to be addressed. The present chapter is thus intended as an introduction to key issues which apply across Chapters 8–11.

To begin, let us consider the question of whether everyone who kills another human being is a murderer. The obvious answer is no, even setting aside moral excuses or justifications such as self-defence. The action of one person on a construction site might kill another person without anyone being thought criminally responsible. (The question of negligence is returned to below.) The point is that the objective or factual act of killing is not enough: we will only call someone a murderer if the killing was blameworthy in a particular way. The killer must be *culpable*.[1] We will usually judge this question of culpability by referring not only to what a person objectively did or physically caused but also the person's *subjective* intention or their *mental* state.

In general, then, we conceive of a crime as having two components: prohibited conduct (which may be called the objective, material or 'real' element of the crime or its *actus reus*) and a culpable mental state (which may be called the subjective, or mental element of the crime or its *mens rea*). This is, of course, an oversimplification. In some legal systems it is common to see:

> several different material elements combining with appropriate mental *elements* (plural) to form "the offence" while other legal systems 'tend to see *the* material element, a global "thing", and a single intent/knowledge mental element which gets attached to that thing'.[2]

---

[1] In this context Honoré instead uses the terms responsibility and liability and distinguishes between them on the basis that while we are responsible for all the direct and indirect outcomes of our actions—both willed and unwilled—we will be held liable or sanctioned only in a smaller set of cases according to principles of law or morality: T Honoré, *Responsibility and Fault* (Hart 1999) 121.

[2] RS Clark, 'The Mental Element in International Criminal Law: The Rome Statute of the International Criminal Court and the Elements of Offences' (2001) 12 Criminal Law Forum 291, 303.

The first approach may be called an 'element analysis', the second an 'offence analysis'.[3] The Elements of Crimes under the Rome Statute of the International Criminal Court (ICC) tends to take the first approach: a crime is made up of a combination of material elements with defined mental elements attaching to each.

In addition to material and mental elements, certain international crimes may also require a *contextual* element. That is, some international crimes may require that the prohibited act occurs in or has a relationship to a particular set of circumstances: for example, a war crime must be closely connected with an armed conflict. This contextual element is sometimes also called a nexus requirement.

 Learning aims

By the end of this chapter you should be able to:

- explain the basic ideas of mental elements and material elements;
- be able to compare common law ideas of criminal recklessness with civil law concepts of *dolus indirectus*;
- discuss the role of the requirement that the accused act with 'intent and knowledge' in proving the required mental elements under the ICC Statute; and
- identify the role of a 'contextual element' in the core international crimes.

In light of these objectives, this chapter explores three main issues:

- Section 7.2 looks at the extent to which a contextual element is a common or necessary feature of international crimes.
- Section 7.3 considers the material element of international crimes.
- Section 7.4 examines what the mental element requirements are for international crimes.

The latter is particularly difficult because international law has drawn on both common law and civil law traditions in defining the mental element required for international crimes. Different commentators, sources, and judgments will use different terminology. While some roughly equivalent concepts can be determined, it is important to understand that lawyers both from the common law tradition and civil law tradition often 'attempt to interpret' mental element provisions in international criminal law 'as conforming to their own national biases'.[4] Given the diversity within both the common law and civil law traditions, let alone between them, this may be perilous. The issues involved are complicated and, as always, the present book

---

[3] ME Badar, 'The Mental Element in the Rome Statute of the International Criminal Court: A Commentary from a Comparative Criminal Law Perspective' (2008) 19 Criminal Law Forum 473, 476.

[4] JD Van Der Vyer, 'Prosecutor v Jean-Pierre Bemba Gombo' (2010) 104 American Journal of International Law 241, 247.

is intended as an introduction to them rather than as an exhaustive exposition of the relevant law and theory.

7.2 Contextual elements or thresholds

It is commonly suggested that international crimes, by definition, must share some quality that sets them apart from national crimes. The most common suggestion is that they involve a special context (for example, crimes committed on a massive scale or as part of an 'atrocity'). While intuitive, this is not strictly correct. Certain of the 'core' international crimes may be thought of as requiring some contextual elements or thresholds, but not all of them. Their only truly common feature is that they are defined by customary international law as acts resulting in individual criminal responsibility[5] and that there have been historical examples of international tribunals set up to prosecute them.

 Counterpoint

Antonio Cassese and his co-authors have suggested that international crimes are distinct from crimes in national law because international crimes have a number of special characteristics:

- they violate a rule of international law that entails individual criminal responsibility;
- they may be committed by officials or private persons;
- they may by definition require an ordinary crime defined at national law to be committed in a particular context (i.e. the war crime of murder is murder committed with a nexus to an armed conflict); or
- 'they are somehow connected with a state policy or at any rate with "system criminality"', i.e. crimes committed on a massive scale within an organized structure.[6]

This is less than entirely convincing. Only the first point is true in all cases. However, rules of international law entailing individual criminal responsibility is a category much wider than the 'core crimes' we will examine in this book.[7] It would include, for example, the offences stipulated under

---

[5] Although this is not unique to the 'core' crimes: torture, slavery, piracy, and other offences might qualify. See discussion in Chapters 1 and 2 for acts thought to be crimes contrary to *jus cogens* and/or subject to universal jurisdiction. Further, the fact a crime is subject to universal jurisdiction does not necessarily mean the act has been prohibited under international law, simply that all States have been given jurisdiction to repress it: A Cassese et al, *Cassese's International Criminal Law* 3rd ed (Oxford University Press 2013) 19 and R O'Keefe, *International Criminal Law* (Oxford University Press 2015) 51 (discussing piracy).

[6] A Cassese et al, *Cassese's International Criminal Law* 3rd ed (Oxford University Press 2013) 37. A slightly different list is offered in: A Cassese et al, *International Criminal Law: Cases and Commentary* (Oxford University Press 2011) 113–114, focussing on: (1) international customary rules; (2) international values; (3) a universal interest in repression; and (4) the official capacity of perpetrators.

[7] O'Keefe suggests that an 'inclusive' definition of international crimes covering both cases where conduct is directly subject to criminal prohibition under international law and those cases where international law simply provides jurisdiction for national criminalization is the most coherent approach to take: O'Keefe, *International Criminal Law*, 50–56.

the suppression treaties discussed in Chapter 2, section 2.5. The second point, while true, is no different from the situation at national law: both officials and private persons can commit crimes. The third point is true of at least crimes against humanity and war crimes; it is less clear that the law of genocide as a strict and formal matter requires a contextual element. The fourth point is likely to be *factually* correct in many cases: genocide and crimes against humanity will typically occur as a result of 'system criminality' involving a State or organization. However, a single *unlawful* killing in an armed conflict may constitute the war crime of murder without any element of 'system criminality'.

Such attempts to define the core features of international crimes reveal more about our assumptions than legal definitions: we expect international crimes will usually be committed through numerous offenders, on a mass scale, and in a context of 'system criminality' where one leader (or a group operating through a military or political structure) is 'pulling the strings'.[8] These may not, however, be strict legal requirements in all cases.

When we come to look in detail at the definitions of the core crimes in later chapters we will note that:

- war crimes require a close connection or nexus with an armed conflict (a contextual element or threshold);

- crimes against humanity must be committed as part of a widespread or systematic attack against a civilian population (a contextual element);

- genocide requires that prohibited acts such as murder must: (a) be carried out with the intent to destroy a racial, ethnic, or religious group in whole or in part as such (a requirement of a special intent or *dolus specialis*); and (b) there is some authority under the ICC Elements of Crimes for the proposition that this must occur within a manifest pattern of similar conduct (i.e. a contextual element);[9] and

- the crime of aggression is a 'leadership crime': it can only be committed by those officials in a position to control the political or military action of a State (a highly restricted class of perpetrator).

Thus most of the 'core' international crimes have a contextual or nexus requirement: war crimes and crimes against humanity certainly do, and genocide possibly does as well. Genocide is also distinguished from national crimes by its additional mental element: the *dolus specialis* or special intent requirement. Aggression, strictly, requires neither a contextual element nor a *dolus specialis*. It is distinct from ordinary crimes by virtue of the fact that only a limited class of perpetrators can commit it.

---

[8] E van Sliedregt, 'System Criminality at the ICTY' in H van der Wilt and A Nollkaemper (eds), *System Criminality in International Law* (Cambridge University Press 2009) 183.

[9] This reflects our common-sense intuition that a single racially motivated killing committed by a lone perpetrator could not constitute genocide, even if that lone killer sincerely (but unrealistically) believed they would go on to kill many other members of that racial group.

7.3 Material element

As noted above, the material element (or elements) of a crime is the physical conduct (either an act or omission) prohibited by a rule of international criminal law. We will examine the material elements of each of the core crimes in following chapters. What we should note for the moment is that the Rome Statute contemplates three different types of material element: conduct, consequence, and circumstance elements. Piragoff and Robinson offer the following definitions of each:

- conduct includes 'a prohibited action or prohibited omission that is described in the definition of a crime';
- consequences 'can refer either to a completed result, such as the causing of death, or the creation of a state of harm or risk of harm, such as endangerment'; and
- circumstances 'qualify the conduct and consequences. They may, for example, describe the requisite features of the persons or things mentioned in the conduct and consequence elements'.[10]

The importance of these distinctions is that a different mental element may attach to each,[11] as discussed further in section 7.4.3. Of these, the concept of circumstances may require slightly more elaboration. 'Circumstances' describes a state of affairs which must exist for conduct to be considered criminal.[12] It is a situation which exists in fact or law, and need not be something the defendant has brought about. Thus, the material element requiring that war crimes be committed in the context of an armed conflict may be considered a 'circumstance'.

7.4 Mental element

7.4.1 General meanings and forms

As noted, the generally accepted definition of the mental element (*mens rea*) of a crime is that it is the guilty or culpable mental state accompanying a prohibited act. Acts are generally only criminal if accompanied by such a culpable mental state: we are usually reluctant to punish persons for consequences they did not intend. However, this raises a preliminary problem: what do we mean by 'intend' or 'intention'? Different legal systems take different approaches, and all legal systems recognize that there are 'different *gradations* or *degrees* of intent'.[13] Commentators in this context tend to contrast

[10] D Piragoff and D Robinson, 'Article 30: Mental Element' in O Triffterer (ed), *Commentary on the Rome Statute of the International Criminal Court: Observers' Notes, Article by Article*, 2nd ed (Beck 2008) 852.

[11] See e.g.: *Katanga*, ICC Trial Chamber, 7 March 2014, para 774.

[12] S Finnin, 'Mental Elements under Article 30 of the Rome Statute of the International Criminal Court: A Comparative Analysis' (2012) 61 International and Comparative Law Quarterly 325, 338.

[13] Finnin, 'Mental Elements under Article 30', 328.

'common law' and 'civil law' approaches. These labels are obviously much too broad. As Roger Clark has put it:

> The civil law is not a monolith; the common law is not a monolith. Matters that I think obvious are hotly disputed by other common lawyers. They are equally debated among civilians. Even basic terminology is not always agreed upon.[14]

The examples commonly contrasted in the literature are taken from Anglo-American common law and Romano-Germanic civil law.[15] Even then, these examples involve broad generalizations and are often based more on scholarly than judicial approaches to the concepts involved.

Put very simply, the common law recognizes several potentially culpable mental states:[16]

- 'Intent' or 'direct intent': where a person intended the outcome achieved or the result that followed from his or her act or omission. We might call this mental state '*dolus directus*' in civil law systems.

- 'Oblique intent': where a person acts to achieve one goal but knows with virtual certainty that a criminal consequence (which is not directly intended) will come about as a result.[17] An example would be an assassin who plants a bomb to kill a governmental leader knowing that other people (who are not his or her target) will be killed as a result. The assassin intends to kill his target and has 'oblique intent' regarding the other victims' whose death or injury is almost certain to come about. We might call this mental state '*dolus indirectus*' in civil law systems.

- 'Recklessness': which 'consists of the state of mind of a person who does not intend to cause a harmful result but takes an unjustifiable risk of which he [or she] is aware, thus causing an unlawful result.'[18] Recklessness thus involves both 'foresight and a volitional act' and can be thought of as deliberately taking an unacceptable risk.[19] A difficult question in discussing recklessness is how likely the risk in question must be. Common law systems vary on this point and may require either foresight of a probable outcome or simply of a possible outcome.[20] However, in some conceptions recklessness will also cover failing to

---

[14] Clark, 'The Mental Element in International Criminal Law', 294–295; compare Finnin, 'Mental Elements under Article 30', 328–9.

[15] See e.g. A Vallini, 'Intent' in A Cassese (ed), *The Oxford Companion to International Criminal Justice* (Oxford University Press 2009) 376–78.

[16] The following discussion draws upon: 'Paper prepared by the International Committee of the Red Cross relating to the mental element in common law and civil law systems' (15 December 1999), Preparatory Commission for the International Criminal Court, Doc No. PCNICC/1999/WGEC/INF/2/Add.4, reproduced in: K Dörmann, *Elements of War Crimes under the Rome Statute of the International Criminal Court* (Cambridge University Press 2003) 487–498 ('Red Cross Paper').

[17] D Ormerod et al, *Smith and Hogan's Criminal Law* 13th ed (Oxford University Press 2011) 107, 202, and 405 ff.

[18] Red Cross Paper, 489.   [19] Cassese et al, *Cassese's International Criminal Law*, 46.

[20] Finnin, 'Mental Elements under Article 30', 335.

give an obvious and unjustifiable risk any thought ('wilful blindness'). In a civil law context we might call this mental state *dolus eventualis*.[21]

- 'Negligence' or 'criminal negligence': describes a mental state where a person *should* have foreseen the consequences of his or her act irrespective of whether he/she actually did foresee those consequences or not. Whereas recklessness requires some conscious advertence to the risks involved in one's behavior, 'criminal negligence' will cover situations even where a person is unaware of the risk. Here, 'the conduct is criminalized because it constitutes a wanton disregard, or a substantial departure from the standard of care that a reasonable person would observe.'[22] It is thus judged objectively and without reference to what the individual knew or intended. We might call this mental state *culpa* in the civil law tradition. In the common law tradition gross negligence may be sufficient for a criminal conviction. In the civil law tradition, mere negligence—however outrageous—is usually *never* sufficient for a criminal conviction.

The civil law tradition has a different taxonomy and conception of culpable mental states which might form the mental element of a crime. Briefly, these may be termed:[23]

- *Dolus directus* (sometimes called *dolus directus* of the first degree): where the outcome is *intended* by the person. In such a case it does not matter if the outcome was 'foreseen as certain or only being possible'. This has obvious similarities to 'intent' in the common law tradition.

- *Dolus indirectus* (sometimes called *dolus directus* of the second degree): where the accused was indifferent to the outcome but knew it to be a 'certain or highly probable' consequence of his or her action. This seems similar to 'oblique intention' in common law but does not require foresight of virtual certainty.

- *Dolus eventualis*: where the accused person 'foresees the result as being reasonably probable or at least possible as the consequence of his [or her] acts' and accepts or reconciles himself or herself to the fact that this may occur. If the person 'wrongfully believes' the result will not come about he or she is merely grossly negligent and not punishable in law.

There is obviously considerable potential for overlap and confusion between these categories. Nonetheless, a serious debate in international criminal law concerns which mental states should suffice for serious crimes under international law. There is widespread agreement that mere negligence, however gross, is usually not enough. Any further conclusions require an assessment of both the case law of the ad hoc Tribunals and of the International Criminal Court.

Before turning to that case law, we should note the concept of *dolus specialis*: special intent. This phrase is used to describe the required mental element for genocide. It is

---

[21] Though some would suggest there are real differences between the two concepts: Finnin, 'Mental Elements under Article 30', 335–6. The most important point is that the definition of recklessness does not always require showing a defendant reconciled themselves to the risk they were taking in contrast to *dolus eventualis*.

[22] Red Cross Paper, 490.   [23] Red Cross Paper, 491–92.

enough to be convicted of a war crime such as murder, if one *intends* to kill a person and also has knowledge of the relevant context (i.e. the existence of an armed conflict). Genocide requires that the prohibited act (such as murder) was carried out with the intent to destroy a protected group, in whole or in part, as such. There is thus a further intentional requirement (*dolus specialis*): the special intent not only to commit the prohibited act but also to destroy the group. This may be thought of as an aggravated form of intent.[24]

7.4.2 The ICTY and ICTY approach

The International Criminal Tribunal for the Former Yugoslavia (ICTY) and the International Criminal Tribunal for Rwanda (ICTR) have both held that under customary international law the required mental element for international crimes at customary international law may be satisfied either by intent (*dolus directus*) or a lesser form of intent greater than negligence. It is not always easy to categorize what the ad hoc Tribunals consider to be the acceptable alternative to intent. It is common in the literature to suggest the ICTY and ICTR case law in particular will accept recklessness or *dolus eventualis* as sufficient.[25] Certainly there are cases that would appear to support the contention. The ICTY Trial Chamber in *Stakić* said:[26]

> Turning to the *mens rea* element of the crime, the Trial Chamber finds that both a *dolus directus* and *dolus eventualis* are sufficient to establish the crime of murder...German law takes *dolus eventualis* as sufficient to constitute intentional killing. The technical definition of *dolus eventualis* is the following: if the actor engages in life-endangering behaviour, his killing becomes intentional if he 'reconciles himself' or 'makes peace' with the likelihood of death.... [K]illings that would be classified as reckless murder in the United States would meet the continental [i.e. civil law] criteria of *dolus eventualis*. The Trial Chamber emphasises that the concept of *dolus eventualis* does not include a standard of negligence or gross negligence.

Similarly, in *Musema* the ICTR Trial Chamber said that for the crime of murder the required mental element was that:[27]

> [a]t the time of the killing the Accused ... had the intention to kill or [had the intention to] inflict grievous bodily harm on the deceased having known that such bodily harm is likely to cause the victim's death, and is reckless as to whether or not death ensues.

On this approach it is sufficient that the prohibited act was carried out either: (a) with intent (*dolus directus*) or (b) recklessly (with *dolus eventualis*). However, some decisions

---

[24] Cassese et al, *Cassese's International Criminal Law*, 119.
[25] Ibid, 48–49; R Cryer 'General Principles of Liability' in R Cryer, H Friman, D Robinson, and E Wilmshurst, *An Introduction to International Criminal Law and Procedure* 3rd ed (Cambridge University Press 2014) 382. See further, Vallini, 'Intent', 377–8.
[26] *Stakić*, ICTY Trial Chamber, 31 July 2003, para 587.
[27] *Musema*, ICTR Trial Chamber, 27 January 2000, para 215.

of the ad hoc Tribunals appear to refer to a slightly different standard: 'indirect intent'. In *Strugar* the ICTY Trial Chamber suggested that widespread use of the term *dolus eventualis* may have obscured the degree of risk required by the Tribunal, and that the preferable term was 'indirect intent':

> to prove murder, it must be established that death resulted from an act or omission of the accused, committed with the intent either to kill or, in the absence of such a specific intent, in the knowledge that death is a probable consequence of the act or omission. In respect of this formulation it should be stressed that knowledge by the accused that his act or omission might possibly cause death is not sufficient to establish the necessary *mens rea*. The necessary mental state exists when the accused knows that it is probable that his act or omission will cause death.[28]

In terms of the simplified taxonomy outlined above, this notion of 'indirect intent' would seem closer to *dolus indirectus* than *dolus eventualis*. In common law terms the standard envisaged by this use of 'indirect intent' would probably fall within most definitions of recklessness and would certainly not be as strict as the definition of oblique intent given above. Similarly, in *Delić* an ICTY Trial Chamber held: 'indirect intent comprises knowledge that the death of a victim was a "probable" or "likely" consequence of [the] act or omission' of the defendant.'[29] It also noted that '[n]egligence and gross negligence do not form part of indirect intent.'[30]

It may therefore be that describing the ICTY approach to the mental element required for international crimes as encompassing recklessness or *dolus eventualis* is somewhat misleading, at least in so far as those terms might (in some national systems) encompass mental states wider than the ICTY concept of 'indirect intent'. ICTY 'indirect intent' appears to require knowledge that a (prohibited) outcome of one's actions or omissions is at least probable.

7.4.3 The ICC approach: intent and knowledge are required (unless otherwise provided)

The general rule

The fundamental rule on the required mental element before the ICC Statute is found in Article 30 of the Rome Statute. Article 30 sets out the default or general rule: it applies 'unless otherwise provided'. Thus, other provisions of the statute might set a higher or lower mental element requirement for a particular offence. Article 30 is worth quoting in full.

1. Unless otherwise provided, a person shall be criminally responsible and liable for punishment for a crime within the jurisdiction of the Court only if the material elements are committed with intent and knowledge.

---

[28] *Strugar*, ICTY Trial Chamber, 31 January 2005, para 235–36.
[29] *Delić, Rasim*, ICTY Trial Chamber, 15 September 2008, para 48.
[30] Ibid.

2. For the purposes of this article, a person has intent where:
   (a) In relation to conduct, that person means to engage in the conduct;
   (b) In relation to a consequence, that person means to cause that consequence or is aware that it will occur in the ordinary course of events.
3. For the purposes of this article, 'knowledge' means awareness that a circumstance exists or a consequence will occur in the ordinary course of events. 'Know' and 'knowingly' shall be construed accordingly.

On its face, this seems simple enough: a crime must be committed with intent (either as to conduct or a consequence) *and* knowledge (either of a circumstance or a consequence).[31] Thus, Article 30 could encompass several conceptions of intent. Article 30(2)(a) certainly covers 'direct intent' or '*dolus directus*'. Article 30(2)(b) would also appear designed to cover 'oblique intent' or *dolus indirectus* ('is aware that [a consequence] will occur in the ordinary course of events').[32] Indeed, the ICC Trial Chamber in *Katanga* held precisely that Article 30(2)(b) corresponds to 'oblique intention' and requires that the consequences foreseen are a virtual certainty not a mere possibility.[33] Some commentators suggest the required standard is very high indeed: that the consequence would occur 'unless extraordinary circumstances intervened'.[34] Whether the ICC will take this approach remains to be seen.

Very peculiarly, the Pre-Trial Chamber in *Lubanga* held that Article 30(2)(b) could encompass some forms of *dolus eventualis*.[35] This approach was, entirely correctly, not accepted by the Trial Chamber judgment in *Lubanga* which held that Article 30 clearly excludes *dolus eventualis*.[36] The exclusion of recklessness and *dolus eventualis* follows from two points:

- First, the definition of knowledge embodies a higher standard of *mens rea* than recklessness or *dolus eventualis* requires. The perpetrator must have known not that an outcome was likely or probable but that 'a consequence *will occur* in the ordinary course of events'.[37] This seems much closer to knowing that an outcome was almost inevitable rather than merely likely or probable and would appear to correspond to concepts such as 'oblique intent' or *dolus indirectus*.

- Second, intention is *always* required (unless the Statute specifies otherwise) in addition to knowledge. So even if the Article 30 standard for knowledge was the same as the standard for recklessness or *dolus eventualis*, it could not substitute for proof of intention.

---

[31] See the useful table in: Finnin, 'Mental Elements under Article 30', 341.

[32] Finnin, 'Mental Elements under Article 30', 343.

[33] *Katanga*, ICC Trial Chamber, 7 March 2014, paras 775–76. The Lubanga Trial Chamber simply observed: 'A low risk will not be sufficient': *Lubanga*, ICC Trial Chamber, 14 March 2012, para 1012.

[34] Finnin, 'Mental Elements under Article 30', 344.

[35] *Lubanga* (Decision on the Confirmation of Charges), ICC Pre-Trial Chamber, 29 January 2007, para 352.

[36] *Lubanga*, ICC Trial Chamber, 14 March 2012, paras 1009–11.

[37] Although one can certainly argue the level of certainty involved in the ICC Statute's 'will occur in the ordinary course of events' standard is less than the 'practically certain' or 'virtually certain' standard found in some common law jurisdictions: Finnin, 'Mental Elements under Article 30', 332.

The Trial Chamber in *Lubanga* expressly confirmed that the intention in the drafting of Article 30 was to exclude both *dolus eventualis* and recklessness from having any place within the Statute.[38]

Must there always be both intent and knowledge?

The idea that every crime requires both intent *and* knowledge is difficult for those with common law training to accept. Common lawyers would tend to think of intent and knowledge as potentially overlapping but separate types of mental element, and that the appropriate one to apply in a given case would depend on the exact definition of the elements of the offence. A crime might require intent in relation to some elements, knowledge in relation to others, or both. The words 'unless otherwise provided' perhaps provide some scope for this approach.

The effect of the requirement for intent *and* knowledge is perhaps also diluted somewhat by the Elements of Crimes, insofar as they provide guidance on the interpretation of the Statute.[39] The 'General Introduction' to the Elements of Crimes notes two important points for present purposes. First, while re-stating that criminal liability under the Statute only arises 'if the material elements are committed with intent and knowledge' it further notes that:

> Where no reference is made in the Elements of Crimes to a mental element for any particular conduct, consequence or circumstance listed, it is understood that *the relevant mental element, i.e., intent, knowledge or both, set out in article 30 applies* (emphasis added).

This may suggests that the mental elements of a crime could include intent, knowledge, *or* both which might suggest the 'and' in Article 30 can sometimes be read as an 'or'.[40] Nonetheless, its precise effect is uncertain. In practice it may be enough that most international crimes will require intent regarding some elements and knowledge regarding others: therefore, taken as a global whole, the crime will only be able to be committed with intent *and* knowledge. An example is given below.

Second, the 'General Introduction' to the Elements of Crimes provides that the '[e]xistence of intent and knowledge can be inferred from relevant facts and circumstances.' Crucially, this means that a prosecutor does not literally have to prove what a perpetrator was thinking in order to make out the mental element of a crime, the *mens rea* can be inferred from the relevant facts and circumstances

---

[38] *Lubanga*, ICC Trial Chamber, 14 March 2012, para 1011. See also: *Bemba Gombo* (Confirmation Decision), ICC Pre-Trial Chamber, 15 June 2009, para 360.

[39] Under Art 9(1), ICC Statute the Elements of Crimes 'shall assist the Court in the interpretation and application' of the substantive crimes set out in the Statute. This might suggest the Elements of Crimes are strictly non-binding. However, under Art 21(1)(a), ICC Statute the Court 'shall apply' the Elements of Crimes as part of its applicable law. The correct interpretation is likely that while the Court must 'apply' the Elements of Crimes (under Article 21) it applies them as an interpretative aid only (Article 9). They thus cannot override the Statute and the Court may, in theory, depart from them.

[40] Cassese agreed with this approach, saying that a purely grammatical approach must sometimes give way to logical necessity if the object and purpose of a rule and the principle of effectiveness require it: Cassese et al, *Cassese's International Criminal Law*, 57.

proven in the case.[41] Realistically, absent a confession, the mental state of a defendant in relation to a crime will normally have to be inferred from circumstantial evidence.

 Example

Applying the mental element requirements to the ICC Elements of Crimes

According to the ICC Elements of Crimes, the crime against humanity of murder requires the prosecutor to prove the following elements (footnotes omitted):

1. The perpetrator killed one or more persons.
2. The conduct was committed as part of a widespread or systematic attack directed against a civilian population.
3. The perpetrator knew that the conduct was part of or intended the conduct to be part of a widespread or systematic attack against a civilian population.

There is thus 'a conduct element in the first paragraph (or if you like, a consequence element), a circumstance or a contextual circumstance element in the second and a "particular" mental element ("knowledge") required' in the third.[42] This is called an 'elements analysis approach'.[43] Equally, one could interpret Article 30 as requiring that the killing occurs with *intent* and that the accused has *knowledge* of the context. The crime thus requires, as a whole, both intent and knowledge—but in relation to separate elements and not every element.[44] In practice, then, Article 30 may not be as difficult or complex as it might at first seem to common lawyers.

Exceptions where the ICC Statute has 'otherwise provided'

We will see in later chapters that there are cases under the Statute where the *mens rea* required is less than 'intent and knowledge'. For example, under the provisions on superior responsibility, criminal liability may attach to a military superior where he or she *should* have known his or her subordinates were committing crimes, or had information before them suggesting such crimes might be occurring, and failed to take further action. There are also cases of special intent where additional mental elements must be proved: the *dolus specialis* of genocide is an obvious example.

---

[41] On the use of circumstantial evidence more generally, see for example: *Prosecutor v Lubanga*, Judgment (ICC Trial Chamber, 2012), para 111. ('When, based on the evidence, there is only one reasonable conclusion to be drawn from particular facts, the Chamber has concluded that they have been established beyond reasonable doubt.') Strictly, *mens rea* was not being discussed in this paragraph.

[42] Clark, 'The Mental Element in International Criminal Law', 328.

[43] Finnin, 'Mental Elements under Article 30', 337.

[44] Ibid, 336–37; see also Piragoff and Robinson, 'Article 30: Mental Element', 854.

> ### →← Counterpoint
>
> Is the mental element required under the ICC Statute too high in some contexts? Finnin gives the example of roadside improvised explosive devices, as used in many conflicts involving rebel armed groups.[45] Such devices are notoriously unreliable and may fail to detonate a majority of the time. In such cases can it be said that the person planting a bomb foresees that a criminal 'consequence will occur in the ordinary course of events'? In the ordinary course of events, such bombs may not detonate at all.

7.5 Summary and conclusions

We have considered a number of important issues in this chapter concerning the structure of international crimes. First, we have noted that it is not easy to define precisely what constitutes an international crime. We focus in this book on the 'core crimes' (war crimes, crimes against humanity, genocide, and aggression). These are generally regarded as 'core' for the pragmatic reason they all fall within the jurisdiction of international criminal tribunals. However, this is simply a fact of history, it is not a requirement of law that an 'international tribunal' has jurisdiction over all such crimes.[46] We can suggest that the core crimes typically involve a 'contextual element', and the suggestion would have some truth. War crimes and crimes against humanity certainly have contextual or nexus requirements. As we shall see in Chapter 10, genocide does have a contextual element under the ICC Elements of Crimes and may do under customary international law despite the silence of the Genocide Convention on the issue. Aggression does not (unless one counts the fact of bringing about a war or a use of force in inter-State relations as a contextual element). It may therefore be inaccurate to say all 'core' crimes involve a contextual element.

The chapter has also discussed the straightforward idea that a crime has two components: a prohibited act or omission (the material element or *actus reus*) and a culpable mental state (the mental element or *mens rea*). Material elements may involve conduct, consequences, or circumstances. The more difficult question is the requisite mental element for international crimes. Broadly speaking, direct intent is always sufficient: acting with the intent to bring about the crime. The jurisprudence of the ad hoc Tribunals and the Statute of the ICC vary as to what further mental states may be sufficient. The case law of the ICTY in particular indicates that 'indirect intent' may suffice: acting in the knowledge that an international crime occurring is a probable result of one's act or omission. The standard of 'intent and knowledge' found in Article 30 of the ICC Statute is higher: at the least a defendant will have to act in the knowledge that the consequences foreseen are a virtual certainty not a mere possibility. In practice, international crimes are divided into 'elements' (as we shall see in later chapters) and different mental

---

45 Ibid.   46 See further: O'Keefe, *International Criminal Law*, 60.

states may be required of each element depending on whether it involves conduct, a consequence or a circumstance.

Useful further reading

R CLARK, 'The Mental Element in International Criminal Law: The Rome Statute of the International Criminal Court and the Elements of Offences' (2001) 12 Criminal Law Forum 291.
One of the most important articles written on these questions, which benefits from a clear and accessible style—as well as providing insights into the process of negotiating the Rome Statute from the point of view of a delegate.

S FINNIN, 'Mental Elements under Article 30 of the Rome Statute of the International Criminal Court: A Comparative Analysis' (2012) 61 International and Comparative Law Quarterly 325.
An exceptionally clear and useful treatment of the concepts involved in interpreting Article 30.

D PIRAGOFF and D ROBINSON, 'Article 30: Mental Element' in O Triffterer (ed), *Commentary on the Rome Statute of the International Criminal Court: Observers' Notes, Article by Article*, 2nd ed (Beck 2008) 849.
A short but detailed and scholarly exposition of the drafting history of Article 30 and the ideas relevant to its interpretation.

A VALLINI, 'Intent' in A Cassese (ed), *The Oxford Companion to International Criminal Justice* (Oxford University Press 2009) 376.
A concise and useful overview of the key concepts discussed in this chapter.

8

War crimes

8.1 Introduction

The law of war crimes is now a significant part of international criminal law. Indeed, it is common to refer to international criminal tribunals as 'war crimes tribunals' even when they also have jurisdiction over other offences. The place of war crimes in international criminal law, and their complexity, is reflected in Article 8 of the International Criminal Court (ICC) Statute which lists no less than 50 different war crimes. In interpreting and applying this law we must pay careful attention to the law governing the conduct of warfare, or as it is now typically called 'the law of armed conflict'. Some authors suggest that one of the great achievements of international criminal law is that it is now used to enforce the law of armed conflict, and that those who violate it can expect to be held to account before national and international courts.[1] Such statements must be treated with caution for at least two reasons. First, the prosecution of war crimes remains disappointingly rare and often frustratingly complex. Second, not every violation of the laws of armed conflict is a crime—only some violations attract criminal sanction. Correctly applying and interpreting the law of war crimes requires us to have some understanding of the history and principles of the law of armed conflict.

Efforts to regulate the conduct of war through law expanded significantly throughout the nineteenth and twentieth centuries. This may be attributed, at least in part, to the changing scale and character of warfare. Major mediaeval battles could involve only a few tens of thousands of people and would have been inaudible to the civilian population a few kilometres away, and (other than matters of taxation and conscription) would not necessarily have greatly disrupted civilian life.[2] The rise of the modern State from the beginning of the nineteenth century allowed mass conscription and the creation of much larger armies than ever seen before. Industrialization also produced more effective weapons. Inevitably, the combination of larger armies and

---

[1] G Werle and F Jessberger, *Principles of International Criminal Law*, 3rd ed (Oxford University Press 2014) 402.

[2] That said, in mediaeval Europe a common means of economic warfare was the deliberate destruction of towns, villages, and agricultural land ('laying waste') which could inflict extraordinary hardship on civilians through famine: M Strickland, *War and Chivalry: The Conduct and Perception of War in England and Normandy, 1066–1217* (Cambridge University Press 1996) 261–78.

better weapons brought vastly greater casualties on the battlefield.[3] Industrial warfare also brought an increasing exposure to the hazards of war for civilians.

It is now accepted that, as a basic principle, a combatant's choice of means and methods of warfare is not unlimited.[4] The major sources of written law commonly referred to (although there are many others) in the field are now:

- National military manuals stipulating the law of armed conflict to be followed by a State's military forces. These have a long history, going back to (at least) the 1863 Lieber Code issued during the US Civil War. They are generally taken to constitute statements of *opinio juris* as to the content of the laws of armed conflict.

- The Hague Conventions of 1899 and 1907 and the Regulations on War on Land annexed to the latter (often called the 'Hague Regulations').

- The first through fourth Geneva Conventions of 1949 (referred to in this book as 'GC I', 'GC II', 'GC III', and 'GC IV', respectively).

- The 1977 first Additional Protocol to the Geneva Conventions, providing additional rules governing *international* armed conflicts (hereafter, 'AP I').

- The 1977 second Additional Protocol to the Geneva Conventions, providing additional rules governing *non-international* armed conflicts (hereafter, 'AP II').

The four Geneva Conventions in particular are treaties with effectively universal membership. Not all States are parties to the two Additional Protocols, though many rules therein are accepted as customary law.

The law of armed conflict is thus usually divided into two branches:

- the law governing the methods and means of warfare (i.e. prohibited weapons and tactics), sometimes called 'Hague law' (after the Hague Convention and Regulations); and

- the law governing the treatment and protection of civilians taking no part in hostilities and combatants placed out of combat due to injury or having been captured (*hors de combat*), sometimes called 'Geneva law' (after the Geneva Conventions and Additional Protocols).

As both these branches of law aim at minimizing 'unnecessary suffering' they may be referred to as international humanitarian law (IHL). It is common to use IHL to mean the same thing as the law of armed conflict (LOAC).

Historically, the majority of this law applied only to international armed conflicts between States. States resisted the legal regulation of civil wars or conflicts with guerrillas or insurgencies ('non-international armed conflicts'), in part because this was thought an internal matter for sovereign States and in part to avoid conferring any legal

---

[3] French and Russian losses in the First World War or 'Great War' of 1914–1918 were staggering. Russia mobilized an army of 12 million, with 1.7 million killed and a further 5 million wounded; France mobilized more than 8 million, of whom 1.3 million were killed and more than 4 million wounded: see www.pbs.org/greatwar/resources/casdeath_pop.html.

[4] Art 23(e), Hague Conventions of 1899 and 1907 and the Regulations on War on Land annexed to the latter (Hague Regulations) Art 35(2), First Additional Protocol to the Geneva Conventions (AP I).

status or privileges upon civil war insurgents. To understand modern LOAC one must grasp this basic historical fact: States have been very reluctant to submit the conduct of non-international conflicts to legal regulation and the law applicable to such conflicts has expanded only slowly. Some minimal provisions applicable to non-international armed conflicts are found in Common Article 3 of the Geneva Conventions. Common Article 3, as the name suggests, is an identical provision in each of the four Geneva Conventions set-ting out a set of minimum standards to be observed in non-international armed conflicts. Common Article 3 is significant because, as we shall see, it has been held to: be a statement of customary international law; contain rules also applicable in international armed con-flict; and give rise to rules of criminal law. Common Article 3, as a body of rules applying to non-international armed conflicts, was later supplemented by the terms of AP II.

As the majority of armed conflicts around the world are now non-international armed conflicts (NIACs), the limited regulation of them by treaty law is increasingly problem-atic. A trend commenced by the ICTY was to find that many treaty-based rules applicable to international armed conflicts (IACs) have also become applicable to NIACs.[5] As this 'convergence' between the LOAC applicable to both types of conflicts continues, some have questioned the value of maintaining the distinction. Nonetheless, the distinction remains as a matter of law[6] leading to some important differences in the law applicable to IACs or NIACs.[7] The most important difference for our purposes is to note that it remains the case that a narrower range of conduct is criminalized in NIACs than in IACs. Therefore, before we can apply the law of war crimes to a conflict it will be important to categorize the conflict. Some controversies arise, however, as to whether transnational conflicts with non-State actors should be classified as IACs (because they cross a border) or NIACs (because one party is not a State). The problem is discussed further below.

It is important to bear in mind that the majority of LOAC was originally drafted as rules to be followed *by States*. With the exception of a limited class of 'grave breaches' in the Geneva Conventions,[8] most rules of LOAC did not originally entail individual criminal responsibility. ICTY case law paved the way in finding that many of these rules were now rules of individual criminal responsibility under customary international law. This was perhaps initially controversial, but the ICC Statute indicates that in a very short time much of the ICTY case law had been accepted by States as stating customary international law. Once again, though, it is important to point out that not every breach of LOAC is a crime of individual responsibility.

---

[5] R Kolb and R Hyde, *An Introduction to the International Law of Armed Conflicts* (Hart Publishing 2008) 69; R Mullerson, 'International Humanitarian Law in Internal Conflicts' (1997) 2 Journal of Armed Conflict Law 109, 116; *Tadić* (Decision on Jurisdiction), ICTY Appeals Chamber 1995, paras 119–36.

[6] *Tadić* (Decision on Jurisdiction), ICTY Appeals Chamber, 2 October 1995, para 126; K Ambos, *Treatise on International Criminal Law* (Oxford University Press 2013), Vol 2, 120 n 28.

[7] For example, the full law governing the status of prisoners of war only apply in IACs; persons detained in NIACs are protected by Common Article 3 of the Geneva Convention and AP II. See further: International Committee of the Red Cross, 'Prisoners of war and detainees protected under international humanitarian law' (2010): www.icrc.org/eng/war-and-law/protected-persons/prisoners-war/overview-detainees-protected-persons.htm.

[8] The relevant treaty provisions are: Arts 49 and 50, GC I; Arts 50 and 51, GC II; Arts 129 and 130, GC III; Arts 146 and 147, GC IV; Art 85, AP I.

If finding that there was a broad range of crimes applicable in IACs was controversial, one would have expected still greater controversy in the case of NIACs. As noted, the provisions of Common Article 3 of the Geneva Conventions are considered customary international law, applicable to both international and internal conflicts. In the *Nicaragua Case* the International Court of Justice (ICJ) said:

> Article 3...defines certain rules to be applied in...armed conflicts of a non-international character. There is no doubt that, in the event of international armed conflicts, these rules also constitute a minimum yardstick, in addition to the more elaborate rules which...apply to international conflicts; and they are rules...[reflecting] 'elementary considerations of humanity'.[9]

While these rules were thus widely accepted as minimum rules of conduct binding on States, they were not widely thought to be rules of criminal law before:

- first, their inclusion as such by the Security Council in Article 4 of the ICTR Statute in 1994; and

- second, the finding of the ICTY in the *Tadić* case in 1995 that violations of Common Article 3 constituted war crimes.[10]

This acceptance of Common Article 3 as part of customary international *criminal* law is also now also reflected in the ICC Statute.[11] More broadly, the ICC Statute also indicates a general acceptance by States that many more criminal rules apply to both international and non-international armed conflicts than had perhaps previously been thought.

 Learning aims

By the end of this chapter you should be able to:

- distinguish between the law of war crimes and international humanitarian law;

- discuss the basic principles of legitimate military objectives, target differentiation, and proportionality;

- discuss the differing tests for establishing the existence of international or non-international armed conflicts (IACs and NIACs) and the consequences of that classification;

- identify how a war crime must be related to the contextual element;

- distinguish between grave breaches of the Geneva Conventions and other serious violations of the laws and customs of war; and

- apply the law, including the ICC Elements of Crimes, to a hypothetical scenario.

---

[9] *Case concerning Military and Paramilitary Activities in and against Nicaragua (Nicaragua v USA)*, 1986 ICJ Reports 14, para 218 ('*Nicaragua Case*').

[10] *Tadić* (Decision on Jurisdiction), ICTY Appeals Chamber, 2 October 1995, paras 126–29.

[11] Art 8(2)(c), ICC Statute. See further: D Robinson, 'War Crimes' in R Cryer et al, *An Introduction to International Criminal Law and Procedure*, 3rd ed (Cambridge University Press 2014) 268–69.

Following from these aims, the chapter is structured as follows:

- Section 8.2 introduces the basic principles of the law of armed conflict: distinction and proportionality.
- Section 8.3 deals with the distinction between international and non-international armed conflicts.
- Section 8.4 outlines the contextual element and mental element required for war crimes.
- Section 8.5 provides an overview of the prohibited acts that may form the conduct underlying a war crimes.
- Section 8.6 examines select war crimes in more detail.

The chapter concludes with a table comparing the range of offences applicable under the ICC Statute to NIACs and IACs; as well as providing a hypothetical scenario to which you can apply the law.

8.2 Basic principles of LOAC: distinction and proportionality

We noted above that interpreting and applying the law of war crimes requires not only some understanding of the origins and history of LOAC but also of its principles. Two of the most fundamental are the principles of distinction and proportionality. They are addressed here in some detail not only because of their general importance but also because they apply in both IACs and NIACs and their violation may form the basis of war crimes (as further discussed in section 8.6).

The principle of distinction involves the difference between civilians and civilian objects and military personnel and military objects. Only military persons and objects may be targeted during war. Such attacks on military targets may cause incidental damage or death to civilians, but cannot proceed if that damage would be disproportionate to legitimate military aims.

These principles may be expressed as:

(a) only combatants and other military objectives are lawful targets; the civilian population and 'civilian objects' may not be made the *direct* target of attack (the principle of *distinction*); and

(b) even military objectives may not be attacked if an attack is likely to cause civilian casualties or damage which would be *excessive* in relation to the concrete and direct military advantage which the attack is expected to produce (the principle of *proportionality*).[12]

---

[12] C Greenwood, 'The Law of War (International Humanitarian Law)' in M Evans (ed), *International Law* (Oxford University Press 2003) 797 (footnotes omitted and emphasis added).

Though called principles, because of their general nature, these are binding rules of customary international law. They are also codified in Article 48 (distinction) and Articles 51(5)(b) and 57 (proportionality) of AP I. Distinction may also have a second meaning under LOAC: at a minimum in NIACs LOAC requires combatants to *distinguish* themselves from (i.e. not disguise themselves as) civilians by openly carrying their weapons during military operations; and LOAC may further require that in IACs combatants take further measures to *distinguish* themselves from civilians such as wearing a distinctive emblem which is visible at a distance.[13] Distinction in this second sense is largely irrelevant to international criminal law.

The principle of distinction as a rule of targeting raises the question of what counts as a military objective. Certainly, enemy forces may be attacked. In respect of objects, Article 52(2) of AP I states:

> military objectives are limited to those objects which by their nature, location, purpose or use make an effective contribution to military action and whose total or partial destruction, capture or neutralization, in the circumstances ruling at the time, offers a definite military advantage.

The test in Article 52(2) obviously has two parts: the object must make an effective contribution to military action; and its total or partial destruction must offer a definite military advantage. This is now the generally accepted definition of legitimate military objectives[14] and it *potentially* covers a wide range of objects beyond obvious military equipment. Many objects may be 'dual-use' items or facilities capable of civilian or military use.[15] A bridge the enemy can advance (or retreat) over could 'make an effective contribution to military action'. The destruction of that bridge might therefore offer 'a definite military advantage'. The important test is 'in the circumstances ruling at the time': a bridge that was useful to the enemy yesterday might be of no use to them today. In such a case it is no longer a legitimate military objective.[16] The test is thus heavily contextual and situation dependent.[17]

 Example

Eritrea v Ethiopia (Western Front, Aerial Bombardment and Related Claims, Partial Award), Eritrea-Ethiopia Claims Commission

Several useful examples of the application of distinction and proportionality are provided by the jurisprudence of the Eritrea-Ethiopia Claims Commission.[18] This was an international arbitration

---

[13] See: Art 44(3), AP I; Art 4(A)(2)(b), GC III.
[14] W Fenrick, 'Targeting and Proportionality during the NATO Bombing Campaign against Yugoslavia' (2001) 12 European Journal of International Law 489, 494.
[15] Ibid.   [16] Greenwood, 'The Law of War', 797.
[17] Fenrick, 'Targeting and Proportionality', 494.
[18] *Eritrea v Ethiopia (Western Front, Aerial Bombardment and Related Claims, Partial Award)*, Eritrea-Ethiopia Claims Commission, 19 December 2005, 27 UN Reports of International Arbitral Awards 291, http://legal.un.org/riaa/cases/vol_XXVI/291-349.pdf.

panel established to deal with matters of State responsibility for war damage, not international criminal law. Nonetheless, in order to assess whether compensation was due for illegal war damage the Commission had to consider the law of targeting. Two examples assist us here: the Commissions' findings regarding the bombing of a reservoir and a power plant.

First, Eritrea claimed Ethiopia's aerial bombing of the Harsile Water Reservoir was illegal because it was the primary source of water for the large port city of Assab.[19] Ethiopia claimed the air strikes were made to deprive the Eritrean military of water. The Commission found the attacks illegal: despite the claim by Ethiopia that it believed a few military units drew water from the reservoir, it was obvious it was an object indispensible to the survival of the civilian population (including a refugee camp) in an arid and hot region. Further Eritrean military units had in fact their own separate water supplies. The Commission found a violation of the principle of *distinction*—the reservoir was only used for civilian purposes. Even if some military units had used water from the reservoir the Commission might still have found a violation of *proportionality*—depriving a large city of water could be considered excessive in relation to the military advantage of depriving a few army units of water.

Second, Eritrea claimed Ethiopia's bombing of the Hirgigo Power Station was unlawful.[20] Construction of this power station had only just finished at the time of its bombing and Eritrea claimed its purpose was to supply power to nearby cities, including the port city of Massawa which housed a naval base. The existing power supply for Massawa was considered old and 'on its last legs'. The Commission, by a majority, found that a facility supplying electricity to the naval base and port at Massawa would make an effective contribution to the Eritrean war effort and its destruction would offer a definite military advantage. Therefore targeting it did not violate the principle of distinction. One Arbitrator, however, considered that the damage done to the civilian population through loss of a new power station constructed at great expense was disproportionate to the aim of impairing port facilities which could have been achieved by other means.[21] The difficulty of assessing disproportionate damage is discussed further at section 8.6.10.

 Counterpoint

Can new war-fighting technologies adequately comply with the principle of distinction?

A great deal has been written in recent years about the increasing use of weapon-carrying unmanned aerial vehicles, so-called 'drones', in modern armed conflicts, especially NIACs.[22] Some drones may even be automated but with a 'human in the loop', in the sense that they patrol an area and identify targets—but do not fire without a human operator making a final decision (or having the power to over-ride any automatic targeting).[23] Such automated drones are an attractive weapon system in that a number of drones could be managed by one operator, thus allowing

[19] Ibid, paras 98–105.   [20] Ibid, paras 117–21.
[21] Ibid, separate opinion of Arbitrator van Houtte.
[22] See e.g.: P Bergen and D Rothenberg (eds), *Drone Wars: Transforming Conflict, Law, and Policy* (Cambridge University Press 2015).
[23] H Scheltema, 'Lethal Automated Robotic Systems and Automation Bias', EJIL: Talk!, 11 June 2015, www.ejiltalk.org/lethal-automated-robotic-systems-and-automation-bias/#more-13393.

a single individual to effectively patrol a large area. Significant concerns have been raised about the risks to the principle of distinction in such an approach. Heko Scheltema raises the concern that humans often suffer from 'automation bias': a tendency to trust computerized decisions over their own judgment.[24] There is thus a risk operators might make fatal errors through not exercising sufficient care in deciding a suspicious person or vehicle identified by a drone is actually a military target which can be attacked with lethal force. Of course, not every drone is automated in this manner: many are remotely piloted by a single operator.

Conversely, Michael Lewis and Emily Crawford have suggested that drones were actually developed as a means of complying with distinction and proportionality.[25] That is, it is increasingly common (especially during NIACs) for armed groups to conceal themselves among a civilian population. Attacking them with conventional forces may thus risk massive and disproportionate casualties. Drones, however, arguably have the potential to allow armed forces to target individuals very precisely and actually minimize the risk to nearby civilians in such situations. In this sense one would expect them to cause fewer civilian casualties than planes or missiles and to minimize the risk of disproportionate damage. Whether they achieve this result in reality is, of course, a separate question and one which can be surprisingly difficult to answer.[26]

8.3 International armed conflicts and non-international armed conflicts

8.3.1 **The distinction**

As noted above, different rules may apply in international armed conflicts (IACs) and non-international armed conflicts (NIACs). It is thus often important to classify an armed conflict before asking whether war crimes have been committed.

The existence of an international or non-international armed conflict is a question of fact. As stated by the ICTY Appeals Chamber in the *Tadić* case (1995 Decision on Jurisdiction):

> an armed conflict exists whenever there is a resort to armed force between States or protracted armed violence between governmental authorities and organized armed groups or between such groups within a State.[27]

Thus the type of conflict is defined by the nature of the parties. An IAC occurs between *States*; a NIAC occurs between a State and an organized armed group or between such armed groups.

On this basis, an IAC occurs whenever there is recourse to violence between States;[28] a NIAC requires 'protracted armed violence' involving armed groups organized along

---

[24] Ibid.
[25] MW Lewis and E Crawford, 'Drones and Distinction: How IHL Encouraged the Rise of Drones' (2013) 44 Georgetown Journal of International Law 1127.
[26] F Mégret, 'The Humanitarian Problem with Drones' (2013) 5 Utah Law Review 1283, 1296.
[27] *Tadić (Decision on Jurisdiction)*, ICTY Appeals Chamber, 2 October 1995, para 70.
[28] See further the discussion in the text related to n 43.

military lines. The two requirements for a NIAC are thus that there is a sufficient level of violence and the armed groups involved have a sufficient level of (military) organization. The case law has established that in assessing whether violence is protracted a court must consider: 'the seriousness of attacks..., their spread over territory and over a period of time, the increase in the number of government forces, the mobilisation and the distribution of weapons among both parties to the conflict' and whether the United Nations Security Council has considered the conflict and if so whether it has passed any resolutions on point.[29] Situations such as riots, 'isolated and sporadic acts of violence',[30] mere 'banditry', or even an 'unorganized and short-lived insurrection' will not constitute NIACs.[31] The requirement of organization is addressed further in section 8.3.4.

This does not resolve all questions, such as:

- Are national liberation movements engaged in a struggle for self-determination against an alien or colonial regime engaged in a non-international conflict (because the forces involved are not both States) or an international conflict (given the foreign nature of the regime)?

- If one State organizes irregular forces within another State to fight, is such a 'proxy force' enough to trigger an IAC?

- In NIACs, what are the requirements to be an 'organized armed group'? This question is more than academic: many criminal gangs, such as those in a number of South American countries, may be sufficiently armed and organized that they can challenge local government.[32] Are government operations against them governed by the law of law-enforcement or the law of NIAC?

- Is it significant if a confrontation between a State and a non-State armed group *crosses a border*? Will this transform what would otherwise be a NIAC into an IAC?

- Finally, if the law applicable to IACs and to NIACs is converging, how much difference does the distinction continue to make?

These questions are addressed in turn below.

8.3.2 National liberation movements

Generally speaking, one would expect armed conflicts involving liberation movements struggling against colonial regimes to be classified as NIACs, as liberation movements will by definition be non-State groups. Under AP I, however, Article 1(4) international armed conflicts include: 'armed conflicts which peoples are fighting against colonial domination and alien occupation and against racist regimes in the exercise of their

---

[29] *Lubanga*, ICC Trial Chamber I, 14 March 2012, para 538 quoting *Mrkšić et al.*, ICTY Trial Chamber, 27 September 2007, para 407.

[30] Art1(2), AP II; Art 8(2)(d) and (f), ICC Statute.

[31] J Pictet, *Commentary on the Geneva Conventions of 12 August 1949* (International Committee of the Red Cross 1952) vol I, 50.

[32] E.g. D Rodgers and R Muggah, 'Gangs as Non-State Armed Groups: The Central American Case' (2009) 30 Contemporary Security Policy 301.

right of self-determination'. This is referred to here as the 'expanded definition' in AP I. Whether this expanded definition is customary international law is open to question, but the general view is that it is not yet customary international law. The expanded definition therefore applies only to the parties to AP I.

This expanded definition is not expressly referred to in the ICC Statute. However, Article 21(1)(b) of the ICC Statute includes within the Court's applicable law: 'where appropriate, applicable treaties and the principles and rules of international law, including the *established* principles of the international law of armed conflict'. Whether the expanded AP I definition of international armed conflict applies under the ICC Statute would appear then to hinge on whether this is an *established* rule.[33] This could in turn depend on whether the rule is accepted as custom. Given the dubious status of the expanded definition as a rule of customary international law, the most likely outcome therefore is that the expanded AP I definition does not apply under the ICC Statute.

8.3.3 The question of proxy forces and IACs

An armed conflict occurring in the territory of a single State may seem, at first, purely a NIAC. However, it may become an IAC if either another State intervenes or 'where some participants in the internal armed conflict [in fact] act on behalf of this other State'.[34] Thus, if one can factually show a sufficient legal link between an organized armed group which is a party to the conflict and a foreign State, then that link 'confers an international nature upon an armed conflict which initially appears internal'.[35]

This link required is one of *attribution*: the act of the proxy force must legally be attributable to the intervening foreign State. In the case of 'organised and hierarchically structured' groups such as military units or armed bands of irregulars participating in a conflict the ICTY Appeals Chamber in the *Tadić* case applied a test for attribution of 'overall control'.[36] That is, if certain armed groups were under the 'overall control' of an outside State, then the conflict would be classified an IAC. In *Tadić*, it was found that the Federal Republic of Yugoslavia (FRY), as it then was, had overall control of certain Serbian militia forces in Bosnia on the basis of considerations including:

- the fact that some members of FRY forces had remained in Bosnia after the official withdrawal of all FRY troops in 1992 and continued to fight with or alongside the Serb forces;

- indeed, some of these troops who stayed behind served as officers in the Serb militias, and such officers continued to be paid by the FRY; and

- the relationship of complete dependence of Serb forces in Bosnia on the FRY for funding and equipment;

---

[33] One should also note the reference in Art 8(2)(b) ICC Statute to 'the established framework of international law'.

[34] *Blaškić*, ICTY Trial Chamber, 3 March 2000, para 76.   [35] Ibid.

[36] *Tadić*, ICTY Appeals Chamber, 15 July 1999, paras 117–20.

- the fact that the irregular forces in Bosnia joined the FRY delegation to peace conferences and the FRY undertook to ensure their respect for the Dayton Accord (a peace agreement).[37]

Such facts made it obvious that the FRY had control over the irregulars, at least to the extent that if it withdrew material support their effective fighting capacity would be ended or greatly limited. The ICTY expressly noted that 'overall control' required more than an outside State simply equipping and financing an armed group but requires a degree of involvement in planning and supervising military operations.[38] In effect, where 'overall control' is present then, under the *Tadić* test, such armed groups will be treated as an arm of the State which has 'overall control'.

However, the 'overall control' test has proved controversial. In the earlier *Nicaragua* case the ICJ held that a State was only responsible at public international law for the acts of armed groups under a State's 'effective control'.[39] This is a harder standard to satisfy. The ICJ was clear that even a relationship of complete dependence would not satisfy this stricter test, instead individual missions had to be planned and ordered by the responsible State. The ICTY Appeals Chamber in *Tadić* rejected the *Nicaragua* test as too strict, leaving a conflict between the two legal authorities.[40]

In the *Genocide Case* the ICJ suggested the two tests were not contradictory, but rather that they could logically be different tests used for different purposes:

- 'effective control' is the test in public international law litigation between States where the question is the responsibility of the State itself;

- 'overall control' is the test used in international criminal law to establish certain facts (i.e. whether an IAC exists).[41]

Put another way, an international criminal trial is concerned only with individual responsibility. It has no power to rule on issues of State responsibility: the finding of an IAC in *Tadić* did not require the FRY to pay compensation, for example, to Bosnia. It is therefore acceptable that international criminal law might use a different legal test from that used in State-to-State litigation. Some find this logic unconvincing and suggest that as a matter of common sense it is untenable to say that a State could be responsible for the acts of an armed group for international criminal law purposes but not for the purposes of State responsibility.[42] Which approach the ICC will take to the issue remains to be seen.

8.3.4 **The definition of 'organized armed groups' in NIACs**

When considering the application of the laws of armed conflict and war crimes to a NIAC two crucial threshold questions arise. What types of groups count as 'organized

---

[37] Ibid, paras 146–157.   [38] Ibid, para 145.   [39] *Nicaragua Case*, para 115.
[40] *Tadić*, ICTY Appeals Chamber, 15 July 1999, para 115.
[41] *Application of the Convention on the Prevention and Punishment of the Crime of Genocide (Bosnia and Herzegovina v Serbia and Montenegro)* (2007) ICJ Reports 43, paras 399–407.
[42] A Cassese, 'The Nicaragua and *Tadić* Tests Revisited in Light of the ICJ Judgment on Genocide in Bosnia' (2007) 18 European Journal of International Law 649.

armed groups' to which the laws of NIACs apply? And what constitutes a sufficient intensity of violence?

Several tests are available. Article 1(1), AP II sets a high standard. It refers to 'organized armed groups' which are 'under responsible command' and which 'exercise such control over a part of [a State's] territory as to enable them to carry out sustained and concerted military operations and to implement this Protocol.' There must therefore be: (1) sufficient organization that there is a responsible commander capable of ensuring respect for LOAC; and (2) control over territory enabling sustained military operations.[43] AP II is also clear that the rules of NIACs do not apply 'to situations of internal disturbances and tensions, such as riots, isolated and sporadic acts of violence'.[44] Such situations are not armed conflicts.

The AP II standard is likely higher than that required by customary international law. Neither the *Tadić* case (as quoted above) nor the ICC Statute or case law require control over territory.[45] Indeed, in modern 'asymmetric' warfare many non-State actors do not necessarily seek to establish territorial control. The critical question thus seems to be a sufficient degree of organization and responsible command.

Article 8(2)(f) of the ICC Statute defines NIACs as 'armed conflicts that take place in the territory of a State when there is protracted armed conflict between governmental authorities and organized armed groups or between such groups' and excludes from this definition 'situations of internal disturbances and tensions, such as riots, isolated and sporadic acts of violence'. It thus adopts a mixed approach combining the test in *Tadić* and the definition found in AP II of circumstances which fall below the threshold of an armed conflict.

NIACs thus require:

- a protracted armed conflict, which excludes riots, isolated and sporadic acts of violence; and

- involving organized armed groups (under responsible command).

The test of whether an armed conflict is 'protracted' is discussed in section 8.3.1.

8.3.5 Is a conflict between a State and a non-State organized armed group an IAC if the violence crosses an international border?

It is sometimes claimed that a conflict between a State and an armed group *which crosses an international border* should be treated as an IAC.[46] For example, Israel in 2006

---

[43] Although arguably the plain words of Common Article 3 to the GCs do not require either responsible command or territorial control and simply apply to all *parties* to a NIAC the famous Red Cross commentary holds responsible command and territorial control are nonetheless required for a NIAC: Pictet, *Commentary on the Geneva Conventions*, vol I, 50–51.

[44] Art 1(2), AP II.

[45] Ambos, *Treatise*, vol. 2, 128; *Lubanga*, ICC Trial Chamber 2012, para 536 (agreeing with *Tadić*).

[46] *The Public Committee against Torture in Israel v The Government of Israel* (The Supreme Court of Israel) (2007) 46 ILM 375. The conclusions in this case are generally regarded as wrong: see e.g. the case note by O Ben-Naftali and K Michaeli (2007) 101 American Journal of International Law 459.

conducted military operations against Hezbollah (an organized armed group conducting hostilities against Israel) on the territory of Lebanon. Was this an IAC or NIAC?
The question, as a matter of the law of armed conflict, is an important one. To take only
one example, in an IAC formal prisoner of war (POW) status exists and combatants
captured by either side must be treated as POWs. In a NIAC any person detained by
parties to the conflict (including combatants) is protected by the minimum guarantees
of Common Article 3 and AP II.[47] Why should members of an armed group suddenly
become eligible for POW status because they cross a border? Just as importantly, why
should such a group suddenly be treated as an organization capable of administering
POW camps or facilities and, indeed, obliged to do so?[48] The correct conclusion must
be that where one party to a conflict is not a State, the conflict is a NIAC. As the US
Supreme Court has put it in *Hamdan v Rumsfeld*: '[t]he term "conflict not of an international character" is used...in contradistinction to a conflict between nations.'[49] The
question is not one of geography but of the parties to the conflict.

It may seem absurd, however, to say that Israel invading Lebanon to confront
Hezbollah had no legal consequences for the applicable law. This, however, may not
be the case. While there is a minimum threshold of violence required for NIACs,
the general view is that any violence between States is sufficient to trigger an IAC.[50]
Indeed, even the occupation of part of another State's territory which meets no armed
resistance can be an IAC.[51] Further, the invasion of a State or the temporary occupation of its territory is considered an act of aggression (i.e. an illegal act of war).[52] If
State A's troops enter State B's territory without State B's consent, there is therefore
arguably an IAC automatically existing between them. There will certainly be an IAC
if State A assumes control over some part of State B's territory (i.e. becomes an occupying power under GC IV). On this basis, returning to the example given above of
the 2006 Israel/Hezbollah conflict, Israel's incursion into Lebanon may mean Israel
was automatically engaged in an IAC *with Lebanon*. Thus, if in military operations
against Hezbollah (a NIAC) it encountered Lebanese troops or occupied territory
inhabited by Lebanese civilians it would have been bound by the laws of IAC in
relation to those troops and those civilians.[53] This would not have changed the law
applicable to the conflict between Israel and Hezbollah, which would have remained
a NIAC. Nonetheless, the question remains unsettled.

---

[47] See further: International Committee of the Red Cross, 'Prisoners of war and detainees protected under
international humanitarian law' (2010), www.icrc.org/eng/war-and-law/protected-persons/prisoners-war/
overview-detainees-protected-persons.htm.

[48] N Lubell, *Extraterritorial Use of Force against Non-State Actors* (Oxford University Press 2010) 103.

[49] *Hamdan v Rumsfeld*, 548 US 557, 630 (2006).

[50] There is some debate on point but this is clearly the majority view. See e.g.: Robinson, 'War Crimes'
in Cryer et al, *Introduction*, 3rd ed, 275 (n 79) and 279; UK Ministry of Defence, *The Manual of the Law of
Armed Conflict* (Oxford University Press 2004), para 3.3.1; and C Byron, 'Armed Conflicts: International or
Non-International?' (2001) 6 Journal of Conflict and Security Law 63, 81.

[51] Art 2, GC IV.

[52] Art 3, Definition of Aggression annexed to UN General Assembly Resolution 3314 (XXIX), 1974.

[53] See further: D Guilfoyle, 'The *Mavi Marmara* Incident and Blockade in Armed Conflict' (2011) 81 British
Yearbook of International Law 171, 187–88.

8.3.6 **The narrowing distinction between IACs and NIACs**

As noted above, there is an increasing convergence between the law applicable in IACs and NIACs. A great move in this direction was made by the ICTY Appeals Chamber in the 1995 Decision on Jurisdiction in the *Tadić* case. As noted above, this decision found that violations of Common Article 3 gave rise to criminal sanction. It also found that a number of criminal prohibitions had passed from the law applicable to IACs into the law of NIACs. However, the Appeals Chamber made two important points about this extension of IAC rules to NIACs: first, it applies to 'only a number of rules'; and second, this extension of rules does not involve 'a full and mechanical transplant' of the relevant rules, instead only 'the general essence of those rules, and not the detailed regulation they may contain' applies in NIACs.[54] Put simply, the gradual extension of treaty provisions by customary international law is likely to occur on a rule-by-rule basis and one cannot assume that a customary rule will contain all the precise detail of a treaty rule.

This, however, leaves us with a new question: what test tells us when a particular violation of LOAC in a NIAC has become punishable under international criminal law? The Appeals Chamber in *Tadić* held that such LOAC violations gave rise to individual criminal liability where:

- there is 'clear and unequivocal recognition' of the relevant rule in international law; and

- there is 'State practice indicating an intention to criminalize the prohibition', including actual cases of punishment by national courts or by military tribunals; and

- 'No one [could] doubt the gravity of the acts at issue, nor the interest of the international community in their prohibition.'[55]

The necessary result of the *Tadić* approach is that the international criminal law of NIACs is more limited in the number of applicable rules and those rules are likely to be more general and less detailed than the equivalent rules applicable in IAC. Thus, despite increasing overlap between the two bodies of law, they remain distinct. Accepting this broad approach, the distinction between IACs and NIACs was preserved in the ICC Statute. Antonio Cassese criticized this as 'being too obsequious to State sovereignty'.[56]

 Pause for reflection

Maintaining the distinction between IACs and NIACs does have, however, real consequences beyond simply identifying the applicable law. Prosecutors may prefer to issue charges based on the law of NIACs where non-State armed groups are concerned. Trying to apply the law of IACs to

---

[54] *Tadić*, ICTY Appeals Chamber, 15 July 1999, para 126.
[55] *Tadić* (Appeal on Jurisdiction), ICTY Appeals Chamber, 2 October 1995, para 128–29.
[56] A Cassese, *International Criminal Law*, 2nd ed (Oxford University Press 2008) 95–97.

the actions of organized armed groups would involve the added complication for a Prosecutor of having to prove the involvement of a State in the conflict.

This arose as an issue in the ICC *Lubanga* trial (a case concerning the war crime of recruiting child soldiers in the Ituri region of the Democratic Republic of the Congo),[57] with the Pre-Trial Chamber originally concluding the conflict varied between being a NIAC and IAC. That is, the Pre-Trial Chamber considered that in the period 2002–2003 Uganda was in occupation of Ituri and this gave the conflict there an international character. At least on its face this created problems. Mr Lubanga was alleged to be part of a non-State rebel group. The offence of recruiting child soldiers in a NIAC refers to the enlistment and conscription of children under 15 'into armed forces or groups'.[58] However, the equivalent offence in an IAC applies to the enlistment and conscription of children under 15 'into the national armed forces'.[59] Could Mr Lubanga thus not be charged with a crime during the period of Ugandan occupation because he was not part of State forces? The Pre-Trial Chamber, oddly, interpreted 'national' forces to have a meaning broader than 'State' forces.[60] The issue was resolved when the Trial Chamber re-characterized the conflict (once again) as being a NIAC throughout the relevant period.

8.4 The nexus requirement and mental element of war crimes

To constitute a war crime, a prohibited act must have:

(1) a connection to an armed conflict (a nexus or contextual requirement);

(2) been committed against a protected person or object under LOAC; and

(3) been committed with the relevant mental element.

These requirements are discussed in turn below.

8.4.1 The nexus requirement

The ICTY Appeals Chamber in the *Tadić* Decision on Jurisdiction held it was enough that the alleged crimes were 'closely related to the hostilities occurring in the territories controlled by the parties to the conflict'.[61] The ICC Elements of Crimes require that a war crime be committed 'in the context of and associated with' an armed conflict.[62] What does this mean in practice?

A more precise test was articulated by the ICTY in *Kunarac*: 'the existence of an armed conflict must, at a minimum, have played a substantial part in the perpetrator's ability to commit [the crime], his decision to commit it, the manner in which it was

---

[57] See for example: M Happold, '*Prosecutor v Thomas Lubanga*, Decision of Pre-Trial Chamber I of the International Criminal Court' (2007) 56 International and Comparative Law Quarterly 713, at 718–22.

[58] Art 8(2)(e)(vii), ICC Statute.   [59] Art 8(2)(b)(xxvi), ICC Statute.

[60] *Lubanga* (Decision on the Confirmation of Charges), Pre-Trial Chamber, 29 January 2007, paras 202–4.

[61] *Tadić* (Decision on Jurisdiction), ICTY Appeals Chamber, 2 October 1995, para 70.

[62] Art 8, ICC Elements of Crimes (this language is used in the second last element of each individual crime).

committed or the purpose for which it was committed.'[63] Factors a court may take into account in making this assessment include the fact that:

- 'the perpetrator is a combatant';
- 'the victim is a non-combatant';
- 'the victim is a member of the opposing party';
- 'the act may be said to serve the ultimate goal of a military campaign'; and
- 'the crime is committed as part of or in the context of the perpetrator's official duties.'[64]

It is thus enough that 'the perpetrator acted in furtherance of or under the guise of the armed conflict'.[65] This would cover, for example, cases involving abuse of power or authority such as soldiers looting a town they have captured or an official in charge of a detention camp during an armed conflict using his position to carry out unlawful medical experiments on the inmates.

The perpetrator need not be a military official, civilians can commit war crimes.[66] However, can any civilian commit a war crime? Imagine two neighbours (A and B) in a disputed borderland where an armed conflict is taking place. A takes advantage of the chaos attendant on the conflict to settle an old grudge by murdering B and stealing B's land. Under the *Kunarac* test, the existence of the conflict has probably played a significant role in A's decision to commit the crime and ability to commit the crime. However, if A claims no status or connection with one of the parties to the conflict, he is not acting 'in furtherance of or under the guise of the armed conflict'. Thus, if 'during an armed conflict, a person kills another person in a strictly private interpersonal conflict', the act is not 'associated' with the conflict and therefore not a war crime.[67]

The post-Second World War case law tends to confirm the idea that there must be some reasonably close connection between the civilian perpetrator and one party to the conflict. The *Engister* case involved a civilian prisoner who had worked as a concentration camp policeman (or 'Kapo') and had viciously abused other prisoners.[68] This connection was sufficiently close to allow him to be convicted of war crimes. The *Roechling* case concerned a civilian industrialist involved in forced-labour programmes as war crimes.[69] Roechling also held official

[63] *Kunarac*, ICTY Appeals Chamber, 12 June 2002, para 57.
[64] *Katanga* (Decision on Confirmation of the Charges), ICC Pre-Trial Chamber I 30 September 2008, para 382; endorsing *Kunarac*, ICTY Appeals Chamber, 12 June 2002, para 59.
[65] *Kunarac*, ICTY Appeals Chamber, 12 June 2002, para 58.
[66] See in particular: *Akayesu*, ICTR Trial Chamber, 2 September 1998, para 631 (finding that some official status is needed to commit a war crime); and compare it with *Akayesu*, ICTR Appeals Chamber, 1 June 2001, paras 430–45 (overturning the Trial Chamber and finding there is no requirement of official status).
[67] M Bothe, 'War Crimes' in A Cassese, *The Rome Statute of the International Criminal Court: A Commentary* (Oxford University Press 2002), vol 1, 388.
[68] See case extracts in: Cassese et al., *Cases and Materials*, 127–32.
[69] Ibid, 122–6.

administrative posts and, though a civilian, had close ties to the government. This would seem a sufficiently close connection but his conviction at trial for war crimes was, however, overturned on appeal.[70] Civilians are still often involved in the running of prison camps in armed conflicts and may, as noted above, commit war crimes against those detained there.[71]

In this context we should also note that international criminal law is equally applicable to those serving in the forces of a non-State armed group, such as Hezbollah or the so-called 'Islamic State' organization which controls areas in Iraq and Syria. Such organized armed groups are clearly capable of being 'parties to a conflict' (see section 8.3.4). Therefore any act committed by members of their forces (or acts committed by civilians which are sufficiently closely connected to their cause) is capable of being a war crime if it breaches the applicable law. Such groups are sometimes referred to as 'illegal', 'unlawful', or 'unprivileged' combatants in cases where they do not comply with the principle of distinction (in the sense of distinguishing themselves from civilians). Even if this characterization is correct, it does not change the law applicable to their actions.

8.4.2 Protected persons/objects

The *actus reus* of war crimes requires a prohibited act (as discussed below) committed against a protected person or object. Those persons protected under LOAC in international armed conflicts are:

- sick and wounded combatants in the field (under GC I);
- sick, wounded, and shipwrecked at sea (under GC II);
- prisoners of war or 'POWs' (under GC III);
- civilians in the hands of a party to the conflict of which they are not nationals (under GC IV); and
- the wounded and medical or religious personnel in international conflicts (under AP I).

Those persons protected under LOAC in non-international armed conflicts are:

- civilians, the wounded, and those *hors de combat* as well as medical and religious personnel (under AP II).

In the case of offences under Common Article 3 of the Geneva Conventions protected persons are 'those taking no active part in hostilities.' This has been interpreted to cover civilians, those *hors de combat*, and those not fighting at the time of the offence.[72]

[70] The acquittal of numerous German industrialists of war crimes in post-1945 trials was, however, controversial: G Baars, 'Capitalism's Victor's Justice: The Hidden Story of the Prosecution of Industrialists Post-WWII' in G Simpson and K Heller (eds), *Untold Stories: Hidden Histories of War Crimes Trials* (Oxford University Press 2012), Chapter 8.
[71] Bothe, 'War Crimes', 388; *Tadić*, ICTY Trial Chamber, 7 May 1997, para 575.
[72] *Tadić* (Decision on Jurisdiction), ICTY Trial Chamber, 2 October 1995, paras 615–16.

8.4.3 The mental element for war crimes: issues of intent and knowledge

Under the ICC Statute the material elements of an international crime must be 'committed with intent and knowledge'.[73] The concepts of intent and knowledge in international criminal law were discussed in Chapter 7. For present purposes it is enough to note that war crimes, like crimes against humanity, require *intent* to commit a particular prohibited act and *knowledge* of relevant facts or contextual elements. Here the perpetrator must have knowledge of the factual circumstances establishing both the existence of an armed conflict *and* the victims' protected status.

The ICC Elements of Crimes addresses the question of the standard of knowledge a perpetrator must have of the existence of an armed conflict. In particular they note that the perpetrator need not make a 'legal evaluation as to the existence of an armed conflict' or its classification as an IAC or NIAC; the requirement is only for an 'awareness of the factual circumstances that established the existence of an armed conflict'.[74] The idea that a perpetrator need only be aware of the factual circumstances that establish the existence of an armed conflict is consistent with the ICTY case law.

We should also note two further points. First, war crimes may be committed in a variety of ways including by aiding, abetting, instigating, or ordering an international crime or one may be found guilty as a superior for failing to prevent or punish war crimes. These issues are discussed as 'modes of participation' in Chapter 12. Second, this section has only outlined the general rule governing the mental element required for war crimes, some specific offences may require further elements be proved. In particular, the war crime of attacks causing excessive civilian damage requires the perpetrator actually come to a value judgement that an attack would be disproportionate before proceeding to attack.

We turn now to the substantive law of war crimes.

8.5 The substantive law of war crimes: the prohibited acts

For anyone new to the subject (and even to those who have studied it for some time) the law of war crimes can be a complex and dauntingly detailed field. Ultimately, no textbook is any substitute for a detailed reading of Article 8(2) of the ICC Statute and the relevant Elements of Crimes. These form a useful starting point for several reasons. First, Article 8(2) serves as evidence of the acts the great majority of negotiating States were prepared to accept as war crimes and therefore of *opinio juris*. Second, the offences set out in Article 8(2) usually draw upon ICTY and ICTR case law and may generally be accepted as an attempt to codify customary international law. Thus Article 8(2) forms the basis of our study of substantive war crimes.

---

[73] Art 30, ICC Statute.   [74] Art 8, Introduction, ICC Elements of Crimes.

Two special features of Article 8 should, however, be noted:

- First, Article 8(1) states: 'The Court shall have jurisdiction in respect of war crimes in particular when committed as part of a plan or policy or as part of a large-scale commission of such crimes.' This has been called a 'non-threshold threshold'. It does not limit the ICC's jurisdiction to cases involving a 'plan or policy', it simply indicates that the Court should (not must) focus its efforts on such cases. These words are therefore 'a guide rather than a requirement'.[75]

- Second, both Articles 8(2)(b) and (e) refer to 'Other serious violations of the laws and customs applicable in armed conflict, *within the established framework of international law*' (emphasis added). What do the words 'within the established framework of international law' mean? Cassese suggested this means that the ICC must satisfy itself that these offences are also part of customary international law before applying them.[76] This has not been the approach of the ICC in practice and is unlikely to have been the intent of the drafters. It is far more likely these words were intended to suggest that the broader rules of LOAC are relevant in interpreting and applying these crimes. For example, AP I lists the precautions which should be taken before launching an attack which may harm civilians—if these precautions are not complied with it may be easier to infer there was a *deliberate* attack on civilians.

Turning to the offences listed in Article 8(2), even a brief glance at the Article can be confusing. Article 8(2)(a) lists eight crimes applicable in international armed conflicts; Article 8(2)(b) adds a further 26. Article 8(2)(c) lists four offences applicable in non-international armed conflicts and Article 8(2)(e) adds 12 more. Under the ICC Statute there are therefore 34 potential war crimes in international armed conflicts and 16 in non-international armed conflicts—and the two lists of offences do not necessarily perfectly overlap (as we would expect given the approach in *Tadić*). Studying 50 separate offences is thus a daunting task.

Why was Article 8 organized in this complex fashion? As noted above, while it is generally accepted that the law applicable to IACs and NIACs is converging to some extent, States do not yet accept they have perfectly converged into a single body of law. In addition to different crimes applying in different types of conflicts, the crimes themselves may have different sources—in treaty and custom.[77] Table 8.1 considers the different types of armed conflicts and the different sources of law; we can see that the drafting of Article 8 reflects these considerations.

---

[75] Robinson, 'War Crimes' in Cryer et al, *Introduction*, 3rd ed, 284.

[76] Cassese, *International Criminal Law*, 2nd ed, 94–5.

[77] The International Committee of the Red Cross (ICRC) has an ambitious project to codify all the customary rules of IAC and NIAC (irrespective of whether they attract criminal sanction). The ICRC International Humanitarian Law database presently lists 161 rules of armed conflict: www.icrc.org/customary-ihl/eng/docs/v1_rul. The entry for each rules specifies whether it applies in IAC or NIAC (generally the ICRC takes the view most rules apply in both types of conflict). The database is likely to be influential in the work of international courts but is controversial in some quarters: WH Parks, 'The ICRC Customary Law Study: A Preliminary Assessment' (2005) 99 Proceedings of the Annual Meeting (American Society of International Law) 208–12.

Table 8.1 Legal source of the prohibition

Type of conflict	Treaty law	Customary law
International	Grave breaches of the GCs: Art 8(2)(a), ICC Statute.	Other serious violations of the laws and customs of war applicable in international armed conflict: Art 8(2)(b), ICC Statute.
Non-international	Breaches of Common Article 3 of the GCs and AP II: Art 8(2)(c), ICC Statute.	Other serious violations of the laws and customs of war applicable in **non-**international armed conflict: Art 8(2)(e), ICC Statute.

Most textbooks cover this subject in a very limited way. The effort here will be to look at only a selection of crimes which have rough equivalents in both NIACs and IACs. The aim is to:

- actually allow you to study a selection of crimes in detail, rather than just read about them in general terms;
- to simplify a large amount of material to be covered; and
- to illustrate where there are (and are not) significant differences between the international criminal law applicable in IACs and NIACs.

Given these goals, we start with the offences found in Common Article 3(1) of the Geneva Conventions which (as noted above) are applicable in *both* IACs and NIACs. These crimes are:

(a) violence to life and person, in particular murder of all kinds, mutilation, cruel treatment and torture;
(b) taking of hostages;
(c) outrages upon personal dignity, in particular humiliating and degrading treatment;
(d) the passing of sentences and the carrying out of executions without previous judgment pronounced by a regularly constituted court, affording all...[internationally recognized] judicial guarantees.

After looking at these and two other important crimes (sexual violence and attacks on civilians), we will consider a table of roughly equivalent offences for the other crimes in the ICC Statute. This will give you a more complete picture of where 'gaps' between the international criminal law applicable to IACs and NIACs remain. Notably while there are a number of crimes punishable in IACs which have no direct equivalent in NIACs, the opposite is not true. This is because the law applicable to IACs provides the 'higher standard' of protection.

8.6 Select war crimes

8.6.1 Introduction

The discussion of the individual crimes below is intended as a general guide which should be supplemented by reading the ICC Statute and Elements of

Crimes. Indeed, the elements of each offence are taken directly from the Elements of Crimes, though any notes or footnotes are usually omitted. After listing the elements which must be proven in respect of each offence, a short explanatory commentary is offered.

Two points are applicable to all offences. First, there is always a difference in the category of protected persons under either the law of IAC or NIAC. In an IAC protected persons are those covered by one of the four Geneva Conventions. In each case in a NIAC those protected are persons who are *hors de combat* and 'civilians, medical personnel, or religious personnel taking no active part in the hostilities.' We should note that the express inclusion of medical and religious personnel in the ICC Elements of Crimes are in addition to those categories of persons expressly protected under Common Article 3, represents a potential expansion of the range of protected persons in NIAC. Second, where an IAC crime constitutes a grave breach of the Geneva Conventions it will attract mandatory universal jurisdiction. That is, every State is obliged to seek out those on its territory suspected of the offence (see Chapter 2, section 2.5). In all other cases of IAC and NIAC offences universal jurisdiction is permissive: States *may* investigate and prosecute suspected perpetrators but have discretion whether to do so (see Chapter 2, section 2.4.1).

8.6.2 Murder (NIAC) and wilful killing (IAC)

Table 8.2 Elements to be proven in respect of murder and wilful killing

ICC Statutory Provisions and Elements	
NIAC	IAC
Article 8(2)(c)(i): 'Murder'	Article 8(2)(a)(i): 'Wilful killing'
Elements: 1. The perpetrator killed one or more persons.	**Elements:** 1. The perpetrator killed one or more persons.
2. Such person or persons were either *hors de combat*, or were civilians, medical personnel, or religious personnel taking no active part in the hostilities. 3. The perpetrator was aware of the factual circumstances that established this status.	2. Such person or persons were protected under one or more of the Geneva Conventions of 1949. 3. The perpetrator was aware of the factual circumstances that established that protected status.
4. The conduct took place in the context of and was associated with an armed conflict not of an international character. 5. The perpetrator was aware of factual circumstances that established the existence of an armed conflict.	4. The conduct took place in the context of and was associated with an international armed conflict. 5. The perpetrator was aware of factual circumstances that established the existence of an armed conflict.

The ICTY Trial Chamber in *Delalić* held that murder (causing death with the required intent) under Common Article 3 (applicable in NIACs) was indistinguishable from the offence of wilful killing as a grave breach of the Geneva Conventions (applicable in IACs).[78] The ICC Elements of Crimes take the same approach on this point, as the *actus reus* for both offences is that: 'The perpetrator killed one or more persons'; the Elements further note that the term 'killed' is interchangeable with the term 'caused death'.[79]

As noted above and in Table 8.2, the ICC Elements for the NIAC offence indicate a potentially broader range of protected persons than the Common Article 3 offence of murder. The same consideration applies for all the offences discussed below.

8.6.3 Mutilation

Table 8.3 Elements to be proven in respect of mutilation

ICC Statutory Provisions and Elements	
NIAC	IAC
Article 8(2)(c)(i)-2: 'Mutilation'	Article 8(2)(b)(x)-1: 'Mutilation'
Elements: 1. The perpetrator subjected one or more persons to mutilation, in particular by permanently disfiguring the person or persons, or by permanently disabling or removing an organ or appendage. 2. The conduct was neither justified by the medical, dental, or hospital treatment of the person or persons concerned nor carried out in such person's or persons' interests. 3. Such person or persons were either *hors de combat*, or were civilians, medical personnel, or religious personnel taking no active part in the hostilities. 4. The perpetrator was aware of the factual circumstances that established this status. 5. The conduct took place in the context of and was associated with an armed conflict not of an international character. 6. The perpetrator was aware of factual circumstances that established the existence of an armed conflict.	**Elements:** 1. The perpetrator subjected one or more persons to mutilation, in particular by permanently disfiguring the person or persons, or by permanently disabling or removing an organ or appendage. 2. The conduct caused death or seriously endangered the physical or mental health of such person or persons. 3. The conduct was neither justified by the medical, dental or hospital treatment of the person or persons concerned nor carried out in such person's or persons' interests. 4. Such person or persons were in the power of an adverse party. 5. The conduct took place in the context of and was associated with an international armed conflict. 6. The perpetrator was aware of factual circumstances that established the existence of an armed conflict.

---

[78] *Delalić*, ICTY Trial Chamber, 16 November 1998, paras 421–4.
[79] Art 8, n 31, ICC Elements of Crimes.

Article 8(2)(b)(x) actually covers two offences in IACs only one of which is listed here: in addition to mutilation it prohibits 'medical or scientific experiments'. Medical or scientific experiments are defined in a separate offence in the Elements of Crimes with the same elements as those above, with the exception that paragraph 1 reads '[t]he perpetrator subjected one or more persons to a medical or scientific experiment'. Prima facie, then, such medical or scientific experiments are not prohibited in NIACs. This could lead to the disturbing conclusion such experiments might be lawful. Two points should be made: first, the absence of criminal sanction is not the same thing as conduct being permitted; second, such experimentation could still potentially be charged as mutilation (if it involved disfiguring or disabling the victim, or removing an organ) or cruel or inhuman treatment (as discussed below).

As shown in Table 8.3, notably absent from the Elements of Crimes for the IAC offence is any reference to the victim being protected under one of the Geneva Conventions. This follows from the fact that offences under Article 8(2)(b) are taken to derive from customary international law. This has no obvious consequences under the ICC Statute.

8.6.4 **Torture**

Table 8.4 Elements to be proven in respect of torture

ICC Statutory Provisions and Elements	
NIAC	IAC
Article 8(2)(c)(i): 'Torture'	Article 8(2)(a)(ii): 'Torture'
Elements:	**Elements:**
1. The perpetrator inflicted severe physical or mental pain or suffering upon one or more persons.	1. The perpetrator inflicted severe physical or mental pain or suffering upon one or more persons.
2. The perpetrator inflicted the pain or suffering for such purposes as: obtaining information or a confession, punishment, intimidation or coercion, or for any reason based on discrimination of any kind.	2. The perpetrator inflicted the pain or suffering for such purposes as: obtaining information or a confession, punishment, intimidation or coercion, or for any reason based on discrimination of any kind.
3. Such person or persons were either *hors de combat*, or were civilians, medical personnel, or religious personnel taking no active part in the hostilities.	3. Such person or persons were protected under one or more of the Geneva Conventions of 1949.
4. The perpetrator was aware of the factual circumstances that established this status.	4. The perpetrator was aware of the factual circumstances that established that protected status.
5. The conduct took place in the context of and was associated with an armed conflict not of an international character.	5. The conduct took place in the context of and was associated with an international armed conflict.
6. The perpetrator was aware of factual circumstances that established the existence of an armed conflict.	6. The perpetrator was aware of factual circumstances that established the existence of an armed conflict.

The definition of torture as a war crime under the ICC Statute varies from the definition of torture in general international law. The Convention Against Torture (CAT),[80] Article 1 defines torture as:

- an act or omission causing severe pain or suffering whether physical or mental;
- committed for a prohibited purpose (such as obtaining information or a confession, punishment, intimidation/coercion, or discrimination);
- which has an official element ('when such pain or suffering is inflicted by or at the instigation of or with the consent or acquiescence of a public official or other person acting in an official capacity').

While the CAT definition of torture is generally accepted as customary international law, it is obvious that the war crime of torture as defined under the ICC Statute and Elements of Crimes is different. The key question is whether torture must be officially sanctioned, given that war crimes can be committed by persons who are not military officials. As shown in Table 8.4, the ICC Elements include only the first two requirements of the CAT listed above: the requirement of the infliction of severe pain or suffering for a prohibited purpose. The ICTY case law agrees that no element of official involvement is required for torture as a war crime.[81] (The rationale for this approach is that war crimes may be committed by persons other than State officials such as civilians lacking official status or members of organized armed groups.) We can thus conclude torture has a separate meaning as a war crime.

Indeed, torture has a separate definition again when committed as part of a crime against humanity (as discussed in Chapter 9, section 9.4.6). The definition of torture as a crime against humanity requires that the victim be in the custody or under the control of the perpetrator. The absence of such a requirement in the case of war crimes is explained on the basis that element 3 of the crime (at least in respect of IACs) requires that victims must be protected persons under one of the Geneva Conventions.[82]

Note also that Article 8(2)(a)(ii) refers to the war crime in IACs of '[t]orture or inhuman treatment, including biological experiments' thus covering a wider range of offences than just torture.

---

[80] Convention Against Torture and Other Cruel, Inhuman or Degrading Treatment or Punishment 1984, adopted 10 December 1984, entered force 26 Jun 1987, 1465 UNTS 85.
[81] *Delalić*, ICTY Trial Chamber, 16 November 1998, para 459; and *Kunarac*, ICTY Trial Chamber, 22 February 2001, para 485.
[82] Art 8, n 35, ICC Elements of Crimes.

8.6.5 **Cruel or inhuman treatment**

Table 8.5 Elements to be proven in respect of cruel or inhuman treatment

ICC Statutory Provisions and Elements	
NIAC	IAC
Article 8(2)(c)(i): 'cruel treatment'	Article 8(2)(a)(ii): 'inhuman treatment'
Elements:	**Elements:**
1. The perpetrator inflicted severe physical or mental pain or suffering upon one or more persons.	1. The perpetrator inflicted severe physical or mental pain or suffering upon one or more persons.
2. Such person or persons were either *hors de combat*, or were civilians, medical personnel, or religious personnel taking no active part in the hostilities.	2. Such person or persons were protected under one or more of the Geneva Conventions of 1949.
3. The perpetrator was aware of the factual circumstances that established this status.	3. The perpetrator was aware of the factual circumstances that established that protected status.
4. The conduct took place in the context of and was associated with an armed conflict not of an international character.	4. The conduct took place in the context of and was associated with an international armed conflict.
5. The perpetrator was aware of factual circumstances that established the existence of an armed conflict.	5. The perpetrator was aware of factual circumstances that established the existence of an armed conflict.

In 1998 in *Delalić* the ICTY Trial Chamber described the offence of cruel treatment as encompassing: 'all acts against a protected person which causes serious mental or physical suffering or injury, and which at the same time constitute a serious attack on human dignity.'[83] We can therefore ask whether an 'attack on human dignity' is a separate element to be proved. The State parties to the Rome Statute did not appear to consider it a separate requirement as the subsequent ICC Elements of Crimes require only 'severe physical or mental pain or suffering' (as shown in Table 8.5).

Thus cruel or inhuman treatment is a broad offence, and the same conduct could be charged under other heads. That is, according to the facts of the case, an offence of cruel treatment might also be charged as:

- torture (where there is a prohibited purpose); or
- the crime against humanity of inhumane acts (where there is a widespread or systematic attack).

Where this occurs, a conviction will only be entered for the most precise offence made out (i.e. the one with the more specific and detailed elements) and this

---

[83] *Delalić*, ICTY Trial Chamber, 16 November 1998, para 443.

conviction will subsume the lesser more general offence. Thus, a perpetrator could not be convicted of both torture and cruel treatment—as torture has more elements to prove it would subsume cruel treatment and a conviction would be entered only for torture. The point is discussed in more detail in Chapter 9.

8.6.6 **Hostage taking**

Table 8.6 Elements to be proven in respect of hostage taking

ICC Statutory Provisions and Elements	
NIAC	IAC
Article 8(2)(c)(iii): 'War crime of taking hostages'	Article 8(2)(a)(viii): 'War crime of taking hostages'
Elements: 1. The perpetrator seized, detained, or otherwise held hostage one or more persons. 2. The perpetrator threatened to kill, injure, or continue to detain such person or persons. 3. The perpetrator intended to compel a State, an international organization, a natural or legal person, or a group of persons to act or refrain from acting as an explicit or implicit condition for the safety or the release of such person or persons. 4. Such person or persons were either *hors de combat*, or were civilians, medical personnel, or religious personnel taking no active part in the hostilities. 5. The perpetrator was aware of the factual circumstances that established this status. 6. The conduct took place in the context of and was associated with an armed conflict not of an international character. 7. The perpetrator was aware of factual circumstances that established the existence of an armed conflict.	**Elements:** 1. The perpetrator seized, detained, or otherwise held hostage one or more persons. 2. The perpetrator threatened to kill, injure, or continue to detain such person or persons. 3. The perpetrator intended to compel a State, an international organization, a natural or legal person, or a group of persons to act or refrain from acting as an explicit or implicit condition for the safety or the release of such person or persons. 4. Such person or persons were protected under one or more of the Geneva Conventions of 1949. 5. The perpetrator was aware of the factual circumstances that established that protected status. 6. The conduct took place in the context of and was associated with an international armed conflict. 7. The perpetrator was aware of factual circumstances that established the existence of an armed conflict.

Under Article 34 of GC IV, '[t]he taking of hostages is prohibited.' The definition of the offence codified in the ICC Statute is, however, derived from the International Convention Against the Taking of Hostages 1979.[84] Article 1(1) of that Convention

---

[84] International Convention against the Taking of Hostages (adopted 17 December 1979, entered into force 17 December 1979) 1316 UNTS 206.

defines hostage taking as seizing or detaining a person and threatening 'to kill, to injure or to continue to detain' that person:

> in order to compel a third party, namely, a State, an international intergovernmental organization, a natural or juridical person, or a group of persons, to do or abstain from doing any act as an explicit or implicit condition for the [hostage's] release.

In *Blaškić*, Croatian forces detained over 2,000 local Muslims and threatened to kill them if a Bosnian Muslim military unit did not halt its advance. These facts were found to make out the offence of hostage taking. In discussing the applicable law the ICTY Trial Chamber noted that the defendant was charged with hostage taking during an IAC as a grave breach of the Geneva Conventions;[85] yet the law it examined was that of Common Article 3 applicable in NIACs.[86] This suggests that the applicable law is the same for both offences, an approach also taken by the ICC Elements of Crimes (see Table 8.6). *Blaškić* defined hostages as 'persons unlawfully deprived of their freedom, often wantonly and sometimes under threat of death' and noted that hostage taking required using detainees 'to obtain some advantage' or to force 'a belligerent, other person or other group of persons enter into some undertaking'.[87]

8.6.7 **Denial of fair trial rights**

Table 8.7 Elements to be proven in respect of denial of fair trial rights

ICC Statutory Provisions and Elements	
NIAC	IAC
Article 8(2)(c)(iv): 'War crime of sentencing or execution without due process'	Article 8(2)(a)(vi): 'War crime of denying a fair trial'
Elements: 1. The perpetrator passed sentence or executed one or more persons.	**Elements:** 1. The perpetrator deprived one or more persons of a fair and regular trial by denying judicial guarantees as defined, in particular, in the third and the fourth Geneva Conventions of 1949.
2. Such person or persons were either *hors de combat*, or were civilians, medical personnel, or religious personnel taking no active part in the hostilities. 3. The perpetrator was aware of the factual circumstances that established this status.	2. Such person or persons were protected under one or more of the Geneva Conventions of 1949. 3. The perpetrator was aware of the factual circumstances that established that protected status.

(Continued)

---

[85] *Blaškić*, ICTY Trial Chamber, 3 March 2000, para 158.
[86] Ibid, para 187.   [87] Ibid.

Table 8.7 Continued

ICC Statutory Provisions and Elements

NIAC	IAC
Article 8(2)(c)(iv): 'War crime of sentencing or execution without due process'	Article 8(2)(a)(vi): 'War crime of denying a fair trial'
4. There was no previous judgment pronounced by a court, or the court that rendered judgment was not 'regularly constituted', that is, it did not afford the essential guarantees of independence and impartiality, or the court that rendered judgment did not afford all other judicial guarantees generally recognized as indispensable under international law.	4. The conduct took place in the context of and was associated with an international armed conflict.
5. The perpetrator was aware of the absence of a previous judgment or of the denial of relevant guarantees and the fact that they are essential or indispensable to a fair trial.	5. The perpetrator was aware of factual circumstances that established the existence of an armed conflict.
6. The conduct took place in the context of and was associated with an armed conflict not of an international character.	
7. The perpetrator was aware of factual circumstances that established the existence of an armed conflict.	

As Table 8.7 shows, the essential difference between the two crimes is that the broader IAC offence does not require the imposition of a sentence or penalty.[88] Thus is a crime is committed if the trial is unfair, even if the victim is acquitted. The generally recognized essential elements of a fair trial for a defendant under either crime would include under the International Covenant on Civil and Political Rights (ICCPR):[89]

- the right to counsel (e.g. Article 14(3)(b), ICCPR);
- the right to be informed of the charges (e.g. Article 14(3)(a), ICCPR);
- the right to prepare a defence and present evidence and witnesses (e.g. Article 14(3)(b) and (e), ICCPR);
- the right to trial before an independent and impartial court (e.g. Article 14(1), ICCPR); and
- the right to an interpreter (e.g. Article 14(3)(f), ICCPR),[90]

[88] K Dörmann, *Elements of War Crimes under the Rome Statute of the International Criminal Court: Sources and Commentary* (Cambridge University Press 2003) 100.
[89] International Covenant on Civil and Political Rights (adopted 16 December 1966, entred into force 23 March 1976) 999 UNTS 171.
[90] See also: Dörmann, *Elements of War Crimes*, 104–5.

but a much longer and more detailed list could easily be offered of 'all other judicial guarantees generally recognized as indispensable under international law'.[91] Some of these rights and their implications for a fair trial were discussed in Chapter 6.

8.6.8 **Rape and other sexual violence**

Table 8.8 Elements to be proven in respect of rape and other sexual violence

ICC Statutory Provisions and Elements	
NIAC	IAC
Article 8(2)(e)(vi): 'Committing rape, sexual slavery, enforced prostitution, forced pregnancy…, enforced sterilization, and any other form of sexual violence also constituting a serious violation of article 3 common to the four Geneva Conventions'	Article 8(2)(b)(xxii): 'Committing rape, sexual slavery, enforced prostitution, forced pregnancy…, enforced sterilization, or any other form of sexual violence also constituting a grave breach of the Geneva Conventions'
Elements of rape: 1. The perpetrator invaded the body of a person by conduct resulting in penetration, however slight, of any part of the body of the victim or of the perpetrator with a sexual organ, or of the anal or genital opening of the victim with any object or any other part of the body. 2. The invasion was committed by force, or by threat of force or coercion, such as that caused by fear of violence, duress, detention, psychological oppression or abuse of power, against such person or another person, or by taking advantage of a coercive environment, or the invasion was committed against a person incapable of giving genuine consent. 3. The conduct took place in the context of and was associated with an armed conflict not of an international character. 4. The perpetrator was aware of factual circumstances that established the existence of an armed conflict.	**Elements of rape:** 1. The perpetrator invaded the body of a person by conduct resulting in penetration, however slight, of any part of the body of the victim or of the perpetrator with a sexual organ, or of the anal or genital opening of the victim with any object or any other part of the body. 2. The invasion was committed by force, or by threat of force or coercion, such as that caused by fear of violence, duress, detention, psychological oppression or abuse of power, against such person or another person, or by taking advantage of a coercive environment, or the invasion was committed against a person incapable of giving genuine consent. 3. The conduct took place in the context of and was associated with an international armed conflict. 4. The perpetrator was aware of factual circumstances that established the existence of an armed conflict.

[91] Dörmann, *Elements of War Crimes*, 410–38.

The crime of rape in international criminal law is discussed more extensively in the next chapter on crimes against humanity (in section 9.4.7). Only a brief account of the applicable law is offered here.

As Table 8.8 shows, under the ICC Elements of Crimes dealing with rape as a war crime it is noted that '[t]he concept of "invasion" is intended to be broad enough to be gender-neutral' and second that '[i]t is understood that a person may be incapable of giving genuine consent if affected by natural, induced or age-related incapacity.'[92] Two difficulties arise with this approach. First, the focus on 'invasion' or physical penetration may risk being quite narrow and may exclude other serious acts of a sexual nature. Second, the focus on consent requires the court to examine the mental state of the victim *and* the perpetrator: that is, it must be proved both that the victim did not consent and the perpetrator *knew* the victim did not consent. While this may be consistent with the common definitional of rape in national legal systems, no other international crime takes this approach and arguably it weakens the protection of 'protected persons' from sexual violence.[93]

On the first question of narrowness of definition, in *Stakić* an ICTY Trial Chamber suggested that international criminal law should address 'all serious abuses of a sexual nature inflicted upon the integrity of a person by means of coercion, threat of force, or intimidation in a way that is humiliating and degrading to the victim's dignity.'[94] Such an approach would have had the advantage of providing a general offence of sexual violence focussed on the conduct of the perpetrator and not the consent of the victim. However, the ICTY has generally taken a narrower approach more in line with the ICC Statute definition of rape.[95] To some extent the ICC Statute addresses this concern by listing other offences as well, including 'sexual slavery, enforced prostitution, forced pregnancy,... enforced sterilization, or any other form of sexual violence also constituting a grave breach of the Geneva Conventions'. In particular, the offence of 'other forms of sexual violence' may have a breadth comparable to the *Stakić* approach. The requirement in the ICC Statute that other serious sexual violence also constitute a violation of Common Article 3 or a grave breach of the Geneva Conventions should be easily satisfied as rape could also be charged as cruel or inhuman treatment (as rape inherently involves severe physical or mental suffering and will always suffice for the *actus reus* of torture).[96]

As regards the lack of consent of the victim, the approach in ICTY case law has been to hold that '[t]he Prosecution can prove non-consent beyond reasonable doubt by proving the existence of coercive circumstances under which meaningful consent

---

[92] Art 8, nn 50–51 and 62–63, ICC Elements of Crimes.
[93] See generally: P Weiner, 'The Evolving Jurisprudence of the Crime of Rape in International Criminal Law' (2013) 36 Boston College International & Comparative Law Review 1207.
[94] *Stakić*, ICTY Trial Chamber, 31 July 2003, para 757.
[95] *Kunarac*, ICTY Appeals Chamber, 12 June 2002, para 127.
[96] Ibid, paras 149–52; and as discussed in Chapter 9, section 9.4.7.

is not possible'.[97] The use of force against the victim is not a requirement *per se*, but where it is present it will prove the absence of consent.[98] Similarly, the ICC Elements of Crimes generally require for all sexual offences that the prohibited conduct: 'was committed by force, or by threat of force or coercion, such as that caused by fear of violence, duress, detention, psychological oppression or abuse of power, against such person or another person, or by taking advantage of a coercive environment, or... [the sexual conduct was] against a person incapable of giving genuine consent.' The question of consent in the law applicable to the crime of rape is further discussed in Chapter 9, section 9.4.7.

As noted above the ICC Statute and Elements of Crimes also specifically elaborate separate crimes of sexual slavery, enforced prostitution, forced pregnancy and enforced sterilization. There will often be overlap between these specific offences and rape. While this might suggest a single offence of serious sexual violence would be preferable, there is merit to creating individual crimes in each case given that these are undoubtedly serious crimes to which women historically have been—and continue to be—subjected during armed conflicts. Such precise offences serve an expressive function: they make clear that the international community condemns all forms of sexual violence during war. There is, however, always a potential 'dark side to detailed codification': the risk that detailed enumeration of multiple 'gender crimes' may create more 'loopholes' for skilled defence lawyers to argue over.[99]

8.6.9 Direct attacks upon the civilian population

Table 8.9 Elements to be proven in respect of direct attacks upon the civilian population

ICC Statutory Provisions and Elements	
NIAC	IAC
Article 8(2)(e)(i): 'Intentionally directing attacks against the civilian population as such or against individual civilians not taking direct part in hostilities'	Article 8(2)(b)(i): 'Intentionally directing attacks against the civilian population as such or against individual civilians not taking direct part in hostilities'
Elements:	**Elements:**
1. The perpetrator directed an attack.	1. The perpetrator directed an attack.
2. The object of the attack was a civilian population as such or individual civilians not taking direct part in hostilities.	2. The object of the attack was a civilian population as such or individual civilians not taking direct part in hostilities.

(Continued)

---

[97] *Gacumbitsi*, ICTR Appeals Chamber, 7 July 2006, para 155.

[98] *Kunarac*, ICTY Appeals Chamber, 12 June 2002, para 129.

[99] W Schabas, *An Introduction to the International Criminal Court*, 4th ed (Cambridge University Press 2011) 126.

Table 8.9 Continued

ICC Statutory Provisions and Elements

NIAC	IAC
Article 8(2)(e)(i): 'Intentionally directing attacks against the civilian population as such or against individual civilians not taking direct part in hostilities'	Article 8(2)(b)(i): 'Intentionally directing attacks against the civilian population as such or against individual civilians not taking direct part in hostilities'
3. The perpetrator intended the civilian population as such or individual civilians not taking direct part in hostilities to be the object of the attack. 4. The conduct took place in the context of and was associated with an armed conflict not of an international character. 5. The perpetrator was aware of factual circumstances that established the existence of an armed conflict.	3. The perpetrator intended the civilian population as such or individual civilians not taking direct part in hostilities to be the object of the attack. 4. The conduct took place in the context of and was associated with an international armed conflict. 5. The perpetrator was aware of factual circumstances that established the existence of an armed conflict.

As shown in Table 8.9, this is precisely the same crime in IACs and NIACs. It embodies the principle of distinction (as discussed above): the basic proposition being that neither the civilian population itself (nor civilian morale) are legitimate military objectives.[100] The requirement is that civilians are the object of the attack *as such*: incidental civilian casualties are not prohibited.

Excessive civilian casualties will constitute a violation of the principle of proportionality in both NIACs and IACs. However, the ICC Statute only expressly criminalizes attacks contrary to the principle of proportionality in IACs, as detailed below.

 Example

Gotovina et al, ICTY Trial Chamber and Appeals Chamber

Gotovina et al[101] concerned crimes against the Serbian civilian population of the Krajina region of the former Yugoslavia allegedly committed by Croatian forces. In part, the case concerned evidence of indiscriminate shelling of towns which, if accepted, could show an intention to attack the civilian population as such. The Trial Chamber conducted an 'impact analysis' of shell fire on four towns and took it to be a reasonable inference that any shell falling within 200 metres of a legitimate target was intended to hit that target. After 'subtracting' such shell damage, on review of the rest of the evidence, the Trial Chamber was convinced that there was evidence that the

---

[100] Fenrick, 'Targeting and Proportionality', 497.
[101] *Gotovina et al*, ICTY Trial Chamber, 15 April 2011 and ICTY Appeals Chamber, 16 November 2012.

towns themselves were the object of attack—as so many shells appeared to have been directed at areas containing no military targets.

On appeal, however, the Appeals Chamber found that the Trial Chamber did not explain how it had derived the '200 metre standard' and that its application excluded the possibility of fire upon 'mobile targets of opportunity' such as tanks or trucks. It therefore found the Trial Chamber had not sufficiently justified its conclusions and that this was a sufficiently serious error as to invalidate its analysis of the facts. The Appeals Chamber decision was controversial because it neither specified what it thought the correct standard to be nor did it conduct a complete review of the evidence in the case de novo.[102] It simply quashed the Trial Chamber's findings.

One might have some sympathy for the Trial Chamber's approach, which could have been thought to generously discount rocket fire which was plausibly aimed at a legitimate target before assessing the rest of the evidence.

Consider also whether the same pattern of facts could have supported a conclusion that this was an attack contrary to the principle of proportionality.

8.6.10 Attacks contrary to the principle of proportionality (IAC)

Table 8.10 Elements to be proven in respect of attacks contrary to the principle of proportionality and relevant provisions of Additional Protocol I to the Geneva Conventions 1949

Comparison of API and ICC Statute and Elements	
AP I Provisions (relevant to interpreting the ICC offence)	ICC Statutory Provisions and Elements (applicable in IACs only)
Article 57(2)(a)(iii): 'those who plan or decide upon an attack shall…refrain from deciding to launch any attack which may be expected to cause incidental loss of civilian life, injury to civilians, damage to civilian objects, or a combination thereof, which would be excessive in relation to the concrete and direct military advantage anticipated'	Article 8(2)(b)(iv): 'Intentionally launching an attack in the knowledge that such attack will cause incidental loss of life or injury to civilians or damage to civilian objects or widespread, long-term and severe damage to the natural environment which would be clearly excessive in relation to the concrete and direct overall military advantage anticipated'
See also: Article 51(5)(b), AP I – such attacks are also prohibited as indiscriminate;	**Elements:** 1. The perpetrator launched an attack.

(Continued)

---

[102] See: M Milanovic, 'The Gotovina Omnishambles', EJIL: Talk!, 18 November 2012, www.ejiltalk.org/the-gotovina-omnishambles; JN Clark, 'Courting Controversy: the ICTY's Acquittal of Croatian Generals Gotovina and Markac' (2013) 11 Journal of International Criminal Justice 399.

Table 8.10 Continued

Comparison of API and ICC Statute and Elements

AP I Provisions (relevant to interpreting the ICC offence)	ICC Statutory Provisions and Elements (applicable in IACs only)
Article 57(2)(a)(iii): 'those who plan or decide upon an attack shall…refrain from deciding to launch any attack which may be expected to cause incidental loss of civilian life, injury to civilians, damage to civilian objects, or a combination thereof, which would be excessive in relation to the concrete and direct military advantage anticipated'	Article 8(2)(b)(iv): 'Intentionally launching an attack in the knowledge that such attack will cause incidental loss of life or injury to civilians or damage to civilian objects or widespread, long-term and severe damage to the natural environment which would be clearly excessive in relation to the concrete and direct overall military advantage anticipated'
Article 57(2)(b), AP I – if it becomes apparent an attack is having such effects it must be cancelled; and	2. The attack was such that it would cause incidental death or injury to civilians or damage to civilian objects or widespread, long-term and severe damage to the natural environment and that such death, injury or damage would be of such an extent as to be clearly excessive in relation to the concrete and direct overall military advantage anticipated.
Article 85(3)(b), AP I – 'launching an indiscriminate attack affecting the civilian population or civilian objects in the knowledge that such attack will cause excessive loss of life [etc]' is a grave breach of AP I to which the grave breaches regime of the GCs apply.	3. The perpetrator knew that the attack would cause incidental death or injury to civilians or damage to civilian objects or widespread, long-term and severe damage to the natural environment and that such death, injury or damage would be of such an extent as to be clearly excessive in relation to the concrete and direct overall military advantage anticipated. 4. The conduct took place in the context of and was associated with an international armed conflict. 5. The perpetrator was aware of factual circumstances that established the existence of an armed conflict.

The principle of proportionality is profoundly important to protecting civilians in times of armed conflict; it is also very difficult to apply in practice. Robinson notes that weighing military advantage against civilian casualties will be particularly difficult under conditions of war, where outcomes are uncertain, and decisions must be taken with urgency. Further, the comparison is 'even more challenging' given that military advantage and civilian damage 'are entirely unlike properties with no common unit of measurement'.[103] That is, no precise formula can tell us that so much military advantage justifies this number of civilian deaths. A 'human rights lawyer and an experienced combat commander' are 'unlikely to assign the same relative values to military advantage and injury to non-combatants'; indeed, military commanders with different national backgrounds, training, and levels of experience may disagree 'in close cases'.[104] This, in part at least, may explain the relative rareness of prosecutions for excessive civilian damage.[105] Further, the requirement that such damage be 'clearly excessive' indicates a considerable margin of appreciation is left to armed forces.[106] We should also carefully bear in mind that the fact of civilian casualties proves nothing of itself. Even a pattern of high levels of civilian death or injury over the course of a military campaign will generally only be prima facie evidence of violations of the principle of proportionality. A contextual assessment of individual attacks, and possibly of the campaign as a whole, will always be necessary. Civilian casualties may result from a lawful attack because of:

- intelligence errors (the wrong target was hit);
- weapons malfunctions;
- the right target being hit and proportionate collateral damage resulting;
- weapons hitting the wrong target because of enemy intervention (e.g. 'aircraft being shot down or missiles deflected by countermeasures'); or
- the right target being hit but the presence of civilians not being known at the time.[107]

Whether these are acceptable reasons for civilian casualties may be contextually dependent. If, for example, over the course of a military campaign it becomes apparent that a particular weapon system has a high failure rate then its use against legitimate targets near civilian population centres may no longer be acceptable. Similarly, intelligence failures leading to accidental civilian deaths will not be acceptable if only cursory attempts at proper target identification were conducted.

Military advantage

The ICC Elements define 'concrete and direct overall military advantage' as referring to 'a military advantage that is foreseeable by the perpetrator at the relevant time.'[108] The advantage foreseen need not be 'temporally or geographically related to the object of the attack':[109] that is, striking at a particular target here and now may produce a military advantage elsewhere and later.

[103] Robinson, 'War Crimes' in Cryer et al, *Introduction*, 3rd ed, 294.

[104] Fenrick, 'Targeting and Proportionality', 497.

[105] H Durham, and T McCormack, 'Aerial Bombardment of Civilians: The Current International Legal Framework' in Y Tanaka and MB Young, *Bombing Civilians: A Twentieth-Century History* (New Press 2009), Chapter 10.

[106] Robinson, 'War Crimes' in Cryer et al, *Introduction*, 3rd ed, 294.

[107] Fenrick, 'Targeting and Proportionality', 499–500.

[108] Art 8(2)(b)(iv), n 36, ICC Elements of Crimes.   [109] Ibid.

Mental element

In the context of this crime, the ICC Elements (as in Table 8.10) require: 'that the perpe-trator make the value judgment as described therein. An evaluation of that value judg-ment must be based on the requisite information available to the perpetrator at the time.' Bothe suggests this approach is 'highly problematic' and risks making the perpetrator 'the judge in his own cause': it seems to suggest that if the perpetrator did not think the attack was excessive, he or she cannot be convicted.[110] On this basis, Robinson suggests 'there are grave reasons to doubt its compatibility with general principles and hence the ICC Statute' and that the Court might disregard it (that is, the ICC is only obliged to fol-low the Elements of Crimes to the extent they are compatible with the ICC Statute).[111]

We should not lose sight however of the fact that there is a legal obligation to conduct such an assessment[112] and a court is not obliged to accept a defendant's account of his or her own mental state if it is wholly incredible. That is, if a defendant suggests they mis-takenly concluded damage would not be disproportionate a court could nonetheless reject such an explanation if it 'did not have an air of reality to it.'[113] Similarly, Dörmann also notes that on certain facts, where there is clearly excessive injury, a defendant's suggestion that he/she had concluded the damage would not be excessive would lack credibility. The Court could then infer the required mental element 'based on that lack of credibility.'[114]

Further, Dörmann suggests that during the negotiation of the ICC Elements of Crimes there was agreement among States that this definition should not lead to 'exon-erating a reckless perpetrator' who conducted no evaluation of possible incidental damage or injury and whether it would be excessive.[115] Indeed, during the negotiations it was argued 'that by refusing to evaluate the relationship between military advantage and the incidental damage ... he/she has made the value judgment required.'[116]

8.7 Corresponding offences between IACs and NIACs in the ICC Statute

Table 8.11 Corresponding offences between IACs and NIACs in the ICC Statute

Offence	NIAC	IAC	Notes
Common Article 3			
Murder	Art 8(2)(c)(i)	Art 8(2)(a)(i) ['wilful killing']	

(Continued)

---

[110] Bothe, 'War Crimes', 400.
[111] Robinson, 'War Crimes' in Cryer et al, *Introduction*, 3rd ed, 297.
[112] Art 57(2)(ii) and (iii), AP I; and see Fenrick, 'Targeting and Proportionality', 498.
[113] W Schabas, *Introduction*, 4th ed, 242.   [114] Dörmann, Elements of War Crimes, 165.
[115] Ibid.   [116] Ibid.

Table 8.11 Continued

Offence	NIAC	IAC	Notes
Mutilation	Art 8(2)(c)(i)	Art 8(2)(b)(x)	Art 8(2)(b)(x) covers mutilation along with medical experiments
Cruel treatment	Art 8(2)(c)(i)	Art 8(2)(a)(ii) ['inhuman treatment']	Art 8(2)(a)(ii) also covers torture and experiments
Hostage taking	Art 8(2)(c)(iii)	Art 8(2)(a)(viii)	
Executions without due process	Art 8(2)(c)(iv)	Art 8(2)(a)(vi)	Art 8(2)(a)(vi) also concerns fair trials more generally.
Outrages upon personal dignity (including rape)	Art 8(2)(c)(ii)	Art 8(2)(b)(xxi)	See also: 'sexual violence', below.
Prohibited methods of warfare			
Direct attacks on civilian population and individuals not taking part in hostilities	Art 8(2)(e)(i)	Art 8(2)(b)(i)	
- use of human shields	?	Art 8(2)(b)(xxiii)	
- deliberate starvation	?	Art 8(2)(b)(xxv)	
Attacks contrary to the principle of proportionality	?	Art 8(2)(b)(iv)	
Direct attacks on civilian objects	?	Art 8(2)(b)(ii)	
Direct attacks on undefended buildings	?	Art 8(2)(b)(v)	
Treacherous killing or wounding	Art 8(2)(e)(ix)	Art 8(2)(b)(xi)	
Ordering that there shall be no survivors	Art 8(2)(e)(x)	Art 8(2)(b)(xii)	
Destruction of property not 'imperatively demanded by the necessities of war/conflict'	Art 8(2)(e)(xii)	Art 8(2)(b)(xiii)	
Attacks on specially protected persons/objects			
Attacks against marked medical personnel, units and transport	Art 8(2)(e)(ii)	Art 8(2)(b)(xxiv)	
Attacks against humanitarian or peacekeeping missions	Art 8(2)(e)(iii)	Art 8(2)(b)(iii)	
Direct attacks on civilian objects 'dedicated to religion, education, art, science or charitable purposes, historic monuments, [and] hospitals'.	Art 8(2)(e)(iv)	Art 8(2)(b)(ix)	

(Continued)

Table 8.11 Continued

Offence	NIAC	IAC	Notes
Human rights violations			
Mutilation and medical/ scientific experiments	Art 8(2)(e)(xi)	Art 8(2)(b)(x)	Note also overlap with Art 8(2)(a) (ii) ('inhuman treatment')
Sexual violence	Art 8(2)(e)(vi)	Art 8(2)(b)(xxii)	
Conscripting or enlisting children	Art 8(2)(e)(vii)	Art 8(2)(b)(xxvi)	
Displacement of the civilian population	Art 8(2)(e)(viii)	Art 8(2)(b)(viii)	
Pillage	Art 8(2)(e)(v)	Art 8(2)(b)(xvi)	
Extensive destruction/ appropriation of property	?	Art 2(a)(iv)	
Unnecessary seizure or destruction of property	?	Art 8(2)(b)(xiii)	
Other offences found only in international conflict			
Wilfully causing (1) great suffering or (2) injury to body or health	?	Art 8(2)(a)(iii)	Note possible overlap with Art 8(2)(a) (ii) ('inhuman treatment')
Compelled service	?	Arts 8(2)(a)(v) and 8(2)(b)(iv)	
Deprivation of fair trial rights; declarations limiting access to courts	?	Arts 8(2)(a)(vi); 8(2)(b)(xiv)	
Unlawful deportation, transfer or confinement	?	Art 8(2)(a)(vi)	Note overlap with Art 8(2)(b)(viii) ('displacement of civilian population')
Killing or wounding a combatant who has surrendered	?	Art 8(2)(b)(vi)	
Improper use of symbols and uniforms	?	Art 8(2)(b)(vii)	
Use of prohibited weapons	?	Arts 8(2)(b)(vii)-(xx)	

Table 8.11 shows corresponding offences between IACs and NIACs in the ICC Statute.[117] Note that offences marked '?' have no obvious equivalent in a NIAC.

---

[117] The categories used in this table are largely drawn from Bothe, 'War Crimes'.

Pause for reflection

How would you apply the law to the following scenario?

Alpha is a military commander in the State of Entropia which is engaged in fighting an organized armed group. The armed group is led by Zeta. The armed group retreats across the border into the State of Dystopia.

Zeta orders his men to split up into small three–five man units and to hide among the population of Dystopia city. Zeta's men use small mortars and rockets to make a sustained attack on Alpha's troops in Entropia. Alpha is told by a helicopter surveillance team that most of the mortar shells originate from an apartment block roof. The helicopter drops leaflets on the neighbourhood warning residents to leave.

Alpha orders three heavy mortar shells to be fired at the tower-block roof. One misses by 300 metres, one by 100 metres and one destroys the top five floors of the tower block. The shells that miss cause 10 casualties, and the hit on the tower-block kills 20 people. It is later found that the mortar position was elsewhere.

Consider whether Alpha or Zeta may be guilty of war crimes.

8.8 Summary and conclusions

By this stage the following general principles are, hopefully, obvious:

- the law of war crimes draws on a number of key principles from the law of armed conflict including the idea of 'protected persons' during hostilities and the basic principles of legitimate military objectives, target differentiation, and proportionality;

- the laws of armed conflict have a long and complex history, but it remains clear that there is a key distinction between international and non-international armed conflicts (IACs and NIACs) of continuing legal significance;

- IACs are essentially conflicts between States (for which there is no threshold of violence); NIACs involve 'protracted' violence between 'organized armed groups' or between a State and an organized armed group;

- the distinction between IACs and NIACs remains important because historically States were reluctant to extend the law applicable in IACs to NIACs;

- while the gap between the two bodies of law has closed to some extent, they have not completely converged: the law of NIACs remains a subset of the law of IACs;

- irrespective of whether we are discussing the law of NIACs or IACs it is important to remember that *not every breach of the law of armed conflict is a crime*—for example, attacks inflicting disproportionate civilian damage are prohibited in both IACs and NIACs but there is only an applicable crime in the case of IACs under the ICC Statute.

In applying the law of war crimes you should always recall that:

- because of the difference in applicable law it may be important to classify a conflict as an IAC or a NIAC before proceeding to consider what crimes may have been committed (although Common Article 3 offences will always apply in both types of conflict);

- the contextual element of war crimes requires that the existence of an armed conflict must play a substantial role in a perpetrator's ability or decision to commit the crime or the manner in or purpose for which it was committed (*Kunarac*);

- the perpetrator need not be a military official, a civilian may commit a war crime (*Akayesu*) but the perpetrator must still be closely linked to a party to the conflict (*Engister*).

In considering where or if alleged war crimes may be prosecuted it is important to recall the limitations on the jurisdiction (and resources) of the ICC as discussed in Chapter 4. Even if a State party to the ICC Statute has passed a modern war crimes law reflecting the ICC Statute offences, that is no guarantee it will assert universal jurisdiction over the offences of foreign nationals committed on foreign territory (see Chapter 4). Only the grave breaches provisions of the Geneva Conventions applicable in IACs expressly require States to seek out and either prosecute or extradite persons suspected of having committed those offences.[118]

Useful further reading

M Bothe, 'War Crimes' in A Cassese, *The Rome Statute of the International Criminal Court: A Commentary* (Oxford University Press 2002), Vol. 1.
An excellent and concise treatment of the crimes found in the ICC Statute.

A Cassese, 'The *Nicaragua* and *Tadić* Tests Revisited in Light of the ICJ Judgment on Genocide in Bosnia' (2007) 18 European Journal of International Law 649.
In this article Cassese argued against the distinction between 'overall control' in the ICTY case law and 'effective control' under the ICJ approach.

E Crawford, 'Unequal before the Law: The Case for the Elimination of the Distinction between International and Non-international Armed Conflicts' (2007) 20 Leiden Journal of International Law 441.
A useful treatment of the continuing legal distinction between IACs and NIACs and its consequences.

K Dörmann, *Elements of War Crimes under the Rome Statute of the International Criminal Court: Sources and Commentary* (Cambridge University Press 2003).
An authoritative and incredibly useful book prepared under the auspices of the International Committee of the Red Cross. It covers the drafting history of each set of elements of crimes as well as their relationship to relevant international treaty law and case law.

R Kolb and R Hyde, *An Introduction to the International Law of Armed Conflicts* (Hart Publishing 2008), Chapters 10 and 32.
This book provides an accessible introduction to LOAC more generally. The recommended chapters examine the concept of, and law applicable, in NIACs.

---

[118] Essentially being those listed in Art 8(2)(a), ICC Statute.

9

Crimes against humanity

9.1 Introduction

The first prosecution for crimes against humanity occurred before the Nuremberg International Military Tribunal (IMT) in 1945–46. Under Article 6(c) of the London Charter the Nuremberg IMT had jurisdiction over crimes against humanity. An obvious inspiration for including such a crime in the Charter was the use of the term 'crimes against civilization and humanity' in the 1915 Joint Declaration of France, Great Britain and Russia in condemning the massacre of Armenians in Turkey during the First World War.[1]

Following the First World War, the Allies established a 15 member panel, the Commission on the Responsibility of the Authors of the War to consider the possibility of war crimes trials. The Commission recommended that there be trials for both war crimes and crimes against humanity. However, at the time the US took the view that 'crimes against humanity' was too vague and uncertain a concept to found criminal prosecutions and no such prosecutions occurred.[2]

The 1915 Joint Declaration is thus a weak historical precedent, and the modern law must be taken to commence with the Nuremberg IMT (and to a lesser extent the Tokyo IMT for the Far East). In drafting the offence,[3] the Allies had two concerns:

- the need for an offence that covered crimes against the civilian population in Germany (such crimes committed in occupied territories would be war crimes); and

- creating a link between crimes against humanity and other war-related offences (either war crimes or aggression) in the IMT Charter.

---

[1] Hundreds of thousands of Armenians were killed in Turkey in 1915–1917. For a detailed historical account see: VN Dadrian, 'Genocide as a Problem of National and International Law: The World War I Armenian Case and Its Contemporary Legal Ramifications' (1989) 14 Yale Journal of International Law 221, 255–278.

[2] A Cassese et al, *Cassese's International Criminal Law*, 3rd ed (Oxford University Press 2013) 85; B Van Schaack, 'The Definition of Crimes against Humanity: Resolving the Incoherence' (1998–1999) 37 Columbia Journal of Transnational Law 787, 797.

[3] The term 'crimes against humanity' was chosen at the suggestion of Cambridge scholar Hersch Lauterpacht. See: M Koskenniemi, 'Hersch Lauterpacht and the Development of International Criminal Law' (2004) 2 Journal of International Criminal Justice 810.

The link to other offences was seen as necessary for at least two reasons. First, international law had previously placed few limitations on what States could do to their own nationals; thus, the 'exercise of international jurisdiction over acts committed by Germans against other Germans' was considered an extraordinary innovation and a considerable incursion into State sovereignty.[4] The 'war link' helped limit the scope of crimes against humanity to situations where the offences had some impact on other States and therefore some international dimension.[5] Second, concerns that this was a novel crime, being retrospectively applied may also help explain the desire to 'link' crimes against humanity with the clearly established category of war crimes.[6]

 Learning aims

By the end of this chapter you should be able to:

- identify how the definition of a crime against humanity has evolved through the statutory law of the major tribunals;

- discuss the contextual element of the offence, including whether the attack must be both 'widespread and systematic' or simply 'widespread or systematic';

- define the main prohibited acts that may form part of a crime against humanity and their elements; and

- discuss or explain some of the historical and theoretical reasons which justify having crimes against humanity as a separate category from war crimes and genocide.

Given the learning aims, the rest of this chapter concerns the definition of crimes against humanity, its underlying offences, and some of the historical and theoretical issues surrounding the offence. The chapter is structured as follows:

- Section 9.2 outlines the evolution of the legal definition of crimes against humanity.

- Section 9.3 deals with the 'contextual element' of the offence.

- Section 9.4 considers the prohibited acts that may form the conduct underlying a crime against humanity, with the exception of the complex crime of persecution.

- Section 9.5 examines the crime of persecution (which, as noted, though it logically forms part of the material covered in 9.4 has been given a separate section for convenience).

---

[4] B. Van Schaack, 'The Definition of Crimes against Humanity', 791 and 798–807; see also G Boas, JL Bischoff, and NL Reid, *International Criminal Law Practitioner Library*, vol 2 (Cambridge University Press 2009) 24.

[5] Cassese et al, *International Criminal Law*, 86. Cynically, one may also suggest that absent such a restriction the Allies could have faced difficulties regarding the treatment of their own national minorities or colonies.

[6] Ibid, 87; Boas, Bischoff, and Reid, *Practitioner Library*, vol. 2, 25.

- Section 9.6 re-considers the question *why* should there be a separate category of crimes against humanity?

9.2 The evolution of the definition of crimes against humanity

Almost uniquely, the concept of crimes against humanity is one which has evolved through the statutes of international criminal tribunals (and Control Council Law No. 10). It is therefore useful to review the definitions in historical order. While there has never been a subject-specific treaty defining crimes against humanity and affirming the responsibilities of State to prevent and punish such crimes, in 2013 the International Law Commission (ILC) placed the issue on its agenda.[7] It has not, however, commenced work on the subject and a specialized treaty on point still seems a distant prospect.

9.2.1 The Nuremberg IMT Charter

The definition of crimes against humanity found in Article 6(c) of IMT Charter is:

> murder, extermination, enslavement, deportation, and other inhumane acts committed against any civilian population, before or during the war, or persecutions on political, racial or religious grounds in execution of or in connection with any crime within the jurisdiction of the Tribunal, whether or not in violation of the domestic law of the country where perpetrated.

The words 'in execution of or in connection with any crime within the jurisdiction of the Tribunal' (i.e. aggression or war crimes) were read as a limitation applying to the whole list of underlying offences ('the nexus requirement'). The inclusion of this nexus requirement provided the limitation on the scope of the crime desired by the Allies in drafting the Charter. That said, crimes against humanity under this definition could still have occurred 'before or during the war' so long as there was a connection with the war. The IMT, however, entered no convictions for crimes against humanity committed before the outbreak of the war.[8]

The words 'whether or not in violation of the domestic law of the country where perpetrated' reflect the fact that the Nazi regime changed the laws of Germany to permit many of its actions, and the US acknowledged that the extent to which Nazi outrages in the period 1933–1939 'may have been in violation of German law, as changed by the Nazis, is doubtful'.[9]

---

[7] See the ILC website: http://legal.un.org/ilc/.

[8] On the surprising ground it had been presented with no evidence such crimes were committed: Cassese et al, *International Criminal Law*, 87–88.

[9] See Memorandum to President Roosevelt from the Secretaries of State and War and the Attorney General, January 22, 1945 ('The Yalta Memorandum'), as discussed in Chapter 3, section 3.3.3.

9.2.2 **Allied Control Council Law No. 10**

As noted in Chapter 3, Control Council Law No. 10 was the law passed by the Allies as the occupying powers of Germany passed in 1945 allowing the occupying authorities (France, the Soviet Union, the UK, and the US) to conduct war crimes trials in their various zones of control. Control Council Law No. 10 had a slightly different formulation of crimes against humanity from that of the Nuremberg Charter:

> Atrocities and offenses, including but not limited to murder, extermination, enslavement, deportation, imprisonment, torture, rape, or other inhumane acts committed against any civilian population, or persecutions on political, racial or religious grounds whether or not in violation of the domestic laws of the country where perpetrated.

Notably, there are two main differences between the Control Council Law No. 10 definition of crimes against humanity and the IMT Charter definition. First, there is no limiting nexus requirement that the offences must be connected with war crimes or aggression; and second, imprisonment, torture, and rape are expressly added to the list of underlying offences.

9.2.3 **The Statute of the International Criminal Tribunal for the former Yugoslavia**

As was also discussed in Chapter 3, the International Criminal Tribunal for the former Yugoslavia (ICTY) was established as a subsidiary organ of the UN Security Council in 1993 in response to the Yugoslavian wars of dissolution of the early 1990s. These conflicts were characterized by large-scale criminal conduct against civilians, including sexual offences and various crimes of persecution, forced deportation, and murder described as 'ethnic cleansing'. In this context, Article 5 of the ICTY Statute defined crimes against humanity as:

> the following crimes when committed in armed conflict, whether international or internal in character, and directed against any civilian population: (a) murder; (b) extermination; (c) enslavement; (d) deportation; (e) imprisonment; (f) torture; (g) rape; (h) persecutions on political, racial and religious grounds; (i) other inhumane acts.

The main difference to note is that while adopting the Control Council Law No. 10 list of underlying or covered offences, the ICTY Statute retains something close to the Nuremberg IMT requirement that the offences have a nexus to an armed conflict.

9.2.4 **The International Criminal Tribunal for Rwanda**

As discussed in Chapter 3, the International Criminal Tribunal for Rwanda (ICTR) was created by the UN Security Council in 1994 as response to the genocidal massacres of Tutsis by Hutus in Rwanda in that same year and shared a close connection with the ICTY (having the same Appeals Chamber and, until 2003, the same

Prosecutor). While the events of 1994 did not directly involve an armed conflict,[10] they were preceded by campaigns by factions within the Hutu majority to expel Tutsis from Rwanda, resulting in conflicts with an armed Tutsi resistance in 1990–1993. In this context, Article 3 of the ICTR Statute defined crimes against humanity as:

> the following crimes when committed as part of a widespread or systematic attack against any civilian population on national, political, ethnic, racial or religious grounds: (a) murder; (b) extermination; (c) enslavement; (d) deportation; (e) imprisonment; (f) torture; (g) rape; (h) persecutions on political, racial and religious grounds; (i) other inhumane acts.

Notably, under this definition the ICTR Statute requires no nexus to an armed conflict (as there was not one occurring at the time of the 1994 genocide), but introduces two new requirements:

- a contextual requirement that the underlying offences were 'committed as part of a widespread or systematic attack against any civilian population'; and
- a requirement that the underlying offences were committed with a discriminatory motive (i.e. that the population was attacked 'on national, political, ethnic, racial or religious grounds').

Otherwise, the list of covered offences is the same as that found in both the ICTY Statute and Control Council Law No. 10.

9.2.5 Key issues under the ICTR and ICTY Statutes

If we are trying to establish the definition of crimes against humanity as a matter of customary or general international law, the differences in the definition of the offence between the ICTY and ICTR Statutes might be thought significant. Following the discussion above it should be clear that the major questions are whether the definition of crimes against humanity:

- requires a nexus to an armed conflict; and/or
- requires a contextual element of a 'widespread or systematic attack against any civilian population'; and/or
- requires that the underlying offence be committed with a discriminatory motive?

The question of the requirement that the offence be committed as part of a 'widespread or systematic attack' is returned to at 9.3. The other issues will be dealt with briefly here.

9.2.6 No nexus to an armed conflict is required

Despite the wording of the ICTY Statute, the ICTY Appeals Chamber found in 1995 that 'customary international law no longer requires any nexus between crimes against

---

[10] The definition of international and non-international armed conflict was discussed in Chapter 8, section 8.3.

humanity and armed conflict' and that Article 5 was intended by the Security Council to 'reintroduce' this nexus requirement only for the purposes of the ICTY.[11] (This presumably reflects the role of armed conflict in the former Yugoslavia in the decision to establish the Tribunal.) In reaching this conclusion the ICTY looked to Control Council Law No. 10, the ICTR Statute, and the International Law Commission's 1996 draft Code of Crimes Against the Peace and Security of Mankind. In addition the Secretary General's report that led to the ICTY's creation had concluded that: 'Crimes against humanity are aimed at any civilian population and are prohibited regardless of whether they are committed in an armed conflict, international or internal in character'.[12] This approach was borne out in the negotiation of the ICC Statute, which also rejects the need for any nexus with an armed conflict.

9.2.7 No discriminatory motive required

Again the discriminatory motive requirement was found to be a requirement applying uniquely under the ICTR Statute, despite the fact it was also found in some national (French and Canadian) case law.[13] The ICTY Appeals Chamber in *Tadić* reasoned as follows:

- *none* of the basic textual definitions in the London Charter of the IMT, the Charter of the Tokyo IMT, and in Control Council Law No. 10 contained a discriminatory motive requirement;
- these texts form the basis or origin of the customary law rule;
- adding a discriminatory motive requirement would *narrow* the customary law rule;
- to accept that customary law had changed and become more restricted, 'uncontroverted evidence would be needed' in the form of judicial decisions and consistent State practice (which it found lacking, despite some national case law); and
- the ILC's draft Code of Crimes Against the Peace and Security of Mankind and the ICC Statute both rejected any discriminatory motive requirement.[14]

The last point is particularly convincing. If the 147 States involved in drafting the ICC Statute (or the 120 which voted in favour of the final text) had believed as a matter of *opinio juris* that a discriminatory motive was a customary international

---

[11] *Tadić*, ICTY Appeals Chamber, Appeal on Jurisdiction, 2 October 1995, para 78.

[12] 'Report of the Secretary General pursuant to paragraph 2 of Security Council Resolution 808' (3 May 1993), para 47, available at: www.icty.org/sections/LegalLibrary/StatuteoftheTribunal.

[13] See the discussion of the historical development of the crime in *Akayesu*, ICTR Trial Chamber, 2 September 1998, paras 563–77. In particular, the Supreme Court of Canada held that: 'with respect to crimes against humanity the additional element is that the inhumane acts were based on discrimination against or the persecution of an identifiable group of people' (*R v Finta* [1994] 1 SCR 701, 813). See also footnote 350 in *Tadić*, ICTY Appeals Chamber, 15 July 1999.

[14] *Tadić*, ICTY Appeals Chamber, 15 July 1999, para 290.

law requirement for a crime against humanity, it would surely have been included in the Statute.

9.2.8 **The ICC Statute**

Once again, we need to bear in mind the difference in origin of the ICC compared to the ICTY and ICTR. It is a court of limited treaty-based jurisdiction, reliant on the consent of State parties (or the support of the Security Council) to operate. Nonetheless, we can, with due caution, deduce something about the attitude of those States who negotiated the Statute towards the definition of crimes against humanity from the text that they concluded.[15]

Article 7(1) of the ICC Statute provides:

> For the purpose of this statute, 'crime against humanity' means any of the following acts when committed as part of a widespread or systematic attack directed against any civilian population, with knowledge of the attack: (a) murder; (b) extermination; (c) enslavement; (d) deportation or forcible transfer of population; (e) imprisonment or other severe deprivation of physical liberty in violation of fundamental rules of international law; (f) torture; (g) rape, sexual slavery, enforced prostitution, forced pregnancy, enforced sterilization, or any other form of sexual violence of comparable gravity; (h) persecution...; (i) enforced disappearance of persons; (j) the crime of apartheid; (k) other inhumane acts of a similar character intentionally causing great suffering, or serious injury to body or to mental or physical health.

Articles 7(2) and (3) contain further, more detailed definitions of the relevant prohibited acts. There are several notable features of the ICC Statute definition. First, the definition is provided 'for the purpose of this statute'. We should not, however, conclude the drafters understood their definition to be different from customary international law. Indeed, it is generally accepted that the intention of the drafters of the Rome Statute was to reflect customary international law in their definitions of the crimes covered by the Statute.[16] Second, it adopts the ICTR Statute's contextual requirement that the prohibited act be committed 'as part of a widespread or systematic attack directed against any civilian population' but adds the words *'with knowledge of the attack'*. Third, the definition expands the range of crimes of sexual violence expressly covered beyond rape. Fourth, it adds enforced disappearances and apartheid to the list of prohibited acts. Fifth, it contains an expanded definition of persecution (discussed further below). Finally, the category of 'other inhuman acts' creates a residual class of crimes not otherwise expressly covered. This makes the list non-exhaustive and open to expansion through judicial interpretation.

---

[15] On the relationship between treaty law and custom see Chapter 1, section 1.5.
[16] A Zimmermann, 'Article 5', in O Triffterer (ed), *Commentary on the Rome Statute of the International Criminal Court* (2008) para 1.

9.3 The contextual element: 'as a part of a widespread or systematic attack directed against any civilian population with knowledge of the attack'

Having reviewed the historical origins of crimes against humanity it is apparent that the vital part of the definition is not a nexus requirement but a contextual element. All the covered acts in the definitions above are crimes in themselves, they become a crime against humanity when committed 'as a part of a widespread or systematic attack directed against any civilian population with knowledge of the attack'. This has four elements requiring further examination, being the requirements that the perpetrator's action forms *'part of'* a *'widespread or systematic attack'* directed against *'any civilian population'* with *'knowledge of the attack'*. These are dealt with in turn below.

9.3.1 'Any civilian population'

The words 'any civilian population' address who can be the victims of a crime against humanity. The word 'any' includes enemy nationals (in time of armed conflict), one's own nationals (in times of armed conflict or peace), and stateless persons. 'Population' implies collective crimes, but the entire population need not be targeted according to ICTY case law.[17]

What is required by the word 'civilian'? Technically, the word only strictly has meaning in times of armed conflict, thus making its use in the definition of a crime that applies in time of both war and peace somewhat problematic. Nonetheless, the following propositions are established in the case law:

- That the target population is predominantly civilian is enough, the presence of some military personnel will not deprive a population of its civilian character.[18] In assessing whether a 'population' is 'civilian' the relative proportion of civilians and military personnel will be important; in this assessment military personnel who are *hors de combat* (i.e. the wounded, disabled, etc) will not count as civilians.[19]

- However, the civilian population must be the primary object of attack, therefore attacks on legitimate military objectives which comply with the law of armed conflict do not qualify as crimes against humanity.[20]

- It is possible for military personnel and members of resistance movements when they are *hors de combat* (i.e. the wounded, disabled, etc.) to qualify as *victims* of crimes against humanity.[21] That is, simply because the relevant prohibited act

[17] *Tadić*, ICTY Trial Chamber, 7 May 1997, para 644; *Kunarac*, ICTY Trial Chamber, 22 February 2001, para 424.

[18] *Tadić*, ICTY Trial Chamber, 7 May, para 638; *Kordić*, ICTY Trial Chamber, 26 February 2001, para 180; *Kupreškić*, ICTY Trial Chamber, 14 January 2000, para 549.

[19] R O'Keefe, *International Criminal Law* (Oxford University Press 2015) 142.

[20] *Kunarac*, ICTY Appeals Chamber, 12 June 2002, para 91.

[21] *Kupreškić*, ICTY Trial Chamber, 14 January 2000, para 549 and 568 (quoting *Barbie* and *Touvier*).

(e.g. killing a person) is committed against a member of a military force does not mean it cannot be charged as a crime against humanity.

 Pause for reflection

Can an act which is legal in war be charged as being an 'attack' constituting a crime against humanity?

There is the distinct possibility that an act which is lawful under the law of armed conflict could equally be characterized as unlawful if viewed only as a question of law of crimes against humanity. The classic example is the idea of a forced transfer of persons or forced deportations.[22] As noted below (at 9.4.4), the law of armed conflict expressly contemplates that in certain cases a civilian population might be moved for a range of legitimate military purposes. These could include protecting civilians from harm by removing them from the theatre of combat.

The question of whether legitimate military operations could result in a crime against humanity of forced deportation was an issue before the ICTY in *Popovic et al*. The case concerned, among other crimes, the genocidal attack by Bosnian-Serb forces against the Bosnian-Muslim enclaves in Srebrenica and Žepa. The ICTY Trial Chamber found that the crimes committed in Srebrenica and Žepa were part of a wider criminal plan to forcibly remove the Bosnian-Muslim civilian population from the enclaves. Controversially, the Trial Chamber held that Bosnian-Muslim combatants who ultimately fled the fighting at Žepa and crossed the border into Serbia were not to be considered retreating soldiers but were victims of the crime of forcible deportation.[23] Indeed, the Trial Chamber did not distinguish in its analysis between civilians and combatants who fled across the river.

The Appeals Chamber held that while it is possible for combatants to be among the victims of a crime against humanity (so long as the targeted population is predominantly civilian), nonetheless: (1) there was a week's gap between the main attack on Žepa and the movement of men across the river; and (2) it was not clear that those men who fled across the river included any civilians. It was thus not possible to conclude that the movement of men across the river was related to the main attack.[24] Further, the Appeals Chamber also noted that 'forcible displacement of enemy soldiers is not prohibited' under the law of armed conflict.[25]

While this may seem to suggest that conduct which is lawful under the law of armed conflict should not be regarded as a crime against humanity, the judgment is not entirely clear if this should always be the inevitable result.[26]

---

[22] See: P Akhavan, 'Reconciling Crimes Against Humanity with the Laws of War: Human Rights, Armed Conflict, and the Limits of Progressive Jurisprudence' (2008) 6 Journal of International Criminal Justice 21.

[23] *Popovic et al.*, ICTY Trial Chamber, 10 June 2010, para 956.

[24] *Popovic et al.*, ICTY Appeals Chamber, 10 June 2015, para 956.

[25] *Popovic et al.*, ICTY Appeals Chamber, 10 June 2015, para 774.

[26] See further: R Bartels, 'Two Cheers for the ICTY Popovic et al. Appeals Judgement: Some Words on the Interplay Between IHL and ICL', EJIL: Talk!, 4 February 2015, www.ejiltalk.org/two-cheers-for-the-icty-popovic-et-al-appeals-judgement-some-words-on-the-interplay-between-ihl-and-icl/#more-13008.

9.3.2 'Widespread or systematic attack directed against...'

The word '*or*' makes this requirement disjunctive, not cumulative: an attack can be *either* widespread *or* systematic; it does not need to be both widespread *and* systematic.[27] There was some opposition to this approach during the drafting of the ICC Statute on the basis that a disjunctive test would allow conduct which was widespread and merely random (such as a crime wave) to be a crime against humanity.[28] The answer to this is that either the word 'attack' or the words 'directed against' must exclude sporadic or merely random and unrelated events, no matter how widespread.[29] As an ICC Pre-Trial Chamber has put it, an attack is something which is 'planned, directed or organised' and this excludes 'spontaneous or isolated' acts of violence.[30]

The key ideas are that:

- 'widespread' is a question of scale of the attack and number of victims,[31] but it does not involve a mathematical minimum;
- 'systematic' refers to an attack that is (to some degree) organized or methodical, and not merely random.[32]

In interpreting 'widespread' the question arises whether the requirement of scale could be met by a single devastating attack of sufficient magnitude or whether there must be multiple acts of a similar nature. The ICC Elements of Crimes take 'widespread' to mean 'a course of conduct involving the multiple commission' of prohibited acts.[33] The ICTY case law, however, takes the view a single attack of sufficient magnitude would be sufficient.[34]

In addition, the words 'attack directed against' could be taken to suggest that there must be some governmental or organizational policy to commit the attack (i.e. without a policy an attack cannot be 'directed'). The ICTY has tended to reject this approach. The ICTY Appeals Chamber said in *Kunarac*:

> It may be useful in establishing that the attack was directed against a civilian population and that it was widespread or systematic (especially the latter) to show that there was in fact a policy or plan [but it is not necessary].[35]

---

[27] Boas, Bischoff, and Reid, *Practitioner Library*, vol 2, 52.

[28] D Robinson, 'Crimes Against Humanity' in R Cryer et al, *Introduction to International Criminal Law* 3rd ed (Oxford University Press 2014) 237.

[29] Ibid and Cassese, *International Criminal Law*, 91–2. Compare, W Schabas, *An Introduction to the International Criminal Court*, 4th ed (Cambridge University Press 2011) 111.

[30] *Bemba* (Decision on Confirmation of Charges), ICC Pre-Trial Chamber II, 15 June 2009, para 81

[31] *Kunarac*, ICTY Trial Chamber, 22 February 2001, para 428; see also *Akayesu*, ICTR Trial Chamber, 2 September 1998, para 580.

[32] *Tadić*, ICTY Trial Chamber, 7 May 1997, para 648; *Kunarac*, ICTY Trial Chamber, 22 February 2001, para 429.

[33] ICC Elements of Crimes, Introduction to Article 7, para 3.

[34] *Kordić and Čerkez*, ICTY Trial Chamber, 26 February 2001, para 176; *Blaškić*, ICTY Trial Chamber, 3 March 2000, para 206; Robinson, 'Crimes Against Humanity' in Cryer et al, *Introduction*, 235.

[35] *Kunarac*, ICTY Appeals Chamber, 12 June 2002, para 98: Followed in *Kordić and Čerkez*, ICTY Appeals Chamber, 17 December 2004, para 98. See also *Kupreškić*, ICTY Trial Chamber, 14 January 2000, para 543. *Blaškić*, ICTY Appeals Chamber, 29 July 2004, para 120.

The ICTY has thus seen the existence of a policy not as an element of the crime in itself but as useful evidence going to the required elements of an attack directed against a civilian population, which is widespread or systematic.

However, in ICTY case law a policy does not need to be expressly formulated[36] and can itself be inferred from the widespread or systematic commission of prohibited acts.[37] It thus does not need to be a policy in the sense of an official, written government or organizational document.

The ICC Elements of Crimes require that: 'The conduct was committed as part of a widespread or systematic attack directed against a civilian population'; but further stipulate that the attack must be: 'pursuant to or in furtherance of a State or organizational policy to commit such attack.' If ICC member States in their national law and implementing legislation follow the ICC approach, then State practice and *opinio juris* is likely to support the policy requirement. While some expressed concern that the early case law of the ICC might be applying a policy requirement too strictly,[38] it seems clear that ICC case law now accepts (in line with ICTY case law) that the 'policy need not be formalised' and therefore 'an attack which is planned, directed or organized' will satisfy the policy requirement.[39]

Moreover, on inferring the existence of a policy, the ICC Elements of Crimes provide, somewhat confusingly:

> Such a policy may, in exceptional circumstances, be implemented by a deliberate failure to take action, which is consciously aimed at encouraging such attack. The existence of such a policy cannot be inferred solely from the absence of governmental or organizational action.

Darryl Robinson explains this by saying it acknowledges both the possibility of a policy of 'passive encouragement' *and* that there may be reasons for inaction other than a policy to commit crimes against humanity, such as 'lack of knowledge of crimes, lack of ability [to prevent them]'. As a result, a policy 'should not be inferred without considering alternative explanations.'[40] Gerhard Werle and Florian Jessburger characterize what is required in cases based on such of lack of action as a 'purposeful "looking away" and a [deliberate] refusal to take measures to protect the attacked population.'[41]

The question remains as to how the ICC will apply the 'State or organizational policy' requirement. In practice, it appears the ICC may have adopted a very broad view of the types of organization capable of carrying out an attack against a civilian population. The crucial case so far is the 2010 *Decision Authorizing an Investigation into the Situation in the Republic of Kenya*.[42] (We should note this is a decision of an ICC

---

[36] *Kupreškić*, ICTY Trial Chamber, 14 January 2000, para 551.

[37] *Tadić*, ICTY Trial Chamber, 7 May 1997, para 653.

[38] Robinson, 'Crimes Against Humanity' in Cryer et al, *Introduction*, 239–40; LN Sadat, 'Crimes against Humanity in the Modern Age' (2013) 107 American Journal of International Law 334, 359 and 376.

[39] *Bemba* (Decision on Confirmation of Charges), ICC Pre-Trial Chamber II, 15 June 2009, para 81; *Gbagbo* (Decision on Confirmation of Charges), ICC Pre-Trial Chamber I, 12 June 2014, para 215.

[40] Robinson, 'Crimes Against Humanity' in Cryer et al, *Introduction*, 239, n 69.

[41] G Werle and F Jessberger, *Principles of International Criminal Law*, 3rd ed (Oxford University Press 2014), 345–346, para 910.

[42] 'Decision Pursuant to Article 15 of the Rome Statute on the Authorization of an Investigation into the Situation in the Republic of Kenya', ICC Pre-Trial Chamber II, 31 March 2010, ICC-01/09-19-Corr., www.icc-cpi.int/iccdocs/doc/doc854562.pdf.

Pre-Trial Chamber and a different view could be taken at trial or on appeal.) In this Decision the Chamber made several significant findings about the kind of 'organization' that may (through a policy) carry out a crime against humanity. The Chamber noted that some commentators have argued that only State-like organizations should be considered capable of committing crimes against humanity. The Chamber, however, rejected such an approach, seemingly on the basis that a wider range of groups may be able 'to perform acts which infringe on basic human values'.[43] Ultimately, it saw the question of whether a particular group is an 'organization' under the ICC Statute as an assessment to be made case-by-case. In making this assessment considerations to be taken into account include:

> (i) whether the group is under a responsible command, or has an established hierarchy; (ii) whether the group possesses, in fact, the means to carry out a widespread or systematic attack against a civilian population; (iii) whether the group exercises control over part of the territory of a State; (iv)whether the group has criminal activities against the civilian population as a primary purpose; (v) whether the group articulates, explicitly or implicitly, an intention to attack a civilian population; (vi) whether the group is part of a larger group, which fulfils some or all of… [these] criteria.[44]

The Chamber noted that these were *considerations* to assist a Chamber in reaching a determination, not strict legal *criteria* which need to be 'exhaustively fulfilled'.[45] On this basis it held that 'various groups including local leaders, businessmen and politicians associated with the two leading parties, as well as with members of the police force' in Kenya could constitute organizations for the purposes of the policy requirement for a crime against humanity.[46] If an 'organizational policy' can be the plan of a group of businessmen or politicians it would not appear to be a particularly demanding threshold in practice.

The Decision in the Kenyan situation is open to criticism on the basis that, given the concept's history, the value protected by the idea of crimes against humanity is protecting populations which depend upon living within a State for their security from attacks by the State apparatus itself.[47] Given those origins, some would argue for a narrower view: that—at most—the relevant concept of 'organization' should be expanded to include armed rebel groups or *de facto* governments during a civil war. The broad view is preferable if one considers the policy element only exists to exclude random, unrelated occurrences occurring at the same time (e.g. a crime wave) constituting a crime against humanity.[48]

Nonetheless, there is now clearly a divergence in the authorities. The ICTY and its case law (which should be treated as strong evidence of customary international

---

[43] Ibid, para 90.   [44] Ibid, para 93.   [45] Ibid, para 93.   [46] Ibid, para 117.

[47] C Kress, 'On the Outer Limits of Crimes Against Humanity: The Concept of Organization within the Policy Requirement—Some Reflections on the March 2010 ICC Kenya Decision, 2010', (2010) 23 Leiden Journal of International Law 855, 866; D Luban, 'A Theory of Crimes against Humanity' (2004) 29 Yale Journal of International Law 85. See also the Dissenting Opinion of Judge Kaul appended to the Decision, *supra* n 42, paras 50–70.

[48] Robinson, 'Crimes Against Humanity' in Cryer et al, *Introduction*, 240.

law) hold that a policy is *not* an element of crimes against humanity. The ICC Statute (which constitutes good evidence of the *opinio juris* of many States) holds that it is, but the ICC case law seems to suggest the threshold is not a high one. It is possible to contend that the two different approaches aim at the one result, excluding attacks which are merely random,[49] but as a formal matter the different requirements remain.

9.3.3 The perpetrator's participation in the attack: 'as part of ... the attack' and with knowledge of the attack

The acts of the accused must form 'part of' the attack to be a crime against humanity. To this end we should note that:

- the accused's prohibited act must objectively fall within wider attack;[50]
- the accused's acts need not be widespread or systematic;[51] and
- the accused need not be a State official.[52]

The perpetrator's participation in the attack: with knowledge of the attack

Finally, the accused must have knowledge of the factual context of a widespread or systematic attack against a civilian population of which his or her attack forms a part. What is required is that the accused knew their plan fitted into a broader attack, this is an objective test and the knowledge may be inferred from the evidence.[53] The personal motives of the accused are irrelevant: if a perpetrator takes advantage of the broader attack to achieve some personal goal it is still a crime against humanity.[54] To this end, according to the ICTY, it is enough that the accused was 'wilfully blind' or 'knowingly took the risk' that their act would fit within this context.[55]

By contrast, the ICC Elements of Crimes require: 'The perpetrator *knew* that the conduct was part of or *intended* the conduct to be part of a widespread or systematic attack against a civilian population' (emphasis added).[56] Thus the accused does not need to have the intended his conduct to be part of the attack, mere knowledge that his or her conduct objectively falls within wider attack is sufficient. The ICC Elements of Crimes clarify that in relation to cases of knowledge the Elements do not require 'proof that the perpetrator had knowledge of all characteristics of the attack or the precise details of the plan or policy of the State or organization.'[57]

---

[49] Ibid.   [50] *Tadić*, ICTY Appeals Chamber, 15 July 1999, paras 248, 271–72.

[51] *Kuanarac*, ICTY Appeals Chamber, para 96.

[52] *Kupreškić*, ICTY Trial Chamber, 14 January 2000, para 555.

[53] *Tadić*, ICTY Trial Chamber 1997, paras 656–59.

[54] *Tadić*, ICTY Appeals Chamber, 15 July 1999, paras 271–72.

[55] *Tadić*, ICTY Trial Chamber 1997, para 657; the Canadian Supreme Court reached a similar conclusion in: *Finta* [1994] 1 SCR at 819–20.

[56] ICC Elements of Crimes, Article 7 (see the last element of each offence).

[57] ICC Elements of Crimes, Introduction to Article 7, para 2.

Pause for reflection

Consider the terrorist attacks in the United States on 11 September 2001. This involved the simulta-
neous hijacking of four commercial passenger aircraft by 19 men who were later found to be associated with the Al-Qaida terrorist network. Notoriously, two aircraft were crashed into the World
Trade Center in New York, causing approximately 3,000 deaths. A third hijacked aircraft crashed into
the Pentagon and a fourth crashed in a field in Pennsylvania. Was this a crime against humanity?

Many of the features of the attack appear to satisfy the elements of the offence: as regards the
attacks on the World Trade Center, this was clearly an attack directed against civilians; while there
is no numerical minimum requirement 3,000 deaths must surely qualify as a 'widespread' attack;
alternatively, if the multiple commission of acts is required there were four attempted and three
successful acts of mass killing; and the attack involved a prohibited act (murder, discussed below).

This leaves the question of whether these attacks were systematic or directed by a policy to commit such an attack? It was certainly a highly organized attack committed pursuant to an Al-Qaida
policy (or ideology) calling for terror attacks on civilians in western States.

The only grounds for suggesting these attacks were not a crime against humanity is to suggest that
crimes against humanity may only be committed by States or State-like entities with some degree
of territorial control (as discussed in section 9.3.2).

9.4 The underlying prohibited acts and their definitions

9.4.1 Murder

Murder is usually defined as unlawfully and intentionally causing death. The conduct
element is the same as the war crime of wilful killing. In *Kupreškić*, the ICTY held: 'The
requisite *mens rea* of murder . . . is the intent to kill or the intent to inflict serious injury
in reckless disregard of human life.'[58]

As noted, in the ICC Statute, Article 30 requires a crime be committed with 'intent
and knowledge'. Thus far the ICC has not interpreted 'intent' to include 'reckless disregard' as a *mens rea* for murder remains to be seen, but it would appear unlikely (see
Chapter 7, section 7.4.3).

9.4.2 Extermination

Extermination requires mass killings. An act of extermination could also be a single act
of killing within a pattern of mass killings. Under the ICC Elements of Crimes to Article
7(1)(b), extermination requires that:

- 'The perpetrator killed [directly or indirectly] one or more persons, including by
  inflicting conditions of life calculated to bring about the destruction of part of a
  population [e.g. through deprivation of access to food and medicine]'; and

---

[58] *Kupreškić*, ICTY Trial Chamber, 14 January 2000, para 561; see also *Akayesu*, ICTR Trial Chamber,
2 September 1998, para 589.

- The conduct constituted, or took place as part of, a mass killing of members of a civilian population [which includes the initial murders in a mass killing].'

In the absence of relevant case law, the approach taken in the ICC Elements to the definition of extermination was adopted by an ICTY Trial Chamber in 2001 in *Krštić*.[59] As to the requirement that the killing constituted part of a pattern of mass killing, the ICTY had held that the killings must form part of the same incident, taking into account such factors as: 'time and place, the selection of the victims, and the manner in which they were targeted.'[60]

As regards mass killing through the infliction of conditions of life designed to bring about the destruction of part of a population, the *Stakić* case is illustrative. The case concerned the head of a municipal assembly 'crisis staff' with alleged responsibility for concentration camps. In *Stakić* the ICTY held that the *actus reus* of 'killing on a large scale' could be satisfied by 'subjecting a widespread number of people or systematically subjecting a number of people to conditions of living that would inevitably lead to death.'[61] The *mens rea* required is that the accused 'intended, by his acts or omissions, either killing on a large scale' or the subjection of persons 'to conditions of living that would lead to their deaths.'[62]

Note, however, that the *mens rea* does not require a discriminatory intent (this is the main difference between crimes against humanity in general and the crime of persecution) and that a single act of killing within a larger patter of extermination will suffice.

9.4.3 Enslavement

In general international law there is a difference between slavery and 'practices similar to slavery'. Slavery in the strict sense involves exercising rights of ownership over a person, as set out in the 1926 Slavery Convention.[63] The 1956 Supplementary Convention on the Abolition of Slavery (1956 Supplementary Slavery Convention) prohibited a wider range of 'practices similar to slavery'.[64] These include practices such as serfdom (i.e. a system where persons may be indentured to work a particular piece of land), debt bondage (i.e. entrapping someone in forced labour),[65] etc. The question is whether 'enslavement' should follow the narrow approach focussed on asserting rights of ownership over another person or whether it should encompass the broader concept of practices similar to slavery.

---

[59] *Krštić*, ICTY Trial Chamber, 2 August 2001, para 498.
[60] *Krajišnik*, ICTY Trial Chamber, 27 September 2006, para 716.
[61] *Stakić*, ICTY Appeals Chamber, 22 March 2006, para 259.   [62] Ibid.
[63] Slavery Convention, adopted 25 September 1926, entered into force 9 March 1927, 60 LNTS 254.
[64] Supplementary Convention on the Abolition of Slavery, the Slave Trade, and Institutions and Practices Similar to Slavery, adopted 7 September 1956, entered into force 30 April 1957, 266 UNTS 3.
[65] Debt bondage is entrapping someone in a system of forced labour by imposing a continually accruing debt upon them and paying them too little to ever realistically 'work off' the debt.

Example

Kunarac, ICTY Trial Chamber

Kunarac[66] concerned the detention of young women by soldiers who were confined to an apartment, sexually abused, and forced to perform domestic labour. In *Kunarac* the ICTY took the broad approach and held that a wider category of acts could constitute 'enslavement' than might constitute 'slavery' in the strict sense. The essence of enslavement is found in the absence of the victim's consent or free will and their exploitation. Thus, indicia of enslavement include: 'elements of control and ownership; the restriction or control of an individual's autonomy, freedom of choice or freedom of movement', exploitation, forced labour, and sexual exploitation or abuse.[67] As this list of indicia indicates, it is difficult to exhaustively define 'enslavement' at customary international law. Control may be exercised over the victim through force, coercion, violence, deception, abuse of power, 'detention or captivity' or 'the victim's position of vulnerability.'[68]

The ICC approach is potentially more restrictive than that taken in *Kunarac*. The Elements of Crimes require the perpetrator to exercise rights of ownership over the victim 'such as by purchasing, selling, lending or bartering such a person or persons, or by imposing on them a similar deprivation of liberty.'[69] This focus on powers associated with rights of ownership is obviously closer to the traditional definition of *slavery* rather than any broader concept of *enslavement*. However, the elements do refer to the alternative case of imposing on the victim 'a similar deprivation of liberty'.[70] A note to the Elements further explains that this includes 'trafficking in persons, in particular women and children' and may also 'in some circumstances' include 'forced labour or otherwise reducing a person to a servile status' as defined in 1956 Supplementary Slavery Convention. The reference to 'in some circumstances' and the 1956 Supplementary Slavery Convention could therefore allow this provision to be interpreted in the more expansive *Kunarac* sense.

9.4.4 **Deportation or forcible transfer of population**

Deportation refers to the forced movement of persons across an international border. Forced transfer refers to the movement of people *within* a State.[71]

Forcible transfer as a separate crime against humanity was first established by ICTY as an example of 'other inhumane act' (see 9.4.10), although one should note the

---

[66] *Kunarac*, ICTY Trial Chamber, 22 February 2001.

[67] *Kunarac*, ICTY Trial Chamber, 22 February 2001, para 543; see also *Kunarac*, ICTY Appeal Chamber, 12 June 2002, para 119.

[68] *Kunarac*, ICTY Trial Chamber, 22 February 2001, paras 541–3.

[69] Art 7(1)(c), para 1, ICC Elements of Crimes.   [70] Ibid.

[71] *Stakić*, ICTY Appeals Chamber, 22 March 2006, para 317.

prohibition on 'mass forcible transfers' from occupied territory during an international armed conflict.[72]

The key ideas from the case law[73] are that:

- the persons displaced must have no genuine choice;
- the accused need not intend the victim's movement to be permanent;[74]
- the movement involved must *not* be something generally permitted by international law.

As regards the last point, governments are allowed to expel aliens and humanitarian law may allow for total or partial evacuations of a given area if 'imperative military reasons so demand' (e.g. to remove civilians from a zone of fighting).[75] Such movements will be lawful and therefore are not deportations.

Similar ideas are found in the ICC Elements of Crimes.[76] These require that the perpetrator 'deported or forcibly transferred' one or more persons 'by expulsion or other coercive acts'. This must have occurred 'without grounds permitted under international law' and the persons in question must have been 'lawfully present in the area from which they were . . . deported or transferred'. On the meaning of 'forcibly' a note to the ICC Elements clarifies that the term is not limited to physical force, but includes threats and coercion, 'such as that caused by fear of violence, duress, detention, psychological oppression or abuse of power' or through 'taking advantage of a coercive environment'. The essence of a forcible transfer is thus that it is *coercive* not that it is *violent*.

9.4.5 **Imprisonment or other severe deprivation of physical liberty**

Kordić and Čerkez clarified that the crime against humanity of imprisonment requires that the detention involved is unlawful. It therefore involves imprisonment without due process of law; or detention that continues once there is no longer a lawful excuse (i.e. keeping someone in prison after they have served their sentence or failing to release prisoners of war at the end of a conflict).[77] The ICC Elements of Crimes further require that: '[t]he gravity of the conduct was such that it was in violation of fundamental rules of international law'.[78] This seems to indicate that some unlawful detentions will not be capable of forming part of a

---

[72] Art 49, Geneva Convention IV 1949, adopted 12 August 1949, entered into force 21 October 1950, 75 UNTS 287.

[73] See: *Krštić*, ICTY Trial Chamber, 2 August 2001, paras 519–32; *Krajišnik*, ICTY Trial Chamber, 27 September 2006, paras 722–32; *Stakić*, ICTY Appeal Chamber, 22 March 2006, paras 278 ff.

[74] *Stakić*, ICTY Appeals Chamber, 22 March 2006, para 317.

[75] Art 49, Geneva Convention IV 1949.

[76] Art7(1)(d), paras 1 and 2 and n 12, ICC Elements of Crimes.

[77] *Kordić and Čerkez*, ICTY Appeals Chamber, 17 December 2004, para 116.

[78] Art 7(1)(e), para 2, ICC Elements of Crimes.

crime against humanity. Under the ICC Elements of Crimes the perpetrator must further have been 'aware of the factual circumstances that established the gravity of the conduct.'[79]

9.4.6 **Torture**

The crime of torture under the Convention against Torture (CAT) and customary international law was discussed in Chapter 2, section 2.5 and Chapter 8, section 8.6.4. There it was noted that all the distinctive elements of torture under the CAT (consisting of the infliction of severe pain or suffering, with the involvement of a State official, for a prohibited purpose)[80] are not necessarily included in the definitions used when torture forms part of other international crimes.

In the case law of the ICTY torture as a crime against humanity under customary international law requires:[81]

(1) the infliction, by an act or omission, of severe pain or suffering, whether physical or mental;

(2) that the act or omission must be intentional; and

(3) that the act or omission must aim at obtaining information or a confession, or at punishing, intimidating or coercing the victim or a third person, or at discriminating, on any ground, against the victim or a third person (the 'prohibited purpose' requirement).

Most notably, the requirement of the involvement or acquiescence of a State official found in the CAT is absent. This is perhaps best explained on the basis that crimes against humanity can clearly be committed by non-State organizations such as rebel armed groups or by individuals acting as 'part of' an attack.

As to element (1), what is the standard for 'severe suffering'? Three propositions should be noted from *Kunarac*: (a) the '[e]xisting case-law has not determined the absolute degree of pain required for an act to amount to torture'; (b) however, it need not result in visible suffering long after the event; and (c) rape *inherently* inflicts a degree of suffering sufficient to meet the standard.[82] This does not mean all rape is torture: the offence must still satisfy element (3). Element (3) is a requirement that the severe pain or suffering is inflicted for a prohibited purpose. While that purpose must be present, it need not be the sole or dominant motive.[83]

---

[79] Art 7(1)(e), para 3, ICC Elements of Crimes.

[80] Art 1, Convention Against Torture and Other Cruel, Inhuman or Degrading Treatment or Punishment 1984, adopted 10 December 1984, entered force 26 June 1987, 1465 UNTS 85.

[81] *Kunarac*, ICTY Trial Chamber, 22 February 2001, para 497, reproduced and followed in *Kunarac*, ICTY Appeals Chamber, 12 June 2002, para 142; followed in *Stakić*, Trial Chamber, 31 July 2003, para 750.

[82] *Kunarac*, ICTY Appeals Chamber, 12 June 2002, paras 149–52, following *Kunarac*, Trial Chamber, 22 February 2001, paras 447–56.

[83] *Kunarac*, ICTY Appeals Chamber, 12 June 2002, para 155.

The ICC definition of torture as a crime against humanity departs from that used by the ICTY. Under the ICC Elements of Crimes, torture a crime against humanity requires:

(1) The perpetrator inflicted severe physical or mental pain or suffering upon one or more persons.

(2) Such person or persons were in the custody or under the control of the perpetrator.

(3) Such pain or suffering did not arise only from, and was not inherent in or incidental to, lawful sanctions.[84]

Notably this definition *introduces* a requirement of custody and *excludes* both the requirement of the involvement of a public official and the 'prohibited purpose' element normally found in torture. This would appear to involve a considerable departure from the customary international law definition of torture.[85] Ordinarily, without the involvement of a State the infliction of severe pain or suffering by a private individual does not rise to the level of an international crime. It is the involvement of a State that makes torture an international crime.[86] However, these modifications largely reflect the idea found in the Elements of Crimes that crimes against humanity must be committed 'pursuant to or in furtherance of a State or organisational policy':[87] that is, the custody or control requirement and the absence of the need for a State official to be involved might be taken to reflect the fact that crimes against humanity are not committed exclusively by States.

The reference to 'lawful sanctions' in the third element may also seem confusing. As a starting proposition this must mean sanctions which are lawful under national law, but such sanctions cannot exceed what international law permits.[88] The suffering inflicted by lawful imprisonment (under internationally acceptable conditions) is both serious and carried out by State officials; however, even if it could be considered 'severe' (which seems unlikely), it would not constitute torture.

9.4.7 Rape and other serious sexual offences

Material element

Rape may be defined more narrowly or more broadly. The ICTY Appeals Chamber took a narrow approach in *Kunarac* holding that the *actus reus* of rape in international law involved:

the sexual penetration, however slight: (a) of the vagina or anus of the victim by the penis of the perpetrator or any other object...; or (b) the mouth of the victim by the penis of the

---

[84] Art 7(1)(f), paras 1–3, ICC Elements.

[85] A Cassese, 'Crimes Against Humanity' in Cassese et al (eds), *The Rome Statute of the International Criminal Court: A Commentary* (Oxford University Press 2002), 374. See also Chapter 2, section 2.5 and Chapter 8, section 8.6.4.

[86] Cassese et al, *International Criminal Law*, 3rd ed, 134–35.   [87] Ibid.

[88] UN Special Rapporteur on Torture, Report on the question of the human rights of all persons subjected to any form of detention or imprisonment, UN Doc. E/CN.4/1988/17 (23 February 1988), para 42.

perpetrator; where such sexual penetration occurs without the [voluntarily given] consent of the victim.[89]

Similarly, the ICC Elements of Crimes define rape as requiring the penetration of the victim.[90] A narrow definition focussed on penetration may exclude other serious acts of a sexual nature or may require further sexual offences to be elaborated and defined.

To this end the ICTR Trial Chamber in *Akayesu* defined rape as 'a physical invasion of a sexual nature, committed on a person under circumstances which are coercive.'[91] Similarly, in *Stakić* the ICTY Trial Chamber suggested that under international criminal law 'all serious abuses of a sexual nature inflicted upon the integrity of a person by means of coercion, threat of force or intimidation in a way that is humiliating and degrading to the victim's dignity' are punishable.[92] These broader approaches did not prevail in ICTY case law, as noted above. However, the ICC Statute and Elements of Crimes did embrace a similar approach to *Stakić* in its offence of 'sexual violence': using force, threats, or coercion to commit an act of a sexual nature.[93]

The ICC Elements of Crimes also specifically elaborate separate crimes of sexual slavery, enforced prostitution, forced pregnancy, and enforced sterilization.[94] There will often be overlap between these specific offences and rape. The offence of sexual slavery also overlaps with enslavement. While this might suggest a single offence of serious sexual violence would be preferable, there is merit to creating individual crimes in each case given that these are undoubtedly serious crimes to which women and children (and, to a lesser extent, men) historically have been—and continue to be—subjected as part of attacks on civilian populations. Nonetheless, as noted in the discussion of rape as war crime there may be a risk that detailed enumeration of multiple sexual offences may inadvertently create 'loopholes'[95] while a single offence of serious sexual violence would not.

Mental element: knowledge of lack of consent or coercion?

An important question is whether, in the context of a crime against humanity (or war crime), the crime of rape should require a lack of consent to sexual acts, or force, or threats—or simply the existence of coercive circumstances making genuine consent impossible.[96] That is, must the perpetrator know the victim did not consent, or must he or she simply be aware of the existence of coercive circumstances precluding consent? The difference is important: 'Force, threats, and coercion focus on the acts of the accused, whereas voluntary consent relates to the mental state of the victim.'[97]

[89] *Kunarac*, ICTY Appeals Chamber, 12 June 2002, para 127.
[90] Art 7(1)(f), paras 1–3, ICC Elements of Crimes.
[91] *Akayesu*, ICTR Trial Chamber, 2 September 1998, para 598.
[92] *Stakić*, ICTY Trial Chamber, 31 July 2003, para 757.
[93] Art 7(1)(g)-6, ICC Elements of Crimes.   [94] See: Art 7(1)(g)-2 to 5, ICC Elements of Crimes.
[95] Schabas, *Introduction*, 126. See also Chapter 8, section 8.6.8.
[96] See generally: P Weiner, 'The Evolving Jurisprudence of the Crime of Rape in International Criminal Law' (2013) 36 Boston College International & Comparative Law Review 1207.
[97] Ibid, 1215.

The emphasis in ICTY case law has generally been on the lack of consent of the victim as being the critical element. Thus the ICTY Appeals Chamber in *Kunarac* held 'The *mens rea* is the intention to effect...sexual penetration, and the knowledge that it occurs without the consent of the victim'.[98] This mental element has been described as a two part *mens rea*: it requires intention as to the act *and* knowledge of the victim's lack of consent.[99] On the latter requirement, the approach in ICTY and ICTR case law has been to hold that '[t]he Prosecution can prove non-consent beyond reasonable doubt by proving the existence of coercive circumstances under which meaningful consent is not possible'.[100] The use of force against the victim is not a requirement *per se*, but where it is present it will prove the absence of consent.[101] Nonetheless, the hazard of this approach remains that in principle the mental state of the victim must be proved and a perpetrator may attempt to raise a mistake of fact defence (i.e. that he or she believed the victim to be consenting). Mistake of fact defences are discussed in Chapter 13, section 13.7.1.

The ICC Elements of Crimes require that rape or sexual violence:

> was committed by force, or by threat of force or coercion, such as that caused by fear of violence, duress, detention, psychological oppression or abuse of power,...or by taking advantage of a coercive environment, or...against a person incapable of giving genuine consent.[102]

The ICC approach may be seen as more progressive: it focuses on the acts of the perpetrator and not the mental state of the victim.[103] However, as crimes under the ICC Statute must be committed with both intent and knowledge, the defendant must know the act was committed by force or coercion or that the victim was in capable of giving consent. The defendant may thus attempt, in theory, to raise a mistake of fact defence (e.g. that he or she did not know the circumstances in which the sexual acts took place were in fact coercive).

9.4.8 **Enforced disappearances**

'Enforced disappearance of persons' is defined in Article 7(2)(i) of the ICC Statute as:

> the arrest, detention or abduction of persons by, or with the authorization, support or acquiescence of, a State or a political organization, followed by a refusal to acknowledge that deprivation of freedom or to give information on the fate or whereabouts of those persons, with the intention of removing them from the protection of the law for a prolonged period of time.

The ICC Statute definition was preceded by a 1992 General Assembly resolution on the subject (adopted by consensus) and by a 1994 inter-American convention.[104] The ICC

---

[98] *Kunarac*, ICTY Appeals Chamber, 12 June 2002, para 127.

[99] Weiner, 'The Evolving Jurisprudence of the Crime of Rape', 1213, 1219.

[100] *Gacumbitsi*, ICTR Appeals Chamber, 7 July 2006, para 155.

[101] *Kunarac*, ICTY Appeals Chamber, 12 June 2002, para 129.

[102] Arts 7(1)(g)-1, para 2 and 7(1)(g)-6, para 1, ICC Elements of Crimes.

[103] As, indeed, did the ICTY and the ICTR in: *Akayesu*, ICTR Trial Chamber, 2 September 1998, para 598; and *Stakić*, ICTY Trial Chamber, 31 July 2003, para 757.

[104] UN Declaration on the Protection of All Persons from Forced Disappearance 1992, UN Doc. A/RES/47/133 (adopted without a vote); Art 2, Inter-American Convention for the Protection of All Persons

definition is now closely followed in the definition used in the Enforced Disappearances Convention.[105] Where the same (or a very similar) definition is repeated in a variety of instruments there may be a good argument it is accepted as reflecting customary international law.

The crime was included in the ICC Statute to reflect the experience of victims of the Nazis and various military regimes in Latin America. The Elements of Crimes make it clear that a perpetrator may be responsible for enforced disappearances through various forms of participation in the offence. The elements provide that the *actus reus* may be that a perpetrator either: '[a]rrested, detained or abducted one or more persons'; or '[r]efused to acknowledge the arrest, detention or abduction, or to give information on the fate or whereabouts of such person or persons.'[106] Such acts must be carried out either:

- in the case of arrest, detention or abduction with awareness of the subsequent likelihood of a refusal to give relevant information about the victim; or

- in the case of refusing information, with awareness of the preceding detention (or arrest or abduction).[107]

The offence further requires 'the authorization, support or acquiescence of, a State or a political organization'.[108]

9.4.9 Apartheid

Apartheid was the name given in South Africa to the government policy of residential, social, and economic separation between those inhabitants of European descent and those of non-European descent '([c]oloured or mixed, Bantu, Indian, etc)'.[109] It is now used as the term for such a policy or racial segregation anywhere.

The crime of apartheid is defined in Article 7(2)(h) of the ICC Statute as: 'inhumane acts ... committed in the context of an institutionalized regime of systematic oppression and domination by one racial group over any other racial group or groups and committed with the intention of maintaining that regime'. The Elements of Crimes make it clear that the 'inhumane act' must be one referred to in Article 7(1) of the Statute (i.e. any of the other crimes against humanity such as murder, enslavement or persecution) or be of similar gravity.[110]

Thus, the crime of apartheid is made out by proving some other crime against humanity (or an inhumane act of comparable gravity) coupled with the special intent requirement. The mere fact that a society experiences marked residential, social, and

---

from Forced Disappearance 1994, adopted 9 June 1994, entered force 28 March 1996, OAS Doc. OEA/Ser.P/ AG/Doc 3114/94.

[105] This definition closely follows: Art 2, International Convention for the Protection of All Persons from Enforced Disappearance, adopted 20 December 2006, entered force 23 December 2010, UN Doc. Doc. A/61/448.

[106] Art 7(1)(i), para 1, ICC Elements of Crimes.   [107] Art 7(1)(i), para 3, ICC Elements of Crimes.
[108] Art 7(1)(i), para 4, ICC Elements of Crimes.   [109] Oxford English Dictionary definition.
[110] Art 7(1)(j), para 2, ICC Elements of Crimes.

economic separation between different racial groups (as many do) is insufficient. One of the more likely underlying offences for apartheid might be persecution, as discussed below.

9.4.10 Other inhumane acts

'Other inhumane acts' included as a form of crime against humanity in the ICC Statute,[111] the ICTR Statute,[112] and the ICTY Statute.[113] The ICC Statute defines 'other inhumane acts' as being 'acts of a similar character [to other crimes against humanity] intentionally causing great suffering, or serious injury to body or to mental or physical health'.[114] The ICC Statute definition is very similar to that found in the 1954 ILC Draft Code of Crimes against the Peace and Security of Mankind: 'other inhumane acts which severely damage physical or mental integrity, health or human dignity, such as mutilation and severe bodily harm'.[115] This approach requires that the conduct:

- be of a similar character (i.e. gravity) to other crimes against humanity;
- that it causes great suffering, or serious injury to body or to mental or physical health; and
- that it is intended to cause great suffering or serious injury.

The ICC definition was quoted and applied by the ICTY Trial Chamber in *Tadić*, where severe beatings were found to qualify as 'other inhumane acts'.[116] Another ICTY decision found that the offence was essentially the same as the war crime of cruel treatment, with only the relevant contextual elements being different.[117]

Notably, this residual category allows the recognition—effectively, the creation—of new crimes against humanity. This may raise questions as to whether the provision is so vague as to violate *nullum crimen sine lege*,[118] or at least as to the appropriateness of judges creating substantially new criminal law.[119]

The point is not free from controversy. The ICTY Trial Chamber in *Stakić* was quite reluctant to have recourse to the idea of 'other inhumane acts' to create new offences not previously recognized in and prohibited by international criminal law, in part due to concerns over *nullum crimen sine lege*.[120] The Appeals Chamber disagreed, arguing

---

[111] Art 7(1)(k).   [112] Art 3(i).   [113] Art 5(i).   [114] Art 7(1)(k), ICC Statute.

[115] Yearbook of the International Law Commission, 1996, vol. II (2), 47 (Article 18(k)).

[116] *Tadić*, ICTY Trial Chamber, 7 May 1997, para 729.

[117] *Delalić, Mucić et al (Čelebići)*, ICTY Trial Chamber, 16 November 1998, para 443. On the war crime of cruel treatment see Chapter 8, section 8.6.5.

[118] See, for example: *Kordić and Čerkez*, ICTY Appeals Chamber, 17 December 2004, para 117. In this context Cassese et al draw a distinction between substantive justice and strict legality: *International Criminal Law*, 24–27 (ie substantive justice would prefer to see heinous acts punished even if that violated the principle against retrospective punishment; strict legality would, however, require that all rules of criminal law be declared clearly in advance).

[119] Note Robinson, 'Crimes Against Humanity' in Cryer et al, *Introduction*, 261 (arguing that the requirements of (1) similar character to other crimes against humanity and (2) the threshold of great suffering or serious injury are sufficiently precise to prevent concern).

[120] *Stakić*, ICTY Trial Chamber, 31 July 2003, paras 719–22.

that the idea of other inhumane acts 'cannot be regarded as a violation of the principle of *nullum crimen sine lege* as it forms part of customary international law'.[121]

9.5 Persecution

The crime against humanity of persecution was usefully summarized in the *Krajišnik* case as involving an act or omission which: '(a) discriminates in fact and denies a fundamental human right laid down in international law; and (b) is carried out with the intention to discriminate on one of the listed grounds, namely politics, race, or religion.'[122] While useful, this summary is not entirely comprehensive for two reasons.

First, the underlying act of persecution may be either:

- another crime against humanity; or
- a denial of a fundamental human right.[123]

On the latter point one should note that 'not every denial of a fundamental human right will be serious enough to constitute a crime against humanity'; the act 'committed on discriminatory grounds', must be of the same gravity as other crimes against humanity when considered either in isolation or when committed in conjunction with other acts.[124] Nonetheless, a unique feature of persecution remains that severe deprivations of a fundamental human right may constitute the act underlying the crime against humanity.

Second, the essence of persecution is discriminatory intent. While *Krajišnik* refers to discrimination based on politics, race, or religion the ICC Statute adds to this list discrimination based on national, ethnic, cultural, or gender grounds.

9.5.1 Material element

In light of this, the material element or conduct underlying the crime of persecution may be of two main types:

- the commission of acts which could by themselves constitute crimes against humanity: murder, imprisonment, enslavement, torture, etc;[125] or
- severe deprivations of rights protected by treaty or customary international law.[126]

---

[121] *Stakić*, ICTY Appeals Chamber, 22 March 2006, para 315.
[122] *Krajišnik*, ICTY Trial Chamber, 27 September 2006, para 734.
[123] Ibid, para 734.   [124] Ibid, para 735.
[125] *Kupreškić*, ICTY Trial Chamber, 14 January 2000, para 596 refers for example to 'deportation, slave labour, and extermination' as underlying acts considered by the Nuremberg IMT to make out charges of persecution.
[126] Ibid, para 596 (referring to the severe restriction of economic rights of the Jewish population under Nazi race laws); compare *Kordić and Čerkez*, ICTY Appeals Chamber, 17 December 2004, para 106; *Tadić*, ICTY Trial Chamber, 7 May 1997, para 710.

Several qualifications should be noted. First, in ICTY case law acts constituting war crimes against civilians and their property may also form the underlying offences of persecution.[127]

Second, the ICC Statute definition of is different and narrower. In the ICC Statute persecution refers *only* to the 'intentional and severe deprivation of fundamental rights' on discriminatory grounds and *also* requires that such deprivation of rights occurs in connection with an act prohibited as a crime against humanity, or another crime within ICC jurisdiction.[128] Thus the following forms of persecution under ICTY case law do not fall within the ICC Statute definition:

- acts constituting a crime against humanity of themselves, coupled with a discriminatory intent; or

- severe rights deprivations carried out with a discriminatory intent but which are not connected with another international crime.

While there are similarities between the ICC definition and Article 6(c) of the Nuremberg IMT's London Charter, the ICC definition appears to reject the broader view taken in ICTY case law. Indeed, the ICC definition was not accepted as an accurate statement of customary international law by an ICTY Trial Chamber in *Kupreškić*.[129]

9.5.2 Severity/gravity comparable to other crimes against humanity

Where the underlying conduct is not *per se* a crime against humanity, but instead a deprivation of a fundamental right, then an additional requirement must be met. Either:

- under the ICTY case law (and, arguably, customary international law) the deprivation in question must be of 'the same gravity' as other crimes against humanity;[130] or

- under the ICC Statute the deprivation must be both 'severe' and connected with another act or acts constituting a crime against humanity.

Ultimately, there is no 'comprehensive list' of rights violations that may constitute persecution.[131] Some examples drawn from the case law include:

- hate speech may, in the context of widespread killings already underway, be sufficiently serious to constitute the material element of persecution;[132]

- it has been held that the collective denial of civil rights can amount to persecution, even where the violations in isolation would not be sufficiently serious: thus, 'the denial of freedom of movement, the denial of employment, the denial of the right to judicial process, and the denial of equal access to public services' may not

---

[127] *Kordić and Čerkez*, ICTY Appeals Chamber, 17 December 2004, paras 104–9.
[128] See Art 7(1)(h) and (2)(g), ICC Statute.
[129] *Kupreškić*, ICTY Trial Chamber, 14 January 2000, paras 567–80.
[130] *Krajišnik*, ICTY Trial Chamber, 27 September 2006, para 735.
[131] *Kordić and Čerkez*, ICTY Trial Chamber, 26 February 2001, para 694.
[132] *Nahimana et al (The Media Case)*, ICTR Appeals Chamber, 28 November 2007, paras 983–88.

in isolation be of sufficient gravity but may constitute persecution 'when taken in conjunction with each other';[133] and

- the cumulative effect of abusive treatment in war-time detention camps involving harassment, humiliation, and psychological abuse may constitute persecution. Such treatment may be contrary to the human rights protections of the Geneva Conventions, including the prohibition on 'outrages upon personal dignity, in particular humiliating and degrading treatment'.[134]

9.5.3 Mental element: prohibited discriminatory grounds (politics, race, religion)

The prosecution must prove that the acts were carried out on discriminatory grounds: 'political, racial, national, ethnic, cultural, religious, gender [grounds]' or other grounds 'universally recognized as impermissible under international law', in the words of the ICC Statute.[135] This does not require proof of a specific intent or *dolus specialis* on the part of the accused. That is, what is required is an objective knowledge that *in fact* the conduct fits into a pattern of discrimination; the perpetrator need not *subjectively* intend (or desire) the persecution of a group.[136]

9.6 Why have a separate category of crimes against humanity?

If we already have war crimes and genocide, is there a good reason to have crimes against humanity as a separate category? The easy answer is that governments and other organized groups can commit appalling acts against their own people that fall short of genocide and do not constitute war crimes (either because there is no armed conflict or because the law of war crimes traditionally protected only foreign nationals). As a matter of positive law it cannot be doubted that crimes against humanity exist. However, as the historical evolution of the crime through the documentary sources shows, there has perhaps been more agreement on the existence of the category than its precise content.

It is easy enough to resort to the idea that these crimes should be punished because they, in the worlds of the Supreme Court of Israel in the *Eichmann* case, 'affront the conscience of all civilised nations'.[137] But is such a broad moral intuition a good basis for declaring something criminal? How can it help us find the precise limits of the offence so a fair trial can be conducted? As noted above, at the end of the First World War the US took the view that 'crimes against humanity' was too vague and uncertain a term to

---

[133] *Krajišnik*, ICTY Trial Chamber, 27 September 2006, para 740 (summarizing the approach of the ICTY Trial Chamber in *Brđanin*).

[134] *Kvočka*, ICTY Appeals Chamber 2005, paras 321–25.   [135] Art 7(1)(h), ICC Statute.

[136] See *Kordić and Čerkez*, Trial Chamber, 26 February 2001, para 212; *Kordić and Čerkez*, Appeals Chamber, 17 December 2004, para 111; Art 7, fn 22, ICC Elements of Crimes.

[137] *A-G Israel v Eichmann* (1968) 36 ILR 277 (Supreme Court of Israel), 292.

found criminal prosecutions. The idea of *humanity* involved seemed too subjective and there was a risk its content could vary with the judge.

There remains a debate about whether there is a good theoretical justification for crimes against humanity going beyond a very general (and obvious) moral point that such things are horrifying and should be punished. Another way of asking the same question is to ask where is the dividing line between an ordinary crime (murder under national law) and an international crime (murder as a crime against humanity)? Two broad approaches may be contrasted. For some the essence of a crime against humanity is that it sets limits on what the State—or State-like entities—may do and sees in crimes against humanity a failure to fulfil a 'responsibility to protect' that a State owes its citizens and residents (a state-centred approach).[138] Others see crimes against humanity as protective: the point of crimes against humanity is that individual human beings need protection, irrespective of which entity violates their human rights.[139] Both approaches ask what the role of 'humanity' is within crime against humanity. A brief account of some of these debates will be offered here. The aim is not to present an exhaustive account, but rather to introduce a number of key ideas and representative positions.

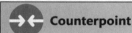 **Counterpoint**

Much of the thinking about crimes against humanity engages with the work of Hannah Arendt. Arendt was a German political philosopher who fled Nazi rule to live in France (and later the US). She was rendered stateless in 1937 when, as a Jew, she was stripped of her German citizenship. Her experience of being left effectively rightless when her citizenship was withdrawn informed her political thought. As she put it, describing the plight of stateless persons: '[t]he world found nothing sacred in the abstract nakedness of being human.'[140] This was the paradox of human rights as a matter of lived experience: stateless people were not *in practice* protected by inherent human rights.[141] Those rights, it appeared to Arendt, could only truly be protected by membership in a political community—having citizenship in a State. However, it was that same State that could become a persecutor of its citizens.

One modern theorist who has engaged with the work of Arendt is David Luban.[142] Luban notes that the theoretical challenge is to identify what makes crimes against

---

[138] Robinson, 'Crimes Against Humanity' in Cryer et al, *Introduction*, 240; compare Cassese et al, *Cassese's International Criminal Law*, 90–92.

[139] G Werle and B Burghardt, 'Do Crimes against Humanity Require the Participation of a State or a "State-Like" Organization?' (2012) 10 Journal of International Criminal Justice 1151, 1153

[140] H Arendt, *The Origins of Totalitarianism* (World Publishing 1958), 299.

[141] A Kesby, *The Right to Have Rights: Citizenship, Humanity and International Law* (Oxford University Press 2012), 3.

[142] D Luban, 'A Theory of Crimes against Humanity' (2004) 29 Yale Journal of International Law 85, 109–123.

humanity different from (or worse than) the worst crimes committed under national law. He acknowledges theories that crimes against humanity attack humanity itself by diminishing human diversity (that is, human diversity is attacked by targeting groups). He thinks such theories are inadequate because humanity is diverse not only in groups but also in individuals. To treat people only as members of groups is not an adequate account of what human diversity means. (Indeed, we might also observe that protecting human diversity in terms of groups is rather the aim of the law of genocide than crimes against humanity.)

Instead, Luban sees crimes against humanity as an attack on the human as a political animal (defined below). Crimes against humanity are not only committed against groups, but by groups. The paradox of human sociability is that to lead full and productive (and safe) lives we are better off as part of organized political communities (i.e. humans are political animals, to be fully human we must live in a *polis*—an organized community). However, there is also the possibility that the same organized political community that protects us could be used to attack us. He describes this as 'politics gone cancerous':[143] when the State starts attacking its own people. Crimes against humanity acknowledge that people live in States and as part of groups and therefore live alongside other groups—but that there is always a risk that politically organized groups can turn against those they live alongside.

One may perhaps criticize Luban's approach as being too focussed on the idea of groups and discriminatory motives. A discriminatory motive is required only for the crime of persecution (and genocide). However, his basic account of crimes against humanity as protecting individuals against the political power of collective groups fits the State-centred approach described above.

In contrast to Luban, Christopher Macleod espouses a more human-centred approach.[144] He suggests that there are advantages in focussing on an explanation of crimes against humanity as being those crimes that *damage* humankind. He distinguishes two meanings of 'humanity': the human race ('humankind'); and some shared special characteristic that makes us all human ('human nature' or 'humaneness'). He examines a number of approaches to crimes against humanity, but focusses on two main ideas: either crimes against humanity are those that *shock the conscience* of humankind; or crimes against humanity are those that *damage* humankind. Macleod also notes that something has to be identified that makes these crimes worse than or different from the worst crimes committed under national law (the 'Arendt test', as he calls it). He suggests we can think of crimes against humanity as those that somehow affect humanity in the sense of affecting literally every human being (a literal collection of all people) or which affect an imagined body of all people. That is, crimes against humanity are those that damage the interests of humankind as a whole. These interests might be damaged when a sufficiently large number of people are killed (thus harming humanity

---

[143] Luban, 'A Theory of Crimes against Humanity', 116.

[144] C Macleod, 'Towards a Philosophical Account of Crimes Against Humanity' (2010) 21 European Journal of International Law 281.

as the literal collection of all human beings). Humankind as a whole might also have an interest in being 'unmarked by moral atrocities' (thus the imagined community of all humanity is morally harmed).[145] That is, there is something so uniquely shocking about these crimes that we can imagine the *body of all people* being shocked (his test does not require that every individual human being is shocked). This approach has its appeal, particularly the idea of the interest of all humanity in being 'unmarked by moral atrocities'. However, we can ask whether it really carries us much further than the *Eichmann* case proposition that crimes against humanity are those that shock the conscience of all humankind. If not, we still lack a theory that tells us anything very precise about where the limits of the crime should fall.

9.7 Summary and conclusions

This chapter started with history, moved through the positive law, and ended with questions of theory. In particular, this chapter has covered:

- how the definition of a crime against humanity has evolved through the statutory law of the major tribunals;
- the contextual element of crimes against humanity, being that such crimes must be 'committed as part of a widespread or systematic attack directed against a civilian population';
- the range of underlying offences which may form part of a crime against humanity; and
- the required mental element, being that a perpetrator intended to commit the elements of the underlying offence and had knowledge that, objectively, his or her conduct would form 'part of' the ongoing 'attack'.

Further, the chapter has addressed:

- the contextual element of crimes against humanity; that is, what is meant by the words 'a widespread or systematic attack', 'directed against', civilian population and, indeed, 'part of';
- whether 'widespread *or* systematic attack' is as disjunctive as it at first appears, given the element of organization implied by the words 'attack' and 'directed against';
- the question of whether a crime against humanity must be committed pursuant to a policy and if so what types of organizations (other than States) can formulate such policies; and
- some of both the historical and theoretical reasons that justify having crimes against humanity as a separate category from war crimes and genocide.

---

[145] Macleod, 'Towards a Philosophical Account', 298.

A number of controversies are thus apparent. One of the most obvious points is that there has never been a treaty on crimes against humanity.[146] A moment's reflection may indicate why this might be so. States typically commit war crimes against other State's citizens. Genocide is so heinous that all States could readily agree that it should criminalized under a treaty. However, historically crimes against humanity have been something that States typically commit against their own citizens. This may leave governments nervous about creating an offence which could be used to impugn elements of their own policy. For example, one Australian Member of Parliament has recently alleged that the Australian government's policy of intercepting boat people on the high seas and subjecting them to compulsory detention amounts to a crime against humanity.[147] (Obviously, a systemic government policy of unlawful detention against a particular 'population' could be a crime against humanity. However, consider whether migration detention is obviously unlawful and whether groups of irregular migrants of disparate nationality moving across the high seas constitute a 'population'.) This leads us to the next major controversy, whether it is a requirement of crimes against humanity that they be committed by a State or State-like organizations. The early jurisprudence of the International Criminal Court on the Kenyan situation seems to indicate that the Court is moving towards a broader view of the types of organizations which can commit crimes against humanity.

Useful further reading

A CASSESE, 'Crimes Against Humanity' in A Cassese et al (eds), *The Rome Statute of the International Criminal Court: A Commentary* (Oxford University Press 2002), Chapter 11, 11.2.
A concise account of the historical development of crimes against humanity as a matter of customary international law, and the relationship of the ICC Statute definition to the customary law definition.

C KRESS, 'On the Outer Limits of Crimes Against Humanity: The Concept of Organization within the Policy Requirement: Some Reflections on the March 2010 ICC Kenya Decision' (2010) 23 Leiden Journal of International Law 855.
This article closely reviews the implications of the Kenyan Situation Decision for the kinds of organizations which can commit crimes against humanity, and the arguments for and against the 'narrow' understanding of organization the author prefers.

D LUBAN, 'A Theory of Crimes against Humanity' (2004) 29 Yale Journal of International Law 85, especially at p 109.
One of the more influential articles examining the idea that crimes against humanity should be understood in terms of how such crimes diminish humanity. He suggests that crimes against humanity should be understood as serving a protective function, one acknowledging the dangers posed to individuals by the fact that we live in organized political groups.

---

[146] See further: LN Sadat (ed), *Forging a Convention for Crimes against Humanity* (Cambridge University Press 2013).

[147] See: S Medhora, 'Asylum seekers: Andrew Wilkie takes Australia to International Criminal Court', The Guardian (Australian edition), 22 October 2014, www.theguardian.com/australia-news/2014/oct/22/asylum-seekers-andrew-wilkie-takes-australia-to-international-criminal-court.

P WEINER, 'The Evolving Jurisprudence of the Crime of Rape in International Criminal Law' (2013) 36 Boston College International & Comparative Law Review 1207.
An excellent account of the development of sexual offences law in international criminal law. The author makes a strong case that the focus on the absence of the victim's consent found in many national jurisdictions is inappropriate for international criminal law (which he proposes should focus on the existence of coercive circumstances).

G WERLE and B BURGHARDT, 'Do Crimes against Humanity Require the Participation of a State or a "State-Like" Organization?' (2012) 10 Journal of International Criminal Justice 1151.
A closely-argued article making a strong case for the 'broader' understanding of the types of organization which can commit crimes against humanity.

10

Genocide

10.1 Introduction

The present chapter introduces the crime of genocide. As the UN Secretary-General noted during the negotiation of the Genocide Convention, genocide is as crime 'almost as old as the world'[1]—even if it was not named as such before the twentieth century. We now most strongly associate the term with the Nazi regime in Germany of 1933–1945, given its systematic and large-scale destruction of certain racial and ethnic groups. Indeed, the term 'genocide' itself was coined by legal academic Raphael Lemkin in 1943–1944 to describe Nazi efforts to destroy national, ethnic, or religious groups.[2] The Nazi regime was responsible for the deaths of approximately six million Jews in the Holocaust, as well as the murder of very large numbers of ethnic Roma, the mentally and physically disabled, and homosexuals.

Nonetheless, genocide was not a crime within the jurisdiction of the Nuremberg International Military Tribunal (IMT). Lemkin in fact lobbied for the inclusion of geno-cide in the IMT Charter but lost to the objections of those who favoured the inclusion of crimes against humanity instead. The debate turned, to some extent, on whether one considered it more important to focus on individuals or groups as the victims of Nazi atrocities.[3] Nonetheless, the term genocide was used by the prosecutors at Nuremberg, if not by the judges.[4]

The prohibition against genocide is now found in treaty and customary law, and is universally accepted as being an international crime 'whether committed in time of peace or in time of war'.[5] In 1946 the United Nations General Assembly affirmed that

---

[1] H Abtahi and P Webb, *The Genocide Convention: The Travaux Préparatoires* (Brill 2009) 35.

[2] R Lemkin, *Axis Rule in Occupied Europe* (1944), 79 ff.

[3] A key proponent of the inclusion of crimes against humanity instead of the crime of genocide was Hersch Lauterpacht, then professor of international law at the University of Cambridge and later a Judge of the ICJ. Both Lemkin and Lauterpacht were Jewish and had radically different ideas as to how law should react to the Holocaust. See further: S Troebst, 'Lemkin and Lauterpacht in Lemberg and Later: Pre- and Post-Holocaust Careers of Two East European International Lawyers', *Transit*, 2013, www.iwm.at/read-listen-watch/transit-online/lemkin-and-lauterpacht-in-lemberg-and-later-pre-and-post-holocaust-careers-of-two-east-european-international-lawyers/.

[4] W Schabas, *An Introduction to the International Criminal Court*, 4th ed (Cambridge University Press 2011), 99.

[5] Art 1, Convention on the Prevention and Punishment of the Crime of Genocide, adopted 9 December 1948, entered into force 12 January 1951, 78 UNTS 277.

genocide was *already* an existing crime under international law in Resolution 96(1). This resolution clearly provides evidence of *opinio juris*. It was followed by the Convention on the Prevention and Punishment of Genocide 1948, which came as a reaction to the Nazi genocide[6] and entered into force on 12 January 1951. Moreover, the International Court of Justice (ICJ) held in 1951 that the Genocide Convention's underlying principles bound all States[7] and in later cases that the prohibition on genocide is a peremptory norm of international law (*jus cogens*).[8] The ICTY has also affirmed in *Krstić* that genocide is a peremptory norm of general international law.[9] The crime, of course, remains one of tragic contemporary relevance, acts of genocide having been committed in the former Yugoslavia in the period 1992–1995 and in Rwanda in 1994.[10] In cases before the ICC, genocide has also been alleged to have been committed in Darfur, west Sudan, in the period since 2003.[11]

 Learning aims

By the end of this chapter you should be able to:

- discuss the role of the protected groups in the definition of the crime of genocide, their correct interpretation, and their limitations;

- explain the 'special intent' requirement in the case law, and distinguish the alternative 'knowledge based approach' proposed in academic literature;

- discuss whether genocide requires (or should require) a 'contextual' element similar to crimes against humanity; and following from the contextual element question, discuss whether there could be a lone *génocidaire*; and

- understand why genocide is a difficult crime to prove.

---

[6] G Werle and F Jessberger, *Principles of International Criminal Law*, 3rd ed (Oxford University Press 2014) 292, para 779.

[7] *Advisory Opinion on Reservations to the Convention on the Prevention and Punishment of the Crime of Genocide*, (1951) ICJ Reports 15, 23. On the consequences of *jus cogens* status see discussion in Chapter 2 and J Wouters and S Verhoeven, 'The Prohibition of Genocide as a Norm of Jus Cogens and Its Implications for the Law of Genocide' (2005) 5 International Criminal Law Review 401. In particular, the fact a norm has *jus cogens* status may not affect in practice questions of State immunity: *Jurisdictional Immunities of the State (Germany v Italy: Greece intervening)*, 2012 ICJ Reports 99, paras 92–97. See further Chapter 14.

[8] *Democratic Republic of the Congo v Rwanda*, 2006 ICJ Reports 6, para 64; *Application of the Convention on the Prevention and Punishment of the Crime of Genocide (Bosnia and Herzegovina v Serbia and Montenegro)*, 2007 ICJ Reports 43, para 161 ('*Bosnian Genocide Case*') both noting again that: the principles underlying the Convention are 'recognized by civilized nations as binding on States' even in the absence of treaty obligations.

[9] *Krstić*, ICTY Trial Chamber, 2 August 2001, para 541.

[10] There have been a significant number of convictions before the ICTR for Genocide and also before the ICTY: LN Sadat, 'Crimes against Humanity in the Modern Age' (2013) 107 American Journal of International Law 334, 343, and 347. See also the condemnation of the Rwandan genocide in UN Security Council Resolution 2150 (2014).

[11] *Al Bashir* (Second Decision on the Prosecution's Application for a Warrant of Arrest), ICC Pre-Trial Chamber I, 12 July 2010.

Many of the essential issues for consideration in this chapter can be unpacked from the text of the Genocide Convention itself and it is worth quoting the relevant provisions in full.

Article 2, Convention on the Prevention and Punishment of the Crime of Genocide 1948

In the present Convention, genocide means any of the following acts committed with intent to destroy, in whole or in part, a national, ethnical, racial or religious group, as such:

(a) Killing members of the group;

(b) Causing serious bodily or mental harm to members of the group;

(c) Deliberately inflicting on the group conditions of life calculated to bring about its physical destruction in whole or in part;

(d) Imposing measures intended to prevent births within the group;

(e) Forcibly transferring children of the group to another group.

We can note the following features of this definition:

- The crime of genocide is limited to acts committed against members of a 'national, ethnical, racial or religious group' ('the protected groups') but does not further define these vital terms.

- On its face the list of protected groups is exhaustive and cannot be broadened to include members of other groups, such as members of a political party or groups defined by sexual orientation.

- The list of prohibited acts is not confined to killing, but does not expressly include efforts to change or extinguish a group's cultural identity ('cultural genocide'), although some of the prohibited acts could have this result.

- The prohibited acts must be committed with the additional 'intent to destroy, in whole or in part,' a protected group 'as such' (the 'special intent' or '*dolus specialis*').

- The Convention includes no express requirement that such acts be committed on a wide scale or as part of a governmental or organizational policy (a 'contextual element', which is obviously a requirement of crimes against humanity).

This last point appears to leave open the possibility that a single act of killing by a lone individual who acted with the required intent could technically be genocide (the 'lone *génocidaire*' question). This issue is returned to later.

In addition, the Genocide Convention makes clear that not only those who physically carry out killing (or other prohibited acts) are guilty of genocide. The Convention expressly contemplates in Article 3 that:

- conspiracy to commit genocide;

- direct and public incitement to commit genocide;

- attempt to commit genocide; and

- complicity in genocide,

are all punishable as 'other acts'.[12] We consider such modes of participation in international crimes (i.e. conspiracy, incitement, attempt, and complicity) in detail in

---

[12] Art 4, Genocide Convention 1948.

Chapter 12. Peculiarly, though, this 'other acts' terminology used in the Genocide Convention necessarily suggest these acts are offences alongside genocide *sensu stricto* rather than being means of committing genocide.

A few observations can be ventured here though about the relationship between these 'other acts' and genocide. First, the 'other act' approach in which conspiracy, incitement, attempt, and complicity are listed as separate crimes is not generally taken in the ICC Statute. Instead, the ICC has a number of general modes of participation in crimes which apply to all crimes equally—with the one exception of limiting 'direct and public incitement' as means of participation in genocide.[13] Second, conspiracy in the common law tradition is the inchoate crime of two or more people agreeing to commit a crime 'even if the crime is never perpetrated'.[14] The drafting history of the Convention shows that 'conspiracy to commit genocide' was intended to be an inchoate crime in the common law sense.[15] (As opposed to conspiracy in the civil law tradition in which liability only follows to the extent that the crime comes about.) Third, the requirements of direct and public incitement to commit genocide are discussed in Chapter 12, section 12.4.4 but it notably is also an inchoate crime, in that a genocide does not have to come about as a result of the incitement. Fourth, there has never been a prosecution for attempt to commit genocide,[16] but the general view is that attempt involves having taken a 'substantial step' towards completion of a crime.[17] It is therefore also an inchoate offence. Finally, complicity refers to the liability of an accomplice and can be taken to have a 'substantially similar' meaning to 'aiding and abetting' as discussed in Chapter 12, section 12.4.2,[18] though it might also cover such forms of participation in a crime as ordering a crime or taking part in a collective criminal plan.[19] These concepts are also separately discussed in Chapter 12.

With these various considerations in mind the present chapter is structured as follows:

- Section 10.2 considers the definition of the protected groups.
- Section 10.3 outlines the legal definitions of the prohibited acts.
- Section 10.4 considers whether there is a 'contextual element' required as part of the crime of genocide and addresses the lone *génocidaire* question.
- Section 10.5 examines the mental element of the crime of genocide and the role of the 'special intent' requirement.

---

[13] Art 25(3), ICC Statute.
[14] Cassese et al, *Cassese's International Criminal Law*, 201.
[15] W Schabas, *Genocide in International Law: The Crime of Crimes*, 2nd ed (Cambridge University Press 2009) 310.
[16] Schabas, *Genocide in International Law*, 337.   [17] E.g. Art 25(3)(f), ICC Statute.
[18] *Semanza*, ICTR Trial Chamber, 15 May 2003, para 394.
[19] See also: Schabas, *Genocide in International Law*, 345–50.

10.2 Protected groups

Genocide requires that a prohibited act is committed against a member of one of the protected groups, being a 'national, ethnical, racial or religious group'. This list is not preceded in the Convention by words suggesting the list is an open one (e.g. 'such as' or 'including'). Therefore the list is closed: only the four listed groups are protected. Social, cultural, sexual-orientation, or political groups, for example, are excluded. During the negotiation of the genocide Convention this issue was debated[20] and the USSR in particular advocated that political groups should be *excluded* on the basis that they lack stability or permanence because their members do not belong to them by birth.[21] (Arguably, it was unsurprising that the USSR took this view given its history of political purges.)[22] A number of scholars have criticized this restrictive aspect of the Convention definition.[23] Further, as noted above, the Convention does not provide the definition of those groups; Antonio Cassese in particular considered this a serious flaw in the Convention.[24]

There is, however, some support for the idea that any stable and permanent group may be a protected group under the Convention, including:

- the 1998 *Akayesu* case before the Trial Chamber of the International Criminal Tribunal for Rwanda;[25] and

- the 2005 Report of the International Commission of Inquiry on Darfur (the 'Darfur Report').[26]

Cassese and his co-authors also appear to support this wider approach. They argue that, on a modern understanding, the concept of national, racial, religious, or ethnic groups are 'subjective cultural constructs rather than fixed biological facts'.[27] Thus they argue that the question of whether a targeted group is protected under the Genocide

---

[20] A good summary of the debates is found in: United Nations Report on the Study of the Question of the Prevention and Punishment of the Crime of Genocide, UN Doc. E/CN.4/Sub.2/416 (4 July 1978), paras 79–87.

[21] M Boot, *Genocide, Crimes Against Humanity, War Crimes: Nullum Crimen Sine Lege and the Subject Matter Jurisdiction of the International Criminal Court* (Intersentia 2002) 426.

[22] A. Cassese et al, *International Criminal Law: Cases and Commentary* (Oxford University Press 2011) 204.

[23] A Cassese et al, *Cassese's International Criminal Law*, 3rd ed (Oxford University Press 2013) 113; J Paoust et al, *Human Rights Module on Crimes Against Humanity, Genocide, Other Crimes Against Human Rights, and War Crimes*, 2nd ed (Carolina Academic Press 2006) 73; J Quigley, *The Genocide Convention: An International Law Analysis* (Ashgate 2006) 83. Contrast, however, W Schabas, 'Genocide and Crimes against Humanity: Clarifying the Relationship', in HG van der Wilt et al (eds), *The Genocide Convention: The Legacy of 60 Years* (Brill 2012) 4 (noting the Convention 'is what it is' and that attempts to cure its 'gaps' are akin to proposing 'improvements' to Picasso's Guernica).

[24] A Cassese, 'International Criminal Law' in M Evans (ed), *International Law* (Oxford University Press 2003) 739.

[25] *Akayesu*, ICTR Trial Chamber Judgment, 2 September 1998, para 516.

[26] The full report is found in UN Doc. S/2005/60. Available via the Security Council web page or www.un.org/news/dh/sudan/com_inq_darfur.pdf.

[27] A Cassese et al, *International Criminal Law: Cases and Commentary*, 204; compare E Wilmshurst, 'Genocide' in R Cryer et al, *An Introduction to International Criminal Law and Procedure*, 3rd ed (Cambridge University Press 2014) 213 ('Groups are often social constructs, rather than scientific facts').

Convention should be one of whether the group has 'stable characteristics'.[28] It is certainly difficult to give the listed groups an objective meaning. For example, one might think of 'ethnic groups' as having distinct languages and cultures. Yet in the Rwandan genocide the different 'ethnic' groups of Hutus and Tutsis shared the same language and culture. Similarly, the Darfur Report noted:

> The various tribes that have been the object of attacks and killings (chiefly the Fur, Masalit and Zaghawa tribes) do not appear to make up ethnic groups distinct from the ethnic group to which persons or militias that attack them belong. They speak the same language (Arabic) and embrace the same religion (Islam). In addition, owing to the high incidence of intermarriage, they can hardly be distinguished in their outward physical appearance from the members of tribes that allegedly attacked them.[29]

The main points of distinction between the tribes were whether they lived sedentary or nomadic lives or whether they spoke only Arabic or their own dialect in addition to Arabic. Such difficulties support arguments for the adoption of the broad 'any stable or permanent group' approach.[30] However, there is no evidence this broad view enjoys widespread support in the *opinio juris* of States and nor has it been followed in subsequent ICTR, ICTY, or ICC case law.[31]

If we accept (as most scholars and international courts do) that the list of protected groups is closed, we must still define 'national, ethnical, racial or religious group'. How then are we to approach this question? The ICTY Trial Chamber in *Krstić* took the view that the four terms cannot be differentiated 'on the basis of scientifically objective criteria' and the list was 'designed more to describe a single phenomenon, roughly corresponding to . . . [the older idea of] "national minorities" '.[32] Schabas refers to this as the 'four corners' approach, where each term helps define the others.[33] While this is a helpful way of thinking about the question, it is does not necessarily provide a legal test which a court could apply.

Given the difficulties of objective definition of groups, it is useful to give some role to the *subjective* view of the perpetrator or victim.[34] On a subjective view, a victim would belong to a group if the perpetrator believed them to be part of that group. This approach reflects the reality that racist persecution may have little basis in fact, and turn largely on perceptions. A focus on whether victims and perpetrators subjectively believe themselves to belong to different groups reduces or eliminates any need to expand the four categories of group protected under the Convention.[35] Referring to

[28] A Cassese et al, *International Criminal Law: Cases and Commentary*, 204; see also A Szpak, 'National, Ethnic, Racial, and Religious Groups Protected against Genocide in the Jurisprudence of the ad hoc International Criminal Tribunals' (2012) 23 European Journal of International Law 155, 163.

[29] Darfur Report, n. 26, para 508.

[30] *Akayesu*, ICTR Trial Chamber Judgment, 2 September 1998, para 516.

[31] Wilmshurst, 'Genocide' in Cryer et al, *Introduction*, 210–11; Schabas, *Introduction to the International Criminal Court*, 105.

[32] *Krstić*, ICTY Trial Chamber, 2 August 2001, para 556.

[33] Schabas, *Genocide in International Law*, 129.

[34] Szpak, 'National, Ethnic, Racial, and Religious Groups', 163; Schabas, *Introduction to the International Criminal Court*, 105.

[35] Schabas, *Introduction to the International Criminal Court*, 105.

the situation in the Sudan, for example, Schabas explains that militias have perse-
cuted various groups not because they perceived those groups as being permanent
and stable, but because they perceived them to be a national, ethnic, racial, or religious
group.[36] A court may thus deem a victim to belong to a group because he or she per-
ceives himself or herself to be a part of the group (self-identification), or because he
or she is perceived as to be a member of the group by the perpetrators (identification
by others).[37]

The approach of the ICTY and ICTR on balance appears to be neither wholly subjective (focussed on the perceptions of victims or perpetrators) nor wholly objective
(focussed on observable group characteristics). A Court will always have to consider issues of both self-identification and identification by others, in light of the
relevant historical, political, social, and cultural context. Of these two subjective
approaches, the view of the perpetrators (identification by others) is probably the
more important.

 Pause for reflection

***How does a court balance issues of self-identification and of identification-by-
others in a given local context?***

This approach of testing the existence of a protected group by looking to questions of identification within the local historical, political, social, and cultural context can be found in ICTR
cases such as *Semanza*,[38] *Kayishema and Ruzindana*,[39] and *Rutaganda*.[40] These cases involved
a mixed approach based on subjective identification but also taking into account objective
contextual factors (including, in the Rwandan case, government issued identity documents
listing whether one was Hutu, Twa, or Tutsi which 'codified subjective perceptions of group
divisions').[41] In *Kayishema and Ruzindana*, this reasoning was made quite explicit: the Court
held that 'an ethnic group is one whose members share a common language and culture; or,
a group which distinguishes itself, as such (self-identification); or a group identified as such
by others'.[42]

10.3 Prohibited acts

Pursuant to Article 2 of the Genocide Convention, there are five categories of underlying prohibited act which may constitute genocide. These acts are generally closely associated with physical or biological destruction, since the negotiators of the Convention

---

[36] Ibid, 106.   [37] Szpak, 'National, Ethnic, Racial, and Religious Groups', 163.
[38] *Semanza*, ICTR Trial Chamber, 15 May 2003, para 317.
[39] *Kayishema and Ruzindana*, ICTR Trial Chamber, 21 May 1999, paras 522–26.
[40] *Rutaganda*, ICTR Trial Chamber Judgment, 6 December 1999, paras 48–62.
[41] Cassese et al, *International Criminal Law: Cases and Commentary*, 207 (also discussing how such group
memberships were in practice fluid and could change over time, including by marriage).
[42] *Kayishema and Ruzindana*, ICTR Trial Chamber, 21 May 1999, para 98.

abandoned the concept of 'cultural genocide' (being the annihilation of the cultural elements, such as the language, of a group).[43]

10.3.1 Killing members of the group

Killing has been characterized as the 'paradigmatic example' of the conduct element of genocide.[44] In this context killing has been interpreted as voluntarily or intentionally causing death.[45] Unplanned and spontaneous acts are unlikely to indicate genocidal intent.[46] Mere recklessness or negligence as to whether one's actions will cause death is not sufficient. (Intention, recklessness, and negligence were discussed in Chapter 7, section 7.4.1).

10.3.2 Causing serious bodily or mental harm to members of the group

Genocide can clearly be carried out by acts other than killing. What constitutes causing 'serious harm' has to be decided on a case-by-case basis.[47] *Krštić* held that serious harm need not be 'permanent and irremediable' but must go 'beyond temporary unhappiness, embarrassment or humiliation'; the harm involved must result in 'a grave and long-term disadvantage to a person's ability to lead a normal and constructive life.'[48] When the US ratified the ICC Statute it entered an 'understanding' to the text stating that mental harm must result in 'permanent impairment'.[49] This is certainly an expression of US *opinio juris* on the issue, but it does not appear to be a view supported by other States or case law. The US subsequently withdrew its ratification and is not presently a party to the ICC Statute in any event.

Examples of serious harm from the case law include:

- the wounds and trauma inflicted on those who survive mass executions;
- sexual violence and rape; and
- deportation.[50]

---

[43] Cassese et al, *International Criminal Law: Cases and Commentary*, 201; for a summary of the drafting and negotiating history see: N Ruhashyankiko, 'Study of the Question of the Prevention and Punishment of the Crime of Genocide' UN Doc. E/CN.4/Sub.2/416 (4 July 1978). The concept of cultural genocide was also rejected by the ICJ in the *Bosnian Genocide Case*, para 344.

[44] R Cryer, 'International Criminal Law', in M Evans (ed), *International Law*, 4th ed (Oxford University Press 2014) 755.

[45] See: *Akayesu*, ICTR Trial Chamber, 2 September 1998, paras 500–01; *Kayishema and Ruzindana*, ICTR Appeals Chamber, 1 June 2001, para 151; *Rutaganda*, ICTR Trial Chamber, 6 December 1999, para 49.

[46] *Rukundo*, ICTR Appeals Chamber 2010, para 236; E-O Chile, *International Law and Sexual Violence in Armed Conflicts* (Brill 2012) 165.

[47] *Kayishema and Ruzindana*, ICTR Appeals Chamber, 1 June 2001, para 110; *Krstić*, ICTY Trial Chamber 2001, para 513.

[48] *Krstić*, ICTY Trial Chamber, 2 August 2001, para 513.

[49] Wilmshurst, 'Genocide' in Cryer et al, *Introduction*, 215.

[50] *Krstić*, ICTY Trial Chamber, 2 August 2001, para 514 (wounds/trauma suffered by survivors of genocidal killing); *Akayesu*, ICTR Trial Chamber, 2 September 1998, para 731 (sexual violence and rape); *Attorney-General*

The ICC Elements of Crimes notes that prohibited 'conduct may include, but is not necessarily restricted to, acts of torture, rape, sexual violence or inhuman or degrading treatment'.[51] Importantly, regarding deportation, where the objective is only 'to displace, but not to destroy' a group this will not constitute genocide; for forced deportation to be genocide the objective must be the death of the deportees.[52] Forced deportation or forced migration may nonetheless constitute other crimes (particularly crimes against humanity as discussed in Chapter 9, sections 9.3.1 and 9.4.4).

10.3.3 Deliberately inflicting on the group conditions of life calculated to bring about its physical destruction in whole or in part

Cassese and his co-authors characterize the measures which aim to inflict on the group conditions of life calculated to bring about its physical destruction in whole or in part as 'slow death measures'.[53] This is an accurate summary of the ICTY and ICTR case law, which has held that deliberately inflicting on the group conditions of life calculated to bring about its physical destruction, in whole or part, includes:

- 'subjecting a group of people to a subsistence diet, systematic expulsion from homes and the reduction of essential medical services below minimum requirement';[54]

- the infliction of such conditions may also occur through 'the deliberate deprivation of resources indispensible for survival, such as food or medical services';[55] and

- '[a]lso included is the creation of circumstances that would lead to a slow death, such as lack of proper housing, clothing and hygiene or excessive work or physical exertion.'[56]

The ICC Elements of Crimes also list 'deliberate deprivation of resources indispensable for survival, such as food or medical services, or systematic expulsion from homes' as means of committing genocide.[57]

The inclusion of forced expulsions from homes raises the question of whether 'ethnic cleansing' can be genocide; that is, driving people from an area in order to create an ethnically homogenous population. The objective of creating an ethnically homogenous area through a policy of forcible expulsions is not necessarily genocide. As noted

---

of the Governent of Israel v Eichmann (Israel Su Ct. 1962) (1968) 36 International Law Reports 238 (deportation). On deportation, see further the discussion of forced migration below.

[51] ICC Elements of Crimes, Art 6(b), n.3.

[52] *Stakić*, ICTY Appeals Chamber, 22 March 2006, para 56. Compare Quigley, *The Genocide Convention*, 200 (arguing the forced displacement of indigenous people should constitute genocide where serious harm is a foreseeable outcome. Foresight of harm, however, is insufficient to prove genocide: see at n 60).

[53] Cassese et al, *International Criminal Law*, 116.

[54] *Akayesu*, ICTR Trial Chamber, 2 September 1998, paras 505–06.

[55] *Kayishema and Ruzindana*, ICTR Appeals Chamber, 1 June 2001, para 115.

[56] *Brđanin*, ICTY Trial Chamber, 1 September 2004, para 498.

[57] Art 6(c), n 4, CC Elements of Crimes.

in Chapter 9, section 9.4.4, crimes committed for 'the sole purpose of driving people away'[58] may constitute a crime against humanity of deportation or forced transfer of population. However, such crimes will not be genocide unless there is intent to destroy the group, as such, in whole or in part.[59] Nevertheless, where an expulsion is deliberately carried out in a manner designed to cause the deaths of those expelled then a campaign of 'ethnic cleansing' will cross the line into genocide; however, merely knowing that some of those expelled will inevitably die because of the methods of expulsion chosen is insufficient.[60]

10.3.4 Imposing measures intended to prevent births within the group

As a means of committing genocide, imposing measures intended to prevent births within the group clearly has its roots in Nazi compulsory sterilization laws.[61] The particular measure must aim to 'prevent the biological reproduction of the group'.[62] The means of prevention vary. The leading case is *Akayesu*, where the ICTR Trial Chamber held that:

- measures intended to prevent births within the group include 'sexual mutilation, the practice of sterilization, forced birth control, separation of the sexes and prohibition of marriages'; and
- that rape may be used as a means of preventing births within the group, either through: (a) the physical forced impregnation of a woman belonging to the group by a man from another group (where group membership is by paternal descent); or (b) where the trauma inflicted results in the victim subsequently refusing to procreate, in the same way that members can be led, through threats or trauma, not to procreate.[63]

Measures intended to prevent births within the group may thus be both physical and mental.

10.3.5 Forcibly transferring children of the group to another group

This form of the crime of genocide has received little judicial consideration.[64] It is also hard to see it as a species of physical or biological destruction. Rather, it must be understood as the only form of cultural genocide included within the Convention definition. In *Akayesu*, the ICTR Trial Chamber noted that 'as in the case of measures intended to prevent births' the crime could be committed not only through 'a direct act of forcible physical transfer' but also through 'acts of threats or trauma' leading to 'the forcible

---

[58] *Brđanin*, ICTY Trial Chamber, 1 September 2004, para 118.
[59] Werle and Jessberger, *Principles*, 313 para 840.
[60] *Stakić*, ICTY Appeals Chamber, 22 March 2006, para 56.
[61] Wilmshurst, 'Genocide' in Cryer et al, *Introduction*, 217.
[62] Cassese et al, *International Criminal Law*, 116.
[63] *Akayesu*, ICTR Trial Chamber, 2 September 1998, at paras 507–08.
[64] Wilmshurst, 'Genocide' in Cryer et al, *Introduction*, 218.

transfer of children from one group to another.'[65] The ICC Elements of Crimes require that the 'perpetrator knew, or should have known, that the person or persons [forcibly transferred] were under the age of 18 years'.[66] It further notes that forcible transfers can be brought about through threats, abuse of power ,and other non-physical forms of coercion.

In national practice, the Australian Human Rights and Equal Opportunities Commission held that Australia violated the Genocide Convention through its historic policies of forcibly transferring indigenous children into non-indigenous families and care institutions (principally in the period 1905–1969).[67] The Commission concluded:

> the predominant aim of [such] indigenous child removals was the absorption or assimilation of the children into the wider, non-indigenous, community so that their unique cultural values and ethnic identities would disappear...Removal of children with this objective in mind is genocidal because it aims to destroy the 'cultural unit' which the Convention is concerned to preserve.[68]

This conclusion was controversial, not least because there was a sincere (though racist) belief on the part of many persons involved in administering the policy that indigenous people would inevitably die out and the removal of children of 'mixed blood' was in their best interests. This casts doubt on whether the policy was in fact *designed* to bring about group destruction, as opposed to such destruction being a likely outcome of a policy implemented for different, misguided reasons. Nonetheless, the underlying idea behind this form of the offence, that a group identity will be lost, can only be sustained if particularly young children are transferred.[69] As William Schabas notes, the ICC threshold that children are those up to 18 seems too high if the concern is that cultural practices, language, and religion would be lost.[70]

10.4 The 'contextual element' of genocide

We normally associate the term 'genocide' with an organized and/or widespread pattern of killings, usually orchestrated in accordance with a governmental or organizational policy. Unlike crimes against humanity, which require the existence of

[65] *Akayesu*, ICTR Trial Chamber, 2 September 1998, para 509.

[66] Art 6(c), Element 6, ICC Elements of Crimes.

[67] There were earlier laws with similar effect dating from 1869. The chronology is complicated by the fact that such removals were often carried out by state governments under state law rather than the federal Commonwealth government. A common state/federal policy of 'absorption' of aboriginal persons 'not of the full blood' was agreed in 1937. See: Australian Human Rights Commission, 'Timeline: History of separation of Aboriginal and Torres Strait Islander children from their families', www.humanrights.gov.au/timeline-history-separation-aboriginal-and-torres-strait-islander-children-their-families-text#date-1952.

[68] Schabas, *Genocide in International Law*, 205, quoting the Australian Human Rights and Equal Opportunities Commission, *Bringing them Home: Report of the National Inquiry into the Separation of Aboriginal and Torres Strait Islander Children from Their Families* (1997), www.austlii.edu.au/au/other/IndigLRes/stolen/.

[69] (1996) ILC Yearbook, vol 2(2), 46.   [70] Schabas, *Genocide in International Law*, 203.

ttttt

systematic attack against a civilian population, the definition of genocide contains no such express provision, nor do the Statutes of the ICTY, the ICTR, or the ICC. In other words, in the case of genocide the emphasis is not on the context but 'is shifted to the *mens rea* in the form of genocidal intent'.[71]

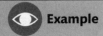 **Example**

Jelisić, ICTY Trial and Appeals Chamber

The question that arises is whether a contextual requirement exists in customary law or whether it is possible for a single person acting alone to be guilty of genocide (a so-called 'lone *génocidaire*'). At one end of the spectrum, the ICTY Appeals Chamber held in *Jelisić* that 'the existence of a plan or policy' is not a legal requirement but that the existence of a plan or policy will often be important in proving intent to commit genocide.[72] That is, the existence of a plan or policy to destroy a group in whole or in part may make it easier to prove that an individual perpetrator (who followed that policy) acted with the special intent required. On this view, a plan or policy is not a necessary legal ingredient, but may be valuable as evidence. Thus, in *Jelisić*, the Trial Chamber also observed that it: 'did not discount the possibility of a lone individual seeking to destroy a group as such.'[73] Other ICTY and ICTR cases have also expressly rejected the proposition that a contextual element is required.[74]

Many would regard the result in *Jelisić* as being an absurd one that contradicts the meaning of the word 'genocide'.[75] It is not inconceivable, however, in the age of weapons of mass destruction that an individual might attempt to destroy a group *in part* through a devastating attack on a particular population centre. In such a case a 'lone *génocidaire*' could have the ability to succeed a total or *partial* destruction of a protected group.[76]

Taking a middle position, Cassese contended that there is no logical problem with the idea of a lone *génocidaire* or the absence of a policy element as certain of the prohibited acts could logically be committed without a greater plan or policy, such as:

- killing members of the group; or
- causing serious bodily or mental harm to members of the group.[77]

[71] Werle and Jessberger, *Principles*, 309 para 826.
[72] *Jelisić*, ICTY Appeals Chamber Judgment, 5 July 2001, para 48.
[73] *Jelisić*, ICTY Trial Chamber Judgment, 14 December 1999, para 100.
[74] E.g.: *Krstić*, ICTY Appeals Chamber, 19 April 2004, para 224.
[75] E.g. W Schabas, 'State Policy as an Element of International Crimes' (2008) 98 Journal of Criminal Law and Criminology 953.
[76] KJ Heller, 'The Majority's Problematic Interpretation of Genocide's Contextual Element' (2009), available at:http://opiniojuris.org/2009/03/06/the-majoritys-problematic-interpretation-of-genocides-contextual-element/.
[77] A Cassese, *International Criminal Law*, 2nd ed (Oxford University Press 2008) 140–141.

These are acts that could be done by one or a few individuals. He contends, however, that certain of the other prohibited acts *by their nature* require 'some sort of collective or even organised action', namely:

- deliberately inflicting on the group conditions of life calculated to bring about its physical destruction in whole or in part;
- imposing measures intended to prevent births within the group; and
- forcibly transferring children of the group to another group.[78]

Similarly, Gerhard Werle and Florian Jessberger conclude that customary law has established that 'an isolated individual acting with specific intent can, through his or her individual conduct, be guilty of the crime of genocide'.[79]

The view that prevailed, however, in the negotiation of the ICC Elements of Crimes is that some 'contextual element' is required. (We should remember that the ICC is to apply the Elements of Crimes in interpreting the ICC Statute but only to the extent they are consistent with the Statute.)[80] The Elements of Crimes require that the:

> conduct took place in the context of a manifest pattern of similar conduct directed against that group or was conduct that could itself effect such destruction.[81]

Notably this is disjunctive. Either the prohibited act must take place 'in the context of a manifest pattern of similar conduct' or the conduct must itself be capable of effecting such destruction. The latter alternative does not rule out the possibility of a lone *génocidaire* capable of making a massive attack, but does rule out one isolated killing by one person (committed with the intent to destroy a protected group) constituting genocide. Where the prohibited act is committed 'in the context of a manifest pattern of similar conduct', this includes an act occurring within 'the initial acts in an emerging pattern'.[82] The Elements of Crimes approach has been upheld in the *Al Bashir* arrest warrant decision of Pre-Trial Chamber I as consistent with the ICC Statute.[83] There is therefore a conflict in the authorities. If the ICTY approach is correct as a matter of customary international law, then the definition applicable under the ICC Statute is narrower than the customary rule. Two views are possible: that this is simply an 'ill-considered' and 'misguided' addition[84] or that despite its wording it is not strictly intended to be an additional element of the crime, but rather to set an adequate objective threshold for the kind of situation in which it will be possible to infer the existence of genocidal intent (see section 10.5).[85]

As discussed in Chapter 7, section 7.4, Article 30 of the ICC Statute requires, as a general rule, that a crime is committed with intent and knowledge. Under the ICC Statute,

---

[78] Ibid, 140–141.   [79] Werle and Jessberger, *Principles*, 309 para 826.
[80] Arts 9 and 21(1), ICC Statute.
[81] Art 6 (a)(4), (b)(4), (c)(5), (d)(5), (e)(7), ICC Elements of Crimes.
[82] Art 6, Introduction, ICC Elements of Crimes.
[83] *Al Bashir*, ICC Pre-Trial Chamber (Decision on Arrest Warrant), 4 March 2009, paras 117–33.
[84] R O'Keefe, *International Criminal Law* (Oxford University Press 2015) 149–50.
[85] See: C Kress, 'The Crime of Genocide and Contextual Elements: A Comment on the ICC Pre-Trial Chamber's Decision in the Al Bashir Case' (2009) 7 Journal of International Criminal Justice 297.

then, the prosecution must show that the defendant either intended his conduct to form part of manifest pattern or knew that it did so.[86]

10.5 The mental element required for genocide

10.5.1 Introduction

As noted in Chapter 7 all crimes consist of a material or conduct element (*actus reus*) and a culpable mental element (*mens rea*). The mental element for genocide is twofold:

- the relevant prohibited act or underlying criminal offence must have been carried out intentionally; and
- it must have been carried out with the 'special intent' to destroy, in whole or in part, a protected group, as such.

In addition, as noted above, under the ICC approach to the contextual element one may have to prove that the accused intended (or knew) his conduct to form part of a 'manifest pattern'.[87]

The important point to note is that intentionally causing or participating in mass killings is not enough: the prohibited act must be carried out with intent to destroy a protected group. Mass killings carried out, for example, with the intent to remove a military threat would not necessarily be genocide. The *Krstić* case concerned the mass killing of Bosnian Muslims in Srebrenica by Serb forces. In *Krstić* the ICTY accepted that General Krstić's intent had been to effect a forcible displacement to remove military aged men who might support the Bosnian Muslims in Srebrenica. Such conduct may still constitute a war crime or crime against humanity, but without the required special intent it is not genocide. In the event, because General Krštić knew some of his subordinates had a genocidal intent, he was convicted of aiding and abetting genocide. Conversely, for genocide to be directly committed by foot soldiers carrying out a genocidal plan, they must personally share in the planners' intention to destroy a protected group. Each individual participant must have the required intent.[88]

This 'intent-based approach' has been criticized as unrealistic: it may seem unlikely that in the course of a wider genocidal campaign 'one individual [will intend] to destroy the group through his own conduct'.[89] It has been suggested as an alternative that a 'knowledge-based approach' should be adopted. On a knowledge-based approach it would be enough that the perpetrator acted with knowledge of and in furtherance of a genocidal campaign planned by others.[90]

---

[86] Art 6, fn 142, ICC Elements of Crimes.   [87] Ibid.

[88] *Krstić*, ICTY Trial Chamber, 2 August 2001, para 549.

[89] Wilmshurst, 'Genocide' in Cryer et al, *Introduction*, 223.

[90] See K Goldsmith, 'The Issue of Intent in the Genocide Convention and Its Effect on the Prevention and Punishment of the Crime of Genocide: Toward a Knowledge-Based Approach' (2014) 5 Genocide Studies and Prevention: An International Journal 238; A Greenawalt, 'Rethinking Genocidal Intent: The Case for a Knowledge-Based Interpretation' (1999) Columbia Law Review 2259.

Another way of putting the same criticism is that if we consider that genocide is normally a collective crime, then:

- while the *mens rea* of genocide (intending to destroy, in whole or in part, a protected group, as such) is one we would normally associate with leaders;
- the prohibited conduct which can make up the *actus reus* (killing, serious harm, forcible transfers, etc) are acts we would normally expect to be carried out by subordinates.[91]

On this basis Kress argues that there is a difference between those who *order* genocide and those who *carry out* the orders: the latter 'will often act without being "personally imbued with [the collective] intention"'.[92] On this approach, formulating the intention element of the crime from a leadership perspective and the material elements from a subordinate's perspective creates problems. Theoretically, one could have a genocidal campaign of killing in which, although the leaders involved have the required specific intent, the foot soldiers who carry out the killings do not. Kress therefore suggests it should be enough that the subordinate perpetrator acted with 'knowledge that the campaign furthered by his acts would destroy, in whole or in part, the group as such'.[93] Kress' formulation could also logically be applied as the test for the contextual element under the ICC Statute.

The idea of a knowledge-based approach also received support from the International Law Commission (ILC). In the commentary to its 1996 Draft Code of Crimes against the Peace and Security of Mankind the ILC remarked that 'genocide requires a degree of knowledge of the ultimate objective of the criminal conduct' rather than comprehensive knowledge of a genocidal master plan.[94] A subordinate is thus 'presumed to know' his superiors' intentions 'when he receives orders to commit the prohibited acts against . . . [members of] a particular group'; and an individual cannot escape 'criminal responsibility by ignoring the obvious'.[95]

Whatever its logical merits, a knowledge based approach has *not* been adopted in the case law. We might also question the assumption of its supporters that subordinates will not share their superiors' intention to destroy a group.

On any approach, absent a confession or documented plan, genocidal intent will have to be inferred from all the circumstances. In such an assessment the acts and utterances of the accused will certainly be relevant; there is some controversy over inferring genocidal intent on the basis of *other* persons' acts and utterances.[96] The better view perhaps is that evidence of the apparent intent of others may provide indirect evidence of the perpetrator's mental state.[97] However, if the prosecution seeks to prove a defendant's

---

[91] See e.g.: K Ambos, 'What Does "Intent to Destroy" in Genocide Mean?' (2009) 91 International Review of the Red Cross 833.

[92] C Kress, 'The Crime of Genocide under International Law' (2006) 6 International Criminal Law Review 461, 496 (quoting the District Court of Jerusalem in the *Eichmann* case).

[93] Ibid, 497.   [94] (1996) ILC Yearbook, vol II(2), 45.   [95] Ibid.

[96] Wilmshurst, 'Genocide' in Cryer et al, *Introduction*, 223.

[97] *Stakić*, ICTY Appeals Chamber, 22 March 2006, para 40.

state of mind by inference, then that inference 'must be the only reasonable inference available on the evidence'.[98] While in many cases 'genocidal intent can be inferred from factors such as the scale of the atrocities committed or the deliberate targeting of victims on account of their membership in a particularly group' it will still be necessary to show the individual defendant shared that intent.[99] Evidentiary issues were discussed in Chapter 5 (particularly in section 5.3.4).

In conclusion, the key points to note from this discussion are that:

- under the intent-based approach the perpetrator of a prohibited act must have personally held the intent to destroy a protected group;
- while under the knowledge-based approach a perpetrator would only need to act with 'knowledge that the campaign furthered by his acts would destroy' a protected group; and
- the case law to date clearly favours the intent-based approach, in accordance with the plain words of the Genocide Convention.

10.5.2 Issues of intent arising from the definition: 'to destroy'

The ILC was clear in its 1996 Draft Code of Crimes against the Peace and Security of Mankind that destruction in this context means the 'material destruction of a group either by physical and biological means and not the destruction of the national, linguistic, religious, cultural or other identity of a particular group'.[100] This approach has been followed by the ICTY and ICTR.[101] Notably, the requirement is *intent* to destroy: actual destruction of the group need not be achieved.[102]

A contrary view, focussing on destruction of a group as a unique and distinctive 'social unit' was taken by the German Federal Court in *Jorgić*, holding that the crime 'does not necessarily require that the perpetrator intended the physical extermination and destruction of the group as such'.[103] The approach taken in *Jorgić* remains, however, very much in the minority.

The case law has generally confirmed that destruction does not encompass cultural destruction. The point was emphasized by the ICTY Trial Chamber in *Krstić* that the concept of ' "cultural" destruction of a group was expressly rejected' by the drafters of the Genocide Convention and therefore an 'enterprise attacking only the cultural or sociological characteristics' of a group in order to destroy its distinct identity would

---

[98] *Vasiljević*, ICTY Appeals Chamber, 25 February 2004, para 120.
[99] G Lewy, 'Can There be Genocide Without the Intent to Commit Genocide?' (2007) 9 Journal of Genocide Research 671.
[100] (1996) ILC Yearbook, vol II(2), 46.
[101] *Krstić*, ICTY Trial Chamber, 2 August 2001, para 580; and *Kamuhanda*, ICTR Trial Chamber, 22 January 2004, para 627.
[102] L Van den Herik, 'The Meaning of the Word 'Destroy' and Its Implications for the Wider Understanding of the Concept of Genocide' in HG van der Wilt et al (eds), *The Genocide Convention: The Legacy of 60 Years* (Brill 2012), 52.
[103] See the translated case as excerpted in: Cassese et al, *International Criminal Law: Cases and Materials*, 288–89.

not constitute genocide.[104] The Trial Chamber noted, however, that the destruction of cultural and religious property as 'symbols of the targeted group' could be evidence of genocidal intent.[105]

10.5.3 Issues of intent arising from the definition: 'in whole or in part'

The meaning of the phrase 'in whole or in part' was clarified by the ICJ in the *Bosnian Genocide* case. The ICJ made three critical points:

- first, 'the intent must be to destroy at least a substantial part of the particular group'; that is, 'the part targeted must be significant enough to have an impact on the group as a whole';
- second, genocide *may* be committed 'where the intent is to destroy the group within a geographically limited area'; and
- third, a qualitative element may be important: certain population centres may be so important to or 'emblematic' of a group that even if they represent only a small percentage of the total group they may nonetheless constitute a 'substantial' part.[106] Thus the intent to destroy in part the population of a city which is particularly culturally important to a group may qualify.

In respect of the second point the ILC has noted that 'it is not necessary to intend to achieve the complete annihilation of a group from every corner of the globe'.[107] Thus, an intent to wipe out a protected group within a particular country or region might suffice. The ICJ in the *Bosnian Genocide* case did however note that defining the relevant group as one within too limited a geographical area would risk distorting the meaning of genocide.[108]

 Counterpoint

Can genocide really be committed against the population of a single city?

While it is accepted that genocide can be the committed by targeting a relevant protected group within a geographically limited area, just how narrow that area can be has proved controversial. For example, the *Krstić* case involved the killing of 7,000–8,000 Bosnian Muslim men at Srebrenica out of a population of approximately 40,000. The ICTY Trial chamber found there was ample evidence of an intent to wipe out the Muslim population of Srebrenica. The plan was to kill all adult males and 'the Bosnian Serb forces had to be aware of the catastrophic

---

[104] *Krstić*, ICTY Trial Chamber, 2 August 2001, para 576.
[105] Ibid, para 580.
[106] *Bosnian Genocide Case*, paras 198–200 and 296. The same position was taken in: *Application of the Convention on the Prevention and Punishment of the Crime of Genocide (Croatia v Serbia)*, International Court of Justice, 3 February 2015, para 142.
[107] (1996) ILC Yearbook, vol II(2), 45.   [108] *Bosnian Genocide Case*, para 199.

impact that the disappearance of two or three generations of men would have on the survival of a traditionally patriarchal society'.[109] There was intent to kill *all* the men and therefore destroy the group (Bosnian Muslims) in part (the Bosnian Muslims of Srebrenica). The fact that 'only' 7,000–8,000 people were killed did not, in the Trial Chamber's view, prevent this being genocide because of the importance of Srebrenica to this group. The ICJ also agreed in the *Bosnian Genocide* case that the massacre at Srebrenica constituted genocide. Other factors helped the Trial Chamber infer that the intent was to achieve 'the physical disappearance of the Bosnian Muslim population at Srebrenica', including: the forcible transfer of women and children, the destruction of homes, the destruction of mosques, and concealment of the dead in mass graves.[110]

The ICJ and ICTY were clear about their reasoning. The critical factor was the third qualitative element noted above. It is not normally open to a court to define the relevant group in a highly geographically restricted way and then hold that mass killings in that area constitute the destruction of a significant part of that geographically limited group. This approach is only justified where a particular population centre is especially important to, or 'emblematic' of, a group as a whole. Nonetheless, there has been criticism of the approach taken in *Krstić* and the *Bosnian Genocide* case on the basis that the reasoning suggests that killing *a part of* a part of a group is enough and that this sets 'too low a threshold' for the genocide.[111]

10.5.4 Issues of intent arising from the definition: 'as such'

The inclusion of the words 'as such' within the definition of genocide may be viewed as puzzling.[112] The distinction drawn here is between intention and motive. Normally criminal law is only concerned with intention: that a perpetrator intended to kill his grandmother and did so is enough to prove murder. Motive is usually irrelevant: it is no part of proving murder that the perpetrator was motivated to kill his grandmother by a desire to inherit her wealth. Genocide is thus commonly seen as an unusual crime where proof of motive is required. As Cassese and his co-authors put it, genocide 'is a crime where the victim is not targeted on account of his or her individual qualities or characteristics, but only because he or she is a member of a [national, ethnic, racial or religious] group'.[113] The point is significant: proof of motive introduces an additional complication to prosecutions. In cases where crimes are clearly directed at members of an ethnic group but it is difficult to prove that the crimes were direct at the group 'as such' it will be easier to charge those crimes as crimes against humanity rather than genocide.[114]

[109] *Krstić*, ICTY Trial Chamber, 2 August 2001, para 595.   [110] Ibid, paras 595–96.
[111] Wilmshurst, 'Genocide' in Cryer et al, *Introduction*, 226.
[112] Schabas, *Introduction to the International Criminal Court*, 106.
[113] Cassese et al, *International Criminal Law*, 118.
[114] Schabas, *Introduction to the International Criminal Court*, 106 and n 166.

Pause for reflection

Is the definition of genocide in the Genocide Convention too narrow?

Issues to consider in answering this question include: the limited range of protected groups; and the limited range of prohibited acts. The definition as it stands excludes political groups as victims and does not list 'cultural genocide' or rape as prohibited acts. Are these restrictions justifiable?

On the first point, one could reflect that:

- The group-limited definition of genocide has been justified on the basis that the protected groups possessed immutable characteristics (i.e. that were beyond their power to change).

- However, nationality and religious affiliation (two of the protected groups) are capable of change and are not immutable.

- Why then are national, ethnic, racial, and religious characteristics more fundamental to an individual's identity or more worthy of protection than political, economic, or social characteristics or affiliations? If no good reason can be put forward for this distinction, should these characteristics not be protected as well?

- On the other hand, one could argue that these limitations are justified by the historical origins of the crime (in particular the response to the Holocaust) and that an over-expansive definition would dilute the seriousness of the crime.

As to the limited range of prohibited acts, one could note that the case law, in particular that of the ICTR, has supplemented the strict wording of the Genocide Convention to include acts not expressly covered, such as rape. This actually falls within the definition of genocide, as the prohibition on 'causing serious bodily or mental harm' is open-ended as to what constitutes serious harm. While the extermination or repression of a culture or language might constitute a 'serious... mental harm', it does not meet the requirement that genocide result in the physical or biological destruction of the group. The cultural destruction of a group is not expressly covered, although the forcible transfer of children as a prohibited act might indirectly cover one form of cultural destruction.

10.6 Summary and conclusions

This chapter aimed to illustrate the following principles:

- the modern law of genocide is principally set out in the Genocide Convention;

- the underlying principles of the Genocide Convention bind all States as customary international law and as norms of *jus cogens* status (according to the ICJ in the *Reservations to the Genocide Convention* and *Bosnian Genocide* cases);

- the crime of genocide involves offences committed with the 'intent to destroy, in whole or in part, a national, ethnical, racial or religious group, as such';

- the four protected groups are a closed list excluding other possible groups (such as groups based on the victims' political views or sexual orientation);

- as there is no objective definition of what constitutes a national, ethnic, racial, or religious group the question must always be assessed in its relevant historical, political, social, and cultural context and questions of self-identification as a group member and especially identification by others as a group member will be important;

- the offence of genocide must be carried out with the 'special intent' to destroy, in whole or in part, a protected group, as such and the individual perpetrator must be shown to have had this intent;

- it is not necessary that the perpetrator intend to wipe out the group from every corner of the globe, some geographical restriction is permissible—though targeting a group in a very restricted area (a single city) will only be genocide if that population is particularly emblematic of the group as a whole (the *Bosnian Genocide* and *Krstić* cases);

- it is theoretically possible to have a 'lone *génocidaire*', at least in cases where a single devastating attack could wipe out a significant part of a group as such;

- however, the ICC Elements of Crimes add a contextual requirement not found in the Convention or the ICTY and ICTR case law that the conduct charged as genocide must have occurred 'in the context of a manifest pattern of similar conduct' directed against a protected group or which was 'conduct that could itself effect such destruction'; and

- the acts prohibited as genocide are focussed on the physical or biological destruction of the group (killing, inflicting serious bodily or mental harm or conditions of life calculated to bring about death, or imposing measures designed to prevent births); in addition the forcible transfer of children to another group is the only accepted form of 'cultural genocide'.

In practice, genocide prosecutions are made difficult by the specific intent requirement. Convictions for war crimes and especially crimes against humanity are thus more frequent.[115]

Useful further reading

K AMBOS, 'What Does "Intent to Destroy" in Genocide Mean?' (2009) 91 International Review of the Red Cross 833.

This article makes an historical and textual argument in favour of the knowledge-based approach.

C KRESS, 'The Crime of Genocide under International Law' (2006) 6 International Criminal Law Review 461.

A thorough and comprehensive article providing a detailed and useful analysis of all elements of the crime of genocide. The author also supports a knowledge-based approach to the intent requirement.

---

[115] Sadat, 'Crimes against Humanity in the Modern Age'.

C KRESS, 'The Crime of Genocide and Contextual Elements: A Comment on the ICC Pre-Trial Chamber's Decision in the Al Bashir Case' (2009) 7 Journal of International Criminal Justice 297.
This article makes the argument that the ICC Elements of Crimes do not strictly add a contextual element but rather set 'an objective point of reference for the determination of a realistic genocidal intent'. That is, absent a 'manifest pattern of similar conduct', it will be difficult to prove such intent.

W SCHABAS, *Genocide in International Law: The Crime of Crimes*, 2nd ed (Cambridge University Press 2009).
The leading scholarly text on the law of genocide, providing a comprehensive account of the history and case law of the crime of genocide.

E WILMSHURST, 'Genocide' in R Cryer, H Friman, D Robinson, and E Wilmshurst, *An Introduction to International Criminal Law and Procedure*, 3rd ed (Cambridge University Press 2014), Chapter 10.
This chapter provides an excellent and concise account of the law of genocide which pays detailed and close attention to the case law of the *ad hoc* Tribunals.

HG VAN DER WILT, J VERVLIET, GK SLUITER, and JTM HOUWINK TEN CATE (eds), *The Genocide Convention: The Legacy of 60 Years* (Brill 2012).
An excellent collection of essays written by experts in the field on a range of related issues including the prosecution of genocide in practice, the legal status of victims of genocide and the controversy surrounding national laws making genocide denial a crime, among other topics.

11

Aggression

11.1 Introduction

Aggression is a 'leadership crime' attaching to those in a position to control the political or military action of a State and who plan, prepare, or initiate an act of aggression. Unlike other international crimes, the crime of aggression links individual criminal responsibility to the wrongful act of a State. Understanding aggression therefore also involves having an understanding of when it is lawful for States to use force in their international relations in order to be able to assess whether aggression has occurred. The crime of waging of an aggressive war was first recognized in the London Charter of the Nuremberg International Military Tribunal (IMT), the Charter of the Tokyo IMT, and Control Council Law No. 10. There have been no convictions for the offence since the prosecutions in Germany and Japan that followed World War II. It has, in practice, been easier to agree that aggression is a crime than it has been to agree a definition itself. This position was reflected in the International Criminal Court (ICC) Statute as it was first drafted. Controversy continues to surround both how the offence should be defined and whether any prosecution for aggression should be subjected to special procedural restraints or safeguards (most notably, whether a prosecution for an act of aggression should only follow a finding of aggression by the UN Security Council). It remains to be seen whether the definition and procedures adopted by ICC State parties at the 2010 Kampala Review Conference (the 'Kampala Conference') can resolve some of the controversies involved.

 Learning aims

By the end of this chapter you should be able to discuss or explain:

- the historical evolution of the offence, including the difficulties in settling a definition for the purposes of the ICC Statute;
- explain the meaning of 'act of aggression' and the limitations upon that term in the ICC Statute definition, including the requirement that the act must be a 'manifest violation of the Charter of the United Nations';

> - the different procedural paths by which the crime of aggression could come before the ICC (i.e. the differences between a Security Council referred, member State referred or prosecutor initiated process); and
> - the controversies that remain after the Kampala review process of 2010.

In light of these aims the rest of this chapter proceeds as follows:

- Section 11.2 concerns the historical development crime of aggression.
- Section 11.3 addresses the question of who can be considered a perpetrator of the crime.
- Section 11.4 outlines the manner in which the crime can be committed.
- Section 11.5 turns to the controversial question of how 'aggression' is to be defined for the purposes of the offence.
- Section 11.6 considers the distinction between aggression and lawful uses of military force in international law.
- Section 11.7 discusses some controversial cases of the use of force and whether they might constitute aggression, including 'humanitarian intervention' or 'anticipatory self-defence'.
- Section 11.8 outlines the mental element required.
- Section 11.9 explains the applicable law before the ICC.
- Section 11.10 explores the possibility of prosecuting acts of aggression before national courts.

11.2 Historical development

Prior to World War II there was certainly law about the conduct of war (including war crimes), but the law had little to say about when States could go to war.[1] War was an acceptable instrument of policy for States. So much is reflected in both the 1919 League of Nations Covenant and the 1928 Kellogg-Briand Pact. The League of Nations Covenant did not renounce war, but provided for compulsory dispute settlement procedures and instituted a 'three-month cooling-off period'[2] before war could be declared in situations where war seemed likely. Going slightly further, the Kellogg-Briand Pact was a treaty that renounced, as among the parties to it, 'recourse to war for the solution of international controversies'.[3] Implicitly, however, absent the treaty—or in their relations with non-parties—the member States of the Kellogg-Briand Pact enjoyed an unfettered right to go to war. In sum, neither the League Covenant nor the Kellogg-Briand Pact

---

[1] See generally: V Lowe, *International Law* (2007), Chapter 8.   [2] Ibid, 269.
[3] 225 Consolidated Treaty Series 195. The full text is also available via: www.yale.edu/lawweb/avalon/imt/kbpact.htm.

contained any declarations that war was generally prohibited. One attempted to impose procedural restraints on going to war; the other renounced it as an instrument of policy but only as among a club of European States, the USA, Japan, and the British Empire.

World War II constituted the turning point, with the Nuremberg IMT conducting the first trial in modern times for the crime of aggression, which was prosecuted under the title of 'crimes against peace'. Article 6(a) of the London Charter gave the IMT jurisdiction over crimes against peace:

> namely, planning, preparation, initiation or waging of a war of aggression, or a war in violation of international treaties, agreements or assurances, or participation in a common plan or conspiracy for the accomplishment of any of the foregoing.

An almost identically-worded offence was included in both the Tokyo IMT Charter and in Control Council Law No. 10.

Both IMTs ruled that aggressive war had been made an international crime by the 1928 Kellogg-Briand Pact. While it is true to say that the Kellogg-Briand Pact had renounced the use of war as an instrument of national policy among the parties to it, it contained no express criminal provisions. (The problem with the retrospective creation and application of new criminal offences in a manner that may violate the *nullum crimen sine lege* principle was discussed in sections 1.4 and 3.3.3.)

Nonetheless, UN General Assembly Resolution 95(I) affirmed that the principles recognized in the London Charter and the Nuremberg judgment were part of international law. In 1974, the United Nations General Assembly in Resolution 3314 (XXIX) (the 'Definition of Aggression'), acknowledged the dual nature of aggression by stating that aggression as a wrongful act was both: (1) a crime of individual responsibility; and (2) an act of State responsibility. The crime of aggression was also recognized in Article 16 of the 1996 ILC Draft Code of Crimes against the Peace and Security of Mankind.[4]

However, while all of these sources clearly supported the idea that aggression was a crime under customary international law, none of them provided a precise definition of aggression as a crime of individual responsibility. In particular these sources lacked detail regarding who may commit the crime, what acts are prohibited, and what mental state is required. Thus it is hard to argue that as at 1996 there was any generally agreed definition. This, in turn, makes it hard to argue there was a clearly defined crime of aggression at customary international law. This brings us to consider the ICC Statute—and while the Statute may have provided progress on the question of a definition, we must as always be cautious about whether any such definition is accepted as custom.

At the 1998 Rome Conference that drafted the ICC Statute, there was a failure to agree a definition of aggression, reflecting the controversy that still surrounded the crime. Such controversies included:

- whether a crime of aggression should be included in the ICC Statute at all (a view that clearly did not prevail at the time);

---

[4] A longer account of these developments and sources is found in: Y Dinstein, *War, Aggression and Self-Defence*, 4th ed (Cambridge University Press 2005), Chapter 5.

- how to define the crime, i.e. whether it should be limited to 'wars of aggression' or broad enough to cover all 'acts of aggression' and what role concepts drawn from the UN Charter and relevant General Assembly Resolutions should play in such definition; and
- what role the UN Security Council should have, e.g. should prosecutions be limited to cases where the Security Council had already found a State had committed an act of aggression, or should a trial for aggression require the positive authorization of the Security Council before prosecution commenced, etc?[5]

Instead of agreeing a definition, the Rome Conference included Article 5(2) in the ICC Statute, stipulating that, as a formal matter the ICC had jurisdiction over the crime of aggression, but could not exercise it until such time as a definition was added to the Statute through the amendment process. It was not until 2010 that an amended definition of aggression was adopted at the Kampala Conference, but it will be some time before that definition is activated and comes into force. This issue (and the ICC Statute more generally) will be discussed further below.

11.3 Perpetrators

The words 'waging...a war of aggression' in the IMT Charter definition of aggression are very broad. They are broad enough to capture the conduct not only of generals and civilian officials, but all military personnel, including foot soldiers.

In practice however, the class of potential perpetrators has been given a more restrictive interpretation. The American Military Tribunal constituted under Control Council Law No. 10 said in the *High Command Case*:

> the criminality which attaches to the waging of an aggressive war should be confined to those who participate in it at the policy level.[6]

Therefore, in contrast to other international crimes, which may be committed by individuals of all levels of seniority, aggression is a 'leadership' crime.[7] Responsibility is limited to those at the upper echelons of the civilian government and the military. As the *High Command Case* makes clear, however, for the latter category, holding high military rank is not enough. One must be in a position to exercise control at the policy level. This may mean that in fact it will often be the politicians and not the generals who will be responsible.

The definition of aggression in the Kampala Conference amendments to the ICC Statute refers to 'a person in a position effectively to exercise control over or to direct

---

[5] A Cassese et al, *Cassese's International Criminal Law*, 3rd ed (Oxford University Press 2013), 138–9; Dinstein, *War*, 122–3.

[6] *US v von Leeb et al* (*High Command Case*), US Military Tribunal Sitting in Nuremberg, 27 October 1948; excerpted in A Cassese et al, *International Criminal Law: Cases and Commentary* (Oxford University Press 2011), 244–47 at 244.

[7] R O'Keefe, *International Criminal Law* (Oxford University Press 2015), 158, para 4.96.

the political or military action of a State'.[8] The crucial element is the ability of effective control or leadership, not the legal position of the individual.[9]

This idea of 'control' seems narrower than the idea of 'participate...at the policy level'. So, whereas the ICC definition seems limited to the highest level civilian and military leaders who exercise actual control, the *High Command Case* definition could, in theory, extend to senior advisors who, while lacking the direct authority to give orders, effectively participate in policy formation at the highest level.

The difference in approaches is worth bearing in mind. If the *High Command Case* reflects customary international law, then the ICC category of perpetrators is narrower. The consequence of potential differences between the ICC definition of aggression and the definition at customary international law is returned to below.

11.4 Prohibited conduct

Such persons can commit aggression by, in the language of Article 6 of the London Charter, participating in the 'planning, preparation, initiation or waging of a war of aggression' or through 'planning, preparation, initiation or execution of an act of aggression' according to the ICC definition.

According to the Nuremberg IMT there was little difference between 'planning, preparation,...or participation in a common plan' to commit aggression on the one hand or 'conspiracy' to commit aggression on the other. The essence of this mode of participation in the crime was '[p]articipation in the formulation of aggressive plans'.[10] One should note, however, that the planning of and preparation for 'a war of aggression are only criminal if they actually result in' hostilities commencing.[11]

The question remains, however, as to what actually counts as aggression for this purpose.

11.5 Defining aggression

11.5.1 Defining aggression under customary international law

If we are asking what the definition of aggression is under customary international law, the starting points are few. We might begin by recalling that the Nuremberg IMT Charter and judgment were accepted in General Assembly Resolution 95(I), which may be taken as an expression of States' *opinio juris* regarding the crime. This may support a conclusion that the definition found in the Nuremberg IMT Charter should

---

[8] Article 8*bis*(1), ICC Statute.

[9] G Werle and F Jessberger, *Principles of International Criminal Law*, 3rd ed (Oxford University Press 2014) 542, para 1459.

[10] D Robinson, 'Aggression' in R Cryer et al, *An Introduction to International Criminal Law and Procedure*, 3rd ed (Cambridge University Press 2014), 314.

[11] Werle and Jessberger, *Principles of International Criminal Law*, 544, para 1463.

be accepted as a statement of customary international law. If the definition of crimes against peace found in the Nuremberg and Tokyo IMT Charters may be accepted as the basic statement of a customary international law rule regarding aggression, then the crime of aggression is limited to cases involving a 'war of aggression', being a war contrary to international law. However, moving on from the IMT Charter wording, we no longer commonly speak of 'war' in international law and formal declarations of war are a thing of the past. Instead, we speak of 'armed conflicts' or 'uses of force', which may be lawful or unlawful under international law (a point discussed further below).

Turning to other possible sources, Article 5(2) of the Definition of Aggression adopted by the UN General Assembly distinguishes between:

- aggression, 'giv[ing] rise to [the] international responsibility' of a State; and

- a *war of* aggression, being 'a crime against international peace' for which there is individual criminal responsibility.[12]

While all aggression is outlawed under the Definition of Aggression, only the narrower category of a 'war of aggression' is criminalized. The result for customary international law would appear to be that 'not every unlawful use of force by a State comes within the concept of aggression [as a crime],' instead 'only large-scale and serious instances' do.[13]

11.5.2 Defining aggression under the ICC Statute

At the 2010 Kampala Conference a definition of aggression was adopted as an amendment to the ICC Statute in Resolution RC/Res.6. This was inserted after Article 8 and is numbered Article 8*bis*, although it will not come into force for some time (see the discussion below). The text reads in part:

1. For the purpose of this Statute, 'crime of aggression' means the planning, preparation, initiation or execution, by a person in a position effectively to exercise control over or to direct the political or military action of a State, of an act of aggression which, by its character, gravity and scale, constitutes a manifest violation of the Charter of the United Nations.
2. For the purpose of paragraph 1, 'act of aggression' means the use of armed force by a State against the sovereignty, territorial integrity or political independence of another State, or in any other manner inconsistent with the Charter of the United Nations ...

Paragraph 2 further includes a list of acts drawn from the Definition of Aggression that 'qualify as an act of aggression'. These include: invasion, occupation, or annexation by the armed forces of a State of the territory of another State; the use of weapons 'by a State against the territory of another State'; blockade of ports or coastlines; an attack by one State's armed forces upon those of another; where armed forces are present in another State's territory by consent—using those forces in contravention of that agreement or

---

[12] See Dinstein, *War, Aggression and Self-Defence*, 125.
[13] Robinson, 'Aggression' in R Cryer et al, *An Introduction to International Criminal Law*, 2nd ed (Cambridge University Press 2010), 321. This phrase appears to have been omitted from the current edition.

extending the presence in that State's territory beyond the life of the agreement; and the 'sending by or on behalf of a State of armed bands, groups, irregulars or mercenaries, which carry out acts of armed force against another State' of comparable gravity to the other listed acts.

The Article 8*bis* definition does not refer to a 'war of aggression' but instead to 'an *act* of aggression'. While the words 'act of aggression' are potentially very broad, they are limited by the Article's further requirement that the act be of such a 'character, gravity and scale' that it 'constitutes a manifest violation of the Charter of the United Nations'. These words require further interpretation in light of the law on the use of force under the UN Charter, a point discussed further below.[14]

If, as would seem to be the case, the ICC Statute definition is broader than the customary international law definition, this has two possible consequences: (1) it may be evidence of State practice and *opinio juris*, that could in time lead to a broader customary definition of aggression; or (2) this broader rule is only binding upon State Parties to the ICC Statute and could not be validly used as a definition for the purposes of prosecuting the crime under customary international law pursuant to universal jurisdiction (e.g. if a national court were to prosecute a head of government or a military leader from a State that is not party to the ICC Statute).

More importantly, how will the words of limitation in Article 8*bis* of the Statute be interpreted? Are there three separate tests of character, gravity, and scale (i.e. is it enough to prove one of the three) or are they cumulative (i.e. must you prove all three)? Further, is 'manifest violation' a separate requirement?

 Pause for reflection

What would be the effect of treating the words 'manifest violation' as imposing a separate requirement in addition to 'character, gravity and scale'? If it is an additional requirement, an act might be of sufficient character, gravity, and scale to constitute aggression but one could still raise a defence that it was not a *manifest* violation of the UN Charter. For example, consider a leader who orders military intervention in a foreign civil war to prevent crimes against humanity being committed. Assume this leader has government legal advice stating such humanitarian intervention is legal.[15] Could such a leader argue his or her action was therefore not manifestly a violation of the UN Charter and therefore would not constitute aggression? Humanitarian intervention and other issues regarding lawful and unlawful uses of force are discussed further below.

---

[14] This renvoi (referral) to a body of law external to the ICC Statute has been criticized for its potential vagueness. For a discussion of the possible problems that arise see: M Milanović, 'Aggression and Legality: Custom in Kampala' (2012) 10 Journal of International Criminal Justice 165.

[15] For example, in 2013 it was the UK's position that unilateral humanitarian intervention in Syria would have been lawful (though this did not occur): 'Chemical weapon use by Syrian regime: UK government legal position', 10 August 2013, www.gov.uk/government/publications/chemical-weapon-use-by-syrian-regime-uk-government-legal-position.

A plain reading of the text suggests that:

- the requirement that an act must be of sufficient character, gravity, and scale is a cumulative test, so all three elements must be proved or satisfied on an overall assessment of the facts;[16] and

- whether a violation is 'manifest' is a result of its character, gravity, and scale (i.e. that 'manifest violation' is the standard to which 'character, gravity and scale' must rise).[17] It is not a separate element allowing for a defence of the type described above.

This reading is supported by Resolution RC/Res.6 that contains in its Annex III a series of 'understandings'. These are non-binding, but form part of the preparatory works that may be referred to if the provision is ambiguous.[18] Understanding 7 notes:

> It is understood that in establishing whether an act of aggression constitutes a manifest violation of the Charter of the United Nations, the three components of character, gravity and scale must be sufficient to justify a 'manifest' determination. No one component can be significant enough to satisfy the manifest standard by itself.

So, how is this threshold test to be applied? In particular, can single acts of State violence falling far short of what we might usually consider war constitute an act of aggression? The ideas of character, gravity, and scale have been discussed in a number of ICJ cases, including the following in the context of a right of self-defence:

- in the *Nicaragua Case*[19] the ICJ held that for an incursion by armed bands or mercenaries to be an 'armed attack' giving rise to a right of self-defence (and being equivalent to an act of aggression) their actions had to be (1) of the same gravity as an armed attack by regular forces and (2) be of sufficient 'scale and effects' to prevent it being classified as a 'mere frontier incident' (which would not be of sufficient gravity to be classified as an armed attack);[20] and

- in *Oil Platforms* the ICJ, reiterated the *Nicaragua* distinction between grave and less grave uses of force, but did not exclude the possibility that the mining of a single warship, or an attack by a single missile on a flag vessel, could constitute an armed attack.[21]

---

[16] Chatham House, 'The International Criminal Court: Reviewing the Review Conference' (24 June 2010), 6, www.chathamhouse.org/sites/files/chathamhouse/public/Research/International%20Law/il240610summary.pdf.

[17] O'Keefe, *International Criminal Law*, 159, para 4.100.

[18] Following the rules of interpretation in Article 32(a) of the Vienna Convention on the Law of Treaties, as discussed in Chapter 2.

[19] *Case concerning Military and Paramilitary Activities in and against Nicaragua (Nicaragua v USA)*, 1986 ICJ Reports 14, para 195.

[20] The ICJ's requirement that an armed attack meet a certain threshold of gravity has attracted criticism on the basis that States should be able to respond in self-defence to any use force, but it has been upheld by the ICJ and other international tribunals such as the Eritrea/Ethiopia Claims Commission: C. Gray, *International Law and the Use of Force*, 3rd ed (Cambridge University Press 2008), 147–48. Compare: 'Chatham House Principles of International Law on the Use of Force by States In Self-Defence' (2006) 55 ICLQ 963, 966 n 13.

[21] *Case Concerning Oil Platforms (Islamic Republic of Iran v United States of America)*, 2003 ICJ Reports 161, paras 51, 62, and 72.

These cases suggest that a degree of armed violence (crossing the *Nicaragua* threshold of gravity) is required to constitute an armed attack and therefore to qualify as both: (1) a manifest breach of the UN Charter; and (2) an act of aggression under the ICC Statute. Nonetheless, the threshold of violence or force that must be crossed is lower than war on the scale tried by the Nuremberg IMT. The examples given in paragraph 2 of the ICC Statute definition support this view, referring to 'the use of *any* weapons by a State against the territory of another State' and '*[a]n* attack by the armed forces of a State on the land, sea or air forces, or marine and air fleets of another State' (emphasis added). The plain wording covers even single attacks and therefore, the single use of a mine or missile could be enough to constitute an act of aggression, as *Oil Platforms* suggests. The ICC Elements of Crimes provides further support for such a conclusion, clearly stating that: '[i]t is understood that any of the acts referred to in article 8*bis*, paragraph 2, qualify as an act of aggression'.

11.6 Aggression or lawful use of force?

The international criminal law applicable to aggression and the rules relating to when States may use force (known as the *jus ad bellum*) are closely linked. It is necessary therefore to be able to identify issues that relate to whether a use of force by a State is legal (and therefore not aggressive) or whether it is unlawful and may therefore constitute an act of aggression.

Paragraph 2 of Article 8*bis* of the ICC Statute in defining aggression refers to 'the use of armed force by a State against the sovereignty, territorial integrity or political independence of another State, or in any other manner inconsistent with the Charter of the United Nations.' This reference to the UN Charter (and the use of language very similar to Charter provisions) makes a brief review of the Charter law on the use of force necessary.

The basic law on the use of force under the UN Charter is found in three provisions. First, a general prohibition on the use of force is found in Article 2(4):

> All member States shall refrain in their international relations from the threat or use of force against the territorial integrity or political independence of any State, or in any other manner inconsistent with the Purposes of the United Nations.

This general prohibition is subject to only two express exceptions under the UN:

- The first and most important exception is found in Article 51, which provides for the 'inherent right of individual or collective self-defence following an "armed attack"'. Notably, under customary international law, to be legal, any action in individual or collective self-defence must be both *necessary* and *proportionate*. These requirements are objectively judged.

- The second exception is found in Article 42, located within Chapter VII of the UN Charter, which provides for use of force authorized by the UN Security Council. As the UN has no standing army, UN Security Council Resolutions under Article 42 usually call upon States to take relevant military action. This is sometimes called a Chapter VII authorization to use force.

Therefore, any use of force by a State in violation of Article 2(4), which is not: (a) a necessary and proportionate act of self-defence; or (b) an action authorized by the Security Council, will in principle be in breach of the UN Charter and customary international law and may therefore constitute aggression. The question is whether there are any further arguable exceptions to this basic principle, a point we turn to next.

 Example

Was Russia's 2014 intervention in Crimea an act of aggression?

In the period November 2013–February 2014 there was unrest and eventual revolution in Ukraine, resulting in Ukrainian President Viktor Yanukovych being deposed by a vote of the Parliament on 22 February 2014. Mr Yanukovych then fled to Russia. Throughout this period there was also increasing evidence of Russian military intervention in the Crimea region of Ukraine, and by March it was obvious that Russian forces had control of the Crimean peninsula. On 16 March 2014 the Crimean regional authorities held a referendum on whether to secede from Ukraine and join the Russian Federation. On 18 March 2014 Ukrainian authorities met with the Russian government to formalize Russia's annexation of Crimea.

Using government troops to detach territory from another State and incorporate it into your own territory is prima facie a grave use of force against the 'territorial integrity' of another State contrary to the UN Charter. Three arguments that appear to have been put by Russia in support of its action are:

- self-defence under Article 51 of the UN Charter (either in respect of its military forces stationed in Crimea or to protect Russian nationals in Crimea);
- it was invited to intervene by President Yanukovych; and/or
- the citizens of Crimea had a right to secede from the Ukraine and choose to join Russia.

As noted above, self-defence may be invoked in cases of an armed attack against a State's military units which are outside its territory, including its warships (*Oil Platforms*). There is little evidence, however, of any attacks on Russian troops or the Russian fleet in Crimea let alone attacks rising to the scale of 'armed attacks' (*Nicaragua Case*). Action to protect nationals abroad as a species of self-defence is controversial,[22] but could in any event only be justified on the basis that the incursion was temporary and for a limited purpose. Such 'limited purpose' arguments could not justify the annexation of territory and have in any event been rejected by the ICJ (see section 11.7.5).

It is generally accepted that foreign troops may be invited or permitted into a receiving State's territory and that this does not constitute aggression (so long as their acts while within the territory remain within the scope of their permission to be there). This is consistent with the provision of the definition of aggression discussed above that deals with foreign troops stationed abroad by consent. The question then is whether President Yanukovych could represent the government for

---

[22] Contrast: Dinstein, *War*, 231–4 (citing State practice in support of such a right); Gray, *International Law and the Use of Force*, 156–60 (noting that such claims are controversial).

the purpose of requesting Russian military assistance. While one could debate whether he was validly deposed as a matter of Ukrainian constitutional law, international law is normally only concerned with the question of identifying the *effective* government of a territory. It is clear that the Ukrainian parliament did not approve of Russia's intervention in Crimea and Crimea's detachment from its territory.

Russia's final argument is that the citizens of Crimea had a right to declare their independence from Ukraine and, once independent, had a right to join another State such as the Russian Federation. The existence of such a right of succession is deeply controversial in international law,[23] but even if it exists would it justify Russian intervention? At best this would be a species of the humanitarian intervention argument (discussed at 11.7.3): intervention to support a (supposed) right for regions or federal entities to unilaterally secede from their parent State.

After reading the further material below in section 11.7 reflect on whether or not you consider the Russian intervention in Crimea could be characterized as an act of aggression.

11.7 Controversial cases of the use of force—lawful or unlawful?

The fact that lawful uses of force by a State will not constitute aggression poses significant difficulties for international criminal law in those instances where the *jus ad bellum* is either unclear or its precise boundaries are controversial. Any grey areas may provide an opportunity for States and their leaders to make a case justifying the use of force, thereby constituting a possible defence to a claim that they have committed the crime of aggression. Relevant debates and controversies that may affect our assessment of whether an act of aggression has occurred are outlined below.

11.7.1 Unlawful reprisals

While an 'armed attack' gives rise to a right of self-defence under Article 51 the response must be necessary and proportionate. Where there is a significant delay between a completed attack and a military response it is hard to say that response is *necessary*. It is not relevant to claim a counter-attack is needed to deter future attacks: such a 'punitive rather than a defensive' use of force is undoubtedly an illegal reprisal.[24]

11.7.2 Pre-emptive self-defence

Is self-defence limited to only taking action *after* an armed attack has occurred, or may force be used to repel future attacks? In brief, the academic consensus appears to be

---

[23] Significant controversy surrounds the declaration of independence of Kosovo from Serbia in 2008. See: *Accordance with international law of the unilateral declaration of independence in respect of Kosovo (Request for Advisory Opinion)*, 2010 ICJ Reports 403; and M Milanović and M Wood (eds) *The Law and Politics of the Kosovo Advisory Opinion* (Oxford University Press 2015).

[24] Gray, *International Law and the Use of Force*, 197.

that force may be used to repel an attack that is (a) ongoing or (b) imminent, meaning that there is no moment for deliberation and no time to take alternative non-forcible measures, such as further negotiations.[25] This may be called 'interceptive' or 'anticipatory' self-defence. The idea that force may be used to prevent a *possible* future attack that has not yet materialized ('pre-emptive or preventative self-defence') is highly controversial.

Anticipatory self-defence in response to imminent attacks is widely accepted by academics, provided that such anticipatory action remains both necessary and proportionate.[26] A clear cut example is shooting down an incoming missile or even, perhaps, incoming aircraft on a bombing run.[27] After all, it would be unfair to require that States passively sit by to await the actual effects of an attack, which is clearly and manifestly about to be launched or felt, before responding to it.[28] In contrast, preventative self-defence refers to merely possible or feared future threats and very few States have ever supported this broader doctrine.[29]

11.7.3 Humanitarian intervention or the 'responsibility to protect'

Can a State use force to prevent egregious human rights violations occurring in another State if the UN Security Council fails to act? The existence of such a right of humanitarian intervention is controversial. While some advocate such a right in circumstances such as the genocide in Rwanda or the present conflict in Syria, humanitarian intervention is not expressly recognized by the UN Charter as a justification to use force and prima facie it would constitute a breach of the Article 2(4) prohibition. Furthermore, it is doubtful whether such a right has emerged as customary international law. Humanitarian motivations have occasionally been invoked by some States to justify such military actions as the 1999 NATO bombings of Serb forces in the contested territory of Kosovo. See the following example for a discussion of one such argument.

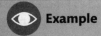 **Example**

United Kingdom statement to the UN Security Council in respect of NATO action in Kosovo

In the early 1990s civil war saw the federal State of Yugoslavia dissolve into a number of newly recognized States. These new States were generally formed within the borders of the previous six 'republics' which had constituted Yugoslavia. A problem that remained

---

[25] Lowe, *International Law*, 276.

[26] Ibid; Gray, however notes that most States in their expressions of *opinio juris* appear literalists who would confine the right of self-defence exclusively to cases where a prior attack has actually occurred: *International Law and the Use of Force*, 160 and 165.

[27] Dinstein, *War*, 190–192.   [28] Lowe, *International Law*, 276.

[29] Ibid, 209–27. The strongest supporter of such a doctrine has been the US.

was the status of certain autonomous territories within those republics, especially that of Kosovo which had previously been administered as a special autonomous (largely Islamic Albanian) territory within Serbia. Violence between Serb and Kosovar forces reached a peak in 1999, prompting NATO intervention against Serbia within what was widely considered at the time to be Serbian territory. In 1999 the UK made the following statement in justification of its participation in NATO bombing of Serbian armed forces within Kosovo:[30]

> The action being taken is legal. It is justified as an exceptional measure to prevent an overwhelming humanitarian catastrophe. Under present circumstances in Kosovo, there is convincing evidence that such a catastrophe is imminent. Renewed acts of repression by the authorities of the Federal Republic of Yugoslavia would cause further loss of civilian life and would lead to displacement of the civilian population on a large scale and in hostile conditions. Every means short of force has been tried to avert this situation. In these circumstances, and as an exceptional measure on grounds of overwhelming humanitarian necessity, military intervention is legally justifiable. The force now proposed is directed exclusively to averting a humanitarian catastrophe, and is the minimum judged necessary for that purpose.

This may well be a statement of the UK's *opinio juris* that such action is legal. It does not, however, provide any detailed argument as to *why* such action should be considered legal other than as a matter of policy. No source of law, doctrine, precedent, or provision of the UN Charter is cited by the UK in support of the conclusion presented.

Distilling clear State practice and *opinio juris* from 'humanitarian intervention' situations is very difficult, as different States may give a variety of justifications for their conduct and often base those justifications on political or moral grounds having little to do with strict legality.[31] The UN General Assembly has certainly not endorsed a unilateral right of States to intervene in other States on humanitarian grounds. In the 2005 World Summit Outcome document, adopted by consensus in the General Assembly, UN member States committed themselves only to taking collective action, through the Security Council, to address genocide, war crimes, ethnic cleansing, and crimes against humanity.[32] This vision of a 'responsibility to protect' emphasizes the duty of territorial States to prevent crimes and the duty of the international community (collectively) to respond to them. However, in practice, States have not rushed to take collective action through the UN system in cases such as the Syrian civil war. (Those States participating in 2014–2015 bombing campaigns against the non-State actor 'Islamic State' in Syria have tended to justify their actions on the basis of collective self-defence in response to 'Islamic State' attacks on Iraq.[33])

---

[30] UN Doc S/PV.3988 (24 March 1999) 12.   [31] Lowe, *International Law*, 42–43.
[32] UN Doc. A/Res/60/1 (24 October 2005), para 139.
[33] S Sengupta and C Savage, 'US Invokes Iraq's Defense in Legal Justification of Syria Strikes', *New York Times*, 23 September 2014, www.nytimes.com/2014/09/24/us/politics/us-invokes-defense-of-iraq-in-saying-strikes-on-syria-are-legal.html?_r=0.

Pause for reflection

Consider the following fictional scenario. The government of Remorra is using its army to commit genocide against a minority ethnic group within its own borders. The President of Arden orders his air force to bomb the Remorran troops to prevent the genocide from continuing. Has he committed aggression?

11.7.4 Action against non-State actors

This issue most commonly arises in the context of terrorism where a State has been the victim of an attack from terrorists operating from foreign territory. The legal question here has three parts: (1) following an armed attack by non-State actors against a State (2) does that State have a right to strike defensively against such persons or groups present in another State's territory (3) if that 'host' State is unable or unwilling to take action against them? The relevant State practice remains limited. For example, while the international community generally supported US action in Afghanistan against Al Qaida, following the events of 11 September 2001 there was controversy as to the legality and proportionality of Israel's actions against Hezbollah in Lebanon in 2006. While a right of self-defence against non-State actors is now generally acknowledged, a right to take action against them on another State's thus territory remains controversial. (The exception is in cases where that territorial State has 'effective control' of the armed group, in which case the 'host' State itself is responsible for the attack and action against its territory is clearly permissible.[34])

11.7.5 Armed intervention with a limited purpose

Particularly in the case of purported humanitarian intervention and self-defence against non-State actors, a State may attempt to claim its actions are not inconsistent with the UN Charter because they are not intended to be 'against the sovereignty, territorial integrity or political independence of another State' under Article 2(4). It may argue that the intention of such actions is not to conquer the State or change its government, but to take temporary action that does not compromise its territorial integrity or (arguably) its political independence. While popular with some academics, such arguments have little *opinio juris* or State practice to support them.[35] The purpose of Article 2(4) was to create a rule of 'territorial inviolability'[36] and it is hard to see why a majority of States would favour the introduction of exceptions that would allow a number of great powers to intervene with armed force in

---

[34] See discussion in Chapter 8, section 8.3.3. See further: Dinstein, *War*, 203; S Talmon, 'The Responsibility of Outside Powers for Acts of Secessionist Entities' (2009) 58 International and Comparative Law Quarterly 493–517.

[35] Gray, *International Law and the Use of Force*, 65–66, 191–209, and 237–44.

[36] H Lauterpacht (ed), *Oppenheim's International Law*, 7th ed (Cambridge University Press 1952), vol 2, 154.

their territory. Further, the ICJ has not favoured 'limited purpose' arguments (see the following example).

 Example

Armed Activities (Democratic Republic of the Congo v Uganda), International Court of Justice

In *Armed Activities (Democratic Republic of the Congo v Uganda)*, Uganda claimed before the ICJ that it had only sent troops into the Democratic Republic of the Congo to prevent cross-border raids by armed groups hostile to Uganda. Thus Uganda argued that in response to an untenable security situation in the DRC:[37]

> it made a decision on 11 September 1998 to augment its forces in eastern Congo and to gain control of the strategic airfields and river ports in northern and eastern Congo in order to stop the combined forces of the Congolese and Sudanese armies as well as the anti-Ugandan insurgent groups from reaching Uganda's borders.

Irrespective of this ostensibly limited, defensive purpose (Uganda in fact occupied large swathes of DRC territory) the ICJ found Uganda's actions to constitute violations of Article 2(4).[38]

11.7.6 Conclusions

It is easy for examples such as these to create the impression that the law on the use of force under the UN Charter is highly uncertain. It is not.[39] While there are marginal controversial cases, there is a clear settled core to the rule: the prohibition on the use of force is absolute, subject only to self-defence and Security Council authorized action. Article 2(4) enshrines a principle of territorial inviolability that leaves little or no room for 'limited intervention' arguments.[40] Further exceptions or deviations from these foundational principles need to be very clearly evidenced in State practice and *opinio juris*. However, the consequences of this discussion for the crime of aggression are not clear cut. Under UN Charter law the scope of 'acts of aggression' may be wide. However, for such acts to be held to constitute the crime of aggression they must be accompanied by the mental element set out in section 11.8. Without it, there may be situations

---

[37] *Armed Activities on the Territory of the Congo (Democratic Republic of the Congo v Uganda)*, (2005) ICJ Reports, 168, para 39 (and see also paras 35–38).

[38] Ibid, para 153.

[39] See in particular: M O'Connell and M Niyazmatov, 'What is Aggression?: Comparing the Jus ad Bellum and the ICC Statute' (2012) 10 Journal of International Criminal Justice 189, 201–3.

[40] O'Connell (at 201) suggests an intervention to rescue nationals in danger abroad could involve so little force that it does not even violate Article 2(4). Compare Werle and Jessberger, *Principles of International Criminal Law*, 540, para 1454. Nonetheless, the doctrine of intervention to protect nationals abroad is controversial as it is often used as a pretext for toppling a foreign government. It is therefore in practice supported by very few States: Gray, *International Law and the Use of Force*, 88–92, 156–60.

that clearly constitute an *act* of aggression but which do not rise to being a *crime* of aggression.

11.8 Mental element

In considering the mental element or *mens rea* required for the crime of aggression we need once again to distinguish between the crime as defined at customary international law and under the ICC Statute. For the purposes of customary international law, the post-World War II case law suggests the mental element required is: 'an intent to participate in the aggressive act'; this standard also covers cases where the defendant knew of the 'collective intent to initiate and wage aggressive war' and participated anyway.[41] It is also sometimes suggested this must be coupled with a further special aggressive intent: to conquer territory, gain economic advantage, or topple a foreign government, for example.[42]

For the purposes of the ICC however, the ICC Elements of Crimes adopted at the Kampala Conference are significantly different. Under the Elements the perpetrator must have: (a) planned, prepared, initiated, or executed an act of aggression (defined as the use of armed force by a State against the sovereignty, territorial integrity, or political independence of another State) with intent to do so; and (b) must have been 'aware of the factual circumstances' establishing both that the use of armed force involved was inconsistent with the UN Charter and also that the use of force was a 'manifest violation' of the UN Charter. It is not required that the perpetrator made a legal evaluation that the act was either inconsistent with the UN Charter or a manifest violation of it.

 Pause for reflection

Could one argue that a political leader lacked the intent to commit an act of aggression if he or she had advice that a use of force was legal?

This question is more than hypothetical.[43] For example, certain governments took the highly controversial view that the invasion of Iraq in 2003 was implicitly authorized by a series of prior Security Council Resolutions.[44] If in similar circumstances in the future it was argued that such an invasion was authorized by the Security Council then, if that was a correct interpretation of the relevant Resolutions, there would be no act of aggression. This, however, would be a question of

---

[41] Robinson, 'Aggression' in Cryer et al, *Introduction*, 322; Cassese et al, *Cassese's International Criminal Law*, 141.

[42] Cassese et al, *Cassese's International Criminal Law*, 142; compare K Ambos, *Treatise on International Criminal Law* (Oxford University Press 2014), vol 2, 201; Werle and Jessberger, *Principles of International Criminal Law*, 539, para 1453.

[43] See e.g. Ambos, *Treatise*, vol 2, 201.

[44] The argument was roundly rebutted in academic commentary. For a concise summary see V Lowe, 'The Iraq Crisis: What Now?' (2003) 52 International and Comparative Law Quarterly 859, 865–866; and Lowe, *International Law*, 273.

fact for the Court. A mistaken belief that there was a legal justification would not, on the plain text of the Elements, exclude liability. There would still be: (a) the intentional planning and initiation of a use of force against a foreign State; (b) factual knowledge of the invasion and its enormous scale. Whether those facts establish a 'manifest violation' of the Charter is a question for the Court. It is not required to show that the perpetrator held a specific intent to act contrary to the UN Charter, or had knowledge that the attack was contrary to the UN Charter, or had made any other legal evaluation. Thus, it is sufficient a leader chose to 'lead his country into a conflict' with knowledge of the surrounding circumstances; knowledge that the conflict was unlawful is not required.[45]

11.9 Aggression before the ICC

First, we should note that, controversially, the amendments adding a definition of aggression to the ICC Statute were added by the Article 121(5) amendment procedure. This means that the aggression amendment will only come into force among those States that ratify or accept the amendment. The ICC cannot therefore prosecute aggression committed on the territory, or by a national, of a State that has not ratified or accepted the aggression amendment.[46] Thus, if a State that has not ratified the amendment commits aggression on the territory of a State that has ratified it, the leaders of the aggressor State *cannot* be prosecuted before the ICC as a consequence of Article 121(5). An alternative procedure under Article 121(4) would have required seven-eighths of all State parties to ratify the amendment, but one year after that the amendment would have been binding on all State parties. What has been chosen for aggression (uniquely among the crimes covered by the ICC Statute) is an 'opt in' system. This 'opt in' system does not have immediate effect (see below).

Second, as aggression is an act committed by a State and engaging State responsibility, while also giving rise to individual criminal responsibility, how do these different legal questions relate to each other (if at all)? One approach would suggest that prosecution of an individual should not commence before there has been a finding of aggression against a State. Such a finding could be made by the Security Council (which has primary responsibility for international peace and security),[47] the General Assembly (which may consider questions of international peace and security in parallel to the Security Council),[48] or the ICJ (which may rule on issues of State responsibility). Some would suggest that the question of aggression is so serious that only the Security Council should be able to authorize an investigation. However, due to the five permanent members' right of veto,[49] this has not been a popular option. Prosecutions could

---

[45] Robinson, 'Aggression' in Cryer et al, *Introduction*, 322.

[46] Unless there is a Security Council referral, as discussed below.   [47] Article 24(1), UN Charter.

[48] *Legal Consequences of the Construction of a Wall in the Occupied Palestinian Territory*, Advisory Opinion (2004) ICJ Reports 36, para 27.

[49] That is, on all but procedural matters decisions of the Security Council require the concurring votes of China, France, Russia, the United Kingdom, and the US (the permanent members): Art 27, UN Charter. In practice only a negative vote is interpreted as blocking a decision or resolution. See further: M Shaw, *International Law*, 7th ed (Cambridge University Press 2014), 877.

be stymied by the Security Council failing to act, or by permanent members shielding their allies. Furthermore, as the Security Council and General Assembly are political bodies, and the ICJ is not concerned with individual criminal cases, it could be seen as damaging the right to a fair trial to have UN organs ruling on questions relevant to the trial of an individual. That said, State aggression does have implications for individual criminal responsibility, as may be seen by the approach taken in drafting the ICC Statute definition (see the discussion of Article 15*ter*, below).

Concerning the questions of which member States would be bound by the aggression amendments (and when) and what role the Security Council should play, the Kampala Conference voted to add two new articles following Article 15 of the ICC Statute: Articles 15*bis* and 15*ter* (in that order). Critically, Article 15*bis* provides the Court will have no temporal jurisdiction over acts of aggression until one year after the date on which the 30th State party accepts or ratifies the amendment incorporating the definition of aggression.[50] Even then, the Court may not exercise that jurisdiction until a further decision is taken by the State parties at some point after 1 January 2017 to 'activate' it.[51] Thus there will be two different 'start dates' for the Court's jurisdiction: the first day from which the Court has temporal jurisdiction over the crime of aggression; and the first day the Court can exercise that jurisdiction. Article 15*bis* also completely excludes from the Court's jurisdiction cases of aggression committed by or on the territory of a non-State party to the ICC Statute. Without such a provision cases concerning aggression committed by a State party against a non-State party could fall within the Court's jurisdiction irrespective of the territorial State's consent.[52]

Very oddly, Article 15*bis*(4) also provides that the Court may 'exercise jurisdiction over a crime of aggression, arising from an act of aggression committed by a State Party' *unless* that State party has lodged with the Court a declaration stating that 'it does not accept such jurisdiction' over such acts. As has widely been observed, this 'opt out' provision in Article 15*bis*(4) conflicts with, or contradicts, the Article 121(5) 'opt in' procedure.[53] That is, given that a State must opt into jurisdiction under Article 121(5) it is not obvious why Article 15bis(4) was thought necessary. Indeed, the Article 15*bis*(4) 'opt out' provision appears to create a one-sided exclusion: State A may accept the Court's jurisdiction over aggression under Article 121(5) but if it then exercises the opt out its nationals cannot be prosecuted for aggression, but the nationals of other States (that have accepted the amendment) could still be prosecuted for acts of aggression committed against State A.[54]

Probably the only satisfactory way to reconcile Articles 121(5) and 15*bis* is to conclude that the ICC will (eventually) have jurisdiction over aggression when the alleged act has occurred: (a) on the territory of a State party that has accepted the amendment; (b) was committed by an alleged aggressor State party that has accepted the amendment; and (c) that alleged aggressor State has not opted out under

[50] Article 15*bis*(2), ICC Statute.   [51] Article 15*bis*(3), ICC Statute.

[52] A non-State party can still accept the jurisdiction of the Court in relation to a particular 'situation': see Chapter 5, section 5.3.

[53] Robinson, 'Aggression' in Cryer et al, *Introduction*, 324.

[54] Milanović, 'Aggression and Legality', 180.

Article 15*bis*.[55] Article 15*bis* also places a number of limitations on the power of the Prosecutor to commence an investigation into a crime of aggression on his or her own initiative. The ICC Prosecutor may initiate an investigation into a case of aggression *proprio motu* where: (1) the Security Council has determined that an act of aggression has taken place, or (2) where the ICC Prosecutor has notified the UN Secretary General of the situation before the Court and no Security Council determination is made within six months.[56] The usual requirements of Pre-Trial Chamber approval to open an investigation and the possibility of the Security Council deferring an investigation for 12 months apply.[57] A determination of aggression by the Security Council (or any other body) does not prejudice the Court's own determination of the issues.[58]

Article 15*ter* provides that the Security Council may also refer a situation of aggression to the ICC for investigation and trial. This could allow acts of aggression committed by non-parties to the Statute to be prosecuted before the Court. It is subject to the same limitation of temporal jurisdiction as found in Article 15*bis* and the same restriction that the Court may not exercise its jurisdiction until a decision is taken to 'activate' that power at some point after 1 January 2017.

Should we judge these amendments a success or failure? That there is now a permanent international criminal tribunal that may one day have jurisdiction over the crime of aggression is a major achievement.[59] It is also probably a victory for the independence of the Court that there is no strict requirement that a determination of aggression be made by the UN Security Council before the Court can prosecute aggression.[60] Nonetheless, the Court in its future case law will face a number of challenges including defining what constitutes a 'manifest' violation of the UN Charter, whether controversial cases such as humanitarian intervention constitute a breach of the Charter, and the correct way to resolve the seeming contradiction between the Article 121(5) 'opt in' and the Article 15*bis* 'opt out' jurisdictional provisions.[61]

11.10 Aggression before national courts

A separate question is whether national courts currently have universal jurisdiction for crimes of aggression over other States' political leaders present in their territory. The first problem for national courts in prosecuting crimes of aggression is divining the precise customary international law definition of aggression. Even if they can ascertain one, a national court will be reluctant to 'invent' a definition of the crime for the first time for national law purposes. Thus, in *R v Jones* the UK House of Lords concluded

---

[55] Milanović, 'Aggression and Legality', 181; Robinson, 'Aggression' in Cryer et al, *Introduction*, 324.

[56] Article 15*bis*(6)–(8), ICC Statute.   [57] Articles 15 and 16, ICC Statute.

[58] Article 15*bis*(9), ICC Statute.

[59] Although some would suggest aggression is a dangerous concept to criminalize and it should not have been codified in the ICC Statute: E Creegan, 'Justified Uses of Force and the Crime of Aggression' (2012) 10 Journal of International Criminal Justice 59–82.

[60] M Politi, 'The ICC and the Crime of Aggression: A Dream that came through and the Reality Ahead' (2012) 10 Journal of International Criminal Justice 267, 287. See also: Ambos, *Treatise*, Vol. 2, 212.

[61] Politi, 'The ICC and the Crime of Aggression', 283–88.

that aggression was a crime under customary international law and subject to universal jurisdiction, but that as a matter of constitutional law it could not be prosecuted in the United Kingdom without a national statute providing for its criminalization.[62] If there is a statutory crime of aggression, this could resolve the definition problem from the perspective of a national judge. However, even if this were the case national courts tend to exercise great restraint in reviewing matters of foreign affairs or national defence, or may consider such questions beyond their jurisdiction entirely.[63] A decision to go to war against another State would likely rank high in the category of government acts that courts would be reluctant to review. Furthermore, prosecuting a foreign head of State or other senior official for aggression before a national court could be diplomatically embarrassing, and have potential consequences in international relations. It would also likely raise issues of State immunity, as discussed in Chapter 14.

In the end, this may leave a greater role to the complementary jurisdiction of the ICC. If national courts are unable to prosecute aggression due to the lack of a national law, then aggression can only (and some would argue should only) be prosecuted at the international level.[64]

11.11 Summary and conclusions

This chapter has attempted to highlight the following key concepts:

- the complex history of efforts to outlaw aggressive war, and the important difference between a legally prohibited *act of aggression* and individual responsibility for *a crime of aggression*;
- the possible difference between the definition of a crime of aggression at customary international law and under the ICC Rome Statute (or the possibility that the Rome Statute might be evidence that customary law is changing);
- what it means to describe aggression as a 'leadership crime' and who might constitute the relevant categories of leaders (or what legal test will tell us who is a leader capable of committing aggression);
- the meaning of 'act of aggression' and the limitations upon that term in the ICC Statute definition, including the requirement that the act must be by its 'character, gravity and scale' a 'manifest violation of the Charter of the United Nations';
- the controversies that remain after the Kampala Conference amendments to the ICC Statute;
- among those controversies whether a 'humanitarian intervention' would constitute aggression;

---

[62] On the theory that it would be a violation of the separation of powers for the courts to create a new crime, that task being normally the preserve of Parliament: see *R v Jones* [2006] UKHL 16.

[63] See for example the UK case: *Abbasi v Secretary of State for Foreign and Commonwealth Affairs* [2002] EWCA Civ 1598, paras 51–67 and 85 (not ruling out judicial scrutiny of the actions of foreign governments, but citing case law suggesting decisions about making war are generally not justiciable).

[64] See generally: B Van Schaack, '*Par in Parem Imperium Non Habet*: Complementarity and the Crime of Aggression' (2012) 10 Journal of International Criminal Justice 133–164.

- the complex limitations upon the ICC's jurisdiction over aggression including the two limitations on a 'start date' for that jurisdiction and the complexity created by use of the jurisdictional 'opt-in' under Article 121(5) of the ICC Statute and the jurisdictional 'opt-out' under Article 15*bis*(4) of the Statute; and

- whether having government legal advice stating that an invasion or other act of aggression is lawful will in itself provide any defence against a charge of aggression.

Finally, you might consider whether the long, tortuous debate on the crime of aggression has amounted to much. It does not seem especially likely that national courts will ever try the crime of aggression and there will be a number of delays before the ICC's jurisdiction over the crime is 'activated' (if it ever is) and even then there will be serious limitations upon its exercise.

Useful further reading

Books and articles

Y DINSTEIN, *War, Aggression and Self-Defence*, 4th ed (Cambridge University Press 2005), especially Chapters 5 and 7.
Along with Gray (below) this is one of the pre-eminent texts on the use of force in international law. It is also one of the very few to focus on the relationship between the crime of aggression and the law of self-defence.

C GRAY, *International Law and the Use of Force*, 3rd ed (Oxford University Press 2010), Chapters 2, 4, 6.
This is the pre-eminent text on the use of force by States in international law, though it does not directly consider the crime of aggression.

C KRESS and L VON HOLTZENDORFF, 'The Kampala Compromise on the Crime of Aggression' (2010) 8 Journal of International Criminal Justice 1179.
A useful historical account of how the Kampala definition of aggression was drafted, including an insightful account of the issues at stake and the controversy over the amendment procedure chosen.

M MILANOVIĆ, 'Aggression and Legality: Custom in Kampala' (2012) 10 Journal of International Criminal Justice 165.
This article provides a detailed and complex examination of the extent to which the definition of aggression arrived at in the Kampala compromise might conflict with the *nullum crimen sine lege* principle or other principles of legality (such as the requirement that crimes be sufficiently clearly defined).

UN Documents

The following documents are useful in interpreting the meaning of 'acts of aggression':

The Friendly Relations Declaration, UN General Assembly Resolution 2625 (XXV), 1970.

Definition of Aggression, UN General Assembly Resolution 3314 (XXIX), 1974.

PART IV

Defendants
in international
criminal trials

12

Modes of participation in crimes and concurrence of crimes

12.1 Introduction

International crimes often involve large numbers of people acting over large areas. We may have a strong moral intuition that the general or president who plans or directs war crimes or crimes against humanity is more responsible or more culpable than the soldier who 'pulls the trigger' and kills an individual victim. In national legal systems, however, we would probably think of the person who physically commits a crime as the person most responsible and those who encouraged or planned the crime as less responsible.

This leaves us with a problem: in international criminal law people physically distant from the crimes may be those we consider most responsible. Indeed, in international criminal law it may be that the degree of responsibility of an individual for a crime may grow rather than diminish with distance from the crime.[1] The International Criminal Tribunal for the Former Yugoslavia (ICTY) Appeals Chamber noted the same point in *Tadić*: because an international crime is often the result of collective criminality moral responsibility for the crime does not stop with the person who commits a physical act such as murder; indeed, the moral gravity of participating in or facilitating such a crime may be no different to actually carrying it out.[2] Nonetheless, this presents particular challenges for international criminal law as a discipline.

An important principle in criminal law generally is *fair labelling*: accurately describing someone's role in an offence. However, as international criminal tribunals have worked to elaborate legal principles capable of accurately describing an offender's role in a crime, they have also had to address other principles such as the requirement for legal certainty. That is, there may be a tension between having a doctrine sufficiently flexible to capture the responsibility of leaders who are physically remote from a crime but at the same time making sure such a doctrine is sufficiently clearly defined that a fair trial can be conducted.

---

[1] G Werle and F Jessberger, *Principles of International Criminal Law*, 3rd ed (Oxford University Press 2014), 221–22, para 581.

[2] *Tadić*, ICTY Appeals Chamber, 15 July 1999, para 191.

In this chapter we will consider the idea of commission of crimes: who do we hold directly responsible for crimes (principals) and who do we label as having simply assisted a crime without having committed it (accessories)?[3] We will consider a range of ways of being involved in crimes, called 'modes of participation in crimes' in this chapter, such as: aiding and abetting; ordering or inciting crimes; or being responsible for crimes as a superior.

Further, two special doctrines of 'commission' have grown up before international tribunals to describe the involvement of leaders as principals (i.e. being just as culpable as those who 'pull the trigger') in international crimes. These are called joint criminal enterprise and co-perpetration, respectively.

Finally, we will consider a somewhat different issue: what happens when the one set of facts might satisfy the elements of several different international crimes (i.e. it could equally be charged as a war crime or crime against humanity)? This gives rise to issues of concurrence of crimes.

 Learning aims

By the end of this chapter you should be able to:

- explain the distinction between a principal and an accessory, and the concept of 'fair labelling';
- identify the major modes of participation and define their legal elements;
- identify the elements of superior responsibility, and discuss the extent to which the doctrine distinguishes between civilian and military leaders;
- compare the doctrines of joint criminal enterprise and (direct or indirect) co-perpetration and discuss their relative merits or weaknesses as tools for prosecuting mass atrocities and, indeed, whether such doctrines are necessary; and
- explain when the same facts may result in charges for different crimes (and how this should affect sentencing).

With these objectives in mind the rest chapter is structured as follows:

- Section 12.2 outlines the distinction between principals and accessories.
- Section 12.3 introduces the concept of committing a crime as a principal, including commission through inaction, conspiracy, or as part of a group.
- Section 12.4 considers the general forms of secondary or accessorial participation, such as aiding and abetting, instigation, ordering and planning crimes.
- Section 12.5 discusses the law of command or superior responsibility.

---

[3] The principals/accessories distinction is not expressly found in many modern international criminal tribunal statutes but is present in Art II(2), Control Council Law No. 10.

- Section 12.6 explains the doctrine of 'joint criminal enterprise'.
- Section 12.7 outlines the recent development of the doctrine of co-perpetration at the International Criminal Court (ICC).
- Section 12.8 considers other ways in which a person may be convicted of participation in a group crime under the ICC Statute.
- Section 12.9 deals with the question of concurrence of crimes, a concept relevant in situations where is the same proven facts might give rise to more than one offence.

12.2 The liability of principals and accessories

12.2.1 Introduction

When a crime occurs, there is an important question about how far criminal liability should extend. Consider a killing using a hand gun: do we blame the person who pulled the trigger; the person who gave the killer the gun; the manufacturer of the gun itself? A basic distinction is that between principals and accessories. In our example the perpetrator who pulls the gun trigger, deliberately killing another, has committed murder. He is liable as the *principal* or *perpetrator*. The person who gave him the gun knowing it would be used for that purpose, or who stood lookout while the murder took place, may be considered an *aider and abettor* who is liable as an *accessory*. We would not, typically, assign any degree of criminal responsibility to the manufacturer.[4]

Though both the principal and accessory will be held guilty of the same offence (murder), it is generally assumed that the accessory is less culpable and should receive a lesser sentence.[5] In some jurisdictions the accessory *must* receive a lesser sentence.[6] The distinction between principals and accessories is preserved in international criminal law, but has no formal consequence for sentencing. That is, in international criminal law the same maximum sentence is theoretically available for both principals and accessories, though as we noted in Chapter 5, section 5.4.4 the mode of liability or participation in the crime usually influences sentencing in practice.

Put in more formal terms:

- a crime is committed by a person who completes the material element with the requisite *mental element*, this person (the 'principal' or 'perpetrator') bears *primary* responsibility for perpetrating the crime;

---

[4] Though some would suggest we can consider the arms industry itself as a collective principal wrongdoer to which many individual human agents may be accessories: J Gardner, 'Complicity and Causality' (2007) 1 Criminal Law and Philosophy 127, 140–41.

[5] See e.g.: G Werle, 'Individual Criminal Responsibility in Article 25 ICC Statute' (2007) 5 Journal of International Criminal Justice 953, 955.

[6] A Cassese et al, *Cassese's International Criminal Law* 3rd ed (Oxford University Press 2013), 162.

- further, a group of persons may share primary responsibility for the same acts (for example, a firing squad that executed civilians in an armed conflict may all be principals or co-perpetrators, as might a group that kicked a person to death); but alternatively

- a person may bear secondary responsibility for a crime if they participated in it in a prescribed manner (for example, by assisting the executions without directly killing). This may be called 'being an accessory' or 'accessorial liability'.

Why do we bother with such distinctions? The underlying reason is the role of the principle of fair labelling in criminal law: 'The fair labelling principle aims to ensure that the label describing criminal conduct accurately reflects its wrongfulness and its severity.'[7] The correct label for an offence should sum up the crime committed. Relevant considerations will include: the interests affected (e.g. harm to people or harm to property), 'the gravity of the harm', and the mental state of the perpetrator.[8]

A challenge for international criminal law, then, is how to adequately label—in legal terms—the responsibility of highest-ranking leaders, often far removed from the actual killing.[9] If the usual distinction is between the person who directly committed a crime (the perpetrator or principal) and a person who assisted in the commission of the crime less directly (an accessory); then these distant leaders are not obviously principals guilty of directly committing the crimes. Applying the terminology with which we are familiar as a matter of national criminal law would often result in situations where 'the real villain' behind a crime would be labelled 'the accomplice' while the 'principal offender' as a matter of law would simply be 'a small cog in the machine'.[10]

This prospect clearly troubled the ICTY Appeals Chamber in *Tadić*, where it noted that convicting participants in a common plan to commit an international crime 'only as an aider and abettor might understate the degree of their criminal responsibility.'[11] Similarly, the ICC Trial Chamber noted in *Lubanga* that 'the notion of principal liability' expresses 'the blameworthiness of those persons who are the most responsible for the most serious crimes of international concern'.[12]

---

[7] D Nersessian, 'Comparative Approaches to Punishing Hate: The Intersection of Genocide and Crimes Against Humanity' (2007) 43 Stanford Journal of International Law 221, 255–6.

[8] Ibid.

[9] Much of the analysis in this chapter draws on: D Guilfoyle, 'Responsibility for Collective Atrocities: Fair Labelling and Approaches to Commission in International Criminal Law' (2011) 64 Current Legal Problems 255.

[10] W Schabas, *Genocide in International Law: The Crime of Crimes*, 2nd ed (Cambridge University Press 2009), 340.

[11] *Tadić*, ICTY Appeals Chamber 1999, para 192.

[12] *Lubanga*, ICC Trial Chamber, 14 March 2012, para 999.

→← **Counterpoint**

Given the truth-telling function of international criminal trials, judges appear to feel a strong compulsion to label leaders as direct perpetrators who have committed the crime itself and not as accessories who have ordered or incited or failed to prevent it. Indeed, Gideon Boas, James Bischoff, and Natalie Reid have gone so far as to say that at the ICTY and International Criminal Tribunal for Rwanda (ICTR) there appears to be:

a growing obsession…with finding senior-level accused responsible for *committing* crimes, instead of describing their responsibility as a superior, orderer, planner, instigator, or aider and abettor.[13]

This might suggest that the concept of commission risks crowding out other forms of liability such as aiding and abetting.

Labelling distant leaders as principals requires an *expanded theory of commission*. This raises some important questions. Once we uncouple the idea of commission from the direct physical perpetrator, where do the boundaries of commission fall? If our basic moral intuition is that describing the leadership of a regime that commits atrocities as mere accessories is to under-state their culpability, then the challenge is to devise a theory of criminal responsibility that appropriately describes their role but which also places sufficiently clear boundaries on the concept of commission. A theory of commission that is too wide may inappropriately catch 'small fish', labelling them as being just as culpable as high-ranking leaders.

Two different efforts to construct such an expanded theory of commission are:

- joint criminal enterprise of 'JCE' (as adopted at the ICTY, the ICTR, and the Special Court for Sierra Leone in particular); and

- co-perpetration and indirect co-perpetration (as adopted by the ICC Pre-Trial Chambers but not yet applied in a Trial Chamber judgment).

Both of these theories are complex and potentially confusing.

JCE has underpinned the majority of convictions at the ICTY. Co-perpetration may yet play an equally important role at the ICC. A vital question, however, is what they add to 'ordinary' concepts of perpetration or accessorial liability. Therefore we will first turn to commission by perpetration and accessorial forms of liability, before considering JCE and co-perpetration.

12.2.1.1 A final point: material and mental elements (*actus reus* and *mens rea*)

Each mode of participation in a crime involves a defined form of conduct (though not necessarily physical acts) and an intentional element. These are commonly referred to as the material and mental elements (or the *actus reus* and *mens rea*) of the mode of

---

[13] G Boas, J Bischoff, and N Reid, *International Criminal Law Practitioner Library* (Cambridge University Press 2007), vol 1, 89.

participation. This is perhaps not entirely accurate as these terms, strictly speaking, only apply to crimes themselves. Nonetheless, the use of terminology is common and acceptable.

12.3 Liability by perpetration/commission

12.3.1 Perpetration under the Statutes

The idea of commission or direct perpetration is found in all the major tribunal Statutes. Article 7(1) of the Statute of the ICTY states:

> A person who…committed…a crime referred to in articles 2 to 5 of the present Statute, shall be individually responsible for the crime.

This definition does not contain much by way of explanation of what will constitute 'commission'. The same absence of a definition can be seen in Article 6 of the Nuremberg IMT Charter and Articles 1 and 3 of the Genocide Convention. The essential idea is obvious enough: a person who performs the material element of an offence with the required mental state has committed or directly perpetrated a crime. However, the concept of commission does not necessarily stop with the man or woman who pulls the trigger of a gun or who commits some other overt physical act. The question then is how far the term 'commission' may legitimately extend.

Article 25(3)(a) of the ICC Statute contains rather more detail, providing for the liability of a person who: 'Commits such a crime, whether as an individual, or through another person, regardless of whether that other person is criminally responsible'. Article 25(3)(a) thus covers four types of commission:[14]

- commission as an individual;

- joint commission;

- perpetration through an 'innocent agent'; that is, through a legally incapable person (such as a child) or a person lacking the required mental element;[15] and

- 'perpetration through a guilty agent'—i.e. the principal liability of a 'mastermind' or indirect perpetrator for the criminal actions of others directed by him or her.

Similar concepts have been used in decisions of the ICC Pre-Trial Chambers. These concepts, often with origins in German legal theory and therefore given different labels, include:

- 'co-perpetrator' or 'co-perpetration' (covering 'joint perpetration' above);

---

[14] Werle, 'Individual Criminal Responsibility', 958–64; and R Cryer, 'General Principles of Liability' in R Cryer et al, *An Introduction to International Criminal Law*, 3rd ed (Cambridge University Press 2014), 355.

[15] This would cover not only children or the mentally incompetent, but theoretically those lacking the required mental element to commit the crime (e.g. A wants to kill B at a dinner party by poison, so A asks C to give B a glass of poisoned wine; if C does not know the wine is poisoned, he or she is the innocent agent of A's attempt at murder).

- 'indirect perpetrator' or 'indirect perpetration' (covering 'commission through another person' above); and

- 'indirect co-perpetrators' or 'indirect co-perpetration' (involving a combination of joint perpetration and commission through a guilty agent).

All of these concepts will be discussed in further detail below. In particular it will be worth comparing the idea of indirect co-perpetration with joint criminal enterprise.

12.3.2 Some complications

The concept of commission may now be beginning to seem quite complicated. Unfortunately the case law of international criminal tribunals throws up a number of further complications. Two are worth considering here. First, can one *commit* a crime without engaging in any over physical act? Second, can one commit a crime through *inaction*—that is, by failing to act?

Commission without any overt physical act

 Example

Seromba, ICTR

Seromba[16] concerned a Rwandan priest (Seromba), who during the course of the 1994 genocide in Rwanda, accepted the decision of local community authorities to destroy with bulldozers the parish church in which approximately 1,500 members of the Tutsi ethnic minority were sheltering. He pointed out the weakest wall of the church to a bulldozer driver. The driver asked him three times if he should really bulldoze the church with people inside and Seromba replied in the affirmative, telling him demons had entered the church and it should be destroyed.

There was little doubt that Seromba was in some sense involved in the Rwandan genocide. However, had he *committed* genocide or simply assisted it in some other manner? It was held by the ICTR Appeals Chamber in *Seromba* that committing genocide and the crime against humanity of extermination does not require direct, physical perpetration.[17] It was considered sufficient that the acts of an accused are 'as much an integral part of the genocide as were the killings which [they] enabled'.[18]

This was an extraordinarily controversial finding (a strong dissent was attached to the judgment by Judge Liu), for two reasons:

- the 'integral part' test is vague and no guidance was given in the judgment as to what this might mean in other cases; and

[16] *Seromba*, ICTR Appeals Chamber, 12 March 2008.
[17] Ibid, para 161 ff.   [18] Ibid, para 161.

- the facts appeared much more consistent with a conviction for aiding and abetting, ordering or incitement (as discussed below). Indeed, Seromba was originally
convicted on this basis and the Prosecutor appealed on the ground that he should
have been considered to have committed genocide and received a higher sentence
accordingly.

The approach does not appear to have been followed in subsequent cases.

Conviction for commission on the basis of a failure to act

A person in a position of authority may, exceptionally, be able to commit crimes
through a failure to act. Normally, this requires a clear rule of *criminal* law which specifies a positive duty to act.[19]

As we shall see when we discuss superior responsibility, a superior may be responsible for the crimes of his or her subordinates if he or she failed either to prevent
them or punish them. This clearly implies a duty to take preventative action ahead
of time or to punish those responsible afterwards. In the *Delalić* case the defendant was the person effectively in charge of a prison camp in the village of Čelebići.
He was aware of the crimes being committed by his subordinates against detained
civilians and did nothing to stop them. He was thus guilty of the war crime of cruel
treatment.[20]

However, in addition, he committed crimes through failing to provide detainees
with adequate food and facilities. That is, the appalling conditions at the Čelebići
camp were sufficient of themselves to make him guilty of the war crime of cruel
treatment or the commission of acts of genocide through causing serious bodily harm to his victims. This result appears just but is slightly harder to explain in
strict law. It is certainly prohibited under international criminal law to actively treat
non-combatants detained during an armed conflict cruelly (e.g. by beating them); it
is less obvious that a failure to comply with rules concerning the humane treatment
of detainees (e.g. by neglecting to provide adequate food and facilities) breaches a
rule of *criminal* law. Nonetheless, *Delalić* and other cases make it clear that crimes
based on causing suffering (such as cruel treatment or torture) can be committed by
omission.[21]

12.3.3 Inchoate offences: attempts and conspiracy

Attempts and conspiracy are examples of preparatory or initiating acts which are
punishable irrespective of whether the relevant crime was committed or completed.[22]
As the intended crime remains incomplete these are called 'inchoate offences'.

---

[19] Cassese et al, *Cassese's International Criminal Law*, 181.

[20] *Delalić, Mucić et al (Čelebići)*, ICTY Trial Chamber, 16 November 1998, para 1123 and compare paras
1092–96, 1101–05.

[21] Werle, 'Individual Criminal Responsibility', 964–66.

[22] Cassese et al, *Cassese's International Criminal Law*, 193; Cryer 'General Principles of Liability' in Cryer
et al, *Introduction*, 379.

Attempt

Attempt is a relatively obvious idea, but is harder to define concisely: a defendant with the relevant mental state who acted with the intention of completing the material elements of a crime, but who failed to do so, has attempted to commit the crime. That attempt is punishable even though the crime was not completed. The ICC Statute makes it clear that such attempts are punishable only when the action taken amounts to a 'substantial step' but 'the crime does not occur because of circumstances independent of the person's intentions'.[23] An attempted execution which fails only because a weapon jams, for example, would constitute an attempt. The ICC Statute also makes it clear that a person may abandon 'the effort to commit the crime' or prevent its completion and in such cases their responsibility is excluded and they may not be convicted of attempt.[24]

The key points to note are the requirements for a 'substantial step' and whether the effort to complete the crime is frustrated 'because of circumstances independent of the person's intentions'. There is, however, little modern case law on point: prosecutors at the ICTY have tended to charge different offences with less onerous elements (e.g. 'inhumane acts') rather than charge attempts of more serious offences (e.g. attempted murder).[25]

Conspiracy

Conspiracy is usually considered to be the inchoate crime of two or more people agreeing to commit a crime, 'even if the crime is never perpetrated'.[26] Under international criminal law it is *not* a crime to conspire to commit war crimes or crimes against humanity (but where such crimes have occurred consider whether planning, inciting, or abetting would be available).[27]

Originally, it was not clear if inchoate conspiracy was punishable at international law. Article 6 of the International Military Tribunal (IMT) Charter covered engaging in a 'conspiracy or common plan' to wage a war of aggression but *only* in cases where such a war came about. In convicting on the basis of a conspiracy to commit crimes against the peace the Nuremberg IMT said: '[t]he conspiracy must be clearly outlined in its criminal purpose. It must not be too far removed from the time of decision and action.'[28]

The only clear rule of international law which presently criminalizes conspiracy as an inchoate is found in the Genocide Convention.[29] That it is a crime to conspire to commit genocide was accepted in both the ICTY Statute and ICTR Statute.[30] An example of a conviction for conspiracy to commit genocide is provided in *Musema*.[31] Mr Musema was accused of helping lead and organize various attacks in the Bisesero area

---

[23] Art 25(3)(f), ICC Statute.

[24] Werle, 'Individual Criminal Responsibility', 973; compare Werle and Jessberger, *Principles*, 264–66.

[25] Cryer 'General Principles of Liability' in Cryer et al, *Introduction*, 380.

[26] Cassese et al, *Cassese's International Criminal Law*, 201.

[27] See: Werle and Jessberger, *Principles*, 262 para 696; Cassese et al, *Cassese's International Criminal Law*, 202.

[28] *Judgment of the International Military Tribunal (Nuremberg)* (1947) 41 American Journal of International Law 172, 222.

[29] Art 3(b), Convention on the Prevention and Punishment of the Crime of Genocide 1948, 78 UNTS 277; see further: Schabas, *Genocide in International Law*, 310 ff.

[30] Art 4(3)(b), ICTY Statute; Art 2(3)(b), ICTR Statute.

[31] *Musema*, ICTR Trial Chamber, 27 January 2000, paras 187–92.

of Rwanda as part of the 1994 genocide. In *Musema* the ICTR held that the *mens rea* for conspiracy includes the *dolus specialis* of the primary offence: one cannot conspire to commit genocide unless one agreed to bring about the destruction of a protected group in whole or in part.[32]

We should note, however, conspiracy to commit genocide is not covered by Arts 6 or 25 of the ICC Statute and thus is *not* a crime in the Court's jurisdiction.[33] Article 25(3)(d) of the ICC Statute does contain a rule on liability for contribution to a group crime, which is discussed further at section 12.8. While this might sound a great deal like conspiracy,[34] it does not cover inchoate offences—the crime must actually have come about.

12.3.4 Common-purpose or common-plan liability as a form of commission as a principal

Where multiple persons act pursuant to a common plan that involves the commission of an international crime, it is possible that they will each be held jointly responsible for the acts of other members of that group. However, the correct way to formulate a test for such common-plan liability and how to place limits upon it are controversial. Despite this, common-plan doctrines of liability in various forms have been the cornerstone of many international criminal law prosecutions. Because of their complexity the two major doctrines on point, joint criminal enterprise and co-perpetration, are discussed only after the secondary or accessorial modes of participation outlined in section 12.4.

It is also useful to consider secondary modes of participation first in order that we can ask whether common-purpose or common-plan liability usefully adds anything to them. Why convict someone as a member of a joint criminal enterprise if one could as equally convict on the basis that they aided or abetted a crime?

12.4 General forms of secondary participation

The following discussion is based largely on ICTY and ICTR case law and ICC Statute. This section will discuss aiding and abetting, ordering, instigating, and planning or preparing. In the next section we will consider the doctrine of superior responsibility. Before turning to these modes of participation, the question arises as to what mental state or *mens rea* a secondary participant must have. Must he or she intend the crime to come about? Or is it sufficient they foresee that it is likely the crime will come about? Or is reckless indifference to whether their actions contribute to a crime sufficient? This is an important general question and the ICTY case law and ICC Statute have taken different approaches to answering it.

---

[32] See further: *Popović* et al, ICTY Trial Chamber, 10 June 2010, paras 867–76.

[33] See Arts 6 and 25, ICC Statute.

[34] Werle sees it as a form of conspiracy rule: Werle, 'Individual Criminal Responsibility', 970; compare Werle and Jessberger, *Principles*, 219.

12.4.1 What mental element is required for the secondary forms of participation?

In Chapter 7 we discussed the point that the question of culpability—whether someone *should* be held guilty of committing an offence—inherently raises issues of the required mental element for a crime. We noted in Chapter 7 that:

- before ICTY and ICTR it is generally sufficient that the material elements of the offence (the prohibited act or *actus reus*) were carried out either: (a) with intent (*dolus directus*) or (b) with 'indirect intent' (recklessly or with *dolus eventualis*); but

- under the ICC Statute the material elements of the offence must be committed with 'intent and knowledge' unless 'otherwise provided' (Article 30).

In particular the ICTY has held that a person who instigates, aids, abets, or orders 'an act or omission with the *awareness of the substantial likelihood* that a crime' will consequently be committed 'has the requisite *mens rea* for establishing responsibility'.[35] This is because acting 'with such awareness has to be regarded as accepting that crime'.[36] This is now established in the ICTY jurisprudence as being the mental element required at customary international law for most modes of secondary participation. If this is correct, then it would appear the ICC Statute may set a higher standard for the required mental element for conviction as an accessory than is required under customary international law.

At the time of writing, there have been two convictions at the ICC, entered in the *Lubanga* and *Katanga* cases. Mr Lubanga was convicted as a co-perpetrator (a principal) of the war crime of conscripting children into an armed force. Mr Katanga was convicted of having 'contributed' to the commission of a crime 'by a group of persons acting with a common purpose' (that is, as an accessory).[37] In *Katanga* it was held that this form of accessorial liability required: that the defendant made a significant contribution to a crime; that contribution was intentional; and, the contribution was made in full knowledge of the criminal intention of the group which committed the crime.[38] This seems consistent with the proposition that *dolus eventualis* is not included within the ICC Statute: the liability of the accessory does not extend to the crimes they foresaw as being a likely consequence of their acts, it is limited to the planned crimes to which he or she directly contributed.[39] However, the *mens rea* requirement under the ICC Statute will vary according to the mode of liability charged as we shall see below. One should thus be cautious about drawing too many general conclusions about the requirements of accessorial liability from this early case law.

---

[35] *Kordić and Čerkez*, ICTY Appeals Chamber, 17 December 2004, paras 30, 31, and 32; following *Blaškić*, ICTY Appeals Chamber, 29 July 2004, para 42 (emphasis added).
[36] *Kordić and Čerkez*, ICTY Appeals Chamber, 17 December 2004, para 32.
[37] Art 25(d), ICC Statute.   [38] *Katanga*, ICC Trial Chamber, 17 March 2014, para 1620.
[39] Ibid, para 1619.

12.4.2 Aiding, abetting (encouraging), or otherwise assisting

This mode of participation is found in the ad hoc Tribunal Statutes and that of the Special Court for Sierra Leone (SCSL), which provide that: 'A person who...aided and abetted in the planning, preparation or execution of a crime...shall be individually responsible for the crime.'[40] It is also provided for in Article 25(3)(c) of the ICC Statute.

Aiding and abetting has long been recognized as a form of liability in trials for international crimes. Among the subsequent Nuremberg trials under Control Council Law No. 10 was the 1946 *Schonfeld Case*, which concerned a group of men who killed three Allied airmen who were being hidden in a house by members of the Dutch resistance. In this case a British Military Court held that a defendant could aid and abet a crime if he acted as a lookout to prevent his companions being surprised or to assist their escape, or was positioned ready to come to his companions' assistance if needed, and this 'was calculated to give [them] additional confidence' in committing the crime.[41] The important point is that mere presence (even mere presence nearby) can constitute aiding and abetting, so long as it has a substantial effect on the commission of the crime.[42] The contribution need not be causal (in the sense that without it the crime would not have occurred) or even physical, but the aider/abettor must know or assume that it has some effect on the principal.

12.4.2.1 The case law of the ad hoc Tribunals and the Special Court for Sierra Leone

The elements of aiding and abetting at customary international law were stated in the *Tadić Case* as follows:[43]

- The material element (*actus reus*) of aiding and abetting requires that the defendant (i) 'carries out acts specifically directed to assist, encourage or lend moral support to the perpetration of a certain specific crime' and (ii) that 'this support has a substantial effect upon the perpetration of the crime'.

- The mental element (*mens rea*) of aiding and abetting requires that the defendant has: 'knowledge that the acts performed by the aider and abettor assist the commission of a specific crime by the principal.'

The most influential formulation of aiding and abetting liability in ICTY case law, however, was the earlier 1998 Trial Chamber judgment in *Furundžija* which stated:

> the *actus reus* [of aiding and abetting] consists of practical assistance, encouragement, or moral support which has a substantial effect on the perpetration of the crime. The *mens rea* required is the knowledge that these acts assist the commission of the offence.[44]

---

[40] See: Art 7(1), ICTY Statute; Art 6(1), ICTR Statute; Art 6(1), SCSL Statute.

[41] *Trial of Franz Schonfeld and others* (1946) 11 Law Reports of Trials of Major War Criminals 64, 70.

[42] See: K Ambos, *Treatise on International Criminal Law* (Oxford University Press 2013), vol 1, 128; *Tadić*, ICTY Trial Chamber, para 687.

[43] *Tadić*, ICTY Appeals Chamber, 15 July 1999, paras 190–92, 229

[44] *Furundžija*, ICTY Trial Chamber, 10 December 1998, para 249; endorsed in *Furundžija*, ICTY Appeals Chamber, 21 July 2000, paras 117 ff.; *Delalić et al*, ICTY Appeals Chamber, 20 February 2001, para 352.

The requirement that the assistance has a 'substantial' effect on the commission of a crime might seem a high threshold. In practice, it is not. Certainly, it signals that there must be some relationship between the assistance and the crime, but this is obviously not the same thing as say 'but for' the assistance the crime would not have occurred.[45] Indeed, the requirement has been described as meaning any contribution which is more than *de minimis*.[46] Put another way, the ICTY case law appears to distinguish between the nature of the support (which might be merely 'moral encouragement') and the effect it has on the crime (the support must make a significant difference).[47] Thus aiding and abetting involves 'practical assistance, encouragement, or moral support which has a substantial effect on the perpetration of the crime'.[48] This leaves the crucial limiting factor as being the 'substantial effect' requirement. The meaning of these words, however, remains rather vague and is settled on a case by case basis.[49] It is established that one can aid or abet an international crime by omitting to perform a duty. In *Mrkšić and Šljivančanin*, for example, one of the defendants was found guilty of aiding and abetting torture through his failure to ensure adequate protection for detained persons under his control.[50]

Note that, at least in the jurisprudence of the ad hoc Tribunals, the mental element required for aiding and abetting is a knowledge-based standard: there is no requirement that the principal perpetrator and the aider or abettor shared a common intention.[51] The aider or abettor need only be aware of the 'essential elements' of the crime and that his or her conduct assists that crime.[52] Even in the case of a crime of specific intent, such as genocide, an aider or abettor need only have knowledge of the principal's specific intent. It is also enough if the accused 'is aware that one of a number of crimes will probably be committed, and one of those crimes is in fact committed'.[53]

In the case law there has been recent controversy over whether this *mens rea* standard is too broad. One may call this the 'arms dealer' or 'assistance to rebels' problem. If the President of a country (or arms dealer) provides weapons to a State army or non-State armed group, and it is generally known that the fighting force in question is committing war crimes, can the weapons supplier be convicted of aiding and abetting any future war crimes committed by that force? On a strict knowledge based standard the answer would appear to be 'yes'. The case law, and in particular the case law of the ICTY Appeals Chamber, briefly 'fragmented' on whether this is the correct answer.[54]

On the extent to which it was commonly followed in later cases see: G Boas, J Bischoff, and N Reid, *International Criminal Law Practitioner Library* (Cambridge University Press 2007), vol 1, 305.

[45] Ambos, *Treatise*, vol 1, 128.

[46] Cryer 'General Principles of Liability' in Cryer et al, *Introduction*, 371.

[47] Ambos, *Treatise*, vol 1, 128.

[48] *Furundžija*, ICTY Trial Chamber, 10 December 1998, para 249; and references at n 44.

[49] Ambos, *Treatise*, vol 1, 130.

[50] *Mrkšić and Šljivančanin*, ICTY Appeals Chamber, 5 May 2009, para 134.

[51] *Vasiljević*, ICTY Trial Chamber, 29 November 2002, para 71; *Krnojelac*, ICTY Appeals Chamber, 17 September 2003, para 52.

[52] *Tadić*, ICTY Appeals Chamber, 15 July 1999, para 164; *Orić*, ICTY Trial Chamber, 30 June 2006, para 288.

[53] *Furundžija*, ICTY Trial Chamber, 10 December 1998, para 246.

[54] M Milanovic, 'The Self-Fragmentation of the ICTY Appeals Chamber', EJIL: Talk!, 23 January 2014, www.ejiltalk.org/the-self-fragmentation-of-the-icty-appeals-chamber/.

The *Perišić* case before the Appeals Chamber of the ICTY concerned war crimes and crimes against humanity committed by armed groups in Croatia. These groups were extensively supported, in particular through the provision of weapons, by the Yugoslav Army. Perišić was chief of the General Staff of the Yugoslav Army and oversaw the provision of weapons. Did this make him an aider and abettor of the war crimes and crimes against humanity carried out by the groups he supported? The ICTY Appeals Chamber held, relying on certain words used in *Tadić*, that there was a requirement of 'specific direction': that is, the assistance must be *specifically directed* to assist a particular crime.[55] (Very oddly, despite the clear volitional element involved it found this requirement to be part of the material element and not the mental element of aiding and abetting.[56]) Thus, at least in cases where the accused is remote from the commission of the relevant crimes, *Perišić* held 'specific direction' must be proved. On the facts the ICTY Appeals Chamber held that a policy of assisting an armed group's general war effort was not evidence that the assistance was *specifically directed* to aid crimes being committed in particular regions. The decision attracted serious criticism[57] and there were good grounds for thinking the requirement (if it was one) had not been applied in previous ICTY case law with any consistency.[58]

The reasoning in *Perišić* was first rejected by the Appeals Chamber of the Special Court of Sierra Leone (SCSL) in the *Taylor* case. Charles Taylor, former President of Liberia, was accused of selling weapons to rebel forces in neighbouring Sierra Leone in exchange for 'blood diamonds' during his term of office. It was known that these forces had committed war crimes and crimes against humanity and it appeared likely they would continue to do so. The SCSL Appeals Chamber found that the requirements for aiding and abetting were that the acts of 'assistance, encouragement and/or moral support had a substantial effect on the commission of the crimes' and the perpetrator was aware of the substantial likelihood that his acts would assist the commission of the crimes (and that he was aware of the essential elements of the crimes actually committed).[59] On this basis, Taylor's trade in weapons for diamonds made him an aider and abettor of war crimes and crimes against humanity. An additional requirement of 'specific direction' in the case of 'remote' leaders was expressly rejected.[60] The case has, however, been criticized on the basis that the SCSL should have conducted a more detailed assessment of whether the impact of the weapons provided by Taylor was, in fact, *substantial*.[61] (The argument being that this should have required some qualitative assessment of the impact of different sources of weapons on the crimes committed.[62])

[55] *Perišić*, ICTY Appeals Chamber, 28 February 2013, para 53.

[56] See the separate and dissenting opinions to *Peršić* in which: Judges Meron and Agius hold 'specific direction' is really a question of the required mental element (para 4); Judge Liu suggests it is at best a circumstance relevant to mental element (fn 7); and Judge Ramaroson disagrees that it is part of the material element (para 1).

[57] Cryer 'General Principles of Liability' in Cryer et al., *Introduction*, 373; JG Stewart, 'The ICTY Loses its Way on Complicity', Opinio Juris, 3 April 2013, http://opiniojuris.org/2013/04/03/guest-post-the-icty-loses-its-way-on-complicity-part-1/.

[58] *Perišić*, ICTY Appeals Chamber, 28 February 2013, Dissenting Opinion of Judge Liu, paras 2–3.

[59] *Taylor*, SCSL Appeals Chamber, 26 September 2013, paras 482–83.   [60] Ibid, para 480 and 533.

[61] K Ambos and O Njikam, 'Charles Taylor's Criminal Responsibility' (2013) 11 Journal of International Criminal Justice 789, 801.

[62] Ambos and Njikam, 'Charles Taylor's Criminal Responsibility', 801.

Similarly, in 2014 in the *Sainovic* case a differently constituted bench of ICTY Appeals Chamber judges held that specific direction was *not* a requirement of aiding and abetting at customary international law and endorsed the requirements set out in *Furundžija*.[63] Indeed, it 'unequivocally rejected' the approach in *Perišić* on the basis that it conflicted with the established case law. This was quite an extraordinary development.[64]

There do appear to be strong historical arguments to suggest that 'specific direction' is not well-founded in the case law. However, some have made the argument that there was always an *implicit* element of 'specific direction' analysis in ICTY case law and the requirement serves a valuable function in making sure there is a close, culpable link between the assistance offered and the relevant crime.[65] On this view 'specific direction' is best understood as a question of *mens rea* which can often be inferred when the accused (and the assistance he or she provided) was close to crime scene but may need to be expressly proved in other cases.[66] Nonetheless, if the ICTY Appeals Chamber considered it necessary to limit the scope of aiding and abetting liability other options were available: one could focus on the type of knowledge required (i.e. the degree of likelihood that crimes would be committed);[67] or one could more closely define the substantial contribution requirement.

In any event, the recent ICTY Appeals Chamber judgment in *Popović* may be taken to have settled the matter. It too rejected *Perišić*[68] and we can assume it is now settled that 'specific direction' is not regarded as a requirement of aiding and abetting under customary international law.

12.4.2.2 The ICC Statute definition of aiding and abetting

In any event, a higher mental element is certainly required under the ICC Statute, Article 25(3)(c) of which provides that a person is individually criminally responsible if he or she:

> *[f]or the purpose* of facilitating the commission of such a crime, aids, abets or otherwise assists in its commission or its attempted commission, including providing the means for its commission (emphasis added).

Notably, there is no express requirement that the contribution made be *substantial*. Nonetheless, an ICC Pre-Trial Chamber has indicated that a substantial contribution may form part of the material element required under Article 25(3)(c).[69]

---

[63] *Sainovic et al*, ICTY Appeals Chamber, 23 January 2014, paras 1649–50.

[64] Milanovic, 'The Self-Fragmentation of the ICTY Appeals Chamber'.

[65] Ambos and Njikam, 'Charles Taylor's Criminal Responsibility', 805–06.

[66] Ibid, 807.

[67] Judge Moloto criticized the Trial Chamber findings in *Peršić* on the basis that, in his view, it had not been shown Peršić actually knew of the occurrence of crimes only that he had enough information that he had reason to know. The latter is an appropriate *mens rea* for superior responsibility but not for aiding and abetting. *Peršić*, ICTY Trial Chamber 2011, dissenting opinion of Judge Moloto, para 38.

[68] Indeed, it did so in a cursory paragraph which simply quoted *Sainovic et al*: *Popović*, ICTY Appeals Chamber, 30 January 2015, para 1758.

[69] *Mbarushimana*, ICC Pre-Trial Chamber, 16 December 2011, para 279; see also: Werle, 'Individual Criminal Responsibility', 969.

Note that the words 'for the purpose of facilitating' would not appear to require a shared intention between perpetrator and an aider or abettor, but they would seem to require that the aider acts with more than just knowledge that his or her acts will assist a crime.[70] That is, what the aider or abettor must intend is to *facilitate* a specific crime; the objective contribution to the crime can remain, as under ICTY and ICTR case law, quite low.[71] What precisely is meant by an intention to facilitate has not been the subject of much commentary or any case law. One possibility is, of course, that it might be interpreted to mean something similar to 'specific direction' in the *Perišić* sense.

12.4.3 **Ordering**

Ordering is listed as a mode of liability in all the major international criminal tribunal Statutes, although it is included without a definition.[72] We therefore need to look to the case law to determine its elements. It was said in *Kordić and Čerkez*:

> The *actus reus* of 'ordering' means that a person in a position of authority instructs another person to commit an offence. A formal superior-subordinate relationship...is not required.[73]

The required *mens rea* has been held to be direct intent to issue the order with awareness of the substantial likelihood of the resultant crime.[74] While ordering is provided for under the Statute of the ICC there is no relevant case law as yet.[75]

12.4.4 **Instigating, soliciting, inducing, and inciting (i.e. prompting, urging, and encouraging)**

The requirements of this form of participation are the same, irrespective of the precise label applied. In *Orić* it was said that instigation required more than mere facilitation of the crime, it 'requires some kind of influencing the principal perpetrator by way of inciting, soliciting or otherwise inducing him or her to commit the crime'.[76] There is a requirement for a nexus between this influence and the commission of the crime:

> it suffices to prove that the instigation of the accused was a substantially contributing factor for the commission of the crime.[77]

This same 'substantially contributing factor' standard was applied in *Kordić and Čerkez*,[78] while the term 'clear contributing factor' was used in *Blaškić*.[79]

---

[70] Cryer 'General Principles of Liability' in Cryer et al, *Introduction*, 377.

[71] Ambos, *Treatise*, vol 1, 166.

[72] Art 7(1), ICTY Statute; Art 6(1), ICTR Statute; Art 6(1), SCSL Statute; Art 25(3)(b), ICC Statute.

[73] *Kordić and Čerkez*, ICTY Appeals Chamber, 17 December 2004, paras 28–30.

[74] See also: *Galić*, ICTY Appeals Chamber, 30 November 2006, para 152; *Ntagerura*, ICTR Appeals Chamber, 7 July 2006, para 365.

[75] Art 25(3)(b), ICC Statute.   [76] *Orić*, ICTY Trial Chamber, 30 June 2006, paras 271–79.

[77] Ibid.   [78] *Kordić and Čerkez*, ICTY Appeals Chamber, 17 December 2004, para 27.

[79] *Blaškić*, ICTY Trial Chamber, 3 March 2000, para 270.

It was also noted in *Orić* that:

- instigation is not the same as ordering, because no superior-subordinate relationship is needed; and

- in cases where the principal perpetrator has already 'definitely decided to commit the crime' instigation is not possible but 'further encouragement or moral support' may still constitute aiding and abetting.[80]

A three-step approach to the required mental element was set out in *Orić*:

- the instigator must be aware of his influence on the principal;

- the instigator must be aware of and agree to principal's commission of the crime; and

- 'the instigator, when aware that the commission of the crime will more likely than not result from his conduct, may be regarded as accepting its occurrence'.[81]

Instigation or incitement is not ordinarily an inchoate crime: a crime must have been committed before the instigation can be prosecuted. The one exception is that direct and public incitement to genocide can be committed as an inchoate crime.[82] Strictly speaking the act of incitement will be a completed crime of public endangerment in itself; it is only an inchoate crime 'with regard to genocide as the main offence'.[83] Thus numerous commentators consider incitement to genocide not to be a means of committing genocide but a special offence in itself.[84] Nonetheless, incitement to genocide has been held by the ICTR in *Akayesu* and in the *Media Case* to require:

- a call to a large number of people in a public place or a broadcast/publication to the public at large;

- that call must be a 'direct' call for genocide to be committed—although what constitutes 'direct' may vary with cultural context (*Akayesu*);[85] and

- there is a double mental element—the defendant must have both the *dolus specialis* for genocide and the intent to produce in their audience a particular state of mind necessary to commit the crime (*Media* case).[86]

12.4.5 Planning and preparing

The ad hoc Tribunal Statutes and that of the SCSL all provide that: 'A person who ... [participated] in the planning, preparation or execution of a crime ... shall be individually responsible for the crime.'[87] There is, however, no equivalent in the ICC Statute.

---

[80] *Orić*, ICTY Trial Chamber, 30 June 2006, para 271.
[81] *Orić*, ICTY Trial Chamber, 30 June 2006, para 279.
[82] As listed in: Art 3(c), Genocide Convention; Art 4(3)(c), ICTY Statute; Art 2(3)(c), ICTR Statute; Art 25(3)(e), ICC Statute.
[83] Ambos, *Treatise*, vol 1, 132.   [84] Ibid; Werle and Jessberger, *Principles*, 321–24.
[85] *Akayesu*, ICTR Trial Chamber, 2 September 1998, para 562.
[86] *Nahimana et al* (the '*Media Case*'), ICTR Trial Chamber 2003, paras 1000–12.
[87] Art 7(1), ICTY Statute; Art 6(1), ICTR Statute; Art 6(1), SCSL Statute.

The required mental element is that 'a person who plans an act or omission with the awareness of the substantial likelihood that a crime will be committed in the execution of that plan, has the requisite *mens rea* for establishing responsibility... Planning with such awareness has to be regarded as accepting that crime'.[88]

12.5 Command or superior responsibility

Superior responsibility is an unusual type of duty in criminal law as it involves a positive duty to act to prevent another's crime. It is therefore a type of omission liability, whereas most criminal law focuses on punishing a person's wrongful act. Indeed, superior responsibility may be seen as an 'original creation of international criminal law'.[89] Anyone studying superior responsibility would therefore be wise to begin by reading Article 7(3) of the Statute of the ICTY and Article 28 of the Statute of the ICC to gain a sense of how it has been defined. Essentially, though, superior responsibility has three required elements under the ICTY case law:

- a superior/subordinate relationship;
- a mental element; and
- that the superior failed to take reasonable measures to prevent or punish international crimes committed by a subordinate or subordinates.

The ICTY has held these to be the essential elements of the mode of liability as a matter of customary international law. Under the ICC Statute an additional element of *causation* is required. That is, the ICC Statute requires that the crime came about 'as a *result* of' the superior's failure to act.[90] Each of these four elements is discussed below.

12.5.1 Superior/subordinate relationship

Whether a relationship of superior and subordinate exists is a factual test of *effective* control, merely having substantial influence over another person is insufficient.[91] Obedience (or disobedience) to orders will be good evidence of effective control (or the lack of it), as will any legal authority held by the superior. A legal duty to obey on the part of subordinates is not required as this would mean superiors in rebel armies or organized armed groups could not be held responsible as superiors.

Nor is a military relationship required: civilian superiors may be liable under the doctrine where they have a similar degree of control over subordinates as military commanders, even if that control or authority might be exercised in a different way.[92] The ICC Statute

---

[88] *Kordić and Čerkez*, ICTY Appeals Chamber, 17 December 2004, para 31.
[89] Werle and Jessberger, *Principles*, 221 quoting K Ambos, *Der Allgemeine Teil des Volkerstrafrechts* (2002) 667.
[90] Art 28(a) and (b), ICC Statute.
[91] *Delalić, Mucić et al ('Čelebići')*, ICTY Appeals Chamber, 20 February 2001, paras 256, 266.
[92] *Bagilishema*, ICTR Appeals Chamber, 3 July 2002, para 52.

distinguishes military commanders who exercise 'effective command and control'[93] from cases of other superior/subordinate relationships based on 'effective authority and control'.[94] Despite this difference in wording, the idea of effective control clearly underlies both provisions. Gerhard Werle and Florian Jessberger suggest that civilian superiors will need to be shown to have 'de facto control' of subordinates of 'an intensity and degree of hierarchical integration and stability' comparable to military commanders.[95]

Under the ICC Statute, in the case of a civilian superior the relevant crimes must have 'concerned activities that were within the effective responsibility and control of the [civilian] superior.'[96] In situations outside that sphere of 'effective responsibility' civilians will not treated as a responsible superior.[97] For example, a Minister of Transport might be responsible for subordinates in his or her ministry who plan and carry out the war crime of forced deportation. The same Minister could not be responsible if his subordinates—while off duty, off Ministry premises, and not using any powers or equipment put at their disposal by the Ministry—participated in other crimes. Such acts would occur beyond his sphere of effective authority and control as a civilian.

There is controversy as to whether customary international law requires that the superior has effective control *at the time* of the offences: that is, whether their duties extend to events before they took up command ('prior acts'). In the *Hadžihasanović* case a narrow majority of the ICTY Appeals Chamber held that there was no command responsibility for prior acts (largely on the basis that there was no relevant case law regarding such cases).[98] The controversy stems from the fact that command responsibility is a duty either to prevent *or* to punish. While one cannot prevent acts that have already occurred, one can logically punish prior acts and this might be thought to reasonably fall within the scope of a superior's responsibilities. Indeed, the SCSL in *Sesay* held that it is not necessary the superior had effective control 'at the time' of the offence. Thus in respect of prior acts a superior has 'the duty to punish the perpetrators from the moment he assumes effective control'.[99] An ICC Pre-Trial Chamber has, however, said that under the ICC Statute 'the suspect must have had effective control at least when the crimes were about to be committed'.[100] This result is said to follow from the causation requirement (unique to the Statute) which is discussed below. As a result, the state of customary international law on point is at best uncertain and commentators differ as to what the correct rule is or should be.[101]

---

[93] Art 28(a), ICC Statute.   [94] Art 28(b), ICC Statute.

[95] Werle and Jessberger, *Principles*, 227–28.   [96] Art 28(b)(ii), ICC Statute.

[97] The ICC Statute wording reflects the idea that civilian authority 'is normally limited in place and time to his or her official function': Werle and Jessberger, *Principles*, 228. See also R Arnold and O Triffterer, 'Article 28: Responsibility of commanders and other superiors' in O Triffterer, *Commentary on the Rome Statute of the International Criminal Court*, 2nd ed (Beck, Hart and Nomos 2008), 840–41 marginal notes 127 and 129.

[98] See further *Hadžihasanović* (Decision on Command Responsibility), ICTY Appeals Chamber 2003, paras 37–56 and the Dissenting Opinion of Judge Hunt.

[99] *Sesay et al (RUF Case)*, SCSL Trial Chamber, 25 February 2009, para 299. See generally: V Oosterveld, 'Prosecutor v. Issa Hassan Sesay' (2010) 104 American Journal of International Law 73.

[100] *Bemba Gombo* (Decision on the Confirmation of Charges), ICC Pre-Trial Chamber, 15 June 2009, paras 418–19.

[101] E van Sliedregt, *Individual Criminal Responsibility in International Law* (2012) 187–89; Cryer 'General Principles of Liability' in Cryer et al, *Introduction*, 388; Ambos, *Treatise*, vol 1, 220.

Pause for reflection

Should a responsible superior be criminally responsible for failure to punish international crimes committed before he or she assumed command? Why or why not? Consider the following scenario.

So-called 'water-boarding' (simulated drowning) is generally agreed to constitute torture, and was a technique used by US military officials on detainees in Guantanamo Bay, Cuba in 2002–2003. These persons were detained in the course of an armed conflict and acts of torture committed against them could, therefore, be war crimes. Investigations into, and prosecutions of, any, offences committed by military officials were not commenced by the President or Defence Secretary at the time.

Inaugurated in January 2009, President Barack Obama has decided that no prosecutions will occur. Does this make Obama responsible for failing to punish any crimes committed before he entered office? Should it?[102]

12.5.2 **Mental element**

Superior responsibility is always engaged where the superior has *actual* knowledge of his or her subordinate's crime. However, the doctrine also covers other cases. Two standards for the mental element could be suggested. In cases other than actual knowledge liability might logically follow either in:

- cases of negligence (the superior *should* have known, but fell short of the standard of a competent superior); or
- cases of constructive knowledge or a failure of due diligence (the superior had some degree of information indicating a risk that crimes would be or had been committed; and this information triggered a duty of further investigation).

The case law and statutes make it clear that it is the second standard (constructive knowledge) that applies. A superior will be responsible if he or she has either actual knowledge or knew enough that they should have made further inquiries.

The ICTY Statute, in Article 7(3), refers to superiors who 'knew or had reason to know' of a subordinate's crime. It was said in *Delalić* (the Čelebići detention camp case) that under this provision a superior has the required mental element where either:

- 'he had actual knowledge, established through direct or circumstantial evidence, that his subordinates were committing or about to commit [international] crimes'; or

---

[102] Note that there is also a rule of international law under the Convention Against Torture requiring that those suspected of committing torture must be investigated and, if the evidence warrants it, prosecuted. This rule does not, however, make it an offence not to commence such investigations/prosecutions: Art 7, Convention Against Torture and Other Cruel, Inhuman or Degrading Treatment or Punishment 1984, adopted 10 December 1984, entered into force 26 Jun 1987, 1465 UNTS 85.

- 'where he had in his possession information of a nature, which at the least, would put him on notice of the risk of such offences by indicating the need for additional investigation in order to ascertain whether such crimes were committed or were about to be committed...'[103]

Either approach is based on the information the defendant actually had at the relevant time: negligent failure to acquire such information will not be sufficient to make out the mental element.[104] This is the standard that has prevailed at the ICTY despite academic criticism.[105] A broader test was formulated by the ICTY Trial Chamber in *Blaškić* emphasizing that a responsible superior had a 'duty of due diligence' to acquire information about the conduct of his or her subordinates and that 'where the absence of knowledge is the result of negligence' then superior responsibility could still be made out.[106] This approach was rejected on appeal.[107]

The ICC, however, requires a different mental element in the case of military or non-military superiors respectively. Essentially, a stricter standard applies to military superiors:

- under Article 28(a)(i) of the ICC Statute, military commanders may be liable under the doctrine if they: 'knew or, owing to the circumstances at the time, should have known that the forces [under their control] were committing or about to commit such crimes';

- under Article 28(b)(i), all other superiors only have the required *mens rea* if they: 'either knew, or consciously disregarded information which clearly indicated, that the subordinates were committing or about to commit such crimes'.

The ICC Statute's required mental element for military superiors (knowledge or constructive knowledge 'owing to circumstances at the time') is a notable exception to the usual principle that under the ICC Statute offences must be committed with 'intent *and* knowledge'.[108] The question is how this standard is to be interpreted.

It could be interpreted to mean much the same thing as the standard set in *Delalić* (actual possession of information putting a commander on notice of a risk and the need for further investigation) or in the *Blaškić* sense of encompassing a duty of due diligence to seek such information out. An ICC Pre-Trial Chamber in the *Bemba Gombo* confirmation of charges decision took the *Blaškić* approach.[109] It noted the words 'should have known' in the ICC Statute can be taken to support the existence of 'an active duty on the part of the superior to take the necessary measures to

---

[103] *Delalić, Mucić et al ('Čelebići')*, ICTY Appeals Chamber, 20 February 2001, para 223.
[104] Ibid, para 226.   [105] Cryer 'General Principles of Liability' in Cryer et al, *Introduction*, 289.
[106] *Blaškić*, ICTY Trial Chamber, 3 March 2000, para 332.
[107] *Blaškić*, ICTY Appeals Chamber, 29 July 2004, para 63.
[108] Art 30, ICC Statute (emphasis added).
[109] *Bemba Gombo* (Decision on the Confirmation of Charges), ICC Pre-Trial Chamber, 15 June 2009, para 432.

secure knowledge of the conduct of his troops'.[110] Thus, under the ICC Statute liability under the doctrine of command responsibility in the case of military leaders can arise through negligence or failures of due diligence.

In *Bagilishema* the ICTR Appeals Chamber (and remember the ICTY and ICTR Appeals Chamber are the same body of judges) has rejected the more restrictive ICC Statute test for civilian superiors and has held there is only one test of superior responsibility at customary international law.[111] If this is correct, then the ICC test is unique to its Statute. Of course, it is open to argue that the ICC Statute is itself potential evidence of States' *opinio juris* and should have been given more weight in *Bagilishema*.

12.5.3 Failure to take necessary and reasonable measures to prevent or punish

A superior may be liable either for a failure to prevent a crime *or* a failure to punish it. Liability can arise on either basis, however, and taking steps after the fact to punish an offence will not absolve a superior of having failed to prevent a crime.[112]

Articles 28(a)(ii) and (b)(iii) of the ICC Statute require that the superior 'failed to take all necessary and reasonable measures within his or her power to prevent or repress…commission [of the crimes] or to submit the matter to the competent authorities for investigation and prosecution'.

The ICTY has held that what is required of a superior is commensurate with the degree of control the superior exercises, which is always a question of evidence.[113] How should this be assessed? The *Orić* case suggests there are four factors to take into account:

- first, 'the kind and extent of measures to be taken ultimately depend on the degree of effective control [a superior has] over the conduct of subordinates'; that is, different superiors may have different degrees of power, this will affect what measures they can be expected to take;

- second, 'a superior must undertake all measures [within their powers] which are necessary and reasonable to prevent subordinates from planning, preparing or executing the prospective crime';

- third, 'the more grievous and/or imminent the potential crimes of subordinates appear to be' then the 'quicker the superior is expected to react'; and

- fourth, a superior is 'not obliged to do the impossible.'[114]

---

[110] Ibid, para 433. See further: R Cryer, 'Command Responsibility at the ICC and ICTY: In Two Minds on the Mental Element?', EJIL: Talk!, 20 July 2009, www.ejiltalk.org/command-responsibility-at-the-icc-and-icty-in-two-minds-on-the-mental-element/.

[111] *Bagilishema*, ICTR Appeals Chamber, 3 July 2002, paras 26–37.

[112] Werle and Jessberger, *Principles*, 231 para 604. See also *Blaškić*, ICTY Trial Chamber, 3 March 2000, para 336.

[113] *Blaškić*, ICTY Appeals Chamber, 29 July 2004, para 72.

[114] *Orić*, ICTY Trial Chamber, 30 June 2006, para 329 (footnotes omitted).

Failure to maintain discipline may be enough to satisfy these criteria.[115]

The case law was also usefully summarized in *Milutinović*:

> It is primarily the accused's degree of effective control—that is, his material ability to prevent and/or punish the crimes or underlying offences of his subordinates—that guides a Chamber in determining whether he took measures that were necessary and reasonable in the circumstances. 'Necessary' measures are those appropriate for the superior to discharge his obligation, evincing a genuine effort to prevent or punish, and 'reasonable' measures are those reasonably falling within the material powers of the superior. Although a superior is 'not obliged to perform the impossible', the Appeals Chamber has held that he is obliged to take all measures that are within his material possibility. In addition, a superior's duty cannot be discharged by the issuance of 'routine' orders, and any measures taken by him should be specific and closely linked to the acts that they are intended to prevent.[116]

One possible way of measuring what is 'necessary and reasonable' is to consider the duties imposed on armed forces by international humanitarian law. This might require training in the laws of war and the establishment of systems of supervision, reporting, and a system of sanctions and punishment for breaches.[117]

12.5.4 Causation

The case law of the ICTY clearly takes the view that the prosecutor need not prove that 'a superior's failure to take the necessary and reasonable measures...caused [the] crimes' in order to establish superior responsibility.[118] Indeed, as superior responsibility encompasses a responsibility to prevent (before the fact) and punish (after the fact), it is hard to see how failure to punish conduct after it has occurred could be said to have caused the conduct in the first place.[119]

However, as we have noted, the ICC Statute provides under Article 28(a) and (b) that a superior 'shall be criminally responsible for crimes within the jurisdiction of the Court committed by subordinates under his or her [command and control or] effective authority and control, *as a result of* his or her failure to exercise control properly over such subordinates...' (emphasis added).

It is hard to see how a failure to act can cause something else to happen. There was some debate over how to interpret this provision, but the first ICC decision on point in *Bemba Gombo* held that:

> There is no direct causal link that needs to be established between the superior's omission and the crime committed by his subordinates. Therefore, the Chamber considers that it is

---

[115] *Orić*, ICTY Trial Chamber, 30 June 2006, para 336.

[116] *Milutinović*, ICTY Trial Chamber Judgment, 26 February 2009, para 122.

[117] Werle and Jessberger, *Principles*, 231–32 para 606.

[118] See: *Milutinović*, ICTY Trial Chamber Judgment, 26 February 2009, para 122; *Orić*, ICTY Trial Chamber 2006, para 338; *Blaškić*, ICTY Appeals Chamber, 29 July 2004, paras 75–7; and *Hadžihasanović*, ICTY Appeals Chamber 2008, paras 38–42 (all holding that causation is not a necessary element).

[119] See: Cryer 'General Principles of Liability' in Cryer et al, *Introduction*, 392 (causation in this context is 'difficult, but not impossible, to apply'); Werle and Jessberger, *Principles*, 233–4 paras 611–14 (doubting that the question is strictly one of causation); *Blaškić*, ICTY Appeals Chamber, 29 July 2004, para 77.

only necessary to prove that the commander's omission increased the risk of the commission of the crimes charged in order to hold him criminally responsible under article 28(a) of the Statute.[120]

This clearly adopts the position advocated by Kai Ambos: 'it is sufficient that the supervisor's failure of supervision increases the risk that the subordinates commit certain crimes'.[121] The only alternative is to consider that a superior has a duty to exercise proper control which may be shown to have been violated before the crime occurred, and that such a failure to exercise proper control resulted in the crimes.[122]

12.5.5 Conceptualizing command responsibility

Finally, we should note that there are different understandings of what the responsible commander may be guilty of: the question is whether responsibility makes him or her guilty of the crimes of subordinates (as a form of complicity or accessorial liability); or whether he or she is guilty of a separate dereliction of duty offence. The point is not trivial: in the first case one would expect a superior's sentence to reflect the gravity of the crimes actually committed; in the second case one would expect a superior's sentence to reflect how far short they fell in carrying out their duties.

Two different approaches have been taken:

- the ICC Statute makes it clear that the superior is responsible for the crimes of their subordinates; but
- the ICTY and ICTR case law has been inconsistent: sometimes suggesting a superior is responsible for the underlying crimes, sometimes suggesting he or she is liable only for their own failure to act and most recently suggesting that the seriousness of a failure to act can be measured by the gravity of the ensuing crimes.[123]

As a result we cannot say that the position at customary international law is entirely clear.

12.6 Joint criminal enterprise (JCE)

12.6.1 Introduction: prosecuting a group with a common plan/purpose

As noted above, where multiple persons act pursuant to a common plan that involves the commission of an international crime, it is possible that they will each be held jointly

---

[120] *Bemba Gombo* (Decision on the Confirmation of Charges), ICC Pre-Trial Chamber, 15 June 2009, para 452.

[121] K Ambos, 'Superior Responsibility' in A Cassese, P Gaeta, and J Jones (eds), *The Rome Statute of the International Criminal Court: A Commentary* (Oxford: Oxford University Press 2002), vol 1, 860; and Ambos, *Treatise*, vol 1, 215.

[122] Werle and Jessberger, *Principles*, 232–34.

[123] Cryer 'General Principles of Liability' in Cryer et al, *Introduction*, 393–5; referring to *Ntabazuke*, ICTR Appeals Chamber, 8 May 2012, para 282. See also: Werle and Jessberger, *Principles*, 222–23 para 583.

responsible for the acts of other members of that group. At the ICTY and the ICTR the doctrine that has developed to cover such situations is joint criminal enterprise or 'JCE'. JCE is a form of conspiracy liability where you may become responsible for the acts of others. It is also common to refer to participants in a common plan as 'members of a JCE'. JCE can thus refer to either a doctrine of liability or the group sharing a common plan in a particular case. The ICTY in cases such as *Furundžija* and *Tadić* found (rather controversially and on a limited survey of trials conducted after World War II) that JCE is a form of liability established in customary international law.[124] The doctrine has since been adopted at other international tribunals including the SCSL. JCE can be a powerful prosecutorial tool as it may make each member of the JCE liable for the acts of all other members (or their agents). It has thus been joked that JCE really stands for 'just convict everybody'.[125]

While it is obviously useful and morally justifiable to have a doctrine that can connect high leaders with foot soldiers, there is an important question about what degree of connection is needed to link the leader with the crime. Put another way: what limits could be put on any doctrine of common-plan liability to stop it catching too many people with varying degrees of involvement and blameworthiness in one net?

A number of possible limitations on any doctrine might include:

- a requirement of causation or a high 'contribution' threshold: a court could require that every participant in the common plan must make a necessary (or at least important) contribution to the success of the plan without which it cannot succeed;

- a court could restrict the application the doctrine to small, closed, or identifiable groups—thus requiring: (1) a close connection between all participants; and (2) that prosecutors list those involved in a JCE and precisely explain their role in order to allow defendant to prepare their case.

However the case law of both the ICTY and ICTR have rejected such limitations. In particular it was held in *Karemera* that JCEs can emerge among participants who have never met and cover crimes committed over vast areas. An accused can thus be liable for crimes which are 'structurally or geographically remote from the accused'.[126] In addition, the plan involved need not be premeditated or expressly agreed but can arise spontaneously and be inferred from the evidence.[127] This has led to criticisms that the doctrine is too broad.

---

[124] *Furundžija*, ICTY Trial Chamber 10 December 1998 and *Tadić*, ICTY Appeals Chamber, 15 July 1999. See Boas, Bischoff and Reid, *International Criminal Law Practitioner Library*, vol 1, 10–28. The doctrine originates in the common law and (perhaps in part for that reason) has proved controversial with civilian criminal law scholars: H Olásolo, *The Criminal Responsibility of Senior Political and Military Leaders as Principals to International Crimes* (Hart 2009), 5–7 and n 19.

[125] G Sluiter, 'Foreword' (2007) 5 Journal of International Criminal Justice 67, 67.

[126] *Karemera* (JCE Appeal Decision), ICTR Appeals Chamber, 12 April 2006, para 14.

[127] *Tadić*, ICTY Appeals Chamber, 15 July 1999, para 227; and *Stakić*, ICTY Appeals Chamber, 22 March 2006, para 64.

In considering the case law we should ask whether it clearly answers the following questions:

- What level of contribution must an accused make to a crime to be a participant in a JCE?
- Can the JCE doctrine capture people who make no material contribution to the crime at all?
- How do you define who is in a JCE: what degree of connection or relationship is required between participants?

If these questions cannot be clearly answered significant doubts about the fairness of the doctrine must be entertained.

12.6.2 The material element of JCE

According to the ICTY Appeals Chamber in *Tadić* a JCE requires:

- a plurality of persons (i.e. more than one person, but not necessarily a military or organizational structure);
- the existence of a common plan, design or purpose involving the commission of a crime under the statute (which can 'materialize extemporaneously' or 'be inferred from the fact that a plurality of persons acts in unison'); and
- the participation of the accused in the common design involving the perpetration of one of the crimes (this must only involve 'performing acts...in some way...directed to the furtherance of the common plan or purpose', the accused does not have to personally commit a specific criminal act).[128]

While the requirement that more than one person be involved is perhaps obvious, the common plan and participation requirements need further scrutiny.

12.6.2.1 The plan: can it change?

According to the International Criminal Tribunal for the Former Yugoslavia case law it is indeed possible for the relevant plan to change. In such cases a participant in the original plan will not be liable for acts committed pursuant to any new plan, unless he or she has agreed to the new plan. Of course, a defendant will remain liable for any crimes falling within the scope of the original plan to which he or she did agree.[129] This approach raises the possibility of an 'inner circle' within a larger JCE group who have a separate plan of more limited membership.

12.6.3 Participation in the plan: how do we test JCE membership?

A vital question is to know who will be liable as a member of the JCE and who will not be. We could answer 'anyone who has expressly agreed to the plan' is a JCE member,

---

128 *Tadić*, ICTY Appeals Chamber, 15 July 1999, para 227.
129 See: *Blagojević and Jokić*, ICTY Trial Chamber, 7 January 2005, para 700 and n 2157.

but the ICTY Appeals Chamber in *Tadić* instead preferred a test of *participation*. That participation requirement is potentially low: lower even than that which is required for aiding and abetting. The ICTY Appeals Chamber in *Tadić* noted that:

> an aider and abettor carries out acts specifically directed to assist, encourage or lend moral support to the perpetration of a certain specific crime (murder, extermination, rape, torture, wanton destruction of civilian property, etc.), and this support has a substantial effect upon the perpetration of the crime. By contrast, in the case of acting in pursuance of a common purpose or design, it is sufficient for the participant to perform acts that in some way are directed to the furthering of the common plan or purpose.[130]

This implies that 'performing acts' in some way 'directed to the furtherance of the common plan or purpose' can involve acts having a less than 'substantial' effect. Indeed, later cases make it clear that:

- participation in a JCE may be by act or omission (at least where there is a duty to act);[131]

- the accused need not be present at time or place of the crime's commission;[132]

- the accused's participation need not be a *sine qua non* without which the crime could or would not have been committed (called a 'necessary contribution' below);[133]

- the *Kvočka* case suggested that while the accused's participation or contribution need not be 'substantial', nonetheless a substantial contribution might help prove the mental element required;[134] and

- some cases suggest a very low standard for participation: notoriously in *Mpambara* it was said that 'there is no minimum threshold of significance or importance' and 'the *actus reus* [of JCE] may be satisfied by any participation, no matter how insignificant'.[135]

This potentially casts the net very wide in terms of who will be considered a member of the JCE. The question then becomes whether more recent jurisprudence has introduced a more demanding standard. No ICTY judgment has yet expressly over-ruled the proposition in *Kvočka* that the participation of the accused need not be 'substantial'. However, subsequent Appeals Chamber and Trial Chamber judgments have implicitly rejected the sweeping statements in *Mpambara* and have held that while the contribution 'need not be necessary or substantial, it should at least be significant'.[136]

---

[130] *Tadić*, ICTY Appeals Chamber, 15 July 1999, para 229.
[131] *Milutinović*, ICTY Trial Chamber Judgment, 26 February 2009, paras 103–05.   [132] Ibid.
[133] *Tadić*, ICTY Appeals Chamber 1999, paras 191, 199; *Kvočka et al.*, ICTY Appeals Chamber, 28 February 2005, paras 98, 193.
[134] *Kvočka et al.*, ICTY Appeals Chamber, 28 February 2005, paras 97, 104, and 187.
[135] *Mpambara*, ICTR Trial Chamber, 12 September 2006, paras 13 and 14.
[136] *Milutinović*, ICTY Trial Chamber, 26 February 2009, paras 104–05, quoting the *Brđanin* Appeals Chamber, 3 April 2007, para 430; and *Kvočka et al.* Appeals Chamber, 28 February 2005, paras 101, 192. See also *Popović* Trial Chamber, 10 June 2010, para 1027.

What is a 'significant' contribution? In *Milutinović* the following propositions were distilled from the jurisprudence of the ICTY:

- a contribution that goes to the efficiency, effectiveness and smooth running of the plan may be considered significant. Relevant factors to consider include: 'the size of the enterprise, the functions performed by the accused and his efficiency in performing them, and any efforts made by the accused to impede the efficient functioning of the joint criminal enterprise';
- '[a]n accused's leadership status and approving silence likewise militate in favour of a finding that his participation was significant'; and
- 'in most situations the accused will not be someone readily replaceable'.[137]

From this it appears a very low standard applies to leaders (approving silence may be a significant contribution), but a higher level of contribution will be required before a readily replaceable subordinate is considered a participant in a JCE. Thus:

- failure to investigate or follow-up reports of crimes may be sufficient to be a participant in a JCE, even where that failure cannot be shown to be causally connected to a crime;[138] and
- Antonio Cassese considered that merely voting in favour of a criminal plan is sufficient to become a JCE participant.[139]

The *mental element* will vary according to the type of JCE involved which are discussed below.

12.6.4 Mental element and the three types of JCE

In *Tadić* it was established that JCE comes in three forms, each defined by a different mental element. In each case, however, the material element remains the same—there must always be:

- a plurality of persons;
- the existence of a common plan among them; and
- the participation of the accused in that plan.

JCE Type 1

The first type of JCE ('JCE 1' in the cases) involves a form of 'co-perpetration, where all participants in the common design possess the same criminal intent to commit a crime (and one or more of them actually perpetrate the crime, with intent)'.[140] The core

---

[137] *Milutinović*, ICTY Trial Chamber, 26 February 2009, paras 104–05.

[138] *Krajišnik*, Trial Chamber, 27 September 2006, para 1121.

[139] A Cassese, *International Criminal Law*, 2nd ed (Oxford University Press 2008) 191.

[140] *Tadić*, ICTY Appeals Chamber, 15 July 1999, paras 199–220 and 228. The emphasis on common intent over making a necessary or causal contribution has led to JCE being described as a 'subjective

requirement is the common intent to commit a certain crime, which is then carried out. For example in the *Furundžija* case Furundžija interrogated the victim, who was kept naked while the other accused, Brano, used a knife to threaten her with sexual violence.[141] Furundžija had the mental element for torture (inflicting severe pain and suffering to extract information) and shared a common criminal intent with Brano. The acts constituting torture were divided between them: Furundžija interrogated, Brano inflicted severe psychological suffering. Both performed integral parts of the offence and, vitally, they shared the same criminal intent.[142] It does not matter that their *motives* may have varied (for example, if Brano participated in the acts only to gratify sadistic impulses and Furundžija only wished to extract information).[143] Therefore they are both liable as principals for the entire offence.

JCE Type 2

The second type of JCE ('JCE 2') consists of the 'so-called "concentration camp" cases, where the requisite *mental element* comprises knowledge of the nature of the system of ill-treatment and intent to further the common design of ill treatment'.[144] In such cases intent to further the system of ill-treatment may be directly proved or inferred 'from the nature of the accused's authority within the... organisational hierarchy'.[145]

One should note that in JCE 2 cases it is easier to tell who is, and is not, in the JCE. The outer possible bounds of the JCE are the bounds of the camp or organization. Under such conditions could a camp guard or organization member show that they were not part of the JCE? Cassese et al suggest one would either have to ask to be relieved of one's duties or to have been genuinely ignorant of both the crimes being carried out and one's role in that system.[146]

Sadly such cases are not rare in international criminal law. The major cases include the *Dachau Concentration Camp Case* and the *Auschwitz/Belsen Concentration Camps Case* prosecuted under Control Council Law No. 10;[147] and subsequent ICTY detention camp cases including *Krnojelac* and *Kvočka*.[148]

One may also fairly suggest that JCE 2 involves the proof of an additional material element: the existence of a system for mistreating prisoners and committing international crimes.[149]

approach' to liability: *Lubanga* (Confirmation of Charges), ICC Pre-Trial Chamber, 29 January 2007, para 329.

[141] *Furundžija*, ICTY Appeals Chamber, 21 July 2000, para 113. See also A Zahar and G Sluiter, *International Criminal Law: A Critical Introduction* (Oxford University Press 2008), 224.
[142] See *Tadić*, ICTY Appeals Chamber, 15 July 1999, para 199.
[143] On the irrelevance of motive see: *Krnojelac*, ICTY Appeals Chamber, 17 September 2003, paras 99–100.
[144] *Tadić*, ICTY Appeals Chamber, 15 July 1999, paras 220 and 228.   [145] Ibid.
[146] Cassese et al, *Cassese's International Criminal Law*, 166.
[147] *Gottfried Weiss and Others, Dachau Trial* (1945) 11 Law Reports of Trials of War Criminals 5–16; *Kramer and Others, Belsen Trial* (1945) 2 Law Reports of Trials of War Criminals 1–125.
[148] *Krnojelac*, ICTY Appeals Chamber, 17 September 2003; *Kvočka et al.*, ICTY Appeals Chamber, 28 February 2005.
[149] Werle and Jessberger, *Principles*, 203 para 534.

JCE Type 3

Type 3 JCE or 'JCE 3' is an expanded theory of commission.[150] It is often referred to as the expanded form of JCE liability because under JCE 3 an accused who:

- participated in a common plan; and
- can be convicted of crimes (as a principal) going beyond that plan;
- provided that those crimes were a *foreseeable* consequence of the plan.

For example, it might be foreseeable that murders or rapes would occur in the course of a war crime of forced deportation.

Two mental element requirements must be met for JCE 3 liability to be applied: 'responsibility for a crime other than the one agreed upon in the common plan arises only if... (i) it was foreseeable that such a crime might be perpetrated by one or other members of the group and (ii) the accused willingly took that risk'.[151]

While (i) appears to be an objective test ('foreseeable' not 'foreseen'), it should be read consistently with the subjective element in (ii). That is, the further crimes must have been objectively foreseeable and also *actually foreseen* and *accepted* by the accused.[152]

The test is ultimately one of subjective recklessness (*dolus eventualis*): the defendant foresaw the risk and willingly took it. Indeed the ICTY Appeals Chamber in *Tadić* expressly refers to '*dolus eventualis*' or 'advertent recklessness'.[153]

Later cases tended to formulate the 'foreseeability' standard slightly differently. For example the ICTY Appeals Chamber in *Kvočka* referred to JCE 3 responsibility: 'for crimes which were not part of the common criminal purpose, *but which were nevertheless a natural and foreseeable consequence of it*' (emphasis added).[154] This might seem a high standard, but the trend of later cases appears to confirm that it is only necessary the defendant foresaw that such crimes were 'possible'.[155]

The critical element is obviously that the accused has foreseen and accepted the possibility of the further crimes. Such acceptance is indicated by nevertheless continuing to act to further the JCE's common purpose.

12.6.5 Criticisms of JCE 3

Criticisms based on applying the doctrine to vast groups

Early JCE cases involved groups of relatively few people or defined groups, for example the *Tadić* case itself concerned crimes committed by a military unit. Thus, on the facts, in the early case law there was always a close link between members of the JCE. Thus,

---

[150] *Tadić*, ICTY Appeals Chamber, 15 July 1999, paras 220 and 228.

[151] Ibid, para 228.

[152] See Cassese et al, *Cassese's International Criminal Law*, 166–72; Boas, Bischoff, and Reid, *International Criminal Law Practitioner Library*, vol 1, p 73; *Stakić*, ICTY Appeals Chamber, 22 March 2006, para 65; *Brdanin*, ICTY Appeals Chamber, 3 April 2007, para 365.

[153] *Tadić*, ICTY Appeals Chamber, 15 July 1999, para 228.

[154] *Kvočka et al.* Appeals Chamber, 28 February 2005, para 83.

[155] Boas, Bischoff, and Reid, *International Criminal Law Practitioner Library*, vol 1, p 82; see further Ambos, *Treatise*, vol 1, 126–27.

many commentators[156] and some Trial Chambers of the ICTY became uneasy with the 'expansion' of JCE3 to cover:

- persons very remote from the commission of a crime and having only attenuated links with the physical perpetrators; or
- persons who made little or no obvious direct contribution to the physical commission of the crimes.

Thus a number of Trial Chambers attempted to impose new limits to the doctrine which were invariably rejected on appeal. For example, an ICTY Trial Chamber in *Brđanin* held that there must be some *mutual* understanding or arrangement among JCE members *including* the relevant physical perpetrators. The concern of the Trial Chamber arose from its view that the fact that leaders and perpetrators all espouse a common political plan is not enough: two different groups of people could, independently of each other, decide to commit crimes to achieve the same political goals. The fact that different members of the same political group committed crimes does not necessarily prove a common plan among all members of the group.[157] The Trial Chamber thus emphasized the need for mutual understanding within a JCE and that the JCE should include the perpetrators. More significantly, the ICTY Trial Chamber in *Stakić* attempted to discard JCE 3 entirely for a theory of co-perpetrators, *each* of whom must make an important contribution to the crime (this follows the 'control of the crime' approach discussed below). Such attempts at imposing a requirement of 'mutual understanding' or an 'important' contribution were rejected on appeal.

 Pause for reflection

Have the risks of vast or expanded JCEs been reduced by the introduction of a requirement that the accused make a 'significant' contribution, discussed above?

Criticisms of JCE 3 based on the mental element

JCE 3 has been criticized for allowing the conviction of a person for specific intent crimes which they *foresaw* but for which they did not themselves possess the required *mental element*. Nonetheless, the ICTY Appeals Chamber held in a preliminary appeal in *Brđanin* that under JCE 3 it is *not* necessary to prove the mental element of

---

[156] Among many critics see: JD Ohlin, 'Three Conceptual Problems with the Doctrine of Joint Criminal Enterprise' (2007) 5 Journal of International Criminal Justice 69–90; H Olásolo, 'Joint Criminal Enterprise and Its Extended Form: A Theory of Co-Perpetration Giving Rise to Principal Liability, a Notion of Accessorial Liability, or a Form of Partnership in Crime?' (2009) 20 Criminal Law Forum 263–287; Zahar and Sluiter, *International Criminal Law*, 221–57; Boas, Bischoff and Reid, *International Criminal Law Practitioner Library*, vol 1, 104.

[157] *Brđanin*, ICTY Trial Chamber, 1 September 2004, para 351.

the underlying offences, and that the prosecutor may enter a charge for genocide on this basis.[158]

Thus JCE 3 could permit a conviction for genocide where the defendant lacked the specific intent to destroy a group in whole or in part, but foresaw that crimes committed with that intent were a possible outcome of the agreed JCE. Consequently, arguments are sometimes made that JCE 3 allows for the 'dilution' of the required mental element of serious offences.[159]

 Pause for reflection

Krštić Case, ICTY

We should stop to consider whether, in many cases, JCE is actually needed to secure a conviction. The *Krštić Case*[160] is used here as an example.

In *Krštić* the Trial Chamber found two JCEs existed as part of a plan to rid Srebrenica of its Bosnian-Muslim inhabitants: one JCE concerned the removal of Bosnian-Muslim women and children from the region, another JCE concerned the removal of the Bosnian-Muslim men.

The first JCE aimed to transfer by bus Muslim women and children out of the town of Potočari to Bosnian-Muslim held territory. The defendant Krštić organized the buses, ordered the transfers, secured roads, and supervised the operation as then Deputy Commander of the 'Drina Corps'. Shortly afterwards he was promoted to the head of the Corps.

Krštić was held responsible under JCE 1 for the forced transfers and under JCE 3 for the 'the incidental murders, rapes, beatings and abuses committed in the execution of this [primary] criminal enterprise'.[161]

Regarding the men, Krštić knew they were being separated and detained in appalling conditions without any form of prisoner of war screening. He knew thousands of Muslim men had been captured within his zone of responsibility. He also knew mass killings were taking place. Nonetheless, he helped organize further troops for operations, and these troops were involved in further killings. He was convicted of these killings based on JCE 3.

Do we need a theory of joint criminal enterprise to convict for these crimes? What other doctrine (or doctrines) could make Krštić responsible for these crimes?

12.6.6 Summary of joint criminal enterprise as a form of commission

Table 12.1 summarizes the underlying material element involved in any joint criminal enterprise and outlines the mental element required for each of the three different 'types' of joint criminal enterprise. Where the relevant material and mental elements are made out a defendant may be convicted as a perpetrator of the relevant offence.

---

[158] *Prosecutor v Brđanin*, Case No. IT-99-36-A, Decision on Interlocutory Appeal on JCE, 19 March 2004, para 6.

[159] Cassese, one of the judges in *Tadić* to create JCE3, has argued that its application to genocide cases is inappropriate: Cassese et al, *Cassese's International Criminal Law*, 172–73.

[160] *Krštić*, ICTY Trial Chamber, 2 August 2001.   [161] Ibid, para 617.

Table 12.1 Joint criminal enterprise as a form of commission

The **material element** involves: (1) a plurality of persons (not necessarily a military or organizational structure); (2) the existence of a common plan, design, or purpose involving the commission of a crime under the Statute; (3) participation of the accused in the common design involving the perpetration of one of the crimes (*Tadić*, Appeals Chamber 1999, para 227). Participation requires: 'acts that in some way are directed to the furthering of the common plan or purpose' (*Tadić*, Appeals Chamber 1999, para 229). As regards that participation: the contribution to the common design 'need not be necessary or substantial, [but] it should at least be a significant [one]' (*Brđanin* Appeals Chamber 2007, para 430).

The **mental element** required for participation in a JCE will vary according to the 'type' of JCE (below).

Type 1 or basic form	Type 2 or systemic form	Type 3 or extended form
'Co-perpetration'* where all participants in the common design possess the same criminal intent to commit a crime (and one or more of them actually perpetrate the crime, with intent)' (*Tadić*, Appeals Chamber 1999, para 220). * Note that co-perpetration as a form of JCE should not be confused with the term as used in ICC case law (or by the ICTY Trial Chamber in *Stakić*).	'Concentration camp' cases, where the required mental element comprises knowledge of the nature of the system of ill-treatment and intent to further the common design of ill treatment. Intent may be directly proved or inferred 'from the nature of the accused's authority within the ... organisational hierarchy' (*Tadić*, Appeals Chamber 1999, para 220).	'... what is required is the intention to participate in and further the criminal activity or the criminal purpose of a group and to contribute ... [to] the commission of a crime by the group. In addition, responsibility for a crime other than the one agreed upon in the common plan arises ... [if], (i) it was foreseeable that such a crime might be perpetrated by one or other members of the group and (ii) the accused willingly took that risk' (*Tadić*, Appeals Chamber 1999, para 228). Each JCE member is thus responsible as a perpetrator for further crimes committed in carrying out a JCE if those crimes were both foreseeable and actually foreseen.

12.7 Commission by co-perpetration or indirect co-perpetration

12.7.1 Introduction: a false start at the ICTY?

As noted above, the ICTY Trial Chamber in *Stakić* proposed an alternative theory of common-purpose liability. It suggested that for:

> co-perpetration it suffices that there was an explicit agreement or silent consent to reach a common goal by coordinated co-operation and joint control over the criminal conduct ... [Typically] one perpetrator possesses skills or authority which the other ... does not.

These... [are] shared acts which when brought together achieve the shared goal based on the same degree of control over the execution of the common acts.[162]

Several points should be noted about this approach:

- the theory requires that each participant brings some necessary skill or authority the other (or others) lack;

- this means that the common plan would fail (or at least could not proceed in the same way) if any participant withdrew their efforts; and

- this means in turn each participant could frustrate the plan and therefore each has a common degree of control over whether the crime goes ahead.

This can be described as the 'control of the crime' approach.[163] Obviously, this sets a high—but relatively clear—threshold for who can be held criminally responsible on the basis of common-purpose or common-plan liability. As noted, the idea was rejected by the ICTY Appeals Chamber. Nonetheless it is a common concept in German and Latin American legal systems and has proved influential at the ICC.

12.7.2 Co-perpetration at the ICC

Despite the fact that Article 25(3)(d) of the ICC Statute expressly includes a form of common-purpose liability, ICC Pre-Trial Chambers in the *Lubanga*, *Katanga* and *Bemba Gombo* cases[164] have held the words '[c]ommits...jointly with another, or through another person' in Article 25(3)(a) may be interpreted to include a 'control of the crime' form of co-perpetration.

Three possible forms of common-purpose liability thus arise:

- co-perpetration (where two or more people act together);

- indirect perpetration (one person acting through another agent, as discussed above at 12.2.1); and

- indirect co-perpetration (where two or more people act together to bring about their criminal plan by using other persons as their agents).[165]

Unlike JCE in the ICTY and ICTR, co-perpetration before the ICC requires that the accused makes an *essential* contribution to the common plan, capable of frustrating

---

[162] *Stakić*, ICTY Trial Chamber, 31 July 2003, para 440.

[163] See in particular: JD Ohlin, E Van Sliedregt, and T Weigend, 'Assessing the Control-Theory' (2013) 26 Leiden Journal of International Law 725–746.

[164] *Lubanga* (Confirmation of Charges), ICC Pre-Trial Chamber, 29 January 2007, paras 322–67; *Katanga and Ngudjolo Chui* (Confirmation of Charges), ICC Pre-Trial Chamber, 30 September 2008, paras 480–539; *Bemba Gombo* (Decision on the Confirmation of Charges), ICC Pre-Trial Chamber, 15 June 2009, paras 346–71.

[165] There is a controversy about whether the ICC Statute allows the Court to combine co-perpetration and indirect perpetration, which are separately provided for in Article 25(3)(a): Ohlin, Van Sliedregt, and Weigend, 'Assessing the Control-Theory', 735–37; *Lubanga*, ICC Trial Chamber, 14 March 2012, Concurring Opinion Judge Van den Wyngaert, para 44.

the commission of the crime if it was withdrawn. This is often called 'joint control', as any co-perpetrator could frustrate the crime. This control of the crime approach will treat those who control *whether* and *how* a crime is committed as the principals.[166] In essence:

> Co-perpetration based on joint control over the crime involves the division of essential tasks between two or more persons, acting in a concerted manner, for the purposes of committing that crime.[167]

This approach becomes slightly more complex where *indirect co-perpetration* is alleged. Obviously, many international crimes which are committed on a large scale involve control over organizations, government, or other power structures. Where indirect co-perpetration is alleged through control of an organization or an 'apparatus of power' the existence of such an organization must be proven. In *Katanga* the Pre-Trial Chamber said this required:

- an organization 'based on hierarchical relations between superiors and subordinates';
- the 'organization must also be composed of sufficient subordinates to guarantee that superiors' orders will be carried out, if not by one subordinate, then by another'; and
- the leader must 'exercise authority and control over the apparatus and...his authority and control' must be 'manifest in...compliance with his orders'.[168]

In such an organization there must be almost automatic compliance with orders (i.e. sufficient discipline), which in turn requires either a sufficient pool of replaceable or interchangeable subordinates (so that if orders are disobeyed by one they will be carried out by another) or alternatively such compliance might be secured 'through intensive, strict and violent training regimes'.[169] The organization must be of such a kind that the 'highest authority...through his control over the organisation, essentially decides whether and how the crime would be committed'.[170] The idea of commission through control over an organization could have an obvious role to play in international criminal law, if one believes that many 'cases involving governmental or similarly organized atrocities' necessarily involve 'multiple higher-level government or rebel officials' collaborating to commit crimes through the organization under their command.[171] One can hold that this is different from superior responsibility as it is a form of *indirect perpetration*:[172] one is being held responsible for committing crimes, not for what one failed to prevent.[173]

---

[166] *Lubanga* (Confirmation of Charges), ICC Pre-Trial Chamber, 29 January 2007, paras 330; *Katanga and Ngudjolo Chui* (Confirmation of Charges), ICC Pre-Trial Chamber, 30 September 2008, paras 485.
[167] *Katanga and Ngudjolo Chui* (Confirmation of Charges), ICC Pre-Trial Chamber, 30 September 2008, para 521.
[168] Ibid, paras 512–13.   [169] Ibid, paras 518 and 547.   [170] Ibid, para 518.
[171] Ohlin, Van Sliedregt, and Weigend, 'Assessing the Control-Theory', 735.
[172] Ibid, 'Assessing the Control-Theory', 734.
[173] *Lubanga*, ICC Trial Chamber, 14 March 2012, para 1221.

However, it is not obvious that the ICC will always apply the test of control of an organization as strictly as the *Katanga* Pre-Trial Chamber suggested. The Pre-Trial Chamber in the *Bemba Gombo* confirmation of charges decision did not find it necessary to discuss the point at all.[174] (This could pose problems for the trial, if defence lawyers do not know what the Prosecutor needs to prove in order to make out control over an organization.) More importantly, in *Lubanga* the defendant was convicted of the crime of the conscription and use of children as combatants through his control over an organization. That is, Lubanga was said to be the President of the rebel group the Union des Patriotes Congolais and its military wing the Force Patriotique pour la Libération du Congo (referred to collectively in the case as the 'UPC/FPLC') and to have used that organization to carry out a plan with others to recruit and use child soldiers. However, rather than follow the strict test set out in *Katanga* the *Lubanga* Trial Chamber seemed content to review evidence of:

- Lubanga's position and authority within the UPC/FPLC;
- the general hierarchy and structure of that organization;
- whether it had internal lines of reporting and means of communication;
- meetings of its leadership (and the role of Lubanga in these meetings).[175]

The significance of the evidence was that it demonstrated there was an organization capable of carrying out a plan to recruit child soldiers and that Lubanga was in a position to 'shape policies' within the organization and played a key role in organizing 'logistical support' for its operations.[176] Therefore, his contribution to the common criminal plan was essential in that it could not have occurred without his policy and logistical support.

We can note the following critical features of the doctrine commission by indirect co-perpetration from the *Lubanga* judgment.[177] The material elements of individual co-perpetration required involve:

- a common plan or agreement among the co-perpetrators;
- that plan must involve at a minimum a 'critical element of criminality', that is 'a sufficient risk that, if events follow the ordinary course, a crime will be committed';[178]
- the contribution made by the accused to the common plan must be 'essential' (rather than 'more than *de minimis*' or 'substantial');[179]
- the accused need not be present at the scene of the crime.

---

[174] *Bemba Gombo* (Decision on the Confirmation of Charges), ICC Pre-Trial Chamber, 15 June 2009, para 350.
[175] *Lubanga*, ICC Trial Chamber, 14 March 2012, paras 1137–1223.　　[176] Ibid, para 1270.
[177] See generally the discussion in: Ambos, *Treatise*, vol 1, 152–54.
[178] *Lubanga*, ICC Trial Chamber, 14 March 2012, para 984.　　[179] Ibid, para 993.

The mental elements required are that:

- the accused must have intended the crime or been aware that, as a result of the common plan, it would occur in the ordinary course of events; and
- the accused must have been aware that his contribution to the common plan was essential.

A third mental element was proposed by the Pre-Trial Chamber in *Bemba Gombo*: that the accused 'be aware of the factual circumstances enabling him to control the crimes jointly with the other co-perpetrator'.[180] This was not applied by the Trial Chamber in *Lubanga* and therefore would not appear to be part of the doctrine at the ICC (at least at present).[181]

 Example

Summary of co-perpetration based on control of the crime through an organization

See *Katanga and Ngudjolo Chui* (Confirmation of Charges), ICC Pre-Trial Chamber, 30 September 2008, paras 512–39; and *Lubanga*, ICC Trial Chamber (Judgment), 14 March 2012, 976–1018

1. **Objective elements of committing a crime through an organization:** Article 25(a) of the Rome Statute is interpreted in these cases to include indirect co-perpetration which also includes commission through control of an organised apparatus of power. Note that the test below was *not* applied strictly in *Lubanga*.

   (a) There must be an organised and hierarchical apparatus of power

   This requires: (i) 'the organisation must be based on hierarchical relations between superiors and subordinates'; (ii) the 'organisation must also be composed of sufficient subordinates to guarantee that superiors' orders will be carried out, if not by one subordinate, then by another'; (iii) leader must 'exercise authority and control over the apparatus and…his authority and control' must be 'manifest in…compliance with his orders.' (*Katanga*, paras 512–13)

   (b) Control over the organisation. Is the accused a leader exercising control?

   (c) The execution of crimes is secured by almost automatic compliance with orders

   'The leader's ability to secure this *automatic compliance with his orders* is the basis for his principal—rather than accessorial—liability. The highest authority does not merely order the commission of a crime, but through his *control* over the organisation, essentially decides whether and how the crime would be committed.' (*Katanga*, para 518. Emphasis added.)

---

[180] *Bemba Gombo* (Decision on the Confirmation of Charges), ICC Pre-Trial Chamber, 15 June 2009, para 351.

[181] Ambos, *Treatise*, vol 1, 154.

This requires: (1) sufficient 'fungible' or 'replaceable' subordinates, making it irrelevant if any one disobeys; **or** (2) sufficient discipline, e.g. 'intensive, strict and violent training regimens.' (*Katanga*, para 518)

2. **Objective elements of co-perpetration generally**

(a) **Existence of an agreement or common plan between two or more persons**

This requires: 'an agreement or common plan between the persons who physically carry out the elements of the crime or between those who carry out the elements of the crime through another individual.' Participating in crimes which lack coordination falls outside co-perpetration. (*Katanga*, para 522). The agreement or common plan need not be explicit, and the existence of the agreement 'can be inferred from circumstantial evidence' (*Lubanga*, para 988). Such evidence might include 'the subsequent concerted action of the co-perpetrators.' (*Katanga*, para 523)

(b) **Coordinated essential contribution by each co-perpetrator resulting in the realisation of the objective elements of the crime**

'When the objective elements of an offence are carried out by a plurality of persons acting within the framework of a common plan, only those to whom essential tasks have been assigned—and who, consequently, have the power to frustrate the commission of the crime by not performing their tasks—can be said to have joint control over the crime.' (*Katanga*, para 525)

'Designing the attack, supplying weapons and ammunitions, exercising the power to move…troops…; and/or coordinating and monitoring the[ir] activities…, may constitute [essential] contributions' whether they happen 'before or during the execution stage of the crime'. (*Katanga*, para 526)

3. **Subjective elements co-perpetration generally**

(i) '[T]he accused and at least one other perpetrator meant [the crime to occur]…or they were aware that in implementing their common plan this consequence "will occur in the ordinary course of events";' and

(ii) 'the accused was aware that he provided an essential contribution to the implementation of the common plan.' (*Lubanga*, para 1013)

12.8 Other forms of participation in a group crime at the ICC

Article 25(3)(d) of the ICC Statute provides for individual criminal responsibility where a person in 'any other way contributes to the commission or attempted commission of such a crime by a group of persons acting with a common purpose'. Such a contribution must be made either (i) 'with the aim of furthering the criminal activity or criminal purpose of the group' or be made (ii) 'in the knowledge of the intention of the group to commit the crime'. The relevant crime must, of course, be one within the ICC Statute.

Article 25(3)(d) seems clearly to be an accessorial form of liability: it does not equate *contributing* to a crime with *committing* the crime. It is therefore likely to be less popular with prosecutors and judges concerned with 'fair labelling' who would prefer to see those most responsible for a crime labelled as principals who have committed the offence, not merely contributed to it.

Nonetheless, one of the first convictions under the ICC Statute has been on the basis of contributing to a criminal plan rather than by committing it through indirect co-perpetration. This occurred in the *Katanga* case. Katanga's case was originally joined with that of a co-defendant Ngudjolo Chui. In that joined case, *Katanga and Ngudjolo Chui*, it was alleged that each defendant controlled a different rebel organization. The Prosecution case was that in the course of conflict along ethnic lines in the Democratic Republic of the Congo in 2003 the two accused attacked the village of Bogoro with the intention to 'wipe out' it and its ethnically Hema population, and that this common plan involved or resulted in war crimes and crimes against humanity.[182] They were co-perpetrators because the attack involved the coordination of their separate forces. Charges were confirmed against both accused men as indirect co-perpetrators acting through an organized apparatus of power on the basis of Article 25(3)(a).

However, at trial there was found to be insufficient evidence to establish the leadership role of either of the two men. The Trial Chamber severed proceedings against Ngudjolo Chui and acquitted him. It then proceeded in *Katanga*, very controversially and after the presentation of the evidence had closed, to use the Court's power to re-characterize the charges alleged against Katanga.[183] As a result, Katanga was convicted under Article 25(3)(d) and on the basis of a mode of liability that neither his defence lawyers nor the Prosecutor had addressed at trial.[184] The properness of this approach will not be tested on appeal, as both prosecution and defence lawyers have withdrawn appeals in the case.[185]

In the event Katanga was convicted under Article 25(3)(d)(ii) of the ICC Statute which was held to require:

- that a crime within the jurisdiction of the Court had been committed;
- the persons who committed the crime were part of a group of persons acting in concert in pursuit of a common plan;
- the accused made a significant contribution to the commission of the crime;
- that contribution was intentional;
- the contribution of the accused was made in full knowledge of the intention of the group of persons to commit the crime.[186]

The common plan required is very similar to that required for conviction as a co-perpetrator under Article 25(3)(a): it must involve an element of criminality, in that the members of the group either intend the crime to come about or know it will occur

---

[182] *Katanga and Ngudjolo Chui* (Confirmation of Charges), ICC Pre-Trial Chamber, 30 September 2008, para 35.

[183] Regulation 55, ICC Regulations. See discussion in Chapter 5, section 5.3.4.

[184] See generally: C Stahn, 'Justice Delivered or Justice Denied? The Legacy of the *Katanga* Judgment' (2014) 12 Journal of International Criminal Justice 809.

[185] Ibid, 810–11.

[186] *Katanga*, ICC Trial Chamber, 17 March 2014, para 1620.

in the ordinary course of events.[187] The 'significant' contribution must affect either the occurrence of the crime or its manner of commission.[188] The contribution may be to an intermediate step in the plan (one does not have to be able to trace a direct line from the contribution to the commission of the crime by a principal) and what will constitute a 'significant' contribution will need to be assessed on a case by case basis.[189] The contribution need not be criminal in itself.[190] There is no requirement that the accused be present at the crime scene or be in a particularly 'proximate' relationship to the crime.[191] (On proximity, consider the debate over 'specific direction' and aiding and abetting discussed above in section 12.4.3.)

On the facts, the majority of the Trial Chamber (Judge Van Den Wyngaert dissenting) found the following facts sufficient to make out a significant contribution, that the accused:

- had a role in establishing a coalition with regional authorities and in devising a military strategy with them;
- impressed upon those regional authorities the importance of fighting with the various militias against the Hema ethnic group;
- had a role facilitating good communications between soldiers, local commanders, and regional authorities; and
- had a 'role in receiving, stockpiling and distributing weapons and ammunitions'.[192]

Judge Van Den Wyngaert in particular criticized the majority for (in her view) finding on the basis of very weak evidence that Katanga was 'president' of a group of fighters rather than merely acting as a 'middle man' between various factions and the regional authorities.[193] In her view, his contribution to any crimes was, at best, indirect.[194]

One difficulty that may arise in such cases is whether the evidence is likely to fit rigid, pre-conceived theories. The control of the crime approach, especially when it involves commission through an organization, seems to presume that international crimes occur when a group of leaders direct the actions of 'foot soldiers' through a vertical, hierarchical organizational structure.[195] This may be an apt description of crimes committed by States apparatuses. However, in chaotic civil war situations we may see much looser horizontal networks of power and influence which cut across formal structures.[196] The result in *Katanga* may actually suggest that the relatively loose, flexible, and horizontal framework of JCE could perhaps better describe the manner in which international

---

[187] Ibid, para 1627.   [188] Ibid, para 1633; Stahn, 'Justice Delivered or Justice Denied?', 826 n 184.

[189] *Katanga*, ICC Trial Chamber, 17 March 2014, paras 1632 and 1635.

[190] Stahn, 'Justice Delivered or Justice Denied?', 826.

[191] *Katanga*, ICC Trial Chamber, 17 March 2014, para 1636.

[192] Ibid, para 1671 (in French); translation based on that of the Dissenting Opinion of Judge Van Den Wyngaert, para 293.

[193] *Katanga*, ICC Trial Chamber, 17 March 2014, para 1671, Dissenting Opinion of Judge Van Den Wyngaert, para 302; Stahn, 'Justice Delivered or Justice Denied?', 828.

[194] Ibid.   [195] Guilfoyle, 'Responsibility for Collective Atrocities', 256.   [196] Ibid, 264.

crimes are committed. Whether that makes JCE a fair or legally justifiable doctrine remains a separate question.

 Pause for reflection

Comparing joint criminal enterprise and indirect co-perpetration

Read the hypothetical scenario below and then consider the questions posed.

Alpha is a relatively minor official within a revolutionary movement (the RM) in the district of Rossum. Rossum lies within a country torn by violent ethnic conflict. Beta is the local chief of police. Gamma is a charismatic national politician who is resident within Rossum and seen as influential the wider RM.

Alpha, Beta, and Gamma all sit on the local organizing committee of the RM.

Gamma opens a session of the local organizing committee, with a long speech about the rightful dominance of their shared ethnic group and the need for purity and harmony in Rossum. He then leaves the meeting to take a long phone call from the movement's national leadership.

The local organizing committee proceeds to vote to expel all members of rival ethnic groups from the capital of the Rossum district at gunpoint. (Presume this constitutes forced deportation as a war crime or crime against humanity.) In the course of the debate Alpha votes against the proposal and Beta votes for it. Alpha, taking the minutes, records the vote and the decision to leave the organization of the deportations to Beta. Gamma returns late in the meeting after the vote and sits in silence for the rest of it.

The committee also requires all RM organizing committee members to contribute weapons to a common store. Alpha contributes 20 single-action rifles to a store of 200 weapons.

The deportations are carried out by 'volunteer police' (a mix of policemen out of uniform and other RM members) organized by Beta: 150 men armed from the common store with repeating weapons. Alpha's rifles are not distributed. In the course of the deportations, scores of civilians are shot and killed (presume this constitutes murder as a war crime, or murder or extermination as a crime against humanity).

Questions

Consider the criminal liability of Alpha, Beta, and Gamma under both joint criminal enterprise and as indirect co-perpetrators. Would any of them be found *not* to be perpetrators under one doctrine or the other? Is one doctrine better or fairer than the other?

Are there additional or more appropriate modes of liability under which they could be charged which would still accurately describe their role in these crimes?

12.9 Concurrence of crimes

A separate liability issue arises when the one act may give rise to multiple crimes. No such issue arises where a defendant commits different conduct against different people. To borrow Cassese's example a soldier in a detention camp may beat up one prisoner of war, rape another, and take part in a firing squad that executes a person not properly sentenced.[197] Each of these acts constitutes a *separate* war crime (murder, rape, and unlawful execution): each would be charged separately, and each would attract a separate sentence.

Sometimes one course of conduct or one transaction will include closely related offences where one has more specific requirements than the other. In such cases the *greater or more specific offence subsumes the lesser offence*. For example, a soldier could beat a prisoner extensively and mercilessly (cruel treatment) before killing them (murder); or a soldier might sexually humiliate and intimidate someone (an outrage on their dignity) before raping them. If both offences were proved a conviction would only be entered for the murder or the rape, and similarly, only one sentence would be imposed (though it would reflect the gravity of the whole course of conduct). A similar example is the distinction between the war crimes of:

- cruel treatment, which involves the infliction of severe pain; and
- torture, which requires the infliction of severe pain for a prohibited purpose (such as obtaining information or a confession).

The latter contains a further element not found in the former. As torture is thus a more *specific* offence it subsumes cruel treatment and only one conviction is entered. Another way of putting it is that every war crime of torture would also always give rise to cruel treatment: so cruel treatment is a *lesser included offence* that does not justify a separate sentence.

Sometimes, however, one course of conduct may give rise to two different international crimes. This occurs because 'various rules [cover] the same subject matter'.[198] Rape, for example, can be committed as both a war crime and a crime against humanity, or as the *actus reus* of genocide (at least at customary international law under the International Criminal Tribunal for Rwanda jurisprudence). A good example is that given in the *Kupreškić* Trial Chamber Judgment at para 679:

> Consider for example the shelling of a religious group of enemy civilians by means of prohibited weapons (e.g. chemical weapons) in an international armed conflict, with the intent to destroy in whole or in part the group to which those civilians belong. This single act contains an element particular to . . . genocide to the extent that it intends to destroy a religious group, while the element particular to . . . war crimes lies in the use of unlawful weapons.[199]

In such a case, the same facts may make out all of the elements required of two different crimes (genocide and a war crime). Therefore, the prosecutor should charge both offences (cumulative charging) and the Court should enter a separate conviction for each. However, as the crimes result from one act the sentences for each crime should be served concurrently (i.e. at the same time).

---

[197] Cassese, *International Criminal Law*, 2nd ed, 179.   [198] Ibid, 180.
[199] *Kupreškić*, ICTY Trial Chamber, 14 January 2000, para 697.

12.10 Summary and conclusions

This chapter has explored a number of difficult concepts in international criminal law. The essential question which has been posed is: 'when is someone responsible for an international crime?' The answer involves two different concepts neither of which is simple. The first is 'system criminality', the idea that international crimes are typically committed as acts of systematic organized violence. The second is the distinction between principals and accessories. This distinction can be thought of as either normative or purely descriptive/analytical. That is, we might describe principals as those who are most responsible for crime and accessories as those who play other, less culpable roles. This involves a moral or normative element (the idea of those 'most responsible'). A purely descriptive approach might limit the idea of principals to the direct physical perpetrator of the crime and describe all other persons who contribute in any manner to a crime as accessories. In national law the principal normally will be the direct physical perpetrator, although all national legal systems acknowledge there are situations where joint acts will make a number of people equally liable as principals. Indeed, national legal systems may even acknowledge situations where the mastermind of a crime should be described as a principal or indirect perpetrator rather than as an accessory, even if he or she carries out no physical element of the crime. Nonetheless, in national law such situations will normally involve a degree of *proximity*. Principals who are not direct physical perpetrators will normally be members of a relatively small group of people and will likely stand in a close physical or causal relationship to the crime which occurs. The difficulty arises when in international criminal law we try and apply these national law notions to a context of massive system criminality. Suddenly, our moral intuition (or doctrines such as fair labelling) requires us to come up with a theoretical account of why leaders who are often physically or structurally remote from a particular crime should be described as principals. A large part of this chapter, therefore, has been dedicated to the rival theories of joint criminal enterprise and 'control of the crime' (indirect co-perpetration) both of which represent *extended* theories of commission. (That is, they label people other than the direct physical perpetrator as having committed the crime.)

Joint criminal enterprise has attracted a great deal of academic criticism and has not, so far, been applied under the ICC Statute. Equally, however, the contours of the doctrine of 'control of the crime' theory or indirect co-perpetration at the ICC do not yet seem to be fully settled. From the point of view of practicality, the flexibility of joint criminal enterprise has been praised as a useful and necessary tool for prosecutors; while the collapse of charges based on 'control of the crime' in *Katanga* may show that it will not always be as easy to apply in practice as one might have thought. Still, while practicality is important in a criminal trial, fairness to the defendant should be paramount. Joint criminal enterprise has certainly been criticized as an unfair and over-broad doctrine and many theorists seem to prefer the 'control of the crime' approach. Whether you consider one doctrine better or fairer than the other may depend on your national background: common lawyers are generally more comfortable with joint criminal enterprise; civil lawyers are generally more comfortable with 'control of the crime'. In reaching a conclusion you might care to consider factors such as:

- clarity (does one theory make it clearer who is a principal?);
- contribution (is it better to have a high or low standard of contribution?);
- leaders (does one theory make it easier or harder to find leaders guilty?);
- breadth and fair labelling (is there the risk that an over-broad doctrine will capture relatively replaceable 'small fish' and label them as principals?); and
- whether the theories risk rendering redundant other theories of liability (should a sensible system of ICL leave meaningful work to be done by doctrines such as command responsibility, ordering, inciting, and aiding and abetting? One might think giving such distinctions meaning work to do would help and not hinder fair labelling).

Indeed, one could ask whether such theories are really necessary, given the existence of the doctrine of superior responsibility, now applicable both to military commanders and to civilian superiors. The answer would appear to be that international criminal tribunals are reluctant to rely only on superior responsibility as it may 'under-label' the role of some accused persons. That is, because superior responsibility is a form of omission liability, then convicting someone 'only' as a responsible superior is seen as less morally serious than convicting someone is a principal.

A further difficulty that may arise, however, is gathering evidence about the role of the accused person. Indirect co-perpetration in particular is a theory which is easiest to apply to organizations that are hierarchical and disciplined. Many conflict and atrocity situations in the world now occur in complex civil wars and may not involve organizations as clearly and hierarchically structured as the conventional army of a national government. Further, evidence gathering in such environments—particularly when a conflict is continuing—may be very challenging. We can therefore expect to see prosecutors making use of other secondary or accessorial modes of liability, which may enable a conviction in cases where the evidence is insufficient to establish someone's guilt as a principal perpetrator, even under expanded theories of commission.

Useful further reading

A CASSESE, 'The Proper Limits of Individual Responsibility under the Doctrine of Joint Criminal Enterprise' (2007) 5 Journal of International Criminal Justice 109.
An important article by a major figure arguing that it would be inappropriate to use JCE 3 to convict someone of a special intent crime such as genocide without evidence that he or she had the required *dolus specialis* for genocide.

GP FLETCHER, 'The Theory of Criminal Liability and International Criminal Law' (2012) 10 Journal of International Criminal Justice 1029.
This article provides an introduction to some of the major challenges faced by international criminal law in terms of having a coherent approach to some of the major theoretical questions any system of criminal law must confront.

D GUILFOYLE, 'Responsibility for Collective Atrocities: Fair Labelling and Approaches to Commission in International Criminal Law' (2011) 64 Current Legal Problems 255.

This article presents an expanded version of some of the arguments made in this chapter concerning fair labelling, the principal/accessory distinction, and the tendency of expanded theories of commission or perpetration to 'crowd out' other descriptively useful modes of participation in international crimes.

J OHLIN, E VAN SLIEDREGT, and T WEIGEND, 'Assessing the Control-Theory' (2013) 26 Leiden Journal of International Law 725.

An excellent critical review of the early ICC case law on co-perpetration, especially in light of the re-characterization of the mode of participation in *Katanga*.

H OLÁSOLO, 'Joint Criminal Enterprise and Its Extended Form: a Theory of Co-Perpetration Giving Rise To Principal Liability, a Notion of Accessorial Liability, or a Form of Partnership In Crime?' (2009) 20 Criminal Law Forum 263.

An excellent article contrasting control over the crime and joint criminal enterprise.

E VAN SLIEDREGT, *Individual Criminal Responsibility in International Law* (Oxford University Press 2014).

An exceptionally clear account of the principles of both defences and modes of participation in offences in international criminal law. In particular, it is an excellent resource when trying to navigate differences in common law and civil law approaches to these questions.

G WERLE, 'Individual Criminal Responsibility in Article 25 ICC Statute' (2007) 5 Journal of International Criminal Justice 953.

This article makes the (somewhat controversial) argument that Article 25 paragraphs (a), (b), (c), and (d) should be interpreted as setting out four levels of participation in crimes which should be construed as a hierarchy (with subsequent implications for sentencing).

13

Defences or grounds for excluding criminal responsibility

13.1 Introduction

'Defences' is used here as an overall term for matters excluding criminal responsibility. The present chapter does not cover matters relevant only to mitigation of sentence (with the exception of diminished mental capacity). Defences are sometimes divided into justifications and excuses.[1] This categorization can have, in some legal systems, important consequences for defendants and victims.

A defendant in a criminal trial is entitled to raise legal reasons why they should not be convicted (that is, certain reasons other than lack of evidence or alibi evidence). These are generally called 'defences', although, as noted, some jurisdictions distinguish between 'justifications' and 'excuses'. Justifications consist of reasons why the defendant's conduct should be considered lawful. 'Excuses' might be thought of as arguments that a defendant's conduct was not blameworthy because they lacked free will or a free moral choice (insanity or acting under duress might provide examples).

Justifications are pleas that conduct was inherently lawful, and hence not criminal. An example of this is killing another person in self-defence. Provided the rules on self-defence are satisfied, such a killing is an act permitted by law and thus not unlawful homicide (murder, manslaughter, etc). In national systems, a successful justification may be a bar to other actions: for example, accessorial actions brought against other parties (i.e. one cannot be criminally liable for aiding and abetting a lawful act) or private liability (i.e. in civil systems where alleged victims may sue the defendant for compensation as part of the criminal trial).[2] A defendant raising an excuse does not contest that the conduct was wrongful, but instead asserts that circumstances made the defendant's conduct not blameworthy. For example, a person who participates in a robbery because a relative is being held hostage by the robbers has no claim that their acts are lawful. Their acts are, however, not blameworthy

---

[1] A Eser, 'Justification and Excuse' (1976) 24 The American Journal of Comparative Law 621, 621–22; A Cassese et al, *Cassese's International Criminal Law* 3rd ed (Oxford University Press 2013) 209.

[2] R Cryer, 'Defences/Grounds for Excluding Criminal Responsibility' in R Cryer et al, *An Introduction to International Criminal Law*, 3rd ed (Cambridge University Press 2014) 399.

because they had no real moral choice. Generally excuses do not create further procedural bars in national law. The usefulness of such distinctions in international criminal law is questionable. While there is a clear theoretical difference between the two categories, no obvious consequences attach to the distinction in international criminal practice.

Finally we should note the idea of a 'failure of proof' defence. Strictly speaking this is not a separate ground for excluding responsibility. It is simply a claim that the prosecution has not made out an essential element of the crime. For example, the absence of the victim's consent is normally considered an element of sexual offences and could also be required for the offence of deprivation of liberty (i.e. holding someone against their will).[3] If a defendant can show the prosecutor has not demonstrated the absence of the victim's consent (or can prove consent), this would raise a 'lack of proof' defence. Factors vitiating the victim's consent (or ability to consent) include: force, coercion, detention, or where the victim was a person incapable of giving genuine consent.[4] The difficulties created by approaches which focus on the victim's consent rather than the conduct of the perpetrator were discussed in Chapter 9, section 9.4.7.

Defence counsel may also prefer to challenge the jurisdiction of an international criminal tribunal, or the admissibility of a case before it, rather than raise one of the defences listed below. Such challenges might go to the personal, material, or temporal jurisdiction of a tribunal as discussed in Chapter 4. (That is, a case could not logically proceed if—for example—defence counsel could show the events complained occurred at a time outside the tribunal's temporal jurisdiction.) A more radical approach is to challenge the legality of a tribunal's existence by contending that it is not 'established according to law' as required under Article 14(1) of the International Covenant on Civil and Political Rights as discussed in Chapter 6, section 6.2.2. Such challenges have not succeeded in practice. More realistically, before the International Criminal Court (ICC) challenges to the admissibility of a particular case are to be expected, as the system of complementarity established under Articles 17 and 19 expressly allows affected individuals and States to make such challenges. An admissibility challenge does not strictly deny the jurisdiction of the Court, it is simply an argument that the Court under its own Statute is obliged to decline to exercise its jurisdiction because another (national) court is dealing with the case. A separate question is whether a tribunal otherwise having jurisdiction should (or could, or must) decline to exercise it if a defendant is brought before it illegally. This question was considered in section 6.4 (the conclusion being there is no clear rule of international law on point). Such challenges to jurisdiction and admissibility are not further considered here.

---

[3] K Ambos, 'Defences in International Criminal Law' in BS Brown (ed) *Research Handbook on International Criminal Law* (Elgar 2011) 328.

[4] See, for example, the ICC Elements of Crimes at Art 8(2)(b)(xxii-1).

Learning aims

By the end of this chapter and the relevant readings you should be able to:

- explain the difference between justifications and excuses, and whether this distinction has any relevance for international criminal law;
- identify the major defences to international crimes and define their legal elements;
- distinguish mistake of fact, mistake of law, and superior orders as defences;
- explain whether international criminal law should include controversial defences such as duress and superior orders; and
- apply the law to hypothetical scenarios.

Therefore the principal defences discussed in this chapter are (appearing in the order they are found in the ICC Statute):[5]

- Section 13.3 discusses mental incapacity.
- Section 13.4 covers intoxication.
- Section 13.5 concerns self-defence.
- Section 13.6 covers duress and necessity.
- Section 13.7 explain mistake of fact and law.
- Section 13.8 covers superior orders.

In addition two defences are discussed which arise under the law of war crimes:

- Section 13.9 covers reprisals and '*tu quoque*'.
- Section 13.10 covers military necessity.

Some of these defences may overlap. Superior orders, for example, is a special type of mistake of law defence. We should also question whether certain defences *should* be permitted. Duress and superior orders, for example, are often considered highly controversial.

13.2 Defences before international criminal tribunals

13.2.1 Defence practice in the ICTY and ICTR

This book addresses those defences available under the ICC Statute and in general international criminal law theory. There are few detailed studies on actual defence

---

[5] See Arts 31–33, ICC Statute.

practice before the ad hoc Tribunals. Nonetheless, we can observe that in many cases in the ad hoc Tribunals the raising of defences (in the sense of justifications or excuses) is less frequent than arguments regarding *nullum crimen sine lege* or failure of proof arguments including:

- challenges to witness testimony (i.e. claims that the testimony is uncorroborated or unreliable);
- challenges based on a lack of physical or documentary evidence;
- raising an alibi (e.g. casting doubt that the defendant could have been in the place the crimes were committed at the relevant time); and
- appeals on the basis that a Trial Chamber drew invalid inferences from circumstantial evidence.[6]

These types of defence arguments will not be examined in any detail in this book.

13.2.2 Defences under the ICC Statute

As noted above, available defences under the ICC Statute include: mental incapacity; intoxication; self-defence; duress; mistake of fact and mistake of law; and superior orders.[7] These are further discussed below. However, we should note the effect of Article 31(3):

> At trial, the Court may consider a ground for excluding criminal responsibility other than those [expressly listed]...where such a ground is derived from applicable law as set forth in article 21.

The Statute's list of defences is thus *not* exhaustive, and reference may be made to other sources of law under Article 21. It is possible that other defences could, therefore, be found in applicable rules of international law or 'general principles of law derived by the Court from national laws of legal systems of the world'.[8]

Further, on the basis of Article 21, in the context of war crimes there may be a limited scope for justifications such as the law of reprisals and military necessity within the ICC Statute either:

- as a consequence of other sources of law under Article 21; or
- due to the requirement that the law of war crimes be interpreted 'within the established framework of international law' under Articles 8(2)(b) and (e) of the Statute.

These are considered below in sections 13.9 and 13.10.

---

[6] A Zahar and G Sluiter, *International Criminal Law: A Critical Introduction* (Oxford University Press, 2008), Chapter 11.
[7] Arts 31, 32, and 33, ICC Statute.   [8] Art 21(b) and (c), ICC Statute.

13.3 Mental incapacity

13.3.1 Case law of the ICTY

ICTY case law has addressed two forms of mental incapacity defence: 'insanity' and
diminished mental capacity. The approach of the Tribunal is illustrated by reference to
the cases *Delalić, Mucić et al* and *Vasiljević*.

The *Delalić, Mucić et al* case concerned the Čelebići detention camp. One of the
accused, Landžo, was sentenced to 15 years imprisonment by the ICTY Trial Chamber
for participating in the murder and abuse of persons detained there in his role as a
prison guard. Lawyers for Landžo claimed that he was unfairly sentenced as he suffered from diminished mental capacity.[9] The Appeals Chamber distinguished between
'insanity' (a defence, or a complete defence) and diminished mental capacity (a matter
not relevant to guilt or innocence, but which might justify a lesser sentence). To understand the case we must distinguish a plea of insanity (which would preclude guilt) and
a plea of diminished mental capacity (which would not preclude being found guilty but
might be considered in mitigation of sentence).

In *Delalić* the ICTY Appeals Chamber held that *insanity* may be a complete defence,
but that the defendant must establish on the balance of probabilities that 'at the time of
the offence he was labouring under such a defect of reason, from disease of the mind,
as not to know the nature and quality of his act or, if he did know it, that he did not
know that what he was doing was wrong'[10] (quoting the famous English judgment in
M'Naghten's Case).[11] Thus, when raising an insanity defence the defendant bears the
onus of proof, but only a balance of probabilities (more likely than not) standard.

Diminished mental capacity, in mitigation of sentence only, was found to be available in international criminal law also. But it is, once again, for the defence to prove on
the balance of probabilities that the condition existed at the relevant time. What do we
mean by diminished mental capacity? In *Delalić* the ICTY Trial Chamber in discussing
diminished responsibility adopted the test found in s 2(1) of the UK Homicide Act:[12]

> ...the accused must be suffering from an *abnormality of mind* which has *substantially
> impaired* his mental responsibility for his acts or omissions. The abnormality of mind must
> have arisen from a condition of arrested or retarded development of the mind, or inherent
> causes induced by disease or injury. These categories clearly demonstrate that the evidence
> is restricted to those which can be supported by medical evidence (emphasis added).

Thus, what is required is a medically provable, physical cause. In the event the Trial
Chamber concluded that Landžo did have a personality disorder, but was capable of
controlling his actions. This was insufficient to make out diminished mental capacity.
The Appeals Chamber upheld this conclusion.

---

[9] *Delalić, Mucić et al (Čelebići detention camp)*, ICTY Appeals Chamber, 20 February 2001, paras 572 ff.
[10] Ibid, para 582.   [11] (1843) 8 ER 718 (House of Lords).
[12] *Delalić, Mucić et al (Čelebići detention camp)*, ICTY Trial Chamber, 16 November 1998, paras 1166, 1172.

In *Vasiljević*, the ICTY Trial Chamber formulated a slightly different test for diminished mental capacity:[13]

> The Trial Chamber is satisfied that an accused suffers from a diminished mental responsibility where there is *an impairment* to his capacity to appreciate the unlawfulness of or the nature of his conduct or to control his conduct so as to conform to the requirements of the law [emphasis added].

The ICTY rejected the plea on the facts of the case, despite supporting psychiatric evidence from just one month after relevant crimes. The idea that diminished mental capacity will usually be quite difficult to prove is reinforced by the ICTY decisions in *Jelisić*. In that case the Trial Chamber held:

> [T]he expert diagnosis indicated that Goran Jelisić suffered from personality disorders, had borderline, narcissistic and anti-social characteristics. Still, though this does speak in favour of psychiatric follow-up, the Trial Chamber concurs with the Prosecution and does not agree that such a condition diminishes Goran Jelisić's criminal responsibility.[14]

The Appeals Chamber agreed, further explaining:

> [T]here is no per se inconsistency between a diagnosis of the kind of immature, narcissistic, disturbed personality…and the ability to form an intent to destroy a particular protected group. Indeed,…it is the borderline unbalanced personality who is more likely to be drawn to extreme racial and ethnical hatred than the more balanced…individual without personality defects.[15]

A personality disorder might thus help explain why someone committed a crime, but falls short of the kind of physical abnormality or injury that precludes a person appreciating the unlawful nature of his or her conduct. Factually, Vladimir Kovačević was the only ICTY defendant found lacking the mental capacity to stand trial.[16] The ICTY transferred him to Serbia where he was confined in a psychiatric institution.

13.3.2 **The ICC Statute**

The ICC Statute does not refer to a defence of insanity, but rather one of 'mental disease or defect'. Article 31(1)(a) of the ICC Statute requires that: '[t]he person [raising the defence] suffers from a mental disease or defect that *destroys* that person's capacity to appreciate the unlawfulness or nature of his or her conduct, or capacity to control his or her conduct to conform to the requirements of law' (emphasis added). Note the use of the word *destroys* and not *impairs* or *diminishes*. The standard set here is very high: the idea is that the relevant mental capacity must be destroyed completely and not merely in part. However, if proven, this defence then entirely excludes criminal responsibility (providing a defence and not merely a matter relevant to mitigation of sentence).

---

[13] *Vasiljević*, ICTY Trial Chamber, 29 November 2002, paras 282–83.
[14] *Jelisić*, ICTY Trial Chamber, 14 December 1999, para 125.
[15] *Jelisić*, ICTY Appeals Chamber, 5 July 2001, para 70.
[16] Zahar and Sluiter, *International Criminal Law*, 441.

However, the ICC defence might better be called one of 'mental incapacity'. The phrase 'mental disease or defect' sounds similar to the terms used in *Delalić* in discussing diminished responsibility as a matter relevant to mitigation of sentence. However, this is misleading as the ICC defence has nothing in common with *Delalić*. The ICC defence requires much more than mere abnormality or impairment of mind and, as noted, completely excludes criminal responsibility rather than going to mitigation of sentence.

Article 31(1)(a) on its face covers situations where:

- the defendant is unable to understand nature of his/her conduct; or
- the defendant cannot understand the unlawfulness of his/her conduct; or
- cases of an 'irresistible impulse' where the defendant may have conscious knowledge that their act is wrong, but cannot control their behaviour.[17]

 Pause for reflection

Is the ICC able to take the *Kovačević* approach and confine a person needing treatment, or must it release them? On their face the ICC provisions on prisoner transfer could not apply to a person *acquitted* on the basis of their mental capacity (see Articles 103 and 104 of the ICC Statute as discussed in Chapter 6, section 6.6.2).

13.4 Intoxication

13.4.1 Case law of the ICTY

ICTY case law has not found intoxication to be any form of defence. In *Vasiljević* the ICTY considered and rejected a defence case of incapacity through alcoholism.[18] (Although strictly speaking incapacity through chronic alcoholism is obviously not the same thing as incapacity through intoxication at a given time.) In *Kvočka* the ICTY held that intentional consumption of alcohol 'in contexts where violence is the norm and weapons are carried' may be an *aggravating* factor in sentencing.[19] That is, wilful or deliberate intoxication could justify a higher and not a lesser sentence.

There is no case law on *involuntary* intoxication. In this context one might consider the known cases in which child soldiers are administered drugs to increase their willingness to kill or harm others.

[17] Famously someone once wrote as graffiti in a New York subway 'Stop me before I kill again' (almost certainly as a dark joke); a more plausible example might be the pyromaniac who knows it is wrong to destroy property but feels uncontrollably compelled to light fires. See generally: K Vihvelin, 'Stop me before I kill again' (1994) 5 Philosophical Studies 115–148.

[18] *Vasiljević*, ICTY Trial Chamber, 29 November 2002, para 294.

[19] *Kvočka*, ICTY Trial Chamber, 2 November 2001, para 706; and Appeals Chamber, 28 February 2005, paras 707–08.

13.4.2 **The ICC Statute**

Article 31(1)(b) of the ICC Statute requires that:

> [t]he person [raising the defence] is in a state of intoxication that *destroys* that person's capacity to appreciate the unlawfulness or nature of his or her conduct, or capacity to control his or her conduct to conform to the requirements of law, *unless* the person has become voluntarily intoxicated *under such circumstances* that the person *knew*, or *disregarded* the risk, that, as a result of the intoxication, he or she was likely to engage in *conduct constituting a crime* within the jurisdiction of the Court [emphasis added].

The three points to note here are: (1) the emphasis on destruction of capacity; (2) the definition covers both voluntary and involuntary intoxication; and (3) this is a complete defence which entirely excludes criminal responsibility.

Under the ICC Statute, intoxication must destroy either the defendant's appreciation of the unlawfulness of his/her actions or the 'capacity to control' his/her conduct. Again, this is a high standard excluding merely impaired or diminished understanding.[20]

In a case of involuntary intoxication all the defendant must show is that the 'state of intoxication' *destroyed* his or her capacity to appreciate or control his or her conduct. As noted, involuntary intoxication is particularly common in the case of child soldiers. Antonio Cassese also suggests a hypothetical example in which a solider receiving medical treatment is administered powerful drugs 'which seriously alter his mental state'.[21]

Voluntary intoxication is only a defence in limited circumstances under the ICC Statute. This result follows from the fact that there was controversy during the Statute's negotiation as to whether voluntary intoxication should ever be a defence, due to the different positions taken in different national legal systems.[22] Thus, under the Statute voluntary intoxication is *not* a defence in circumstances where the defendant has knowledge of, or disregards, the 'risk' of the relevant criminal 'conduct'. This embodies a recklessness standard.[23] But what risk does one have to have known of or disregard if recklessly becoming drunk? There are two possible approaches:

- on a broad view, the risk which is known or disregarded could encompass any act which could constitute the material element of a crime in the ICC Statute;
- on a narrow view, the act anticipated must be the one with which the accused was actually charged.

For example, consider a scenario where there is evidence that a defendant (who was head of detention camp during an armed conflict) said 'if I get any more drunk I'll just go kill one of the prisoners'. After becoming more intoxicated the defendant then

---

[20] G Werle and F Jessberger, *Principles of International Criminal Law*, 3rd ed (Oxford University Press 2014) 256 para 679.

[21] A Cassese, *International Criminal Law*, 2nd ed (Oxford University Press 2008) 266.

[22] Werle and Jessberger, *Principles of International Criminal Law*, 257. On different national approaches see: E van Sliedregt, *Individual Criminal Responsibility in International Law* (Oxford University Press 2014) 230–33.

[23] Ambos, 'Defences in International Criminal Law', 306. Compare Werle and Jessberger, *Principles of International Criminal Law*, 257 (referring to this as an 'aggravated form of negligence').

sexually assaulted one of the hostages. On the broad view outlined above no defence
is available; on a narrow view the defence might be available, as the evidence points
to foresight of a crime other than the one committed. There is some ambiguity as to
whether the 'conduct' which must be foreseen includes the relevant contextual elements
of international crimes.[24] This could perhaps be covered by the words 'under such circumstances' (i.e. the defendant had knowledge of the contextual elements, and under
those circumstances became intoxicated).

We should note that in common law systems a plea of intoxication would usually
result in conviction of a lesser offence (i.e. the defendant would be found guilty on a
lesser charge of manslaughter instead of murder).[25] Under the ICC Statute, if success-
fully proved it is a 'complete' defence and the accused will be acquitted.

13.5 Self defence

13.5.1 Introduction

In this instance, the ICTY case law and ICC Statute may be taken together: in *Kordić
and Čerkez* the ICTY adopted the ICC Statute definition as a statement of customary
law.[26] Art 31(1)(c) of the ICC Statute permits a defence of self defence where:

> [t]he person acts *reasonably* to defend himself or herself or another person or, in the case of
> war crimes, property which is essential for the survival of the person or another person or
> property which is essential for accomplishing a military mission, against *an imminent and
> unlawful use of force* in a manner *proportionate* to the degree of danger to the person or the
> other person or property protected. The fact that the person was involved in a defensive
> operation conducted by forces shall not in itself constitute a ground for excluding criminal
> responsibility [emphasis added].

The elements for consideration are obviously: (1) an 'imminent and unlawful use of
force' against oneself, others, or mission essential property; and (2) that the response is
reasonable and proportionate.

What is 'imminent' will always have to be judged in context on the facts of the case.
However, it is clear that a person does not have to 'wait for someone else to strike the
first blow'.[27] Anyone who acts at the last possible moment to avert danger will clearly
have acted in the face of an 'imminent' threat; however, this does not mean that earlier
action could not be justified on the facts of a case.

A useful example of imminence is provided by the Control Council Law No. 10 case
Erich Weiss and Wilhelm Mundo of 1945.[28] A captured US airman was handed over

---

[24] Cryer, 'Defences/Grounds for Excluding Criminal Responsibility' in Cryer et al, *Introduction*, 403.
[25] Ibid, 404.   [26] *Kordić and Čerkez*, ICTY Trial Chamber, 26 February 2001, paras 449–51.
[27] Cryer, 'Defences/Grounds for Excluding Criminal Responsibility' in Cryer et al, *Introduction*, 405.
[28] (1945) XIII Law Reports of Trials of War Criminals 149–150. Excerpted in A Cassese et al, *International
Criminal Law: Cases and Commentary* (Oxford University Press 2011) 461–62; also available via: www.loc.gov/
rr/frd/Military_Law/pdf/Law-Reports_Vol-13.pdf.

to two German policemen. There was no evidence they searched him for weapons. The policemen became surrounded by a hostile crowd demanding the airman's death. When the airman suddenly reached into his right pocket, both policeman fired at him and he was killed. They believed he was about to draw a weapon and that their lives were in danger. The defence was upheld and the two policemen were acquitted.

What is interesting about *Erich Weiss and Wilhelm Mundo* is that this would appear to be a case of *mistaken* self-defence. Although the full case report does not make it clear,[29] it seems possible the airman did not have a gun at all. The drafting of the ICC definition of the defence does not expressly appear to allow for violent action taken on the basis of an honest and reasonable mistake. Indeed, a common view of the ICC Statute definition is that it requires the threat of force to be objectively imminent: the situation must actually exist and 'not only in the actor's mind'.[30]

Other than *Weiss and Mundo* one might consider a situation where a soldier on patrol is shot at by enemy forces from an apartment block and the soldier shoots back at the figure he believes to be the gunman. If this figure is in fact a civilian standing in the window of the next apartment, has the soldier committed the war crime of attacking a civilian? Defences based on mistakes of fact are discussed further at 13.7.1.

As to the requirement that force be 'unlawful', the point is obviously that one cannot claim self-defence against lawful action (e.g. an occupying power during armed conflict has a duty to maintain order and could use force for that 'policing' purpose). Cryer suggests, however, this does not mean the action must necessarily be *criminal* to invoke self-defence.[31] Self-defence against violence which lacks lawful authority, but for which the perpetrator may not be criminally responsible (due to insanity, intoxication, etc) should obviously be permissible.

It is generally accepted in national legal systems that a person may defend not only themselves but other people from unlawful violence. The addition of mission essential property is perhaps novel though it is not entirely without precedent. For example, the UN Rules of Engagement for peacekeeping forces allow the use of weapons to defend property which is essential to a mission.[32] Nonetheless, the extension of the defence to property has caused some controversy. Cassese objects that this defence could be used abusively to excuse war crimes in a way that undermines the law of armed conflict.[33] Consider a scenario in an international armed conflict where mission essential equipment is about to be attacked by enemy combatants, and a commander orders his men to attack those enemy combatants—but to do so using poisonous gases. This is a war crime under the ICC Statute[34]—could the commander justifiably plead defence of mission essential property? The answer to Cassese's objection is that this (and similar scenarios) would fail to be *reasonable* and *proportionate* responses to the threat.

---

[29] Ibid.   [30] Ambos, 'Defences in International Criminal Law', 307.

[31] Cryer, 'Defences/Grounds for Excluding Criminal Responsibility' in Cryer et al, *Introduction*, 405.

[32] Ibid, 405. For a major study on point see: T Findlay, *The Use of Force in UN Peace Operations* (Oxford University Press 2002) especially at 15, 113, 120, 183, 186, and 420.

[33] Cassese et al, *Cassese's International Law*, 213.   [34] Art 8(2)(b)(xviii), ICC Statute.

Pause for reflection

Consider whether a military force should be able to defend its base or vehicles from acts of sabo-tage by civilians. Is a separate defence—at least in times of armed conflict—necessary or is it argu-able that a civilian sabotaging military vehicles has become a participant in the conflict and has lost their right to protection?

Two final questions need to be addressed regarding the requirements governing the use of force in self defence: (1) was it reasonable given the facts of the case to respond with force; and (2) if so, was the force used proportionate? The ICC Statute gives limited guidance as to the applicable tests or standards to be applied in answering these questions. One would expect that there must be some margin of appreciation given. That is, the Court should not view the facts on the basis of 20-20 hindsight nor a strict objective test based on a perfect understanding of the facts. However, while a defendant should be given the benefit of some margin of appreciation, the word 'reasonable' makes it clear that the subjective appreciation of the defendant cannot be determinative. Ambos suggests the test of proportionality is that one 'may not cause disproportionately greater harm than that sought to be avoided' and therefore killing an aggressor would be acceptable as a last resort to avert one's own death.[35] Note that the formulation 'not . . . disproportionately greater' does not require a precisely equal use of force.

Pause for reflection

Interesting questions arise where the person exercising self-defence is armed and their attacker is not. Consider first whether it would be proportionate to shoot an unarmed attacker: does an armed soldier in such a case have to throw their gun aside? Second, in the same case, what of shooting an attacker armed with a machete?

No sensible law of self-defence should require the soldier in the first scenario to throw their weapon away. Using it might, however, not be proportionate if there were other less lethal and effective means of averting the danger available to him or her. For example, one might expect in the first scenario that a militarily trained 'defender' would use escalatory force, e.g.:

- first, a threat of force (e.g. a warning shot or calling 'stop or I shoot');
- then, disabling fire (e.g. at legs); and
- only finally, shots directed at the head or torso,

[35] Ambos, 'Defences in International Criminal Law', 308; in accord Werle and Jessberger, *Principles of International Criminal Law*, 238 para 628.

> but *only if* this could be done without endangering the defender. Less precision would be expected of a person untrained in the use of firearms.
>
> In the second scenario responding to potentially lethal force with lethal force should generally be considered permissible: perfect equality of weapons is not required by proportionality.

13.6 Duress and necessity

13.6.1 Introduction

Duress covers situations where a defendant's act was not lawful but a claim is raised that their will is overpowered by the actions of another person, leaving them with no moral choice. Consider for example the situation of a person who participates in a robbery because a relative is being held hostage and threatened with grave harm or death by the robbers. In this national law example a threat to life is easy to balance against a property crime: the harm the person acting under duress does is less than the threatened harm to the hostage. However, should duress ever be a defence to international crimes—especially those involving killing? Most controversially, can a soldier threatened with death by a superior officer excuse their act of killing civilians? While duress is caused by other human actors, necessity is taken to arise from objective circumstances beyond a defendant's control, in particular forces of nature.[36]

13.6.2 The case law of the ICTY

In the ICTY case of *Erdemović* the Appeals Chamber found that duress was not a complete defence at international criminal law, at least in cases where *a soldier* is charged with killing an innocent person.[37] However, the decision was a split one, with only three of five judges supporting this conclusion. The *Erdemović* majority found that duress can never be a defence to the killing of innocents (although it could be considered in mitigation of sentence). They came to this conclusion by laying down an *absolute moral postulate* justified by considerations of public policy. That is, if the law says that duress is never a defence to murder or killing, then such a clear rule protects society because otherwise criminals could confer immunity on their agents by threatening their lives. This line of reasoning echoes that of the common law in England.[38] Logically, the majority decision in *Erdemović* does not foreclose the possibility that duress is available as a defence in cases *not* involving soldiers and/or the killing of innocents.

Judge Cassese in his dissenting opinion in *Erdemović* points to a critical problem in the majority's reasoning. The majority acknowledge that as a general rule duress is acknowledged as a defence across many national legal systems. Further, the majority was unable to point to a consistent rule across national criminal law systems as to

---

[36] Werle and Jessberger, *Principles of International Criminal Law*, 239 para 633.
[37] *Erdemović*, ICTY Appeals Chamber, 7 October 1997.
[38] Ibid, Joint Separate Opinion of Judges MacDonald and Vohkah, paras 32, 73–88.

whether there are cases where duress is *never* available (i.e. for murder). Some systems do allow a plea of duress to murder, others do not. Because the majority could find no consistent rule in State practice, it decided to invent a rule that it considered desirable on policy grounds. However, the absence of uniform rule could equally argue for the application of the unmodified general rule. That is, if national systems agree on a general rule (duress is a defence) but not on exceptions or limitations (it is not available for murder), then it would be equally logical to argue that State practice supports the general rule. On Cassese's approach then, duress would always be available as a defence as a matter of customary international law (or general principles of law) unless consistent State practice proves an exception.[39]

Cassese formulated the test or requirements of duress as being:

(1) there must be an immediate threat of severe and irreparable harm to life or limb;

(2) there was no adequate means of averting this harm;

(3) the act was not disproportionate to the threat (the act was the lesser of two evils); and

(4) the duress situation was no voluntarily brought about by the person coerced.[40]

The *Erdemović* dissenting opinions of Judges Cassese and Judge Stephen in 1997 were vindicated by ICC Statute as adopted in 1998—although note that the Statute makes proportionality a *subjective* question as discussed immediately below.

Later references to the defence of duress in ICTY case law are few and unclear. For example, in *Kvočka*, the Chamber at first appeared to claim that the defence is never available in cases of war crimes or crimes against humanity (misconstruing the scope of the narrow principle decided in *Erdemović*),[41] but then nonetheless appeared to consider how the defence might apply on the facts of the case.[42]

13.6.3 **The ICC Statute**

Article 31(1)(d) of the ICC Statute requires that:

> The conduct...alleged to constitute a crime...has been caused by duress resulting from a threat of imminent death or of continuing or imminent serious bodily harm against that person or another person, and the person acts necessarily and reasonably to avoid this threat, provided that the person does not intend to cause a greater harm than the one sought to be avoided. Such a threat may either be: (i) Made by other persons; or (ii) Constituted by other circumstances beyond that person's control.

The elements of this formulation are: (1) the need for an imminent threat; (2) necessary and reasonable actions in response; (3) an element of causation; and (4) a mental element (intending only the lesser of two evils). Each is considered below.

---

[39] Ibid, Separate and Dissenting Opinion of Judge Cassese, paras 11–12.
[40] Ibid, para 16.
[41] *Kvočka*, ICTY Trial Chamber, 2 November 2001, para 403.   [42] Ibid, para 427.

Imminent threat of death or bodily harm

Art 31(1)(d) requires: 'a threat of imminent death or of continuing or imminent serious bodily harm against [the defendant] or another person'. The points to note are that:

- the threat must be real;
- imminence may not have the same meaning as in the law of self-defence (i.e. it need not be as immediate; consider, for example, a threat to allow a hostage at an undisclosed location to starve to death);
- the harm must be very serious; and
- no relationship is required between the defendant and the person threatened.

Necessary and reasonable actions

Not all acts can be excused by duress. It is generally accepted that for duress to be available as a defence there must not have been another adequate means for averting the harm. What, then, will constitute necessary and reasonable actions? Consider the hypothetical of Judge Cassese in his dissent in *Erdemović*:

> An inmate of a concentration camp, starved and beaten for months, is then told, after a savage beating, that if he does not kill another inmate, who has already been beaten with metal bars and will certainly be beaten to death before long, then his eyes will, then and there, be gouged out. He kills the other inmate as a result. Perhaps a hero could accept a swift bullet in his skull to avoid having to kill, but it would require an extraordinary—and perhaps impossible—act of courage to accept one's eyes being plucked out. Can one truly say that the man in this example should have allowed his eyes to be gouged out and that he is a criminal for not having done so? This example, and one can imagine still worse, is one of those rare cases, in my opinion, where duress should be entertained as a complete defence.[43]

As Ambos puts it: '[r]ecognition of the defence of duress rests on the assumption that the ordinary person is too weak to refuse an order to kill if there is a risk he [or she] will be killed'.[44] Consider also, from the Control Council Law No. 10 prosecutions in occupied Germany, the *Einsatzgruppen Case*:[45]

> Let it be said at once that there is no law which requires that an innocent man must forfeit his own life or suffer serious harm in order to avoid committing a crime which he condemns. The threat, however, must be imminent, real and inevitable. No court will punish a man who, with a loaded pistol at his head, is compelled to pull at lethal lever. Nor need the peril be that imminent in order to escape punishment.

In the *Einsatzgruppen Case* case the defence was found to be available, but in the case of most defendants it failed upon the facts: where defendants approved of orders to kill Jews, they acted under no compulsion. A threat of death has no force if you are already willing to carry out the order.

---

[43] *Erdemović*, ICTY Appeals Chamber, 7 October 1997, Separate and Dissenting Opinion of Judge Cassese, para 47.

[44] Ambos, 'Defences in International Criminal Law', 315.

[45] (1948) IV Trials of the War Criminals 3, 480.

Cassese further suggested that duress will not be available where 'a person ... *freely and knowingly* chooses to become a member of a unit, organisation or group institutionally bent upon actions contrary' to international law.[46] This might be a fair summary of the post-World War II case law, including cases such as *Einsatzgruppen*. It seems unlikely to be a special rule of ICL however, and may simply be an example of a situation where a person has voluntarily brought about the situation causing duress or is under no duress because they agree with the organization's actions and policies.

Causation

Threats must have caused defendant's conduct, but must the threats be a cause or *the* cause? Cryer holds that nothing in the ICC Statute requires the ICC 'to take the view that the relevant threat needs to be the sole cause of the conduct'.[47] There is no defence if the accused would have so acted anyway, or voluntarily brought about the situation leading to duress.[48] It may also be relevant to take into account situations where persons are expected to engage in risk taking and have been 'trained for life-threatening situations'.[49] Soldiers are expected to voluntarily assume a high degree of risk and this may preclude claims of necessity or duress in certain cases.

Mental element: proportionality, lesser of two evils

The requirement of proportionality appears as a limitation on the defence in the ICC Statute: 'provided that the person does not intend to cause a greater harm than the one sought to be avoided'. The defendant must thus have intend to cause the lesser of two evils and have weighed the act committed against the threat averted. But how does one engage in such balancing in practice? Does the word 'intend' in the ICC formulation create a distinction between *actions* and *consequences*? If so, one does not take into account the 'unintended excessive consequences of necessary and reasonable actions'.[50] This would seem the fairest result. If not, one must balance actual consequences against those the accused sought to avoid.

In *Erdemović* the defendant's case was that irrespective of his participation 1,200 civilians were going to be executed. He personally killed between 10 and 100, but there is no suggestion these victims would have lived had he not acted. How does one weigh this? Was Erdemović obliged by law to disobey the order and surrender his life? Judge Stephen (in his dissent in *Erdemović*) said:

> If ... the evidence should prove to be consistent with the Appellant's ... statements, namely
> that the choice open to him was not that of the victims' deaths or his own but, rather, that

---

[46] Cassese et al, *Cassese's International Criminal Law*, 216.

[47] Cryer, 'Defences/Grounds for Excluding Criminal Responsibility' in Cryer et al, *Introduction*, 409.

[48] *Erdemović*, ICTY Appeals Chamber, 7 October 1997, Separate and Dissenting Opinion of Judge Cassese, paras 16.

[49] Werle and Jessberger, *Principles of International Criminal Law*, 244 para 645. This statement still leaves some ambiguity as to whether those who voluntarily expose themselves to danger in other cases have voluntarily brought about a situation of distress or necessity.

[50] Cryer, 'Defences/Grounds for Excluding Criminal Responsibility' in Cryer et al, *Introduction*, 409.

of their deaths or their deaths together with his own, the whole question of proportionality... [would be] meaningless; ... the choice, if it can be described as a choice, would be between many lives or many lives plus one, his own. The Appellant was but one member of a firing squad and, according to his statements, no other member supported... his protest.[51]

To similar effect Judge Cassese suggests plea of duress to a crime involving the killing of innocent persons might only ever succeed on such extreme facts.[52]

Such an analysis is, however, rejected by some scholars. John Morss and Mirko Bagaric point out that Erdemović *did* refuse to participate in certain later killings and was supported by colleagues in his refusal at that time; on this basis one might re-consider whether a genuine moral choice was available in the case of the earlier killings.[53]

 Pause for reflection

How would the ICC definition apply to the facts alleged by the defendant in *Erdemović*?

Consider the following:

(1) Was there a threat to the defendant of 'imminent death or... serious bodily harm'?

(2) Were the defendant's actions in killing 10–100 people 'necessary and reasonable', at least in the sense there was no alternative means of averting the harm available?

(3) How should we weigh whether the acts caused a greater harm or avoided a greater harm?

On the last point is it better to say the defendant caused more harm than he avoided (i.e. he caused at least 10 deaths instead of his death alone); or that if he refused to act the consequences would have been no different or involved more deaths (i.e. the inevitable deaths plus his own)?

13.7 Mistake of fact and law

13.7.1 Mistake of fact

Article 32(1) of the ICC Statute provides: 'A mistake of fact shall be a ground for excluding criminal responsibility only if it negates the mental element required by the crime.' A mistake of fact is thus only a defence if it goes to show the person lacked the requisite mental element or *mens rea*. There is no express requirement in the ICC Statute that the mistake be a reasonable one.[54] While Cassese suggested the mistake involved must

---

[51] *Erdemović*, ICTY Appeals Chamber, 7 October 1997, Dissenting Opinion of Judge Stephen, para 19.

[52] Ibid, Dissenting Opinion of Judge Cassese, paras 12 and 42–44.

[53] J Morss and M Bagaric, 'The Banality of Justice: Reflections on Sierra Leone's Special Court', (2006) 8 Oregon Review of International Law 1, 20–24.

[54] Strictly, as a matter of logic an unreasonable mistake can negate *mens rea*: van Sliedregt, *Individual Criminal Responsibility*, 278.

be honest and reasonable, he appears to do this to exclude totally incredible claims.[55] William Schabas suggests instead that a court would simply be unlikely to consider a defence of mistake which 'did not have an air of reality to it.'[56]

To take an easy example of a mistake of fact which negates the required mental element, consider the law of attacks on civilians or civilian objects as a war crime: the mental element required would be absent if the defendant had mistakenly identified the target as a military one.[57] Similarly, consider a military recruiter charged with recruiting children under the age of 15 who claims he believed the children were older. If he or she did not know or believe them to be under 15, the mental element required would also be absent.[58]

Consider, however, the following case of mistaken self-defence: a soldier who intentionally fired at a civilian might claim that he or she honestly and reasonably believed that the attacked civilian had fired at him or her first and that they were acting in self-defence. While such a mistake might suggest the soldier is not morally blameworthy it might be thought that it does not negate the mental element involved in the crime of intentionally attacking a civilian. Clearly, the soldier *did* intend to attack the civilian. How should we approach this?

Some suggest that Article 32(1) does not encompass a mistake of fact—which if true—would raise a *separate defence*.[59] This is a narrow approach that follows, to some extent, from the common-law view that crimes consist only of mental element and physical element with no separate consideration of blameworthiness or moral culpability (in German, *Schuld*). This approach to Article 32 could perhaps exclude claims of mistaken self-defence, such as that above. The conclusion on our example would then be that the mistake of fact made by the solider does *not* negate the required mental element. All we can say is that his or her mistake would only (if true) have raised a separate defence, but that this scenario is not covered by Article 32(1). This seems a very harsh result, but the extent to which it is likely to arise in practical cases is considered below.

On another view mistake of fact cases typically involve mistaking one person or object for another; the mistake does not go to intention in the narrow sense (the mental element or *mens rea*) but goes instead to broader issues of culpability.[60] Such a broader approach, found especially in German law, would allow a plea of mistaken self-defence.

In the end, one does not need to take a view in the abstract. One should instead closely examine the relevant elements of crimes and ask if the mistake in question did preclude the required mental element.

---

[55] Cassese, *International Criminal Law*, 2nd ed, 290.

[56] W Schabas, *An Introduction to the International Criminal Court*, 4th ed (Cambridge University Press, 2011), 242.

[57] Ambos, 'Defences in International Criminal Law', 318.   [58] Schabas, *Introduction*, 242.

[59] Cryer, 'Defences/Grounds for Excluding Criminal Responsibility' in Cryer et al, *Introduction*, 410; Werle and Jessberger, *Principles of International Criminal Law*, 246 para 652.

[60] See further: ME Badar, 'Mens Rea—Mistake of Law & Mistake of Fact in German Criminal Law: A Survey for International Criminal Tribunals' (2005) International Criminal Law Review 203, 235.

Pause for reflection

Consider the mistaken self-defence controversy: what crime would it be charged as under the ICC Statute? Let us take the war crimes of wilful killing, murder, or attacking civilians as set out in the ICC Elements of Crimes, Articles 8(2)(a)(i), 8(2)(b)(i), 8(2)(c)(i), and 8(2)(e)(i). The crime of attacking civilians, for example, requires an intent to attack an individual civilian 'not taking a direct part in hostilities'. In practice, then, a soldier's mistaken belief the he or she was acting in self-defence *against a civilian taking part in hostilities* could negate this essential part of the mental element. That is, in our scenario the soldier would have believed they were attacking a civilian who was attacking combatants and therefore was taking a direct part in hostilities. This is a mistake of fact that directly negates the mental element required, not a mistake which indirectly raises a separate defence.

13.7.2 Mistake of law

Usually a mistake of law defence is conceived of as covering situations where an accused is fully aware of all the circumstances surrounding his or her actions but either:

- does not believe his or her actions constitute an offence;
- believes the offence does not count as criminal behaviour in the circumstances; or
- acts under the mistaken assumption his or her conduct does not fall within the scope of the criminal provision (i.e. he or she is aware of the offence but believes their act falls outside the prohibited material element).[61]

It is controversial as a defence because it allows ignorance of the law to be an excuse. This is rejected on policy grounds in many States. For example, it is usually said in common law systems that ignorance of the law is not an excuse (because it would encourage deliberate ignorance of the law).

Article 32(2) of the ICC Statute provides:

A mistake of law as to whether a particular type of conduct is a crime within the jurisdiction of the Court shall not be a ground for excluding criminal responsibility. A mistake of law may, however, be a ground for excluding criminal responsibility if it negates the mental element required by such a crime, or as provided for in article 33 [on superior orders].

First, it is obvious this definition excludes ignorance of the law. Cassese suggested a broader rule existed in the post-World War II case law and that a defendant could plead they lacked *mens rea* because they were unaware that the conduct was criminal.[62] The

---

[61] Badar, 'Mens Rea', 235–6.
[62] Cassese et al, *Cassese's International Criminal Law*, 220–221 (on the basis that the lack of clarity of some international law rules justifies a more liberal approach than national courts might take to a claim of ignorance of the law). He suggests, however, courts would dismiss out of hand a claim of ignorance of clear and

ICC Statute plainly rejects this approach. To invoke this defence one must show the defendant lacked the required mental element of the offence as a consequence of the mistake. What does this mean in practice? There has been little ICC case law on point, although the Pre-Trial Chamber in *Lubanga* did characterize the effect of this provision (rather opaquely) as meaning that a:

> defence of mistake of law can succeed him under article 32 of the statute only if… [the defendant] was unaware of a normative objective element of the crime as a result of not realizing its social significance (its everyday meaning).[63]

This is difficult to untangle. It appears to reflect the idea that mistakes of fact go to *objective* circumstances while mistakes of law involve a *normative* question in respect of elements of the crime which are legally defined (such as the crime of denying a fair trial) or which involve mixed legal-factual judgements (such as disproportionate damage).[64] What is required in such cases is not the precise understanding of a lawyer but a 'parallel layman's evaluation': a layman need not know (normatively) that medical experiments on prisoners are specifically prohibited by law in order to know they are impermissible (as a matter of 'social significance' or 'everyday meaning').[65] Put more plainly: it does not take a lawyer to know attacks on Red Cross vehicles are prohibited, even a layman 'knows what the symbol of the Red Cross means'.[66] The defence of mistake of law is thus best understood as applying in cases where a legal evaluation was required and mistaken.[67] Examples might include cases involving accusations of unlawful confinement as a war crime or unlawful imprisonment as a crime against humanity where the accused believed the victim had been lawfully sentenced or detained.

This approach, however, might be thought to raise a different question: can a mistaken belief in a positive rule negate the mental element for a crime? For example, imagine a case where a defendant mistakenly believed a population had lost its civilian character because military forces were hiding within it and therefore the ordinary rules of distinction and proportionality did not apply.[68] The point is not hypothetical. Cassese raises historic cases where a defendant thought they had positive legal authority to carry out the prohibited act. For example, in the *B Case* an untrained Dutch resistance leader thought, on the basis of British radio broadcasts, it was positively lawful to kill a Nazi collaborator without trial.[69]

---

universally recognized rules. See also Ambos, 'Defences in International Criminal Law', 320 on mistakes as to elements of an offence under the ICC Statute.

[63] *Lubanga* (Decision on Confirmation of Charges), ICC Pre-Trial Chamber, 29 January 2007, para 316.

[64] Ambos, *Treatise*, vol. 1, 289–90.

[65] A Eser, 'Mental Elements: Mistake of Fact and Mistake of Law', in A Cassese, P Gaeta, and JRWD Jones (eds), *The Rome Statute of the International Criminal Court: A Commentary* (Oxford University Press 2002), vol 1B, 924–25.

[66] Sliedregt, *Individual Criminal Responsibility*, 272.

[67] Cryer, 'Defences/Grounds for Excluding Criminal Responsibility' in Cryer et al, *Introduction*, 410.

[68] Sliedregt, *Individual Criminal Responsibility*, 272.

[69] Cassese et al, *Cassese's International Criminal Law*, 221 n 40; and case note by C Burchard in A Cassese (ed), *Oxford Companion to International Criminal Justice* (Oxford University Press 2009), 591.

So, should the defence be allowed:

(1) only in cases where a legal evaluation is required;

(2) in cases where one honestly and mistakenly believed the conduct was positively allowed by law (mistaken belief in a justification); or

(3) in any case where the accused was genuinely ignorant of the law?

Option (1) is clearly within the wording of the ICC Statute; and option (3) is equally clearly excluded by the wording of the ICC Statute. Could we consider option (2) as negating *mens rea*, at least in a broad sense?

Most commentators would hold that the ICC Statute does not extend so far and has only a narrow scope of application.[70] Cryer, for example, considers that Article 32(2) cannot include a mistaken belief that a defence exists.[71] That is, a belief in the existence of a defence which would *excuse* or *justify* an action which is otherwise a crime does not actually go to the mental element required by that crime. Logically, excuses and justifications are only relevant after the crime has already been established. One looks *only* to the elements of the relevant crime in applying the test for mistake of law.

 Pause for reflection

Consider the following two scenarios:

(1) A soldier decides to lure the enemy into his line of fire by using a flag of truce. He does not know such use is prohibited. Does he have a mistake of law defence? (See the ICC Elements of Crimes, Article 8(2)(b)(vii)-1.)

(2) Consider the facts of the *B Case*. Would a mistaken belief that you had a right to summarily execute a collaborator under the laws of war be a mistake of law negating the mental element for relevant war crimes? Consider the example of a civilian taking no active part in hostilities but passing information to the enemy. (See the ICC Elements of Crimes on Article 8(2)(a)(i) and (vi) regarding the crimes of wilful killing or denying a fair trial.)

In scenario (1), under the Elements the accused must have known, 'or should have known', such use was prohibited. Requiring knowledge of the law as part of the *mens rea* might appear to allow ignorance of the law to raise a mistake of law defence. What do we make of 'should have known'? It *might* be that a higher standard is expected of officers (who should be better trained).[72] It would certainly seem to suggest the Court will take into account all relevant facts to determine if a defendant had enough information to understand such conduct was prohibited. Theoretically, a defence of ignorance of the law would appear to be available but one would expect it to be quite hard to make out on the facts of a given case.

---

[70] Werle and Jessberger, *Principles of International Criminal Law*, 247–48; Cryer, 'Defences/Grounds for Excluding Criminal Responsibility' in Cryer et al, *Introduction*, 3rd ed, 410. For a contrary view see: KJ Heller, 'Mistake of Legal Element, the Common Law, and Article 32 of the Rome Statute: A Critical Analysis' (2008) 6 Journal of International Criminal Justice 419.

[71] Cryer, 'Defences/Grounds for Excluding Criminal Responsibility' in Cryer et al, *Introduction*, 410.

[72] Sliedregt, *Individual Criminal Responsibility*, 273.

In scenario (2), the executed victim was a civilian not taking a direct part in hostilities at the time when they were killed. He or she was thus out of combat (*hors de combat* in Geneva law) and he or she was therefore a protected person under the Geneva Conventions. The war crime of murder or wilful killing requires no legal evaluation, just knowledge of the facts making a person a protected person. The legal mistake ('I believed I had a right to kill him') would not appear to negate the mental state required for murder or wilful killing.

On the charge of denying a fair trial, given that crimes under the ICC Statute must be committed with intent and knowledge, the Elements of Article 8(2)(a)(vi) might appear to suggest that the accused needs to know the victim was entitled to a trial under the Geneva Conventions. Indeed, Dörmann suggests that this a crime which must be committed 'wilfully and knowingly' based on the post World War II case law.[73] However, in the cases he surveys all the victims were given trials—just blatantly unfair trials failing to meet essential judicial guarantees (an impartial tribunal, access to evidence, a right to defence counsel, etc). Some would conclude that this is a mistake of law covered by the Statute, so long as the defendant thought (wrongly) that sufficient judicial guarantees had been given.[74]

13.8 Superior orders

13.8.1 Introduction

A defence of superior orders involves the idea that where a subordinate is given an order by a superior which they are legally obliged to obey, then they should have a defence (at least in some cases or under certain conditions) if that conduct was unlawful.[75] This is often pejoratively referred to as the defence of 'I was only following orders' or even as 'the Nuremberg defence'. Notably it only applies to an order to commit an illegal act (hereafter, for brevity, 'an illegal order').

It is commonly said that the defence of superior orders was effectively abolished or ended by the judgment of the Nuremberg International Military Tribunal (IMT). This is not, in fact, correct and many national legal systems continue to recognize such a defence in some form. It is true that the Nuremberg IMT held that superior orders are never a defence, and may only go to mitigation of sentence. But in reaching this conclusion the Tribunal was simply following the clear wording of its own Charter which excluded the defence from being raised.[76] It is sometimes suggested that the Nuremberg Charter was not meant to be reflective of a general rule that superior orders were *never* a defence but instead to reflect the rank of the defendants (i.e. if the defence was available to Hitler's inner circle, all guilt could be sheeted home

---

[73] K Dörmann, *Elements of War Crimes under the Rome Statute of the International Criminal Court* (Cambridge University Press 2003), 100–105.

[74] Werle and Jessberger, *Principles of International Criminal Law*, 248 para 656.

[75] A good short treatment of the international law issues is found in: S Wallerstein, 'Why English law should not incorporate a defence of superior orders' (2010) Criminal Law Review 109. The definitive study is: Y Dinstein, *The Defence of 'Obedience to Superior Orders' in International Law* (Oxford University Press 2012).

[76] See the Judgment of the Nuremburg International Military Tribunal, (1947) 41 American Journal of International Law 172, 221.

to Hitler, who was dead).[77] We should note that there is little case law on point from international tribunals since the Nuremberg IMT. We thus have to deal with issues of legal theory (should superior orders ever be a defence?) and older national case law.

The best justification for allowing a defence of superior orders is what is sometimes called the soldier's dilemma which arises if: (1) national law requires obedience to orders; and (2) international law requires disobedience to illegal orders.[78] In the case of an illegal order, therefore, the solider is placed in a 'lose-lose' position. There is thus a tension between national and international legal perspectives as to a soldier's duty. From a national perspective obedience to orders is vital to military discipline and the efficient functioning of armed forces. From an international perspective, blind obedience to orders is undesirable as it may make international crimes easier to commit or graver in scale. International law might prefer less efficient armed forces. Many national legal systems, perhaps hypocritically, uphold the defence for their own national forces but then exclude the defence and apply a rule of absolute liability in the case of war crimes committed by enemy nationals.[79]

There are three logical possible responses to the idea of a defence of superior orders. Superior orders could constitute:

(1) an unconditional defence (i.e. subordinates bear no criminal responsibility and only the superiors giving the orders are liable);

(2) a conditional defence (which is only available if certain conditions are met);

(3) no defence at all.[80]

Generally, the idea that it should be an unconditional defence is now rejected. In the case of an illegal order, that leaves us to consider whether there should be absolute liability or a conditional defence.

 Pause for reflection

Will subordinates always need a defence of superior orders?

Contrast the facts of the two Leipzig Trial cases on point (discussed in Chapter 3, section 3.2):

- The *Dover Castle* case involved an attack on a hospital ship by a German vessel, normally a war crime. However, there was a mistaken belief that a hospital ship was being used as troop transport and the defence therefore succeeded.

- In the *Llandovery Castle* case the order to fire upon survivors after sinking a hospital ship was considered *manifestly illegal* and the defence failed.

---

[77] NR Doman, 'The Nuremberg Trials Revisited' (1961) 47 American Bar Association Journal 260, 263; Werle and Jessberger, *Principles of International Criminal Law*, 249.

[78] Dinstein, *The Defence of 'Obedience to Superior Orders'*, 5–6.

[79] See: P Gaeta, 'The Defence of Superior Orders: The Statute of the International Criminal Court versus Customary International Law' (1999) 10 European Journal of International Law 172, 179 and n 22 who gives as examples the law of France, Belgium, Norway, Netherlands, and the US.

[80] Gaeta, 'The Defence of Superior Orders', 174–175; Wallerstein, 'Why English law', 111–113.

Did *Dover Castle* actually require a defence of superior orders to acquit those accused? If the accused were innocent in *Dover Castle*, it is because there the required mental element was absent: they acted under a mistake of fact.[81]

13.8.2 **Tribunal Statutes**

International tribunal statutes have often rejected the defence (but acknowledged that it may be raised in possible mitigation of punishment).[82] The ICC Statute acknowledges a conditional defence in Article 33, which reads:

(1) The fact that a [Rome Statute] crime...has been committed by a person pursuant to an order...shall not relieve that person of criminal responsibility unless: (a) The person was under a legal obligation to obey...; (b) The person did not know that the order was unlawful; and (c) The order was not manifestly unlawful. (2) For the purposes of this article, orders to commit genocide or crimes against humanity are manifestly unlawful.

The elements of the defence are thus:

- a legal obligation to obey;
- lack of knowledge that the order was unlawful; and
- the order was not manifestly unlawful.

Note there is a presumption *against* the defence being available: 'an order...*shall not* relieve that person of criminal responsibility *unless*...' (emphasis added). This wording imposes a high threshold for the defendant to pass. The mistake involved in following an unlawful order must be both honest ('did not know') and reasonable ('was not manifestly'), and it thus contains both subjective and objective elements. Article 33 therefore provides a narrow, cumulative test which could only apply to war crimes and aggression but *never* to crimes against humanity and genocide. We can ask whether this is a justifiable distinction (war crimes could be as grave as crimes against humanity; a war of aggression could kill as many people as a genocide).

The defence of superior orders is effectively a species of mistake of law (note in particular Article 33(1)(b)), which makes it worth asking whether a separate defence of superior orders is really needed.

13.8.3 **Legal obligation to obey**

The existence of a legal obligation to obey is a question of what duties are imposed by national law. Soldiers may be under a duty to obey military superiors; civilians would usually not be. The obligation involved must be a *legal* obligation: therefore it seems

---

[81] See: Ambos, 'Defences in International Criminal Law', 324 (arguing that superior orders will seldom be an autonomous defence but usually a form of mistake defence).

[82] Art 8, London Charter of the Nuremberg IMT; Art 6, Tokyo IMT Charter; Art 2(4)(b), Control Council Law No. 10; Art 7(4), ICTY Statute; Art 6(4), ICTR Statute.

likely the defence cannot apply to rebel forces in an internal conflict (whose disciplinary structures will not be enforced by law).

The defence does not appear to encompass a mistaken belief that one was under a legal obligation to obey (for example, a civilian obeying a general during war time, etc). Such a mistaken belief certainly would not raise a mistake of law defence. It would not negate the mental element of a crime to have committed it under a mistaken belief one had been legally ordered to commit it. One would still have intended to kill, torture, etc.

13.8.4 Knowledge of unlawfulness

Such knowledge will obviously preclude reliance on the defence. Proof, however, of what the defendant knew may be difficult. In *Kappler et al* (an Italian case of 1948) a former German soldier entered a plea of superior orders in respect of an order to kill 320 Italian civilians in reprisal for the death of 32 German soldiers.[83] That plea was upheld. The court was not convinced the defendant knew the order to be illegal, given that it came directly from the head of State (who can be presumed to know the law) and given that the defendant was aware such orders had been given and carried out in other theatres of the war. While all of this may be the case, it is hard to accept this was not a case of manifest illegality. One would not expect the same result to follow if a modern court heard a case on similar facts.

13.8.5 Manifest illegality

The defence is not available where an order was manifestly unlawful. This is quite a high standard, but the cases are rather vague.[84] A number of examples can be drawn from the case law:[85]

- The Control Council Law No. 10 *High Command* case discussed the idea in terms of an order which is 'criminal on its face'.[86]
- The *Eichmann* case used the metaphor of an order so obviously illegal it is as though a 'black flag' is flying over it.[87]
- The *Finta* case referred to outrageous and manifest illegality.[88]
- *Csihas et al* held the standard was that 'the order was not obviously illegal and contrary to the principles of humanity'.[89]

---

[83] The case is usefully excerpted in: Cassese et al, *International Criminal Law: Cases and Commentary*, 468–9.

[84] MJ Osiel, *Obeying Orders: Atrocity Military Discipline and the Law of War* (Transaction Publishers 2009), 77–83.

[85] See: Cryer, 'Defences/Grounds for Excluding Criminal Responsibility' in Cryer et al, *Introduction*, 414; and Cassese et al, *International Criminal Law: Cases and Commentary*, 466–71.

[86] *Von Leeb and Others (The High Command Trial)*, (1948) XII Law Reports of Trials of War Criminals 1, 74.

[87] *Eichmann v Attorney General for Israel* 36 ILR 275 (Supreme Court of Israel, 1962), 227

[88] *R v Finta* (1994) SCR 701 (Supreme Court of Canada), 828–46.

[89] The case was heard before a US Military Commission in Hungary (1946): excerpted in Cassese et al, *International Criminal Law: Cases and Commentary*, 467.

- In *Mahmud et al* the stresses of armed conflict and the alleged lack of clarity inherent in the laws of war were not accepted as factors showing an order to kidnap, detain, and beat civilians was not manifestly illegal. The Supreme Court of Israel (perfectly properly) held: 'Conduct of this kind is an outrage to any civilised person, and no obscurity or lack of clarity can shield them…'[90]

One might suggest the standard should be applied differently as between soldiers and officers. The latter should presumably be better trained, especially in the law of armed conflict.

13.8.6 Relationship to other defences: duress, mistake of fact, mistake of law

As noted earlier, superior orders may itself be a type of mistake of law defence. Where duress is raised, it supersedes a plea of superior orders: one is acting under compulsion, not the order.[91]

An order may also contain an assertion of fact leading the accused to believe that their conduct is not unlawful. Again, military targeting provides a convenient example. An order might come to an officer to bomb a weapons depot. This contains a statement of fact: the target *is* a weapons depot. An officer might then bomb the target believing (on the basis of the order) it to be a legitimate military objective. If in fact it is a civilian object the officer has a defence of either superior orders or mistake of fact (negating the required mental element).

13.8.7 Evaluating superior orders: duress, mistake of fact, mistake of law

Should there be a defence of superior orders at all? Above we noted three possible answers:

(1) There should be an unconditional defence of superior orders—i.e .only superiors are liable.

(2) There should be a conditional defence of superior orders.

(3) There should be no such defence at all.

Some suggest an absolute defence is appropriate as the solider is simply a cog in a greater machine; or that the individual soldier is compelled to obey by force of military discipline. The first argument suggests that a soldier is not a reasoning moral agent who should be held accountable for his or her own acts (contrary to one of the key bases or justifications for criminal law).[92] The second argument equates military discipline with

[90] Supreme Court of Israel (1989): excerpted in Cassese et al, *International Criminal Law: Cases and Commentary*, 470–71.
[91] *Erdemović*, ICTY Appeals Chamber, 7 October 1997, Dissenting Opinion of Judge Cassese, para 15.
[92] Wallerstein, 'Why English law', 116.

a defence of duress—which usually requires threat to life or serious injury (and, as we have noted, may not be available for murder). An unconditional defence does not seem morally defensible on either ground.[93]

The argument for there being no such defence would be that subordinates as rational agents should only be allowed to follow legal orders. This certainly avoids treating soldiers as tools with no moral choices open to them. However, it does impose a very high standard, showing little concern for the 'soldier's dilemma' and presuming—perhaps—a significant knowledge of the law.[94]

A conditional defence may be justified by the need to resolve or provide for the 'soldier's dilemma': But we can ask whether a separate defence is needed to do this. Note that the dilemma only exists in cases of uncertainty and does not apply to cases of manifest illegality. Prima facie a soldier could reasonably assume that the great majority of orders given within a responsible military hierarchy will be legal: especially where judgments are made on complex issues by trained officers.

Some legal systems do not recognize a defence of mistake of law at all: everyone is presumed to know the law. This approach upholds the objectivity of the law, encourages knowledge of the law, and avoids the risk of a broad defence of ignorance of the law resulting in an unequal application of criminal law (i.e. those who know more are held to higher standards). On similar grounds it is arguable that there should be no defence of superior orders—but if this is correct there should be no defence of mistake of law either.

As noted, superior orders may itself be a type of mistake of law defence; and some orders may lead to mistakes of fact. We might then ask if a separate defence of superior orders is simply redundant. In any case covered by a mistake of law defence, the standard required under the ICC Statute is:

> A mistake of law may, however, be a ground for excluding criminal responsibility if it negates the mental element required by such a crime ...[95]

This refers only to the defendant's mental state without any further objective or qualifying test (such as manifest illegality). Thus it could be *easier* to make out a defence of mistake of law than a defence of superior orders. As noted, mistake of fact cases can also negate the *mental element* required for an offence.[96] Similarly, in mistake of fact cases there is no requirement the mistake be both honest and reasonable. The test is purely subjective.

However, note the narrow views taken of mistakes of fact and law under the ICC Statute taken by some (discussed at 13.7.1 and 13.7.2). If one takes a narrow view of the scope of mistake of fact and mistake of law, does the defence of superior orders then become useful? The point is examined in the activity below.

---

[93] Wallerstein, 'Why English law', 115–16.

[94] *The Peleus (Re Eck and Others)* 13 International Law Reports 248 (Hamburg, British Military Court 1945), 249 ('no soldier and no sailor can carry with him a library of international law').

[95] Art 32(2), ICC Statute.   [96] Art 32(1), ICC Statute.

Pause for reflection

Consider the following scenarios:

(1) During an international armed conflict a solider is ordered to take a civilian's jeep, on the basis that no other vehicle is available, to take vital information back to headquarters. In fact, many such vehicles are available but the soldier's superior prefers not to use them.

(2) An artillery commander is ordered to fire at an enemy command post and hits it. The building is in fact a school.

(3) A firing squad of soldiers is ordered to shoot a person sentenced to death under the laws of occupation by a military tribunal. In fact, there was no trial and the soldiers were unaware of the true facts.

(4) During an IAC a soldier at a checkpoint is told that the approaching vehicle is a truck-bomb packed with explosives, driven by a suicide bomber. He is ordered to shoot to kill. The driver turns out to be an ordinary civilian, a mistaken identification having occurred.

Which defences may be implicated in each scenario?

Scenario (1) may involve a war crime against property not justified by military necessity: see ICC Statute, Article 8(2)(b)(xiii). The Elements of Crimes make it clear that the perpetrator must know it was civilian property, but do not expressly require knowledge that the seizure was not justified by military necessity. The mistake may not negate the mental element for seizing property; but there is an order, a duty to obey, no obvious knowledge of the illegality, and the order is not on its face manifestly illegal. Thus superior orders might be a better defence than mistake of law.

In scenario (2), a mistake of fact *does* negate the required mental element (intention to attack a civilian target). The defence of superior orders adds nothing further.

Arguably, scenario (3) involves a mistake as to the factual status of the person shot: the order induced a belief that the victim had had a proper and regular trial. This scenario could be covered by mistake of fact. There is also an order, a duty to obey (provided this is a regular military force), no obvious knowledge of the illegality on the part of the firing squad, and the order is not on its face manifestly illegal.[97] Thus superior orders would also be available as defence if there is any doubt about whether the scenario can be classed as a mistake of fact.

In scenario (4), if it was true that the driver was a suicide bomber, then attacking the driver would not be a crime as the suicide bomber would be a civilian taking part in hostilities. The mistake of fact negates the mental element for crimes such as intentionally attacking a civilian under Article 8(2)(b)(i) of the ICC Statute as here there was no intention to attack a civilian *not taking a direct part in hostilities* as required under the Elements of Crimes. Similarly, under ICC Statute Article 8(2)(a)(i) on the war crime of wilful killing the soldier was not aware of victim's protected status, e.g. as a civilian taking no part in hostilities. The defence of superior orders is not needed. However, if it was relied on, then the assertion of fact contained in the order ('the driver is a suicide bomber') prevents the order from being manifestly illegal.

[97] Ambos, 'Defences in International Criminal Law', 323.

13.9 Reprisals and '*tu quoque*'

Reprisals are illegal acts of war that respond to a prior illegality by opposing forces, with the aim of inducing those forces to resume fighting using lawful methods of war.[98] For example, if the enemy deliberately attacks civilian population centres then reprisals might involve the use of prohibited weapons.[99] Such an act, ordinarily a war crime, could be defended on the basis of lawful reprisals. '*Tu quoque*' (literally 'you also') is an attempt to defend one's unlawful conduct on the basis that the adversary committed similar crimes first.[100] It does not involve an assertion that the conduct was committed in order to induce the adversary to resume compliance with their obligations. *Tu quoque* is not accepted as a defence in customary international law.[101]

Reprisals and *tu quoque* were both discussed by the ICTY in *Kupreškić*. In that case the Trial Chamber laid out four criteria for reprisals to be lawful:

- 'they must be a last resort in attempts to impose compliance by the adversary' with the laws of armed conflict and thus they require prior warning be given;

- there is an 'obligation to take special precautions before implementing them' and as a result the decision to take reprisals must be made at the highest level and not by local commanders;

- reprisals must comply with the principle of proportionality; and

- reprisals must respect 'elementary considerations of humanity'.[102]

As a consequence of the last criterion, reprisals may not be conducted against persons protected by Geneva law: the sick and wounded, the shipwrecked, prisoners of war, and civilians either in occupied territories or who have been interned.[103] It is not yet clear that other categories of civilians are protected from reprisals as a matter of customary international law.[104] Nonetheless, the scope for conducting legal reprisals in an international or non-international armed conflict is severely limited.[105]

The *Kupreškić* Trial Chamber also described the *tu quoque* principle as 'the argument whereby the fact that the adversary has also committed similar crimes offers

---

[98]   Werle and Jessberger, *Principles of International Criminal Law*, 258–259 para 658.

[99]   A Cassese, 'Justifications and Excuses in International Criminal Law' in Cassese, Gaeta, and Jones (eds), *The Rome Statute of the International Criminal Court*, vol 1B, 951.

[100]   F Harhoff, '*Tu Quoque* Principle' in A Cassese (ed), *Oxford Companion to International Criminal Justice* (Oxford University Press 2009) 533; see further: Sliedregt, *Individual Criminal Responsibility*, 263–4.

[101]   Werle and Jessberger, *Principles of International Criminal Law*, 260–61 para 691.

[102]   *Kupreškić*, ICTY Trial Chamber, 14 January 2000, para 535.

[103]   Art 46, GC I; Art 47, GC II; Art 13, GC III; Art 33, GC IV. See further: Cryer, 'Defences/Grounds for Excluding Criminal Responsibility' in Cryer et al, *Introduction*, 417; M Henckaerts and L Doswald-Beck, *Customary International Humanitarian Law: Volume 1: Rules* (International Committee of the Red Cross/ Cambridge University Press 2009) 519–24.

[104]   Henckaerts and Doswald-Beck, *Customary International Humanitarian Law*, Vol 1, 520–521.

[105]   Ibid, 519–29.

a valid defence to the individuals accused' before noting such arguments have been universally rejected.[106] Nonetheless, it noted that a *tu quoque* argument might:

> amount to saying that such breaches, having been perpetrated by the adversary, legitimise similar breaches by a belligerent in response to, or in retaliation for, such violations by the enemy. Clearly, this second approach to a large extent coincides with the doctrine of reprisals.[107]

Thus, '*tu quoque*' is not accepted as a separate defence but only to the extent it is covered by the stricter conditions of the law of reprisals.[108]

13.10 Military necessity

13.10.1 Introduction

Military necessity is no longer acknowledged as a *general* defence (i.e. the idea that anything done in the course of winning a war is lawful). Nonetheless, certain acts of 'detention, displacement and property damage' may be justified where military reasons or reasons of security so demand[109] under both Geneva Convention IV (applying to international armed conflicts)[110] and the ICC Statute. How 'necessary' or vital must be the advantage gained? It is clear that a defence of military necessity requires more than 'mere military advantage, but falls short of requiring absolute necessity'; however Geneva law may further qualify this by use of terms such as 'imperative' military necessity or 'urgent' military necessity.[111] The standard is thus high, but falls short of requiring proof that the action was absolutely vital to the war effort.

13.10.2 Detention or internment of protected persons

Relevant provisions of Geneva Convention IV include (emphasis added):[112]

- 'The internment . . . of protected persons may be ordered only if the security of the Detaining Power makes it *absolutely necessary*'.[113]
- 'The Occupying Power shall not detain protected persons in an area particularly exposed to the dangers of war unless the security of the population or *imperative military reasons* so demand'.[114]

---

[106] *Kupreškić*, ICTY Trial Chamber, 14 January 2000, para 515.   [107] Ibid.

[108] Ambos, 'Defences in International Criminal Law', 326.

[109] H van der Wilt, 'Justifications and Excuses in International Criminal Law: an Assessment of the Case-law of the ICTY' in B Swart, A Zahar, and G Sluiter (eds) *The Legacy of the International Criminal Tribunal for the Former Yugoslavia* (Oxford University Press 2011), 287; compare van Sliedregt, *Individual Criminal Responsibility*, 264–7.

[110] Geneva Convention (IV) Relative to the Protection of Civilian Persons in Time of War 1949, 75 UNTS 287 ('Geneva Convention IV').

[111] Zahar and Sluiter, *International Criminal Law*, 431–32.   [112] Ibid, 430.

[113] Art 42, GC IV.   [114] Art 49, GC IV.

- 'If the Occupying Power considers it necessary, *for imperative reasons of security*, to take safety measures concerning protected persons, it may, at the most, subject them to...internment'.[115]

The ICC Statute contains no direct equivalent, but these provisions of Geneva law might be relevant in interpreting the war crime of unlawful confinement (i.e. detention justified under Geneva Convention IV should not be considered unlawful).

13.10.3 Displacement (evacuation of protected persons, including beyond occupied territory)

Article 49 of Geneva Convention IV prohibits '[i]ndividual or mass forcible transfers, as well as deportations of protected persons from occupied territory', unless in a given area 'the security of the population or *imperative military reasons* so demand' (emphasis added). The ICC Statute adopts the same wording in respect the crime of displacement of civilians in a non-international armed conflict.[116]

The defence was considered in *Krštić* where it was argued by the defence that there was no war crime of forced displacement (regarding the expulsion of the Muslim population of Srebrenica in 1992) because military necessity required Serbian forces to evacuate the civilian population. The argument failed on the facts of the case:

> In this case no military threat was present following the taking of Srebrenica. The atmosphere of terror in which the evacuation was conducted proves, conversely, that the transfer was carried out in furtherance of a well organised policy whose purpose was to expel the Bosnian Muslim population from the enclave. The evacuation was itself the goal and neither the protection of the civilians nor imperative military necessity justified the action.[117]

13.10.4 Destruction of private property

Geneva Convention IV prohibits the destruction of private property except where it is 'rendered absolutely necessary by military operations'.[118] Indeed, it is expressly criminalized as a grave breach of the Geneva Conventions (which covers destruction of property 'not justified by military necessity').[119]

The ICC Statute lists several war crimes against property which incorporate a military necessity exception:

- Article 8(2)(a)(iv) prohibits in an international armed conflict the '[e]xtensive destruction and appropriation of property, not justified by military necessity and carried out unlawfully and wantonly'.[120]

---

[115] Art 78, GC IV.   [116] Art 8(2)(e)(viii), ICC Statute.
[117] *Krštić*, ICTY Trial Chamber, 2 August 2001, para 527.   [118] Art 53, Geneva Convention IV.
[119] Art 147, Geneva Convention IV.   [120] Art 2(d), ICTY Statute.

- Article 8(2)(b)(xiii) prohibits in an international armed conflict '[d]estroying or seizing the enemy's property unless such destruction or seizure be imperatively demanded by the necessities of war'.

- Article 8(2)(e)(xii) prohibits in a non-international armed conflict '[d]estroying or seizing the property of an adversary unless such destruction or seizure be imperatively demanded by the necessities of the conflict'.

Such war crimes were considered in *Kordić and Čerkez*.[121] The case involved the deliberate destruction of mosques in a non-international armed conflict which were not being used in any way by hostile forces and thus were not legitimate military targets. The Trial Chamber held that in a non-international armed conflict only the unjustified destruction of property specifically protected under Geneva law was a war crime. The destruction of mosques not being used for military purposes was sufficient (because places of worship have a protected status in the law applicable to non-international armed conflicts);[122] but destruction of homes and businesses was not. This is consistent with the general position that only a more limited range of war crimes applies in non-international armed conflicts. It is not obvious, however, whether this narrow view would apply under the broadly drafted offence found in Article 8(2)(e)(xii) of the ICC Statute.

13.11 Summary and conclusions

This chapter has provided an outline of one of the more contentious issues in international criminal law: the extent to which a defendant should be able to plead that there are circumstances excusing or justifying what will invariably be appalling crimes.[123] As a preliminary matter, we noted that while the distinction between justifications and excuses is known in a number of national legal systems, it is of no direct relevance to international criminal law. The distinction does, however, provide a useful tool for thinking about defences as either raising a plea that conduct was inherently lawful (a justification) or as being, in effect, an admission that the conduct occurred but was not blameworthy (an excuse).

The defences available under the customary international law and the Rome Statute of the ICC can be grouped into a number of rough categories. First, the common underpinning of the defences of mental incapacity or intoxication is that the condition in question must *destroy* the accused person's ability to appreciate the unlawfulness of their conduct or to control their behaviour. In practice, this will be an exceptionally difficult burden of proof to meet. In addition, there is no available defence of intoxication

---

[121] *Kordić and Čerkez*, ICTY Trial Chamber, 26 February 2001, paras 803–9.

[122] See: Art 16, Protocol Additional to the Geneva Conventions of 12 August 1949, and relating to the Protection of Victims of Non-International Armed Conflicts 1977, 1125 UNTS 609.

[123] On the general lack of sympathy towards those accused of international crimes see Cryer, 'Defences/Grounds for Excluding Criminal Responsibility' in Cryer et al, *Introduction*, 398.

if the defendant became recklessly intoxicated in circumstances where they knew that an international crime might result.

Second, we can see a certain overlap between the law of self defence, necessity, and duress. In each situation the essence of the plea is that the defendant did not have a free choice in their action and was responding to external circumstances beyond their control. Such circumstances may be constituted by the threat posed by another person or by a force of nature. The defendant will have to show that they faced a serious and imminent threat and took only reasonable and proportionate measures in response.

Third, the defences of the mistake of fact, mistake of law, and superior orders will tend to overlap in practice. The easiest of the three to understand is the concept of a mistake of fact which negates the mental element of the crime. The example used a number of times in this chapter was that of a combatant who shoots a civilian believing him or her to be a participant in hostilities. That belief means that the combatant lacks the required mental element: knowledge of the victim's protected (civilian) status. Whether a mistake of law can raise a defence is controversial. We are all familiar with the ideas that ignorance of the law should be no excuse. However, there may be some cases where a particular legal evaluation is required as part of an offence. For example, consider a case of unlawful detention in the course of an armed conflict which followed a grossly unfair trial. The officer who conducted that trial may have believed that the trial had in fact fulfilled all the essential judicial guarantees guaranteed under the law of armed conflict. In such a case there would be a mistake of law defence to a charge of the war crime of unlawful imprisonment. Superior orders, the so-called 'Nuremberg defence', is probably the most contentious of defences in international criminal proceedings. The best justification for it is that it attempts to resolve the 'soldier's dilemma'. That is, a person may be placed in a situation where national law requires obedience to an order and international law directs them to disobey because the order would result in an international crime. In such cases, a subordinate may have a defence where he or she is under a legal obligation to obey so long as the order in question was not manifestly illegal. This is the so-called conditional defence approach. However, under the Rome Statute superior orders can never be a defence to charges of genocide or crimes against humanity which are always presumed to be manifestly illegal. Thus, carrying out orders resulting in genocide or crimes against humanity will result in unconditional or absolute liability. In practice, however, as we have seen, superior orders are often likely to raise the question of mistake of fact negating the mental element. That is, an order may contain a statement of fact which if it were true would mean the conduct was not unlawful. In such cases, so long as the defendant has no reason to believe the statement of fact contained in the order is untrue, a defence of either superior orders or mistake of fact might be made out.

Fourth, we also noted in this chapter that some war crimes are defined in such a way that they contain within them an exception allowing for urgent and necessary military action. For example, where civilians have to be removed from the theatre of conflict for their own protection no war crime of forcible deportation will be committed as a result. We have also noted that there is a very limited exception in the law of war crimes allowing, under strict conditions, for reprisals: a reprisal being an otherwise illegal act under the law of armed conflict taken in response to the prior illegal act of the adversary and designed to persuade that opposing force to resume compliance with its legal obligations.

In practice, however, such defences may not be greatly used before the ICC if the experience of the ICTY is anything to go by. In particular, it is unusual for international criminal tribunals now to hold a separate hearing on sentencing. Thus, a team of defence lawyers cannot mount a separate legal strategy and introduce the question of defences only after their client has been found guilty. On this basis many may be reluctant to make arguments about defences at trial, if there is a risk that those arguments might be seen as implicitly conceding that the wrongful conduct in fact occurred and was committed by their client. A defendant may be more likely to make their case by challenging the quality of the prosecution evidence in one of the manners noted in section 13.2.1.

Useful further reading

K AMBOS, 'Defences in International Criminal Law' in BS Brown (ed) *Research Handbook on International Criminal Law* (Elgar 2011).
A concise overview of the field by an acknowledged expert.

Y DINSTEIN, The Defence of 'Obedience to Superior Orders' in International Law (Oxford University Press 2012).
The leading monograph on the question of superior orders.

P GAETA, 'The Defence of Superior Orders: The Statute of the International Criminal Court versus Customary International Law' (1999) 10 European Journal of International Law 172.
This article argues that the ICC Statute's adoption of a conditional liability approach is a departure from customary international law, which the author contends supports absolute liability.

E VAN SLIEDREGT, *Individual Criminal Responsibility in International Law* (Oxford University Press 2014).
An exceptionally clear account of the principles of both defences and modes of participation in offences in international criminal law. In particular, an excellent resource when trying to navigate differences in common law and civil law approaches to these questions.

S WALLERSTEIN, 'Why English law should not incorporate a defence of superior orders' (2010) Criminal Law Review 109.
A useful article which, while focussed on the question of English law, provides an accessible account of the debates surrounding the 'soldier's dilemma'.

14

Jurisdictional immunities

14.1 Introduction

We noted in Chapter 4 that one of the revolutionary aspects of the Charter of the Nuremberg IMT was that it provided for the trial of *individuals* for what previously would have been thought of as *acts of State*. That is, it was widely presumed before 1945 that if a State official carried out an act on behalf of his or her State, that he or she would be *completely immune* from the civil or criminal jurisdiction of foreign courts for that conduct. The theory was that such acts were *sovereign* and the courts of one sovereign State cannot judge the acts of another sovereign State (in Latin, *par in parem non habet imperium*). It would contradict the sovereign equality of States if one State could sit in judgment on the acts of another.

The immunity that State officials enjoy from the jurisdiction of foreign courts may be of two types:

- *functional immunity* prevents a current or former State official being brought before the courts of a foreign State in respect of his or her official acts (also called immunity *ratione materiae*);
- *personal immunity* is held by certain high officials for the duration of their office and covers both their private and official acts (also called immunity *ratione personae*). Once they leave office they will still enjoy functional immunity for their official acts only.

Personal immunities are often said to rest on a different rationale from functional immunities. That is, some suggest that while functional immunities are grounded in the *par in parem* principle, personal immunities exist only to preserve the ability of States to operate on the international plane by protecting the ability of high-ranking officials to carry out their representative functions. The idea of such a distinction gains support from the *Arrest Warrant* case, discussed below.[1]

The question then arises whether these immunities are available in the case of international crimes. In respect of functional immunity, at least, some hold that it is a feature

---

[1] States are divided in their *opinio juris* as to whether the basis of immunities is protecting States' functions or emanates from sovereign equality (i.e. *par in parem*): 'Preliminary Report on immunity of State officials from foreign criminal jurisdictions by of the Special Rapporteur Ms. Concepción Escobar Hernández', UN Doc. A/CN.4/654 (2012), para 34.

of international crimes that States are simply barred from claiming functional immunity in respect of international offences.[2] This may be a desirable outcome and it might be the way the law is developing: however, the case law is at best ambiguous. At least as regards personal immunities, numerous courts have upheld the idea that State immunity is available even to individuals charged with crimes violating a rule of *jus cogens*. There is, however, contrary case law. If State immunity is the general rule, then clear and uniform State practice should be required to demonstrate that a new exception has arisen to that rule. You will need to consider after reading this chapter whether the case law supports such a conclusion.

The idea that there could be immunity for crimes contrary to *jus cogens* will likely strike you as contradictory: if *jus cogens* rules 'trump' all other rules of international law, why do they not override pleas of State immunity? The arguments made by courts on this point are considered further below.

Another argument, frequently raised, is that pleas of State immunity bind only national courts and therefore by definition are not available before international courts. Once again, the practice is ambiguous. While the Special Court for Sierra Leone and a Pre-Trial Chamber of the International Criminal Court (ICC) have endorsed such an argument, on its face the ICC Statute expressly prohibits persons being transferred to it in violation of the rules on State immunity.

 Learning aims

By the end of this chapter you should be able to:

- explain the difference between personal and functional immunities;

- discuss the controversies surrounding issues of State immunity and international crimes, including whether immunity means impunity;

- discuss the different approaches taken to the question of functional immunity taken in the case law, especially *Pinochet (No 3)*;

- compare the position before national and international courts, especially the ICC; and

- evaluate whether State immunity is available in cases involving crimes contrary to *jus cogens* and give a reasoned view on whether immunity *should be* available in such cases.

These issues are addressed in turn below after a brief introduction of the relevant historical and theoretical issues.

The rest of this chapter therefore proceeds as follows:

- Section 14.2 provides an overview of the law of state immunity in general international law.

---

[2] A Cassese et al, *Cassese's International Criminal Law* 3rd ed (Oxford University Press 2013) 320.

- Section 14.3 considers the immunities enjoyed by individual officials in criminal cases, with a particular emphasis on the law that applies before national courts.
- Section 14.4 considers the applicable law before the ICC, and the controversial question of which immunities (if any) are available to the officials of States that are not party to the ICC Statute.

14.2 Introduction to the theory and history of State immunity

The classic theory of State immunity is that:

- a State is absolutely immune from the jurisdiction of foreign courts (the general rule);
- unless an exception applies.

This proposition is discussed in more detail below. We then ask why the rule extends not just to States but to individual officers of the State.

14.2.1 The general rule

As noted above, it follows from the sovereign equality of States that one sovereign State cannot exercise power (including judicial power) over another. Chief Justice Marshall of the US Supreme Court put it this way in *Schooner Exchange v McFadden*:

> One sovereign being in no respect amendable to ... the jurisdiction of another, can be supposed to enter a foreign territory only under an express license, or in the confidence that the immunities belonging to his independent sovereign station ... will be extended to him.[3]

Chief Justice Marshall starts from the *par in parem* principle: as a sovereign is 'in no respect amendable to' another's jurisdiction, any exercise of jurisdiction over another State would be unlawful. The 'license' he refers to is simply a presumption that local State organs (such as courts) will refrain from exercising any powers they might have under national law incompatibly with international law. It is a guarantee that nothing will be done, not an assertion that without such a 'license' being granted foreign sovereigns would be subject to jurisdiction.

Thus it was said in the UK case *Holland v Lampen-Wolfe* that the doctrine of State immunity is a rule of customary international law which 'derives from the equality of sovereign states'.[4] Therefore, it is not a voluntarily adopted rule of national

---

[3] *Schooner Exchange v McFadden* (1813) 11 US (7 Cranch) 116, 136. Some suggest the *par in parem* principle provides a basis only for functional immunity: D Robinson, 'Immunities' in R Cryer et al, *An Introduction to International Criminal Law and Procedure*, 3rd ed (Cambridge University Press 2013) 545. It is apparent from the quote above that it was clearly conceived of as stating the rule of personal inviolability of the sovereign as well.

[4] *Holland v Lampen-Wolfe* [2000] UKHL 40 per Lord Millett.

law, it is a limitation 'upon the sovereignty of the United Kingdom' following from international law.[5]

14.2.2 Exceptions

What then are the exceptions to this general rule? The most obvious exception is when the foreign State consents to jurisdiction or waives its immunity. Further, in *commercial* cases it has generally been accepted that States cannot claim immunity in respect of non-sovereign commercial activities any ordinary person could perform (the doctrine of 'restrictive immunity').[6] There is still some controversy about whether the test of immunity should focus upon:

- the nature of the transaction (e.g. no obligations arising under a contract enjoy immunity because entering a contract is something any person can do); or

- the purpose of a transaction (e.g. a contract to buy a battleship should be immune as naval defence is a sovereign function).[7]

How might such distinctions apply to questions of *criminal* law? It is sometimes suggested that committing an international crime, for example torture, is not a legitimate sovereign function and therefore should not benefit from State immunity. If generally accepted this would extend a form of restrictive immunity from national commercial cases to international criminal law. The extent to which case law supports such an approach is discussed below.

The most important point to note in the criminal context is that State immunity is generally treated as a *procedural bar* to a court's jurisdiction: if it can be overcome through an exception, the case may be heard. The importance of this is that a claim of immunity does not extinguish criminal liability: it simply asserts that this particular court cannot hear this particular case at this particular time.[8] The criminal liability of the accused person remains (with the consequence they might be able to be tried before another court at another time). This concept is further explored below, along with criticisms of it.

---

[5] Ibid.

[6] J Foakes, *The Position of Heads of State and Senior Officials in International Law* (Oxford University Press 2014) 16–17.

[7] The approach in the UK has usually upheld an approach based on denying immunity where the transaction has a commercial nature (even if it was done for a sovereign purpose). See, for example: *Trendtex Trading v Bank of Nigeria* [1977] QB 532; and the UK State Immunity Act 1978, s 1(1) (setting out a general presumption of State immunity) and s 3 (introducing a very broad exception for commercial acts, including all contracts). See to similar effect Articles 5 and 10, UN Convention on the Jurisdictional Immunities of States and their Property 2000. The position in the US is more complex: while there is a Foreign Sovereign Immunities Act of 1976 (which does not apply to individual State officers, see: *Samantar v Yousuf*, US Supreme Court, 1 June 2010), States designated under the Anti-Terrorism Act 2005 (ATA) may lose immunity from civil claims.

[8] *Case Concerning the Arrest Warrant of 11 April 2000 (Democratic Republic of the Congo v Belgium)*, 2002 ICJ Reports 3 (*Arrest Warrant Case*), paras 60–61.

14.2.3 Why extend State immunities to individual officers of the State?

The answer to this question can be put quite simply. States are artificial legal persons: they can only act through State agents. State immunity would be completely undermined if its employees or officials 'could be sued as individuals for matters of State conduct' where the State itself would enjoy immunity.[9]

14.3 Immunities enjoyed by individual State officials in criminal cases

14.3.1 Personal immunities (immunity *ratione personae*)

Personal immunities before national courts

'Personal immunities' describes those immunities enjoyed by certain high officials by virtue of their office. It is an *absolute* immunity protecting a narrow class of actors while they remain in office from all exercises of foreign jurisdiction. Importantly, however, this immunity belongs to the State, not the individual: therefore the State may waive it and allow a trial to proceed. (In most cases, however, this is unlikely.)

The classic example is a head of State. A head of State is entitled to complete personal inviolability (i.e. he or she may not be arrested or detained in any manner) and absolute immunity from criminal jurisdiction. (The immunity of a head of State from civil jurisdiction is more complex and is not discussed here.[10])

The International Court of Justice (ICJ) in the *Arrest Warrant Case* found that serving heads of government and foreign ministers enjoy the same immunities as heads of State, so long as these immunities are necessary to carry out their functions.[11] The *Arrest Warrant Case* has held that as foreign ministers must travel to fulfil their functions, they must be immune from the criminal jurisdiction of foreign courts (otherwise this could affect their ability or willingness to travel). On this basis, it makes no difference if travel is for official purposes or personal reasons. A foreign minister arrested while in another State on holiday is just as impaired in fulfilling his or her functions as if he or she had been arrested travelling on official business. The ICJ's logic may also apply to other officials involved in international relations who need to travel abroad as part of their work.

It is sometimes suggested that there is no immunity of any kind for international crimes. An example is provided in *Prosecutor v Blaškić*. In *Blaškić* the ICTY Appeals Chamber discussed the 'general rule' of State immunity and then turned to 'exceptions' that:

> arise from the norms of international criminal law prohibiting war crimes, crimes against humanity and genocide. Under these norms, those responsible for such crimes cannot

---

[9] E.g. *Propend Finance v Sing* (English Court of Appeal, 1997) 111 International Law Reports 611, 699.

[10] In UK law a foreign head of State is immune for all their official, but not their personal, acts: s 20, State Immunity Act 1978. The issue is not covered by the UN Convention on State Immunity (see Art 3(2)).

[11] *Arrest Warrant Case*, para 53.

invoke immunity from national or international jurisdiction even if they perpetrated such crimes while acting in their official capacity.[12]

Taken literally, *Blaškić* is simply wrong. The *Arrest Warrant Case* concerned allegations that a foreign minister had been involved in international crimes. The ICJ finding that Belgium's circulation of an Interpol 'red notice' violated this immunity necessarily means that personal immunities apply *even if* the crimes alleged are contrary to *jus cogens*. Any suggestion to the contrary must explain why we should ignore the ICJ decision when ICJ judgments are usually taken as authoritative statements of international law.

Obviously, this result may not seem principled. Why should the international law of immunities protect those accused of international crimes? The ICJ emphasized that the personal immunities held by high-ranking serving officials 'does not mean that they enjoy impunity in respect of [international] crimes'.[13] The court emphasized, as outlined above, that:

> While jurisdictional immunity is procedural in nature, criminal responsibility is a question of substantive law. Jurisdictional immunity may well bar prosecution for a certain period or for certain offences; it cannot exonerate the person to whom it applies from all criminal responsibility.[14]

The ICJ went on to note that such persons may still be prosecuted: (1) before the courts of their own country; (2) by foreign courts if immunity is waived by their sending State; (3) once they have left office in respect of 'acts committed prior or subsequent to his or her period of office, as well as in respect of acts committed during that period of office in a private capacity'; and (4) before 'certain international criminal courts, where they have jurisdiction'.[15] We may question how convincing these arguments are. If an individual enjoys the support of the State he or she serves, prosecution before national courts or a waiver of immunity may be unlikely. The third point made by the ICJ notably says nothing about crimes committed *in an official capacity while in office*. This may suggest that immunity remains available for such crimes. This would be a case of *functional immunity*, addressed below.

The ICJ's final claim, that serving officials might still be prosecuted before international criminal courts needs to be read carefully. The ICJ refers to 'certain' courts that 'have jurisdiction': an international court might have jurisdiction over persons otherwise having immunity where that immunity has been waived under a treaty or over-ridden, in effect, by a Chapter VII resolution of the Security Council. The ICJ's statement does not necessarily assert a general rule that there can never be claims of immunity before international courts. The point is discussed further below. We should note that the ICJ subsequently upheld the procedure/substance distinction in the *Germany v Italy Case*.[16] There, in a case concerning civil proceedings brought by

---

[12] *Prosecutor v Blaškić*, ICTY Appeals Chamber, Judgment on the Request of the Republic of Croatia for the review of the decision of Trial Chamber II of 18 July 1997, 29 October 1997, para 41.

[13] *Arrest Warrant Case*, 26 at para 60.   [14] Ibid.   [15] *Arrest Warrant Case*, 26–27 at para 61.

[16] *Jurisdictional Immunities of the State (Germany v Italy: Greece intervening)*, 2012 ICJ Reports 99.

victims of war crimes committed on Italian territory, it was found that there was no exception to State immunity following from the *jus cogens* nature of the offences in question.[17]

Irrespective of criticism, this same approach has been taken in other international and national cases. Similar reasoning was followed in the earlier European Court of Human Rights case in *Al-Adsani v UK*.[18] While *Al-Adsani* is a civil case and not a criminal case, the logic of the decision remains instructive. Al-Adsani attempted to use the UK court system to sue the Sheik and Government of Kuwait for unlawful assault and detention (in effect, torture). UK courts denied his claim and upheld State immunity. Al-Adsani claimed this violated his right to a fair trial under Article 6 of the European Convention on Human Rights. The Court divided nine judges to eight on the issue. The majority found that the grant of State immunity was proportionate to the UK's obligation to comply with the international law of State immunity.[19] The impediment this created to Al-Adsani's access to UK courts was thus permissible. The European Court of Human Rights found that while the International Law Commission (ILC) had considered arguments that there should not be immunity for severe human rights violations breaching *jus cogens* in its work on State immunity, in a majority of such cases before national courts such immunity had actually been afforded. The Court found that immunity is only a procedural bar, it does not extinguish substantive legal liability therefore there is no conflict with *jus cogens*. The minority held, simply, that if the prohibition on torture is *jus cogens* it should logically override any inconsistent rule of international law including immunity.

In national law, and on the basis of the *Arrest Warrant Case*, the UK has recognized the availability of personal immunity in respect of serving high officials in the case of a visiting Israeli defence ministers accused of war crimes in *Re General Shaul Mofaz* and a visiting Chinese minister of commerce accused of torture in *Re Bo Xilai*.[20] On the basis of this and other case law (such as the dismissal of a case against President Fidel Castro of Cuba in Spain in 1999) it is generally accepted that personal immunities are available before national courts where international crimes are alleged.[21]

However, UK cases such as *Mofaz* and *Bo Xilai* show that the functional approach to personal immunities in *Arrest Warrant* may significantly widen the number of persons protected by personal immunities. Traditionally such immunities have been enjoyed only by the 'big three': the serving head of State, head of government, and foreign minister.[22] However, focussing on protecting State functions such as the conduct of international relations may allow a much wider range of high-ranking officials to enjoy personal immunities while they are in office.

---

[17] For a critical view of the reasoning involved see: A Mills and K Trapp, 'Smooth Runs the Water Where the Brook is Deep: The Obscured Complexities of Germany v Italy' (2012) 1 Cambridge Journal of International and Comparative Law 153.

[18] *Al-Adsani v The United Kingdom*, Application No. 35763/97, European Court of Human Rights, 2001.

[19] Ibid, paras 52–67.   [20] (2004) 128 ILR 709 and (2005) 128 ILR 713.

[21] Robinson, 'Immunities' in Cryer et al, *Introduction*, 552–553; Cassese et al, *Cassese's International Criminal Law*, 320.

[22] *Arrest Warrant Case*, para 51.

Pause for reflection

Are the four reasons the ICJ gave in the *Arrest Warrant Case* as to why a grant of personal immunity does not necessarily result in impunity convincing?

As we have noted the ICJ suggested a person charged with international crimes who benefits from personal immunities could still be prosecuted: (1) before the courts of their own State; (2) by foreign courts if immunity is waived by their sending State; (3) once they have left office in respect of 'acts committed prior or subsequent to his or her period of office, as well as in respect of acts committed during that period of office in a private capacity'; and (4) before international criminal tribunals having jurisdiction.

An official enjoying personal immunity is likely to have a large degree of political power and support in their home State. This would seem to make options (1) and (2) unlikely. As there is no truly universal international criminal tribunal option (4) relies on, in effect, the official's home State being party to a relevant treaty or the UN Security Council granting jurisdiction to an international court through use of its Chapter VII powers. Option (3) might be thought unhelpful, as it necessarily suggests that official acts committed while in office will continue to be covered by functional immunity (which could cover all international crimes committed pursuant to a government policy).

Do you find the technique of distinguishing between procedural and substantive law in *Arrest Warrant* and *Al-Adsani* a convincing way of reconciling any conflict between international law rules on immunity and *jus cogens*?

There is no correct answer to this. You will either consider that this is a rational and comprehensible, if perhaps regrettable, approach to the law; or you may consider this a use of a purely formal distinction to prevent the law achieving its purpose. The best arguments in favour of such distinction might include: (1) it allows the business of diplomatic relations to continue smoothly, which might be an important part of ending the conflicts that give rise to international crimes; (2) it prevents unfounded or politically-motivated claims being brought against unpopular officials or regimes; and (3) it prevents universal jurisdiction being abused and becoming a tool whereby some (typically wealthy, powerful western) States prosecute the officials of less powerful States while refusing to take action in relation to allegations of international crimes made against their own officials.

Irrespective of whether you think the decision has merit, it is hard to suggest there is consistent case law which supports a rule of non-immunity for international crimes.

Personal immunities before international courts

It is sometimes argued that international law prohibits a plea of personal immunity before 'international courts'. After all, such immunities were specifically excluded in:

- Article 7 of the Nuremberg IMT Charter ('The official position of defendants, whether as Heads of State or responsible officials in Government Departments, shall not be considered as freeing them from responsibility or mitigating punishment');

- Article 6 of the Tokyo IMT Charter ('the official position...of an accused...shall [not], of itself, be sufficient to free such accused from responsibility for any crime');

- Article 4 of the Genocide Convention 1948 ('Persons committing genocide...shall be punished, whether they are constitutionally responsible rulers, public officials or private individuals');

- Principle 3 of the International Law Commissions' 1950 'Nuremberg Principles' ('The fact that a person who committed an act which constitutes a crime under international law acted as Head of State or responsible Government official does not relieve him from responsibility under international law');

- Article 7(2) of the ICTY Statute 1993 ('The official position of any accused person, whether as Head of State or Government or as a responsible Government official, shall not relieve such person of criminal responsibility nor mitigate punishment'); and

- Article 6(2) of the ICTR Statute 1994 (using the same language as the ICTY Statute).

However, the issue is not so clear cut. The Nuremberg IMT was a court established by an occupying power over a defeated enemy and was justified as actually being grounded in German sovereignty as a consequence of the surrender. Its Charter therefore was not necessarily a reflection of general international law. The ICTY and ICTR gain their compulsory powers from Chapter VII of the UN Charter (which prevails over other rules of international law).

Nonetheless, in the *Charles Taylor Case* the Special Court for Sierra Leone (SCSL) held it could issue a warrant for the arrest of serving president of Liberia, Charles Taylor, irrespective of any claim of personal immunity.[23] It did so on the basis that: (1) it considered itself an international court; (2) the passage in *Arrest Warrant* discussed above suggests that personal immunities are not available before international courts; and (3) the rule of international law regarding personal immunity applies *horizontally* between equal States and not *vertically* between a State and a court established on the international plane. (A very similar argument was made by an ICC Pre-Trial Chamber in the *Al-Bashir* case and is discussed below.)

Each step in the SCSL's argument is doubtful.[24] First, the SCSL is a court established under a treaty between a State and the United Nations, and operates within the national judicial system of Sierra Leone. It was not directly created by the compulsory Chapter VII powers of the Security Council in the manner of the ICTY and ICTR. Saying that the Special Court is an 'international court' in the same manner as the ICTY and ICTR is plainly wrong. Second, as discussed above, it is unlikely that the ICJ's reference to immunity not being available before 'certain' international courts in *Arrest Warrant* was intended to lay down a general rule. The reference was to international courts *having*

---

[23] *Charles Taylor Case* (Decision on Jurisdiction) SCSL Appeals Chamber, 31 May 2004, paras 41–59.
[24] Nonetheless, it finds support in some of the literature: Cassese et al, *Cassese's International Criminal Law*, 320–22.

jurisdiction. As noted, sometimes immunity might be waived by consent to a treaty or over-ridden by a compulsory resolution of the Security Council under its Chapter VII powers thus giving a court *personal jurisdiction* over a defendant who would otherwise enjoy immunity. The mere fact of an international court having *subject matter jurisdiction* over international crimes does not make otherwise applicable immunities inapplicable.[25] Third, the argument that a court is not a State and therefore the rules that apply as between States do not bind a court is at best 'rather facile'.[26] Put simply, it is clear—following the *Arrest Warrant Case*—that France, the UK, and Germany (for example) may not ignore the personal immunities of high-ranking foreign officials charged with *jus cogens* crimes before their courts. However, could France, the UK, and Germany instead establish by treaty among themselves the 'International Court for African War Crimes' with jurisdiction over grave breaches of the Geneva Conventions committed in Africa and providing in its statute that no-one before it may benefit from State immunity? On the argument of the *Charles Taylor Case* it would appear so. However, it is a basic proposition of law that States cannot do something collectively that they may not do individually.[27] In the event, by the time there was a judgment in the case Mr Taylor was no longer President of Liberia, so personal immunities were not relevant. (That is, they were only relevant in arrest warrant proceedings.)

The International Criminal Court Statute might be thought to be ambiguous on point and is discussed further below.

14.3.2 Functional immunity (immunity *ratione materiae*)

Functional immunity describes the immunity from foreign jurisdiction attaching to all official State acts. It protects a wide class of actors but only in respect of their official conduct. Once high officials leave office they will no longer enjoy personal immunity but will continue to enjoy functional immunity in respect of all their past official conduct.

The question then is how such principles apply in criminal cases. Can committing a war crime or crime against humanity be an official act? We might be tempted to answer no as a matter of principle, but if a crime against humanity must be committed pursuant to a State or organizational policy, doesn't it follow that what is done as a matter of State policy is prima facie an official act? Arguments that illegal acts or acts going beyond the lawful powers of a State official (*ultra vires* acts) can never be governmental functions would greatly undercut the role and extent of State immunity in cases going well beyond international crimes. After all, the very situation when immunity will be most relevant is when a State official has acted illegally or beyond their powers. Overall, if one accepts the distinction between procedural and substantive law outlined in *Arrest Warrant* in relation to personal immunity it is hard to see why the same logic should not apply when functional immunity is at issue.

---

[25] Ibid, 320–21.   [26] Robinson, 'Immunities' in Cryer et al, *Introduction*, 563.

[27] Ibid and W Schabas, *An Introduction to the International Criminal Court*, 4th ed (Cambridge University Press 2011), 80.

The counter-argument is that from the time of the Nuremberg IMT Charter and the General Assembly's acceptance of the Nuremberg principles, official capacity has been irrelevant to one's responsibility for international crimes.[28] On this approach not to see international criminal law as an exception to the usual rule of functional immunity is a mistake that could lead the structure of international law to collapse.[29] States, it is argued, have *jus cogens* obligations to prosecute international crimes and this obligation cannot be set aside or made discretionary by rules of immunity.[30] The argument is, on any balanced appraisal, optimistic. First, it presumes State courts will not follow the lead of the ICJ and use the procedural/substantive distinction to uphold immunity. Second, it assumes there is an overriding duty to prosecute international crimes as a matter of *jus cogens*. As we saw in our discussion of jurisdiction in Chapter 4 there is no evidence States have uniformly exercised jurisdiction over international crimes. Third, the evidence that national courts consistently hold functional immunity to be inapplicable is, at best, ambiguous (as discussed below). Such arguments from first principles are arguments about what the law *should be* and must be carefully tested against actual State practice. Clearly, a rule that no functional immunities apply in such cases would be desirable. As lawyers, however, we should be cautious about assuming that what the law should be already is.

Along these lines a UK judge has held, in a civil case:

> there is no evidence that states have recognised or given effect to an international law obligation to exercise universal jurisdiction over claims arising from alleged breaches of peremptory norms of international law [thus setting aside immunity] ... But this lack of evidence is not neutral: since the rule on immunity is well-understood and established, and no relevant exception is generally accepted, the rule prevails ...[31]

While this statement should give us pause, it is distinguishable on the basis it was said in a civil case. Indeed, it might well be the case that there is little or no evidence of an exception to immunity in civil cases where, for example, a victim of torture tries to sue a foreign government for damages.[32] Nonetheless, an argument could be made that a different rule might apply to criminal cases. We should ask ourselves, however, if national courts are *unwilling* to set aside functional immunity when only money and embarrassment to a foreign government is at stake, why should they be willing to do so when it would involve sending a former (or current) government official to prison?

Finally, before turning to the actual case law in criminal proceedings, we should recall that the immunity belongs to the State, not the individual, and the State may waive it. It is also up to the State to invoke it if local authorities do not appear to be respecting it.[33]

---

[28] Cassese et al, *Cassese's International Criminal Law*, 247–8.   [29] Ibid, 248.   [30] Ibid, 248.
[31] *Jones v Minister of the Interior, Saudi Arabia and Aziz* [2006] UKHL 26, per Lord Bingham at paras 27 and 28.
[32] See: K Parlett, 'Immunity in Civil Proceedings for Torture: The Emerging Exception' (2006) European Human Rights Law Review 49, 58; note also the discussion of *Al-Adsani*, earlier. In US law functional immunity is available in civil cases alleging international crimes against former government officials: *Matar v Dichter*, United States Court of Appeals, Second Circuit, 16 April 2009 and Cassese et al, *Cassese's Criminal Law*, 246 n 57.
[33] *Certain Questions of Mutual Assistance in Criminal Matters (Djibouti v France)* 2008 ICJ Reports 177, para 196.

Functional immunity in criminal cases: the Pinochet Case

The most famous national case on point is *R v Bow Street Magistrate, Ex parte Pinochet (No. 3)*. Senator Pinochet was the former head of State of Chile. While Pinochet was present in the United Kingdom for medical treatment a Spanish court sought his extradition to Spain to stand trial for acts of torture he was alleged to have ordered while in office as the head of State. As he was no longer head of State Pinochet could only plead that his conduct while in office was covered by functional immunity. The case had a complex procedural history and was, unprecedentedly, re-heard several times by the UK House of Lords (hence the 'No. 3' in the case name).

Pinochet No. 3 is a notoriously complex case as it involved difficult questions of both extradition law and universal jurisdiction under the Convention against Torture. Neither of these points is relevant to the present discussion. What is relevant here is that if Pinochet enjoyed functional immunity for the official acts alleged to constitute torture, then he could not be extradited to Spain. Two further complications were that:

- torture under the Convention against Torture is clearly an official act. Article 1(1) defines torture as the infliction of severe pain or suffering, for a prohibited purpose 'at the instigation of or with the consent or acquiescence of *a public official or other person acting in an official capacity*' (emphasis added); and
- most of the judges of the House of Lords agreed that the general rule was that if immunity is to be waived by a treaty that waiver must be made in express language. No such express language is found in the Convention against Torture which is, in fact, silent on questions of State immunity.

Six of the seven judges who heard *Pinochet No. 3* concluded that Pinochet did not enjoy functional immunity and could be extradited to Spain.[34] Generally, most scholars and commentators take one of two views of the decision in *Pinochet No. 3*:

- on a narrow reading the case stands only for the proposition that the Convention against Torture removes functional immunity in respect of torture (an immunity that would otherwise exist at customary international law); and
- on a broad reading the case is sometimes taken to support the proposition that as a matter of customary international law no plea of functional immunity is permissible in respect of any violation of *jus cogens*.

Which view is correct is not necessarily easy to establish: the seven judges in *Pinochet No 3* each issued separate opinions and the logic of these is not always consistent. Lord Browne-Wilkinson's view is usually taken as the most persuasive. Lord Browne-Wilkinson paid a great deal of attention to the 'extradite or prosecute'

---

[34] Although the House of Lords held, for reasons of extradition law, he could only be extradited on a narrow selection of charges. In the end, Pinochet was not extradited on grounds that his health was such that he was not fit to stand trial.

obligations under the Convention Against Torture (as discussed in Chapter 2). He found that the Convention must exclude functional immunity or 'the whole elaborate structure of universal jurisdiction over torture committed by officials is rendered abortive and one of the main objectives of the Torture Convention—to provide a system under which there is no safe haven for torturers—will have been frustrated'.[35] Thus, unless the 'extradite or prosecute' obligations were to be rendered useless the structure of the Convention had to exclude functional immunity. The logic of the other judges is worth considering briefly:

- Lord Hope held that State immunity is itself a rule of *jus cogens*, and can normally only be waived by express language. He found, however, that there is no immunity in international law for 'international crimes' committed on a widespread scale. In this case, the torture alleged amounts to a crime against humanity—thus, there can no immunity under customary international law.[36]

- Lord Hutton found that the Convention meant 'torture is not a function of a head of state' and therefore immunity does not arise.[37] On his view this was simply a result of the Convention in criminal cases; immunity in civil cases for damages would remain.

- Lord Saville saw torture as an official act, but found that immunity was waived as a result of the express terms of the convention.[38]

- Lord Millett held that to grant functional immunity in respect of torture would be 'inconsistent with the aims and object of the Convention' and therefore Chile 'must be taken to have assented' to the exercise of criminal jurisdiction by foreign courts. He expressly acknowledged, however, that *personal* immunity would still be available under the Convention.[39]

- Lord Phillips made a rather complex argument which comes down to the idea that while functional immunity is a long-established rule of international law, the law of international crimes arose later and so is not limited by the earlier rule. (This type of interpretation or argument is sometimes called *lex posterior derogat priori*: the law that is later in time derogates from the earlier law.) Nonetheless, he held that functional immunity might still be available in civil proceedings for damages; and any waiver of personal immunity would still have to be express.

- Lord Goff argued (in dissent) that any waiver of immunity by treaty must be by express language. As there is no such language in the Convention Against Torture, functional immunity remains available unless waived.

If we look to the position of the judges in the majority overall we find: Lords Browne-Wilkinson, Hutton, Saville, and Millett all base their reasoning on an interpretation the Convention; and Lords Hope and Phillips rely on (very different) interpretations of customary international law. What proposition of law does the case stand for

---

[35] *Commissioner of Police for the Metropolis and Others, Ex Parte Pinochet* [2000] 1 AC 147, 205.
[36] Ibid, 243–48.   [37] Ibid, 263–4.   [38] Ibid, 266–7.   [39] Ibid, 277.

then? The most likely answer is that the House of Lords found that functional immunity was not available under the Convention against Torture either because:

- immunity is implicitly or necessarily waived as part of the obligations under the Convention; or
- the Convention has the consequence that torture cannot be regarded as an official act.

On either view, it is hard to extend the effect of the decision to cases where the international crime in question is not covered by a treaty that includes duties to prosecute.

Thus, Lord Bingham said in *Jones v Saudia Arabia* that the 'Torture Convention was the mainspring of the decision' in *Pinochet (No. 3)* because 'international law could not without absurdity require criminal jurisdiction to be assumed and exercised where the Torture Convention conditions were satisfied and, at the same time, require immunity to be granted to those properly charged'.[40] If this is a fair summary, then the logic of *Pinochet (No. 3)* only applies as regards the Convention Against Torture and in other cases involving treaty-based duties to prosecute. An example of the latter might be the clear treaty law obligation upon State parties to the Geneva Conventions to seek out and bring before their own courts persons alleged to have committed 'grave breaches' of those Conventions.[41] Recent UK case law has upheld the proposition that functional immunities do not apply in criminal cases where breaches of the Convention Against Torture are alleged.[42]

Functional immunity in criminal cases: a broader reading of *Pinochet*?

A close reading of *Pinochet (No. 3)* suggests the case is confined to those involving international crimes defined in a treaty and including an 'extradite or prosecute' provision. Nonetheless, there is international practice supporting the 'broader reading' that suggests there is no immunity for international crimes. The logic of this is summed up in the idea that it is absurd for international law to outlaw conduct and then provide immunity for it.

Support comes from a number of sources. First, as noted above, Principle 3 of the ILC's Nuremberg Principles states clearly that acting in an official capacity does not relieve one of responsibility for an international crime. These Principles were affirmed by the UN General Assembly.[43] Some case law also supports the idea that there can be no functional immunity for international crimes including:

- the decision of the Supreme Court of Israel in *Eichmann* in 1968;[44]
- in *Bourtese* the Netherlands Court of Appeal held in 2000 that the former head of State of Suriname could be tried for acts of torture committed in 1982 as such

---

[40] *Jones v Minister of the Interior, Saudi Arabia and Aziz* [2006] UKHL 26, para 19.

[41] E.g. Art 49, Geneva Convention I of 1949. This would not apply to all war crimes, only grave breaches.

[42] 'Prince Nasser of Bahrain torture ruling quashed', BBC News, 7 October 2014, www.bbc.co.uk/news/uk-29521420 (High Court decision holding the Prince did not enjoy immunity).

[43] Resolution 95(I), 1946.   [44] (1968) 36 ILR 277, 308 ff.

acts: were contrary to customary international law (the Convention Against Torture not yet being in force); and, could not constitute official functions;[45]

- the Supreme Court of Belgium ruled in 2003 in *Sharon and Yaron* that the serving Prime Minister of a foreign State (Sharon) benefitted from *personal* immunity and could not be prosecuted while another senior official (Yaron) enjoying only *functional* immunity could not plead that immunity in respect of international crimes;[46] and

- the African Union Committee of Eminent African Jurists, appointed to consider the *Hissène Habré* case, concluded that Habré could not be shielded by the immunities attaching to a former head of State in a trial for torture.[47]

Some eminent writers in the field thus conclude that the trend towards protecting 'human dignity' has 'shattered the shield of immunities'[48] or, more moderately, suggest that there is a clear trend in the case law and authorities even if a few judgments leave open the 'possibility of doubt'.[49] Either seems an optimistic evaluation of the very limited State practice in the period since 1945.[50] It remains hard to point to many actual *prosecutions* before national courts where functional immunities have expressly been found not to apply. Indeed, prosecutions often do not proceed even in cases where functional immunity is expressly found not to be available.[51] On this basis one eminent scholar suggests there is 'hardly any support from State practice' supporting an exception to functional immunity regarding international crimes;[52] another considers arguments for such an exception 'wishful thinking'.[53]

The issue has also proved remarkably controversial among commissions of experts. Views in the ILC have proved sharply divided.[54] One would not expect the question to be so controversial among a group of eminent experts if the question were as clearly settled as some suggest. On the other hand, while the AU Committee of Eminent African

[45] Robinson, 'Immunities' in Cryer et al, *Introduction*, 550; JHM Willems, 'Treatment of Customary International Law and Use of Expert Evidence by the Dutch Court in the *Bouterse Case*' (2004) 4 Non-State Actors and International Law 65.

[46] A Cassese, 'The Belgian Court of Cassation v. the International Court of Justice: The Sharon and Others Case' (2003) 1 Journal of International Criminal Justice 437.

[47] Report of the Committee of Eminent African Jurists on the Case of Hissène Habré, African Union, 2006, www.hrw.org/legacy/justice/habre/CEJA_Repor0506.pdf.

[48] Cassese et al, *Cassese's International Criminal Law*, 246.

[49] Robinson, 'Immunities' in Cryer et al, *Introduction*, 551.

[50] See in particular: R O'Keefe, *International Criminal Law* (Oxford University Press 2015) 459.

[51] For example, in *Bouterse* the Supreme Court of the Netherlands found the prosecution could not proceed on jurisdictional grounds: Robinson, 'Immunities' in Cryer et al, *Introduction*, 550 n 76. Senator Pinochet was famously not extradited to face trial in Spain and died before national proceedings in Chile against him were concluded.

[52] H Huang, 'On Immunity of State Officials from Foreign Criminal Jurisdiction' (2014) 13 Chinese Journal of International Law 1, 5 (Professor Huang is the Chinese member of the ILC).

[53] O'Keefe, *International Criminal Law*, 459.

[54] Ibid, 4–5. See further: 'Preliminary report on immunity of State officials from foreign criminal jurisdictions by of the Special Rapporteur Ms. Concepción Escobar Hernández', UN Doc. A/CN.4/654 (2012), para 34. The ILC has not concluded any draft text dealing with the question of exceptions to functional immunity and internal debate continues: UN Doc A/70/10 (2015), paras 193–199.

Jurists had no trouble concluding functional immunities were not available, it did not explain its reasoning in any detail beyond stating that the 'rejection of impunity' for international crimes was incompatible with immunity existing.

The argument that it is absurd for international law to outlaw conduct and then provide immunity for it is certainly compelling. However, this argument based on values, if correct, should not only dispense with functional immunities: it should also logically dispense with personal immunities. Indeed, many of the sources commonly relied upon to support the idea that there should be no functional immunity for international crimes—such as Principle 3 of the ILC's Nuremberg Principles—apply both to *functional* and *personal* immunities. Nonetheless, as we have seen, personal immunities are, in fact, invariably upheld by national courts. The best attempt to justify this difference of treatment is to claim that functional immunity only protects a State's official conduct from being judged in a foreign forum while personal immunity preserves the ability of a government to function on the international plane.[55] Advocates of this distinction, however, do not explain why preserving the smooth functioning of international diplomacy at the level of senior officials is a value so important that it 'trumps' the values protected by international criminal law.

As a matter of State practice we can say there are isolated examples of national courts setting aside functional immunities in criminal cases concerning international crimes. However, personal immunities are invariably upheld (and potentially for an expanding category of officials) and even functional immunities are usually upheld in civil cases (e.g. victims of torture suing a foreign government for compensation). It is thus hard to see a general trend away from the application of immunities before national courts in cases involving international criminal law. We can perhaps be optimistic, but we should be slow to blame national courts for failing to be more radical given the equivocal state of the law.[56]

14.4 The ICC and the immunity of the officials of non-State parties

14.4.1 Introduction to Articles 27 and 98

The ICC Statute might be thought to be ambiguous as regards the role of State immunity. Article 27 of the ICC Statute is entitled 'Irrelevance of official capacity' and states that 'official capacity as a Head of State or Government, a member of a Government or parliament, an elected representative or a government official' does not 'exempt a person from criminal responsibility' under the Statute. This might be thought an entirely unambiguous statement that no immunities can apply under the Statute. However, Article 98 provides that the ICC cannot request that a State party surrender a suspect

---

[55] Robinson, 'Immunities' in Cryer et al, *Introduction*, 550; Cassese et al, *Cassese's International Criminal Law*, 318.

[56] R O'Keefe, 'State Immunity and Human Rights: Heads and Walls, Hearts and Minds' (2011) 44 Vanderbilt Journal of Transnational Law 999 (discussing civil immunity).

to the Court if doing so would 'require the requested State to act inconsistently with its obligations' either:

- 'under international law with respect to the State or diplomatic immunity of a person'; or
- under treaties requiring 'the consent of a sending State ... to surrender a person of that State to the Court'.[57]

The first category seems a straightforward prohibition on the ICC requesting the surrender of a suspect who enjoys State or diplomatic immunity.[58] The second category concerns specific treaty arrangements having the effect of prohibiting the surrender of a person to the Court without the consent of a specific 'sending' State. Such obligations would typically arise under agreements governing the stationing of military forces abroad (Status of Forces Agreements or SOFAs) which regulate criminal jurisdiction over visiting forces. For example, under a SOFA a foreign soldier ('sent' to serve in another country) might stand trial in a local court for offences against national law, but still benefit from a treaty prohibition on the territorial State extraditing him or her to face charges in other countries. In either case, the immunity (or treaty provision) could be waived by the relevant State that 'sent' its official to the territory of State party.

The important question is how we reconcile these provisions with Article 27. One possible interpretation is that one applies Article 98 before Article 27. That is, the Court may not obtain jurisdiction over a person in violation of State immunity. However, once it has jurisdiction over a person—i.e. once a defendant is before the Court—immunities become irrelevant. This could be held to follow because either:

(1) the defendant is an official of an ICC State party and Article 27, in effect, constitutes an implicit waiver of State immunity by State parties (on the logic of *Pinochet (No. 3)*); or

(2) the defendant is an official of a State that is *not* a party to the ICC Statute but their immunity has already been waived by the relevant State to allow transfer under Article 98.

On its face, the combination of Articles 27 and 98 does *not* result in the ICC Statute removing the immunity applicable to officials from non-State parties and was not intended to achieve that result.[59] Nonetheless, in the *Al Bashir* case an ICC Pre-Trial Chamber in 2009 concluded President Al Bashir of Sudan (a non-party to the ICC Statute) did not enjoy any immunity from being surrendered to the Court by a State party—despite the fact he would ordinarily enjoy *personal* immunity under customary international law.[60] Fuller reasons were given supporting this conclusion in the 2011 'Malawi Decision', in which the question was asked whether Malawi (a State party to

---

[57] See Art 98(1) and (2), ICC Statute.   [58] The statute does not use the term 'extradition'.
[59] Schabas, *Introduction*, 78–80; Cassese, 'The Belgian Court of Cassation,' 442–43.
[60] *Al Bashir* (Decision on the Prosecution's Application for a Warrant of Arrest against Omar Hassan Ahmad Al Bashir), ICC Pre-Trial Chamber I, 4 March 2009, paras 41–44.

the ICC Statute) should have surrendered President al Bashir to the Court.[61] The ICC Pre-Trial Chamber essentially adopted the logic of *Charles Taylor*: the ICC is an international court and 'the principle in international law is that immunity of either former or sitting Heads of State' does not apply to international courts.[62] The problems with the *Charles Taylor* case reasoning were discussed above. The Malawi Decision in *Al Bashir* has attracted significant criticism for the same reasons. Further, even if it were true there was a rule precluding personal immunity from applying before *international courts* that still would not free *national authorities* from respecting rules on personal immunities that are binding upon States.[63] However, if one accepts the customary international law *binding on States* has changed, then Article 98 would no longer prevent suspects being surrendered to the Court. The Malawi Decision, however, does not attempt to make that argument and could not plausibly do so. As discussed above, personal immunities are still universally upheld by national courts and even the ICJ. A *third* decision on President Bashir's immunities was made in 2014 (the 'Democratic Republic of the Congo Decision'), discussed below.

This discussion does not resolve all questions of immunity arising under the ICC Statute. Two more are explored below:

- the position of officials of a non-party State in cases where the Security Council has referred a situation to the ICC; and
- the legal effect of non-parties to the ICC Statute entering treaties that have the sole purpose of preventing the surrender of their nationals to the ICC.

14.4.2 Immunity before the ICC and Security Council referrals

As noted, the UN Security Council used its compulsory Chapter VII powers to refer the situation in Darfur, Sudan to the ICC. In the *Al Bashir* case the better argument for the ICC Pre-Trial Chamber might have been to focus on the fact of this Security Council referral.[64] Akande suggests that two arguments are available:[65]

- First, one could argue in general that 'whenever the Security Council refers a situation to the ICC, the State concerned is bound by the provisions of the Statute as if it were a party to the Statute', thus Article 27 operates to waive State immunity. Essentially, this is the argument that if the Security Council could (under Chapter VII) set up the ICTY and ICTR and abolish pleas of State immunity before those bodies, then nothing prevents a referral to the ICC having the same

---

[61] *Al Bashir* (Decision Pursuant to Article 87(7) of the Rome Statute on the Failure by the Republic of Malawi to Comply with the Cooperation Requests Issued by the Court with Respect to the Arrest and Surrender of Al Bashir), ICC Pre-Trial Chamber I, 12 December 2011.

[62] Ibid, para 36–42.

[63] See P Gaeta, 'Does President Al Bashir Enjoy Immunity from Arrest?' (2009) 7 Journal of International Criminal Justice 315.

[64] Robinson, 'Immunities' in Cryer et al, *Introduction*, 562; D Akande, 'ICC Issues Detailed Decision on Bashir's Immunity (At long Last) But Gets the Law Wrong', EJIL: Talk!, 15 December 2011, www.ejiltalk.org/icc-issues-detailed-decision-on-bashir%E2%80%99s-immunity-at-long-last-but-gets-the-law-wrong/.

[65] Akande, 'ICC Issues Detailed Decision on Bashir's Immunity'.

effect. A weakness in this argument might be that the lifting of the immunity has to be *implied* from the combined effect of both the referral and the Statute.

- Second, he suggests that because Security Council Resolution 1593 *decides* that 'Sudan must cooperate with the Court' this (again implicitly) requires Sudan to waive claims of immunity.

An alternative possibility is that Al Bashir's immunity is waived by the Genocide Convention 1948 to which Sudan is a party. This follows because Article IV of that Convention requires the punishment of those who commit genocide 'even if they are constitutionally responsible rulers'.[66]

In 2014, an ICC Pre-Trial Chamber was asked to rule on the question of whether the Democratic Republic of the Congo (DRC) had failed in its duties under the Statute to arrest President Al Bashir and transfer him to the Court. In its Decision the Pre-Trial Chamber appeared to abandon arguments based on the *Charles Taylor* case and to adopt similar reasoning to Akande. It concluded that in deciding Sudan shall cooperate with the ICC: 'the SC implicitly waived the immunities granted to Omar Al Bashir under international law and attached to his position as a Head of State', and this removed any horizontal obstacle between the DRC and Sudan which would prevent President Al Bashir's surrender to the Court.[67] Gaeta challenged the persuasiveness of such reasoning in a 2009 article discussed below.

 Counterpoint

P Gaeta, 'Does President Al Bashir Enjoy Immunity from Arrest?' (2009) 7 Journal of International Criminal Justice 315

Gaeta reviews most of the arguments that President Al Bashir lacks immunity and finds them wanting. First she notes that arguments based on Article 27 of the ICC Statute (taken in isolation) or the *Charles Taylor* case, to the effect that there is no plea of immunity before international criminal tribunals, is of little help. This is a rule directed to international tribunals and not to national authorities. Simply because there is no immunity available once a defendant is before an international tribunal does not mean that national authorities may ignore the rules prohibiting them from arresting or detaining a person who benefits from personal immunities. Further, even if one could make a *Pinochet (No 3)*-type argument that Article 27 waives personal immunities as among the States parties to the ICC Statute that, again, does not assist in the present case because Sudan is not a party to the Statute. Indeed, Article 98(1) expressly preserves the rights of *non-parties* to the Statute as regards State and personal immunity, and therefore the ICC lacked authority to issue an arrest warrant in respect of President Al Bashir.

---

[66] This, again, involves a *Pinochet (No 3)*-type argument that such a requirement is incompatible with immunity and a State party to the Convention must be taken to have waived immunity.

[67] *Prosecutor v Omar Hassan Ahmad Al Bashir* (Decision on the Cooperation of the Democratic Republic of the Congo Regarding Omar Al Bashir's Arrest and Surrender to the Court), Pre-Trial Chamber, 9 April 2014, para 29.

Gaeta does conclude that the UN Security Council could have waived the immunity of Al Bashir when it referred the situation in the Sudan to the ICC under Resolution 1593 (2005). To do this, however, it would have had to *decide* that *all States* must cooperate with the ICC investigation and prosecution. This would have had the effect of creating an obligation under Article 103 of the UN Charter that would prevail over other rules of international law—including the obligation to respect personal immunity. However, Resolution 1593 did no such thing. It only decided that the Sudan and parties to the conflict must cooperate with the ICC. Other states were merely *urged* to cooperate with the ICC.

One might nonetheless argue that Sudan is therefore obliged to waive Al Bashir's immunity. However, that is something that only Sudan can do. If it fails to do so, as it has done to date, then it would still be internationally wrongful for a State to seize Al Bashir in violation of his immunities. The argument here is that the Security Council did *not* direct all States to ignore Al Bashir's immunity but at best (arguably) required Sudan to waive it. Sudan's failure to do so may put it in breach of an obligation owed to the Security Council but that would not change the duties other States owed to Sudan.

According to Gaeta's argument it follows, then, that States such as Malawi and DRC were right in their interpretation of Article 98 of the ICC Statute and the ICC was wrong in law to find they should have arrested Al Bashir and surrendered him to the Court.

14.4.3 Agreements prohibiting surrender of foreign nationals to the ICC

The other possible exclusion under Article 98 of the ICC Statute is that a State party is prevented from surrendering a suspect to the ICC because of treaty commitments to a non-State party. As noted, treaties do exist that guarantee State officials 'sent' on their official duties to a 'receiving' State will not be surrendered to a third party for prosecution. The US has controversially entered into over 100 such 'Article 98 agreements' with the express purpose of preventing State parties to the ICC Statute transferring US citizens to the ICC.[68] Entering such agreements was often made a precondition to the US continuing certain aid programmes or military ties. Several ICC State parties refused to conclude such agreements and lost US aid as a result.

These agreements usually contain provisions in the following terms (the articles below are taken from the US-Tunisia Article 98 Agreement 2003):[69]

1. For the purposes of this agreement, 'persons' are current or former government officials, employees or military personnel or nationals of one party.
2. Persons of one Party present in the territory of the other shall not, absent the express consent of the first Party, (a) be surrendered or transferred by any means to the International Criminal Court for any purpose …

A major source of controversy is that this agreement extends to cover *all* US nationals. The wording of Article 98(2) only covers persons *sent* by the State they *serve* to another country. This is consistent with traditional understandings of State immunity (e.g. as discussed in *Arrest Warrant*). A private citizen, who has never been in government

---

[68] Schabas, *Introduction*, 29–30.   [69] See www.state.gov/documents/organization/152187.pdf.

service, has not been *sent* by the US if they visit an ICC State party on holiday or private business.

Any ICC State party entering such an agreement could thus be in a difficult position concerning US nationals who are covered by an agreement with the US but who are not covered by Article 98(2). Consider the following example:

 Example

A person holding US nationality enters an ICC State party (State A). An ICC arrest warrant has been issued against them, alleging they participated in crimes against humanity in the territory of another ICC State party. State A has entered a US Article 98 agreement in the terms above.

What does State A do if the US will not consent to the transfer? Quite simply, it must choose which obligation it will break. It cannot refuse to surrender the person under the terms of Article 98 and it cannot surrender them under the agreement with the US.

Is entering such an Article 98 agreement inconsistent with the ICC Statute? The answer is slightly complicated. In respect of people actually *sent* by their government: no, technically not. Agreements covering such persons fall within Article 98(2). As regards persons not sent by their government, the preferable view is State parties to the ICC Statute should avoid entering such agreements as they are not consistent with the object and purpose of the Statute (which aims to prevent impunity for international crimes).[70]

In practice, no US citizen has been indicted before the ICC and the Article 98 agreements have so far had no practical relevance.

 Pause for reflection

Consider the following scenario. A is a US soldier. The US deployed her as part of a UN peace-keeping mission in Dystopia in 2008. Dystopia is an ICC State party and was at the time of the peace-keeping mission. It is later alleged A committed war crimes while serving as part of that mission. A claims these allegations are unfair and politically motivated and all her actions were within the scope of her duties. The ICC nonetheless issues a warrant for A's arrest in 2010. A travels to Utopia, an ICC State party, as a tourist in 2011. Utopia has refused to sign an Article 98 agreement with the US. Consistent with the ICC Statute, can A be arrested and transferred to the ICC without the US's consent?

On its face, Article 98(1) could prohibit such a result. A was sent into Dystopia by the US military. Prima facie she acted as an official of the US and would enjoy functional immunity. She may

---

[70] See further: J Crawford, P Sands, and R Wilde, 'Bilateral agreements sought by the United States under Article 98(2) of the [ICC] Statute', 5 June 2003, www.iccnow.org/documents/SandsCrawfordBIA14June03.pdf (legal advice given to the Lawyers' Committee on Human Rights and the Medical Foundation for the Care of Victims of Torture).

therefore not be surrendered to the Court as this would be inconsistent 'with [Utopia's] obligations under international law with respect to the State...immunity of a person...of a third State'.

The only exception might be if she was suspected of a grave breach of the Geneva Conventions
(a limited class of war crimes applying only in international armed conflicts). As there is a treaty
obligation requiring States to seek out and prosecute those suspected of grave breaches of the
Geneva Conventions, there could be a *Pinochet (No 3)* argument that this would prevent a claim
of immunity. (The US is a party to the Geneva Conventions.) Absent such an exception, A could
not be arrested or transferred to the ICC without the consent of the US.

Note that Article 98(2) is not relevant on these facts: A was not sent by the US to Utopia.

14.5 Summary and conclusions

This chapter has:

- explained the traditional history of State immunity as a doctrine of absolute
  immunity, grounded in the *par in parem* principle;
- noted the rise, first in civil cases, of a restrictive approach to immunity, where certain exceptions are available;
- explained the distinction between functional and personal immunities, and the
  different role each type of immunity might play before national or international
  courts;
- as regards personal immunity before national courts it has noted that these immunities are always upheld (as discussed in *Arrest Warrant*);
- as regards functional immunity before national courts it has discussed the leading
  case of *Pinochet (No 3)* and the broad and narrow readings of that case;
- examined the difficult question of whether personal immunities are available
  before international courts and noted the controversial decision in *Charles Taylor*
  that there is a rule of international law that such immunities are never available
  before international courts.

In addition it has considered several questions that arise in relation to the ICC Statute:

- the correct understanding of the relationship between Articles 27 and 98 of the
  Statute;
- whether, or under what circumstances, the head of State of a non-party to the
  ICC Statute can invoke personal immunities to prevent his or her surrender to
  the Court; and
- the legal effect of bilateral 'non-surrender' or 'Article 98' agreements.

The conclusion to be drawn is that jurisdictional immunities are a complex field. While
it might be desirable to say that international moves to end impunity have resulted in
there being no immunities in cases where international crimes are alleged, the state of
the law in reality is clearly much more nuanced and uncertain. In many cases where one

might as a matter of principle expect immunities not to be found available, they have in fact been upheld by national and international courts.

Useful further reading

D AKANDE, 'International Law Immunities and the International Criminal Court' (2004) 98 American Journal of International Law 407.

The classic article on the relationship between Articles 27 and 98 of the ICC Statute and the general international law regarding immunity.

A CASSESE, 'The Belgian Court of Cassation v. the International Court of Justice: The Sharon and Others Case' (2003) 1 Journal of International Criminal Justice 437.

An important piece suggesting that in Belgian case law at the time functional immunity provided no immunity in respect of charges of genocide, crimes against humanity, and grave breaches of the Geneva Conventions. As noted in this chapter there is some other case law in support of such a conclusion. However, in respect of charges of genocide and grave breaches of the Geneva Conventions one could argue the relevant treaties have the effect of waiving immunity.

J FOAKES, *The Position of Heads of State and Senior Officials in International Law* (Oxford University Press 2014).

An excellent, balanced, and recent study covering (among other topics) the issues discussed in this chapter in greater detail.

P GAETA, 'Does President Al Bashir Enjoy Immunity from Arrest?' (2009) 7 Journal of International Criminal Justice 315.

An excellent and detailed argument that avoids making sweeping conclusions about the effect of Security Council resolutions in ICC referral cases by giving detailed thought to the different legal relationships involved.

Index